Textbook on Land Law

Textbook on
Land Law

....

Tenth Edition

Judith-Anne MacKenzie
LLM, AKC, Barrister

and

Mary Phillips
MA, LLM, Barrister

OXFORD
UNIVERSITY PRESS

OXFORD

UNIVERSITY PRESS

Great Clarendon Street, Oxford OX2 6DP

Oxford University Press is a department of the University of Oxford.
It furthers the University's objective of excellence in research, scholarship,
and education by publishing worldwide in

Oxford New York

Auckland Bangkok Buenos Aires Cape Town Chennai
Dar es Salaam Delhi Hong Kong Istanbul Karachi Kolkata
Kuala Lumpur Madrid Melbourne Mexico City Mumbai Nairobi
São Paulo Shanghai Taipei Tokyo Toronto

Oxford is a registered trade mark of Oxford University Press
in the UK and in certain other countries

Published in the United States
by Oxford University Press Inc., New York

First published Blackstone Press 1999

© Judith-Anne MacKenzie and Mary Phillips 2004

British Library Cataloguing in Publication Data

Data available

Library of Congress Cataloging in Publication Data

Data applied for

ISBN-13: 978–0–19–926162–8
ISBN-10: 0–19–926162–8

3 5 7 9 10 8 6 4

Typeset in ITC Stone Serif and ITC Stone Sans
by Re neCatch Limited, Bungay, Suffolk
Printed in Great Britain by
Ashford Colour Press Ltd,
Gosport, Hampshire

OUTLINE CONTENTS

Preface   xii
Table of Cases   xiv
Table of Statutes   xxv
Table of Statutory Instruments   xxxiii

PART I   Introduction

1   Estates and interests in land   3

PART II   Acquisition of estates in land

2   Buying a house   23
3   The contract   29
4   Unregistered land   50
5   Registered land   66
6   Acquisition of an estate by adverse possession 113

PART III   Legal estates

7   The freehold estate   139
8   The leasehold estate   145
9   Obligations of landlord and tenant   182
10 Remedies for breach of leasehold covenants   221
11 Commonhold   238

PART IV   Trusts and proprietary estoppel

12 Trusts: an introduction   257
13 Trusts of land   264
14 Settled Land Act settlements   304
15 Perpetuities and accumulations   326
16 Co-ownership   345
17 Resulting and constructive trusts   366
18 Propriety estoppel   382

PART V Licences

19	Nature of a licence	399
20	Enforcement of a licence	415

PART VI Third-party rights

21	Mortgages and charges	433
22	Easements and profits à prendre	493
23	Covenants relating to freehold land	533

PART VII In conclusion

24	The family home	563
25	What is land?	573

Bibliography	583
Glossary	584
Index	591

DETAILED CONTENTS

Preface   xii
Table of Cases   xiv
Table of Statutes   xxv
Table of Statutory Instruments   xxxiii

PART I   Introduction

1   Estates and interests in land   3

1.1 Introduction *3*
1.2 Estate in fee simple absolute in
     possession *5*
1.3 Term of years absolute *7*
1.4 Interests in land *7*
1.5 Legal interests *8*

1.6 Equitable interests *10*
1.7 Legal interests and equitable
     interests compared *15*
1.8 A multiplicity of rights *18*
1.9 Classification of property *18*
1.10 Human Rights Act 1998 *19*

PART II   Acquisition of estates in land

2   Buying a house   23

2.1 The properties *23*
2.2 Two systems of title *23*

2.3 Outline of the conveyancing
     process *26*

3   The contract   29

3.1 Introduction *29*
3.2 Contracts made on or after 27
     September 1989 *29*
3.3 Contracts made before 27
     September 1989 *37*
3.4 Part performance after the 1989
     Act *40*

3.5 Effect of the contract: passing
     of the equitable interest *45*
3.6 Remedies for breach of contract *46*
3.7 Application to 3 Trant Way *48*

4   Unregistered land   50

4.1 Introduction *50*
4.2 Ownership of the estate *50*
4.3 Checking for encumbrances *51*
4.4 Land charges *51*
4.5 Legal or equitable interests
     which are not land charges *59*

4.6 Summary of searches to be made
     in relation to unregistered land *63*
4.7 The conveyance *63*
4.8 Application for first registration *63*

5   Registered land   66

5.1 Introduction *66*
5.2 Need for reform *66*
5.3 What can be registered? *69*

5.4 First registration *71*
5.5 Registering title *73*
5.6 Dealings with a registered estate *82*

5.7 Buying a house with registered
     title *83*
5.8 Interests protected by entries on
     the register *84*
5.9 Interests that override a
     registered disposition *88*
5.10 Interests of persons in actual
     occupation *92*

5.11 Discovering encumbrances:
     searches and enquiries *102*
5.12 Alteration of the register and
     indemnity *104*
5.13 Transfer and completion by
     registration *107*
5.14 Electronic conveyancing *109*
5.15 Purchasers of other interests *111*

6   Acquisition of an estate by adverse possession   113

6.1 Introduction *113*
6.2 Establishing adverse possession *116*
6.3 Adverse possession of
     unregistered land *122*
6.4 Adverse possession of registered
     land under LRA 1925 *127*

6.5 Adverse possession of registered
     land under LRA 2002 *130*
6.6 Adverse possession and HRA
     1998 *133*

PART III   Legal estates

7   The freehold estate   139

7.1 Introduction *139*
7.2 Fee simple *139*
7.3 Absolute *140*

7.4 In possession *142*
7.5 Intervention of public policy *143*

8   The leasehold estate   145

8.1 Introduction *145*
8.2 Basic requirements for a lease *148*
8.3 Creation of leases *153*
8.4 Disposition of leases and
     reversions *160*
8.5 Determining a lease *162*
8.6 Determination by discharge of
     contract *168*

8.7 Determination by joint tenants *172*
8.8 'Contractualisation' of leases *173*
8.9 Effect on subtenant of
     determination of head lease *174*
8.10 Some more types of lease *176*

9   Obligations of landlord and tenant   182

9.1 Introduction *182*
9.2 Express covenants *185*
9.3 Implied and usual covenants *195*
9.4 Enforcement of covenants *199*
9.5 Position of original parties after
     transfer of lease and/or reversion *200*
9.6 Position of new landlord and/or
     tenant after transfer of lease
     and/or reversion *207*

9.7 Enforcement of covenants in the
     Trant Way tenancies *214*
9.8 Effect on a subtenant of
     covenants in the head lease *216*

10   Remedies for breach of leasehold covenants   221

10.1 General contractual remedies *221*
10.2 Tenant's remedies against a
     defaulting landlord *224*

10.3 Landlord's remedies against a
     defaulting tenant *225*

11 Commonhold   238

11.1 Introduction *238*
11.2 The commonhold scheme *240*
11.3 Creating commonhold *244*
11.4 Managing a commonhold
     property *246*

11.5 Nature of a unit holder's interest *247*
11.6 Ending commonhold *250*
11.7 Evaluation *251*
11.8 Updating this chapter *253*

PART IV Trusts and proprietary estoppel

12 Trusts: an introduction   257

12.1 Nature and creation of trusts *257*
12.2 A short historical background *259*

12.3 Trusts of Land and Appointment
     of Trustees Act 1996 *262*

13 Trusts of land   264

13.1 Introduction *264*
13.2 Definition of a trust of land *266*
13.3 Appointment of trustees *267*
13.4 Powers of trustees of a trust of
     land *270*
13.5 Limitation of trustees' powers *272*
13.6 Delegation of trustees' functions *276*

13.7 The rights of beneficiaries *279*
13.8 Powers of the court *282*
13.9 Protection of purchasers *288*
13.10 When will a trust of land arise? *292*
13.11 Comparison of old and new law *296*
13.12 The future *303*

14 Settled Land Act settlements   304

14.1 Introduction *304*
14.2 Types of settlement *306*
14.3 Tenant for life *309*
14.4 Trustees *309*
14.5 Creating a settlement *310*
14.6 Powers of a tenant for life *314*
14.7 Giving notice and obtaining
     consent *317*

14.8 A tenant for life is trustee of his
     powers *318*
14.9 Defective dispositions *319*
14.10 Role of trustees of settlements *321*
14.11 End of a settlement *325*

15 Perpetuities and accumulations   326

15.1 Introduction *326*
15.2 The common law rules *326*
15.3 Reforms made in 1925 *333*
15.4 Perpetuities and Accumulations
     Act 1964 *334*
15.5 Summary of common law rules
     and legislation *337*

15.6 To which other situations do
     the perpetuities rules apply? *338*
15.7 Accumulations *340*
15.8 Reform of the law *342*

16 Co-ownership   345

16.1 Background *345*
16.2 Introduction *345*
16.3 Two types of co-ownership *346*

16.4 Severance of a joint tenancy *352*
16.5 Relationship between co-owners *358*
16.6 Position of a purchaser *363*

17   Resulting and constructive trusts   366

17.1 Introduction   *366*
17.2 Resulting trusts   *366*
17.3 Constructive trusts   *368*
17.4 Trusts arising from contribution   *371*

17.5 Establishing the claim to a share in the beneficial interest   *373*
17.6 Quantifying the share   *379*

18   Proprietary estoppel   382

18.1 Introduction   *382*
18.2 Nature of proprietary estoppel   *382*
18.3 Criteria for proprietary estoppel   *385*
18.4 Satisfying the equity   *389*
18.5 Nature of the equity arising from estoppel   *392*

18.6 Situations in which there is 'no room' for proprietary estoppel   *393*
18.7 Relationship between proprietary estoppel and constructive trusts   *394*

PART V   Licences

19   Nature of a licence   399

19.1 Introduction   *399*
19.2 Distinguishing a lease from a licence   *400*

19.3 Distinguishing an easement or profit from a licence   *413*

20   Enforcement of a licence   415

20.1 Introduction   *415*
20.2 Enforcement against the licensor   *417*
20.3 Enforcement against successors of the licensor   *420*

20.4 Are licences becoming interests in land?   *428*
20.5 Trant Way   *429*

PART VI   Third-party rights

21   Mortgages and charges   433

21.1 Background   *433*
21.2 Introduction   *433*
21.3 What is a mortgage or charge?   *434*
21.4 Legal mortgages   *436*
21.5 Equitable mortgages   *439*
21.6 Rights of the mortgagor   *440*
21.7 Rights of the mortgagee   *446*
21.8 Mortgagees' remedies   *449*
21.9 Right of certain third parties to redeem   *457*
21.10 Liability of mortgagees, receivers and valuers for fraud or negligence   *458*

21.11 Terminating a mortgage   *462*
21.12 Priorities   *463*
21.13 Priorities of mortgages of an equitable interest   *464*
21.14 Priorities of mortgages of the legal estate   *466*
21.15 Priorities of three or more mortgages   *475*
21.16 Mortgagee's right to tack further advances   *476*
21.17 Interests prior to the mortgage: a cause for concern to the mortgagee   *478*

22   Easements and profits à prendre   493

22.1 Introduction   *493*

22.2 What is an easement?   *495*

22.3 What is a profit à prendre? *503*

22.4 Easements and profits may be legal or equitable *504*

22.5 Acquisition by express grant or reservation *507*

22.6 Acquisition by implied grant or reservation *507*

22.7 Acquisition by express grant by virtue of LPA 1925, s. 62 *511*

22.8 Acquisition by prescription *515*

22.9 Remedies *526*

22.10 Extinguishment of easements and profits *528*

22.11 Law reform *529*

23 Covenants relating to freehold land   533

23.1 Introduction *533*

23.2 Trant Way *533*

23.3 Enforceability of covenants: original parties *534*

23.4 Enforceability of covenants: successors of the original parties *537*

23.5 The problem of positive covenants *551*

23.6 Remedies *555*

23.7 Discharge of covenants *557*

23.8 Reform of the law relating to burdens running with the land *558*

PART VII   **In conclusion**

24 The family home   563

24.1 Introduction *563*

24.2 Right to a share in the value of the house *564*

24.3 Right to remain in occupation *566*

24.4 Reform *570*

25 What is land?   573

25.1 The statutory definition *573*

25.2 Earth, minerals, buildings and fixtures *574*

25.3 Hereditaments *576*

25.4 Real and personal property (or, realty and personality) *577*

25.5 Flying freehold *579*

Bibliography   583

Glossary   584

Index   591

PREFACE

This new edition has been produced largely as the result of two major changes to key areas of land law.

One of these changes has not yet been fully implemented but is expected to take effect some time in the Summer of 2004. This is the Commonhold and Leasehold Reform Act 2002, which introduces new arrangements for land-holdings of land in multiple occupation (such as blocks of flats). The Act also makes a number of detailed changes to landlord and tenant law, (most of which are outside the scope of this book) all of which should also be in force by the Summer of 2004.

The other change is far more far-reaching and arises from the coming into force, in October 2003, of the Land Registration Act 2002. This Act has made major changes to the land registration system, that are designed to ensure that in future the register will represent a more accurate reflection of the majority of interests affecting a registered estate. However, while dealing with registration issues this Act has also had an impact on the nature of interests in land and their acquisition and thus you should not assume that it is simply about the recording of those interests that already existed in unregistered land. The 2002 Act makes substantive changes to land law and is the most extensive reform since the reforms introduced in 1926. In this text we deal with the new land registration system in detail and only refer to the pre-2003 registered land system where this is necessary for clarity.

The Land Registration Act 2002 also provides for the introduction of electronic conveyancing but this has not yet been implemented in full. The Land Registry is, however, already very 'e-friendly' and you will find a wealth of helpful information on their excellent web site at **www.landreg.gov.uk**. We have been very grateful during the preparation of this text for the assistance of the Land Registry staff and are grateful to the Registry for their permission to reproduce their forms.

As usual, we also cover in this new text any other developments since the last edition, including, notably, the latest cases on orders for sale of co-owned property and sections 14 and 15 of the Trusts of Land and Appointment of Trustees Act 1996 and those on mortgages and undue influence.

Both of us have been fascinated by land law ever since our first encounters with the subject as undergraduates. Accordingly, we have always been disappointed to note that the majority of law students (and many practitioners) regard the subject with dislike. We feel that one source of confusion, and often boredom, in the student was produced by the traditional method of teaching land law, in which the historical background to the subject was heavily emphasised. Whilst we find the history of the subject both intriguing and informative, we are well aware that most modern students are interested primarily in the law as it is, rather than as it was. As a result, during the years in which we taught together we developed a new approach to the subject, which concentrates on its modern and practical aspects. However, we found our efforts hampered by the lack of a text which suited our methods, and were therefore pleased to be offered the opportunity to present our style of teaching in book form in our earlier book, *A Practical Approach to Land Law*. Over the years we have been pleased to see that many teachers have also come to approach this subject in a more accessible way. We hope that this text will continue to encourage an interest in a lively and important subject and that it will, perhaps, prove to be a comfort to the confused and the faint-hearted.

Trant Way, Mousehole, in the county of Stilton is a purely fictional street and so are its inhabitants, and the other characters and institutions in this book are all inventions and bear no relation to any real persons or bodies, living or dead. We enjoyed inventing Trant Way, and its inhabitants have provided light relief for many of our students. We hope that they will assist you in understanding land law and demonstrate that the subject is not as 'stuffy' as some may have you believe.

Judith-Anne MacKenzie continues to work in the Government Legal Service and is currently Head of the Legislative Unit in the Office of the Deputy Prime Minister. As a member of the Civil Service, she wishes to point out that any opinions expressed in this book are purely personal opinions and have no official weight. Also, they have not been arrived at on the basis of any 'insider information'.

Mary Phillips, since her retirement from the post of Dean on the Inns of Court School of Law, has continued her interest in the teaching of land law, currently at the University of Surrey.

We hope that this new edition will proved as popular as its predecessors. As always, we are happy to receive any comments and suggestions for improvements; which may be sent to us via our publishers.

The law is stated as at 31 March 2004. For later developments (including decisions in several House of Lords cases published too late for this book) see our companion web site at **www.oup.com/uk/booksites/law/land**.

Judith-Anne Mackenzie
Mary Phillips

TABLE OF CASES

Abbahall Ltd v Smee [2003] 1 All ER 465 ... 580–1

Abbey National Building Society v Cann [1991] 1 AC 56; [1989] 2 FLR 265 ... 96, 97, 98, 99, 103, 180

Abbeyfield (Harpenden) Society Ltd v Woods [1968] 1 WLR 374 ... 403

Acklom, Re [1929] 1 Ch 195 ... 318

Actionstrength Ltd v International Glass Engineering IN.GL.EN SpA [2003] 2 AC 541 ... 44–5

Addiscombe Garden Estates Ltd v Crabbe [1958] 1 QB 513 ... 404

AG Securities v Vaughan [1990] 1 AC 417 ... 403, 408, 409

Agra Bank Ltd v Barry (1874) LR 7 HL 135 ... 472

Aldin v Latimer Clark, Muirhead & Co. [1894] 2 Ch 437 ... 187, 188

Aldred's Case (1610) 9 Co Rep 57b ... 498

Alefounder's Will Trusts, Re [1927] 1 Ch 360 ... 313, 324

Allcard v Skinner (1887) 36 ChD 145 ... 480, 482, 484

Ames, Re [1893] 2 Ch 479 ... 318

Amsprop Trading Ltd v Harris Distribution Ltd [1997] 1 WLR 1025 ... 219, 535

Anderson v Midland Railway Co. (1861) 3 El & El 614 ... 177

Andrews v Partington (1791) 3 Bro CC 401 ... 332

Antoniades v Villiers [1990] 1 AC 417 ... 407, 408–9

Appah v Parncliffe Investments Ltd [1964] 1 WLR 1064 ... 149, 401, 402

Arkwright v Gell (1839) 5 M & W 203 ... 516, 526

Armstrong and Holmes Ltd v Holmes [1993] 1 WLR 1482 ... 30, 53

Ashburn Anstalt v Arnold [1989] 1 Ch 1 ... 149, 152, 423, 424, 427, 428–9, 430, 478

Ashworth Frazer Ltd v Gloucester CC [2001] 1 WLR 2180 ... 191, 192

Aslan v Murphy (Nos 1 and 2) [1990] 1 WLR 766 ... 406–7

Attorney-General v Blake [2001] AC 268 ... 555

Attwood v Bovis Homes Ltd [2001] Ch 379 ... 497–8, 500

Austerberry v Corporation of Oldham (1885) 29 ChD 750 ... 539, 541

Bailey (C H) Ltd v Memorial Enterprises Ltd [1974] 1 WLR 728 ... 173–4

Bailey v Barnes [1894] 1 Ch 25 ... 451

Bailey v Stephens (1862) 12 CB NS 91 ... 497

Bakewell Management Ltd v Brandwood [2004] 2 WLR 955 ... 516

Ballard's Conveyance, Re [1937] Ch 473 ... 545

Banco Exterior Internacional SA v Thomas [1997] 1 WLR 221 ... 490

Bank of Baroda v Dhillon [1998] 1 FLR 524 ... 360, 452, 479

Bank of Credit and Commerce International SA v Aboody [1990] 1 QB 923 ... 481, 482, 483

Bank of Ireland Home Mortgages Ltd v Bell [2001] 2 FLR 809 ... 283, 284, 286–7, 360, 452, 479, 566

Bankers Trust Co v Namdar [1997] NPC 22 ... 41

Bannister v Bannister [1948] 2 All ER 133 ... 369

Barclays Bank Ltd v Bird [1954] Ch 274 ... 455

Barclays Bank Ltd v O'Brien [1994] 1 AC 180 ... 480, 481, 482, 485, 486, 488, 489

Barclays Bank plc v Alcorn [2002] All ER (D) 146 ... 454

Barclays Bank plc v Boulter [1998] 1 WLR 1 ... 487

Barclays Bank plc v Zaroovabli [1997] Ch 321 ... 107

Barrett v Halifax Building Society (1995) 28 HLR 634 ... 451

Barrett v Morgan [2000] 2 AC 264 ... 176

Basham, Re [1986] 1 WLR 1498 ... 383–4, 386, 388, 389

Batchelor v Marlow [2003] 1 WLR 764 ... 500, 501

Bates v Donaldson [1896] 2 QB 241 ... 193

Baxter v Four Oaks Properties Ltd [1965] Ch 816 ... 549

Beard, Re [1908] 1 Ch 383 ... 143

Beardman v Wilson (1869) LR 4 CP 57 ... 162

Bedson v Bedson [1965] 2 QB 666 ... 355

Beesly v Hallwood Estates Ltd [1960] 1 WLR 549 ... 188

Benn v Hardinge (1992) 66 P & CR 246 ... 529

Berkley v Poulett (1976) 242 EG 39 ... 574

Berkshire v Grubb (1881) 18 ChD 616 ... 515

Beswick v Beswick [1966] Ch 538 ... 536

Bettison v Langton [2002] 1 AC 27; [2000] Ch 54 ... 503, 504

BHP Petroleum Ltd v Chesterfield Ltd [2002] Ch 194 ... 204–5

Bickel v Duke of Westminster [1977] QB 517 ... 191

Biggs v Hoddinott [1898] 2 Ch 307 ... 444

Bignold, Ex parte (1834) 4 Deac & Ch 259 ... 455

Billson v Residential Apartments Ltd [1992] 1 AC 494 ... 232, 233

Binions v Evans [1972] Ch 359 ... 369–70, 420, 422, 424, 429

Bird v Syme-Thomson [1979] 1 WLR 440 ... 100

Birmingham Citizens Permanent Building Society v Caunt [1962] Ch 883 ... 447, 453

Birmingham Midshires Mortgage Services Ltd v Sabherwal (2000) 80 P & CR 256 ... 290, 301, 393–4

Bond v Nottingham Corporation [1940] Ch 429 ... 527

Borland's Trustee v Steel Bros & Co Ltd [1901] 1 Ch 279 ... 339

Borman v Griffith [1930] 1 Ch 493 ... 499, 510, 515

Borwick, Re [1933] Ch 657 ... 143

Boston's Will Trusts [1956] Ch 395 ... 324

Boustany v Pigott (1995) 69 P & CR 298 ... 487

Boyer v Warbey [1953] 1 QB 234 ... 182, 211, 212

Boyle's Claim, Re [1961] 1 WLR 339 ... 106

BP Properties Ltd v Buckler (1987) 55 P & CR 337 ... 124

Brace v Duchess of Marlborough (1728) 2 P Wms 491 ... 472

Bradburn v Lindsay [1983] 2 All ER 408 ... 527–8

Bradley v Carritt [1903] AC 253 ... 444

Breams Property Investment Co v Stroulger [1948] 2 KB 1 ... 150, 166, 209–10

Brent LBC v Cronin (1997) 30 HLR 43 ... 401

Bridges v Mees [1957] Ch 475 ... 115

Bridgett & Hayes's Contract [1928] Ch 163 ... 324

Bridle v Ruby [1989] QB 169 ... 516, 519, 525

Brikom Investments Ltd v Carr [1979] QB 467 ... 387

Bristol and West v Bartlett [2003] 1 WLR 284 ... 453

British General Insurance Co Ltd v Attorney-General (1945) 12 LJNCCR 113 ... 453

British Railways Board v Glass [1965] Ch 538 ... 498

British Telecommunications plc v Department of the Environment [1996] NPC 148 ... 233

Broomfield v Williams [1897] 1 Ch 602 ... 513, 515

Brown v Wilson (1949); (unreported) ... 175

Browne v Flower [1911] 1 Ch 219 ... 186

Brunner v Greenslade [1971] Ch 993 ... 550

Bruton v London & Quadrant Housing Association [2000] 1 AC 406; [1998] QB 834 ... 146, 174, 178, 179, 399, 405, 408, 409–12, 412

Buchanan-Wollaston's Conveyance, Re [1939] Ch 738 ... 287–8

Buckinghamshire County Council v Moran [1990] Ch 623 ... 117–18, 120–1, 122

Buckland v Butterfield (1820) 2 Brod & Bing 54 ... 574

Bull v Bull [1955] 1 QB 234 ... 281, 347, 348, 351, 359, 361

Bull v Hutchens (1863) 32 Beav 615 ... 56

Bullock v Dommitt (1796) 2 Chit 608 ... 195

Burgess v Rawnsley [1975] Ch 429 ... 356

Burnett (Marjorie) Ltd v Barclay [1981] 1 EGLR 41 ... 189

Burns v Burns [1984] 1 Ch 317 ... 374, 376–7, 378, 565

Burrows v Lang [1901] 2 Ch 502 ... 502

Bury v Pope (1588) Cro Eliz 118 ... 518

Byford, Re [2004] 1 FLR 56 ... 362

Calisher v Forbes (1871) LR 7 Ch App 109 ... 465

Campbell v Griffin [2001] EWCA Civ 990; [2001] W & TLR 981 ... 385, 387, 389

Campbell v Holyland (1877) 7 ChD 166 ... 450

Cannan v Grimley (1850) 9 CB 634 ... 167

Cardiothoracic Institute v Shrewdcrest Ltd [1986] 1 WLR 368 ... 155

Carl-Zeiss Stiftung v Herbert Smith & Co. (No 2) [1969] 2 Ch 276 ... 368

Carter v Wade (1877) 4 ChD 605 ... 450

Cattell, Re [1914] 1 Ch 177 ... 341

Caunce v Caunce [1969] 1 WLR 286 ... 61, 290

Celsteel Ltd v Alton House Holdings Ltd [1985] 1 WLR 204 ... 90, 505, 527

Central London Commercial Estates Ltd v Kato Kagaku Co Ltd [1998] 4 All ER 948 ... 117, 128

Central London Property Trust Ltd v High Trees House Ltd [1947] 1 KB 130 ... 119–20, 382

Centrovincial Estates plc v Bulk Storage Ltd (1983) 46 P & CR 393 ... 206

Chaffe v Kingsley [2000] 79 P & CR 404 ... 499, 511

Chandler v Kerley [1978] 1 WLR 693 ... 416

Charter v Mortgage Agency Services Number Two Ltd [2003] 15 EG 138 (NS) ... 492

Chartered Trust plc v Davies (1997) 76 P & CR 397 ... 172, 173, 188

Chelsea Yacht and Boat Club Ltd v Pope [2000] 1 WLR 1941 ... 576

Cheltenham & Gloucester Building Society v Norgan [1996] 1 WLR 343 ... 454

Cheltenham & Gloucester plc v Krausz [1997] 1 All ER 21 ... 451, 453

Chester v Buckingham Travel Ltd [1981] 1 WLR 96 ... 199

Chhokar v Chhokar [1984] FLR 313 ... 98

China & South Sea Bank Ltd v Tan Soon Gin [1990] 1 AC 536 ... 459

Chowood Ltd v Lyall [1930] 2 Ch 156 ... 105–6

Chowood's Registered Land, Re [1933] Ch 574 ... 106

Church of England Building Society v Piskor [1954] Ch 553 ... 178, 180

CIBC Mortgages v Pitt [1994] 1 AC 200 ... 483, 484–5

Cinderella Rockerfellas Ltd v Rudd [2003] 3 All ER 219 ... 576

Citibank International plc v Kessler (1999) EGCS 40 ... 446

Citro, Re [1991] Ch 142 ... 285

City and Metropolitan Properties Ltd v Greycroft Ltd [1987] 1 WLR 1085 ... 211

City of London Brewery Co Ltd v Tenant (1873) LR 9 Ch App 212 ... 499

City of London Building Society v Flegg [1988] AC 54 ... 101, 289–90, 301, 351, 393, 479

City of London Corporation v Fell [1994] 1 AC 458 ... 202, 207, 209

City Permanent Building Society v Miller [1952] Ch 840 ... 90

Cityland and Property (Holdings) Ltd v Dabrah [1968] Ch 166 ... 438, 444

Clore v Theatrical Properties Ltd [1936] 3 All ER 483 ... 421

Coatsworth v Johnson (1886) 55 LJ QB 220 ... 157

Colls v Home & Colonial Stores Ltd [1904] AC 179 ... 499

Commission for the New Towns v Cooper (Great Britain) Ltd [1995] Ch 259 ... 31, 34–5, 37

Commonwealth of Australia v Verwayen (1990) 170 CLR 394 ... 391

Congleton Corporation v Pattison (1808) 10 East 130 ... 210

Cooke v Head [1972] 1 WLR 518 ... 375, 380

Coomber, Re [1911] 1 Ch 723 ... 490

Cooper v Henderson (1982) 263 EG 592 ... 227

Co-operative Insurance Society Ltd v Argyll Stores (Holdings) Ltd [1998] AC 1; [1996] Ch 286 ... 222, 224

Copeland v Greenhalf [1952] Ch 488 ... 500

Corbett v Halifax Building Society [2003] 1 WLR 964 ... 462

Cordell v Second Clanfield Properties Ltd [1969] 2 Ch 9 ... 507

Cornish v Brook Green Laundry Ltd [1959] 1 QB 394 ... 157

Cory v Davies [1923] 2 Ch 95 ... 508

Cottage Holiday Associates Ltd v Customs and Excise Commissioners [1983] 1 QB 735 ... 147

Cottey v National Provincial Bank of England Ltd (1904) 20 TLR 607 ... 471

Cowcher v Cowcher [1972] 1 WLR 425 ... 257

Cowell v Rosehill Racecourse Co Ltd (1937) 56 CLR 605 ... 418

Cowper v Laidler [1903] 2 Ch 337 ... 527

Crabb v Arun DC [1976] 1 Ch 179 ... 382, 383, 388, 389

Crago v Julian [1992] 1 WLR 372 ... 161

Crancour Ltd v Da Silvaesa [1986] 1 EGLR 80 ... 401, 407

Credit Lyonnais Bank Nederland NV v Burch [1997] 1 All ER 144 ... 485

Cricklewood Property and Investment Trust Ltd v Leighton's Investment Trust Ltd [1945] AC 221 ... 579

Crow v Wood [1971] 1 QB 77 ... 501, 554

Cuckmere Brick Co v Mutual Finance Ltd [1971] Ch 949 ... 460

Dalton v Angus & Co (1881) 6 App Cas 740 ... 500, 518, 526

Dalton v Pickard [1926] 2 KB 545 ... 167

Daly v Edwardes (1900) 83 LT 548 ... 423

Dance v Triplow [1992] 1 EGLR 190 ... 523

Daniel v North (1809) 11 East 372 ... 517

Dano Ltd v Earl Cadogan [2003] 12 P & CR 10 ... 534–5

Darby v Read (1675) Rep T Finch 226 ... 441

Darling v Clue (1864) 4 F & F 329 ... 518

Das v Linden Mews Ltd [2003] 2 P & CR 4 ... 498

Davey v Durrant (1857) 1 De G & J 535 ... 459

Davies v Du Paver [1953] 1 QB 184 ... 521, 523

Davies v Sweet [1962] 2 QB 300 ... 38

Davis v Lisle [1936] 2 KB 434 ... 416

Davis v Whitby [1974] Ch 186 ... 517

Dawson, Re (1888) 39 ChD 155 ... 331

Dayani v Bromley LBC [1999] 3 EGLR 144 ... 198

Dean, Re (1889) 41 ChD 552 ... 328

Dean and Chapter of the Cathedral and Metropolitan Church of Christ Canterbury v Whitbread (1995) 72 P & CR 9 ... 178

Dearle v Hall (1823) 3 Russ 1 ... 464–6

Debtor, Re (No 13A-10–1995) [1995] 1 WLR 1127 ... 228

Dennis v McDonald [1982] Fam 63 ... 362

Dewar v Dewar [1975] 1 WLR 1532 ... 367

Dewar v Goodman [1909] AC 72 ... 210

D'Eyncourt v Gregory (1866) LR 3 Eq 382 ... 575

DHN Food Distributors v Tower Hamlets LBC [1976] 1 WLR 852 ... 422

Dickinson v Grand Junction Canal Co Ltd (1852) 7 Exch 282 ... 499

Diligent Finance Ltd v Alleyne (1972) 23 P & CR 346 ... 54

Dillwyn v Llewellyn (1862) 4 De GF & J 517 ... 386, 388, 424

Diment v Foot Ltd [1974] 1 WLR 1427 ... 520

Doe d Clarke v Smaridge (1845) 7 QB 957 ... 177

Doe d Gray v Stanion (1836) 1 M & W 700 ... 177

Doe d Hanley v Wood (1819) 2 B & Ald 724 ... 415

Doe d Henniker v Watt (1828) 8 B & C 308 ... 183

Doe d Lockwood v Clarke (1807) 8 East 185 ... 164

Doe d Shore v Porter (1789) 3 TR 13 ... 165

Doe d Wilson v Phillips (1824) 2 Bing 13 ... 227

Dolphin's Conveyance, Re [1970] Ch 654 ... 548, 549

Downsview Nominees Ltd v First City Corporation Ltd (No 1) [1993] AC 295 ... 459

Doyle and O'Hara's Contract, Re [1899] IR 113 ... 194

Drake v Whipp (1995) 28 HLR 531 ... 372, 379, 380–1, 571

Duke of Westminster v Swinton [1948] 1 KB 524 ... 233

Duke v Wynne [1990] 1 WLR 766 ... 406–7

Dunbar v Plant [1998] FLR 157 ... 357

Dunn v Blackdown Properties Ltd [1961] Ch 433 ... 340

Dunraven Securities v Holloway (1982) 264 EG 709 ... 231

Dunwell (P) v Hunt (1996) 72 P & CR D6 ... 405

Duppa v Mayo (1669) Saund 282 ... 228

Dyce v Lady James Hay (1852) 1 Macq 305 ... 495

Dyer v Dyer (1788) 2 Cox 92 ... 367

Earl of Berkeley, Re [1968] Ch 744 ... 342

Earl of Leicester v Wells-next-the-Sea UDC [1973] Ch 110 ... 545

Eaton v Swansea Waterworks Co (1851) 17 QB 267 ... 516

Ecclesiastical Commissioners for England v Kino (1880) 14 ChD 213 ... 529

Ecclesiastical Commissioners for England's Conveyance, Re [1936] Ch 430 ... 535

Edgar, Re [1939] 1 All ER 635 ... 143

Edwardes v Barrington (1901) 85 LT 650 ... 423

Egerton v Harding [1975] QB 62 ... 501

88 Berkeley Road NW9, Re [1971] Ch 648 ... 352

Elias (Emile) & Co Ltd v Pine Groves Ltd [1993] 1 WLR 305 ... 549

Elitestone Ltd v Morris [1997] 1 WLR 687 ... 575

Ellenborough Park, Re [1956] Ch 131 ... 495, 496, 497, 499, 501

Elliott v Johnson (1866) LR 2 QB 120 ... 211

Ellis v Lambeth BC (1999) The Times 28 Sept 1999 ... 115

Elliston v Reacher [1908] 2 Ch 374 ... 549

Errington v Errington [1952] 1 KB 290 ... 400, 403, 421–2, 423, 424, 428, 429

Esso Petroleum Co Ltd v Fumegrange Ltd [1994] 2 EGLR 90 ... 401

Eves v Eves [1975] 1 WLR 1338 ... 370, 375, 380

Expert Clothing Service and Sales Ltd v Hillgate House Ltd [1986] 1 Ch 340 ... 227, 229, 230, 231, 232

Eyre v Marsden (1838) 2 Keen 564 ... 342

Facchini v Bryson [1952] 1 TLR 1386 ... 403, 404, 405

Fairclough v Swan Brewery Co Ltd [1912] AC 565 ... 444

Fairweather v St Marylebone Property Co Ltd [1963] AC 510 ... 126, 128

Falco Finance Ltd v Michael Gough Solicitor's Journal 22 Jan 1999 ... 445

Family Housing Association v Jones [1990] 1 WLR 779 ... 403, 407, 408

Farnol Eades Irvine & Co Ltd, Re [1915] 1 Ch 22 ... 450

Farrar v Farrars Ltd (1888) 40 ChD 395 ... 462

Federated Homes Ltd v Mill Lodge Properties Ltd [1980] 1 WLR 594 ... 546, 547, 550

Fernandez v McDonald [2004] 1 WLR 1027 ... 166

Ferrishurst Ltd v Wallcite Ltd [1999] Ch 355 ... 94

First National Bank v Achampong [2003] unreported ... 360

First National Bank v Syed [1991] 2 All ER 250 ... 453

First National Bank v Thompson [1996] Ch 231 ... 179

First National Securities v Hegarty [1984] 1 All ER 139 ... 355

Firstpost Homes Ltd v Johnson [1995] 1 WLR 1567 ... 35, 40–1

Fitzgerald v Firbank [1897] 2 Ch 96 ... 413

Fitzpatrick v Sterling Housing Association Ltd [2001] 1 AC 27 ... 569–70

Flexman v Corbett [1930] 1 Ch 672 ... 198–9

Footwear Corp Ltd v Amplight Properties Ltd [1998] 3 All ER 52 ... 193

Foster, Re [1938] 3 All ER 357 ... 535

Foster v Robinson [1951] 1 KB 149 ... 167, 403

Four-Maids Ltd v Dudley Marshall (Properties) Ltd [1957] Ch 317 ... 447

Freeguard v Royal Bank of Scotland plc The Times 25 April 2002 ... 461

Friends' Provident Life Office v British Railways Board [1996] 1 All ER 336 ... 168, 206

Fry v Lane (1889) 40 ChD 312 ... 486

Fuller v Happy Shopper Markets Ltd [2001] 2 EGLR 32 ... 226

Fuller's Contract, Re [1933] Ch 652 ... 349

Furness v Bond (1888) 4 TLR 457 ... 149

Gafford v Graham (1998) 77 P & CR 73 ... 556

Gaite's Will Trusts, Re [1949] 1 All ER 459 ... 331

Gardner v Hodgson's Kingston Brewery Co Ltd [1974] 1 WLR 1427 ... 526

Garfitt v Allen (1887) 37 ChD 48 ... 455

Garston v Scottish Widows Fund and Life Assurance Society [1998] 1 WLR 1583 ... 166

Gayford v Moffat (1868) LR 4 Ch App 133 ... 517

Ghaidan v Godin-Mendoza [2003] 2 WLR 478 ... 570

Gilbey v Rush [1906] 1 Ch 11 ... 319

Gillett v Holt [2001] Ch 210 ... 384–5, 387, 388, 389

Gissing v Gissing [1971] AC 886 ... 370, 372, 373–6, 378, 379, 394, 395, 564

Glass v Kencakes Ltd [1966] 1 QB 611 ... 231

Go West Ltd v Spigarolo [2002] 2 WLR 987 ... 193

Godden v Merthyr Tydfil Housing Association [1997] NPC 1 ... 32, 41

Goldberg v Edwards [1950] Ch 247 ... 500, 512

Goodman v Gallant [1986] Fam 106 ... 352

Goodman v J. Eban Ltd [1954] 1 QB 550 ... 35

Gorton v Gregory (1862) 3 B & S 90 ... 210

Gouldsworth v Knights (1843) 11 M & W 337 ... 180

Governor and Company of the Bank of Scotland v Hill and Tudor (No 2) [2002] 29 EG 152 (NS) ... 492

Grand Junction Co Ltd v Bates [1954] 2 QB 160 ... 437

Grant v Edwards [1986] 1 Ch 638 ... 394

Gray v Taylor [1998] 1 WLR 1093 ... 400, 405, 406

Greasley v Cooke [1980] 1 WLR 1306 ... 386–7, 387, 388, 389, 424–5

Great Northern Railway Co v Arnold (1916) 33 TLR 114 ... 164

Green v Ashco Horticultural Ltd [1966] 1 WLR 889 ... 502

Greenwich Healthcare NHS Trust v London and Quadrant Housing Trust [1998] 1 WLR 1749 ... 527

Gregg v Richards [1926] Ch 521 ... 514

Griffiths v Young [1970] Ch 675 ... 38

Grigsby v Melville [1974] 1 WLR 80 ... 500, 501

Grindal v Hooper [1999] EGCS 150 ... 354

Grossman v Hooper [2001] 2 EGLR 82 ... 33

Grundt v Great Boulder Pty Gold Mines Ltd (1937) 59 CLR 641 ... 388

Habermann v Koehler (1996) 73 P & CR 515 ... 424, 426

Habermann v Koehler (No 2) [2000] TLR 825 ... 392, 427

Hadjiloucas v Crean [1988] 1 WLR 1006 ... 407

Hall, In the Estate of [1914] P 1 ... 357

Hall v Ewin (1887) 37 ChD 74 ... 543

Hall v Hall [1982] 3 FLR 379 ... 375–6, 377

Halsall v Brizell [1957] Ch 169 ... 426, 551, 552

Hambro v Duke of Marlborough [1994] Ch 158 ... 316

Hamilton v Geraghty (1901) 1 SRNSW Eq 81 ... 428

Hammersmith LBC v Monk [1992] 1 AC 478 ... 164, 172–3

Hammond v Farrow [1904] 2 KB 332 ... 153

Hammond v Mitchell [1991] 1 WLR 1127 ... 571

Hampden v Earl of Buckinghamshire [1893] 2 ch 531 ... 319

Handel v St Stephen's Close [1994] 1 EGLR 70 ... 500

Hanning v Top Deck Travel Group Ltd (1993) 68 P & CR 14 ... 516

Hannon v 169 Queen's Gate Ltd (1999) The Times 23 Nov 1999 ... 551

Hardwick v Johnson [1978] 1 WLR 683 ... 416

Harmer v Jumbil (Nigeria) Tin Areas Ltd [1921] 1 Ch 200 ... 188

Harrison v Malet (1886) 3 TLR 58 ... 196

Harrow LBC v Qazi [2003] 3 WLR 792 ... 135

Hart v O'Connor [1985] 1 AC 1000 ... 487

Harvey v Pratt [1965] 1 WLR 1025 ... 149

Haskell v Marlow [1928] 2 KB 45 ... 198

Hastings & Thanet Building Society v Goddard [1970] 1 WLR 1544 ... 457

Re Haynes (1887) 37 ChD 306 ... 318

Haywood v Brunswick Permanent Benefit Building Society (1881) 8 QBD 403 ... 541

Haywood v Mallalieu (1883) 25 ChD 357 ... 500

Heathe v Heathe (1740) 2 Ark 121 ... 347

Hemingway Securities Ltd v Dunraven Ltd [1995] 1 EGLR 61 ... 217

Henderson v Eason (1851) 17 QB 701 ... 362

Heslop v Burns [1974] 1 WLR 1241 ... 178, 403, 413

Hewitt v Loosemore (1851) 9 Hare 449 ... 472

Hill v Barclay (1810) 16 Ves Jun 402 ... 223, 224

Hill v Booth [1930] 1 KB 381 ... 152

Hill v Tupper (1863) 2 Hurl & C 121 ... 413, 497

Hillingdon Estates Co v Stonefield Estates Ltd [1952] Ch 627 ... 45

Hodgson v Marks [1971] Ch 892 ... 93, 99, 100, 101, 103, 108, 367

Hodson and Howe's Contract, Re (1887) 35 ChD 668 ... 456

Hoffmann v Fineberg [1949] Ch 245 ... 228, 231

Hoggett v Hoggett (1979) 39 P & CR 121 ... 98

Holbeck Hall Hotel v Scarborough BC [2000] QB 836 ... 500, 528

Holland v Hodgson (1872) LR 7 CP 328 ... 575

Hollins v Verney (1884) 13 QBD 304 ... 517

Holmes, Re (1885) 29 ChD 786 ... 465

Hood v Oglander (1865) 34 Beav 513 ... 143

Hooper v Sherman [1994] NPC 153 ... 34

Hope v Walter [1900] 1 Ch 257 ... 47

Hopgood v Brown [1955] 1 WLR 213 ... 425

Horrocks v Forray [1976] 1 WLR 230 ... 416

Houlder Bros v Gibbs [1925] 1 Ch 575 ... 190, 191

Hounslow LBC v Twickenham Garden Developments Ltd [1971] Ch 233 ... 415, 418

Hudston v Viney [1921] 1 Ch 98 ... 472

Hughes v Cook (1994) *The Independent* 21 March 1994 ... 118

Hughes v Williams (1806) 12 Ves Jr 493 ... 459

Hulme v Brigham [1943] KB 152 ... 575

Hunt v Elmes (1860) 2 De G F & J 578 ... 471

Hunt v Luck [1902] 1 Ch 428 ... 61, 62, 102, 478

Hunter v Babbage [1994] EGCS 8 ... 356

Hunter v Canary Wharf Ltd [1997]AC 655 ... 401

Hurrell v Littlejohn [1904] 1 Ch 689 ... 320

Hurst v Picture Theatres Ltd [1915] 1 KB 1 ... 418, 421

Hussein v Mehlman [1992] 2 EGLR 87 ... 171, 172, 221

Hussey v Palmer [1972] 1 WLR 1286 ... 372, 376

Hyman v Van den Bergh [1908] 1 Ch 167 ... 523, 524

Hypo-Mortgage Services Ltd v Robinson (1997) *The Times* 2 Jan 1997 ... 100

IDC Group Ltd v Clark [1992] EGLR 187 ... 413, 424

Ideal Film Renting Co v Nielson [1921] 1 Ch 575 ... 194

Industrial Properties (Barton Hill) Ltd v Associated Electrical Industries Ltd [1977] QB 580 ... 178, 179, 180

Ingram v IRC [1997] 4 All ER 395 ... 174

Inns, Re [1947] Ch 576 ... 274, 300

International Drilling Fluids Ltd v Louisville Investments (Uxbridge) Ltd [1986] Ch 513 ... 190, 191, 193

Inwards v Baker [1965] 2 QB 29 ... 386, 388, 389, 424, 425

Iron Trades Employers Insurance Association Ltd v Union Land & House Investors Ltd [1937] Ch 313 ... 446

Ironside v Cook (1978) 41 P & CR 326 ... 526

Ives (E R) Investment Ltd v High [1967] 2 QB 379 ... 60, 425–6, 428, 507, 552

Ivimey v Stocker (1866) LR 1 Ch App 396 ... 517

Jaison Property Development Co Ltd v Roux Restaurants Ltd (1996) 74 P & CR 357 ... 190

James v Evans [2000] 3 EGLR 1 ... 43–4

James v Plant (1836) 4 Ad & El 749 ... 515

James v Stevenson [1893] AC 162 ... 529

Jared v Clements [1903] 1 Ch 428 ... 18

Javad v Mohammed Aqil [1991] 1 WLR 1007 ... 155, 178

Jee v Audley (1787) 1 Cox 324 ... 331

Jelson Ltd v Derby County Council [1999] 3 EGLR 1991 ... 35

Jennings v Cairns (2003) *The Times* 16 Nov 2003 ... 492

Jennings v Rice [2003] 1 P & CR 8 ... 385, 390, 391–2

Jeune v Queen's Cross Properties Ltd [1974] Ch 97 ... 223–4, 224

Jones (James) & Sons Ltd v Earl of Tankerville [1909] 2 Ch 440 ... 415

Jones v Challenger [1961] 1 QB 176 ... 288

Jones v Jones (1876) 1 QBD 279 ... 143

Jones v Lavington [1903] 1 KB 253 ... 187

Jones v Morgan [2002] 1 EGLR 125 ... 443

Jones v Pritchard [1908] 1 Ch 630 ... 500, 527

Jordeson v Sutton, Smithcoates & Drypool Gas Co Ltd [1898] 2 Ch 614 ... 500

Joscelyne v Nissen [1970] 2 QB 86 ... 32, 47

Keech v Sandford (1726) Sel Cas T King 61 ... 322

Kelly, Re [1932] IR 255 ... 328

Kelly v Monck (1795) 3 Ridg Parl Rep 205 ... 143

Kenny v Preen [1963] 1 QB 499 ... 186

Keppell v Bailey (1834) 2 My & K 517 ... 540

Keymer v Summers (1769) Bull NP 74 ... 518

Kilgour v Gaddes [1904] 1 KB 457 ... 517, 522

Killey v Clough [1996] NPC 38 ... 379

Killick v Second Covent Garden Property Co Ltd [1973] 1 WLR 658 ... 192

Kinch v Bullard [1999] 1 WLR 423 ... 353–4

King, Re [1963] Ch 459 ... 211

King v David Allen & Sons (Billposting) Ltd [1916] 2 AC 54 ... 421, 423

King's Trusts, Re (1892) 29 LR Ir 401 ... 142

Kingsnorth Finance Co Ltd v Tizard [1986] 1 WLR 783 ... 61–2, 99, 367, 372, 566

Knightsbridge Estates Trust Ltd v Byrne [1939] Ch 441 ... 443

Kreglinger v New Patagonia Meat & Cold Storage Co Ltd [1914] AC 25 ... 441, 444

Lace v Chantler [1944] KB 368 ... 7, 146, 149, 150, 166

Ladies' Hosiery and Underwear Ltd v Parker [1930] 1 Ch 304 ... 155

Lagan Navigation Co v Lambeg Bleaching, Dyeing & Finishing Co Ltd [1927] AC 226 ... 526

Lake v Gibson (1729) 1 Eq Rep 290 ... 348

Lane v Cox [1897] 1 QB 415 ... 196

Langton v Langton (1995) *The Times* 24 Feb ... 480, 486

Lashbrook v Cock (1816) 2 Mer 70 ... 348

Lavender v Betts [1942] 2 All ER 72 ... 186

Leach v Jay (1878) 9 ChD 42 ... 124–5

Lee-Parker v Izzet [1971] 1 WLR 1688 ... 223

Leigh v Jack (1879) 5 Ex D 264 ... 120

Leigh v Taylor [1902] AC 157 ... 574

Leigh's Settled Estates, Re [1926] Ch 852 ... 261

Leverhulme (No 2), Re [1943] 2 All ER 274 ... 329

Levy Estate Trust, Re [2000] CLY 5263 ... 331

Lewen v Dodd (1595) Cro Eliz 443 ... 347

Lewis v Fank Love Ltd [1961] 1 WLR 261 ... 443

Liverpool City Council v Irwin [1977] AC 239 ...
    502, 508

Liverpool Corporation v Coghill & Sons Ltd
    [1918] 1 Ch 307 ... 516

Lloyd v Banks (1868) LR 3 Ch App 488 ... 17

Lloyd v Dugdale [2002] 2 P & CR 167 ... 44, 392,
    424

Lloyds Bank plc v Byrne & Byrne [1993] 1 FLR
    369 ... 285

Lloyds Bank plc v Carrick [1996] 4 All ER 630 ...
    29, 58, 393, 426

Lloyds Bank plc v Rosset [1991] 1 AC 107; [1989]
    Ch 350 ... 103, 377–8, 394, 564–5

Lock v Pearce [1893] 2 Ch 271 ... 228

Lodge v Wakefield City Council [1995] 38 EG 136
    ... 118

London and Blenheim Estates Ltd v Ladbroke
    Retail Parks Ltd [1994] 1 WLR 31 ... 496, 500,
    501

London County Council v Allen [1914] 3 KB 642
    ... 542

Long v Gowlett [1923] 2 Ch 177 ... 512

Long v Tower Hamlets LBC [1998] Ch 197 ... 153

Low v Fry (1935) 51 TLR 322 ... 38

Lurcott v Wakeley [1911] 1 KB 905 ... 195

Lynes v Snaith [1899] 1 QB 486 ... 403

Lysaght v Edwards (1876) 2 ChD 499 ... 45

McCausland v Duncan Lawrie Ltd [1997] 1 WLR
    38 ... 32–3

Macepark (Whittlebury) Ltd v Sargeant [2003] 1
    WLR 2284 ... 498

Macleay, Re (1875) LR 20 Eq 186 ... 144

Maddison v Alderson (1883) 8 App Cas 467 ... 40

Malayan Credit Ltd v Jack Chia-MPH Ltd [1986]
    Ac 549 ... 349

Malory Enterprises Ltd v Cheshire Homes (UK)
    Ltd [2002] Ch 21 ... 96–7

Manchester Airport plc v Dutton [2000] 1 QB 133
    ... 401, 413

Manfield & Sons Ltd v Botchin [1970] 2 QB 612
    ... 150, 155, 178

Mann v Lovejoy (1826) Ry & M 355 ... 177

Mannai Investment Co Ltd v Eagle Star Life
    Assurance Co Ltd [1997] AC 749 ... 165–6

Marcroft Wagons Ltd v Smith [1951] 2 KB 496 ...
    404

Markfield Investments Ltd v Evans [2001] 1 WLR
    1321 ... 124

Markham v Paget [1908] 1 Ch 697 ... 186, 196

Marquess of Zetland v Driver [1939] Ch 1 ... 545

Marten v Flight Refuelling Ltd [1962] Ch 115 ...
    546

Martin v Smith (1874) LR 9 Ex 50 ... 154

Massey v Boulden [2003] 1 WLR 1792 ... 498

Matharu v Matharu (1994) 68 P & CR 93 ... 420

Matthews v Godday (1861) 31 LJ Ch 282 ... 440

Matthey v Curling [1922] 2 AC 180 ... 169

Maughan, Re (1885) 14 QBD 956 ... 158

Mayo, Re [1943] Ch 302 ... 262, 272, 358, 359

Medforth v Blake [2000] Ch 86 ... 461

Mellor v Spateman (1669) 1 Saund 339 ... 503

Mellor v Watkins (1874) LR 9 QB 400 ... 175

Middlemas v Stevens [1901] 1 Ch 574 ... 319,
    323

Midland Bank plc v Cooke [1995] 4 All ER 562 ...
    380, 564, 571

Midland Bank Trust Co Ltd v Green [1981] AC
    513 ... 16, 57, 58, 478

Midland Railway Co's Agreement, Re [1971] 1
    CH 725 ... 149

Mikeover Ltd v Brady [1989] 3 All ER 618 ... 408,
    409

Miller v Emcer Products Ltd [1956] Ch 304 ...
    500

Mills v Silver [1991] Ch 271 ... 519, 523, 525, 526

Milmo v Carreras [1946] KB 306 ... 162

Milverton Group Ltd v Warner World Ltd [1995]
    2 EGLR 28 ... 211

Mint v Good [1951] 1 KB 517 ... 197

Mogridge v Clapp [1892] 3 Ch 382 ... 321

Moody v Steggles (1879) 12 ChD 261 ... 497

Moore, Re (1888) 39 ChD 116 ... 141

Morgan's Lease, Re [1972] Ch 1 ... 321

Morley v Bird (1798) 3 Ves Jun 628 ... 349

Morrells of Oxford Ltd v Oxford United FC Ltd
    [2001] Ch 459 ... 542, 543, 545

Mortgage Corporation v Shaire [2001] Ch 743 ...
    283, 284–6, 359, 360, 566

Moses v Lovegrove [1952] 2 QB 533 ... 119

Moule v Garrett (1872) LR 7 Ex 101 ... 202

Mounsey v Ismay (1865) 3 Hurl & C 486 ... 499

Mount Carmel Investments Ltd v Peter Thurlow
    Ltd [1988] 1 WLR 1078 ... 113

Muller v Trafford [1901] 1 Ch 54 ... 339

Multiservice Bookbinding Ltd v Marden [1979]
    Ch 84 ... 445

Mutual Life Assurance Society v Langley (1886)
    32 ChD 460 ... 465

Nash v Eads (1880) 25 Sol J 95 ... 459

National and Provincial Building Society v Lloyd
    [1996] 1 All ER 630 ... 454

National Carriers Ltd v Panalpina (Northern) Ltd
    [1981] AC 675 ... 169–70, 171, 173

National Provincial Bank v Ainsworth [1965] AC
    1175 ... 423, 567

National Provincial Bank Ltd v Hastings Car
    Mart Ltd [1964] Ch 665 ... 61, 93–4, 423

National Westminster Bank plc v Amin [2002] 1
    FLR 735 ... 488–9

National Westminster Bank plc v Morgan [1985]
    AC 686 ... 483, 484

National Westminster Bank plc v Skelton [1993] 1 WLR 72 ... 447

Neaverson v Peterborough Rural District Council [1902] 1 Ch 557 ... 519

Newton Abbot Cooperative Society Ltd v Williamson & Treadgold Ltd [1952] Ch 286 ... 546

Nicholls v Ely Beet Sugar Factory [1931] 2 Ch 84 ... 113

Nickerson v Barraclough [1981] Ch 426 ... 508

90 Thornhill Road, Re [1970] Ch 261 ... 319

Northchurch Estates Ltd v Daniels [1947] Ch 117 ... 188–9, 189

Northern Counties of England Fire Insurance Co v Whipp (1884) 26 ChD 482 ... 471

Norton, Re [1929] 1 Ch 84 ... 261

Nunn v Dalrymple (1989) 59 P & CR 231 ... 400

Nynehead Developments Ltd v RH Fibreboard Containers Ltd [1999] 1 EGLR 7 ... 172

Oak Co-operative Building Society v Blackburn [1968] Ch 730 ... 54

Ocean Estates Ltd v Pinder [1969] 2 AC 19 ... 122

Oceanic Village Ltd v United Attractions Ltd [2000] Ch 234 ... 217–18

Old Grovebury Manor Farm v W Seymour Plant Sales [1979] 3 All ER 504 ... 194

Oliver v Hinton [1899] 2 Ch 264 ... 472

Olympia & York Canary Wharf Ltd v Oil Property Investments Ltd [1994] 2 EGLR 48 ... 193

Orchard Trading Estate Management Ltd v Johnson Security Ltd [2002] 18 EG 155 ... 554

Owen v Gadd [1956] 2 QB 99 ... 186

P & A Swift Investments v Combined English Stores Group plc [1989] AC 632 ... 210, 538

P & S Platt Ltd v Crouch [2004] 1 P & CR ... 513

Paddington Building Society v Mendelsohn (1985) 50 P & CR 244 ... 101

Paine v Meller (1801) 6 Ves Jr 349 ... 45

Palk v Mortgage Services Funding plc [1993] Ch 330 ... 447, 450, 451, 460

Palmer v Fletcher (1663) 1 Lev 122 ... 187

Paradine v Jane (1647) Al 26 ... 169

Parc (Battersea) Ltd v Hutchinson [1999] 2 EGLR 33 ... 162

Parker v Boggon [1947] KB 346 ... 192–3

Parker v Jones [1910] 2 KB 32 ... 194

Parker v Taswell (1858) 2 De G & J 559 ... 157

Parker v Webb (1693) 3 Salk 5; 91 ER 656 ... 211

Parker's Settled Estates, Re [1928] Ch 247 ... 261

Pascoe v Turner [1979] 1 WLR 431 ... 382, 388, 389, 391, 419–20, 565

Passmore v Morland [1999] 1 EGLR 51 ... 195

Pawlett v Attorney-General (1667) Hadres 465 ... 442

Payne v Inwood (1996) 74 P & CR 42 ... 513, 515

Payne v Webb (1874) LR 19 Eq 26 ... 347

Peace v Morris (1869) Lr 5 Ch App 227 ... 457

Peacock v Custins [2002] 1 WLR 1815 ... 497, 498

Peat v Chapman (1750) 1 Ves Sen 542 ... 347

Peckham v Ellison [2000] 79 P & CR 276 ... 511

Peck's Contract, Re [1893] 2 Ch 315 ... 514

Peel's Release, Re [1921] 2 Ch 218 ... 327–8

Pennell v Payne [1995] QB 192 ... 175–6, 187

Penniall v Harborne (1848) 11 QB 368 ... 195

Perera v Vandiyar [1953] 1 WLR 672 ... 185

Perry Herrick v Attwood (1857) 2 De G & J 21 ... 471

Perry v Fitzhowe (1846) 8 QB 757 ... 526

Pesticcio v Huet (2003) 73 BMLR 57 ... 492

Peter v Russel (1716) 1 Eq Cas Abr 321 ... 471

Pettit v Pettit [1970] AC 777 ... 373, 377, 565

Phené v Popplewell (1862) 12 CB NS 334 ... 167

Phillips v Mobil Oil Co Ltd [1989] 1 WLR 888 ... 53, 215

Phipps v Pears [1965] 1 QB 76 ... 502, 514, 528

Pimms Ltd v Tallow Chandlers Co [1964] 2 QB 547 ... 193

Pinewood Estate, Re [1958] Ch 280 ... 548

Pinnington v Galland (1853) 9 Exch 1 ... 510

Pitt v PHH Asset Management Ltd [1994] 1 WLR 327 ... 31

Plimmer v Wellington Corporation (1884) 9 App Cas 699 ... 419

Port v Griffith [1938] 1 All ER 295 ... 188

Poster v Slough Estates Ltd [1968] 1 WLR 1515 ... 60

Powell v McFarlane (1970) 38 P & CR 452 ... 117, 118, 121

Propert v Parker (1832) 3 My & K 280 ... 198

Prudential Assurance Co Ltd v London Residuary Body [1992] 2 AC 386 ... 146, 149, 152, 166–7, 174, 401, 424, 478

Prudential Assurance Co Ltd v Waterloo Real Estate Inc [1999] 2 EGLR 85 ... 117

Pugh v Savage [1970] 2 QB 373 ... 497, 517, 521

Purchase v Lichfield Brewery Co [1915] 1 KB 184 ... 212

Pye (J A) (Oxford) Ltd v Graham [2000] Ch 676; [2001] Ch 804; [2003] 1 AC 419 ... 121–2, 133–5

R (Beresford) v Sunderland City Council [2003] 3 WLR 1306 ... 520, 526

R v Inhabitants of Hermitage (1692) Carth 239 ... 528

R v Inhabitants of Horndon-on-the-Hill (1816) 4 M & S 562 ... 417

R v Oxfordshire CC, ex parte Sunningwell [2000] 1 AC 335 ... 526

R v Tower Hamlets LBC, ex parte Von Goetz [1999] QB 1019 ... 158

R v Westminster City Council, ex parte Leicester Square Coventry Street Association (1989) 87 LGR 675 ... 540

Race v Ward (1855) 4 El & Bl 702 ... 499

Rainbow Estates Ltd v Tokenhold Ltd [1999] Ch 64 ... 224

Raja v Austin Gray (a firm) [2002] EWCA Civ 1965 ... 459, 462

Raja v Lloyds TSB Bank plc (2001) Lloyds Rep Bank 113 ... 454

Ramsden v Dyson [1866] LR 1 HL 129 ... 383, 386

Ransome, Re [1957] Ch 348 ... 341

Rawlings v Rawlings (1964) P 398 ... 288

Rawlinson v Ames [1925] Ch 96 ... 39

Rawlin's case (1587) Jenk 254 ... 180

Record v Bell [1991] 1 WLR 853 ... 31, 32

Red House Farms (Thornden) Ltd v Catchpole [1977] 2 EGLR 125 ... 117

Rees v Skerrett [2001] 1 WLR 1541 ... 502, 528

Reeve v Lisle [1902] AC 461 ... 443

Regent Oil Co Ltd v J A Gregory (Hatch End) Ltd [1996] Ch 402 ... 543

Regis Property Co Ltd v Redman [1956] 2 QB 612 ... 502

Reid v Bickerstaff [1909] 2 Ch 305 ... 550

Remon v City of London Real Property Co Ltd [1921] 1 KB 49 ... 177

Renals v Cowlishaw (1878) 9 ChD 125 ... 545, 547

RG Kensington Co Ltd v Hutchinson IDH Ltd [2003] 2 P & CR 195 ... 35–6

Rhone v Stephens [1994] 2 AC 310 ... 542, 543, 552, 555

Richards v Rose (1853) 9 Exch 218 ... 510

Richmond v Savill [1926] 2 KB 530 ... 167

Rickett v Green [1910] 1 KB 253 ... 212

Roake v Chadha [1984] 1 WLR 40 ... 547

Robinson v Kilvert (1889) 41 ChD 88 ... 188

Robson v Hallet [1967] 2 QB 939 ... 417

Rochefoucauld v Boustead [1897] 1 Ch 196 ... 369

Rochester Poster Services v Dartford BC (1991) 63 P & CR 88 ... 401

Rodway v Landy [2001] Ch 703 ... 361

Roe v Siddons (1888) 22 QBD 224 ... 496

Rogers v Hosegood [1900] 2 Ch 388 ... 545

Romulus Trading Co Ltd v Comet Properties Ltd [1996] 2 EGLR 70 ... 188

Ropaigealach v Barclays Bank plc [1999] 1 QB 263 ... 447, 454

Royal Bank of Scotland v Etridge [2002] 2 AC 773 ... 481–3, 484, 485, 486, 488, 490, 491, 492

Rudge v Richens (1873) LR 8 CP 358 ... 453

Rugby School (Governors) v Tannahill [1935] KB 87; [1934] 1 KB 695 ... 229, 231

Russel v Russel (1783) 1 Bro CC 269 ... 439

Rye v Rye [1962] AC 496 ... 514

St Helen's Smelting Co Ltd v Tipping (1862) 11 ER 1483 ... 499

Salt v Marquess of Northampton [1892] AC 1 ... 441

Samuel v Jarrah Timber & Wood Paving Co Ltd [1904] AC 323 ... 442

Sanderson v Berwick-upon-Tweed Corporation (1884) 13 QBD 547 ... 187

Saner v Bilton (1876) 7 ChD 815 ... 198

Santley v Wilde [1899] 2 Ch 474 ... 434

Sarson v Roberts [1895] 2 QB 395 ... 196

Saunders v Vautier (1841) 4 Beav 115 ... 269

Savva v Hussein (1997) 73 P & CR 150 ... 231, 232, 235

Sayer's Trusts, Re (1868) LR 6 Eq 319 ... 331

Sayers v Collyer [1885] 28 ChD 103 ... 556

Scala House & District Property Co Ltd v Forbes [1974] QB 575 ... 229, 230, 232, 233

Scott v Bradley [1971] 1 Ch 850 ... 38

Scottish Equitable plc v Thompson [2003] HLR 48 ... 453

Seaman v Vawdrey (1810) 16 Ves Jr 390 ... 529

Sefton v Tophams Ltd [1967] 1 AC 50 ... 543

Segal Securities Ltd v Thoseby [1963] 1 QB 887 ... 227

Shah v Shah [2002] QB 35 ... 44

Shanly v Ward (1913) 29 TLR 714 ... 193

Sharpe, Re [1980] 1 WLR 219 ... 422, 425

Shiloh Spinners Ltd v Harding [1973] AC 691 ... 60

Silven Properties v Royal Bank of Scotland plc [2004] 1 WLR 997 ... 458, 461

Simmons v Dobson [1991] 1 WLR 720 ... 517, 519

Simper v Foley (1862) 2 John & H 555 ... 528

Singh v Beggs (1996) 71 P & CR 120 ... 41

Skipton Building Society v Clayton (1993) 66 P & CR 223 ... 150, 152

Sledmore v Dalby (1996) 72 P & CR 196 ... 390–1

Smallwood v Sheppards [1895] 2 QB 627 ... 147

Smith and Snipes Hall Farm Ltd v River Douglas Catchment Board [1949] 2 KB 500 ... 219, 536, 538

Smith v Brudenell-Bruce [2002] 2 P & CR 4 ... 525

Smith v Lawson [1997] 75 P & CR 466 ... 119

Smith v Marrable (1843) 11 M & W 5 ... 196

Smith v Spaul [2003] QB 983 ... 234

Smith-Bird v Blower [1939] 2 All ER 406 ... 38

Southern Depot Co Ltd v British Railways Board [1990] 2 EGLR 39 ... 194

Southwark LBC v Tanner [2001] 1 AC 1 ... 185, 186

Sovmots Investments Ltd v Secretary of State for the Environment [1979] AC 144 ... 512–13, 513, 515

Spencer's Case (1583) 5 Co Rep 16a ... 209, 210, 211, 215, 216, 218, 538, 543, 552

Spiro v Glencrown Properties Ltd [1991] Ch 537 ... 30

Stafford v Lee (1992) 65 P & CR 172 ... 509

Standard Chartered Bank Ltd v Walker [1982] 1 WLR 1410 ... 459, 460

Starling v Lloyds TSB Bank plc [2000] 2 EGLR 101 ... 446

State Bank of India v Sood [1997] Ch 276 ... 290–1, 479

Steadman v Steadman [1976] AC 536 ... 39

Stock v McAvoy (1872) LR 15 Eq 55 ... 367

Stonebridge v Bygrave [2001] All ER (D) 376 ... 500–1

Strand Securities v Caswell [1965] Ch 958 ... 61, 94, 98, 159

Street v Mountford [1985] AC 809 ... 148, 152, 178, 402, 403, 404, 405, 406, 407, 408, 409, 410, 411, 478

Stribling v Wickham [1989] 2 EGLR 35 ... 409

Stromdale & Ball Ltd v Burden [1952] Ch 223 ... 13

Surrey County Council v Bredero Homes Ltd [1993] 1 WLR 1361 ... 555

Sutton v Mishcon de Raya (2004) *The Times* 28 Jan 2004 ... 564

Sweet & Maxwell Ltd v Universal News Services Ltd [1964] 2 QB 699 ... 194

Sykes v Harry [2001] QB 1014 ... 197

T W G S v J M G [2000] 3 WLR 1910 ... 357

Tanner v Tanner [1975] 1 WLR 1346 ... 416, 430, 567

Target Home Loans v Clothier [1994] 1 All ER 439 ... 451

Taylor v Caldwell (1863) 3 B & S 826 ... 170

Taylor v Dickens [1998] 1 FLR 806 ... 384, 385

Taylor v Russell [1891] 1 Ch 8 ... 473

Taylors Fashions Ltd v Liverpool Victoria Trustees Co Ltd [1982] 1 QB 133 ... 385, 386

Tebb v Hodge (1869) LR 5 CP 73 ... 439

Tehidy Minerals Ltd v Norman [1971] 2 QB 528 ... 523, 524, 525

Texaco Antilles Ltd v Kernochan [1973] AC 609 ... 550, 557

Thamesmead Town Ltd v Allotey (1998) 37 EG 161 ... 552, 553

Thatcher v Douglas (1995) 146 NLJ 282 ... 90, 426

Thelluson v Woodford (1799) 4 Ves 227 ... 340

Thomas v Hayward (1869) LR 4 Ex 311 ... 210

Thomas v Sorrell (1673) Vaugh 330 ... 399

Thorpe v Brumfitt (1873) LR 8 Ch App 650 ... 496

Thursby v Plant (1690) 1 Saund 230 ... 201

Tichbourne v Weir (1892) 67 LT 735 ... 125

Tickner v Buzzacott [1965] Ch 426 ... 155

Tiltwood, Sussex, Re [1978] Ch 269 ... 557

Timmins v Rowlinson (1765) 3 Burr 1603 ... 165

Timson v Ramsbottom (1836) 2 Keen 35 ... 465

Tito v Waddell (No 2) [1977] Ch 106 ... 552

Toomes v Conset (1745) 3 Atk 261 ... 442

Tootal Clothing Ltd v Guinea Properties Management Ltd [1992] 2 EGLR 80 ... 31–2, 33

Total Oil Great Britain Ltd v Thompson Garages (Biggin Hill) Ltd [1972] 1 QB 318 ... 171

Tredegar v Harwood [1929] AC 72 ... 190–1

Trenchard, Re [1902] 1 Ch 378 ... 318

TSB Bank plc v Camfield [1995] 1 WLR 430 ... 489

TSB Bank plc v Marshall [1998] 3 EGLR 100 ... 285, 359

Tse Kwong Lam v Wong Chit Sen [1983] 1 WLR 1349 ... 459

Tulk v Moxhay (1848) 2 Ph 774 ... 217, 218, 220, 235, 540, 541, 542, 543, 549

UCB Corporate Services Ltd v Williams [2002] 19 EG 149 (NS) ... 492

Ungarian v Lensoff [1990] Ch 206 ... 370

Union Lighterage Co. v London Graving Dock Co. [1902] 2 Ch 557 ... 520

Union of London & Smith's Bank Ltd's Conveyance, Re [1933] Ch 611 ... 548

United Bank of Kuwait plc v Sahib [1997] Ch 107 ... 440, 456

University of Westminster, Re [1998] 3 All ER 1014 ... 557

Van Haarlem v Kasner (1992) 64 P & CR 214 ... 231, 233, 240

Vernon v Bethall (1762) 2 Eden 110 ... 442

Verrall v Great Yarmouth BC [1981] 1 QB 202 ... 418

Villar, Re [1928] Ch 471 ... 329

Wakeham v Wood [1981] 43 P & CR 40 ... 556

Walker v Linom [1907] 2 Ch 104 ... 471

Wallis's Caytown Bay Holiday Camp Ltd v Shell-Mex and BP Ltd [1975] QB 94 ... 120

Walsh v Lonsdale (1882) 21 Ch D 9 ... 13, 156–8, 159, 439

Ward v Day (1864) 5 B & S 359 ... 227

Ward v Duncombe [1893] AC 369 ... 465

Ward v Kirkland [1967] Ch 194 ... 510, 515

Ward v Ward (1871) LR 6 Ch App 789 ... 347

Wardle v Brocklehurst (1860) 1 El & El 1065 ... 513

Warmington v Miller [1973] QB 877 ... 157

Warner v Jacob (1882) 20 ChD 220 ... 459

Warner v Simpson [1959] 1 QB 297; [1958] 1 QB 404 ... 233

Warr (Frank) & Co v London County Council [1904] 1 KB 713 ... 423

Warren v Keen [1954] 1 QB 15 ... 198

Wasdale, Re [1899] 1 Ch 163 ... 465

Waterlow v Bacon (1866) LR 2 Eq 514 ... 529

Wayling v Jones (1993) 69 P & CR 170 ... 384, 387

Webb v Bird (1861) 10 CB (NS) 268 ... 500

Webb v Pollmount [1966] Ch 584 ... 93

Webb v Russell (1789) 3 TR 393 ... 538

Webb's Lease, Re [1951] Ch 808 ... 510–11

Wedd v Porter [1916] 2 KB 91 ... 198

Weg Motors Ltd v Hales [1962] Ch 49 ... 182

Westminster City Council v Clarke [1992] 2 AC 288 ... 407–8

Weston v Henshaw [1950] Ch 510 ... 320–1

Weston v Lawrence Weaver Ltd [1961] 1 QB 402 ... 526

Wheaton v Maple [1893] 3 Ch 48 ... 517

Wheeldon v Burrows (1879) 12 ChD 31 ... 507, 509, 510, 511, 514, 515

Wheeler v J J Saunders Ltd [1996] Ch 19 ... 510

Wheelwright v Walker (1883) 23 ChD 752 ... 319

White Rose Cottage, Re [1965] Ch 940 ... 456

White v City of London Brewery Co (1889) 42 ChD 237 ... 459

White v Williams [1922] 1 KB 727 ... 514

Whitgift Homes v Stocks [2001] 48 EG 130 ... 550

Wilkes v Spooner [1911] 2 KB 473 ... 62

Williams & Glyn's Bank Ltd v Boland [1981] AC 487 ... 61, 93, 95, 96, 100, 101, 102, 289, 290, 478, 479, 578

Williams v Earle (1868) LR 3 QB 739 ... 210

Williams v Hensman (1861) 1 John & H 546 ... 354, 355, 356, 357

Williams v Kiley (t/a CK Supermarkets Ltd) [2003] 1 EGLR 47 ... 551

Williams v Morgan [1906] 1 Ch 804 ... 450

Willmott v Barber (1880) 15 ChD 96 ... 383, 385

Wills v Stradling (1797) 3 Ves Jr 378 ... 156

Wilson v Truelove [2003] 23 EG 136 ... 339

Wimbledon and Putney Commons Conservators v Dixon (1875) 1 ChD 362 ... 498

Windeler v Whitehall [1990] 1 FLR 505 ... 371–2

Winter Garden Theatre (London) Ltd v Millennium Productions Ltd [1948] AC 173 ... 418

Wong v Beaumont Property Trust Ltd [1965] 1 QB 173 ... 500, 508

Wood v Leadbitter (1845) 13 M & W 838 ... 417, 418

Wood v Manley (1839) 11 Ad & El 34 ... 415

Woodall v Clifton [1905] 2 Ch 257 ... 210, 215

Woolnough, Re [2002] WTLR 595 ... 356

Woolwich Building Society v Dickman (1996) 72 P & CR 470 ... 492

Worthington v Morgan (1849) 16 Sim 547 ... 61

Wright v Johnson [2002] 2 P & CR 15 ... 362–3

Wright v Macadam [1949] 2 KB 744 ... 500, 501, 512, 515

Wright v Robert Leonard (Developments) Ltd [1994] NPC 49 ... 32, 47

Wright v Stavert (1860) 2 E & E 721 ... 401

Wright v Williams (1836) 1 M & W 77 ... 521

Wrotham Park Estate Co v Parkside Homes Ltd [1974] 1 WLR 798 ... 555

Yaxley v Gotts [2000] Ch 162 ... 36, 41–3, 44, 368, 394–5

TABLE OF STATUTES

Access to Neighbouring Land Act 1992 ... 530–1,
    532
  s1(2) ... 530
  s1(4) ... 531
  s2(4)–(5) ... 531
  s5(1)–(2) ... 531
  s5(5) ... 95
Accumulations Act 1880 ... 340
Administration of Estates Act 1925
  s22(1) ... 324
  s33(1) ... 258
Administration of Justice Act 1970
  s36 ... 451, 452, 453, 454
  s36(2) ... 454
Administration of Justice Act 1973
  s8 ... 453
  s8(3) ... 453
Administration of Justice Act 1982
  s22 ... 296
Adoption Act 1976
  s42 ... 331
Agricultural Holdings Act 1986 ... 162
Agricultural Tenancies Act 1995 ... 162

Coal Industry Act 1994
  s7(3) ... 579
Common Law Procedure Act 1852
  s210 ... 228
Commonhold and Leasehold Reform Act 2002
    ... 162, 240, 581
  Part I ... 164, 238, 253
  Part II ... 253
  s1 ... 241
  s1(2) ... 243–4
  s2 ... 241
  s3 ... 241, 244, 245, 246
  s4 ... 241
  s7(3) ... 245
  s7(3)(d) ... 246
  s8 ... 244, 245
  s9 ... 245
  s9(3)(f) ... 246
  s10 ... 246
  s12 ... 242
  s14 ... 243
  s15(2) ... 248
  s16 ... 248
  s17 ... 248
  s17(3)–(4) ... 248
  s18 ... 249
  s20 ... 249
  s20(3) ... 249
  s20(6) ... 249
  s25(1) ... 242
  s25(2) ... 247
  s31(2) ... 251

  s31(3)–(4) ... 243
  s31(5) ... 243
  s31(5)(a) ... 243
  s31(7) ... 243, 505
  s31(8) ... 247
  s32 ... 242
  s32(1) ... 251
  s33 ... 242
  s34 ... 242
  s34(1)–(2) ... 242
  s35(1)–(2) ... 247
  s35(3)(a) ... 247
  s37 ... 247
  s37(2) ... 248
  s38 ... 243
  s38(1)(b) ... 243
  s39 ... 243
  s41 ... 253
  s43(1)(c) ... 250
  s44–s45 ... 250
  s51 ... 250
  s51(4) ... 250
  s54(4) ... 251
  s168–s169 ... 234
  Sch2 ... 241
    para1 ... 241
  Sch3 ... 242
    para7 ... 242
    para10 ... 242
    para12 ... 242
Commons Registration Act 1965 ... 92, 93, 506
Companies Act 1985
  s1 ... 242
  s1(2)(b) ... 242
Consumer Credit Act 1974
  s94 ... 443
  s138 ... 445
  s173 ... 443
Contracts (Rights of Third Parties) Act 1999 ...
    218, 424, 536
  s7(1) ... 536
Conveyancing Act 1881 ... 547
  s6(2) ... 513
  s10 ... 212
Countryside and Rights of Way Act 2000
  Part I ... 532
  s68 ... 516
County Courts Act 1984
  s138(9A) ... 234
Courts and Legal Services Act 1990
  s104–s107 ... 445
Criminal Justice and Public Order Act 1994
  s72 ... 232
Criminal Law Act 1977
  s5 ... 453

s6 ... 177, 232, 453
s12(3) ... 177

Defective Premises Act 1972
s4 ... 197
Disability Discrimination Act 1995
s22(4) ... 190
s23 ... 190
Domestic Violence and Matrimonial Proceedings
    Act 1976 ... 569

Enterprise Act 2002
s261 ... 452

Family Law Act 1996 ... 54, 430, 567, 568
s30 ... 567
s30(3) ... 457
s31 ... 567, 568
s31(7) ... 568
s31(10) ... 95
s31(10)(a)–(b) ... 567
s33 ... 568
s33(6) ... 568
s33(10) ... 568
s36 ... 568, 569, 570
s36(1)(c) ... 568
s36(3)–(4) ... 568
s36(6) ... 568
s41(2) ... 568
s42 ... 569
s62(1) ... 568
s62(1)(9a) ... 568
s62(3) ... 569
Sch8
    para47 ... 567
Family Law Reform Act 1969
s15 ... 331
Financial Services Act 1986 ... 36
Fines and Recoveries Act 1833 ... 307
Forfeiture Act 1982 ... 357

Housing Act 1974
s125 ... 224
Housing Act 1980 ... 163
Housing Act 1985 ... 70
Part VI ... 225
s610 ... 558
Housing Act 1988 ... 162, 418, 419
Part I ... 165
s27 ... 225
Housing Act 1996 ... 162
Human Fertilisation and Embryology Act 1990
s27–s30 ... 329
Human Rights Act 1998 ... 19–20, 89, 116, 133,
    135, 141, 144, 226, 232
s3 ... 133, 570
s3(1) ... 19
s4 ... 133
s6 ... 134, 226
s6(1) ... 19
s6(3)(a) ... 19
Sch1 ... 19

Inheritance Tax Act 1984 ... 52, 105
Insolvency Act 1986 ... 168, 566
s124 ... 250
s313 ... 452
s335A ... 284, 285, 360
Interpretation Act 1978 ... 573, 574
s7 ... 353
Sch1 ... 573

Land Charges Act 1925 ... 51, 214, 470
Land Charges Act 1972 ... 24, 51, 52, 53, 241,
    470
s1 ... 52, 58
s2 ... 507
s2(4) ... 52
s2(4)(i) ... 469
s2(4)(iii) ... 52, 469
s2(4)(iv) ... 57
s2(5) ... 544
s2(7) ... 567
s4(2) ... 56
s4(5) ... 56, 57, 160, 470
s4(6) ... 57, 159, 160, 544
s4(8) ... 56, 160
s9 ... 56
s10(4) ... 56
s17(1) ... 56
Land Registration Act 1925 ... 24, 66, 67, 70, 71,
    74, 76, 81, 82, 83, 84, 86, 89, 90, 91, 92, 93,
    95, 96, 97, 102, 105, 106, 110, 130, 466
s1(2) ... 71
s1(4) ... 71
s3(viii) ... 573
s24 ... 202, 203
s25(2) ... 438
s44 ... 79
s50(1) ... 544
s52(1) ... 110
s58 ... 554
s70 ... 291
s70(1) ... 67, 89, 90, 95
s70(1)(a) ... 90, 505
s70(1)(f) ... 81, 92, 106, 128, 129, 133
s70(1)(g) ... 44, 92, 93, 94, 95, 96, 97, 98, 99,
    100, 102, 103, 128, 290, 360, 377, 392, 394,
    427
s70(1)(h) ... 92
s70(1)(k) ... 90
s75(1) ... 127, 128, 129
s75(2) ... 127
s77 ... 202
s82(1) ... 105
s82(3) ... 105
s85 ... 438
s86(2) ... 94
s87 ... 438
s93 ... 110
s93(1)–(2) ... 110
s102(2) ... 466
Land Registration Act 1986
s5 ... 466
Land Registration Act 1997 ... 72
s1 ... 25

Land Registration Act 2002 ... 12, 24, 25, 66, 68,
    69, 71, 72, 74, 76, 79, 81, 83, 84, 85, 86, 90,
    91, 94, 103, 104, 106, 107–8, 109, 113, 116,
    129, 130, 135, 153, 154, 178, 213, 214, 290,
    436, 466, 468, 477, 505, 506, 558
s2(a) ... 70, 71
s3 ... 73
s3(1)–(3) ... 70
s3(4) ... 70, 73
s3(7) ... 73
s4 ... 25, 71, 437, 438, 479
s4(1)(a) ... 69, 72
s4(1)(c) ... 69, 72, 154
s4(1)(d)–(e) ... 70
s4(1)(g) ... 438, 456
s4(2) ... 69
s4(2)(b) ... 25
s4(8) ... 438
s6 ... 64
s6(2) ... 438
s7 ... 64
s7(1) ... 72
s7(2)(b) ... 154
s7(4) ... 142
s9 ... 76
s9(2) ... 76
s9(3) ... 76, 77
s9(4) ... 77
s9(5) ... 78
s10 ... 76, 78
s10(2) ... 78
s10(3) ... 79
s11(2)–(5) ... 77
s11(4) ... 77
s11(4)(c) ... 81, 103
s11(5) ... 77
s11(6)–(7) ... 78
s12(3)–(6) ... 79
s14 ... 68
s15–s22 ... 74
s23(1)(a) ... 437
s25 ... 438
s26 ... 302
s26(3) ... 302
s27 ... 88, 91, 98, 107, 437, 506
s27(1) ... 82, 154, 466, 506
s27(2) ... 82, 154
s27(2)(b)(ii)–(iii) ... 70
s27(2)(b)(iv) ... 70
s27(2)(b)(v) ... 70
s27(2)(d) ... 506
s27(2)(f) ... 438, 447, 466
s27(4) ... 553
s27(7) ... 91, 506, 512
s28 ... 103, 111, 112, 466, 467, 468, 469
s29 ... 86, 88, 103, 111, 159, 161, 466, 467,
    468, 469
s29(1) ... 83, 84
s29(2) ... 83, 84, 467
s29(3) ... 86, 88, 91, 468, 506
s30 ... 466, 467, 469
s31 ... 103
s32 ... 506, 544
s32(1) ... 85, 466

s32(3) ... 85
s33 ... 86, 506
s34(3)(c) ... 86
s37 ... 86, 506
s38 ... 85
s40(2)–(3) ... 86
s41 ... 86
s41(1) ... 86
s42 ... 87
s42(2) ... 87
s44(1) ... 87, 351
s46(2) ... 87
s49 ... 477
s49(3)–(6) ... 477
s51 ... 438
s62 ... 79
s62(1) ... 79
s62(2)–(5) ... 80
s65 ... 104
s71 ... 88
s71(a) ... 80
s73 ... 86
s86 ... 103
s91 ... 109–10
s91(4)–(5) ... 110
s91(8) ... 110
s96–s97 ... 130
s98 ... 130, 132
s98(5) ... 132
s107 ... 131
s110(4) ... 131
s111 ... 131
s116 ... 393, 429, 469
s117 ... 91, 487
s118 ... 70
s131 ... 105
s134 ... 84, 88, 202
Sch1 ... 77, 80, 81, 88, 524
    para2 ... 133
    para2(1) ... 312
    para3 ... 506
Sch2 ... 82
    para6 ... 554
    para7 ... 91, 553
    para8 ... 466
Sch3 ... 77, 88, 89, 90, 91, 92, 93, 94, 159, 524
    para1 ... 90, 159, 161
    para2 ... 58, 90, 92, 93, 93–6, 96–102, 133,
    159, 290, 393, 478, 487
    para2(1)(a) ... 312
    para3 ... 90, 91, 103, 506
    para3(1)–(2) ... 91
    para4–para14 ... 89
Sch4 ... 87, 104–5
    para1–para2 ... 104–5
    para3 ... 105
    para3(3) ... 105
    para5 ... 105, 463
    para6 ... 105
Sch5
    para7 ... 111
Sch6 ... 130, 131, 132
    para1(1)–(5) ... 130
    para4(5) ... 132

para5 ... 131, 132
para5(1) ... 132
para5(2)–(4) ... 131
para6–para7 ... 132
para11 ... 130
para11(2) ... 130
Sch8
    para1(a)–(b) ... 106
    para5 ... 106
Sch9 ... 131
Sch11
    para2 ... 79
Sch12
    para1–para2 ... 84
    para7 ... 88, 133
    para8–para10 ... 88
    para11 ... 88, 133
    para12–para13 ... 88
    para18 ... 133
    para20 ... 202

Landlord and Tenant Act 1927 ... 190, 193
    s19(1) ... 193
    s19(1)(a) ... 190

Landlord and Tenant Act 1954 ... 165, 400
    Part II ... 162, 246

Landlord and Tenant Act 1985 ... 400
    s4 ... 153
    s8 ... 196
    s11 ... 196, 409–10, 411
    s12–s14 ... 196
    s17 ... 224

Landlord and Tenant Act 1988 ... 193
    s1(3) ... 193
    s1(6) ... 193
    s4 ... 194

Landlord and Tenant (Covenants) Act 1995 ...
    159, 181, 200, 202, 212, 213, 216, 552
    s1 ... 200
    s1(2) ... 205
    s1(3) ... 160, 200
    s2 ... 216
    s2(1)(a) ... 213
    s3 ... 213, 217
    s3(5) ... 217, 218, 235
    s3(6)(a)–(b) ... 213
    s4 ... 213
    s5 ... 202
    s6 ... 203
    s6(2)(b) ... 205
    s7–s8 ... 204
    s11 ... 204
    s11(1) ... 203
    s11(2)(b) ... 203
    s11(3)(b) ... 204
    s16 ... 203
    s17 ... 205
    s18 ... 205
    s18(2)–(3) ... 205
    s19 ... 205
    s20 ... 205
    s20(6) ... 53
    s21 ... 205

s22 ... 193
s23(3) ... 213
s24(4) ... 205, 211
s28(1) ... 204, 213
s30(2)–(3) ... 203
s30(4) ... 218
s30(4)(a) ... 202
s30(4)(b) ... 213

Law of Distress Amendment Act 1888
    s7 ... 226

Law of Property Act 1922
    s1(1) ... 142
    s145 ... 189
    Sch15 ... 189
        para7 ... 148

Law of Property Act 1925 ... 24, 146, 152, 258,
    266, 289, 290, 291, 301, 302, 326, 358, 435,
    451, 574
    s1 ... 305, 306
    s1(1) ... 4, 10, 140, 141, 146, 147, 150, 292,
        305, 578
    s1(1)(b) ... 7
    s1(2) ... 8, 10, 14, 141, 504, 505, 554
    s1(2)(a) ... 8–9, 82
    s1(2)(b) ... 9, 82
    s1(2)(c)–(d) ... 10
    s1(2)(e) ... 10, 82
    s1(3) ... 6, 10, 14, 140, 141
    s2(1) ... 60
    s2(1)(ii) ... 289
    s4(1) ... 429
    s7(1) ... 140, 141
    s13 ... 439
    s25(1) ... 271, 272, 299
    s25(4) ... 297
    s26(1) ... 273
    s26(3) ... 274, 299, 359
    s27 ... 289, 290, 291
    s27(2) ... 291
    s28 ... 298
    s30 ... 283, 284, 285, 287, 302, 359, 360, 479
    s34 ... 350, 351
    s34(1) ... 350, 352
    s34(2) ... 350, 351
    s35 ... 299, 350, 351
    s36 ... 350, 351
    s36(1) ... 350
    s36(2) ... 352, 354, 357, 364
    s36(3) ... 357
    s36(4) ... 353, 357
    s40 ... 29, 37–40, 48, 58, 156, 356, 368, 423
    s40(1) ... 37
    s40(2) ... 37, 39, 40, 439
    s44 ... 178
    s49(1) ... 47
    s52 ... 182
    s52(1) ... 12, 63, 110, 153, 154, 161, 168, 243,
        368, 411, 505
    s52(2)(c) ... 167
    s53(1) ... 298
    s53(1)(b) ... 36, 257, 366, 368, 369, 374
    s53(1)(c) ... 440
    s53(2) ... 36, 258, 366

s54(2) ... 36, 153, 154, 155, 160, 161, 167, 182, 210, 512, 514
s56 ... 219, 535, 536, 548
s56(1) ... 535
s62 ... 93, 160, 506, 512, 513, 514, 515, 559
s62(1) ... 511
s71 ... 514
s76(6) ... 547
s77 ... 202, 203
s77(5) ... 547
s78 ... 219, 538, 539, 543, 546, 547
s78(1) ... 538, 539
s79 ... 201, 202, 209, 220, 235, 543
s80(3) ... 547
s84 ... 557
s84(2) ... 556
s85 ... 10, 435, 436
s85(1) ... 447
s85(2) ... 436
s86 ... 10, 435, 436
s86(1) ... 447
s86(2) ... 436
s87 ... 10, 435, 437
s87(1) ... 447
s88(1) ... 452, 456
s88(2) ... 450
s89(1) ... 452, 456
s89(2) ... 450
s91(2) ... 450, 451, 456
s93 ... 448
s94 ... 477
s94(2) ... 477
s96(1) ... 447
s97 ... 470
s98 ... 446
s99 ... 445
s99(1) ... 448
s100 ... 446
s101(1)(i) ... 451, 455
s101(1)(ii) ... 448
s101(1)(iii) ... 454, 456
s103 ... 451
s104(1) ... 452
s105 ... 452
s108 ... 448
s109 ... 454
s121(6) ... 340
s136 ... 539
s137 ... 465
s137(3)–(4) ... 465
s141 ... 210, 212, 215, 216, 218
s142 ... 210, 212, 213, 215, 216, 218
s143 ... 213
s146 ... 228, 229, 230, 233, 234, 235
s146(1) ... 228, 232
s146(2) ... 233
s146(4) ... 234, 236, 353, 437
s149(3) ... 147, 152
s149(6) ... 150, 152, 309
s149(8) ... 233
s149(9) ... 233
s150 ... 175
s153 ... 168, 554
s163 ... 334, 335, 337

s163(2) ... 333
s164 ... 341
s164(1) ... 341
s164(2) ... 342
s165–s166 ... 341
s185 ... 168
s187(1) ... 504
s196(3) ... 352, 353
s196(4) ... 352
s198 ... 55, 56, 469
s198(1) ... 55–6
s199(1)(ii) ... 17
s205 ... 364, 514
s205(1)(ix) ... 573, 574, 576, 579
s205(1)(xix) ... 6
s205(1)(xxi) ... 57
s205(1)(xxvii) ... 7, 146, 152
s205(1)(xxix) ... 261, 297
Sch1
Part IV ... 346
Sch5 ... 437

Law of Property Act 1969 ... 556
s23 ... 50
s25 ... 55
s28(4) ... 556

Law of Property (Amendment) Act 1926 ... 140
s1 ... 308
s37 ... 310
Schedule ... 140

Law of Property (Joint Tenants) Act 1964 ... 364
s3 ... 364

Law of Property (Miscellaneous Provisions) Act 1989 ... 13, 29, 36–7, 40, 44, 47, 156, 185, 364
s1 ... 12–13, 28, 44, 154
s2 ... 29–36, 37, 40, 41, 42, 43, 44, 48, 110, 111, 356, 368, 401, 439, 440
s2(1) ... 30, 33, 34, 42
s2(2) ... 30
s2(3) ... 30, 34, 35, 36
s2(4) ... 32
s2(5) ... 36, 42
s2(5)(a) ... 36, 156
s3 ... 46

Leasehold Property (Repairs) Act 1938 ... 223, 224

Leasehold Reform, Housing and Urban Development Act 1993 ... 162, 163

Leasehold Reform Act 1967 ... 162, 163

Limitation Act 1939
s9 ... 413

Limitation Act 1980 ... 77, 78, 81, 93, 94, 114–15, 122, 124, 130, 133, 134, 413
s15 ... 115, 123, 127
s15(2) ... 124
s17 ... 115, 125, 126, 128, 133
s28 ... 123
s32 ... 123
Sch1
  para1 ... 123
  para5 ... 119

para8 ... 123
Local Government and Housing Act 1989 ... 158
Local Land Charges Act 1975 ... 27
s10 ... 27
London Building Acts (Amendment) Act 1939 ...
531

Married Women's Property Act 1882 ... 352
s1 ... 346
s5 ... 346
Matrimonial Causes Act 1973
Part II ... 371
s25(2) ... 371
s25(2)(f) ... 565
Matrimonial Homes Act 1967 ... 54
Matrimonial Homes Act 1983 ... 457
Matrimonial Proceedings and Property Act 1970
... 371
s37 ... 565
Mental Health Act 1983 ... 123, 521

National Trust Act 1937
s8 ... 543

Official Secrets Act ... 231

Party Walls Act 1996 ... 531–2
Perpetuities and Accumulations Act 1964 ... 326,
334, 336, 337
s1 ... 334
s2 ... 338
s2(1)(b) ... 336
s2(2) ... 336
s3(1) ... 334, 335, 336
s3(4) ... 335
s3(4)(b) ... 335
s3(5) ... 335
s4 ... 336, 338
s5 ... 337, 338
s8(1)–(2) ... 338
s9 ... 215, 339
s9(1)–(2) ... 339
s10 ... 339
s13 ... 341
s13(1) ... 341
s14 ... 342
s15(5) ... 338
Prescription Act 1832 ... 515, 518, 519, 522, 523,
525, 529
s1–s2 ... 520, 521
s3 ... 524
s4 ... 522, 523
s7 ... 521, 522
s8 ... 519, 521, 522
Protection from Eviction Act 1977 ... 225
s1(3) ... 225
s1(3A) ... 186, 225
s2 ... 232
s3 ... 177, 419
s3(2A)–(2B) ... 419
s3A ... 165
s5 ... 419

s5(1) ... 165
s5(1A) ... 418

Quia Emptores 1290 ... 143

Race Relations Act 1976
s24 ... 190
Real Property Act 1845
s5 ... 536
Recorded Delivery Service Act 1962
s1 ... 352
Sch1
para1 ... 352
Rent Acts ... 180, 400, 401, 408, 512, 575
Rent Act 1977 ... 162, 163, 569
Sch1
para2 ... 569, 570
para3 ... 569
Rentcharges Act 1977 ... 9, 308, 554
s2 ... 553
Rights of Light Act 1959 ... 524
s2 ... 524
Settled Land Act 1882 ... 260

Settled Land Act 1925 ... 52, 93, 150, 258, 260,
261, 263, 264, 267, 281, 292, 296, 297, 299,
300, 304, 305, 308, 314, 316, 317, 318, 350,
369, 370, 451, 465
s1 ... 306, 308
s1(1)(i) ... 306
s1(1)(ii) ... 306–7
s1(1)(iii) ... 307–8, 322
s1(1)(iv)–(v) ... 308
s1(7) ... 261, 297, 308
s3 ... 325
s4 ... 310
s4(2) ... 311
s4(3) ... 310
s5(1) ... 311
s5(1)(b) ... 311
s6 ... 312
s7(4)–(5) ... 323
s8(4) ... 323
s9(2) ... 311, 312
s12 ... 323
s13 ... 313
s17 ... 324
s18 ... 321
s18(1) ... 314, 319
s18(1)(b) ... 322
s19 ... 309
s20 ... 309
s20(1)(iv)–(vi) ... 309
s20(1)(viii) ... 309
s23–s24 ... 322
s26 ... 309
s30 ... 309
s34 ... 309
s38–s39 ... 315
s41 ... 315, 319
s42 ... 315
s42(5) ... 317
s51 ... 316

s51(2) … 316
s52–s57 … 316
s58 … 316
s58(1)–(2) … 318
s59–s64 … 316
s65 … 316, 317
s65(2) … 317
s66 … 316
s66(1) … 317
s67 … 316
s68 … 316, 322
s69–s70 … 316
s71 … 316, 319
s71(2) … 316
s72 … 314
s72(2) … 314
s73 … 323
s73(1)(i) … 323
s73(1)(xi) … 323
s75 … 322
s75(1)–(2) … 323
s75(4) … 323
s101 … 317
s101(5) … 317
s102 … 298
s104(1)–(2) … 318
s106 … 318
s107 … 319
s110 … 320
s110(1) … 320, 321
s110(2) … 312, 313
s117 … 320
s117(1)(ix) … 573
s117(1)(xxvi) … 309
s117(1)(xxx) … 310
Sch3 … 316
Sex Discrimination Act 1975
s31 … 190
Statute of Frauds 1677 … 39, 111, 369, 401
Statute of Westminster the First 1275 … 518
Supreme Court Act 1981 … 555
s37 … 456
s49(1) … 157, 158
s116 … 324
Supreme Court of Judicature Act 1873 … 15, 158, 212
s25(11) … 157
Supreme Court of Judicature Act 1875 … 15, 158, 212

Town and Country Planning Act 1990
s72 … 555
Trustee Act 1925 … 267
s34 … 310
s34(2) … 267, 351
s36 … 268, 269, 310
s36(1) … 268
s36(6) … 268
s39 … 268, 289, 310
s40–s41 … 268
s44 … 268
s68(6) … 573
s68(18) … 268

Trustee Act 2000
s1 … 278
s3 … 323
s10(1)(a) … 323
s40 … 271
Sch2
para9 … 323
para45(1) … 271
Sch4
para10(1) … 323
Trusts of Land and Appointment of Trustees Act
1996 … 7, 144, 150, 262–3, 264, 265, 266,
267, 269, 270, 272, 273, 278, 279, 285, 289,
292, 294, 296, 297, 299, 300, 301, 302, 303,
304, 305, 307, 313, 314, 316, 317, 350, 358,
361, 452, 578
Part I … 292
Part II … 269
s1 … 295, 308, 351
s1(1) … 266
s1(1)(a) … 266
s1(2)(a) … 266, 267, 294
s1(2)(b) … 266, 295
s2(1) … 267, 292, 304
s2(2) … 313, 314
s2(3) … 314
s2(4) … 325
s2(5) … 292, 304
s2(6) … 267
s3 … 354, 573
s3(1) … 294
s4(1) … 271, 272, 282, 294
s5(1) … 295
s6 … 270, 272, 276, 298, 301
s6(1) … 270, 271, 274, 276, 278, 298
s6(2) … 271, 275
s6(3) … 271, 292
s6(4) … 271
s6(4)(b) … 295, 298
s6(5) … 276
s6(6) … 276, 301
s7 … 270, 271, 272
s7(1) … 363
s7(3) … 271, 363
s8(1) … 270, 272, 274, 276, 318
s8(2) … 273
s9 … 276, 278, 279
s9(1) … 276, 277, 278
s9(2) … 277
s9(7) … 276, 278
s9(8) … 278
s9A … 278
s9A(1) … 278
s9A(2) … 278
s9A(6) … 278
s10 … 281
s10(1) … 273
s10(3) … 274
s11 … 275, 279, 281
s11(1) … 275, 299, 358, 363
s11(2)(a) … 275
s11(2)(b) … 275, 295
s11(3) … 275

s12 ... 279, 281, 282, 283, 361, 479,
 566
s12(1) ... 279
s12(1)(b) ... 279
s12(2) ... 279
s13 ... 280, 281, 283, 361, 362
s13(1) ... 280, 362
s13(2) ... 280
s13(3) ... 280, 362
s13(4) ... 361
s13(5) ... 280, 361
s13(6) ... 280, 362
s13(7) ... 281
s14 ... 273, 274, 281, 282, 284, 286, 302, 359,
 361, 451, 452, 479
s14(1) ... 282, 283
s14(2) ... 283
s15 ... 282, 283, 284, 285, 286, 287, 302, 359,
 452
s15(1) ... 283, 285, 287, 360
s15(1)(a) ... 287, 359
s15(1)(b) ... 287, 288, 359
s15(1)(c) ... 283, 287
s15(1)(d) ... 283
s15(2) ... 283
s15(3) ... 283, 285
s16 ... 289, 301
s16(1) ... 275, 363
s16(4)–(5) ... 291
s16(7) ... 289, 301
s17 ... 291
s17(1) ... 292
s17(5) ... 292
s19 ... 268, 269, 273, 310
s19(1) ... 269
s19(1)(a)–(b) ... 269

s19(2) ... 269
s20 ... 268, 269, 310
s21 ... 268, 269, 310
s21(1) ... 269
s25(2) ... 573
s36 ... 269
Sch1 ... 267
 para1 ... 307
 para4 ... 294
 para5 ... 306
 para5(1)–(2) ... 294
 para6 ... 294, 325
Sch2 ... 295
 para3 ... 350
 para4 ... 350
 para4(3) ... 352
Sch3
 para4(1) ... 289
 para23 ... 284
Sch4 ... 350, 573

European Union legislation

Treaty of Rome (EC Treaty)
 Art48 ... 446
 Art81 ... 195

International Treaties and Conventions

European Convention on Human Rights
 Art6 ... 19, 133, 226
 Art8 ... 19, 144, 226
 Art9 ... 144
 Art14 ... 19, 144, 570
First Protocol
 Art1 ... 19, 133, 134, 226

TABLE OF STATUTORY INSTRUMENTS

Land Charges Rules 1974
    r22 ... 56

Land Registration Rules 1925
    r40 ... 544
    r99 ... 312
    r258 ... 505

Land Registration Rules 2003 (SI 2003/1417) ...
    66, 74, 506
    r2 ... 74
    r21 ... 72
    r28 ... 80
    r35 ... 506, 544

r36 ... 524
r91 ... 87
r103 ... 438
r114 ... 462
r115 ... 462
r164 ... 365
r194 ... 130
r198 ... 130

Public Trustee Rules ... 310

Unfair Terms in Consumer Contracts
    Regulations 1994 ... 445

PART I

Introduction

We would like to begin by introducing you to Trant Way, a road in the fictitious town of Mousehole in the County of Stilton. Since Trant Way exists only in our joint imagination, we must explain that we visualise it as a street on the outskirts of an old county town. The town has grown considerably over the past 50 years (although so far it has avoided a ring road), and many of the outlying houses have been built on land which was once farmland. Thus the houses in Trant Way which are nearest to the centre of the town (e.g., Nos. 1–6) stand in a typically suburban environment, whereas the houses at the further end of the road (number 15 onwards) are in more countrified surroundings and in some cases are still flanked by open farmland.

A very important fact about the whole neighbourhood is that the County of Stilton became an area of compulsory land registration on 1 December 1990. We know that this will not mean a lot to you at the moment, but we will explain in Chapter 2 what it involves.

Throughout the book we will use some of the properties in Trant Way to illustrate the application of land law rules in practical situations. Chapter 1 has to be rather theoretical, because we want to give an outline introduction to the various rights which people can have over land. We are, as it were, getting the chess pieces up on the board, and telling you what they are called and how they move. Once you can recognise these rights, we will work through the process of acquiring title to land in Part II and then spend the rest of the book looking at some of the rights over land in more detail. We will leave the discussion of the question 'What is land?' to the end of the book. It is one of the more technical areas of the subject, and we think you will find it easier to follow at a later stage.

We have not included any general introduction to equity because students often study land law and equity (or trusts) at the same time, and in such a case your studies in equity will provide the background knowledge which is needed for land law. If however, land law precedes equity in your course, or if you are not required to study equity in detail or you are not a law student, we do advise you to read some outline introduction to its history and nature. Some suggested references are given at the end of Chapter 1.

1925 property legislation

Finally, this is a convenient place in which to mention the property legislation which was passed in 1925 and which came into force on 1 January 1926. This legislation consolidated earlier amendments to land law, put into statutory form some common law rules and introduced further reforms. This turning-point in land law was contained in the following statutes:

Settled Land Act 1925
Trustee Act 1925
Law of Property Act 1925
Land Registration Act 1925
Administration of Estates Act 1925
Land Charges Act 1925

These statutes have been amended by later enactments and in some cases are largely superseded by later statutes. For convenience we have used the following abbreviations throughout the book, giving the year in each case, in order to avoid confusion where there are two or more statutes with similar names:

SLA—Settled Land Act
LPA—Law of Property Act
LRA—Land Registration Act
LCA—Land Charges Act

More recently, the Trusts of Land and Appointment of Trustees Act 1996 has introduced major changes to the important area of trusts of land. You will find that Act referred to here as TOLATA 1996.

Note on Bibliography

You will find a Bibliography at p. 583, but may like to note now the abbreviations we use for four main textbooks, which are as follows:

Cheshire and Burn's Modern Law of Real Property, 16th edn., Butterworths, 2000: Cheshire and Burn.
Gray and Gray, *Elements of Land Law*, 3rd edn. (4th edn. due autumn, 2004), Butterworths, 2001: Gray and Gray.
Megarry and Wade, *The Law of Real Property*, 6th edn., Sweet & Maxwell, 2000: Megarry and Wade.
Smith, *Property Law*, 4th edn., Longman, 2003: Smith.

1

Estates and interests in land

1.1 Introduction

1.1.1 Freehold, leasehold and commonhold

Anyone who has looked in the window of an estate agent will have seen advertisements similar in form to the two following examples:

1 Trant Way, Mousehole, Stilton.

Freehold House.

Victorian house on 3 floors, completely modernised throughout. Central heating. Large garden. 3 recep. 2 bedrm. 2 bathrm. sep WC. Large kitchen.

£195,000.

2 Trant Way, Mousehole, Stilton.

Leasehold maisonette. 99-yr lease.

Pleasant maisonette, being ground and first floor of this elegant Victorian property. 2 recep. 2 bedrm. bathrm. sep WC. Spacious kitchen/breakfast room.

£160,000.

As yet, you are unlikely to see any advertisements for commonhold property. This is a new form of land-holding, which is only just being introduced, and it may be some time before it begins to appear in estate agents' windows. We will tell you more about this new development later (see Chapter 11), but for the time being will confine ourselves to explaining the terms 'freehold' and 'leasehold'. Although these terms are in common public use, most members of the public will have no idea of what they mean to a lawyer. In land law, specialised terminology is of great importance, and it is necessary to consider how these layman's terms translate into more legal language.

1.1.2 What am I buying?

The answer to this question, as far as the purchaser is concerned, is usually, 'I'm buying a house'. For the lawyer, however, the answer to the same question is rather different and may at first seem unnecessarily complicated. It is certainly true that the scheme underlying the lawyer's answer is unique to England and Wales. A Scottish lawyer will answer the same question in an entirely different manner because the system of land ownership in Scotland is completely different. Thus this book is concerned only with the law relating to England and Wales.

1.1.3 **Estates and tenure**

The first thing to note about land law is that no subject can own land. Theoretically all land belongs to the Crown and the only person who is capable of owning land is the monarch. This is an idea which dates from the Norman conquest in 1066 and which persists even today. The subject cannot therefore own the land upon which he lives or runs his business, but he is allowed the use of the land by the Crown. What the subject owns is a series of rights and duties in relation to that piece of land. Understandably lawyers have given a name to the interest in land which the subject holds, and that name is an 'estate in land'. So the land belongs to the Crown and the subject owns an estate in the land, which gives him certain rights in relation to it. Thus a freehold owner is said to 'hold land of the Crown'. At one time it was usual for an estate owner to render services to the Crown in return for the right to use the land, but these services are now performed only in the rarest of cases and tend to be regarded as an honour rather than as an obligation (for example, the duty to supply a pair of gloves for the monarch to wear at his coronation).

The relationship between the freehold owner and the Crown is called 'tenure' (from the Latin word *'tenere'* which means 'to hold'). At one time there were many types of freehold tenure, classified according to the nature of the services to be rendered by the estate owner. Today only one of these forms of tenure remains and that is called 'free and common socage'. For all practical purposes the doctrine of tenure has little modern significance, and most freehold owners are completely unaware of their tenurial relationship with the Crown.

In the case of leasehold property, the relationship between a landlord and his tenant is also one of tenure, although it usually involves the payment of rent rather than the performance of services.

You may see references to 'commonhold' as a new form of tenure, but this is not really technically accurate since, as we shall see, owners of units within a commonhold scheme will in fact hold the freehold title to their property. As we shall see in Chapter 11, commonhold is not in fact a separate new form of tenure, but a special mechanism that uses existing concepts of land law and company law in new ways.

1.1.4 **LPA 1925, s. 1(1): the two legal estates**

Today there are only two estates in land which are recognised at law and these are set out in LPA 1925, s. 1(1):

The only estates and interests in land which are capable of subsisting or of being conveyed or created at law are—

(a) an estate in fee simple absolute in possession;

(b) a term of years absolute.

The two terms in paragraphs (a) and (b) correspond to the common terms 'freehold' and 'leasehold' and require further detailed consideration.

1.2 **Estate in fee simple absolute in possession**

The fee simple is the larger of the two legal estates, in that it is of greater duration. The technical name describes the characteristics of the estate as it existed *before* 1 January 1926. As we have explained (see p. 2), at this date a number of statutes passed by Parliament in 1925 came into force and made considerable changes to the law relating to property. As a result, some of the characteristics of the fee simple estate were changed but the old name continues to be used. We have therefore to explain what the words meant under the old law, but we will do this very briefly.

1.2.1 **'Fee simple'**

It is this phrase which really causes the difficulty because of the changes made by the 1925 legislation. The word 'fee' denoted an inheritable interest in land and the word 'simple' tells us that the estate could be inherited by the 'general heirs'. This means that the estate would last as long as there were heirs to inherit. If a man died intestate (without making a will), any fee simple estate which he had owned would pass to his heir—a single individual who was identified according to complicated rules. If the deceased had children, the heir would be his eldest son. If the eldest son predeceased his father but had himself left a son, that grandson would be his grandfather's heir. If there were no sons to inherit, any daughters inherited the estate jointly. If the deceased had no descendants, his heir would be one of his blood relations, found among his brothers or sisters (or their descendants), or more remotely among his uncles, aunts or cousins. At a later stage, one of the deceased's ancestors, such as his father or grandfather, might be entitled to inherit. It might be therefore that the estate would pass to a fairly distant relation, as long as he or she was the closest living relative.

All this is now a matter of history, because the 1925 legislation abolished the old concept of the heir. Instead, new statutory rules of inheritance were imposed (and still apply, with modifications), so really after 1925 one cannot define a fee simple by calling it an estate 'inheritable by heirs general'. What remains true is that the fee simple is an estate which can endure indefinitely, as long as there are persons entitled to take the property under the provisions of the will of the previous owner, or under the statutory rules relating to an intestacy. Very occasionally no person entitled to the estate can be discovered after the rules have been applied. In such cases the estate will at this point come to an end and the land will revert to the Crown. — chancellor

1.2.2 **'Absolute'**

The explanation of the word 'absolute' gives rise to further complications. The word indicates that the fee simple should not be subject to any restriction whereby it may not endure as long as there are persons entitled to inherit. So, if I try to give Fred a fee simple estate 'until he qualifies as a solicitor', the gift cannot be of a fee simple estate. The estate will not necessarily last for ever (as long as there is someone to inherit) because it will end earlier should Fred ever become a solicitor. This sort of arrangement is called a 'determinable fee' and, together with its relative the 'conditional fee', it is considered in detail in Chapter 7.

1.2.3 'In possession'

The final words in the legal term for a freehold estate are 'in possession'. This means that the estate must be current, rather than being one which is to give the owner the use of the land at some time in the future. Thus, if I give Paul an estate to start in five years' time, I have not given him a legal estate. Future interests in land are dealt with in more detail in Chapters 13, 14 and 15.

It should be noted that the estate owner does not have to be in physical possession of the land itself in order to have a legal estate. For example, the property may be let to a tenant, in which case the tenant will be in physical possession of the land, whilst the landlord has the right to receive the rent payable under the lease. In this case the landlord still has a legal estate because LPA 1925, s. 205(1)(xix), says:

'Possession' includes receipt of rents and profits or the right to receive the same, if any.

1.2.4 **Effect of 1925 legislation**

It will be obvious that there are many kinds of arrangement which one may wish to make concerning a piece of land, but which cannot amount to a legal estate in fee simple. Examples of arrangements which fall into this category include: an interest for life; an interest to start at some time in the future—a future interest; and an entailed interest (see below). Before 1926, these were all lesser types of legal estate, but LPA 1925, s. 1(3) provides that interests which do not satisfy the new requirements for a legal estate are to take effect as equitable interests. This means that although arrangements of this sort can still be made, they now have to operate by means of a trust. In such a case, the legal fee simple is held by trustees on trust for those entitled to the equitable interests (see 1.6.2.1 and Part IV).

1.2.4.1 *Entailed interest (or fee tail)*

The 'entailed interest' requires some explanation. If you refer back to our remarks on the fee simple you will recall that that estate was inheritable by general heirs, the heir being drawn from a wide range of relatives of the deceased. In the case of a fee tail, however, the estate was still inheritable (denoted by the word 'fee'), but the heir had to come from a more limited class. This class was the 'heirs of the body', meaning the lineal descendants of the original tenant in tail. Sometimes this class was limited even further, to the 'heirs of the body male' (or, rarely, 'female'). In such a case the estate could not pass to an heir of the wrong sex, nor could it pass to the ascendants or siblings of the original tenant. It would pass only to his direct descendants of the correct sex. The fact that the estate was restricted or 'cut down' in this way led to its being described as a fee 'tail' (from the French verb '*tailler*'—'to cut').

If no heir of the right sort existed the estate would come to an end and the property reverted to the fee simple owner who had originally created this more limited estate (or to his general heir had he died). The person who had this right to recover the property should the entail come to an end was said to have a 'reversion'.

As we shall explain in Chapter 13, major changes in this area of law were intro-duced by the Trusts of Land and Appointment of Trustees Act 1996 and it is now no longer possible to create an entailed interest, even in equity.

1.3 Term of years absolute

The 'term of years absolute' is what is more commonly called a lease. It too is a legal estate but it is inferior to the fee simple estate because it is of limited duration. The essential requirement is that a lease must be for a fixed 'term of years', though this can include periods of less than a year (LPA 1925, s. 205(1)(xxvii)) and can include arrangements such as weekly or monthly tenancies. The word 'absolute' does not seem to add anything to the meaning because a lease does not cease to be a legal estate merely because it will terminate on the occurrence of some event (e.g., if the rent is unpaid).

To give one example of an arrangement which cannot qualify as a legal estate under LPA 1925, s. 1(1)(b), one may consider the case of *Lace* v *Chantler* [1944] KB 368, in which there was an attempt to create a lease 'for the duration of the war'. This was not a legal lease because it was not for a fixed period, since at the time that the lease was granted the length of the war could not be predicted.

It should be noted that the owner of a term of years does not hold the land of the Crown. The leaseholder derives his title from that of his landlord, who will be either the owner of a fee simple estate or of a longer leasehold estate.

The lease is of considerable importance in land law and it is considered in far greater detail in Chapters 8, 9 and 10.

1.4 Interests in land

You will probably realise that the legal estates are not the only rights to land which one might own. Normal daily life often requires that one person should be given a right which is enforceable against the land of another. For example, it is frequently the case that owners of neighbouring land share a common driveway to their houses, the drive being constructed partly on one piece of land and partly on the other. Before either owner can use such a driveway, he must be given a right to use the half of the drive which is on his neighbour's property. Unless each owner has a right which he can enforce against the other's estate, the drive will be useless to both of them.

Another example of a third-party right to land arises when an estate owner borrows money from a building society to finance the purchase of the estate. In order to provide security for the loan, the building society will take a mortgage of the property, which will give it rights over the estate should the borrower fail to repay the debt. Thus the society will have a right which is enforceable against the estate of the borrower and that right is a third-party right in land.

A third example might arise if the purchaser of an estate uses partly his own money and partly the money of a friend. The legal estate in the property may be transferred to the purchaser alone, but it is obviously unfair that he should be allowed to treat the property as wholly his (unless the money was provided as a loan or as a gift). Often this arrangement will be regarded as giving an interest in the property to the friend who provided part of the purchase money. In such a case it is possible for a trust of the estate to arise so that the purchaser becomes a trustee in relation to the property, the beneficiaries under the trust being himself and his friend. Thus the friend would have an interest in the land, even though the legal estate belonged solely to the purchaser.

Such third-party rights are very common and come in a multitude of shapes and sizes. They may all, however, be divided into two important classes:

(a) rights recognised by *law*; and

(b) rights recognised by *equity*.

1.5 Legal interests

1.5.1 LPA 1925, s. 1(2): legal interests

The two legal estates are the largest and the most important of the rights to land which are recognised by law, as opposed to operating in equity. However, there are lesser rights which are accepted at law and which are not relegated to an existence in equity only. These lesser interests are called 'legal interests or charges' and they are listed in LPA 1925, s. 1(2) (in which the words given here in brackets have been repealed):

The only interests or charges in or over land which are capable of subsisting or of being conveyed or created at law are—

(a) An easement, right, or privilege in or over land for an interest equivalent to an estate in fee simple absolute in possession or a term of years absolute;

(b) A rentcharge in possession issuing out of or charged on land being either perpetual or for a term of years absolute;

(c) A charge by way of legal mortgage;

(d) [Land tax, tithe rentcharge] and any other similar charge on land which is not created by an instrument;

(e) Rights of entry exercisable over or in respect of a legal term of years absolute, or annexed, for any purpose, to a legal rentcharge.

What follows is a brief introduction to each of these rights, some of which are considered in greater detail later in the book.

1.5.2 Legal easements, rights or privileges (s. 1(2)(a))

Easements are not easily defined but are easily recognisable once encountered. Essentially, they are rights attached to one piece of land, either entitling its occupants to do something on another's property, or preventing the owner of that other property from interfering with the passage of some benefit to the first piece of land. Thus one may have the right to walk over one's neighbour's land (a right of way), or perhaps the right to prevent the neighbour building so as to block the passage of light to one's windows (a right to light). In each case there is a piece of land which is benefited by the easement and a piece of land which is burdened with it. There are many types of easement, such as rights to storage or drainage, the right to water and a great number of others. A list of common examples is given in Chapter 22.

Related to easements, and also capable of being recognised at law under s. 1(2)(a), are profits à prendre. These are rights to take something from land which belongs to another estate owner; for example, a right to cut wood on another's property. These rights are also considered in detail in Chapter 22.

It should be noted that for either of these rights to be legal, as opposed to being enforceable in equity only, they must be granted for a term equivalent to a legal estate. This means that they must last for the same period as one of the two legal estates: that is, effectively in perpetuity (like a fee simple) or for a fixed period (like a term of years). Accordingly, a right of way given to a neighbour 'until the new road is built' cannot be a legal easement because it is to last for an uncertain length of time. Such an easement may, however, be enforceable as an equitable interest (see 1.6.3).

1.5.3 Rentcharges (s. 1(2)(b))

The first thing to note about the term 'rentcharge' is that it does not refer to rent which is payable under a lease, but to other arrangements whereby land is charged with the payment to someone of an annual or periodic sum. If the money is not paid, the person with the benefit of the rentcharge is entitled to enter upon the land in order to enforce payment.

At one time, and in certain parts of the country, it was rare for an estate in fee simple to be sold for a single payment of money; instead the vendor took a lump sum plus a rentcharge securing an annual payment. However the Rentcharges Act 1977 prevented the creation of any new rentcharges of this type, provided that any existing ones are to end 60 years after the Act came into force, and gave the estate owner of the charged land the right to redeem the rentcharge earlier on the payment of compensation.

The 1977 Act did not, however, abolish rentcharges altogether and they may still be created for certain purposes. Thus it is still possible to leave a property to a person, subject to a rentcharge obliging him to make a periodical payment to your widow or widower, or to some other member of your family, in order to provide for the maintenance of such person. This sort of rentcharge gives rise to a trust of the land and is considered in Chapter 13.

It is also still possible to create 'estate rentcharges', which are used to ensure that the estate owner of the charged land makes a payment towards the upkeep of facilities on other land. An example of this type is the rentcharge obliging the estate owner to pay an annual sum towards the maintenance of a road on his neighbour's property. These rentcharges are a means of providing for the enforcement of positive covenants in freehold land and they are considered further in Chapter 23.

For a rentcharge to be a legal interest in land it must last for the same period as one of the two legal estates; that is, either in perpetuity or for a fixed period.

1.5.4 **Charge by way of legal mortgage (s. 1(2)(c))**

A mortgage is the means whereby an estate in land is charged with the repayment of a debt or the performance of some other obligation. For example, the borrower (who grants the mortgage over his estate and is called the 'mortgagor') provides security for a loan by granting a mortgage to the lender (who becomes the 'mortgagee'). The mortgagee obtains an estate or interest in the mortgaged property by virtue of this arrangement. If the borrower fails to repay the loan, the mortgagee may take the mortgagor's property and sell it to satisfy the debt.

The charge by way of legal mortgage is one of the three types of mortgage recognised by LPA 1925, ss. 85–87. The other two are not mentioned in LPA 1925, s. 1(2), because they are created in a manner which gives the mortgagee a legal estate in the mortgaged property (in fact a lease) and are therefore legal by virtue of s. 1(1). The three types of legal mortgage are described in more detail in Chapter 21.

1.5.5 **. . . and any other similar charge on land which is not created by an instrument (s. 1(2)(d))**

The rather peculiar wording of this section is due to the repeal of the first four words, which originally referred to 'land tax' and 'tithe rentcharge'. The charges in this category are all created by statute and are rarely encountered.

1.5.6 **Rights of entry (s. 1(2)(e))**

This heading includes rights of entry included in leases or annexed to rentcharges. It is usual to include in a lease a clause which allows the landlord to recover, or 're-enter', the property, should the tenant be in breach of any of his obligations under the lease. This right is a legal right in itself under s. 1(2)(e) and is regarded as an interest in land. A similar right is usually included in a rentcharge, so that the owner of the rentcharge may enter and recover the land should the owner of the charged estate fail to pay the sums due.

1.6 **Equitable interests**

Section 1(3) of LPA 1925 provides that any interest in land which does not qualify as a legal interest takes effect as an equitable interest. This means that, if one is claiming an interest in land which does not appear on the list in s. 1(2), the interest will be enforced in equity only.

1.6.1 **Creation of equitable interests**

Equitable interests may be divided into two categories. The 'traditional' ones are equitable because historically equity provided a remedy when the common law would not help. Other interests, which are today equitable, were originally legal but became equitable as a result of the statutory reforms of land law. We have already seen that interests which do not fall within the definitions of legal estates and interests in LPA 1925, s. 1(1) and (2), now exist only in equity.

1.6.2 **Traditional equitable interests**

1.6.2.1 *The interest of a beneficiary under a trust*

Trusts are extremely important in land law and are considered further in Part IV. However, it is not possible to proceed very far with a study of this subject without having a basic idea of what a trust is, and so a brief explanation will be included here.

A trust arises when property is held by a person or persons 'upon trust' for another person or persons. Thus, Anne may hold property upon trust for Bob. Anne is called a 'trustee', whilst Bob is called a 'beneficiary'. It is the trustee's job to hold the property for the benefit of the beneficiary. It is the beneficiary who is entitled to the benefits of the property (called 'the beneficial interest'), whilst the trustee is a bare owner and must not use the estate for his own benefit. It may be easier to understand this idea if one compares the estate with a banana: the trustee is regarded as the owner of the banana-skin, whereas the beneficiary is the owner of the banana inside!

Historically, common law did not recognise such a separation of ownership and enjoyment and would not assist the beneficiary if the trustee used the estate for his own benefit. Equity did, however, protect the beneficiary, who accordingly does have an enforceable right to the property. The rights of the beneficiary are enforceable only in equity and not at law.

Where there is a trust of the legal estate in land there are therefore effectively two owners:

(a) the trustee owns the legal estate; and

(b) the beneficiary owns an equitable interest (i.e., the beneficial interest).

In addition to trusts which are created expressly by the owner of property, there are situations which the courts will interpret as giving rise to a trust, sometimes to give effect to the presumed intention of the owner, but on other occasions very much against his will. We have already seen an example of this in the trust which may arise where the purchaser's friend has contributed to the purchase price (1.4).

Trusts which are recognised by the courts in this way, without express creation, are said to be 'implied', 'resulting' or 'constructive' trusts. We deal with them in more detail in Chapter 17.

1.6.2.2 *Interests under contracts to create or transfer legal estates or interests*

Equitable interests also arise from the special way in which equity treats contracts to create legal estates or interests. If, for example, Victor, the fee simple owner of Blackacre, agrees to sell his estate to Peter, this agreement is protected in two ways if either party breaks the contract. The legal remedy available is that of damages for breach of contract. Equity, however, goes further and may give an order for specific performance of the contract. Specific performance is an order which will make the parties to a contract perform their promises—in our example Victor can be compelled to convey the estate and Peter can be made to pay the purchase price. Specific performance is, of course, a remedy which lies in the discretion of the court, because it is equitable in origin and all equitable remedies are discretionary.

Interestingly, the application of an equitable maxim, that 'Equity regards as done that which ought to be done', produces the result that a contract which can be specifically enforced is regarded as creating an interest in equity. The operation of this rule can best be explained by reference to our example of the sale by Victor to Peter. 'That which ought to be done' is the conveyance of the estate to Peter. From the time that the contract is made, therefore, equity acts as though that conveyance had already been completed. As a result Peter is treated as being the owner in equity from the date that the contract is made, whilst Victor remains the legal owner until the deed conveying the legal estate is made, and until that time is regarded by equity as holding the legal estate upon trust for Peter (see further at 3.5).

This special way in which equity treats contracts to create or convey estates or interests in land leads us on to the third type of equitable interest.

1.6.2.3 *Interests which are not created formally*

(1) *Formal requirements* Usually, in order to convey, transfer or create a legal estate or interest in land it is necessary to use a deed (for cases in which a deed is *not* required, see 8.3.1.1 and 11.2.5). LPA 1925, s. 52(1) provides:

All conveyances of land or any interest therein are void for the purpose of conveying or creating a legal estate unless made by deed.

Additional requirements for the creation or transfer of certain legal estates or interests are imposed by LRA 2002, but we will postpone consideration of these until Chapter 5, and will concentrate here on the nature of a deed.

A deed is a document which has been executed in accordance with certain formalities in order to ensure that its validity can be proved. The nature of the formalities required depends on the date at which the deed was executed.

(*a*) *Deeds executed before 31 July 1990* Deeds made before this date are subject to the traditional rules which required a deed to be signed, SEALED, and delivered. At one time it was a person's seal that was essential in order to prove the authenticity of a document, but for many years the habit of using sealing wax and a real seal had been abandoned and the seal was represented by a red sticker on the document, or even by a printed circle containing the letters 'LS' (from the Latin phrase 'locus sigilli'—'the place of the seal'), if it were shown that it was intended that these should represent a seal. It should be noted that in relation to these older documents no witness was necessary though most deeds were in fact witnessed.

(*b*) *Deeds made on or after 31 July 1990* Since 31 July 1990, the Law of Property (Miscellaneous Provisions) Act 1989, s. 1, has required that to be a deed a document must:

(a) make it clear on the face of the document that it is intended to be a deed; and
(b) be signed—
    (i) by the person executing the deed in the presence of a witness who attests the signature (this means that the witness also signs as such), or
    (ii) by another person at the direction of the person who wishes to execute

the deed in the presence of two witnesses who attest the signature (this is used where for some reason the person executing cannot sign something and he has to ask someone to sign on his behalf); and

(c) be delivered by the person executing or by someone else on his behalf.

So basically the document must be signed, witnessed and delivered.

In the case of both the old and the new rules it is technically necessary for the deed to be delivered formally. Correctly this used to be done by the person concerned placing his hand on the seal on the document and saying, 'I deliver this as my act and deed'. Today formal delivery is usually dispensed with, a practice which was approved in *Stromdale & Ball Ltd* v *Burden* [1952] Ch 223.

(2) *How do you know if a document is a deed?* The changes introduced by the Law of Property (Miscellaneous Provisions) Act 1989 have simplified the creation of deeds for the parties involved, but seem to have made the concept of a deed more difficult for law students to understand! The difference between a deed and a document which is merely 'in writing' is less obvious now, but the distinction between the two is essential, because, as we have said, most legal estates and interests cannot be created or transferred unless a deed is used. Since 31 July 1990 the distinguishing characteristics of a deed are that the signature of the party executing it is witnessed and the document is stated to be a deed (for example, by some phrase such as 'This Deed of Conveyance is made the first day of September 1999', or by the party executing it saying that he is signing it 'as a deed'—see pp. 64 and 108–9). A written document which does not satisfy these requirements is not a deed, and in general will not create or transfer a legal estate.

(3) *Help from equity when formal requirements not observed* At law an attempt to create an estate or interest without a deed will be totally ineffective. It may be, however, that the attempted grant can be treated as a contract to create the estate or interest. Contracts relating to land are now subject to strict formalities (see Chapter 3), but in the earlier law, less formality was required and frequently the courts were able to deduce the existence of a contract from the circumstances surrounding the ineffective grant. Where such a contract could be identified, specific performance of that contract might be available to compel the creation of a legal estate or interest in the proper form, by requiring one party to make a grant by deed. Moreover, as we explained above, the maxim that equity regards as done that which ought to be done might enable equity to treat the person entitled to the grant as already having the interest in equity.

We may illustrate this principle with the following example:

If Len purports to grant a lease of a flat to Tom for 10 years without using a deed, Tom does not obtain a legal term of years. Provided, however, that Tom can satisfy the court that a valid contract for a lease exists, he may seek an order for specific performance to compel Len to grant the lease by deed. Meanwhile, if specific performance could be granted, Tom is regarded by equity as having an equitable lease of the property for the specified period. (See *Walsh* v *Lonsdale* (1882) 21 ChD 9, considered further at 8.3.3.)

A similar process operates to give rise to other rights, such as equitable easements and equitable mortgages, where the correct formalities for granting these interests have not been observed, but the court is able to identify a contract to grant such an interest.

1.6.2.4 *Interests arising under restrictive covenants*

A further example of equity's willingness to provide a remedy when the law would not do so relates to restrictive covenants. These are promises made in a deed by which the promisor, or 'covenantor', undertakes not to do certain things on his land. If, for example, Pip is buying a house he might covenant with the vendor not to carry on a business on the premises. Law will enforce this promise against Pip, the original covenantor, as a matter of contract. If Pip later sells the property to Quentin, law will not enforce the covenant against Quentin, because he was not a party to the original contract. This is the ordinary contractual rule which requires 'privity of contract'. However, in certain circumstances, which are explained in Chapter 23, equity will enforce the covenant against Quentin. The person who is seeking to enforce the covenant will therefore have a right which is enforceable in equity against the owner for the time being of the property. This is a rule which originally arose in situations in which equity, as a matter of conscience, ruled that a purchaser should be bound by the covenant because he knew about it when he bought the property. The issue of 'conscience' has over the years become formalised into a series of rules which govern the position.

1.6.3 **Interests which became equitable as the result of statutory reform**

The equitable interests we have considered so far have been those developed by the Chancellor and his court in circumstances in which the common law courts were not able to provide a remedy. However, the range of equitable interests was enlarged considerably in 1926 by the addition of a number of rights which until then had been legal, but ceased to be so as a result of the statutory reforms. As we saw in para. 1.5, LPA 1925, s. 1(2) lists the very limited number of third-party rights which are now capable of existing at law. For example, the only easements which can take effect as legal interests after 1925 are those granted for a term equivalent to a legal estate. Thus a right of way 'until the new road is built' cannot be a legal easement even if it is granted by deed, and under the terms of s. 1(3) of the Act takes effect as an equitable easement.

1.6.4 **Other rights to equitable relief**

Having told you about some equitable interests, we must mention briefly some more rights which have on occasion been described by the courts as 'mere' equities. A party is sometimes said to have an 'equity' when he has a right to some form of equitable remedy, such as a right to have a transaction set aside for fraud or undue influence, or to have a document rectified for mistake. In some cases, most notably those involving estoppel (see 1.6.5), the courts regard themselves as having a wide discretion to chose the form of relief most appropriate to the circumstances. In the past, these rights to relief appeared to operate only between the parties personally concerned, but increasingly now they are regarded as enforceable against successors in title.

1.6.5 **Equitable estoppel**

Before leaving this introductory account of equitable developments, we must refer briefly to equitable estoppel, which in recent years has come to play an important part in many areas of land law. In general, rules of estoppel operate to prevent a party denying matters which he has previously asserted or represented. The doctrine is used by both law and equity, and we shall see some examples of legal estoppel when we come to consider leases (tenancy by estoppel—8.10.4; and surrender by operation of law—8.5.2.3(2)). At law, the representation must relate to existing fact, but equity, in its traditional role of restraining unconscionable behaviour, applies the concept more widely, and where it considers it to be appropriate may prevent a party from going back on his promise or from taking advantage of another person's mistake about his legal rights. Representations may, of course, take the form of oral or written statements, but they can also be made by conduct, and can include a mere passive acquiescence in the other party's mistaken belief.

We will deal with equitable estoppel in more detail in Chapters 18 and 20. However, you will come across other references to estoppel in the course of reading this book, and in particular should note a possible new application of the principle as a replacement for the old doctrine of part performance of a contract (see Chapter 3).

1.7 **Legal interests and equitable interests compared**

1.7.1 **Discretionary nature of equity**

The fact that a right is recognised only in equity and not at law is of practical significance, since all equitable rights are enforceable only at the discretion of the court. Thus although, since the Supreme Court of Judicature Acts 1873 and 1875, the rules of law and equity have both been administered by the same courts, it is still important to know whether one is dealing with a legal interest or an equitable interest. One has no absolute right to the protection by the courts of an equitable interest—remedies are at the discretion of the court. In this context the old equitable maxim, that 'He who comes to equity must come with clean hands', is of great importance. A person may be able to show that he has an equitable interest in land, but this would be of little use to him if he has 'dirty hands' and accordingly would be refused any remedy by the courts. For example, if he claims to have an equitable easement entitling him to walk across another estate owner's land, he may find that he is refused a remedy to enforce his right of way if he has behaved improperly himself (perhaps by exceeding the limits of his right or by causing damage). Legal rights, however, are enforceable as of right, and once the existence of the right is established it is not really open to the court to consider the merits of the situation before giving a remedy. Thus, if a person with a legal easement causes damage, the land owner may be able to claim compensation but the easement will still be enforced by the courts.

1.7.2 Enforcement against third parties

A major difference between legal and equitable rights used to be found in the rules governing the enforceability of those rights against a third party, for example, against the purchaser of the estate which is subject to the rights. Thus while a legal easement over a piece of land could be enforced against a purchaser of any estate in that land, an equitable easement over the same piece of land might not be enforceable against certain purchasers.

This was a rule which had its origins in the separate evolution of law and equity. Legal rights were said to be rights *in rem*; that is, rights in the land itself ('in the thing', from the Latin word *res*, meaning 'thing') and hence generally could be enforced against any person who acquired an estate or interest in the land. This was expressed by saying that legal rights were 'good against the world'.

By contrast, equitable rights were only rights *in personam*; that is, rights which were enforceable against certain categories of person, because it was considered to be fair or equitable that they should take subject to them. The rule which applies to equitable interests is that they bind everyone who takes the legal estate except a bona fide purchaser for value of that legal estate without notice of the equitable interest. This rule is commonly referred to as the 'notice rule'.

In studying the notice rule, you may find it helpful to note Maitland's brief but memorable account of how it developed (see Maitland, *Equity* (1936) at pp. 112–15). The Court of Chancery is pictured as working through the list of people who might acquire the legal estate from a trustee: which of them, in fairness, should be bound by the beneficiary's rights? Over the years, the court decides that it would be fair to enforce such rights against: those who inherit from the trustee; those who take the property from him as a gift ('donees'); and those who buy the property from him either knowing about the beneficiary's rights or deliberately closing their eyes to them. At the end of this development, there is just one person against whom it would not be fair to enforce the beneficiary's rights: someone who buys the legal estate in ignorance of the fact that it is trust property, despite having made all the appropriate enquiries, i.e., to use the technical phrase, the *bona fide* purchaser of the legal estate for value without notice. You should note, of course, that although Maitland explains the doctrine of notice by reference to the trust, the courts applied it to all equitable interests.

We will now look at the doctrine of notice in a little more detail.

1.7.3 The equitable doctrine of notice

1.7.3.1 *The purchaser must be bona fide*

I.e., the purchaser must act in good faith. This part of the rule seems to be duplicated by the requirement that the purchaser should not have notice of the right, and it is difficult to see what is added by this phrase. However, Lord Wilberforce in *Midland Bank Trust Co. Ltd* v *Green* [1981] AC 513 at p. 528 considered that:

> it would be a mistake to suppose that the requirement of good faith extended only to the matter of notice . . . good faith is a . . . separate test which may have to be passed even though absence of notice is proved.

We cannot point to any cases in which a purchaser without notice has failed the good faith test, but you may like to note the suggestion in Smith at p. 205 that 'perhaps the purchase of land for some improper purpose would prevent the defence [of being a bona fide purchaser, etc.] from being raised'.

1.7.3.2 *The purchaser must give value*

It is necessary for the person who acquires the estate to give value if he is to rely on the notice rule. Thus a donee (or 'volunteer') takes a gift of land subject to any equitable interests that there may be. 'Value' includes money, money's worth and some other forms of consideration, such as marriage.

A person who acquires an estate for value is described as a 'purchaser for value'. This may seem unnecessarily long-winded, since in ordinary speech 'purchaser' means 'buyer' and so includes the notion of taking for value. However, for the lawyer, 'purchaser' has the technical meaning of 'one who takes by act of the parties rather than by operation of law'. This means that he has had the property transferred to him in the appropriate way by the previous owner, rather than having it vested in him automatically by operation of some rule of law, such as that which vests a bankrupt's property in his trustee in bankruptcy or the deceased's property in his personal representatives. In this sense then, even a donee is a purchaser and so in a context like this it is necessary to state specifically that the person acquiring the estate is a purchaser for value.

1.7.3.3 *The purchaser must acquire a legal estate*

The purchaser must buy a legal estate, rather than an equitable interest in the land. Thus, if the purchaser is to be safe, he must have acquired the legal estate before he discovers the equitable interest.

1.7.3.4 *The purchaser must not have notice of the equitable interest*

There are three types of notice: actual notice; constructive notice; and imputed notice.

(a) *Actual notice.* This is quite straightforward and applies where the purchaser has actual knowledge of the existence of the equitable interest. It is not necessary for the purchaser to obtain this information from any particular source and he may even discover the truth from a complete outsider (*Lloyd* v *Banks* (1868) LR 3 Ch App 488).

(b) *Constructive notice.* When the notice rule was first created by the courts of equity, clever purchasers soon realised that they could obtain an advantage if they declined to make any investigations which might lead to the discovery of equitable interests. Equity was quick to extend the rule to prevent purchasers deliberately 'turning a blind eye' in this way, as such behaviour was evidence of a lack of good faith on the part of the purchaser. The means used was to say that the purchasers would be deemed to know of interests which they would have discovered if they had asked the usual questions about the property and so were bound by such interests. This rule is preserved in modern law by LPA 1925, s. 199(1)(ii).

(c) *Imputed notice.* A purchaser is also deemed to have notice of an equitable interest if his agent has either actual or constructive notice of it. This rule is essential, since most purchasers do not conduct their own conveyancing. Thus if a conveyancer obtains actual notice of an equitable interest, his purchaser/client is also regarded as having notice of it (*Jared* v *Clements* [1903] 1 Ch 428).

As a result of major changes introduced by the 1925 legislation, the doctrine of notice is of less importance today, but it can still be of some significance and we will tell you more about this in 4.5.2.2 and 5.11.3.

1.8 A multiplicity of rights

It will be obvious from what we have said so far that one piece of land may be subject to a large number of interests all at the same time. Indeed the doctrine of estates may be responsible for encouraging the development of such multiple interests, because it encourages one to think in terms of owning rights in land rather than of owning the land itself. As we shall see, in England and Wales land law is not really concerned with absolute rights but rather with balancing the relative claims to land which may be made by a number of people. Thus one piece of land could be subject to *all* the following rights at the same time:

(a) a fee simple owned by Amy;

(b) a 99-year lease granted by Amy to Bob;

(c) a weekly tenancy granted by Bob to Carol;

(d) a legal mortgage of the freehold granted by Amy to a building society;

(e) an equitable mortgage of the 99-year lease granted by Bob to his bank;

(f) a right of way over the property granted in perpetuity to David, the owner of the house next door (a legal easement);

(g) an estate rentcharge granted by Amy to Eric, a neighbouring owner, to ensure that Amy contributes to the cost of maintaining a shared drive;

(h) a restrictive covenant enforceable by another neighbour, Fred, which prevents the land from being used for business purposes.

1.9 Classification of property

Although we are leaving questions about the definition of land, and other technical matters, until the last chapter, we must make a brief mention here of the lawyers' classification of property and a few of the technical terms connected with it.

1.9.1 Real and personal property

Property is divided into two main categories: 'real' property and 'personal' property (or 'realty' and 'personalty'). Real property consists of all the estates and interests in land which we will be considering in this book, with the exception of leases which, for historical reasons, are regarded as a form of personal property. The reason for this is explained in Chapter 25.

1.9.2 **Personal property**

Personal property is divided into three categories: choses in possession, choses in action and chattels real.

1.9.2.1 *Choses in possession*

Tangible objects other than land which can be physically possessed (such as cars, books and clothes) are called 'choses in possession'. 'Chose' also means 'thing' but this time lawyers use French rather than Latin.

1.9.2.2 *Choses in action*

Intangible rights, other than those relating to land, of which one cannot take physical possession and which depend for their existence on enforcement by the courts are called 'choses in action'. In this category are placed debts, copyrights and patents, amongst other rights.

1.9.2.3 *Chattels real*

Leases, which are estates in land, but were classified as personal property, are known technically as 'chattels real', because although they are chattels (another name for personal property) they became very like real property, as we explain in Chapter 25.

1.10 **Human Rights Act 1998**

Before ending this chapter, we need to draw your attention to the fact that the Human Rights Act 1998 may well be relevant to various aspects of your study of land law. We will comment on these as we go, but should mention now that the Convention articles most likely to be significant in a land law context are: Art. 6 (right to a fair trial); Art. 8 (right to respect for private and family life); Art. 14 (prohibition of discrimination); and Art. 1 of the First Protocol (protection of property). For the full text of these and the other Convention articles, see the Human Rights Act 1998, Sch. 1.

As you probably know already from other studies, a major uncertainty about the Act, still unresolved, is whether it has 'horizontal' effect; that is, whether the Convention rights are enforceable between private individuals. On the fact of it, the Act protects these rights against the State (the 'vertical' effect), and does this by providing that it is unlawful for a public authority to act in a way which is incompatible with a Convention right (s. 6(1)). The definition of 'a public authority' is, however, a wide one, including 'a court or tribunal' (s. 6 (3)(a)), and many commentators suggest that this imposes a duty on the courts to enforce Convention rights in all proceedings, including those between private individuals.

Further, s. 3(1) provides that:

So far as it is possible to do so, primary legislation and subordinate legislation must be read and given effect in a way which is compatible with the Convention rights. ·

Clearly, this will apply in all cases before the courts, regardless of whether the parties are public authorities or private individuals.

The uncertainty about horizontal effect is obviously highly significant in the land law context, where so many of the questions before the courts are between private individuals, and you might think that until the question has been resolved the Act would have little significance in this area of law. However, it must be remembered that a good deal of land is owned by public authorities (local authorities for example having a major role as landlords of public sector housing), and already issues about Convention rights have been raised in a number of cases involving such landowners. In general, however, such cases are concerned with details of statutory codes and procedures which are beyond the scope of this book, but there are one or two decisions involving more general land law concepts and we will discuss these cases and other relevant matters in the appropriate chapters.

FURTHER READING

Generally

Smith, *Property Law*, 4th edn., Longman, 2003, Chapter 4.

On origins and nature of equity

Hanbury and Martin, *Modern Equity*, 16th edn., Sweet & Maxwell, 2001, Chapter 1 (History and Principles—in particular pp. 3–8, 27–31 and 34–40).

Lawson and Rudden, *The Law of Property*, 3rd edn., Oxford University Press, 2002, pp. 82–8 (equitable rights and remedies).

Maitland, *Equity*, Cambridge University Press, 1936, Lectures 1 and 11 (The Origins of Equity).

Pearce and Stevens, *The Law of Trusts and Equitable Obligations*, 3rd edn., Butterworths, 2002, Chapter 1.

Smith, *Property Law*, 4th edn., Longman, 2003, Chapter 3.

Human rights

Howell, 'The Human Rights Act 1998: the "Horizontal Effect" on Land Law', *Modern Studies in Property Law, Vol.1: Property 2000*, Hart Publishing, 2001, p. 149.

Rook, *Property Law and Human Rights*, Blackstone Press, 2001 (in particular, Introduction and Chapter 3).

PART II

Acquisition of estates in land

Introduction

In this part we intend to concentrate on the acquisition of a fee simple estate in land. Most of what we say will also be relevant to acquiring an existing long lease from the current leaseholder, but details of how such leases are originally created will be dealt with in detail in Chapter 8, in which the term of years absolute is further discussed. Although estates and interests in land may be acquired by way of gift, either in the lifetime of the donor or on his death, we are primarily concerned here with acquisitions for value, and will, in the main, be describing the process by which a purchaser buys an estate in land from a vendor.

Although land law and conveyancing are normally taught separately, they are in fact inextricably linked: the law relating to conveyancing is unintelligible without an understanding of the underlying structure of land law, and land law seems pointless unless one has an appreciation of how the theory of the law is applied in practice. Here we are concentrating on the rules of land law rather than those of conveyancing but we will set the land law rules in their conveyancing context as this will make it easier to appreciate their purpose. To this end we will consider in Chapters 2–5 the steps necessary to purchase two properties, Nos. 1 and 3 Trant Way.

We will also discuss another manner of acquiring an estate, which may occur in circumstances in which the owner of the estate has no intention of transferring the estate to another person. This may happen when the other person takes possession of the land and remains upon it for a prescribed period of time; the title so acquired is commonly known as 'squatter's rights' but is more technically called 'title by adverse possession' and is further explained in Chapter 6. The acquisition of title by adverse possession is not a frequent occurrence but it does happen, and can cause particular problems for a purchaser since the 'paper' owner will have nothing of value to sell, whilst the person with title by adverse possession will not have the usual documentary evidence of ownership.

2

Buying a house

2.1 The properties

2.1.1 1 Trant Way

This property has already been mentioned in Chapter 1. It is a large Victorian house with a garden. The current owner of the fee simple is Victor Venn. Mr Venn bought the property in 1992 but is now obliged to move to another part of the country. Mr and Mrs Armstrong (Arnold and Arriety) are interested in buying the property for £195,000.

2.1.2 3 Trant Way

Number 3 is another large house but it has been divided up so that the top floor provides a separate 'granny flat', with its own internal front door but sharing the street door with the rest of the house and using the internal stairs for access. The current fee simple owner is Victoria Ventnor who bought the property in 1988. Barbara Bell is interested in buying the house for £170,000. Barbara has an elderly father, Bob Bell, and she hopes that he will agree to come and live in the top-floor flat so that she can 'keep an eye on him'.

2.2 Two systems of title

2.2.1 What the buyer wants to know

A prospective purchaser of any property (or normally his solicitor) has two main concerns. First, he must be sure that the vendor of the property is really entitled to sell it. Thus the buyer must insist that the vendor proves that his title to the land is good and that he can pass to the purchaser the estate which he is offering to sell. Secondly, the purchaser will want to know whether any third parties have rights to the land which might interfere with his intended use of it. These third-party rights might include covenants restricting use, rights of way, tree preservation orders or even mortgages obliging the owner of the estate to make payments to a creditor. Concern about these matters will lead the purchaser, or his representatives, to make extensive enquiries before the purchase of the estate is finally concluded.

2.2.2 **Registered and unregistered systems**

Unfortunately for the student of English land law, there are two totally separate systems of proving title to land and investigating third-party rights in it. The newer (and now more common) system is the registered land system; the older system is usually called the unregistered system of conveyancing. The enquiries to be made by a purchaser differ depending on whether the title to the property he wishes to buy is registered or unregistered. For the student this means learning two totally different sets of laws: one governed by statute, the Land Registration Act 2002, which has recently repealed and replaced the earlier Land Registration Act 1925 (see Chapter 5); the other governed by the old rules of common law and equity as amended by statute, chiefly now the Law of Property Act 1925 and the Land Charges Act 1972 (see Chapter 4).

2.2.3 **Which system applies?**

The first thing which you must ascertain when dealing with any piece of land is which system of conveyancing is to be applied to it. In other words you must find out whether the estate in the land is (or should be) registered or not. It may surprise you to find that the old unregistered system of title is still in operation nearly 80 years after the introduction of compulsory registration. This is a result of the policy of phased introduction, which we explain below, but undoubtedly the whole process has taken far longer than was expected in 1925, and recent statutory changes are designed to extend registration of title more quickly.

2.2.3.1 *Areas of compulsory registration*

Although there had been some limited registration of title before 1926, it was LRA 1925 which provided that in future registration of title to land was to become compulsory in areas designated as areas of compulsory registration by central government. As it was not possible to introduce the registration system to the whole country immediately (largely due to cost), the practice was adopted of making only certain places areas of compulsory registration and gradually increasing those areas as time went on. Originally it was thought that the whole country would soon be covered, but economic depression, followed by a war and further recession, held up the extension of the system. However, the last areas, including our imaginary town of Mousehole, became compulsory registration areas on 1 December 1990. Accordingly, now all land in England and Wales stands in an area of compulsory registration and any person dealing with a property simply needs to ask the Land Registry whether the title has in fact been registered.

2.2.3.2 *Has the title to the estate been registered?*

One has to ask this question because estates did not have to be registered as soon as the area in which the land stands became an area of compulsory registration. To require this would have involved estate owners in unexpected costs, for Land Registry fees are payable on all registrations. Instead, estates had to be registered at the time of the first dealing for value with the estate (usually the sale of the freehold or a grant of a long lease) after the area became a compulsory area. Thus in Mousehole all estates which have been dealt with since 1990 should have been registered at the Land Registry. Accordingly the title to 1 Trant Way will be registered (dealing in 1992), whilst the title to 3 Trant Way will not be registered (last dealing in 1988).

Triggering registration
Under s. 1 of LRA 1997, which came into effect on 1 April 1998, the occasions which give rise to compulsory registration were considerably extended. The conveyance of the freehold estate and the grant or assignment of a leasehold estate for more than 21 years became registrable not only on dealings for value, but also on dispositions made: by way of gift; by personal representatives (who transfer the property of any deceased person to those entitled to it); and on a court order. In addition, a legal estate became registrable if the owner created over it a first legal mortgage protected by the deposit of the title deeds (as to which, see 4.4.2.2(1)), even though the owner was not transferring the estate itself.

LRA 1997 has been repealed and replaced by LRA 2002. The events noted above as triggering first registration continue to do so under the new Act (LRA 2002, s. 4), but in addition the Act extends registration requirements to all leases which, at the time of their creation or transfer, have more than seven years to run (s. 4(2)(b)), and to certain leases for shorter periods. We will consider the requirements for first registration more fully in Chapter 5, but you should note now that the extension of events inducing registration must lead to a very real increase in the number of titles coming on to the register.

Voluntary registration
While most registered land has been entered on the register in compliance with the requirements for compulsory registration, there are also cases in which registration is appropriate on a voluntary basis. For example, a developer planning to build a large housing estate on land which is currently unregistered may choose to register the title to the whole estate voluntarily. He can then agree an estate plan for all the new properties with the Land Registry before he starts to sell the individual plots. This makes conveyancing of each plot of land easier once purchasers are found and is convenient for the developer, the purchasers and the Registry. Voluntary registration is also sometimes used to solve a problem which has arisen in relation to the property, for example, if the title deeds have been destroyed in a fire or due to an accident. In these cases voluntary registration can avoid many difficulties when the estate owner comes to sell, because the registry entry will replace the missing deeds.

As we shall see in Chapter 5, it is now considered desirable to extend registration of title as rapidly and thoroughly as possible. Landowners are to be encouraged to seek voluntary registration by offering reduced fees for the process and by drawing attention to the advantages of registered title which, under the new Act, will include improved protection against squatters (see Chapter 6).

How to find out if title has been registered
At present, the result of the gradual introduction of registration is that the title to some pieces of land will be registered, whilst the title to others will not. If you are not sure whether a registration has been made you can find out by making an 'index map search', which will tell you whether the estate has been registered (but which will not reveal any other information, such as the name of the estate owner).

Further details may be obtained by making a full search of the register, which, since 3 December 1990, can be done without the consent of the estate owner.

2.2.3.3 *Unregistered land*

Any land which is not shown as being registered on the Land Registry index map is necessarily unregistered land (even though it is in an area of compulsory registration). As such it is covered by the older system of conveyancing rules which are substantially different, particularly as regards the protection of third party rights. According to a Law Commission Consultative Document published in 1998 (*Land Registration for the Twenty-First Century*, Law Com No. 254, para. 1.6) more than 80 per cent of the estimated number of titles to land in England and Wales was registered at that date and the increase in registrations following LRA 1997 means that unregistered land is rapidly becoming even less common. Nevertheless, it remains necessary to have an understanding of how the older system works, because it is still far from being redundant.

2.3 Outline of the conveyancing process

2.3.1 A two-stage process

Conveyancing is usually conducted in two stages. The parties will first enter into a contract, in which the purchaser agrees to buy, and the vendor agrees to sell, the property. After a period of time, the contract will be performed or completed by the transfer or conveyance of the legal estate by the vendor to the purchaser.

The interval between contract and completion used to be quite long, and was the stage at which the main investigation of the vendor's title took place. Nowadays, however, a full investigation of title usually precedes the exchange of contracts, and as a result the period between contract and completion is often shortened. For land law purposes, we still find it convenient to deal with questions relating to the contract before going on to matters of title, but you should remember that this is not necessarily the order in which these topics will present themselves in real life!

2.3.2 Steps before a contract is concluded

2.3.2.1 *Enquiries before contract*

Before they enter into contracts to buy 1 and 3 Trant Way, Mr and Mrs Armstrong and Miss Bell will want confirmation of certain information about the properties: they will want to know how much the council tax is; whether the price includes any fittings, such as carpets; whether there have been any disputes in respect of the land (e.g., boundary disputes); and, no doubt, a great deal else. In addition, their solicitors may wish to query portions of the draft contract each has received from the vendors' solicitors.

As noted above, it may well be that the full investigation of the vendor's title will be carried out at this stage. However, this process varies according to whether the land is registered or unregistered, and so we will deal with it later in the appropriate chapters (see Chapters 4 and 5).

2.3.2.2 *Local land charges*

Before entering into a contract to buy an estate in land, it is usual also to make a search about the property in the local land charges register. These registers are maintained by the local authorities for the properties in their areas under the Local Land Charges Act 1975. They contain details of a variety of 'charges' (burdens) on the land. Thus you might discover from searching the register that the property is in a smoke control zone, or that a tree in the garden is the subject of a tree preservation order, or that the local authority has a claim against the land because the council tax has not been paid. You might also discover planning restrictions or that the building is listed as being of outstanding architectural or historical importance. As all these matters might have a considerable effect upon the use to which the land can be put, it is essential that a purchaser should make a search.

Oddly, a purchaser of an estate will be bound by any charge which exists, even if it has not been registered. However, a search is still worthwhile because, if a purchaser obtains an official search certificate, compensation can be claimed under the Local Land Charges Act 1975, s. 10 if later a charge is discovered which was not revealed by the certificate. This right to compensation arises whether the search was clean because the charge had not been registered or because the local authority made a mistake when issuing the certificate. The compensation is paid by the local authority, even if the loss is due to the mistake of some third party who has failed to register a charge (the authority may seek to recover from the third party any sums so paid).

In addition to providing an official search of the local land charges register, the local authority will also provide, if asked, a wide range of other information about the property (including, for example, details of any planned local road alterations). Standard forms are used for both searches and for raising extra enquiries with local authorities and a fee is payable for both.

2.3.3 The contract

Once a purchaser is satisfied with the answers to whatever enquiries he is making at this stage, has made any necessary arrangements to finance the transaction, and has had a surveyor's report on the property (if he so wishes), the point will have been reached at which the parties are ready to conclude a legally binding contract. Until a contract is concluded neither party is legally bound to continue with the transaction and either can back out of the negotiations without liability. (It is this freedom from obligation, of course, which leads to the practice of 'gazumping', in which the vendor accepts a higher offer from another purchaser.) However, once a contract has been concluded, each party is legally obliged to give effect to the transaction, unless the other party is in breach of the terms of the contract. The detailed requirements for the creation of contracts relating to land will be considered in Chapter 3.

2.3.4 Investigating title

At some stage in the process of selling his house the vendor must show that he does have the title to the land which he intends to sell to the purchaser. The means by which this is done varies depending upon whether the title to the land is registered or unregistered. Basically, if the title is registered the purchaser will investigate the register, whilst if the title is unregistered he will need to see the title deeds to the property. The methods used to protect third-party rights also differ between the two systems and the searches to be made by the purchaser will accordingly be different.

Thus there are two very different processes ahead of Barbara Bell and the Armstrongs, who respectively are buying 3 Trant Way (unregistered title), and 1 Trant Way (registered title) (see 2.2.3.2) and we will follow their progress and consider the two systems in more detail in Chapters 4 and 5.

2.3.5 **Completing the transaction**

Once both parties have made all the necessary arrangements, the time will have arrived for the purchaser to pay the purchase price and the vendor to transfer the legal estate in the land to the purchaser. The vendor will also be obliged to give possession of the property to the purchaser. This transfer is usually called 'completion'. Obviously it requires a further document, and you will recall from Chapter 1 that the document used to dispose of a legal estate must be a 'deed', a document which is signed, witnessed and delivered (Law of Property (Miscellaneous Provisions) Act 1989, s. 1). If the title to the land is registered the deed used is called a 'transfer', and it must be perfected by being registered at the Land Registry: the legal title will not transfer to the purchaser until registration (see Chapter 5). If the land is unregistered the deed is called a 'conveyance' and it has the effect of conveying the legal estate to the purchaser without the need for further formalities (see Chapter 4).

FURTHER READING

Which? Way to Buy, Sell and Move House, Which Books, Consumers' Association, 2004, Chapter 10 (Conveyancing—the legal side of buying and selling a house).

3

The contract

3.1 Introduction

To some extent, a contract for the sale of an estate or an interest in land is just like any other contract. It must comply with the basic requirements for a contract not made by deed: there must have been an offer and an acceptance, there must be consideration, and the parties must have intended to create a legal relationship. However, due to the considerable value of land, it is not surprising that for many centuries there have been additional rules relating to these contracts which require certain formalities to be observed.

The nature of these formalities will depend upon the date at which the contract was made. New rules for making such contracts were introduced by the Law of Property (Miscellaneous Provisions) Act 1989, and apply to contracts made on or after 27 September 1989. The old rules were contained in s. 40 of the LPA 1925, which was repealed by the 1989 Act. You might think that most contracts made under the old law would by now either have been performed or have come before the courts, but in fact cases could continue to arise for some years yet. One of the reasons for this is that, as we explained in Chapter 1, equity may regard an ineffective grant of a legal estate or interest as a contract to make that grant, giving rise to an equitable interest in the property. Parties who rely on informal arrangements of this type, made before 27 September 1989, may continue to enjoy rights under them for many years before any dispute arises. An example of this is to be found in *Lloyds Bank plc* v *Carrick* [1996] 4 All ER 630, in which the defendant relied upon a contract with her brother-in-law, entered into in the early 1980s. In such a case, it will be necessary to show that the alleged contract satisfied the requirements of the law in force at the date of its creation, and accordingly it seems likely that, for some time to come, one will have to be familiar with the old rules as well as with the new ones. We will start by looking at the new rules, and will then consider the old ones more briefly.

3.2 Contracts made on or after 27 September 1989

3.2.1 Law of Property (Miscellaneous Provisions) Act 1989, s. 2

Any contract relating to land which is made on or after 27 September 1989 must be made in writing, must contain all the terms agreed between the parties and must be signed by each of them.

These requirements are imposed by s. 2 of the Law of Property (Miscellaneous Provisions) Act 1989 (which we will refer to hereafter as 'the 1989 Act').

Section 2(1)–(3) provides:

(1) A contract for the sale or other disposition of an interest in land can only be made in writing and only by incorporating all the terms which the parties have expressly agreed in one document or, where contracts are exchanged, in each.

(2) The terms may be incorporated in a document either by being set out in it or by reference to some other document.

(3) The document incorporating the terms or, where contracts are exchanged, one of the documents incorporating them (but not necessarily the same one) must be signed by or on behalf of each party to the contract.

We will now look at the provisions of s. 2 in some detail.

3.2.2 **Requirements of s. 2**

3.2.2.1 *Contracts for the sale or other disposition of an interest in land*

The effect of this phrase is that s. 2 applies to a wide range of transactions. Obviously the words would cover the sale of a fee simple and of an existing lease, but they also include a contract for the original grant of a lease, and contracts to grant a wide range of other interests in land, such as mortgages and easements.

In general, the meaning of this phrase in the Act seems reasonably clear, but a question about its application did arise in *Spiro* v *Glencrown Properties Ltd* [1991] Ch 537. This case was concerned with an option to purchase land, the issue being whether the notice given by the purchaser to exercise the option needed to comply with s. 2. Some authorities describe the option to purchase as a conditional contract, because the vendor is bound to sell the property if the purchaser performs certain conditions (such as giving notice). Other authorities reject this view, relying on the fact that only one party, the vendor, is bound, and prefer to describe the option as an irrevocable offer, with the contract only coming into existence when the option is exercised. On this basis the purchaser in *Spiro* v *Glencrown Properties Ltd* (who had exercised the option, but then failed to complete the purchase) argued that it is the exercise of the option which is to be regarded as the making of the contract, and which therefore has to satisfy the requirements of s. 2. (We shall see later at 4.4.2.2(4) that a similar question, in relation to the stage at which an option to purchase unregistered land should be registered as a landcharge, was considered in *Armstrong and Holmes Ltd* v *Holmes* [1993] 1 WLR 1482.)

In the *Spiro* case, Hoffmann J (at p. 544) took the view that:

An option is not strictly speaking either an offer or a conditional contract. It does not have *all* the incidents of the standard form of either of these concepts. To that extent it is a relationship *sui generis*. But there are ways in which it resembles each of them. Each analogy is in the proper context a valid way of characterising the situation created by an option. The question in this case is not whether one analogy is true and the other false, but which is appropriate to be used in the construction of s. 2.

In the view of the judge:

Section 2 . . . was intended to prevent disputes over whether the parties had entered into a binding agreement or over what terms they had agreed. It prescribes the formalities for recording their mutual consent. But only the grant of the option depends upon consent. The exercise of the option is a unilateral act. It would destroy the very purpose of the option if the purchaser had to obtain the vendor's counter-signature to the notice by which it was exercised (at p. 541).

The court therefore held that the grant of the option, which satisfied the requirements of s. 2, was a valid contract enforceable against the purchaser.

The only other decisions so far on the nature of the interests falling within s. 2 indicate that an option to surrender a lease is within the terms of the section (*Commission for the New Towns* v *Cooper (Great Britain) Ltd* [1995] Ch 259), and that a lockout agreement, by which a vendor agrees with a prospective purchaser not to negotiate with anyone else for a specified time, falls outside them (*Pitt* v *PHH Asset Management Ltd* [1994] 1 WLR 327).

3.2.2.2 *The contract must be made in writing*

We want to emphasise here that there is no alternative to this requirement. The only way in which a contract relating to land can be made on or after 27 September 1989 is in writing: an oral agreement between the parties will not create a contract.

It seems that equitable concepts such as estoppel or the constructive trust may assist a party who relies on an agreement which does not satisfy the Act's requirements (see 3.4.2) but, even so, this would not give the agreement the force of a valid contract.

3.2.2.3 *The written contract must incorporate all the terms which the parties have expressly agreed*

This requirement is set out in s. 2(1), and s. 2(2) then goes on to provide that the terms agreed by the parties may be incorporated in the contract either by setting them out in it, or by referring to some other document which contains them. Failure to do this will invalidate the contract.

Since the 1989 Act has been in operation, a number of cases have come before the courts in which it has been alleged that a term which forms part of the agreement has not been incorporated in the written contract and that the contract is accordingly void. The attempt by one party to escape from his agreement often appears to be somewhat unmeritorious, and occasionally the court has succeeded in holding him to his bargain.

In some cases the court has done this by treating the missing terms as a separate contract, the omission of which does not invalidate the contract relating to an interest in land. This approach was first adopted in *Record* v *Bell* [1991] 1 WLR 853, where a purchaser failed to complete his purchase and then argued that the contract for sale was invalid because it did not include a condition, agreed between the parties' solicitors, about proof of title.

It was held that in this transaction there had been two contracts: one for the sale of the estate in land and the other a collateral contract that the title to the property would be revealed as described when the necessary paperwork was produced. The collateral contract was not in itself a contract for the sale of an estate or interest in land and thus was not subject to s. 2 and could be concluded orally. The collateral contract had been fulfilled and there was no defect in the contract for sale, which accordingly could be enforced.

The possibility of two separate contracts was also considered in *Tootal Clothing Ltd* v *Guinea Properties Management Ltd* [1992] 2 EGLR 80. Here the agreements were:

(1) for the grant of a lease; and (2) that the tenant would carry out shopfitting works at the premises within 12 weeks and that for this work the landlord would pay £30,000. The contract to grant the lease was fulfilled by the formal grant of a lease and the tenant thereafter carried out the work. However, when the work was done the landlord refused to pay. In this case the Court of Appeal held that s. 2 could not continue to apply to the agreement to grant the lease after the transaction had been completed by the making of the grant and that, in any event, there were two separate contracts here. Thus the agreement for the work did not have to be included in the same document as the agreement for the lease in order to be enforceable. Scott LJ said:

> If parties choose to hive off parts of the terms of their composite bargain into a separate contract distinct from the written land contract that incorporates the rest of the terms, I can see nothing in section 2 that provides an answer to an action for enforcement of the land contract, on the one hand, or of the separate contract on the other hand. Each has become, by the choice of the parties, a separate contract.

Thus, in two cases at least, attempts to invalidate a contract by reference to s. 2 have been met by the device of treating the omitted terms as constituting a separate agreement.

By contrast, however, there have been other decisions in which the court has refused to adopt this approach, and has treated the whole contract as void because certain terms have been omitted. In *Wright* v *Robert Leonard (Developments) Ltd* [1994] NPC 49, the purchaser agreed to buy both a show flat and its furnishings, but the furnishings were not mentioned in the written contract. After completion, the purchaser found that the furnishings had been removed and, when he sought damages for breach of contract, was met with the argument that there was not sufficient writing to satisfy s. 2. It would have been relatively easy for the court to adopt the approach taken in *Record* v *Bell*, construing the agreement as creating two separate contracts. The Court of Appeal, however, declined to do this, taking the view that 'if the contract is all one arrangement, there is no collateral contract, and all the terms in it must be in writing, even those which do not refer to the land'. Here there was only one contract with two elements, and both should have been included in the written document (and note the similar approach adopted by the Court of Appeal in *Godden* v *Merthyr Tydfil Housing Association* [1997] NPC 1).

In *Wright* v *Robert Leonard (Developments) Ltd* the court nevertheless found itself able to assist the purchaser, holding that the case was one in which it was appropriate to grant the equitable remedy of rectification, and awarding the purchaser damages for breach of the rectified contract. It should be noted here that s. 2(4) makes express reference to the possibility of rectification, and it appears from *Joscelyne* v *Nissen* [1970] 2 QB 86 that, as long as there is a pre-existing *agreement*, it is not necessary to establish that there was a pre-existing *contract* in order to obtain rectification. (If this were not so, it would of course be impossible to obtain rectification of a document which failed to satisfy s. 2 and so in consequence was not a valid contract.)

Another case to note on the contents of the written contract is *McCausland* v *Duncan Lawrie Ltd* [1997] 1 WLR 38. Here a written contract which complied with the requirements of s. 2 specified a date for completion which was subsequently varied by agreement in correspondence between the parties. When the purchaser failed to complete on the new date, the vendor issued a notice requiring him to complete and, when this did not happen, sought recission of the contract. The purchaser, who still wished to buy the property, sought specific performance, and the case turned on whether the variation of the original completion date was effective. The purchaser relied upon s. 2, claiming that the variation was ineffective because it did not satisfy the requirements of the Act. The Court of Appeal accepted this argument, holding that a variation of a material term in the contract had to comply with the requirements of s. 2 if either party was to be able to enforce the contract as varied.

The most recent decision on this matter is *Grossman* v *Hooper* [2001] 2 EGLR 82, which concerned an agreement for the transfer of a property from a man to a woman on the breakdown of their relationship. He subsequently claimed that she had undertaken to pay off a debt owed to a third party and that the omission of this from the written agreement invalidated the contract for transfer. The Court of Appeal held that the agreement about the debt was not part of the contract for transfer.

The interest of this decision lies in the court's observations about earlier decisions, and its attempt to explain the process of deciding whether or not an agreed term should be included in the written contract. Schiemann LJ commented (at p. 84), in relation to s. 2(1) of the 1989 Act that:

the terms which the parties have expressly agreed means the terms . . . upon which the parties to the sale or other disposition have agreed that the relevant interest in land shall be sold or otherwise disposed of. The words do not refer to terms upon which the parties have agreed (albeit contemporaneously) that some other transaction should be entered.

The judge sought to illustrate this by reference to a hypothetical agreement that a purchaser should take over a vendor's carpets and curtains. Whether or not a provision to this effect is a term of the contract of sale is a matter of fact in each case. It is for the court to decide whether the parties agreed that the sale of the house was conditional on the sale of the furnishings, in which case the term *is* part of the contract, or whether the agreement was for the sale of the house independently of the furnishings, in which case the agreement about carpets and curtains is not a term.

In the court's view, its task of interpreting agreements of this type was not assisted by the notion of 'collateral contracts', which Sir Christopher Staughton described as 'elusive'. He also disagreed with the view expressed in *Tootal Clothing Ltd* v *Guinea Properties Management Ltd* [1992] 2 EGLR 80 (see above) that parties could 'hive off' part of their composite bargain into a separate contract:

If the parties are allowed, by a simple device, to avoid the effects of s. 2 . . ., what was the point of Parliament enacting it? (at p. 85).

It can be seen from the above that the apparently simple requirement that all the terms of the agreement should be incorporated in the written contract has given rise to some difficulties in practice, and it remains to be seen whether the courts will continue to treat the omitted terms as forming separate contracts, or will follow the stricter approach adopted by the Court of Appeal in more recent decisions.

3.2.2.4 *The written contract may take the form of one document, which both parties sign, or of identical documents, each signed by one party and then exchanged*

This requirement is derived from ss. 2(1) and 2(3). The provision for the exchange of contracts perpetuates the method which conveyancers have developed over the years for concluding contracts for the sale of estates in land. The normal procedure is for two identical copies of the contracts to be prepared. One copy is signed by the vendor and the other by the purchaser, and when the time comes to create a binding contract the parties exchange their copies. As a result of the exchange, each party holds a copy of the contract signed by the other.

Contracts by correspondence

The terms of s. 2(1) and (3) appear to produce the result that it is no longer possible to create what are known as 'contracts by correspondence'. Under the old rules, an enforceable contract could come into existence as a result of a written offer and a written acceptance contained in letters passing between the parties, or through correspondence between them confirming the terms of a previously made oral agreement. There have so far been two cases in which the Court of Appeal has had to consider the effect under the 1989 Act of such 'contracts by correspondence'.

In *Hooper* v *Sherman* [1994] NPC 153 an unmarried couple agreed that the man would transfer his interest in the family home to the woman in return for being released from his mortgage obligations. This arrangement was confirmed by letters between the parties' solicitors, but some delay in proceeding was caused by the mortgagees and eventually the man refused to complete. The Court of Appeal held that, while neither letter by itself constituted a contract, a bilateral contract came into existence through the exchange of the letters. Morritt LJ, in a dissenting judgment, took the view that the letters were no more than con-firmation of the oral agreement, and were not enough for the purposes of s. 2 of the 1989 Act.

In *Commission for the New Towns* v *Cooper (Great Britain) Ltd* [1995] Ch 259 the documents in question again took the form of letters passing between the plaintiff and the defendant, purporting to record and confirm an oral agreement reached at a meeting between the parties. The facts of the case are complicated because the defendant had deliberately planned to mislead the plaintiff and had engineered the discussions at the meeting in such a way that the plaintiff was not aware of the true effect of the proposals to which it agreed. The Court of Appeal found for the plaintiff on a number of grounds, one of them being that the correspondence between the parties did not constitute an exchange of contracts for the purpose of s. 2. In the view of the court the exchange of documents contemplated by the Act cannot take place until agreement between the parties has been concluded by offer and final acceptance; in other words, the parties must agree on the sale and then reduce that agreement to writing, in the form of either one document signed by both parties, or in two documents which are to be exchanged between them. Written offers and acceptances can no longer give rise to a written contract: they are merely the process by which the agreement is reached.

It was only at a late stage of the proceedings in *Commission for the New Towns* v *Cooper (Great Britain) Ltd* that the Court of Appeal was reminded of its recent decision in *Hooper* v *Sherman*. The court was, however, able to find reasons for not following this earlier decision, and held on the facts of the case before it that the exchange of letters did not satisfy s. 2.

3.2.2.5 *The written contract must be signed by both parties*

This requirement of s. 2(3) can be satisfied either by both parties signing the same document, or by each party signing a copy and then exchanging them.

The requirement for signature was considered in *Firstpost Homes Ltd* v *Johnson* [1995] 1 WLR 1567. Here the purchaser prepared a letter to himself from the vendor, in which she agreed to sell him land which was identified 'on the enclosed plan'. The purchaser signed the plan but not the letter, and sent both plan and letter to the vendor, who signed both of them. After the vendor's death, the purchaser sought to enforce the contract against the vendor's personal representatives, but the Court of Appeal held that the requirements of s. 2(3) as to the signature were not satisfied, and accordingly there was no valid contract. The court regarded the letter and the plan as two documents, not one ('Something enclosed with the letter is not . . . the same document as the letter'—per Peter Gibson LJ at p. 1573); it was the letter which set out the terms of the agreement, incorporating the details of the plan by referring to it; and accordingly it was the letter which should have been signed by both parties. The purchaser sought to meet this point by arguing that he was identified as the addressee on the letter and that earlier authorities showed that the typing or printing of the name of a party as addressee, in a document prepared by that party, was a sufficient signature. The Court of Appeal, however, rejected this argument, saying that it was an artificial use of language to describe the typing or printing of a name in this way as a signature, and quoting with approval the words of Denning LJ in *Goodman* v *J. Eban Ltd* [1954] 1 QB 550:

In modern English usage, when a document is required to be 'signed' by someone, that means that he must write his name with his own hand upon it.

In consequence, the court held that the relevant document, the letter, was not signed in accordance with s. 2(3), and accordingly there was no written contract within the provisions of s. 2.

Although it may seem self-evident from the wording of s. 2(3), we need to draw your attention to the fact that it is the *parties* to the contract who are required to sign it. The reason for emphasising this is to be found in two High Court decisions, *Jelson Ltd* v *Derby County Council* [1999] 3 EGLR 1991, and *RG Kensington Co Ltd* v *Hutchinson IDH Ltd* [2003] 2 P&CR 195. In *Jelson*, a developer, seeking permission to develop a site, entered into a written agreement with the local authority that it would allocate part of the site for affordable housing and, when work was completed, would transfer that area to a housing association. The developer subsequently challenged that part of the agreement, claiming that it was void under s. 2 because it had not been signed by the housing association as the prospective purchaser. (For a brief criticism of this decision, in which it is described as 'clearly incorrect', see [2000] Conv 4).

A similar point arose in the *Kensington* case, in which a developer contracted with the first claimant, Caan, that it would sell the developed site to the second claimant, Kensington Management Co. Again, the developer argued that this contract was unenforceable because it had not been signed by the prospective purchaser, but this was rejected by Neuberger J:

The closing words of s. 2(3) require the contract to be signed by 'each party to the contract', not by 'each party to the prospective conveyance or transfer'. . . . Kensington is not a party to the . . . agreement and, as it is not a party to that contract, it seems there is no reason to require it to sign it (at p. 206).

In reaching his decision that the contract was not invalidated by a failure to comply with s. 2, the judge departed from the interpretation adopted in *Jolson*, saying that in his view it could not be supported. Although these two decisions are of equal weight, the later one seems more in accordance with the terms of the statute and, as Neuberger J comments, the interpretation relied on by the developer:

would involve an impermissible re-writing and extension . . . of s. 2(3) [and] would also involve giving s. 2 a greater degree of interference with Common Law rights and freedom to contract than it naturally bears.

3.2.3 Contracts which do not have to satisfy s. 2

Section 2(5) specifies certain types of contract which do not have to comply with the main provisions of s. 2, and which accordingly may be made without a written contract.

(1) *Contracts to grant short leases*
While most leases have to be granted by deed, certain leases for not more than three years may be granted more informally: in writing or even by word of mouth (LPA 1925, s. 54(2)); see 8.3.1.1(1). In these circumstances, it would seem inappropriate to require a written contract to grant a lease when the actual grant does not need writing, and accordingly s. 2(5)(a) excludes such leases from the general requirements of s. 2.

(2) *Contracts made in the course of a public auction*
These contracts have always had their own rules, and we will say no more about them here, other than that essentially the contract is concluded on the fall of the hammer.

(3) *Contracts regulated under the Financial Services Act 1986*
This exclusion covers certain contracts for investments which happen to include an interest of some kind in land. An example might be a unit trust or a debenture (a debenture is a type of charge (mortgage) used over the property of a company and it will usually include a charge over any land which the company has).

(4) *Certain trusts*
Section 2(5) also expressly excludes 'the creation or operation of resulting, implied or constructive trusts'. This is in keeping with the terms of LPA 1925, s. 53(2), which excludes those trusts from the requirement in s. 53(1)(b) that declarations of trust must be in writing (see further Chapter 17).

As we shall see later (3.4.2), this provision plays an important part in the Court of Appeal's decision in *Yaxley* v *Gotts* [2000] Ch 162.

3.2.4 Consequences of the 1989 Act

It is obvious that the changes introduced by the 1989 Act affect the way in which contracts are made for the sale of a fee simple or an existing lease. What we want to emphasise here is that the Act also has a considerable effect on the creation of equitable interests which arise from a contract to grant a legal estate or interest or from a failure to use the correct form of grant (see 1.6.2.2 and 1.6.2.3). In order to treat an agreement or a failed grant as giving rise to an equitable interest there now has to be a document which amounts to a written contract under the 1989 Act. This means that the help equity can give to informal transactions may well be more limited than in the past (see for example the effect which the Act has had on informally created mortgages 21.5.2).

3.3 Contracts made before 27 September 1989

3.3.1 LPA 1925, s. 40

Before 27 September 1989 any contract relating to land could be made orally or in writing, but if made orally was not enforceable unless there was some written evidence of it or some act of part performance.

These requirements were imposed by LPA 1925, s. 40, which provided:

(1) No action may be brought upon any contract for the sale or other disposition of land or any interest in land, unless the agreement upon which such action is brought, or some memorandum or note thereof, is in writing, and signed by the party to be charged or by some other person thereunto by him lawfully authorised.

(2) This section . . . does not affect the law relating to part performance . . .

You will note that these provisions refer to 'any contract for the sale or other disposition of land or an interest in land'. This is substantially the same wording as that used in s. 2 of the Law of Property (Miscellaneous Provisions) Act 1989 ('the 1989 Act'), and thus the same range of transactions is covered by both statutory provisions.

We will now look in a little more detail at the s. 40 requirements, and will try to highlight the points of comparison between them and the new rules which we considered in the previous section.

3.3.2 Requirements of s. 40

3.3.2.1 *Contracts could be made in writing or orally*

(1) *Written contracts* Section 40 provided for the possibility of a written contract, which was normally made in the same way as it would be today (i.e. by both parties signing the same document, or by each signing a copy and exchanging it with the other).

However, it was also possible for a written contract to arise through correspondence between the parties, in a way which *Commission for the New Towns* v *Cooper (Great Britain) Ltd* [1995] Ch 259 suggests is no longer possible under the new rules (see 3.2.2.4).

(2) *Oral contracts* A *valid* contract could be created by oral agreement between the parties. Unlike s. 2 of the 1989 Act, s. 40 did not require writing for the

formation of the contract and this is the most significant difference between the old and new rules. An oral contract, however, was not *enforceable* unless there was some written evidence of it, or some act of part performance.

3.3.2.2 *Oral contracts valid but unenforceable without writing or part performance*

The wording of s. 40 did not render an oral contract either void or voidable: it was merely unenforceable by action in the courts. This may seem like splitting hairs but the distinction could be important, as is illustrated by the case of *Low* v *Fry* (1935) 51 TLR 322. In that case the parties made an oral agreement for the sale of an estate in land and the purchaser gave the vendor a cheque for a portion of the purchase price. Later the purchaser decided not to proceed with the transaction and told his bank to stop payment of the cheque. The vendor was unable to enforce the contract to sell because of s. 40, but was able to recover on the cheque: this was not a case in which a cheque had been issued for a consideration which had totally failed, because the contract, though unenforceable, was valid.

3.3.2.3 *Written evidence of oral contract*

(1) *Form*   Section 40 required a written 'memorandum or note' of the agreement. There was no prescribed form for this, and all that was needed was a written document which showed that an oral agreement had been made and set out its terms.

Accordingly, if an intending purchaser of an estate made an oral contract and then later wrote a letter which stated that he had agreed to buy the property from the vendor at a specified price, the letter could constitute a s. 40 memorandum and be used to prove the contract (even if the purchaser sent his letter to his own solicitor: *Smith-Bird* v *Blower* [1939] 2 All ER 406). A receipt signed by a vendor in return for the purchaser's deposit might also amount to a sufficient note of the contract (*Davies* v *Sweet* [1962] 2 QB 300) even if the vendor did not intend the receipt to have this effect. It was also possible to combine several related documents (e.g., a series of letters) in order to produce the necessary memorandum (*Griffiths* v *Young* [1970] Ch 675).

(2) *Content*   In order to satisfy s. 40, the note or memorandum had to contain certain essential details: the names of the parties (or a description which identified them); a clear description of the property; and the consideration. If any of these was missing from the document, the courts would not enforce the contract. In addition, any other material terms of the contract had to be included; however, if any term was omitted, the party affected might choose either to waive it or to perform it (as appropriate). Having done so, he could then enforce the balance of the agreement (*Scott* v *Bradley* [1971] 1 Ch 850). There seems to be no scope for this approach under the 1989 Act (see 3.2.2.3 for the various ways in which the courts have dealt with omitted terms under the new rules).

(3) *Signature*   The document had to be signed by the person against whom the contract was to be enforced. Thus if a purchaser alone had signed the document, he could not rely on it in suing the vendor—for fairly obvious reasons! There was no requirement that the document should be signed by the person seeking to enforce the contract, and this is another significant difference from the new rules, which require the written contract to be signed by both parties.

3.3.2.4 *An alternative to writing: part performance*

Even if there was no written evidence of an oral contract, it might still be enforceable if the plaintiff could show an act of part performance, that is that he had already performed some of his obligations under the contract.

Part performance was an equitable doctrine which arose fairly soon after the Statute of Frauds 1677 first introduced the requirement for written evidence of contracts relating to land.

The statute was intended to combat the numbers of cases of perjured evidence in cases relating to land by requiring written, rather than oral, evidence of contracts. However, the Statute of Frauds soon caused its own problems since it became possible for a vendor to agree orally to sell land, allow the purchaser to move in and improve the land, and then claim the land back (plus improvements) on the ground that there was no contract enforceable at law. Not surprisingly at this point, equity, the guardian of conscience, intervened. To prevent the statute being used as an instrument of fraud, the equitable doctrine of part performance was developed. This doctrine provided that if a party to a contract had acted on the contract in reliance on the promise of the other party, then the contract would be enforced in equity, despite the lack of a written memorandum. The doctrine was specifically retained in relation to s. 40 cases by subsection (2) of that section.

Requirements for the operation of part performance

In order to use the doctrine of part performance, a plaintiff had to show that acts had been done which pointed clearly to the existence of a contract. In essence the plaintiff was claiming that he would not have acted as he did, had he not had a valid contract. This was a method of using actions as evidence of an agreement and thus those actions must be 'such as must be referred to some contract, and may be referred to the alleged one; . . . prove the existence of some contract, and are consistent with the contract alleged' (Sir Edward Fry, *A Treatise on the Specific Performance of Contracts*, 6th edn., p. 278, approved by the House of Lords in *Steadman* v *Steadman* [1976] AC 536). At the same time, however, the courts emphasised their concern with general equitable principles: it would be unfair for a party to escape from his obligations when the other side had already acted in reliance on the contract. Both of these explanations of the doctrine run throughout the decided cases and, in *Steadman* v *Steadman*, Lord Simon commented on 'the uneasy oscillation between regarding the doctrine as a principle vindicating conscientious dealing and as a rule of evidence' (at p. 560).

It is probably easiest to explain part performance by giving an example of the operation of the doctrine. In *Rawlinson* v *Ames* [1925] Ch 96, the defendant had agreed to take a lease from the plaintiff but had asked the plaintiff to do some work on the land before the defendant moved in. The plaintiff did the necessary work under the defendant's supervision but the defendant then refused to take the lease, relying on s. 40 as there was no written contract. In this case the plaintiff was granted an order for specific performance of the oral contract. The court concluded that the plaintiff would not have carried out the improvements to the land at the defendant's direction had there not been a pre-existing contract.

More generally, in cases of a contract to grant a lease, the tenant's act of taking possession and the landlord's permission for this were regarded as acts of part performance by each party, so that either of them could enforce the contract.

Since part performance was a creation of equity, it was discretionary in its application (as are all equitable principles), and a court would decline to assist a party who relied on the doctrine if this would produce injustice, or if the party relying on the doctrine had 'dirty hands'.

The 1989 Act makes no provision for the continuance of the doctrine of part performance, but equally does not expressly abolish it. There has been some debate as to whether the doctrine may continue to operate in the new system, and whether its place could be filled by the principles of estoppel, and we will consider these points in the next section.

3.4 Part performance after the 1989 Act

3.4.1 Has the doctrine of part performance survived the 1989 Act?

The changes introduced by the 1989 Act to the rules governing contracts relating to land were based on the recommendations of the *Law Commission Report on Formalities for Contracts of Sale etc. of Land 1987* (Law Com No. 164). The view of the Law Commission on part performance was that it should be abolished. It was suggested that the doctrine of estoppel might, in appropriate cases, be relied upon as an alternative:

We see no cause to fear that the recommended repeal and replacement of the present section as to the formalities for contracts for sale or other disposition of land will inhibit the courts in the exercise of the equitable discretion to do justice between parties in individual otherwise hard cases. (Law Com No. 164 (1987), para. 5.5.)

The 1989 Act makes no specific reference to the doctrine of part performance, neither continuing it nor abolishing it. The Act does, of course, repeal s. 40, but as we have seen s. 40(2) merely said:

This section . . . does not affect the law relating to part performance . . .

Accordingly, to repeal s. 40 does not abolish the rule in itself. One must look to the origins of the equitable doctrine to see how it arose and whether it could apply to a case in which no *contract* has been made, because the s. 2 formalities are not satisfied, but in which it is clear that an *agreement* has been made (which falls short of a contract only due to the absence of the required document).

As we have seen above (3.3.2.4), an important aspect of the doctrine was that acts had been done which indicated the existence of a contract (see the remarks of Lord Selborne LC in *Maddison* v *Alderson* (1883) 8 App Cas 467 at p. 476). The remedy given, if part performance was established, was specific performance of that contract. Essentially, the doctrine depended on the principle that contracts which did not comply with the statutory formalities were nevertheless valid contracts, albeit unenforceable ones. The position under s. 2 is, as we have seen, very different: failure to satisfy the section results in there being no contract at all. In those circumstances, it is difficult to see how the doctrine of part performance (of a non-existent contract) could have any part to play.

It should be noted, however, that opinion in the Court of Appeal has been divided on this point. In *Firstpost Homes Ltd* v *Johnson* [1995] 1 WLR 1567 Peter Gibson

LJ stated that the doctrine of part performance 'now has no application', whereas the following year in *Singh* v *Beggs* (1996) 71 P&CR 120 Neill LJ doubted that part performance had been abolished, saying, 'it may be that in certain circumstances the doctrine could be relied upon' (at p. 122). Both of these statements are *obiter dicta*, neither of them being necessary for the decision of the case and more recently in *Yaxley* v *Gotts* [2000] Ch 162 the Court of Appeal accepted without question that part performance had not survived the 1989 Act. If this is so, the question then arises of whether there is any other equitable concept which might be able to take its place.

3.4.2 **What might replace part performance?**

The Law Commission assumed that hard cases could be handled by the rules of estoppel, and there are certainly considerable similarities between these rules and the doctrine of part performance. An estoppel may arise where some representation has been made by one party and relied upon by another (see 1.6.5); where A allows B to act to his detriment in reliance on an agreement which A knows is not a valid contract, it certainly could be argued that A's conduct amounts to such a representation, and that he should be estopped from denying that he is bound by the agreement.

Initially it appeared that opinion in the Court of Appeal was divided on the question of whether estoppel could be used to assist parties who had failed to comply with the requirements of s. 2.

In *Godden* v *Merthyr Tydfil Housing Association* [1997] NPC 1 the court rejected the plaintiff's reliance on estoppel, saying that the doctrine was not to be invoked to render valid a transaction which the legislature had enacted was to be invalid. Just a month later, in *Bankers Trust Co.* v *Namdar* [1997] NPC 22, a differently constituted Court of Appeal held that there was insufficient evidence to deal with a point arising under s. 2, but added that, if *Godden* v *Merthyr Tydfil Housing Association* had held that s. 2 could not be circumvented by estoppel, that did not appear to be correct.

The matter has now been more fully considered in *Yaxley* v *Gotts* [2000] Ch 162. In this case the claimant and the first defendant ('Gotts Senior') had agreed that Gotts Senior would acquire the freehold of a large house, already divided into flats, and that the claimant, a self-employed builder, would carry out the necessary development work on the property and act as managing agent for the defendant. In return, the claimant was to be given the ground floor of the house, which he would divide into two flats and then let. No written contract was made, the claimant being content to rely on what he described as 'a gentleman's agreement'. Matters went ahead as agreed, save that the property was bought by the second defendant ('Gotts Junior'—son of the first defendant) and the property was registered in his name. No interest in the property was granted to the claimant. Some four years later, the parties fell out, and the claimant was excluded from the property. He then sought a declaration that he was entitled to ownership of part of the house.

At first instance, the judge held that on these facts a proprietary estoppel arose, and that it was to be satisfied by a grant to the claimant of a rent-free lease of the ground floor for 99 years. The defendants appealed against the first instance decision, raising for the first time the argument that the agreement in question was a contract for the sale or disposition of an interest in land, and should have been made in writing. The defendant also relied upon what we will call the 'public policy' argument, namely a well-established principle that:

the doctrine of estoppel may not be invoked to render valid a transaction which the legislature has, on grounds of general public policy, enacted is to be invalid (Halsbury's Laws of England, 4th edn. reissue, Vol. 16, pp. 849–50).

The three members of the Court of Appeal agreed in dismissing the appeal and upheld the award to the claimant of the 99-year lease. However they reached this conclusion by different routes, with the result that the decision as a whole is of some complexity, and, far from clarifying the issue, may well create greater uncertainty.

Robert Walker LJ gave great weight to the argument based on public policy. He accepted that:

The doctrine of estoppel may operate to modify (and sometimes perhaps even counteract) the effect of s. 2 of the Act of 1989. The circumstances in which s. 2 has to be complied with are so various, and the scope of the doctrine of estoppel is so flexible, that any general assertion of s. 2 as a 'no-go area' for estoppel would be unsustainable (at p. 174).

However, he went on to identify Parliament's requirement for written contracts as being based on the conclusion that the need for certainty in contracts relating to interests in land outweighed the disappointment of those who made informal bargains in ignorance of the statutory requirements, and concluded that:

If an estoppel would have the effect of enforcing a void contract and subverting Parliament's purpose it may have to yield to the statutory law which confronts it (at p. 175).

In other words, Yaxley could not rely on estoppel to overcome the lack of a written contract. Nevertheless, an alternative way of assisting those who act in reliance on an informal agreement was to be found in another equitable concept, the constructive trust. We consider such trusts in detail in Chapter 17, but, for the present, all you need to know is that a trust may be imposed by the court on a property owner if the court considers that his behaviour has been unconscionable, and that as a result he should be required to hold all or part of his property in trust for some other person. One of the many situations in which a constructive trust may be imposed is that of 'common intention': that is, where the parties have agreed that one will have an interest in property belonging to the other, and the non-owning party has acted to his or her detriment in reliance on that common intention.

There are clear similarities between the concepts of proprietary estoppel and the common intention constructive trust, and the course of dealing between Yaxley and the Gotts family could equally well give rise to an estoppel or justify the imposition of a constructive trust. As we have already noted (3.2.3), s. 2(5) of the 1989 Act expressly excludes 'the creation of resulting, implied or constructive trusts' from the requirement of a written contract imposed by s. 2(1). In the judge's view, this section allowed:

A limited exception . . . for those cases in which a supposed bargain has been so fully performed by one side . . . that it would be inequitable to disregard the claimant's expectations . . . (at p. 180).

Accordingly, Robert Walker LJ upheld the first instance decision, but on the basis of a constructive trust, rather than on the principles of proprietary estoppel.

The other two judges, Clarke and Beldam LJJ, agreed that the claimant could rely on a constructive trust, and that the appeal should be dismissed on that basis. However, in addition, they each expressed views on proprietary estoppel and its possible use in the context of the 1989 Act and both considered that in interpreting the Act greater weight could be given to the views of the Law Commission than was considered appropriate by Robert Walker LJ (see pp. 176, 182 and 190).

Beldam LJ considered that the Law Commission's report made it clear that its proposals were not intended to affect the court's power to give equitable relief through the principles of estoppel and constructive trusts. Moreover the general principle that a party could not rely on an estoppel in the face of a statute depended upon the nature and purpose of the enactment, and the social policy behind it. The 1989 Act was not:

aimed at prohibiting or outlawing agreements of a specific kind, though it had the effect of making agreements which did not comply with the required formalities void. This by itself is insufficient to raise such a significant public interest that an estoppel would be excluded (at p. 191).

Thus, while agreeing that the facts in the present case justified the finding that the first defendant held the property subject to a constructive trust in favour of the claimant, Beldam LJ also considered that the trial judge was entitled to reach the same conclusion by finding a proprietary estoppel.

As we hope you can see from this rather lengthy account of the case, the various judgments provide a good deal of material for analysis and discussion. Some writers regret the extension of constructive trusts into the area of contracts for the sale of land (see Smith (2000) 116 LQR 11), and there is also concern about further erosion of the distinction between proprietary estoppel and constructive trusts, a matter to which we return in Chapter 18 (see 18.7).

A further aspect of the case, which may cause difficulty when later courts come to consider it, is that it is by no means certain that s. 2 of the 1989 Act was relevant to the dispute between the parties. The claimant was seeking to enforce his right to an interest in the property against the *son*, who owned it, but his informal agreement was with the *father*, and at least two of the Court of Appeal judges took the view that there was no agreement between Yaxley and Gotts Junior (see pp. 180 and 188). In these circumstances, it may be that proceedings against the son were correctly based on estoppel (arising from the fact that he allowed the claimant to continue work on the premises believing that they belonged to the father, who would grant him an interest as agreed), and were not an attempt to enforce a contract invalidated by the 1989 Act. Thus, it could be that a later court will consider that the case did not give rise to any question under the Act and that the lengthy judgments on the use of estoppel or constructive trusts to relieve against invalidity under the Act may be no more than *obiter dicta*.

There has as yet been no real consideration of *Yaxley* v *Gotts* by a later court. It was referred to briefly in *James* v *Evans* [2000] 3 EGLR 1, in which a prospective tenant, who had been allowed to go into possession during negotiations which were clearly expressed to be 'subject to contract', sought to rely on proprietary estoppel in the absence of a written contract for the grant of the lease. The Court of Appeal had no difficulty in holding that estoppel could not arise when the claimant knew that discussions about the granting of the lease were subject to contract, and in these circumstances the court did not have to consider whether proprietary estoppel could be used to relieve against the effects of the 1989 Act.

More recently, and more surprisingly, the Court of Appeal has dealt with yet another case on the basis of proprietary estoppel in circumstances which would seem clearly within the terms of the 1989 Act. In *Lloyd* v *Dugdale* [2002] 2 P&CR 167, there was an informal agreement for the grant of a lease, and Dugdale, the prospective tenant, was allowed to go into possession and undertook major alterations to the premises at his own expense. The parties did not enter into a written contract, the owner of the property assuring his future tenant that 'his word was his bond'. No lease was ever executed, although Dugdale and his company continued to occupy the premises, and two years later the owner commenced proceedings for possession. These proceedings were still continuing three years later when the owner died; his executors sold the property, and the purchaser, Lloyd, began the current action for possession. Dugdale defended both actions by claiming rights arising from proprietary estoppel in consequence of his acting on the assurance that a lease would be granted to him.

At first instance, the judge held that proprietary estoppel was established, and that the rights arising from it bound the purchaser. This was because the person entitled to those rights was in actual occupation of the property at the time of the sale to Lloyd, and under LRA 1925, s. 70(1)(g) the rights of a person in actual occupation at that time were said to be overriding and to bind the purchaser (see 5.10.1). Accordingly, the judge ordered that a lease should be executed on the terms originally agreed. Although one would think that an agreement for a lease would fall squarely within the provisions of s. 2 of the 1989 Act, it does not appear that any reference to the Act was made either at first instance or on appeal.

The judgment of the Court of Appeal contains a lengthy analysis and application of the principles of proprietary estoppel. The court concluded that Dugdale did have rights arising from such an estoppel but had not been in actual occupation at the relevant time. As a result, his estoppel rights were not overriding and did not bind the purchaser, and the court allowed the appeal on this ground. There is no apparent reason for the failure to consider the 1989 Act in this case, and the omission is the more surprising because it appears that both the trial court and the Court of Appeal were referred to *Yaxley* v *Gotts*. That decision, however, seems to have been treated as an authority on the principles of proprietary estoppel but apparently did not prompt any consideration of the terms of the Act.

We can only wait with interest for the next contribution from the Court of Appeal on this interesting problem. Meanwhile you may like to note two decisions in which the courts have considered the operation of estoppel in relation to other statutory provisions. In *Shah* v *Shah* [2002] QB 35 the Court of Appeal held that, in the particular circumstances of the case before it, public policy did not prevent the use of estoppel to provide relief from the consequences of failing to comply with the attestation requirements imposed by s. 1 of the 1989 Act (see 1.6.2.3(b)). The other decision, *Actionstrength Ltd* v *International Glass Engineering IN. GL.EN SpA* [2003] 2 AC 541, concerned s. 4 of the Statute of Frauds 1677, which renders an oral guarantee agreement unenforceable, unless supported by some written note or memorandum. *Obiter dicta* of the House of Lords in this case suggest that the statutory requirement could be circumvented by estoppel if the guarantor had given an express assurance that he would not rely on the Statute. On the facts of the case, however, there had been no such assurance, and in the words of Lord Walker (at p. 557):

it would wholly frustrate the continued operation of section 4 in relation to contracts of guarantee if an oral promise [of guarantee] were to be treated, without more, as somehow carrying in itself a representation that the promise would be treated as enforceable.

3.5 Effect of the contract: passing of the equitable interest

3.5.1 Purchaser becomes owner in equity

We have already mentioned the equitable maxim that: 'Equity regards as done that which ought to be done' (1.6.2.2). In the case of a contract to sell an estate in land, 'that which ought to be done' is the completion of the sale by the execution of a deed which conveys the legal estate to the purchaser. Therefore, the application of the maxim means that, as soon as there is an enforceable contract, the purchaser is treated in equity as already having received the benefits of a conveyance, and as being the true owner of the property for all equitable purposes.

This gives rise to a position in which there are two 'owners' of the property. The vendor remains the legal owner until the legal estate has been transferred to the purchaser, but the purchaser becomes the equitable owner as soon as the contract is concluded (*Lysaght* v *Edwards* (1876) 2 ChD 499, 506–10). You will realise from Chapter 1 that the result is to make the vendor a trustee of the legal estate and the purchaser a beneficiary owning the equitable interest. The vendor is, however, an unusual trustee because he has more rights than most trustees (e.g., the right to demand the purchase price), and in fact he usually retains personal use of the land until the sale is completed.

3.5.2 Risk passes to the purchaser

As the purchaser becomes the beneficial owner in equity from the date of the contract, the basic rule is that the risk passes to him at that point and he should protect himself by insuring his interest in the property. It is the equitable interest which is the valuable interest in the land and its owner should insure. Indeed, should the house on the property burn down after contract but before conveyance, the purchaser is still bound to complete the purchase and pay over the purchase price (*Paine* v *Meller* (1801) 6 Ves Jr 349). Again, if the land should become the subject of a compulsory purchase order after contract, the purchaser must still proceed (*Hillingdon Estates Co.* v *Stonefield Estates Ltd* [1952] Ch 627). In practice, however, the contract may provide specifically that the risk remains with the seller until the estate is conveyed or transferred, but if this term is not included the purchaser is at risk and should insure.

3.5.3 **Notional conversion of property**

If you refer back to the brief section on Classification of Property (1.9), you will realise that the process of buying and selling land brings about a significant change in the nature of the property owned by each party. The purchaser, who before completion owned personalty in the form of money, exchanges it for realty, the estate in land, and the vendor makes a corresponding change from realty to personalty. This change of classification is not so significant today, but under the old law it could have far-reaching consequences because, for example, the rules about inheriting realty and personalty were very different. If one of the parties died after the contract had been made but before the estate was conveyed, the question would arise of how his property should be classified and who should inherit it. Was it fair to treat it as being in its original form when it was really subject to a specifically enforceable obligation to convert it into the other kind of property?

Equity's answer to this conundrum was to treat the property as notionally converted from the date of the specifically enforceable contract, so that the purchaser's interest was regarded as realty and that of the vendor as personalty. This notional conversion still occurs today when the contract for sale is concluded, although as we shall see it no longer operates in the case of trusts for sale, the other situation to which it used to apply (see 12.2.2.1 and 13.10.2.1).

3.6 **Remedies for breach of contract**

Once a contract has been concluded both the parties are legally bound to carry out their parts of the contract. Should either party fail to do this, a number of possible remedies are available to the other. These should be familiar to you if you have already studied the law of contract, but in case you need to refresh your memory we provide some references in the further reading section at the end of the chapter.

All we will do here is to draw your attention to the range of remedies which are available, emphasising those which are of most significance in the land law context.

3.6.1 **Damages**

The common law remedy for breach of contract is damages. The usual measure of damages is the loss which the claimant has sustained as a result of non-performance. Accordingly it is usually possible for the wronged party to claim damages for the loss of the bargain. Liability in damages may arise in a number of ways, for example, through refusal by either party to perform the contract or due to misrepresentation by the vendor. The Law of Property (Miscellaneous Provisions) Act 1989, s. 3 has removed old rules which limited the measure of damages in certain cases and now ordinary contractual principles will be applied.

3.6.2 **Specific performance**

For many centuries equity has accepted that in cases concerning land the common law remedy of damages is likely to be inadequate. This is because each piece of land is unique in character, and a thwarted purchaser cannot take any damages that he might obtain and buy another identical property (as he might were the subject of the contract a car or a piece of furniture). Accordingly, equity provided the remedy of specific performance, which can be used to compel the defaulting party to carry out his promise. The remedy is available to either party, so a vendor may also use it to force a purchaser to complete (*Hope* v *Walter* [1900] 1 Ch 257). Being equitable this remedy is discretionary in nature and will be refused if the applicant has 'dirty hands', that is, if he is in some way at fault himself in relation to the obligations under the contract.

As we have already seen, the availability of this remedy underlies a number of equitable interests (see 1.6.2.2 and 1.6.2.3), and accordingly this remedy is of particular importance to your study of land law.

3.6.3 **Rescission**

Rescission is a remedy which either party may elect to use should the other party break a term of the contract which is a condition precedent. An example of this would be if the vendor were unable to prove that he had good title to the land; the purchaser would then normally choose to rescind the contract. Rescission is an optional remedy and the wronged party can choose to affirm the contract instead and to seek damages for breach. It is only available in cases in which *restitutio in integrum* is possible; that is, it must be possible to return the parties to their original position.

Rescission of a transaction on the grounds of fraud, misrepresentation or undue influence will be considered further in relation to mortgages in Chapter 21.

3.6.4 **Rectification**

This remedy is available to correct an inaccurate written record of an oral agreement. The remedy is difficult to obtain as the court will require very strong evidence that the document does not record the oral agreement (*Joscelyne* v *Nissen* [1970] 2 QB 86 at 98). This may become of greater importance now that the Law of Property (Miscellaneous Provisions) Act 1989 is in operation: as we have seen (3.2.2.3), this route was used in *Wright* v *Robert Leonard Developments Ltd* [1994] NPC 49 to rectify a written agreement from which certain terms had been omitted.

3.6.5 **Injunction**

This equitable remedy is available to restrain a threatened breach of contract.

3.6.6 **Declaration**

In certain cases a declaration of the court on an issue may be a useful remedy, and LPA 1925, s. 49(1) provides for an application to be made to the court by vendor or purchaser. This process might, for example, be used if there were a dispute over the exact meaning of a term in the contract, or over a matter of proof of title.

3.7 Application to 3 Trant Way

We have seen that Barbara Bell is thinking of buying 3 Trant Way from Victoria Ventnor. We can illustrate the changes in the law produced by the Law of Property (Miscellaneous Provisions) Act 1989, s. 2, by imagining that the two women have discussed the matter, have agreed that Miss Bell should have the property and have settled the price. Miss Bell, thinking she should have the matter set out clearly before she goes to see her solicitor, has written to Miss Ventnor setting out the terms that have been decided upon.

If these facts occurred before 27 September 1989 the parties would have concluded a contract at the time at which they made their oral agreement. However that agreement would not have been enforceable. When Miss Ventnor received Miss Bell's letter she would have come into possession of a document which satisfied LPA 1925, s. 40, provided that Miss Bell had signed her letter and that it was sufficiently detailed, which is probable. Thereafter Miss Ventnor could enforce the contract against Miss Bell. Miss Bell could not enforce against Miss Ventnor because Miss Ventnor had not signed a s. 40 memorandum.

If these facts occurred on or after 27 September 1989 neither of them would be able to enforce her bargain. The document that exists does not comply with the Law of Property (Miscellaneous Provisions) Act 1989, s. 2 because it is not signed by both parties. In addition it may only purport to record an existing agreement, whereas s. 2 requires that the contract be *made* in writing.

As you can see, the date of the contract makes a considerable difference to the result produced.

FURTHER READING

Formalities for the Contract of Sale, etc. of Land 1987 (Law Com No. 164) Parts IV and V (pp. 12–22).

Howell, 'Informal Conveyances and Section 2 of the Law of Property (Miscellaneous Provisions) Act 1989' [1990] Conv 441.

Steadman v *Steadman* [1976] AC 536—for further information on part performance; in particular, see speech of Lord Simon at p. 556.

Swann, 'Part performance: back from the dead? (note on *Singh* v *Beggs* (1996) 71 P&CR 120)' [1997] Conv 293.

Contractual remedies

Hanbury and Martin, *Modern Equity*, 16th edn., Sweet & Maxwell, 2001, Chapter 24, pp. 715–21; 727–30.

Halson, *Contract Law*, Longman, 2001, Chapter 16, Literal Performance (includes specific performance and injunction).

Replacing part performance

Griffiths, 'Part Performance—Still Trying to Replace the Irreplaceable?' [2002] 66 Conv 216.

Moore, 'Proprietary Estoppel, Constructive Trusts and s. 2 of the Law of Property (Miscellaneous Provisions) Act 1989' [2000] MLR 912.

Tee, 'A Merry-Go-Round For the Millenium' [2000] CLJ 23.

Thompson, 'Oral Agreements for the Sale of Land' [2000] 64 Conv 245.

Smith, 'Oral Contracts for the Sale of Land: Estoppels and Constructive Trusts' (2000) 116 LQR 11.

4

Unregistered land

4.1 Introduction

4.1.1 3 Trant Way

You will remember that Barbara Bell wants to buy 3 Trant Way, the title to which is unregistered (see 2.1.2 and 2.2.3.2). In this chapter, we will look at what Barbara (or, more likely, her professional adviser) will have to do, either before or after exchanging contracts, to ensure that it is safe for her to buy the property.

As we explained in Chapter 2 (2.2.1), Barbara will need to check two things about the property she is planning to buy. She needs to make sure that Victoria Ventnor, the vendor, owns the property she is offering to sell, and that it is free from any encumbrances (third-party rights), other than those which have already been revealed. We will now look at how these two aspects of proving title are dealt with in the unregistered system.

4.2 Ownership of the estate

An owner of an estate in unregistered land proves (or 'deduces') his title to the estate by producing the title deeds to the property. These deeds are the documents by which he and his predecessors have acquired the estate. Typically, they will include documents such as: conveyances on sale; transfers (technically known as 'assents') by the personal representatives of a deceased owner to the person entitled under his will or intestacy; mortgages affecting the property; and trust deeds. From this collection of deeds, it should be possible to show that the estate has been correctly conveyed from one owner to another over the years and that it was last conveyed to ('vested in') the current vendor.

Obviously one cannot hope to produce an unbroken chain of deeds stretching right back to the Middle Ages or beyond, and so the habit began of accepting a title which had been proved for a certain long period of years. The parties to a contract for the sale of an estate may agree specifically on the length of the period which is to apply, but if no special agreement is made a standard provision is implied into the contract. Originally at common law the term implied was that one had to prove the devolution of the title for a period of at least 60 years, but this was reduced progressively and the relevant period is now 15 years by virtue of LPA 1969, s. 23.

In order to deduce title one has to start with a 'good root of title'. This is a document which records a dealing with the whole legal and equitable interest in the land and which contains nothing to cast any doubts on the validity of the title. Usually a conveyancer will insist on a document which evidences a dealing for value, such as a conveyance on sale or a mortgage. The reason for accepting such a document is that one presumes that the purchaser in that transaction had himself investigated the title for the necessary period and that his taking the conveyance or lending money on mortgage indicates that he found no defect. The document taken as a good root of title will be the first document which is as old or older than the title period, that is, now, the first such document which is at least 15 years old. Accordingly, the good root of title might be a document which is 16, 30 or even 100 years old, depending on the dealings that have occurred in relation to the estate.

Once a good root of title has been shown, the vendor must produce every deed after the root of title which has affected the property. If the vendor cannot prove an unbroken chain of title the purchaser may rescind the contract (if he has already entered into it) on the ground that the title is defective. The vendor usually proves his title by sending copies or summaries of the documents (an 'epitome of title' or an 'abstract of title') to the purchaser or his solicitor. These copies are then checked against the originals before completion.

4.3 Checking for encumbrances

Certain encumbrances may be revealed while the purchaser is checking the vendor's title, but he must in addition make a range of other enquiries and inspections. As we shall see, many third-party rights will bind the purchaser whether he knows of them or not, but there are still some other rights which will not bind him if he can show that he has not discovered them, despite making all the right enquiries (see 4.5.2.2). The purpose of making these inquiries is therefore twofold: to inform the purchaser about encumbrances and to enable him to override (take free of) certain rights of which he is unaware.

Making such enquiries can be a complicated and time-consuming business, and to help the purchaser the 1925 legislation introduced a system of registering certain encumbrances as land charges. These are now to be discovered by searching the appropriate register. A number of third-party rights, however, did not become registrable land charges and the purchaser has to rely on the old methods for finding out about them.

In the next two sections we look first at land charges and their registration, and then at the legal and equitable interests which are not registrable as land charges.

4.4 Land charges

4.4.1 Nature of land charges

Land charges consist of those interests in land which are set out in LCA 1972 (which replaced LCA 1925). Only interests which are included on the list in the Act are land charges. Interests which do appear on the list should be protected by registration on the Land Charges Register, which is one of the five different registers kept by the Land Charges Department (LCA 1972, s. 1) (the other four are described briefly at 4.4.6).

4.4.2 **Classes of land charge**

Land charges are divided by the 1972 Act into six classes (A to F) and certain of those classes are further subdivided.

4.4.2.1 *Classes A and B*

These are not particularly common. They consist of charges on land arising under statutory provisions.

4.4.2.2 *Class C*

This class is subdivided into four subclasses. Before considering these in detail it is important to note that rights of a type which fall within this class are registrable as land charges only if they were created on or after 1 January 1926 (the date upon which the 1925 legislation came into force) or, more unusually, if the right was created before that date but was itself transferred to some other holder at a later time.

(1) *Class C(i), the puisne mortgage* The puisne mortgage is defined in LCA 1972, s. 2(4), as a legal mortgage which 'is not secured by a deposit of documents relating to the legal estate affected'. Normally when lending money on the security of a mortgage, a mortgagee will take the deeds to the property away from the estate owner in order to prevent him dealing further with the property. If a legal mortgagee does take the deeds in this way, his mortgage is *not* a registrable land charge. It is supposed not to require registration, because the absence of the deeds is sufficient to alert any prospective purchaser to the possible existence of the mortgage. (As noted at 2.2.3.2, since 1998 the creation of this type of mortgage will normally lead to the compulsory registration of the title to the legal estate which is subject to that mortgage.) If the mortgagee does not take the deeds, the mortgage *is* a puisne mortgage and should be registered as a land charge. The puisne mortgage is a slightly unusual land charge because it is a legal interest in land, whilst most land charges are equitable or statutory interests.

(2) *Class C(ii), limited owner's charge* This is a land charge which arises when a tenant for life or statutory owner under the SLA 1925 (someone who has only a limited interest in the property—see Chapter 14), or another person with a similar interest, has paid inheritance tax under the Inheritance Tax Act 1984. Such persons may have a right to charge the repayment of the tax against the land (i.e., to recover from the rents and profits of the land money which they have paid out of their own pockets) and that right is a land charge.

(3) *Class C (iii), general equitable charge* This class of land charge forms a kind of 'dustbin' category. Into this class fall all equitable charges on property which are not specifically excluded from Class C(iii) by the Act itself. Section 2(4)(iii) excludes from this class:

(a) any charge which is secured by a deposit of documents relating to the legal estate affected; (this means that an equitable mortgagee who does not have the title deeds to the property can register a C(iii) land charge, but an equitable mortgagee who has the deeds cannot do so);

(b) interests arising under trusts; (i.e., a beneficiary under a trust of land cannot register his interest as a land charge);

(c) indemnity charges against rents apportioned or charged on land against the breach of covenants:

(d) any charge which falls into another class of land charge.

(4) *Class C(iv), estate contract*   An estate contract is any contract to convey or create a legal estate in land, or any option to purchase a legal estate or any right of pre-emption in respect of a legal estate (a right of first refusal). Thus in addition to contracts for the conveyance of a fee simple, and contracts for the grant or assignment of a lease, this class of land charges includes options to purchase the fee simple, and options contained in leases (such as options for renewal (*Phillips* v *Mobil Oil Co. Ltd* [1989] 1 WLR 888) and for the purchase of the reversion by the tenant). Various statutes have added to this category of land charges: for example, the Landlord and Tenant (Covenants) Act 1995, s. 20(6), provides that a request for an overriding lease (explained in 9.5.3.1(3)) may be registered under the LCA 1972 as if it were an estate contract.

Even where an option has been registered as a Class C(iv) land charge, it has been suggested that there is a need for further registration of an estate contract after notice has been given to exercise the option. However, it was held in *Armstrong and Holmes Ltd* v *Holmes* [1993] 1 WLR 1482 that there is no need for further registration: the registration of the option gives sufficient warning to any other prospective purchaser of the estate, and any conveyance to such a purchaser will be subject to the estate contract which arises from the option.

4.4.2.3 *Class D*

Class D is divided into three subclasses.

(1) *Class D(i), Inland Revenue charge*   This is a land charge which arises in favour of the Inland Revenue when a liability to pay inheritance tax in respect of land has not been discharged.

(2) *Class D(ii), restrictive covenants*   This class comprises any covenants or agreements which are restrictive of the user of land (other than those between landlord and tenant) and which were created on or after 1 January 1926 (at which date the 1925 property legislation came into force). An example would be a covenant, entered into in 1940, not to keep pigs on a particular property. The same covenant would not be a registrable land charge had it been created in 1920.

(3) *Class D(iii), equitable easements*   This class consists of any easements, rights or privileges affecting land which were created on or after 1 January 1926, and which are equitable only. Equitable profits à prendre fall within this definition. It should be noted that legal easements or profits are not registrable as land charges.

4.4.2.4 *Class E*

These are very rare and consist of annuities created before 1926 and which are not registered on the register of annuities (which is one of the five registers maintained under the LCA).

4.4.2.5 *Class F*

This class consists of 'matrimonial home rights' which were first created by the Matrimonial Homes Act 1967 and are now contained in the Family Law Act 1996. These rights exist only in relation to couples who are legally married and give a spouse, who is not a co-owner of the matrimonial home, the right to occupy the home owned by the other spouse. This right is considered in more detail at 24.3.3.1.

While all these classes of charge are important to a purchaser, who may find that the property which he is purchasing is less attractive or perhaps totally valueless to him because it is subject to a land charge, the ones that you will meet most commonly in your study of land law are classes C, D and F, and you should pay particular attention to these.

4.4.3 **Registration of charges**

The application to register a land charge is made by the person who claims that right.

Registration is not made against the address of the property, but against the name of the person who was the estate owner at the date that the charge was created. This choice of method for registration has caused a number of problems with the system.

4.4.3.1 *Incorrect names*

It is not uncommon for an estate owner to be known by a nickname or abbreviated name. If a registration is made against an incorrect version of a person's name, a search made against the true name may not reveal the entry. Or it may be that the registration has been made correctly but that the searcher searches an incorrect name. Once again such a search may well not reveal the relevant entry. These problems have produced a certain amount of litigation, and examples are to be found in such cases as *Diligent Finance Ltd* v *Alleyne* (1972) 23 P&CR 346 and *Oak Co-operative Building Society* v *Blackburn* [1968] Ch 730. Essentially, the person making a search has to be certain of using someone's full, correct names, in order to be safe.

4.4.3.2 *Searching against the names of all past estate owners*

When an estate changes hands, the existing registrations of land charges are not altered but remain against the name of the original estate owner. Accordingly it is not sufficient to make a search simply against the name of the current estate owner. To be certain of finding all registered charges one must search against the names of all the estate owners since 1925. This is, however, impractical in most cases (though some conveyancers will still ask for the full list of names), because in proving his title a vendor is only obliged to go back to a good root of title, which, as we have seen above, may be only 15 years old.

The difficulties which this might cause may be illustrated by referring back to the title to 3 Trant Way. The history of No. 3 since 1925 has been as follows:

1926 The estate owner at the date at which the 1925 legislation came into force was Bill Brie.
1928 Land charge class D(ii) registered against the name Bill Brie.
1956 Bill Brie sold legal estate to Cathy Camembert.

1963 Land charge class D(iii) registered against the name Cathy Camembert.
1989 Cathy Camembert sold legal estate to Victoria Ventnor.
1989 Land charge class C(i) registered against the name Victoria Ventnor.

You will remember that Barbara Bell is considering buying 3 Trant Way from Victoria Ventnor. If Miss Bell agrees to purchase the estate, Miss Ventnor will produce the conveyance made to her by Cathy Camembert in April 1989 as the good root of title, but will not be required to produce any of the earlier deeds. Miss Bell will already know the name of her vendor, Victoria Ventnor, and will learn of Cathy Camembert from the 1989 conveyance. If she makes land charges searches against these names, she will discover the charges registered in 1963 and 1989. However, she will have no means of knowing that the property once was owned by Bill Brie and so will not discover the class D(ii) land charge registered in 1928. This land charge is a restrictive covenant and it is quite likely that it will still be capable of enforcement by a neighbouring landowner (see Chapter 23). Unfortunately for Barbara Bell, she will be deemed to have notice of this charge and will therefore still be bound by it (LPA 1925, s. 198). This is so even though Barbara had no means of discovering the registration.

This difficulty in the system was not originally envisaged as being of importance, because in 1926 the statutory title period was 30 years and it was expected that the registered title system, which does not use land charges, would be generally in force quite quickly. Delays in the introduction of the registered land system and the reduction of the title period to 15 years exacerbated the problem. As a result in 1969 the law was amended by s. 25 of the LPA 1969, which provides that, should a purchaser of an estate or interest in the land suffer loss due to the existence of a registered land charge prior to the root of title, he may obtain compensation from a central fund administered by the Chief Land Registrar.

Now that we are some years on from this development, it is interesting to note that there has been very little call for compensation (one claim in the first 21 years following the introduction of the scheme: Land Registry Annual Report 1989–1990, p. 11). It seems that the supposed difficulties were more apparent than real. Many land charges (such as mortgages), have a relatively short life, and are unlikely to be effective outside the search period. In the case of interests which may last for longer (such as rights under restrictive covenants), there are several ways in which a prospective purchaser may learn of them from the title deeds or associated papers. Thus conveyances within the period the purchaser is searching may well 'recite' previous dealings with the land and give details of the earlier conveyances which created the encumbrance. There is also the possibility of the purchaser having access to earlier land charge search certificates, which may be kept with the title deeds. It seems that in practice the purchaser does not often find himself bound by an active land charge of which he was not aware (see Smith at p. 215).

4.4.4 Effect of registration

Registering a right as a land charge ensures that anyone taking a later estate or interest in the land (most importantly, any purchaser of the legal estate) will take it subject to that right. This result is brought about by s. 198(1) of the LPA 1925 which provides that:

The registration of any instrument or matter under the provisions of the Land Charges Act, . . . shall be deemed to constitute actual notice of such instrument or matter.

This refers back to the old equitable doctrine of notice (see 1.7.3), and in effect introduces a form of 'statutory notice'.

It should be noticed, however, that the fact that a charge appears on the register does not in any way guarantee that it is an effective charge, for under the Land Charges Rules 1974, r. 22, the Registrar is not concerned to check the accuracy of an application to register a charge. It is also possible that a charge may have been effective originally but is no longer so. Thus it may be that a purchaser can be compelled to continue with a purchase even though his searches reveal registered charges. All that is necessary is that the vendor should show that the apparent encumbrance does not in fact affect his title (*Bull* v *Hutchens* (1863) 32 Beav 615).

4.4.4.1 *Searches*

The practical consequence of LPA 1925, s. 198, is to ensure that a careful purchaser makes a search of the Land Charges Register. Such searches may be made at any time and they do not require the prior consent of the current estate owner. The register is a public record, which is open to anyone who is prepared to pay the search fee (LCA 1972, s. 9). On receipt of a search requisition a search is made and the result is communicated to the searcher in the form of a search certificate.

4.4.4.2 *Protection under a search certificate*

Section 10(4) of LCA 1972 says that a search certificate protects a 'purchaser'. For the purposes of the Act 'purchaser' is widely defined, and includes anyone who takes any interest in the land for valuable consideration (s. 17(1)). This would include mortgagees, lessees and the acquirers of other interests, both legal and equitable.

4.4.5 **Effect of non-registration of a charge**

In general terms, failure to register a land charge may mean that the person entitled to it is unable to enforce it against someone who acquires a later estate or interest in the land. The precise effect of non-registration of a charge depends on the class of charge involved. Basically there are two rules: one for land charges of classes A, B, C(i), (ii) and (iii) and F; another for land charges of classes C(iv) and D(i), (ii) and (iii).

4.4.5.1 *Classes A, B, C(i)–(iii) and F*

The general rule with these land charges (with slight variations for class A) is that, unless they are registered before completion (i.e., the point at which the purchaser pays his money and receives his estate or interest), a purchaser for valuable consideration will take the property free of the charge (LCA 1972, s. 4(2), (5) and (8)). Such a purchaser may be either a purchaser of an estate in the land or a purchaser of any interest in the land. Thus even the purchaser of an equitable interest in the property can take an interest which has priority to an unregistered charge. For example, if A has a puisne mortgage (C(i)) over Blackacre, which he has failed to register, and later the fee simple owner grants an equitable mortgage to B, B will take free of A's rights, or in other words, B's rights will take priority over A's. If the estate has to be sold to pay back the sums due under the mortgages, the debt owed to B will be paid first and A may find that there is not enough money to pay him in full (see Chapter 21).

4.4.5.2 *Classes C(iv) and D(i)–(iii)*

In these cases the rule to be applied is that contained in LCA 1972, s. 4(6). If the C(iv) or D land charge is not registered it cannot be enforced against the purchaser of a legal estate for money or money's worth. This is the only person who can take the land free of the charge and thus the purchaser of any lesser interest in the property will still be bound by the charge. Thus if an estate contract (C(iv)) has not been registered and later an equitable mortgage is created by the fee simple owner the estate contract can be enforced against the equitable mortgagee: the equitable mortgagee is not the purchaser of a legal estate.

'Money or money's worth'

The words 'money or money's worth' do require a certain amount of explanation, particularly as they appear in s. 4(6) but not in s. 4(5), which refers only to a purchaser for value. The effect is to exclude from the benefits of s. 4(6) certain persons who are purchasers for valuable consideration but who have not given a consideration in money or have given it in a form which cannot be computed in financial terms. An example of this is an agreement to convey land in consideration of marriage. This is regarded as valuable consideration (LPA 1925, s. 205(xxi)) but not money or money's worth since it is not possible to put a financial valuation on marriage.

In the case of *Midland Bank Trust Co. Ltd* v *Green* [1981] AC 513, the House of Lords considered the meaning of the words 'money or money's worth' in s. 4(6). Here a father had granted his son an option to purchase a farm for £22,500. This agreement came within the definition of estate contract given in LCA 1972, s. 2(4)(iv), and so was registrable as a land charge. The son failed to register his option. Later his father wished to avoid carrying through his promise and, acting on advice, he conveyed the legal estate in the property to his wife for £500. At the date of this conveyance the farm was actually worth £40,000. In the Court of Appeal, it was held that the sale at such a considerable undervalue was not a sale for 'money or money's worth'. However, the House of Lords reversed this decision, holding that the unregistered land charge was unenforceable against the purchaser, and relying on the contractual rule that the court will not enquire into the adequacy of consideration, as long as the consideration is real. It would therefore appear that a sale for 1p would satisfy s. 4(6), providing that it was not made fraudulently.

4.4.5.3 *Knowledge is irrelevant*

Midland Bank Trust Co. Ltd v *Green* [1981] AC 513 also illustrates a second important point, that a purchaser can take an estate free of an unregistered land charge even if he *knows* that the land charge exists. It was clear that the mother had known about her son's interest, but she was still able to take the estate free of it because he had not registered it.

4.4.5.4 *Comparison with registered land*

When you read Chapter 5 on registered land you will see that the result in *Midland Bank Trust Co. Ltd* v *Green*, would have been very different if the title to the farm had been registered. It appears that the son was in actual occupation of the property and that his interest was known to his mother at the time of her purchase. Consequently, in the registered system, he could have claimed that his option was an overriding interest under LRA 2002, Sch. 3, para. 2 and therefore binding on the purchaser.

A similar illustration of the difference between the two systems is to be found in *Lloyds Bank plc* v *Carrick* [1996] 4 All ER 630. Here, the defendant had sold her house on her husband's death, paid the proceeds to her brother-in-law and moved into a maisonette owned by him, on the understanding that it would become hers. In 1982, when those events occurred, this agreement, supported by part performance, was sufficient to satisfy the requirements of LPA 1925, s. 40 (see 3.3.2), and accordingly there was an enforceable contract between the two parties. The defendant lived in the property for a number of years; the legal estate was never conveyed to her, and predictably she did not protect her position by registering a land charge. During this time her brother-in-law mortgaged the property, without her knowledge, as security for his own debts, and when he defaulted on the repayments, the bank sought possession of the property. The defendant argued that her brother-in-law, having received full payment for the maisonette, held the legal estate in it as a bare trustee for her, and that her interest under this trust was not a registrable land charge and depended on notice (see 1.7.2). The Court of Appeal, however, rejected this argument, as well as others based on constructive trusts and proprietary estoppel (see Chapters 17 and 18), holding that her rights arose from the contract with her brother-in-law. Failure to protect that contract by registration as a class C(iv) land charge meant that it was void against the bank, which accordingly was entitled to enforce its security and take possession. In his judgment Morritt LJ drew attention to the fact that the result would have been very different if title to the maisonette had been registered, but said that it was for Parliament to decide whether this distinction between registered and unregistered land should continue. (For a note on this decision, see Thompson [1996] Conv 295).

4.4.5.5 *Right still enforceable against original owner*

Although the effect of non-registration is that the charge cannot be enforced against the new owner of the estate, the right does still remain enforceable against the original owner who granted it. This may not be so satisfactory for the person entitled; for instance, if he has failed to register an equitable right of way (D(iii)) he will no longer be able to use the right over the land, but he may well have a remedy in contract against the original owner and may be able to recover compensation. This is so even though it is he who is really at fault, through failing to register his land charge.

4.4.6 **Other registers maintained by the Land Charges Department**

The other four registers maintained under LCA 1972, s. 1 contain registrations of: petitions in bankruptcy and pending actions relating to land; certain annuities created before 1926; court orders relating to land, and writs issued for the purpose of enforcing them; and deeds of arrangement between bankrupts and their creditors which affect land.

4.5 Legal or equitable interests which are not land charges

4.5.1 Enforcement of legal interests

A purchaser will automatically be bound by all legal interests in the land which are not land charges (and, as we have seen, most legal interests are not on the land charges list). This rule is usually expressed by saying that 'Legal rights are good against the world'. The reason for this rule is that if common law recognised an interest in the land it was regarded as a right *in rem* ('in the thing') which therefore bound anyone who purchased an estate or interest in the burdened land.

Thus the purchaser will be bound, for example, by rights such as legal easements and legal leases. Similarly if an estate is subject to a legal mortgage which is protected by a deposit of the title deeds, then anyone who buys the estate will buy it subject to the mortgage. (In practice the purchaser would insist that the vendor repay the debt on completion of the sale so that the mortgage is discharged and the purchaser is not affected by it; but if the purchaser did not know about the mortgage, and so did not require that this be done, it would bind him.)

4.5.2 Enforcement of equitable interests against the purchaser of the legal estate

We have already explained in Chapter 1 that the Court of Chancery developed the rule that equitable interests in land bound everyone who took the land except the bona fide purchaser of the legal estate without notice (see 1.7.3). In practice, the doctrine of notice imposed a heavy burden on the purchaser, who had to make exhaustive enquiries in order to avoid being said to have constructive notice of equitable rights which he had failed to discover. A major aim of the 1925 legislation, and of the statutory reforms which preceded it, was to facilitate the sale of land and to make the whole process less onerous for the purchaser. For this purpose, two new statutory procedures were introduced, which had the effect of making considerable inroads into the doctrine of notice.

4.5.2.1 *Reducing the dangers of the doctrine of notice*

The first procedure was that of land charge registration, which we have already discussed. Registration was suitable for equitable rights such as restrictive covenants and easements, which must continue to bind the land if they are to benefit those entitled to them. Land charge registration provides a relatively straightforward method by which a prospective purchaser can discover the existence of rights on the register, while taking free of any which do not appear there, and questions of constructive notice are no longer relevant.

The second procedure is known as 'overreaching'. It was introduced to facilitate the sale of trust property, which previously could be sold only with the consent of all the beneficiaries and which, therefore, presented considerable dangers to a purchaser. The new procedure was based on the idea that the rights of beneficiaries under a trust could be satisfied by money payments (of income or capital), and that they did not need to retain their old rights against the land.

Overreaching   The process was introduced by a series of Acts, culminating in the 1925 legislation (see LPA 1925, s. 2(1)). Under the overreaching procedure, subject to certain safeguards, the interests of beneficiaries under a trust involving land can be lifted from the trust property on its sale, and attached instead to the money paid by the purchaser (i.e., to the capital sum arising from the sale). Depending on the terms of the trust, the trustees will then either distribute the capital money among the beneficiaries, or will invest it so as to provide income for them.

The beneficiaries' interests are safeguarded in this process (in theory although not always in practice) by the statutory provision that any capital money arising must be paid to two trustees, or to a trust corporation. In no circumstances should the money be paid to only one trustee or to the beneficiaries. Provided this requirement is satisfied, the purchaser takes the legal estate free of the beneficiaries' interests, even if he has actual notice of them. However, if the requirements relating to the payment of capital money are not satisfied, the beneficiaries' interests are not overreached, and the purchaser will take subject to them, unless he can prove that he did not have notice of them.

We will discuss this process and the statutory provisions relating to it in more detail at 13.9 and 14.6.1.

4.5.2.2 *Doctrine of notice today*

For purchasers of unregistered land the significance of the notice rules was reduced considerably by the 1925 reforms. However, the doctrine still applies to the following equitable rights:

(a) rights excluded from registration as land charges, such as pre-1926 restrictive covenants and equitable easements, and restrictive covenants made between landlord and tenant (see 4.4.2.3);

(b) beneficiaries' rights under a trust which have not been overreached because the proper procedures were not followed (see above); and

(c) equitable rights which had not been identified by the courts at the time of the 1925 legislation and so are not included in the scheme of land charge registration. These rights include, for example, rights arising from estoppel (see *Ives (E.R.) Investment Ltd* v *High* [1967] 2 QB 379, which we will consider further at 20.3.4.1) and certain rights of entry (*Poster* v *Slough Estates Ltd* [1968] 1 WLR 1515 and *Shiloh Spinners Ltd* v *Harding* [1973] AC 691).

In consequence, it remains essential for a purchaser of unregistered land to make thorough searches and enquiries if he is to avoid being held to have constructive notice of any of these equitable rights.

4.5.2.3 *What searches must a purchaser make to avoid constructive notice?*

The searches required of the purchaser are of two types: first, he must investigate the vendor's title correctly by examining the title deeds, and secondly, he must inspect the land itself.

(a) *Constructive notice of matters revealed by examination of deeds.* A purchaser is bound by any right which he would have discovered had he inspected the vendor's title deeds for the statutory period (e.g., *Worthington* v *Morgan* (1849) 16 Sim 547, in which no investigation was made). As a result of this rule, it is common for the owners of equitable interests to insist that a note of their rights is made on the deeds (e.g., written on the back of a deed) so that future purchasers will have actual notice of their rights if they read the deeds and constructive notice if they omit to do so.

(b) *Constructive notice of matters revealed by inspection of land.* The rule that the purchaser must also inspect the land is commonly called the 'rule in *Hunt* v *Luck*'. In the case of *Hunt* v *Luck* [1902] 1 Ch 428, a purchaser was held to have notice of all the rights of a tenant who was in occupation of the land, but not of the rights of the landlord from whom the tenant derived his title. As a result, a purchaser runs the risk of having constructive notice of any rights belonging to anyone in occupation, and should ensure that enquiries are made of any such person.

Occupation by the owner's spouse There used to be some uncertainty about the application of the rule in *Hunt* v *Luck* to property occupied by married couples. It has become increasingly common over the last 50 years for a wife to contribute to the cost of acquiring the matrimonial home. In consequence, she may have an equitable interest in the property, even though the legal estate is vested only in her husband (see 1.4). At first, however, purchasers did not always think it necessary to enquire whether wives had such an interest. This attitude was accepted in *Caunce* v *Caunce* [1969] 1 WLR 286, in which it was held that a purchaser was entitled to presume that a wife lived in the property because of her relationship with the estate owner, and that her presence did not put the purchaser of the estate upon notice. However, this approach was heavily criticised by the House of Lords in the registered land case of *Williams & Glyn's Bank Ltd* v *Boland* [1981] AC 487 at p. 508 (see 5.10.4.4), and in *Kingsnorth Finance Co. Ltd* v *Tizard* [1986] 1 WLR 783 a wife's occupation of unregistered land was regarded as being separate from that of her husband. Accordingly, the older rule in *Caunce* v *Caunce* should now be regarded as outdated, and is most unlikely to be applied in the future.

Kingsnorth Finance Co. Ltd v *Tizard* is a very interesting case and well worth noting in detail. The facts were that Mrs Tizard had contributed to the purchase price of the original matrimonial home. She therefore had a beneficial interest in a later home, which was bought with the proceeds of sale from the previous property, and conveyed into the sole name of her husband. Accordingly Mr Tizard held the property in trust for himself and his wife. After some years the marriage failed, and the wife left the matrimonial home, but lived nearby and came in each day to care for the children, leaving some clothes and other possessions at the house. Subsequently the husband mortgaged the property without his wife's knowledge, having arranged for the preliminary inspection by the mortgagee's agent to be carried out in her absence. When the mortgage repayments fell into arrears, the mortgagee sought to enforce its security and was opposed by Mrs Tizard, who claimed that the mortgagee had had constructive notice of her beneficial interest in the property and therefore took subject to her rights. The court held that Mrs Tizard had been in occupation of the property at the date at which the agent made his inspection and later when the charge was granted. It was said that occupation need not be exclusive, continuous or uninterrupted. The court did, however, agree that someone inspecting property under the rule in *Hunt* v *Luck* was not obliged to go as far as opening drawers or hunting in cupboards (which, if done, would have revealed the wife's possessions). However, since the agent had been told of the recent separation and the fact that Mrs Tizard still lived in the area, it was felt that the mortgagee was put on notice and should have made further enquiries. The inspection of the property at a pre-arranged date did not amount to making sufficient enquiry.

This case, though only a first-instance decision, is of considerable importance because it widens the concept of occupation beyond its previously presumed limits. The judgment is helpful in giving a detailed indication of the type of investigation which will be needed if a buyer or mortgagee is to be safe from hidden rights, and certainly suggests that in cases in which it is known that a vendor or mortgagor is married it is advisable to insist on obtaining written approval from his or her spouse.

4.5.2.4 *Effect of purchase without notice*

As we have already seen, the *bona fide* purchaser for value of the legal estate will take free of any equitable interests of which he does not have notice. An important consequence of this is that anyone who later acquires the legal estate from that purchaser also takes free of the equitable interest, even if he actually knows about it (*Wilkes* v *Spooner* [1911] 2 KB 473).

Although the equitable interest cannot be enforced against the purchaser without notice or against his successor, it does remain enforceable against the person who originally was subject to it (such as a trustee or a person who created the equitable right), but, as we have noted in the case of unregistered land charges (see 4.4.5.5), the only remedy available is likely to be damages for breach of contract or, where appropriate, an action for breach of trust.

4.5.3 **Enforcement of equitable interests against later acquirers of equitable interests**

Thus far we have only considered the position of those who intend to buy a legal estate and who, if they do so, will take the property free of those equitable interests (which are not land charges) of which they have no notice, or which are overreached on sale. However, it is possible for someone to acquire only an equitable interest in the property, for example, by entering into a contract to buy the legal estate but never taking a conveyance of the legal estate. In such a case the intending purchaser has an equitable right to the land under the contract (see 3.5.1) and the question then arises of the extent to which he is bound by pre-existing equitable interests.

Obviously the bona fide purchaser rule does not protect one who acquires an equitable interest in the property. In this case the rule which applies to interests in unregistered land is that 'Where the equities are equal the first in time prevails'.

Thus a later acquirer of an equitable interest will take priority over an earlier equitable interest only where the 'equities' are not equal. This will only arise if the owner of the earlier equitable interest has been involved in a fraud on the later acquirer or possibly if the earlier equitable owner has been grossly negligent about protecting his interests (see further on this, in relation to mortgages, Chapter 21).

4.6 Summary of searches to be made in relation to unregistered land

To summarise what we have told you so far, Barbara Bell (or her adviser) must make the following enquiries in respect of 3 Trant Way, in order to protect herself:

(a) a local land charges search (see 2.3.2.2);

(b) a land charges search against the names of all the estate owners during the title period;

(c) a thorough examination of the title deeds from the root of title onwards;

(d) an investigation of the occupancy of the land including questioning any occupants as to their rights.

4.7 The conveyance

Once Barbara Bell is satisfied with her enquiries and both parties have made the necessary arrangements, the time will have arrived for the completion of the transaction. She will pay the balance of the purchase price, provided either from her own resources or with money borrowed from a lender, to whom she will mortgage her newly acquired property. Victoria Ventnor, the vendor, will execute the deed (required by s. 52(1) of the LPA 1925), which will convey the legal estate to Barbara. An example of a very simple conveyance of 3 Trant Way is given at p. 64: usually these documents are far longer and decidedly more complex than this example.

At the time of the conveyance the vendor will hand to the purchaser the title deeds to the property (unless he is selling only part of the land covered by the deeds, in which case the vendor will give the purchaser an undertaking to produce the deeds should the purchaser ever require them). The purchaser (or probably his legal adviser) should, of course, check the deeds to ensure that the copies that he has previously seen are true copies of the original documents.

4.8 Application for first registration

Although Barbara is now the legal owner of No. 3, there is still one more thing she must do. You will remember that the system of registered title was finally extended to all parts of the country (including Stilton) in 1990, and so all property, wherever

THIS CONVEYANCE is made the   day of   BETWEEN
VICTORIA VENTNOR of 3 Trant Way Mousehole in the County of
Stilton (hereinafter called "the vendor") of the one part and
BARBARA BELL of Oak Tree Cottage Elmdale in Stilton aforesaid
(hereinafter called "the purchaser") of the other part

WHEREAS the vendor is seised of the property hereinafter
described for an estate in fee simple in possession free from
incumbrances and has agreed with the purchaser for the sale thereof
to her at a price of one hundred and seventy thousand pounds
(£170,000)

NOW THIS DEED WITNESSETH as follows:
In consideration of the sum of one hundred and seventy thousand
pounds (£170,000) paid by the purchaser to the vendor (the receipt
whereof the vendor hereby acknowledges) the vendor with full title
guarantee hereby conveys unto the purchaser all that piece or parcel
of land known as 3 Trant Way Mousehole in the County of Stilton
which for the purposes of identification only is shown and delineated
in red on the plan attached hereto TO HOLD the same unto the
purchaser in fee simple.

IN WITNESS of which the vendor has executed this deed in the
presence of the attesting witness the day and year first before written

Signed and delivered   )
As a deed by   )
the said VICTORIA VENTNOR)
in the presence of   )

Julian Possum

JULIAN POSSUM
198, THE HIGH STREET,
MOUSEHOLE,
STILTON

I.T. CONSULTANT

situated, will now be in an area of compulsory registration. In consequence, any new owner who has taken an estate under the unregistered system of conveyancing must apply to the Land Registry for first registration as registered proprietor.

In order to compel purchasers to apply for first registration, LRA 2002 ss. 6 and 7 provide that, if a registration is not made within two months of the date of the conveyance that conveyance shall become void, with the result that the legal estate that has been conveyed to the purchaser will revert to the vendor, who will hold it on a bare trust for the purchaser.

Thus it is essential that once Barbara Bell has taken the conveyance of the legal estate in 3 Trant Way, she applies for first registration of her title without delay and we will see what this involves in the next chapter.

FURTHER READING

Cheshire and Burn, *Modern Law of Real Property*, 16th edn., pp. 59–66 (doctrine of notice).

Harpum, 'Purchasers With Notice of Unregistered Land Charges' [1981] CLJ 213.

Thompson, 'The Purchaser as Private Detective' [1986] Conv 283.

Yates, 'The Protection of Equitable Interests Under the 1925 Legislation' (1974) 37 MLR 87.

5

Registered land

5.1 Introduction

You may remember from previous chapters that the LRA 1925, which governed the system of registered land, was repealed and replaced by the Land Registration Act 2002 ('LRA 2002'), which in the main came into force on 13 October 2003. In this chapter we will concentrate on the terms of the new Act and the rules made under it (Land Registration Rules 2003—SI 2003 No.1417 ('LRR 2003')), and unless otherwise stated references in this chapter are to sections of LRA 2002. For convenience we will refer to the 'old' and 'new' systems, but we want to emphasise at the outset that although the old Act is completely repealed and replaced, the new Act is careful to maintain the continuity of the registered title system. In other words, it is not a question of abolishing one system and replacing it with another, but rather of continuing and improving the existing system.

5.2 Need for reform

5.2.1 Aim of registration

When compulsory title registration was introduced by LRA 1925, the aim of its creators was to simplify conveyancing by placing all the essential information about an estate in land on a register. Thereafter an intending purchaser would only need to look at the register in order to discover all that he needed to know about the property, including proof of ownership of the estate in the land and details of any rights which third parties had in respect of it. Instead of producing a bundle of title deeds in order to prove his title to the land, a vendor would simply have to produce a copy of the details on the register which the purchaser would check against the register. In theory this is an excellent idea, and indeed is still the aim of modern title registration, but as we will see the original system was subject to various problems.

5.2.2 Consultation

Proposals for major changes to the system of registered title were contained in a consultative document, *Land Registration for the Twenty-first Century*, 1998, Law Com No. 254 ('the Consultative Document'), which was produced in 1998 by a joint working party of the Law Commission and the Land Registry.

The Consultative Document proposed nothing less than the complete replacement of the LRA 1925, a task which it described, understandably, as 'a major undertaking'. Several reasons were given for the need for such sweeping new legislation, the most important of which was the move to electronic conveyancing, which we explain further in 5.2.3 and 5.14.

Other reasons included the complicated and badly drafted character of the 1925 Act, and the need to introduce specific changes to the system. As we mentioned above, the original notion of land registration was that the register would provide a complete record of title, so that the purchaser would be able to buy in reliance on it with the minimum of other enquiries or inspections. However, it was thought necessary to accept that certain third-party interests should continue to bind the estate and be enforceable against the purchaser without appearing on the register. These rights were known as '*overriding interests*', and their existence made it impossible to rely solely on the register. As defined by LRA 1925, s.70(1), certain categories of overriding interests constituted a real risk to purchasers and meant that they still had to undertake a range of enquiries and inspections, in addition to checking the register. The Consultative Document proposed a reduction and redefinition of overriding interests, although it accepted that retaining some of them was unavoidable.

There was also a need to deal with a long-standing difficulty, which stemmed from the original belief that registration of title was merely a matter of conveyancing machinery. As a result, it was thought that the substantive law relating to the ownership of land remained the same in both registered and unregistered systems. In fact it had become increasingly obvious during the 75 years since the introduction of the LRA 1925 that there are real differences between the law relating to registered and unregistered land; a good example is to be found in the rules relating to adverse possession, which we discuss in Chapter 6. Despite its very slow introduction, registered title is now the predominant system of landholding in this country, and the joint working party took the view that, where necessary, substantive law should reflect the realities of this system, rather than being tied to the practice of unregistered conveyancing, which is rapidly becoming obsolete.

5.2.3 Electronic conveyancing

It is clear from the Consultative Document that the real impetus for change came from the move to electronic conveyancing, which is already under way. Although most registered titles have now been computerised, transfer of a registered title is still paper-based and is conducted in stages. For example, when a house with registered title is sold, a transfer is made in the form of a written deed, which is then sent to the registry, so that the transfer can be completed some time later by registration. This is time-consuming, and duplicates work, and problems can arise in the gap between transfer and registration, since the purchaser has only an equitable interest in the property until the transaction has been completed by registration.

Under an electronic system, a written deed would no longer be used. The transfer would be made electronically through a computer link to the Land Registry system, which would simultaneously register the purchaser as the new proprietor.

This would do away with the problem of the 'registration gap', and should be quicker and more cost-effective.

The same system would operate for the creation of new interests in land. For example, a lease over 7 years carved out of a registered freehold would no longer be granted by deed and then registered, but would be created and registered simultaneously by use of computer systems.

The electronic system could also be extended to include the contract as well as transfer and grant. This would mean that a valid contract relating to registered land could be created only by electronic means, thus enabling the registry to record the contract against the registered title at the moment at which it was made.

Despite the advantages of the new proposed system, the working party accepted that there is a limited class of rights which at present arise without any formal creation and which must be left free to do so even after the introduction of electronic conveyancing. Rights which can arise in this way include: an equity arising due to proprietary estoppel; rights under a constructive or resulting trust; squatters' rights; easements arising by prescription or implied grant or reservation; and certain equities, such as a right to set aside a transaction for undue influence. We know that this list may not mean very much to you at the moment, but the various rights will be dealt with at later stages in this book. The common characteristic of these rights is that they all come into existence without any formal grant, and it would therefore be completely inappropriate to say that they could not exist unless created by electronic transfer.

Further, the working party accepted that these informally created rights are most unlikely to be protected in any formal way by entry on the register, and would therefore have to continue to operate as overriding interests, since it would be unreasonable to expect rights which arise informally to be protected by formal methods. (For more information on electronic conveyancing, see 5.14.)

5.2.4 **Result of consultation**

Following a period of consultation on the recommendations contained in the Consultative Document, the joint working party published a major report, *Land Registration for the Twenty-First Century A Conveyancing Revolution*, 2001, Law Com No. 271 ('the Report'). The Report contains an account of the responses on consultation, together with an extensive commentary on the draft Bill, which has now been enacted as the Land Registration Act 2002. Although the Report contains far more detail than you can possibly need for your land law studies, it can be helpful to refer to it for an explanation of specific sections in the Act which may appear confusing (so long as you remember that a few of the provisions it describes did not survive the legislative process and so do not appear in the Act).

5.2.5 **LRA 2002**

The new Act makes major changes in the system of registered land, giving effect to most of the recommendations in the Consultative Document and making provision for the introduction of electronic conveyancing.

One of the principal aims in making these changes was to bring about what is described as 'total registration': that is, to bring all land in England and Wales on to the register as soon as possible. The new Act seeks to speed the process by encouraging voluntary registration and by requiring the compulsory registration of relatively short leases (that is, leases for more than seven years). The Act also provides for the registration of Crown land (see Part 7), but that topic is outside the scope of this book.

Before looking at the detail of the Act, you may like to note its 'fundamental objective' which in the words of the Report (at para. 1.4) is:

that under the system of electronic dealing with land . . . the register should be a complete and accurate reflection of the state of the title of the land at any given time, so that it is possible to investigate title to land on line, with the absolute minimum of additional enquiries and inspections.

Thus, the Act has two main objectives:

(1) to ensure that as many interests in registered land as possible are shown on the register (or, if not on the register, are not binding on purchasers); and

(2) to make arrangements that will allow dispositions of registered land to be handled electronically.

5.3 What can be registered?

The land registration system provides for the registration of ownership of the two legal estates and of certain legal interests.

5.3.1 Registration of freehold and leasehold estates

All freehold estates are capable of being registered, but only certain leasehold ones are registrable, and we need to tell you which these are.

5.3.1.1 *Leases with more than seven years to run*

Under the old system, a leasehold estate was registrable only if the term in question was for more than 21 years. One of the most significant changes made by LRA 2002 is to extend compulsory registration to shorter leases, by requiring registration of all leases which at the date of transfer or grant have more than seven years to run (s. 4(1)(a) and (c), and (2)).

In the past the registration of title to relatively short leases was regarded as undesirable, because of the amount of work involved for the registry in first registering them and then removing them from the register when they expired. The proposed move to electronic conveyancing (see 5.2.3) means that the administrative work involved in dealing with short leases is no longer a significant consideration, and it is possible that when the electronic system is in operation compulsory registration will be extended to even shorter leases—probably all those for more than three years—under powers contained in s. 118.

The extension of registration to shorter leases has been contentious, but will still exclude the periodic leases that are used for many domestic premises (such as monthly tenancies). The change has been made because the average length of commercial leases has become much shorter and these leases are often of very considerable value. Obviously, commercial leases vary considerably in length, but whereas formerly most lasted for more than 21 years, the average period for such leases has dropped now to 15 years (and thus many are shorter than that). Therefore, many have been falling outside the registration period in recent years. In addition, reducing the length of registrable leases is seen as an essential step in the process of bringing all titles onto the register.

5.3.1.2 *Leases which are registrable irrespective of length*

(1) The Act provides for registration of two types of leases under which the tenant may not always be in possession of the property. These are:

- (a) leases which are to take effect in possession more than three months after the date of grant (for more information about leases which take effect in the future, see 8.1.3.4); and

- (b) leases in which the right to possession is discontinuous, for example timeshare arrangements for holiday accommodation, by which tenants are given rights of possession for specified periods each year.

In leases of these types, the fact that the tenant is not necessarily in possession of the land means that there is a real risk that a purchaser might buy the landlord's estate without discovering that it is subject to a lease. In consequence, the Act provides for the registration of title to such leases (which will be accompanied by an entry on the landlord's title) even where the lease is for not more than seven years (ss. 3(1)–(4), 4(1)(d), and 27(2)(b)(ii)–(iii)).

(2) Leases of property which is subject to the 'Right to Buy' provisions of the Housing Act 1985 are also registrable regardless of their length. These leases are outside the scope of this book, and we will say no more about them, except that they were registrable under LRA 1925 (as amended) and continue to be so by virtue of LRA 2002, s. 4(1)(e) and s. 27(2)(b)(iv) and (v).

5.3.2 **Registration of legal interests**

In the words of s. 2(a):

This Act makes provision about the registration of title to –
  (a) unregistered legal estates which are interests of any of the following kinds
      (i)   an estate in land [ie the freehold and leasehold estates discussed above]
      (ii)   a rentcharge
      (iii)   a franchise
      (iv)   a profit à prendre in gross, and
      (v)   any other interest or charge which subsists for the benefit of, or is a charge on, an interest the title to which is registered.

At first sight the language of this subsection may seem puzzling, because it lists 'an estate in land' as being just one of a number of 'unregistered legal estates'. The explanation is to be found in LPA 1925, s. 1(4), which defines an estate in land as including not only the freehold and leasehold estates, but also the legal interests and charges listed in LPA 1925, s. 1(2) (see 1.5.1). Section 2(a) of LRA 2002 is saying therefore that the ownership of interests such as easements, rentcharges and charges by way of legal mortgage can be registered by their owners in the same way as title to the freehold and leasehold estates.

This is not a new development, for title to these legal interests was registrable under LRA 1925, although it seems that in practice only rentcharges were registered with their own titles (see Megarry and Wade, p. 221). However, s. 2(a) does add two further rights, franchises and profits à prendre in gross, to the list of registrable interests, and we need to explain briefly the nature of these two rights.

A *franchise* is a privilege which the Crown has allowed a subject to exercise. It gives the holder some particular right, as for example to collect tolls or to hold a fair or market. Although medieval in origin, these can still be valuable property rights, but until LRA 2002 came into force there was no way of registering title to them.

A *profit à prendre* (see 22.3) is the right to take something (wood, gravel, fish etc.) from another's land. The right may be '*appurtenant*', that is, attached to another piece of land and used for its benefit, or it can be '*in gross*', which means that it exists for the personal benefit of its owner and is not attached to any land. Appurtenant profits may be included in the registration of title to the land which they benefit, but until the new Act there was no provision for the registration of title to profits in gross, although they can be of considerable value.

Rules governing the registration of title to the various legal interests listed in s.2(a) form an important part of the registration system, but in what follows we will concentrate on registration of title to freehold and leasehold estates.

5.4 First registration

First registration is the process by which estates currently outside the registered title system are brought within it. As we explained in Chapter 2, the phased introduction of registration has been very slow, with the result that a number of properties are still subject to the old system of unregistered conveyancing, which we described in Chapter 4. The aim now is to bring these properties into the new system as quickly as possible, and eventually to achieve total registration (that is, to have titles to all estates in land on the register). For this purpose, LRA 2002 makes provision for both *compulsory* and *voluntary* first registration, and we will now look at each of these in a little more detail.

5.4.1 Compulsory first registration

5.4.1.1 *Events which trigger the requirement to register title to an estate*
Section 4 continues the existing system under which first registration is required whenever certain dealings with an unregistered legal estate occur. The dealings specified in s. 4 include:

(a) the transfer of an unregistered freehold estate;
(b) the transfer of an unregistered leasehold estate which at the time of transfer has more than seven years to run;

(c) the grant of a lease out of an unregistered estate for a term of more than 7 years; and

(d) the grant of a lease out of an unregistered estate which is to take effect in possession more than three months from the date of grant (see 5.3.1.2).

When compulsory registration of title was first introduced, estates became registrable only on specified dealings *for value*. As a result of amendments made by LRA 1997, triggers also operated where the dealing was by way of gift or in a range of other circumstances, and these provisions are continued under s. 4(1)(a) and (c).

Thus the transfers and grants we noted above give rise to an obligation to register title to the estate, irrespective of whether they are made for value, as a gift, or on a court order. A transfer also operates as a trigger where it is made by an *assent*. This is a special form of conveyance used by the personal representatives of a deceased person to transfer an estate in land to those entitled under his will or intestacy, and is also used to transfer an estate on to the next person entitled under a SLA settlement (as to which see Chapter 14). The inclusion of such transfers will have the gradual effect of requiring first registration of title to land held within family settlements. Such land is unlikely to come on the market and in consequence, before LRA 1997, seemed likely to remain unregistered for a long time to come.

In addition, LRA 2002 continues the LRA 1997 provision that a freehold estate, or a leasehold estate with more than seven years to run, will become compulsorily registrable if the owner creates over it a first legal mortgage protected by deposit of title deeds (as to which see 4.4.2.2), even although the owner is not transferring the estate itself.

5.4.1.2 *Who has to apply for first registration?*

Where the obligation to register arises on the transfer or grant of an estate, it is the new owner (e.g., the purchaser of a freehold estate or the tenant of a new lease) who must make the application. Where the triggering event is the grant of a mortgage, the application must be made by the mortgagor—the owner of the mortgaged estate (although s. 6(6) and rule 21 of LRR 2003 provide for the mortgagee to act if the mortgagor fails to do so).

5.4.1.3 *Failure to apply for first registration*

In order to compel estate owners to apply for registration, s. 7(1) provides that if registration is not made within two months of the triggering event the transfer or grant of an estate or the creation of a mortgage will become void. Where the event in question was a transfer, the estate will revert to the transferor, who will hold it on a bare trust for the transferee. Where the triggering event was the grant of a lease or the creation of a mortgage, the disposition will take effect as an estate contract (i.e., as a contract to grant the lease or mortgage). In all these circumstances, the person who failed to apply for registration will have to bear the costs of repeating the transaction.

5.4.1.4 *3 Trant Way*

You may remember that we left Barbara Bell at the end of Chapter 4, having just completed her purchase of the unregistered freehold estate in 3 Trant Way. This, of course, was an event which under s. 4 triggered the requirement to apply for first registration of her title, and she must seek registration within two months of the conveyance to her. If she does not do so in time, the conveyance will become void, and the estate will revert to Victoria Ventnor. She will hold it on trust for Barbara, who in due course will have to meet all the expenses involved in re-conveying it to her.

Thus it is essential that Barbara Bell applies for first registration of the title to her new house without delay. However, the registration is deemed to be made on the date at which the application arrives in the registry, provided all is in order, so really all that is necessary is that the application to register should be made within two months of the conveyance.

In the next section, we will see what will happen when Barbara Bell applies for first registration, but first we must look briefly at voluntary registration.

5.4.2 **Voluntary first registration**

In seeking to achieve the goal of total registration, the Act continues the process of voluntary registration, which has always been available for owners who wish to register their titles although they are not yet required to do so.

Section 3 provides for voluntary registration of a range of unregistered legal estates. They include the estates in land which are compulsorily registrable (i.e., the freehold estate and a leasehold estate of which more than seven years remains), and a rentcharge, a franchise and a profit à prendre in gross (for which see 5.3.2). In addition there are two provisions which have the effect of enabling certain leases for not more than seven years to be registered voluntarily:

(1) *section 3(4)* provides that leases for seven years or less may be registered if the right to possession under the lease is discontinuous—see 5.3.1.2;

(2) *section 3(7)* provides that where two leases in respect of the same piece of land are held by the same lessee, one being granted to take effect when the other comes to an end, they are to be treated for the purposes of the section as one continuous term. Thus, if A were granted a lease for four years and a separate lease, also for four years, to start at the end of the first, the overall term would be eight years and both leases would become voluntarily registrable.

It is hoped that the number of voluntary registrations will increase over the next few years. For this purpose Land Registry fees are reduced for voluntary applications, and more publicity will be given to the advantages of having a registered title, which is not only easier to deal with, but also under the new Act protects the owner from losing his title to a squatter (as to which, see Chapter 6).

5.5 **Registering title**

In this section we will outline what happens when Barbara Bell applies for first registration of title to her freehold estate in 3 Trant Way.

5.5.1 **Investigation of title by the registry**

We have seen that one of the purposes of registration is to provide any prospective purchaser with reliable information about the estate he is proposing to buy. He will want to be sure that the vendor owns the property he is offering to sell and that it is free from any encumbrances (third-party rights) other than those which have already been disclosed to him. In dealing with Barbara's application for registration therefore, the registry will need to satisfy itself that she does indeed own the estate she wants to register and that as many third-party rights as possible are recorded on the register. It will do this by repeating the process her solicitor undertook on the purchase of the property, scrutinising the title deeds and the results of searches and enquiries, all of which must be submitted with the application for registration. Indeed, the registry may be even more careful than a purchaser or a professional adviser would be, for the title once registered is guaranteed. Thus if the registry makes a mistake it may have to compensate anyone who suffers a loss as a result. If necessary, the registry will raise queries with Barbara, and may even require her to make additional searches and enquiries to clarify uncertain points.

Cautions against first registration

Where a person claims to have an interest against an estate in unregistered land, he may register a 'caution against first registration', which will ensure that his claim is considered by the registrar when dealing with such an application. This process was available under LRA 1925 and continues under LRA 2002 (ss. 15–22).

We will now go on to consider the form of the register, and the way in which the results of the registry's investigations are recorded on it.

5.5.2 **Form of the register**

The 'register of title' consists of a number of individual registers, one for each estate registered (LRR 2002 r. 2). This means that, since there may be more than one estate in one piece of land (for example, a fee simple and a term of years), there may be several individual registers for the same piece of land.

The individual register for an estate consists of three parts:

the property register;

the proprietorship register; and

the charges register.

The opening words of LRA 2002 are:

There is to continue to be kept a register of title kept by the registrar (s.1(1))

and no changes are made to the structure of the register by the Act or the rules made under it (LRR 2003). ⁓ updated version

We know that it can be difficult to visualise the individual register and its parts, and so we suggest that while reading this section you look at the example of the fictional register entry for the freehold estate of 1 Trant Way, which is shown on p. 75. Each title is allocated a title number by the registry and you will see that ST1234 is the title number for 1 Trant Way.

HM Land Registry

TITLE NUMBER: ST1234

Edition date: **1 March 1992**

Entry No.	A. PROPERTY REGISTER *containing the description of the registered land and the estate comprised in the Title*	*A* *Property Register*
	A STILTON : MOUSEHOLE	
1.	(1 March 1992) The Freehold land shown edged with red on the plan of the above Title filed at the Registry and being 1 Trant Way, Mousehole, (ST14 3JP).	

Entry No.	B. PROPRIETORSHIP REGISTER *stating nature of the Title, name, address and description of the proprietor of the land and any entries affecting the right of disposing thereof* TITLE ABSOLUTE	*B* *Proprietorship Register*
1.	*B* (1 March 1992) Proprietor : VICTOR VENN of 1 Trant Way, Mousehole, Stilton ST14 3JP.	

Entry No.	C. CHARGES REGISTER *containing charges, incumbrances etc. adversely affecting the land and registered dealings therewith*	*C* *Charges Register*
1.	*C* (1 March 1992) A conveyance of the land in this title dated 30 September 1934 made between (1) Mary Brown and (2) Harold Robins contains the following covenants: "The Purchaser hereby covenants with the Vendor for the benefit of her adjoining land known as 15 Trant Avenue to observe and perform the following stipulations and conditions: 1. No building erected on the land shall be used other than as a private dwellinghouse. 2. Nothing shall be done or permitted on the premises which may be a nuisance or annoyance to the adjoining house or to the neighbourhood.	

***** END OF REGISTER *****

NOTE A: A date at the beginning of an entry is the date on which the entry was made in the Register.

NOTE B: This certificate was officially examined with the register on   1 March 1992

5.5.2.1 *Property register*

This part of the register describes the property, including the type of estate ('freehold' or 'leasehold'), and invariably refers to a *filed plan*. The filed plan is prepared from the largest size of ordnance survey map and on the register entry the land concerned is shown edged in red. Usually the description of the property is simply its postal address but a different type of description may sometimes be necessary (for instance, if the registration was of a field with no address).

The property register may also contain details of easements, such as a right of way, which *benefit* the registered estate.

5.5.2.2 *Proprietorship register*

This part of the register shows the class of the title (see 5.5.3), and gives the name of the registered owner of the estate and his address. The owner is described as the 'registered proprietor'. The proprietorship register will also record any restrictions on the power of the proprietor to deal with the land, for example, if he is a trustee or a bankrupt (see 5.8.2.2).

5.5.2.3 *Charges register*

The charges section carries the details of certain encumbrances (i.e., third-party rights) on the estate (see 5.8.2.1).

5.5.3 Classes of title

The property and proprietorship registers, when read together, will tell the purchaser the nature of the property registered and who owns it. The type of estate is clear, since it will be described as either freehold or leasehold land, and rights which benefit the estate (such as easements over adjoining property) are also described.

The register will also indicate how good the proprietor's estate is, by recording a 'class' of title, awarded on first registration and showing how reliable the title is considered to be.

The quality of the titles investigated may vary considerably: one title may prove to be entirely sound; another might be based only on the rights a squatter has established by possession of the land for some years (see Chapter 6 on title by adverse possession); and another may suffer from some technical defect. Accordingly LRA 1925 provided for seven classes of title: three for freehold estates and four for leasehold estates, and these continue unchanged under LRA 2002.

Sections 9 and 10 of LRA 2002 specify the classes of title available for freehold and leasehold land respectively, and prescribe the standards to be applied by the registrar in determining the appropriate class.

5.5.3.1 *Classes of freehold title*

Under LRA 2002, s. 9, the classes of freehold title which can be registered are: absolute freehold title; qualified freehold title; and possessory freehold title.

(1) *Absolute freehold title* Absolute freehold title is the best class of title known to the registered land system and it is very nearly indefeasible (though see 5.12 on alteration of the register).

Section 9(2) provides that absolute title to a freehold estate may be registered where the title to the estate is such:

as a willing buyer could properly be advised by a competent professional adviser to accept.

However, this does not mean that the registrar has to demand a *perfect* title, for s. 9(3) provides that in deciding to register an applicant with absolute freehold title, the registrar may disregard the fact:

that a person's title appears to him to be open to objection if he is of the opinion that the defect will not cause the holding under the title to be disturbed.

Under s. 11(2)–(5), the effect of registration of a freehold estate with absolute title is to vest that freehold estate in the registered proprietor, together with all interests which benefit that estate (e.g., an easement, such as a right of way or a right of drainage, which the estate enjoys over neighbouring land). Section 11(4) provides that on first registration the estate:

is subject only to the following interests –

    (a) interests which are the subject of an entry in the register in relation to the estate

    (b) unregistered interests which fall within . . . Schedule 1, and

    (c) interests acquired under the Limitation Act 1980, of which the proprietor has notice.

We will see later that interests which other people may have over the registered estate should generally be protected by some entry on the register of title to the estate, which will alert prospective purchasers to the existence of those rights. Some interests, however, will bind the estate and the purchaser even if not protected by such an entry. The Act gives two lists of such interests, which are said to be 'interests that override first registration' (in Sch. 1) and 'interests that override registered dispositions' (in Sch. 3). Later on, we will explain the reference to interests acquired under the Limitation Act 1980 and will also tell you why there are two lists (see 5.9.1), but for the moment all you need to know is that in general on first registration the estate is free from all encumbrances except those protected by an entry on the register and any rights not protected in that way which override first registration under Sch.1.

One further point to mention about first registration with absolute title is that a trustee who is registered as first proprietor is also bound by those rights of beneficiaries under the trust of which he has notice, even if they are not protected by entry on the register (s. 11(5)). A purchaser from the trustee would take free of them (unless they were overriding or had been protected by some entry on the register) but the trustee cannot free himself of his obligations to the beneficiaries merely by securing a registration which does not mention their interests.

Since the registrar may accept an imperfect title to an estate for registration with absolute title (s. 9(3)), the registration can have a curative effect and prevent future purchasers concerning themselves with technical, but unimportant, defects. Once a title is registered it is the register alone which matters as evidence of title. (This is one reason why owners sometimes choose to register their estates voluntarily.)

(2) *Qualified freehold title*   Qualified freehold titles are extremely rare ('perhaps one in a hundred thousand registered titles is qualified'—*Ruoff & Roper, Registered Conveyancing*, 1991, para.5-08). Such a title is granted:

if the registrar is of the opinion that the person's title to the estate has been established only for a limited period or subject to certain reservations which cannot be disregarded . . . (s.9(4)).

The details of the defect will be entered on the register. Such a situation might arise if a purchaser of an estate in unregistered land had decided to take the risk of not investigating the title to the property as thoroughly as is usual. As we have seen (4.2), it is normal to search back to a deed which is at least 15 years old. If the purchaser had accepted a deed made only 10 years ago and later applied for first registration, it is likely that he would be registered only with qualified title.

Section 11(6) provides that registration with qualified title has the same effect as registration with absolute title:

> except that it does not affect the enforcement of any estate, right or interest which appears from the register to be excepted from the effect of registration.

Thus any later purchaser will know that he runs the risk of finding that the estate is subject to some defect which was not discovered on the earlier investigation of title.

(3) *Possessory freehold title*   Possessory titles are less good than absolute titles but fortunately are fairly rare, occurring in only about 1 per cent of cases. Such titles are registered in cases in which the ownership of the estate is evidenced purely by the fact that the estate owner is in occupation of the land, or that he is in receipt of the rents and profits from the occupant (s. 9(5)). This situation might arise if the deeds to the property had been lost, or if the estate owner had acquired his rights merely through long use of the land (title by adverse possession—see Chapter 6).

Registration with possessory title has the same effect as registration with an absolute title, save that it is subject to any adverse pre-registration estates, rights or interests (s. 11(7)). Thus the danger of having a title which is possessory only is that someone may appear who has a better claim to the estate (for example, the original owner who has been dispossessed by the squatter). In time, any such rights would be time-barred under the Limitation Act 1980, as we explain in Chapter 6, and so the possessory title would become quite safe from disruption. To take account of this, the system provides for a possessory title to be upgraded to absolute title after it has been registered for 12 years (see 5.5.3.3).

5.5.3.2 *Classes of leasehold title*

Under LRA 2002, s. 10, the classes of leasehold title which can be registered are: absolute leasehold title; good leasehold title; qualified leasehold title; and possessory leasehold title.

Three of these titles are very similar to those discussed above in relation to freehold land; but one, good leasehold title, has no counterpart amongst the freehold titles.

(1) *Absolute leasehold title*   As compared with the purchaser of a freehold estate, the purchaser of a leasehold estate has an extra dimension to consider when checking that the vendor can transfer the estate that he has contracted to give. Like the purchaser of the freehold estate, he will check the devolution of the title to the estate that he is buying, and will want to see that it has been correctly passed from one owner to another until it reached the vendor. However, in addition, the purchaser will often wish to be reassured that the landlord (lessor) who granted the lease was actually entitled to do so. Thus the purchaser really needs to investigate the landlord's title to the superior estate in order to check that he had a good title to that estate and therefore had the right to grant the lease which the purchaser intends to buy.

Under s. 10(2), absolute leasehold title is granted only if the Registrar is satisfied both with the lease and with the superior title from which it is derived. Thus if X, a freehold owner, grants a lease to Y, Y can be registered with absolute leasehold title only if the registrar is satisfied that the lease is good *and* that X's freehold title is good.

Before LRA 2002 came into force, it might not be possible for the leaseholder (Y) to prove that the title of the freeholder (X) was good, since under LPA 1925, s. 44, a prospective leaseholder had no right to require the landlord to prove title to his estate unless this was specifically provided for in any contract preceding the grant of the lease. If the landlord's estate was itself registered with absolute title there was usually little problem and the registrar would register an absolute title for the leasehold estate, even though the leaseholder might have no right to examine the superior title himself. However, where the landlord's estate was not yet registered, the leaseholder might well be unable to satisfy the registrar as to his landlord's title, and in such cases the leasehold estate could be registered only with good leasehold title (for which, see below).

To overcome this difficulty, Schedule 11, para. 2 amends LPA 1925 s. 44, with the result that where the owner of an unregistered estate contracts to grant a lease which will be subject to the requirement of compulsory first registration, the grantor will have to prove his title to the superior estate, unless the contract provides otherwise. It is therefore likely that in the future more leasehold estates will be registered with absolute title.

Registration with absolute leasehold title vests the leasehold estate in the owner subject to the encumbrances described in the case of absolute freehold title and, in addition, to all express and implied covenants, obligations and liabilities imposed by the lease or incidental to the land (s. 12(3)–(5)).

The result of the registration is that the registrar will guarantee that the lease was effectively granted and will also show on the leasehold title any covenants which bind the *freehold* estate and which therefore bind the lease as well as the superior title (see Chapter 23).

(2) *Good leasehold title*   This class of title is granted when the registrar is satisfied that the lease itself is good but where there is no evidence of the quality of the superior title (s. 10(3)). In such cases the registry cannot be absolutely sure that the lease was validly granted by a person with power to grant such an estate. Apart from the fact that the superior title cannot be guaranteed, good leasehold title has the same effect as registration with absolute leasehold title (s. 12(6)). If the superior title is registered at a later date the registrar has power to improve the good leasehold title to absolute leasehold title (see 5.5.3.3).

(3) *Qualified leasehold title*   Qualified leasehold titles are practically unknown. They are similar to qualified freehold titles.

(4) *Possessory leasehold title*   Possessory leasehold titles are very rare. They have the same qualifications as possessory freehold titles. In addition there is no guarantee of the superior title. This class of title may be converted to good leasehold title after it has been registered for 12 years (see 5.5.3.3).

5.5.3.3 *Upgrading title*

Section 62 gives the registrar power in specified circumstances to upgrade any of the titles which are less than absolute.

(1) *Upgrading freehold titles*   Possessory or qualified freehold title may be upgraded to absolute at any time if the registrar 'is satisfied as to the title to the estate' (s. 62(1)). Thus if an applicant was registered with only possessory title because the title deeds to the property were lost, his title may be upgraded to absolute if the

deeds are found. Similarly a qualified title may be upgraded to absolute if the registrar is satisfied that the cause of the original objection is no longer a matter of concern.

In addition, where freehold title has been registered as possessory for at least 12 years, the registrar may upgrade it to absolute if satisfied that the registered proprietor is in possession of the land (s. 62(4)). The reason underlying this provision is that if, at the date of first registration, there was any person with a right to claim ownership of the unregistered estate, that right will very probably have been extinguished under the Limitation Act, 1980 (see Chapter 6), and in consequence it is relatively safe to upgrade the possessory title after that period.

(2) *Upgrading leasehold titles* Under s. 62(2), good leasehold title may be upgraded to absolute if the registrar is satisfied as to the superior title as, for example, he will be if title to the superior estate is registered.

Qualified or possessory leasehold title may be upgraded to good leasehold where the registrar is satisfied as to the title of the estate (i.e., in the sort of circumstances we have noted above with regard to freehold title), and may be upgraded to absolute where the registrar is also satisfied as to the superior title (s. 62(3)).

In addition, possessory leasehold title may be upgraded to good leasehold title after a period of 12 years if the registrar is satisfied that the proprietor is in possession of the land (s. 62(5)). The reason for this is the same as that noted in respect of upgrading freehold possessory title.

5.5.4 Recording encumbrances

As you will know from previous chapters, an estate may be subject to a wide range of third-party rights, including leases, easements, mortgages and rights under trusts, restrictive covenants and estate contracts. On first registration, the registrar will aim to record on the estate's register of title as many as possible of the encumbrances which burden it. Depending on the nature of the right, this will be done either by entering a notice in the Charges Register or by putting a restriction in the Proprietorship Register (see 5.8.2 for an explanation of the nature of these two entries and the circumstances in which each is used).

Although the aim is to note most encumbrances on the register, you will remember from 5.5.3.1 that LRA 2002 Sch. 1 lists certain interests that '*override*' first registration or, in other words, will bind the estate although not entered on the register. The list includes: most leases for not more than seven years; interests of persons in actual occupation; legal easements and profits; and a range of legal and statutory rights. The first of these, short leases, will not be entered on the register because they are of limited duration and, for the time being at least, the registry does not want to clutter the register with them. However, the other interests listed in Sch. 1 *will* be entered on the register if the Registry is aware of them, and s. 71(a) and LRR 2003 r. 28 impose a duty on the applicant to inform the registry of any such interests of which he is aware. Thus Sch. 1 really acts as a safety-net, to preserve those interests which bind the unregistered estate but have not been identified and recorded on first registration.

5.5.5 **First registration of title to the freehold estate in 3 Trant Way**

If all goes well with the registry's investigation, Barbara Bell will be registered with absolute title which, as we have already seen, means that she will hold the freehold estate free of all encumbrances except for registered charges, interests which are the subject of an entry on the register, any rights which override first registration under Sch. 1 and interests acquired under the Limitation Act 1980 of which she has notice. At this point we must briefly explain the reference to rights acquired under the Limitation Act, which relates to what are sometimes called 'squatters' rights'.

5.5.5.1 *Squatters' rights (or the rights of the adverse possessor)*

We will explain the rules about adverse possession and squatters' rights more fully in Chapter 6. All you need to know at this stage is that if the owner of unregistered land loses possession of it to another person, his right to recover the land from the dispossessor may be extinguished after 12 years by the Limitation Act 1980. Once this has happened, the dispossessor (usually called an 'adverse possessor' or 'squatter') is regarded as the legal owner, and once he has acquired ownership in this way, he can go out of possession and still retain ownership. Under LRA 1925, s. 70(1)(f), the rights of the adverse possessor were overriding and bound the estate on first registration and on any subsequent disposition. This meant that if a purchaser had bought the land and secured first registration without being aware of the squatter's rights (as he might if the squatter was not in occupation), he could lose his title to the estate if the squatter subsequently claimed ownership. One of the changes made by LRA 2002 Sch.1 is to reduce the overriding effect of the squatter's rights, so that if he is not in actual occupation of the property his rights do not override first registration.

However, under s. 11(4)(c), the squatter's rights will bind the proprietor if he has notice of them (that is, if he knows or ought to know of them), and in such circumstances the squatter would be able to seek alteration of the register to give effect to his rights. Interestingly, this provision appears to produce the unusual result of first registration invalidating an interest which bound the estate immediately before it was registered, since in the unregistered system the dispossessed owner is subject to rights under the Limitation Act irrespective of notice.

5.5.5.2 *Evidence of registration*

On completion of the registration process, Barbara Bell will receive a 'title information document', which consists of a cover sheet around official copies of the individual register and title plan. Under the old system of registration, she would have been given a more impressive document, called the Land Certificate, containing copies of the register and plan, together with some general information about the registered title system. The fictitious register we show on p. 75 is a copy of Victor Venn's Land Certificate, which he received when registered as owner under the old system. As part of the move towards electronic conveyancing and the paperless, dematerialised system, the Registry has discontinued the practice of issuing Land Certificates. Although the contents of the new document is similar to the old Land Certificate, the essential difference is that it is provided simply for *information*, and does not have to be sent to the registry for amendment on any dealing with the estate.

5.6 **Dealings with a registered estate**

5.6.1 **Dispositions which must be completed by registration**

Section 27(2) sets out a list of *registrable dispositions*, that is the dispositions or dealings with a registered estate which must be completed by registration. They include:

(1) a transfer of the registered estate;

(2) the grant of a lease for a term of more than seven years;

(3) the grant of certain leases irrespective of length, including the future leases and leases providing for discontinuous possession which we described in 5.3.1.2;

(4) the express creation of interests under LPA 1925 s.1(2)(a),(b) and (e), that is:

(i)   a legal easement or profit

(ii)   a legal rentcharge

(iii) a right of entry in respect of a legal lease or a legal rentcharge;

(5) the grant of a legal charge.

Section 27(1) provides that these dispositions do not operate at law until registration requirements are met, and Sch. 2 gives details of these requirements.

5.6.2 **Registration requirements**

A transfer of an estate which is already registered requires the entry of the transferee as proprietor, and we will see this rule in operation later when the Armstrongs complete their purchase of 1 Trant Way (5.13).

A grant of a new registrable estate or interest, such as a lease, rentcharge, or easement, requires the grantee to be registered as proprietor of it. In general, this will involve opening a fresh individual register for the new estate or interest. However, in the case of a right such as an easement, which is not given a separate register, the requirement is that it should be added to the register of the estate which it benefits (where it will appear in the property register—see 5.5.2.1). In addition, and most importantly, where the new estate or interest burdens another registered title, a notice of it must be entered on that title. By contrast, a registered charge (or mortgage) is registered in the Charges Section of the title subject to the charge, so no separate notice of it is required.

5.6.3 **Failure to meet registration requirements**

If these requirements are not met, the transfer or grant does not operate at law, but for the time being will take effect in equity. However, when the electronic conveyancing system is in operation, dispositions which do not meet the requirements will have no effect at all, not even in equity (see 5.14).

5.7 Buying a house with registered title

5.7.1 No. 1 Trant Way

Having followed Barbara Bell's progress in buying a house with unregistered title and applying for first registration, we now need to turn our attention to the other househunters, Mr And Mrs Armstrong, who are planning to buy 1 Trant Way (2.1.1). The title to this property is registered (2.2.3.2), and like any other home-buyer, the Armstrongs will want to check two things about the property. They need to make sure that the vendor, Victor Venn, owns the estate he is offering to sell, and that it is free from any encumbrances other than those which have already been disclosed to them.

5.7.2 Does the vendor own the estate?

As we can see from the specimen land certificate at p. 75 Victor Venn is the registered proprietor of the freehold estate in 1 Trant Way, and is registered with absolute title. This is the best title available (see 5.5.3.1), and the Armstrongs can have reasonable confidence in buying the property, although they need to be aware that the system does provide for subsequent alteration of the register for various purposes, including the correction of mistakes.

Of course it is not safe for the Armstrongs to rely on the land certificate, which is only a copy of the register and may not be up to date. They, or more likely their professional adviser, will need to make an official search of the register, but this is all that needs to be done to satisfy themselves that Victor does truly own the estate. There is no need to investigate title in the old way, described in Chapter 4 in respect to the purchase of unregistered land, which involved checking through past dealings with the property as shown by old title deeds. The register is conclusive of the fact that Victor owns the freehold estate in No. 1.

5.7.3 Are there any encumbrances which bind the property?

The effect of LRA 2002 s. 29(1) and (2) is that the buyer of a freehold estate registered with absolute title takes it free of all encumbrances except for:

registered charges (that is, legal mortgages, which will appear in the Charges Section of the register)

interests protected by notices on the register of the estate

any interest that overrides the disposition under Sch. 3 (that is, which bind the estate without appearing on its register)

You may like to note that under LRA 1925 interests which bound without being on the register were known as *'overriding interests'* (rather than as 'interests that override'), while interests which required protection on the register were called *'minor interests'*, a term not used in the LRA 2002.

If the title to the estate is less than absolute (i.e., qualified or possessory) the purchaser will be subject in addition to any exceptions appearing on the register (see 5.5.3), and where the estate is a leasehold one he will also be bound by obligations imposed by the lease but not noted on the register.

The provisions of s. 29(1) and (2) apply not only to a person who buys the registered estate, but also to those who take under any other registrable disposition for valuable consideration. In what follows, we will explain the rules by reference to the buyer of the registered estate, but they apply equally to a range of other disponees, including legal mortgagees and tenants taking grants of registrable leases.

Victor Venn's land certificate (at p. 75) shows that he is registered with absolute title to a freehold estate, so, provided this is confirmed by an official search, the encumbrances which could affect the Armstongs are limited to rights protected by entries on the register and overriding interests, and we will consider these separately in the next two sections.

5.8 Interests protected by entries on the register

Under LRA 1925 there were four types of entry (notices, restrictions, cautions and inhibitions) which could be used to protect encumbrances and to alert prospective purchasers to them. LRA 2002 provides for two forms only – notices and restrictions – but extends their functions to include matters formerly covered by cautions and inhibitions. Nevertheless, transitional arrangements maintain the effectiveness of existing entries in the old form (LRA 2002 s.134 and Sch.12, paras. 1 and 2), and so we must briefly explain their use and effect.

5.8.1 Entries under LRA 1925

5.8.1.1 *Notices*

A notice was entered in the charges section of the register and anyone who acquired the registered estate (or another interest in it) would be bound by the interest which it protected. Notices were used to protect a wide range of interests, including leases, equitable mortgages, estate contracts and restrictive covenants. The difficulty with using a notice was that it had to be entered on the land certificate as well as on the register (so that the certificate remained an accurate copy of the register) and therefore a person wishing to enter a notice had to produce the land certificate to the registrar. This was not a problem if the registered proprietor agreed to the entry being made, but might well be impossible if he opposed it.

5.8.1.2 *Restrictions*

A restriction was entered in the proprietorship section of the register, and prevented dealings with the registered estate until a specified condition had been met. Typically, restrictions were used when the property was subject to a trust, and the restriction would provide that no dealing with the estate was to be registered unless any capital money arising was paid to two trustees. Applications to impose a restriction had to be made by the registered proprietor, and it was necessary to produce the land certificate.

5.8.1.3 *Cautions*

Where inability to produce the land certificate meant that a notice or restriction could not be entered, the person seeking to protect an interest would have to use a caution (entered in the proprietorship section). The caution gave the cautioner the right to be informed of any proposed dealing with the estate and an opportunity to assert the rights he claimed. It was for the registrar or the court to decide if the claim was valid, and whether it should bind the estate.

It is important to realise that the entry of a caution merely gave a right to notice of any proposed dealing, and did not in itself give protection against later registered dealings.

5.8.1.4 *Inhibitions*

An inhibition was placed on the register (in the proprietorship section) only on the order of the court or the Registrar. It was used to prevent dealings with the estate, either totally, or for a certain period or until a specified event occurred. Inhibitions were used most commonly in cases of bankruptcy, to prevent a bankrupt proprietor disposing of his interest in the land to the detriment of his creditors.

5.8.2 **Entries under LRA 2002**

Under the new system, the only types of entry which can be made are notices and restrictions.

5.8.2.1 *Notices*

Nature and effect
LRA 2002, s. 32(1) defines a notice as 'an entry in the register in respect of the burden of an interest affecting a registered estate or charge'. The fact that an interest is the subject of a notice does not necessarily mean that the interest is valid, but does mean that if it is valid it is protected against a purchaser of the registered estate for valuable consideration (s. 32(3)).

Interests which may or must be protected by notice
Section 33 lists the interests which *cannot* be protected by notice. They include:

(1) interests under a trust of land or SLA settlement, which should be protected by a restriction;

(2) a lease for not more than three years, the title to which is not registered (the proviso that the title to the short lease should not be registered is included because it is possible that a lease for not more than three years could come within one of the categories of short lease which are compulsorily registrable—see 5.3.1.2—and which, on registration, must be protected by an entry on the register of the estate which they bind); and

(3) a restrictive covenant between lessor and lessee, so far as it relates to the demised premises.

Apart from these interests, all other interests *may* be protected by notice, and in a number of cases the Act provides that such an entry *must* be made.

(a) *Circumstances in which a notice must be entered*
The rules about the completion of registrable dispositions out of a registered estate include the requirement that the transaction must be completed by the entry of a notice on the title register of the estate (s. 38; and see 5.6.2).

(b) *Circumstances in which a notice may be entered*
Section 37 provides that the registrar may enter a notice in respect of any interest of which he is aware which would otherwise take effect as an overriding interest. This is in accordance with the overall policy of reducing the number of interests which bind an estate without entry in the register. Once such an entry has been made, the interest in question loses its overriding status (s. 29(3)).

All other encumbrances which are not registrable or overriding interests (and are not specifically excluded by s. 33) may be the subject of a notice, and indeed should be protected in this way if they are not to be lost against a purchaser for valuable consideration of the registered estate (s. 29; and see 5.7.3). At first registration, the registrar will enter notices protecting any such rights of which he is aware. Apart from that, notices are entered on the application of the registered proprietor or the person who claims the right which is to be protected.

Applications for entry of notice
Applications may be made for an *agreed notice* or a *unilateral notice*, and the two forms reflects the distinction between notices and cautions in the old system.

(a) *Agreed notice*
An agreed notice will be entered only on the application or with the agreement of the registered proprietor (although see s. 34(3)(c) for a situation in which the registrar may apparently enter a notice without the consent of the registered proprietor). This reflects the old situation under the LRA 1925, in which the requirement to record the notice on the land certificate meant that it could be entered on the register only with the co-operation of the proprietor.

(b) *Unilateral notice*
A unilateral notice may be entered without the consent of the registered proprietor, although he has to be informed of the entry by the registrar and has the right to apply for its cancellation. This type of notice takes the place of the old caution, in that it can be entered without the co-operation of the registered owner. However, it is more effective than the caution, which did not protect the interest but merely entitled the cautioner to be informed of any proposed dealings and to be given an opportunity at that point to put forward a claim. By contrast, in the absence of an objection by the proprietor, a unilateral notice will protect the interest as adequately as an agreed notice. If the proprietor does object and the person lodging the notice maintains the claim, there will be procedures for determining its validity at that point (see s. 73), so that these questions will no longer arise unexpectedly when some dealing with the estate is proposed.

5.8.2.2 *Restrictions*

Nature and effect
LRA 2002, s. 41(1) defines a restriction as 'an entry in the register regulating the circumstances in which a disposition of a registered estate . . . may be the subject of an entry in the register'. In other words, it is a restriction on dealings with the registered estate. Section 41 provides that, where a restriction is entered in the register, no entry in respect of a disposition to which the restriction applies may be made in the register otherwise in accordance with its terms.

Under s. 40(2) and (3) the restriction may operate indefinitely or for a specified period or until the occurrence of a specified event. It may impose a complete ban on any dealing or may impose conditions that must be met before any dealing will be registered. Thus a restriction can be used to ensure that any necessary consent is obtained for a transaction, or to require that capital money from a dealing with trust property is paid to two trustees or a trust corporation (i.e., that requirements for overreaching the beneficiaries' interests are met). In the latter case, the entry of such a restriction will also have the effect of indicating to a prospective purchaser that the property is subject to a trust.

Standard forms for the most usual restrictions are to be found in LRR 2003 r.91 and Sch. 4.

Under LRA 2002 the scope of the restriction is wide enough to cover all the circumstances in which restrictions or inhibitions were entered under the old system. It appears that little was gained by distinguishing between the two types of entry and accordingly they are replaced by the new form of restriction.

Circumstances in which a restriction must or may be entered
In certain specified circumstances the registrar *must* enter a restriction. Section 44(1) provides that where two or more persons are registered as proprietor, the registrar must enter a restriction designed to secure that interests capable of being overreached on the disposition of the estate *are* overreached. The registrar must also comply with any court order requiring him to enter a restriction.

Under s. 42 the registrar *may* enter a restriction if he considers it necessary or desirable to do so for certain specified purposes, which include protecting a right or claim in relation to a registered estate, preventing invalidity or unlawfulness in relation to any disposition and ensuring that appropriate interests are overreached.

Restrictions may also be entered on the application of the registered proprietor or of any person with a sufficient interest in the making of the entry, with or without the proprietor's consent. Where the application is without consent, the proprietor must be notified of it, and there will be a process for dealing with any objections to the application.

A restriction is not an alternative to a notice
The Act provides that a restriction must not be used to protect an interest which is capable of protection by notice (s. 42(2) and s. 46(2)).

5.8.3 1 Trant Way

If you look back at the land certificate for this property on p. 75, you will see that restrictive covenants contained in an earlier conveyance have been protected by the entry of a notice in the Charges Register. The effect of this notice has been continued by the transitional provisions mentioned earlier, and if the Armstrongs go ahead with their purchase of the house, they will take it subject to these covenants.

There are no other entries on the register, and the Armstrongs might think that this means there are no other third-party rights affecting the property. However, they need to remember that there may well be other encumbrances which will override the transfer to them and will bind the estate in their hands even though there are no other entries referring to these rights on the register.

5.9 **Interests that override a registered disposition**

These interests bind anyone taking under a registered disposition, including a purchaser for valuable consideration, although they are not recorded on the register and so cannot be discovered by inspecting it. The existence of such interests has always been a flaw in the registered title system, preventing the register being the perfect reflection of title which it was originally intended to be (indeed, a standard examination question used to describe the existence of overriding interests under LRA 1925 as 'the crack in the mirror of title!')

LRA 2002 reduces the number of potential overriding interests, by redefining some of them, and by providing that others will lose their overriding status, either immediately or after a period of time. In addition, when dealing with first registration or the registration of a dealing with a registered estate, the registry makes every effort to note on the register any interests which would otherwise have overriding effect, and s. 71 requires applicants for registration to reveal any such interests of which they know. Once an interest has been noted on the register it is no longer capable of taking effect as an interest that overrides (s. 29(3)).

Nevertheless, although categories of overriding interests are reduced for the future, existing overriding interests retain their effect under the transitional provisions of the Act (see s. 134 and Sch.12, paras. 7–13). These provide that any overriding interest which bound an estate immediately before the Act came into force will continue to have overriding effect, either indefinitely or for a prescribed limited period. This means that although for the purposes of your study of land law you will probably concentrate on the new categories of overriding interests and how they compare with those under the old scheme, purchasers like the Armstrongs (and their professional advisers) will need to be aware for many years to come that estates may be subject to overriding interests as defined in the old scheme.

5.9.1 **Why are there two lists of overriding interests in LRA 2002?**

LRA 2002 provides two lists of overriding interests: Sch.1 lists interests which override first registration, and Sch. 3 lists interests which override a registered disposition (i.e., later dealings with the registered estate which under s. 27 have to be completed by registration).

To understand why the Act provides two separate lists, you need to remember that an applicant for first registration already has the legal title to the estate and holds it subject to encumbrances which bind it under the rules relating to unregistered land. First registration does not transfer or alter the title to the estate (it is said to have 'no dispositive effect'); it merely records the state of the title already held by the applicant. By contrast, registering a disposition of a registered estate (either its transfer or the creation of a registrable interest granted out of it) does actually give the new owner a legal title which he did not have before. Questions, therefore, arise as to which encumbrances should bind the property in the hands of the new owner, and, under s. 29, registration can actually alter the encumbrances which bind the estate, as for example by freeing it from those which are not protected in the prescribed way. For a brief explanation of the different effects of first registration and registration of a disposition, see the Report, para. 8.3.

The earlier Act provided only one list of overriding interests (see LRA 1925, s. 70(1)), which did not distinguish between first registration and registration of a disposition, but there is a very real difference between them, and it is for this reason that separate statements about the relevant overriding interests are provided in the two schedules of the new Act. While there is a good deal of overlap between the two lists, there are also significant differences relating to: short leases; the rights of persons in actual occupation; and legal easements and profits.

However, we are concerned here with the interests which would bind the Armstrongs if they buy 1 Trant Way (i.e., are parties to a registered disposition), and so must concentrate on the terms of Sch. 3.

5.9.2 Interests that override a registered disposition under LRA 2002 Sch. 3

As we describe the overriding interests listed in Sch. 3, we will also tell you how they compare with the previous list of overriding interests contained in LRA 1925 s. 70(1). For this purpose, we will divide overriding interests into four groups:

(1) interests which remain overriding

(2) interests which remain overriding for a period of 10 years

(3) interests which are redefined and substantially reduced

(4) interests omitted from Sch.3, which cease to be overriding.

5.9.2.1 *Interests which remain overriding*

Paragraphs 4 to 9 of Sch.3 list various rights which were overriding under LRA 1925 s. 70(1) and which override registered dispositions under the new Act. They include: customary and public rights, local land charges and rights in connection with mines and minerals. You may remember from Chapter 2 that local land charges are recorded in their own register (see 2.3.2.2), and since these charges will override a registered disposition, that register should be checked by anyone buying registered land.

5.9.2.2 *Interests which remain overriding for a period of 10 years*

Paragraphs 10 to 14 of Sch. 3 list a range of interests described as 'miscellaneous', which include a franchise, a manorial right and rights in respect of embankments, sea walls, etc. Again, these were all overriding under the old Act, but they gave rise to concern because they might be difficult to discover and could be burdensome. Their overriding status could not be abolished at once, because there were fears that this might contravene the Human Rights Act 1998 (by depriving the owner of a property right), but under s. 117 they will cease to be overriding ten years after the Act came into force. Meanwhile those entitled to these rights will be able to protect them, free of charge, by entering a notice or, where title to the burdened land is not yet registered, a caution against first registration (see 5.5.1). It is important to realise that these rights will not cease to exist: they merely lose their overriding status but will continue to bind the estate if protected in the appropriate way.

5.9.2.3 *Overriding interests which are redefined and substantially reduced*

Paragraphs 1 to 3 of Sch. 3 cover three types of interests which were overriding under LRA 1925: short leases, rights of persons in actual occupation, and easements and profits. The range of interests within each of these categories is, however, very much reduced.

(1) *A leasehold estate granted for a term of not more than seven years*
Schedule 3, para. 1 shortens the length of a lease which can be overriding from 'not exceeding 21 years' to 'not exceeding seven years'. This change is a consequence of the reduction in the minimum length of a registrable lease. Under LRA 1925, the title to leases for more than 21 years was compulsorily registrable, whereas registration requirements now apply to leases for more than seven years. Thus, para.1 provides that leases which are not independently registrable (and therefore noted on the landlord's title) may take effect as overriding interests binding the landlord's estate.

The special leases which are compulsorily registrable whatever their length (see 5.3.1.2) are specifically excluded by para. 1 from the category of overriding short leases. If title to one of these special leases has been registered as it should be, a notice protecting it will be placed on the register of the superior estate and a purchaser of that estate will take subject to it. If a tenant does not comply with the registration requirements he risks being unable to enforce his lease against a purchaser, and the policy of the Act is to encourage compliance by excluding such leases from the overriding category even if they are for not more than seven years.

This category of interests that override registered dispositions is not expressly limited to *legal* leases, but in interpreting the similar provision in LRA 1925 s. 70(1)(k) it was held in *City Permanent Building Society* v *Miller* [1952] Ch 840 that the use of the word 'granted' excluded equitable leases, because they are not the subject of a grant. It seems likely that this interpretation will apply equally to the terms of para. 1.

(2) *Interests of persons in actual occupation (Sch. 3, para. 2)*
This is such an important and interesting category of overriding interests that it must be considered in some detail and so will be dealt with separately in 5.10.

(3) *Certain legal easements and profits*
Under LRA 1925 s. 70(1)(a) all *legal* easements and profits were overriding. In addition it was held in *Celsteel Ltd* v *Alton House Holdings Ltd* [1985] 1 WLR 204 (based on a provision of the Land Registration Rules 1925), that *equitable* easements could be overriding, and although there was some criticism of this decision, it was accepted and applied by the Court of Appeal in *Thatcher* v *Douglas* (1995) 146 NLJ 282. So all easements and profits, however created, were overriding under the old scheme.

This very wide category of overriding interests is reduced by four provisions of LRA 2002, Sch. 3, para. 3.

(i) Paragraph 3 states at the outset that it applies only to legal easements and profits, so equitable interests of this kind cease to be overriding.

(ii) Rights not registered under the Commons Registration Act 1965 are excluded (or, in other words, rights so registered are overriding).

(iii) As a result of para. 3 and s. 27, easements and profits which are expressly created or reserved cannot be overriding. However, before explaining why this is so, we need to say a brief word about the way in which legal easements and profits are created, although we deal with this in more detail in Chapter 22.

Creation of easements and profits These interests may be created expressly by *granting* another person a right over one's land, or by *reserving* a right over land which one is transferring to another person. In certain cases, where there is no express creation, the law may imply a grant or reservation, so that easements and profits can be created without any express words appearing in the documents relating to the burdened land. In addition, these rights can be created by a long period of use (known as prescription), again without any documentary evidence of their existence. Rights which arise by implication or by prescription can be dangerous to a purchaser because there may be nothing which warns of their existence.

As we saw in 5.6.2, s. 27 provides that an express grant or reservation of an easement or profit must be completed by registration, and that it does not operate at law until the relevant registration requirements are met. These are set out in Sch. 2, para. 7, and include a requirement that a notice of the interest must be entered on the register of title of the estate which is burdened by it. Section 29(3) provides that an interest which has been the subject of a notice in the register is not protected under Sch. 3. Thus, to summarise: a grant or reservation which is *not* completed by registration will not create a legal interest and will, therefore, fall outside the terms of para. 3. If it *is* completed by registration, it must be protected by a notice, and so, although legal, cannot take effect as an overriding interest.

This means that the only easements or profits which can be overriding under para. 3 are those which arise from implied grant or reservation, by prescription or as a result of the operation of LPA 1925, s. 62 (LRA 2002, s. 27(7)—for s. 62 generally, see 22.7). Such interests represent a danger to the purchaser; as overriding interests, they will not be entered on the register and yet may be very difficult to discover from an inspection of the property (as for example in the case of underground drains). To guard against this, the range of easements and profits which can be overriding is reduced even further by a provision set out in para. 3(1).

(iv) An exception in para. 3(1) excludes any easement or profit which at the time of the disposition:
    (a) is not within the actual knowledge of the person to whom the disposition is made, and
    (b) would not have been obvious on a reasonably careful inspection of the land over which the easement or profit is exercisable.

However, this seems to tilt the balance too far in the purchaser's favour, so a further sub-paragraph (para. 3(2)) provides that the exception itself will not apply if the person entitled to the interest can show that it has been exercised in the year preceding the disposition.

In summary, the combined effect of these various provisions is that legal easements arising otherwise than by express grant or reservation will be overriding if:

(1) the person to whom the disposition is made actually knows about them; or

(2) they are obvious on a reasonably careful inspection of the land; or

(3) if they have been used in the year preceding the disposition.

In addition, rights registered under the Commons Registration Act 1965 are overriding.

5.9.2.4 *Interests omitted from Sch. 3 which cease to be overriding*

Schedule 3 omits the following categories of interests which were overriding under LRA 1925, s. 70(1).

(1) *Rights acquired or in the course of being acquired under the Limitation Acts (LRA 1925, s. 70(1)(f))*

LRA 2002 makes major changes to the rules about adverse possession and squatters' rights in relation to registered land. We deal with this more fully in Chapter 6, but for the moment all you need to know is that, under the old law, the right of a registered proprietor to recover his land from someone who dispossessed him used to be extinguished by the Limitation Act 1980 after 12 years. Once this had happened, the adverse possessor was said to have 'acquired rights under the Limitation Act', and could require the registrar to register him in the place of the registered proprietor. Once the squatter had acquired a right to the land in this way, he could go out of possession and yet still retain his right to be registered as owner. This made the overriding nature of his rights under LRA 1925 very dangerous to a purchaser, who would be bound by those rights even although there was no way of discovering them.

Under LRA 2002, the Limitation Act 1980 no longer applies to registered land. A squatter who has been in adverse possession for a prescribed period may apply for registration as owner, but Sch. 3 makes no provision for his rights as an adverse possessor to override a registered disposition. If the adverse possessor is on at the land at the relevant time and can satisfy the other requirements of Sch. 3, para. 2 he may claim that his rights override the disposition by virtue of actual occupation, but there is no longer any risk to a purchaser from a squatter who has left the land.

(2) *Rights of a person in receipt of the rents and profits [of the land] save where enquiry is made of such a person and the rights are not disclosed (LRA 1925, s. 70(1)(g))*

This second limb of LRA 1925 s. 70(1)(g) is not replicated in the new Act, and we will consider the reasons for omitting it later, in 5.10.3.4.

(3) *Rights excepted from the effect of registration with possessory, qualified or good leasehold title (LRA 1925, s. 70(1))h))*

The definitions in LRA 2002, ss. 11 and 12 make it clear that the excepted rights are binding on the registered proprietor, and in consequence it is not necessary to provide separately for those rights to be overriding.

5.10 **Interests of persons in actual occupation**

This is a very important category of interests that override a registered disposition, and requires detailed consideration.

5.10.1 **Statutory provisions**

Under Sch. 3, para. 2 certain interests of persons in actual occupation at the time of a disposition override that disposition and will bind the purchaser, despite the fact that they are not recorded on the register of title. The earlier definition of this group of overriding interests was to be found in LRA 1925 s. 70(1)(g), which classified as overriding:

The rights of every person in actual occupation of the land or in receipt of the rents and profits thereof, save where enquiry is made of such person and the rights are not disclosed.

As we shall see, the new Act makes a considerable reduction in this category of overriding interests, but there is still a good deal of common ground between the old and new provisions, and interpretation of the earlier law will almost certainly continue to be relevant. We will therefore continue to refer to earlier case law, where appropriate, to illustrate how the new law is likely to work.

The terms of Sch. 3, para. 2 are considerably longer and more complicated than those of s. 70(1)(g), and we think it would be helpful to set out the actual wording. Schedule 3, para. 2 provides that a registered disposition is subject to:

An interest belonging at the time of the disposition to a person in actual occupation, so far as relating to land of which he is in actual occupation, except for—

(a) an interest under a settlement under the Settled Land Act 1925;

(b) an interest of a person of whom inquiry was made before the disposition and who failed to disclose the right when he could reasonably have been expected to do so;

(c) an interest –

    (i) which belongs to a person whose occupation would not have been obvious on a reasonably careful inspection of the land at the time of the disposition, and

    (ii) of which the person to whom the disposition is made does not have actual knowledge at that time;

(d) [a future lease which is compulsorily registrable (see 5.3.1.2)] which has not taken effect in possession at the time of the disposition.

5.10.2 **What interests override under para. 2?**

It should be noted that para. 2 does not create any new right to occupy the property, but rather gives overriding effect to any interest already belonging to the occupier, which has not been protected by an entry on the register. Thus if the occupier is a tenant under a lease which gives him an option to purchase the reversion (i.e., the right to 'buy out' his landlord's interest) the option may well be held to be overriding and enforceable against a purchaser of the landlord's estate, although there is no mention of it on the register of that estate (*Webb* v *Pollmount* [1966] Ch 584). Similarly, where a beneficiary under a trust is in actual occupation of the land her rights have been held to be overriding and binding on the purchaser (see, for example, *Hodgson* v *Marks* [1971] Ch 892, and *William & Glyn's Bank Ltd* v *Boland* [1981] AC 487, which we will tell you about in 5.10.4.4).

We must emphasise however that the occupier's rights will be overriding only if they amount to a recognised interest in land. LRA 1925 s. 70(1)(g) spoke of the 'rights' of the person in occupation, and the courts were obliged in several decisions to emphasise that rights could be overriding under that provision only if they constituted a recognised interest in land (*National Provincial Bank* v *Hastings Car*

Mart Ltd [1964] Ch 665 per Russell LJ, at 696, and *Strand Securities v Caswell* [1965] Ch 958—for details of which, see 5.10.4.3). The new Act refers specifically to 'an interest' rather than to 'rights', so emphasising this point may become less important. Nevertheless we do suggest that if you are dealing with a problem concerning this class of overriding interests you should begin by identifying the recognised property interest which the occupier is seeking to enforce.

5.10.2.1 *Exclusion of certain rights*

You should also note that in some instances persons have rights and are in occupation but nonetheless their rights will not override because of a specific statutory exclusion. Thus the right of a spouse to occupy the matrimonial home (see 4.4.2.5 and 24.3.3.1) is not capable of overriding and must be protected by means of an entry on the register if it is to bind a purchaser (Family Law Act 1996, s. 31(10)). Similarly, by virtue of the Access to Neighbouring Land Act 1992, s. 5(5) (see 22.11.2), rights arising from orders made under that Act cannot override. As a result it is necessary to check that there is no specific exclusion for the right that you are considering.

Two further exclusions are added by LRA 2002 Sch. 3, para. (2):

(a) *interests under a SLA settlement* (para. 2(a))

Under LRA 1925, s. 86(2), the rights of a beneficiary under such a settlement had to be protected by an entry on the register, even if he was in actual occupation, and this continues to be the position under the new Act. For details of such settlements, see Chapter 14.

(b) *future leases which are compulsorily registrable (unless they have already taken effect in possession at the time of the disposition)* (para. 2(d))

We have already seen that leases of this type cannot be overriding under Sch. 3, para. 1, and para. 2(d) ensures that they do not become overriding by virtue of actual occupation.

5.10.3 **Comparison of LRA 2002 Sch. 3, para. 2 with LRA 1925 s. 70(1)(g)**

The terms of s. 70(1)(g) were very wide and constituted a real risk for unwary purchasers. The provisions of para. 2 are much narrower. There is no reference to the rights of a person in receipt of rents and profits (see 5.10.3.4), and the range of interests which can bind as a result of actual occupation is considerably reduced. In order to do this, the paragraph sets out a list of requirements which must be satisfied if an interest belonging to a person in actual occupation is to be overriding. The wording of the provision is a little complicated, but in substance it prescribes the following conditions.

5.10.3.1 *The interest must relate to land of which the person is in actual occupation* (see proviso to para. 2)

This requirement is designed to deal with situations such as that in *Ferrishurst Ltd v Wallcite Ltd* [1999] Ch 355, in which an occupier's overriding interest under LRA 1925 s. 70(1)(g) was held to extend to a part of the land comprised in the registered title which he did not in fact occupy.

In this case a registered leasehold title included offices and a garage, each of which was let on a separate sublease to a different tenant. The sublease of the offices gave the sub-tenant an option to purchase his landlord's reversion, i.e., to acquire the registered leasehold title to both the offices and the garage. The lease was assigned to a purchaser for value, and Ferrishurst Ltd, the sub-tenant of the offices, sought to enfore its option against that purchaser. The option was not protected by any entry on the title to the lease, but Ferrishurst Ltd claimed an overriding interest arising from actual occupation. The Court of Appeal held that an occupier relying on subsection (g) need not be in actual occupation of the whole plot comprised in the registered title, and in consequence could enforce an overriding interest against the part which he did not occupy.

Shortly before the decision of the Court of Appeal, the Law Commission had recommended that rights protected by actual occupation should be confined to that part of the land occupied by the claimant (*Land Registration for the Twenty-First Century*, 1998, Law Com No. 254, para. 5.70) and para. 2 gives effect to this recommendation.

5.10.3.2 *If asked about the interest, the person to whom it belongs must not have failed to disclose it 'when he could reasonably have been expected to do so'* (para. 2(b))

This requirement is similar to that in LRA 1925 s. 70(1)(g) ('save where inquiry is made of such person and the rights are not revealed'), although the new version suggests that there could be some circumstances in which failure to disclose might be 'reasonable'. It is thus slightly less draconian than the earlier wording, under which non-disclosure automatically deprived the right of its overriding effect. The new wording seems to provide an opportunity for debate as to when non-disclosure would be reasonable. Would it be reasonable, for example, where a beneficiary under a resulting trust is unaware that contribution to the purchase price gives a share in the beneficial interest in the property?

5.10.3.3 *The occupation must have been obvious on a reasonably careful inspection of the land **OR** the purchaser must have had actual knowledge of the interest* (para. 2(c))

In fact, para. 2(c) states these two requirements in the negative (i.e., occupation must not obvious and interest must not known to the purchaser). Both conditions must be fulfilled if the interest is *not* to take effect as an overriding interest. We have rephrased the provision because we think it is easier for you to remember as positive conditions, and to see that satisfying either of them allows the interest to override the disposition. Do note however that it is the *occupation* which must be obvious, and the *interest* which must be known.

Thus to summarise: an interest which satisfies the other conditions of para. 2 will override a disposition if *either* the purchaser actually knew about it (even if the occupation is not obvious on a reasonably careful inspection of the land) *or* if the occupation is obvious on such an inspection, even though he did not know about the interest. This means that provided the occupation is discoverable, the purchaser may still be bound by an interest of which he does not know. To avoid this, it is essential that any persons seen to be in occupation should be asked whether they have any interests in the property, and in fact doing so has been standard practice since the decision in *Williams & Glyn's Bank Ltd* v *Boland* [1981] AC 487 (for which, see 5.10.4.4).

It is interesting to note that the test of reasonableness comes in again here, having appeared already in para. 2(b) and being used again in para. 3. In other contexts, this notion of reasonableness can cause some difficulty in application (see, for example, the case law which has built up around the question of un-reasonable refusal of consent to assignment of a lease—9.2.2.2(2)), and it will be interesting to see if the use here of this concept causes similar difficulties.

5.10.3.4 *Omission of second limb of s. 70(1)(g)*

Under LRA 1925 s. 70(1)(g), the rights of a person who was not in actual occupation of the land but was in receipt of rents and profits from it were also overriding, but these interests are omitted from para. 2 and cease to be overriding.

The person most likely to be affected by this change is an intermediate landlord, that is a person who holds a lease from the freeholder, out of which he has granted a sub-lease to the person who is now in actual occupation. Under the old rules, such a lease would be an overriding interest by virtue of the landlord's receipt of rent, but under the new Act the lease, if made for more than seven years, will be compulsor-ily registrable and protected by a notice on the title of the superior estate. If the leaseholder fails to register his title, he will be at risk of losing it, but in this regard he is in the same position as all other estate owners who do not comply with registration requirements.

Although the proposal to introduce this change was apparently 'somewhat con-tentious' (see Report para. 8.18), it appears that it was supported by a substantial majority of those who responded on consultation, and in consequence Sch. 3 omits this category from the new list of interests that override a registered disposition.

5.10.4 **Some questions about the operation of Sch. 3, para. 2**

As yet there have been no reported decisions on the application of para. 2, but the new provisions are sufficiently close to the terms of LRA 1925 s. 70(1)(g) to suggest that earlier case law may well be relied upon in interpreting them. In addition, some of these decisions illustrate very well the risk to the purchaser posed by this category of interests that override a disposition, and so we will go on to consider some of the questions which arose on the old Act and the answers given by the courts.

5.10.4.1 *What is meant by 'actual occupation'?*

In the words of Lord Wilberforce in *Williams & Glyn's Bank Ltd* v *Boland* [1981] AC 487 at pp. 504–5, 'it is the fact of occupation that matters' and what is required is 'physical presence on the land and not some entitlement in the law'. The courts have been reluctant to suggest any test for what is 'essentially a question of fact', pointing out in *Abbey National Building Society* v *Cann* [1991] 1 AC 56 at p. 93 that:

. . . 'occupation' is a concept which may have different connotations according to the nature and purpose of the property which is claimed to be occupied.

This is well illustrated by the recent decision of the Court of Appeal in *Malory Enterprises Ltd* v *Cheshire Homes (UK) Ltd* [2002] Ch 216, in which the land in question was awaiting development by Malory Enterprises Ltd, which claimed an overriding interest in respect of it under s. 70(1)(g). In the words of Arden LJ (at p. 236):

If a site is uninhabitable . . . residence is not required, but there must be some physical presence, with some degree of permanence and continuity.

Here the company had maintained fences around the land and taken other physical measures to exclude trespassers, and the court considered that this amounted to 'actual occupation'.

Since 'some degree of permanence and continuity' is required, it seems clear that, for example, a prospective tenant or purchaser who is allowed to enter property to plan alterations or furnishings could not be said to be in occupation.

If occupation is established but the interest claimed was not known to the purchaser, the question will then arise of whether the occupation was 'obvious on a reasonably careful inspection of the land' (Sch. 3, para. 2(c)). It seems possible that in a situation similar to that in *Malory Enterprises Ltd* v *Cheshire Homes (UK) Ltd* the Court might hold that there *was* occupation but that it was not obvious, but this must of course be very much a decision on the facts.

5.10.4.2 *When must the person be in actual occupation?*
LRA 1925 s. 70(1)(g) did not specify when the person claiming the overriding interest should be in occupation. As we have seen (5.2.3), there is a gap in time between the transfer of the estate and the completion of that transfer by registration at the registry, and the question arose of whether someone claiming a right under s. 70(1)(g) had to show that he was in actual occupation at the time of the transfer or at the date of registration.

The matter was considered by the House of Lords in *Abbey National Building Society* v *Cann* [1991] 1 AC 56. Although the facts involve the purchase of a registered estate, it was the concurrent grant by the purchaser of a mortgage which was said to be subject to the overriding interest. The facts were as follows.

Cann bought a property with the aid of a mortgage from the Abbey National, representing to the Society that the house was for his sole occupation, although in fact he intended it to be occupied by his mother and uncle. On the day of the transfer and the creation of the charge, the Canns' furniture arrived at the property some 35 minutes before the charge to the Society took place and at that point there were also removal men on the premises moving in items on the mother's behalf. The charge was not completed by registration until a month later and by that time it was quite clear that Cann's mother and uncle were both in occupation of the premises. Both claimed that they had interests in the property by reason of contribution, and, when Cann defaulted on the mortgage payments, they asserted that their rights had priority to those of the Society (i.e., that their rights were overriding under s. 70(1)(g) and bound the mortgagee).

The House of Lords was of the opinion that the purchaser is bound by all overriding interests in existence at the date of registration. However, there were difficulties in holding that a person who went into occupation between transfer and registration could acquire an overriding interest under s. 70(1)(g), because that section clearly contemplated that the purchaser would make enquiries of any person in occupation, and the proper time for making such enquiries is before the transfer. As a result, the House of Lords took the view that in order to succeed under s. 70(1)(g), a claimant must show he was in actual occupation at the date of the transfer. Any rights he might have would then be capable of being overriding interests, and, if still in existence at the date of registration, would bind the purchaser.

Applying this to the facts of the case, the House of Lords held that the preparatory work of moving in furniture did not constitute actual occupation, and that accordingly the Canns were not in occupation at the time of transfer, when the charge to the society was created.

What is the position under para. 2?

Paragraph 2 appears to deal with this question by describing the interest as 'belonging at the time of the disposition to a person in actual occupation' and speaking of 'an inspection of the land at the time of the disposition'. It seems that 'disposition' refers to the paper transfer (or grant), which has to be completed by registration and does not take effect at law until this is done (s. 27). When electronic conveyancing is fully operational, transfer and registration will occur simultaneously, but until then making a disposition remains a two-stage process and the decision in *Abbey National Building Society* v *Cann* may well continue to be relevant.

5.10.4.3 *What happens if the occupier is absent temporarily from the property?*

There is little direct authority on this point, although one would think it is quite likely that an occupier who is unaware of the vendor's intention to sell or mortgage the property may be away at the relevant time—on holiday, perhaps, or in hospital. An apparent decision in such a case is to be found in *Chhokar* v *Chhokar* [1984] FLR 313, in which a husband, who was seeking to deprive his wife of her equitable interest in the matrimonial home, completed the sale of the property to his accomplice while his wife was in hospital. The husband then absconded with the proceeds of sale, and on her return from hospital the wife was excluded from the house by the purchaser, so that she was not physically present on the property when he was registered as proprietor. Noting that the wife's furniture was in the house on the date of registration, the Court of Appeal said that it had no difficulty in holding that she was in occupation at that date, and went on to describe her right in the property as an overriding interest which bound the purchaser. This would appear to be a clear decision on the point, but unfortunately, although the court described the interest as 'overriding', there is no reference to the provisions of LRA 1925, and the language of the report suggests that the whole transaction may have taken place in the unregistered system of title, i.e., before first registration.

It may be helpful to note that similar questions arise under other statutory provisions requiring occupation (for example, under the Rent Acts), and that in such cases the courts take into account whether the occupier had a continuing intention to return, and whether his or her belongings remained in the property. As the Court of Appeal put it in *Hoggett* v *Hoggett* (1979) 39 P&CR 121 at p. 128:

Going to hospital for a few days could not be regarded as going out of occupation, any more than if the [occupier] had gone on a weekend visit to a friend, or, indeed, gone out shopping for a few hours.

In cases of temporary absence it seems then that the presence of the occupier's belongings on the premises may help to establish actual occupation. However, it was held in *Strand Securities* v *Caswell* [1965] Ch 958 that the presence of belongings alone, without any previous occupation and intention to return, was not enough to establish occupation for the purposes of s. 70(1)(g).

In this case, Caswell had a lease of a London flat. The lease, being for just over 39 years, fell into the category of leases which at that time *could* be registered, but did not *have* to be (a rule which was changed by LRA 1986). In fact, the title to the lease was not registered, nor was it protected by an entry on the landlord's title. Caswell kept some furniture and clothing at the flat but did not live there. The property was occupied by his stepdaughter who had moved in with his permission, because her marriage had broken down. She occupied the flat as a licensee (that is, as someone with permission—a licence—to do so). As we shall see in Chapter 20, the protection given by the law to licensees can vary considerably according to the individual's circumstances, but the general principle, which applied in this case, is that this type of agreement can be terminated at any time and gives the licensee no rights in the land.

The landlord sold its interest in the property, and the new owner claimed that the lease was void against it because it was neither registered nor protected by an entry against the landlord's estate. The Court of Appeal rejected the tenant's claim that he had an overriding interest under s. 70(1)(g), because although he had rights in the property (the lease) he was not in occupation. The presence of his belongings at the property did not amount to occupation for the purposes of the Act.

The stepdaughter was of course in occupation of the property, but unfortunately she did not have any recognised property interest in the flat and so had no rights which were capable of being overriding. The court did suggest that, had she occupied the flat at the request of her stepfather and in order to look after it for him, he might have been regarded as being in occupation through an agent. However, on the facts as they stood, she was clearly there because of her own needs and not as Mr Caswell's agent. The House of Lords has since confirmed, in *obiter dicta* in *Abbey National Building Society* v *Cann* [1991] 1 AC 56, that occupation through an agent is possible; and *Kingsnorth Finance Co. Ltd* v *Tizard* [1986] 1 WLR 783 (see 4.5.2.3), a decision on unregistered land, suggests that in some circumstances keeping one's possessions in the property may help to establish occupation.

Under the new provision, of course, even if the court is satisfied that the presence of belongings is sufficient to establish occupation, there will still be the question of whether such occupation is obvious on a reasonably careful inspection of the land (para. 2 (c)).

Finally, you may like to note that the draft Land Registration Bill provided that 'a person is only to be regarded as in actual occupation of land if he, or his agent or employee, is physically present there' (see Report p. 426 for draft of Sch. 3, para. 2(2)), but this provision did not survive the parliamentary process and is not contained in the new Act.

5.10.4.4 *Can several people be in actual occupation of the property at the same time?*

In the past, particular difficulties arose when the vendor and the person claiming under s. 70(1)(g) were both living in the property. This was the position in *Hodgson* v *Marks* [1971] Ch 892, in which it was held that Mrs Hodgson was to be regarded as being in actual occupation of premises even though she shared the property with the registered proprietor. Mrs Hodgson had been the original owner of the estate and had transferred it to her lodger under an arrangement by which it was clear that she was transferring only the legal title and not the beneficial rights to the property. As a result, he held the legal estate on trust for her. When the former lodger sold the property to a third party (in contravention of his agreement with Mrs Hodgson), the purchaser was held to be bound by Mrs Hodgson's rights to the property. Since she was the true beneficial owner of the property, the purchaser was in the position of a trustee and was compelled to convey the legal estate to her. This case illustrates very well the dangers of the s. 70(1)(g) overriding interest, since the purchaser had bought an estate which in reality was worthless.

Similar difficulties concerning shared occupation used to arise in the case of married women living in houses owned by their husbands. They might well have a beneficial interest arising from contribution, but, as we have already seen in the case of unregistered land (4.5.2.3), their presence in the property was attributed to their marital status, and they were not regarded as being in occupation for the purposes of s. 70(1)(g) (*Bird* v *Syme-Thomson* [1979] 1 WLR 440). However, a more modern approach to the role of the married woman was adopted by the House of Lords in *Williams & Glyn's Bank Ltd* v *Boland* [1981] AC 487. This case involved a wife who had acquired an interest in her husband's property by contributing to the purchase price, and so had become a beneficiary under a resulting trust of the land. She lived in the property with her husband, who was the sole registered proprietor. Mr Boland mortgaged the property to his bank and used the money raised in his business. Later, when he failed to make his mortgage repayments, the bank sought vacant possession of the premises, so that it could sell the estate in order to repay the loan. Mrs Boland then claimed that she had rights in the property and that, as she had been in occupation of the premises when the mortgage was granted, the bank's rights as mortgagee were subject to her prior beneficial interest. The House of Lords considered that the wife's occupation of the premises could be distinguished from that of her husband, and accordingly upheld Mrs Boland's claim that she had an overriding interest which bound the bank.

As a result of *Hodgson* v *Marks* and *Williams & Glyn's Bank Ltd* v *Boland*, it appeared that a purchaser or mortgagee could be bound by the rights of all those occupying the property with the vendor, including any of his relatives. Until recently, it seemed possible that even children would be included in the category of those in actual occupation: they are certainly capable of having a beneficial interest in the property. However, the Court of Appeal held in *Hypo-Mortgage Services Ltd* v *Robinson* (1997), *The Times*, 2 January 1997, that a child cannot be a person in actual occupation for the purposes of s. 70(1)(g). The court made it clear that its ruling applied to all minors, not merely to those of 'tender years' (as in the case before it), explaining that children 'had no right of occupation of their own: they were only there as shadows of occupation of their parent'. No thought appears to have been given to minors over the age of 16, who could be married or cohabiting, and who could have acquired an interest in their homes through contribution. For a critical comment on this decision, see [1997] Conv 84.

5.10.4.5 *How can a purchaser take free of the occupier's rights?*

It has to be recognised that despite *Williams & Glyn's Bank Ltd* v *Boland*, there can be circumstances in which a purchaser can take his interest free of the rights of a person in actual occupation, and we consider three of these situations below.

(1) *Overreaching*

As we explained in Chapter 4 (4.5.2.1) the process known as 'overreaching' enables land subject to certain trusts to be sold free of the beneficiaries' interests, provided that the purchase price is paid to at least two trustees, who hold the money upon trust for the beneficiaries in place of the land. In *Boland*, the mortgage was made and the money received by the sole registered proprietor so that over-reaching could not operate. However, in *City of London Building Society* v *Flegg* [1988] AC 54 mortgage money, which arose when a second mortgage was made, was paid to two legal owners who held the estate upon trust for themselves and the Fleggs. In these circumstances the House of Lords held that the interests of the Fleggs, who were beneficiaries under the trust, were overreached by that payment, even though the beneficiaries had been in occupation of the premises at the date of the charge. The effect of that decision was to allow the mortgagee to get priority over the rights of the Fleggs and to be able to sell the property free of their interests. The beneficiaries were left only with the right to sue the legal owners, their trustees, for breach of trust, since the legal owners had used the mortgage money for their own purposes. This decision is very hard for those placed in the position of the Fleggs, since the legal owners who have entered into this kind of transaction are often bankrupt or have fled the country and it is often a matter of pure chance whether the property has one or two legal owners. However, the decision of the House of Lords is in harmony with the overreaching rules which are fundamental to much of the 1925 property legislation (contrast the view of the Court of Appeal, see [1986] Ch 605.

(2) *Implied agreement*

Even where the property has only one legal owner, it is still possible that the occupier's rights will not prevail against a mortgagee. In *Paddington Building Society* v *Mendelsohn* (1985) 50 P&CR 244 the competition was between a beneficiary under a resulting trust, who was in occupation of the property and who had known that a mortgage advance would be needed in order to purchase the property, and the building society which had granted that mortgage. In such a case the Court of Appeal held that the occupier had impliedly consented to the creation of the mort-gage since the possibility of acquiring an interest in the property was dependent upon that mortgage. Thus the occupier could not claim an interest having priority to the rights of the building society. As a result of this case the *Boland* and *Flegg* issues will usually only arise now in cases of second mortgages or sales.

(3) *Express agreement*

Despite these later limitations on the effect of *Hodgson* v *Marks* and *Boland*, the two decisions still constituted a considerable risk for intending purchasers, and *Boland* in particular caused great concern among professional mortgagees, such as build-ing societies and banks. Conveyancers speedily developed procedures for guarding against the results of that decision, and the practice has evolved of requiring any-one in occupation of the property in addition to the mortgagor to sign documents agreeing that any rights they may have will be subordinated to those of the mort-gagee, although as we shall see later, such consent may sometimes be set aside on the grounds of 'undue influence' (21.17.2).

5.11 Discovering encumbrances: searches and enquiries

Now that we have looked at the way in which encumbrances are classified and protected in the registered title system, we should mention briefly the searches and enquiries which will have to be made by the Armstrongs, the prospective purchasers of 1 Trant Way. Details of the conveyancing process are beyond the scope of this book (and are usually not required in a land law course); if you are interested, however, and want to know more, you will find a very readable account in Abbey & Richards, *A Practical Approach to Conveyancing*, 5th edn., Oxford University Press, 2003).

5.11.1 Searching the register

All we need to say here is that the Armstrongs will of course have to make a search of the register: to satisfy themselves that Victor Venn is the registered proprietor of the estate and to see whether any encumbrances have been noted on the register.

We cannot deal here with the mechanics of searching the register, save to mention that a purchaser who completes within a specified period after an official search (the 'priority period') is not affected by any amendments made to the register in the interval.

5.11.2 Inspecting the land

A physical inspection of the land should be made, from which the purchasers may discover overriding interests such as easements, and the existence of occupiers other than the vendor. Most important, in view of Sch. 3, para. 2, enquiries should be made of any such occupiers as to the nature of their rights and, as we have seen (5.10.4.5.3), the usual practice would be to require them to agree to waive any rights which they might have against the purchaser.

This need to inspect the land and make enquiries of the occupiers may remind you of the rule in *Hunt* v *Luck* [1902] 1 Ch 428, which we have discussed in connection with unregistered land (4.5.2.3). We need therefore to consider briefly whether the doctrine of notice has any role to play in the registered title system.

5.11.3 Do notice rules apply to registered land?

At a quick reading of LRA 1925 s. 70(1)(g), there did appear to be considerable similarities between it and the rule in *Hunt* v *Luck*. Nevertheless, there were significant differences between the two. Under paragraph (g) it was not enough for the purchaser to show that he made all the reasonable enquiries which would protect him from constructive notice in the unregistered system: if the rights existed, he was bound by them, even if he could not reasonably be expected to have discovered them. The only occasion on which he could take free of such rights was if he made enquiries of the occupier and the rights were not disclosed. In this way there were clear differences between the operation of the statutory rule and the doctrine of notice.

This view was expressed by Lord Wilberforce in *Williams & Glyn's Bank Ltd* v *Boland* [1981] AC 487 at p. 504:

In my opinion . . . the law as to notice as it may affect purchasers of unregistered land . . . has no application even by analogy to registered land. . . . In the case of registered land, it is the fact of occupation that matters. If there is actual occupation, and the occupier has rights, the purchaser takes subject to them. If not, he does not. No further element is material.

Surprisingly, however, there were two later decisions of the Court of Appeal (*Lloyds Bank plc* v *Rosset* [1989] Ch 350 and *Abbey National Building Society* v *Cann* [1989] 2 FLR 265) in which the court apparently considered that the question of whether a purchaser could discover the rights through reasonable enquiries was relevant to the application of s. 70(1)(g). Moreover, Purchas LJ in *Rosset* even went so far as to say that the words of the subsection:

clearly were intended to import into the law relating to registered land the equitable doctrine of constructive notice (at p. 403).

On appeal in both these cases, the House of Lords made no reference to this aspect of the judgments in the Court of Appeal (*Abbey National Building Society* v *Cann* [1991] 1 AC 56; *Lloyds Bank plc* v *Rosset* [1991] 1 AC 107).

In the Consultative Document, the Law Commission concluded that 'there should in general be no place for concepts of knowledge or notice in registered land' (para. 3.46), and recommended that the new Act should state that the doctrine of notice has no application in dealings with registered land except where the Act expressly provides to the contrary (para. 3.44). In fact, there is no express statement to this effect in LRA 2002, but the terms of s. 29 (and the basic rules about priorities set out in s. 28—see 5.15) certainly appear to leave no room for the operation of the equitable doctrine of notice. As the Report puts it (at paras. 5.16–17):

As a general principle, the doctrine of notice . . . has no application whatever in determining the priority of interests in registered land. [Apart from a number of very limited situations] issues as to whether [a] disponee had knowledge or notice of a prior interest, or whether he or she acted in good faith, are irrelevant.

The specific situations in which knowledge, notice or good faith *are* relevant under the Act are noted below.

5.11.3.1 *Situations in which knowledge etc is relevant*

(1) On first registration, the registered proprietor takes subject to the rights of an adverse possessor of which he has notice (s. 11(4)(c)—see 5.5.5.1).

(2) The provisions of Sch. 3, paras. 2 and 3 (interests of persons in actual occupation and easements and profits a prendre which override a registered disposition) involve requirements of actual knowledge or a reasonably careful inspection of the property, which may remind you of the rules about actual and constructive notice. However, the Report emphasises that these provisions are not drawn from notice-based principles, but are derived by analogy from the requirement of conveyancing law that a seller must disclose to the buyer certain incumbrances which are not obvious on a reasonably careful inspection of the land and of which the buyer does not have actual knowledge. (Report, para. 5.21.)

(3) There are two special cases, involving Inland Revenue charges under the Inheritance Tax Act 1984 and dispositions by a proprietor who has become bankrupt. In these cases, LRA 2002 follows the pattern of the legislation governing these matters, which does involve the concepts of notice and good faith (ss. 31 and 86).

5.12 **Alteration of the register and indemnity**

5.12.1 **How safe is it to rely on the register?**

We have now seen how a prospective purchaser of registered land, like the Armstrongs, can ascertain who owns the estate and obtain information about the encumbrances binding upon it. We now need to consider how safe it is to rely upon the register. As we have said, there are different grades of title, and if one buys an estate with less than title absolute there will obviously be a degree of risk involved. The Armstrong's vendor is registered with title absolute (see p. 75), but they will want to know exactly how safe an absolute title is. Can they assume that the title is indefeasible and that they will not be disturbed at some date in the future by someone else claiming the estate? Unfortunately one would have to tell them that even an absolute title is not completely safe, for there are circumstances in which the register can be altered, even against a registered proprietor with absolute title.

In some cases a person who suffers loss due to an alteration of the register may apply for financial compensation from a central fund, and it is sometimes said therefore that in the case of registered land the State guarantees the title, because it provides a system of compensation for those who suffer from any deficiencies in the system. The 'State guarantee' concept is not altogether true, however, because, as we shall see, compensation is not available to every individual who suffers a loss.

5.12.2 **Background to the new provisions of LRA 2002**

Under LRA 1925 the whole process of changing entries on the register was known as 'rectification'. While the joint working party had no major criticism of the substance of the Act's provisions about rectification, it commented adversely on the way in which they were drafted, saying that they tended to obscure the real nature of rectification and the manner in which it operated (Report, para. 10.4). It was thought that some of the difficulty was caused by the fact that the term 'rectification' was used to describe all alterations of the register, ranging from removing obsolete entries and remedying minor clerical slips to the correction of major errors which substantially affected existing property rights. In consequence, the provisions in the new Act about changes to the register (to be found in s. 65 and Sch. 4) use a different terminology.

5.12.3 **Redefinition of terms**

The overall process of making changes to the register is now described as '*alteration*' of the register, and '*rectification*' is defined in Sch. 4, para. 1 as a type of alteration which:

(a) involves the correction of a mistake; and

(b) prejudicially affects the title of the registered proprietor.

5.12.4 **Power to alter the register**

Schedule 4, para. 2 provides that the court may order alteration of the register for the purpose of—

(a) correcting a mistake,

(b) bringing the register up to date, or

(c) giving effect to any estate, right or interest excepted from the effect of registration.

Under Sch. 4, para. 5, the Registrar is also empowered to alter the register without a court order on these three grounds and, in addition, is given power to remove superfluous entries.

By contrast, LRA 1925, s. 82(1) attempted to enumerate in detail all the circumstances in which the register could be 'rectified'. This was thought by the joint working party to be unnecessarily complicated and to require replacement by a more general statement of principle. This has been carried through in Sch. 4, para. 2, and its simplified wording is thought to cover all eventualities.

Read on their own, paras. 2 and 5 give extremely wide powers to alter the register, and one can imagine that the Armstrongs might feel that the title they propose to buy is somewhat insecure. However, these provisions are substantially curtailed by paras. 3 and 6, which provide that alterations which amount to rectification (i.e., which correct mistakes *and* prejudicially affect the title of the registered proprietor) may not be made:

without the proprietor's consent in relation to land in his possession unless—

(a) he has by fraud or lack of proper care caused or substantially contributed to the mistake, or

(b) it would for any other reason be unjust for the alteration not to be made.

In the past there has been some difficulty about the circumstances in which a proprietor can be said to be in possession and this is clarified in s. 131.

Subject to the restriction on rectification against a proprietor in possession, an application to the court or registrar for alteration *must* be approved, provided that the relevant body has the power to do so, 'unless there are exceptional circumstances which justify not making the alteration' (Sch. 4, paras. 3(3) and 6(3)). There is thus an element of discretion in the process, but the new Act indicates that the usual practice must be to alter the register.

Paragraphs 3 and 6 may well reassure the Armstrongs, but it is important for them to realise that the protection given to the proprietor in possession does not prevent the register being rectified against him to give effect to overriding interests. This has always been the case, although the statutory reason for it has changed with the redrafting of the provisions.

Under LRA 1925 (s. 82(3)), altering the register to give effect to an overriding interest was specifically excepted from the protection given to the proprietor in possession. Under the new Act (Sch. 4, paras. 3 and 6), that protection applies only to a particular type of alteration—rectification—which as we have seen is limited to an alteration which 'involves the correction of a mistake'. Altering the register to give effect to an overriding interest is not regarded as correcting a mistake because all registration of title is made subject to any overriding interest which may bind the estate. The danger to a purchaser is well illustrated by the case of *Chowood Ltd* v

Lyall [1930] 2 Ch 156 in which the registered proprietor of an estate was held to be bound by the rights of an adverse possessor, which were overriding under LRA 1925, s. 70(1)(f). In consequence, the register was rectified by removing the portion of the property occupied by the squatter from the registered title. The fact that the registered proprietor was in possession did not protect him, because the rectification was made for the purpose of giving effect to the overriding interest.

5.12.5 Indemnity

A person who suffers loss due either to a rectification of the register, or to a refusal to rectify, may be able to claim compensation (an 'indemnity') under LRA 2002, Sch. 8, paras. 1(a) and (b). Compensation may also be paid to the person in whose favour the register is rectified for any loss he has suffered in spite of the rectification.

No compensation is payable where the loss suffered by a claimant is caused wholly or partly by his own fraud, or wholly by his negligence. Where the loss is caused only partly by the claimant's negligence, compensation is reduced to take account of his share in the responsibility (Sch. 8, para. 5).

These new provisions continue the previous rules about indemnity. Both old and new schemes appear to provide fairly generously for compensation, but there has always been a hidden limitation which prevents the payment of compensation when the register is changed to give effect to an overriding interest.

Under the 1925 Act this limitation resulted from the requirement that before an indemnity could be paid it had to be shown that the loss which the applicant suffered was due to the rectification, or due to the refusal to rectify. As a result of this provision it was held in *Re Chowood's Registered Land* [1933] Ch 574, *Re Boyle's Claim* [1961] 1 WLR 339, and *Hodgson* v *Marks* [1971] Ch 892 that where the register was altered to give effect to an overriding interest no compensation would be payable. In such cases the loss was caused by the proprietor acquiring an estate which was subject to an overriding interest. When the register was rectified the alteration gave effect to an existing state of affairs and did not cause any fresh loss (i.e., the loss was not due to the rectification).

Under the new Act indemnity is payable only in respect of loss caused by rectification or refusal to rectify. As we saw above, alteration of the register to give effect to an overriding interest does not constitute 'rectification' in its new sense of correcting a mistake, and so it remains the case that compensation is not payable in these circumstances.

From this one can see just how dangerous overriding interests can prove to be for a purchaser of a registered estate, particularly where, as in *Hodgson* v *Marks*, the effect of the overriding interest is to deprive him of the whole estate. It is for this reason that LRA 2002 makes such efforts to reduce the range of overriding interests which can bind a purchaser and cause him loss in this way, but it remains to be seen how successful this will be.

5.13 **Transfer and completion by registration**

Once the Armstrongs are satisfied with their enquiries and have made any necessary arrangements, the time will have come for the completion of the transaction. They will pay the balance of the purchase price, provided from their own funds or with money borrowed from a lender, to whom they will mortgage the property. Victor Venn will execute a transfer made by deed, using the appropriate Land Registry form. An example of such a transfer is given at pp. 108–9.

The transfer of a registered estate is one of the dispositions which must be completed by registration (s. 27) and does not take effect at law until this is done. This means that a transfer of a registered estate, unlike a conveyance of unregistered land, does not have the effect of conveying the legal title to the purchaser. The vendor remains the legal owner until the transfer has been registered, and meanwhile the purchaser continues to own the property in equity, as he has done since the contract was concluded (see 3.5.1).

It is this period of time between transfer and registration, known as the 'registration gap', which can be so dangerous to purchasers. The risks which they run in not completing their transactions by registration are well illustrated by the decision in *Barclays Bank plc* v *Zaroovabli* [1997] Ch 321. Here the bank had been granted a mortgage by the registered proprietor in 1988, but did not register its charge until 1994. During the intervening six years the mortgage took effect in equity only, and was not protected by any entry on the mortgagor's title. Although the terms of the mortgage provided that the mortgagor should not grant any lease of the property without the bank's consent, the mortgagor did in fact grant such a lease some two months after the creation of the mortgage. In 1995, when the mortgagor was unable to repay the loan, the bank sought possession of the property as a preliminary to selling the house and realising its security. The court held that the restriction on the mortgagor's power to grant leases operated only in the case of a legal mortgage, so that the lease created while the bank had only an equitable mortgage was a valid one. Since that lease had been granted before the mortgage was completed by registration, the tenant's lease, and her rights under the Rent Acts, which she derived from the lease, were binding on the bank when it eventually acquired a legal mortgage on registration. As a result, the tenant was entitled to remain in the property, and the value of the bank's security was considerably reduced by the fact that there was a sitting tenant and the house could not be sold with vacant possession.

Although the decision in *Barclays Bank plc* v *Zaroovabli* concerns the grant of a mortgage, exactly the same principles will apply on the sale of any registered freehold or leasehold estate. If the Armstrongs go ahead with their purchase, it is essential, therefore, that they complete the transaction by registration without delay, and do not risk leaving the legal estate in the hands of Victor Venn. Of course, when electronic conveyancing is in operation, transfer (or grant) and registration will occur simultaneously, and purchasers will no longer have to worry about the registration gap. In the next section, we will look at that part of LRA 2002 which provides for the introduction of this new system.

**Transfer of whole
of registered title(s)**

Land Registry

If you need more room than is provided for in a panel, use continuation sheet CS and attach to this form.

1.	Stamp Duty

Place "X" in the appropriate box or boxes and complete the appropriate certificate.

☐ It is certified that this instrument falls within category ⬚ in the Schedule to the Stamp Duty (Exempt Instruments) Regulations 1987

☒ It is certified that the transaction effected does not form part of a larger transaction or of a series of transactions in respect of which the amount or value or the aggregate amount or value of the consideration exceeds the sum of ☐ £250,000

☐ It is certified that this is an instrument on which stamp duty is not chargeable by virtue of the provisions of section 92 of the Finance Act 2001

2. Title Number(s) of the Property *Leave blank if not yet registered.*
ST1234

3. Property
1 TRANT WAY, MOUSEHOLE, ST14 3JP

4. Date

5. Transferor *Give full names and company's registered number if any.*
VICTOR VENN

6. Transferee **for entry on the register** *Give full name(s) and company's registered number, if any. For Scottish companies use an SC prefix and for limited liability partnerships use an OC prefix before the registered number, if any. For foreign companies give territory in which incorporated.*

ARNOLD ARMSTRONG and ARRIETY ARMSTRONG

Unless otherwise arranged with Land Registry headquarters, a certified copy of the Transferee's constitution (in English or Welsh) will be required if it is a body corporate but is not a company registered in England and Wales or Scotland under the Companies Acts.

7. Transferee's intended **address(es) for service (including postcode) for entry on the register** *You may give up to three addresses for service **one** of which **must** be a postal address but does not have to be within the UK. The other addresses can be any combination of a postal address, a box number at a UK document exchange or an electronic address.*

1 TRANT WAY, MOUSEHOLE, ST14 3JP

8. **The Transferor transfers the Property to the Transferee**

9. Consideration *Place "X" in the appropriate box. State clearly the currency unit if other than sterling. If none of the boxes applies, insert an appropriate memorandum in the additional provisions panel.*

☒ The Transferor has received from the Transferee for the Property the sum of one hundred and ninety-five thousand pounds (£195,000.00).
☐

☐ *Insert other receipt as appropriate.*

☐ The transfer is not for money or anything which has a monetary value

---

10. The Transferor transfers with *Place "X" in the appropriate box and add any modifications.*

    ☒ Full title guarantee   ☐ limited title guarantee

---

11. Declaration of trust *Where there is more than one Transferee, place "X" in the appropriate box.*

    ☒ The Transferees are to hold the Property on trust for themselves as joint tenants

    ☐ The Transferees are to hold the Property on trust for themselves as tenants in common in equal shares

    ☐ The Transferees are to hold the Property *Complete as necessary.*

---

12. Additional provisions *Insert here any required or permitted statements, certificates or applications and any agreed covenants, declarations, etc.*

---

13. Execution *The Transferor must execute this transfer as a deed using the space below. If there is more than one Transferor, all must execute. Forms of execution are given in Schedule 9 to the Land Registration Rules 2003. If the transfer contains Transferee's covenants or declarations or contains an application by the Transferee (e.g. for a restriction), it must also be executed by the Transferee (all of them, if there is more than one).*

Signed as a deed by **Victor Venn**
in the presence of:

Victor Venn

Signature of witness

Name (in BLOCK CAPITALS   MICHAEL MOGGIE

Address   14 The Broadway,
           Mousehole,
           Stilton.

5.14 Electronic conveyancing

We have already explained in very general terms what electronic conveyancing means (see 5.2.3). Part 8 of LRA 2002 contains the provisions which are needed to bring such a system into operation, although the details remain to be completed by rules made under the Act.

5.14.1 Formalities

Section 91 prescribes the formalities required for those documents in electronic form which are to be used for such dispositions as are specified by rules. Such documents must make provision for the time and date when they take effect. They must have the electronic signature of each person by whom they purport to be authenticated, and these signatures must be certified. Further conditions may be prescribed by rules.

An electronic document which satisfies these conditions is to be regarded as being made in writing and signed (or in the case of a corporation, sealed) by the individual or corporation whose signature it bears. The document is to be regarded for the purpose of any enactment as a deed, and requirements of attestation (that is, the witnessing of its execution) will not apply to a document in this form

(s. 91(4),(5) and (8)). This means that an electronic document will be capable of satisfying the requirements of s. 2 of the Law of Property (Miscellaneous Provisions) Act 1989 with regard to a written contract, as well as those of LPA 1925, s. 52(1) in respect of the deed needed to effect the grant or conveyance of a legal estate. These are all important practical matters but the most significant provision of all is to be found in s. 93 which deals with the power to require simultaneous registration.

5.14.2 Simultaneous registration

Section 93(1) provides:

This section applies to a disposition of—
   (a) a registered estate or charge, or
   (b) an interest which is the subject of a notice in the register,
where the disposition is of a description specified by rules.

Under s. 93(2) such dispositions will have effect only if made by a document in electronic form which is electronically communicated to the Registrar. This means that the disposition, its completion by registration and, where necessary, the entry of a notice on the title of the burdened estate will all happen simultaneously, thus removing the present gap between transfer and registration.

In addition, s. 93(2) also requires that *contracts* for the specified dispositions must be made electronically and communicated to the Registrar. When the system is operational, this would mean that a valid contract relating to registered land could be created only by electronic means, thus enabling the registry to record the contract against the registered title at the moment at which it is made.

We must emphasise that it is intended that dispositions and contracts which are not made and communicated electronically will have no effect at all: that is, they will be ineffective in both law *and* equity (although see below for concerns which are already being expressed about the way in which the courts may seek to assist parties in 'hard cases').

These changes will have tremendous significance for the operation of the registered title system. They will not only remove the gap between transfer and registration, which, as we have seen, can cause difficulty, but they will also reduce very considerably the number of interests which can be created 'off the register'. At present, a grant or transfer made by a paper transaction creates a valid equitable interest, even although it is not legally effective until completed by registration. Similarly, as we have seen, equitable interests may arise under any contract for the grant or transfer of a legal estate or interest in land. Where the parties do not go ahead and complete the formalities, interests made 'off the register' in this way may last for many years, and have often been protected as overriding interests by virtue of actual occupation. When the new system is in full operation, equitable interests will no longer arise from registrable but unregistered dispositions, and the creation of estate contracts by electronic means only will ensure that equitable interests arising from them are automatically noted on the register. This will gradually reduce the number of interests which can be created off the register and either take effect as interests that override a registered disposition or require protection by subsequent entry on the register.

Overall these changes, when fully implemented, will be to the purchaser's advantage and will mean that he can buy with greater reliance on the register. Inevitably though, there will be circumstances in which the terms of s. 93(2) will be thought to have a disproportionate effect or in which it will appear unconscionable for one party to rely on the other party's failure to observe the new requirements. We have seen in Chapter 3 that this happened with the Statute of Frauds in 1677, and that equity developed the doctrine of part performance to mitigate its rigours. More recently some courts have been sympathetic to litigants who rely on proprietary estoppel or the constructive trust to avoid the effects of the Law of Property (Miscellaneous Provisions) Act 1989, s. 2 (see 3.4.2). Only time will tell whether the terms of s. 93(2) will be enforced strictly by the courts, but some commentators are already expressing concerns that they may be circumvented by the use of equitable principles (see Dixon [2003] Conv. 136, at 153–5).

In any event, it is likely to be some time before this part of the new Act can be brought into operation. The appropriate electronic communications network has to be developed, detailed rules must be made, and arrangements for licensing practitioners and others to use the network must be put in place. An outline of what has to be done can be found in Sch. 5, which deals with the Land Registry network.

In conclusion, we should mention that those who want to do their own conveyancing will still be able to do so, although in electronic form: Sch. 5, para. 7 imposes a duty on the registrar to make provision for what is described as 'do-it-yourself' conveyancing!

5.15 **Purchasers of other interests**

In describing the Armstongs' purchase of 1 Trant Way we have been concerned with the position of a purchaser who buys a *legal* estate. However, it is necessary to consider as well the position of someone who acquires an *equitable* interest in registered land. Examples of purchasers acquiring such interests can be found in the creditor who lends money on the security of an equitable mortgage or the tenant who has no formal lease but holds under an equitable one. In addition, we have already seen that purchasers like the Armstrongs will have only an equitable interest in the property if they do not complete the disposition by registration.

For purchasers of such equitable interests, questions may arise as to whether they are bound by interests created before their own, and whether in turn their interest will bind any later interest, or, possibly, be postponed to it. We have already considered these questions about the priorities of competing interests in relation to the purchase of a legal estate, but now need to think how they affect the purchaser of an equitable interest.

This is one area in which the LRA 2002 appears to make a complete break with the past, so for once we need not tell you about the earlier rules, except to say that they were complicated and in some cases even uncertain. The new rule about priority is set out in s. 28:

(1) Except as provided by sections 29 and 30, the priority of an interest affecting a registered estate or charge is not affected by a disposition of the estate or charge.

(2) It makes no difference for the purposes of this section whether the interest or disposition is registered.

We have already considered s. 29 (see 5.7.3), which deals with the effect of a registered disposition, and have seen that it *does* affect the priority of interests affecting the estate by providing that the disposition will postpone earlier interests if they are not protected in one of the prescribed ways. Section 30 makes similar provision in respect of a registered charge.

Transactions other than registered dispositions (i.e., those which will create the sort of interests we are considering in this section, such as equitable mortgages and rights under estate contracts) are governed by s. 28, and the effect of that section is said to be that priority depends solely on the date of creation. It is not affected by entries on the register, and most importantly it is not subject to the old rule, which used to be applied to some situations, that 'when the equities are equal, the first in time prevails' (i.e., that interests rank in chronological order, unless the holder of an earlier interest has behaved in such a way that equity considers it would be fair to postpone his interest to that of a later purchaser). Under the new provisions, the first in time will prevail, and it appears that no question will arise as to whether the equities are equal. In describing this basic rule, set out in s. 28, the Report says (at para. 5.5):

In cases that fall within this general rule, the priority of any interest in registered land is determined by its date of creation. Unlike the first in time rule which presently applies to competing minor interest, this rule is an absolute one . . . No question rises as to whether 'the equities are equal'.

Although questions about relative priority can arise in respect of any of the equitable interests we have mentioned, they are most commonly found in connection with successive mortgages of the property—that is, where the estate owner grants several mortgages of the same property—and are considered further in Chapter 21.

FURTHER READING

Cooke, 'The Land Registration Bill 2001' [2002] Conv 11.

Dixon, 'The Reform of Property Law and the Land Registration Act 2002: A Risk Assessment' [2003] 67 Conv 136.

Harpum, 'Property in an Electronic Age', *Modern Studies in Property Law, Vol.1: Property 2000*, Hart Publishing, 2001, p. 4.

Land Registration for the Twenty-First Century A Consultative Document, 1998, Law Com No. 254; in particular: Part I (need for reform); Part IV (overriding interests); and paras. 11.2–11.20 (electronic conveyancing).

Land Registration for the Twenty-First Century A Conveyancing Revolution, 2001, Law Com No. 271; in particular: Part I (objectives of Land Registration Bill); and Part II (summary of changes).

Ruoff and Roper, *Registered Conveyancing*, Sweet & Maxwell, looseleaf edn., Oct. 2003, Pt. 1 General Principles.

Tee, 'The Rights of Every Person in Actual Occupation: An Enquiry into Section 70 (1)(g) of the Land Registration Act 1925' [1998] CLJ 328.

6

Acquisition of an estate by adverse possession

6.1 Introduction

So far we have been dealing only with estates in land which have been acquired in a formal manner. However, as we mentioned in the introduction to Part II, it is also possible to acquire an estate in land by adverse possession. The LRA 2002 makes major changes to the process of acquiring *registered land* by adverse possession. However, the old rules continue to apply to *unregistered land*, and we will begin this chapter by considering their application to another house in Trant Way.

6.1.1 4 Trant Way

The title to 4 Trant Way is not registered. The current inhabitant is Sidney Sorrell. Mr Sorrell moved into the property 15 years ago as a squatter, and has occupied it ever since. Fifteen years ago the house was in a bad state of repair and seemed to have been abandoned by its previous owners. Mr Sorrell has never received any complaints about his occupation of the premises and has made considerable improvements and alterations. He has had the electricity and gas supplies restored and has paid rates in respect of the property.

The original owner of the fee simple in 4 Trant Way was Oscar Oregano, who died six months ago at the age of 98. His entire estate was inherited by his nephew Nicholas Oregano, who has just discovered that his uncle had neglected the property and that it has been taken over by Mr Sorrell.

6.1.2 Importance of possession in English land law

There is an old saying that 'Possession is nine-tenths of the law'. In the case of title to land this saying was particularly true. Since the earliest times, title to land has been based on a form of possession, technically called 'seisin'. If two people had a dispute concerning the ownership of an estate in land, the court would decide the case in favour of the person who could show that he had been seised of the land at the earlier date, or who could show that his predecessors in title had the earlier seisin. Thus prior seisin would decide the issue as between the two claimants.

Technically there is a difference between possession and seisin, but today this is of no real importance, because possession is always regarded as clear evidence of seisin and therefore the two concepts are normally coexistent. A dispute about ownership would therefore be decided in favour of the party who could show prior possession of the property.

6.1.3 **Title was relative**

The result of this emphasis on the fact of possession is that in the past in England title to land has been treated as relative rather than as absolute. Absolute title involves the idea that there can be only one owner, whose title is 'not merely better than other titles: it is good and they are non-existent or at the best bad' (Lawson and Rudden, *The Law of Property*, 2nd edn., p. 45). By contrast, in proceedings in an English court where one person claimed land occupied by another, the court was concerned to determine only which of the two parties before it had the better claim: it was not seeking to identify the one 'true' owner. The system of registered title introduced the concept of absolute title into English land law, but by that time the rules of adverse possession were established on the basis of relative title. Thus in the following situation:

1994	A is the fee simple owner of property
1995	B takes possession of the land
2003	C takes possession of the land

if B sues C in order to recover the land, C cannot defend the claim by saying that A, and not B, is the true owner of the estate. A court will consider only the competing claims of B and C, and will therefore regard B as being the better claimant because he has the prior estate (*Nicholls* v *Ely Beet Sugar Factory* [1931] 2 Ch 84 and *Mount Carmel Investments Ltd* v *Peter Thurlow Ltd* [1988] 1 WLR 1078).

6.1.4 **Application to 4 Trant Way**

If we apply this approach to the position of 4 Trant Way we can see that both Sidney Sorrell and Nicholas Oregano have claims to the property.

Mr Sorrell is currently in possession of the property, and is accordingly presumed to be seised of an estate in fee simple. However, Nicholas Oregano also has a claim to the property because he can show that his uncle Oscar was once in possession of the property, and that therefore his uncle was also seised of an estate in the property. That estate is, of course, an inheritable interest, and Nicholas can show that he has inherited the estate under the terms of his uncle's will. Accordingly Nicholas Oregano has an older estate in the property (and no doubt could produce his uncle's deeds to prove this). As a result one would presume that, in any dispute between Nicholas and Mr Sorrell about the ownership of the property, Nicholas would be regarded as having the better right to the property.

Thus far all seems fairly straightforward, but in fact the dispute between Nicholas and Mr Sorrell is likely to be affected by the provisions of the Limitation Act 1980, so that Nicholas's apparent rights may prove to be worthless.

6.1.5 **Effect of the Limitation Act 1980**

Most legal systems provide that a plaintiff must commence court proceedings within a prescribed time (the 'limitation period') or lose his right to sue. Provisions of this sort are necessary to ensure that claimants bring their cases promptly, while the necessary evidence is available, and that defendants are not harrassed by stale claims, which they may have difficulty in meeting when witnesses have disappeared and recollections have become blurred.

The current limitation provisions are contained in the Limitation Act 1980. Section 15, which now applies only to unregistered land, provides that the limitation period in respect of claims to recover land is 12 years. Thus generally, if someone with a prior estate in land allows it to be occupied by a squatter for 12 years, he will lose his right to recover the property from the interloper. So in our example, although Nicholas Oregano can prove that his uncle was in prior possession of the land, he may not be able to bring a claim to recover the land from Mr Sorrell because the right to sue has been time-barred. At one time the original owner's title continued even after the limitation period had elapsed, so that although he could not sue to recover the land he could rely on his title as a defence if he took possession again without a court action. However, today the rule is that at the end of the limitation period the original owner loses both his right to sue and his title to the property (Limitation Act 1980, s. 17). Thus a layman will sometimes say that if a squatter remains in possession of land for 12 years the land 'becomes his'. It would be more accurate to say that the squatter is deemed to obtain an estate in the land as soon as he moves on to the property but that his estate is subject to attack by a prior owner until 12 years have elapsed.

6.1.6 Justification for adverse possession

It may seem somewhat surprising that our legal system allows one person to take land belonging to another and to keep it as his own, and indeed this is sometimes described as 'land theft'. Cases of this sort always arouse public concern and comment when they hit the headlines (as in the example, widely reported in the press in July 1999, of the squatter who successfully established a claim against Lambeth Council to adverse possession of a house worth £200,000—reported, although without reference to the value of the property, in *Ellis* v *Lambeth BC* (1999), *The Times*, 28 September 1999). The example we have given you is of this type: Sidney Sorrell must have known that he had no right to the house when he moved in, and yet it seems that he may now be regarded as having the better title to it. You should be aware, however, that many claims to title by adverse possession do not arise from a deliberate taking of another's property, but rather through some kind of mistake. Boundaries between neighbouring properties are often far from clear, and one owner may occupy a small strip of his neighbour's land in the genuine belief that it belongs to him. Other cases can arise from mistakes on the part of a vendor, who purports to sell the same piece of land to two different purchasers (as, for example, happened in *Bridges* v *Mees* [1957] Ch 475). In cases such as these, the rules of adverse possession can be beneficial in helping to bring the legal title into line with the position on the ground.

In fact, there are several good reasons for retaining a system which allows title to be acquired in this way (in addition, of course, to the general reasons underlying any form of limitation of claims, which we have noted above at 6.1.5). We cannot deal in any detail here with the justifications for adverse possession, but have included some references at the end of the chapter, if you want to know more.

In outline, there seem to be three main ways in which the system of adverse possession is beneficial, although, of course, they do not all apply in every case. First, adverse possession may assist an innocent party who has spent money and time on land which he believes to be his own, but who cannot establish a claim to proprietary estoppel (see Chapter 18), because there has been no encouragement or acquiescence by the owner. Second, the possibility of acquiring title in this way helps to ensure that land abandoned by its owner is not left to become derelict, or taken out of the property market because its occupier cannot prove title to it. Third, and perhaps most importantly, it is said that the system of adverse possession facilitates and cheapens the investigation of title to unregistered land. This is because, in general terms, a purchaser is probably willing to assume that any claim to the land arising before the statutory period of title (currently a minimum of 15 years—see 4.2) has been barred under the 12-year limitation period, so that he will be safe in taking a title shown for the minimum period. This of course is not a consideration when dealing with registered land, but nevertheless, as we shall see (6.4.2), the Law Commission considered that title by adverse possession still had a useful role to play in the registered system, and provision for it is made in LRA 2002, although in an amended form. However, adverse possession is seen by some as an area of law which could be vulnerable to attack under the Human Rights Act 1998, and we will consider this further in 6.6.

Under LRA 2002 there is now a considerable difference between the rules governing adverse possession of registered and unregistered land. However, the requirements for establishing that a person has been in 'adverse possession' remain the same in both systems of title, and we will deal with these first, before going on to see how the two systems now diverge once adverse possession has been established.

6.2 Establishing adverse possession

In order to claim title by adverse possession, the squatter must show that he has been in possession of the land, and that the possession has been adverse. In this section we will look in a little more detail at each of these requirements, but will start by clarifying some of the terms used.

6.2.1 Terminology

6.2.1.1 'Adverse possessor' and 'squatter'
Either of these phrases can be used to describe the person who has dispossessed the owner, and we use them interchangeably.

6.2.1.2 'Paper owner' or 'documentary owner'
Some writers and judges use one or other of these phrases to describe the dispossessed owner, thus indicating that he has acquired title by formal means. This distinguishes him from the squatter who, as we shall see (6.3.3.2), is also regarded as owning an estate in the land, albeit acquired informally. We shall simply talk about 'the dispossessed owner', but you need to understand the other terms in case you meet them elsewhere.

6.2.1.3 'Estate' and 'title'
You will see that the squatter is sometimes said to acquire 'an estate' in the land, and on other occasions to acquire 'title' to it. In the context of adverse possession,

these terms are used synonymously (*Central London Commercial Estates Ltd* v *Kato Kagaku Co. Ltd* [1998] 4 All ER 948 at p. 958), and you do not need to try to distinguish between them.

6.2.2 **Possession**

The squatter must take possession of the land, either by dispossessing the owner or by entering at some time after the owner has discontinued his own possession. There are two essential elements of possession, both of which must be shown to exist: the fact of possession and the intention to possess (sometimes referred to by the Latin phrase '*animus possidendi*').

6.2.2.1 *The fact of possession*

What is required here is described by Slade J in *Powell* v *McFarlane* (1970) 38 P&CR 452 at p. 471:

what must be shown as constituting factual possession is that the alleged possessor has been dealing with the land in question as an occupying owner might have been expected to deal with it and that no-one else has done so.

What the squatter actually does with the land depends on its nature. If it is a house, he may live in it; if it is a piece of land adjoining his garden, he may fence and cultivate it. In some circumstances more occasional use may be enough, as in *Red House Farms (Thornden) Ltd* v *Catchpole* [1977] 2 EGLR 125, where shooting wildfowl was held to be a sufficient act of possession, because that was the only purpose for which the land could be used. Whatever the nature of the land, the squatter must be able to show that he has *exclusive* possession of it; sharing possession with the owner is not enough.

6.2.2.2 *The intention to possess (animus possidendi)*

As well as taking physical possession of the land, the squatter must have the intention to possess it, defined by Slade J in *Powell* v *McFarlane* (1979) 38 P&CR 452 at p. 471 as:

the intention, in one's own name and on one's own behalf, to exclude the world at large, including the owner with the paper title . . . so far as is reasonably practicable and so far as the processes of the law will allow.

The squatter must not only have this intention; he must make it clear to the world, including the owner (if he is present) that he intends to possess the land. As the Court of Appeal put it in *Prudential Assurance Co. Ltd* v *Waterloo Real Estate Inc* [1999] 2 EGLR 85 at 87:

the claimant must, of course, be shown to have the subjective intention to possess the land, but he must also show by his outward conduct that that was his intention.

Proving the necessary intention
In general, the courts are loath to rely on the claimant's own statement about his intentions, because it may so easily be self-serving, and accordingly, they will tend to look for conduct from which the necessary intention may be inferred.

An example of conduct sufficient to show such an intention is to found in *Buckinghamshire County Council* v *Moran* [1990] Ch 623, in which the adverse possessor had cultivated a piece of the council's land which adjoined his garden, fencing it and installing a gate which he chained and padlocked. In the view of the Court of Appeal (at p. 642), the locking of the gate amounted to a 'final unequivocal demonstration of the defendant's intention to possess the land' and to exclude the owner.

You should note that all that is required here is an intention to *possess*; the squatter does not have to show that he intended to acquire title to the property. Thus in *Buckinghamshire County Council* v *Moran*, the squatter knew that the council had plans for the future use of the land, and made it clear that he intended to keep the land only until the council required it. The Court of Appeal was, however, satisfied that he intended to take possession of the land until that time, and this was sufficient, after completion of the limitation period, to enable him to claim title by adverse possession.

Conversely, it is not fatal to the squatter's claim if he took possession believing that he was entitled to the property, either as a tenant or as the freehold owner. Thus in *Lodge* v *Wakefield City Council* [1995] 38 EG 136 the appellant, a former tenant of the council, had not paid any rent under the tenancy since 1974, but did not become aware of this fact until the late 1980s, believing, in the meantime, that he was in possession of the land as tenant. The Court of Appeal rejected the council's contention that time did not run against it until the possessor became aware of his true position, holding that the former tenant had had the necessary intention to possess the property and that his possession was adverse from the time he ceased to pay rent, even if he himself was not aware of this. Similarly, it appears from the decision in *Hughes* v *Cook* (1994), *The Independent*, 21 March 1994 that title by adverse possession can be acquired where the possessor occupies the land under a mistaken belief that he is already the owner of the estate, and indeed, as we mentioned earlier, such mistakes often form the background to cases of adverse possession. At the same time, it must be remembered that other cases can involve the deliberate taking of property which the squatter knows is not his. The rules of adverse possession impose no requirement of good faith, and bad faith is relevant only in the exceptional case of the owner claiming that the squatter has acted fraudulently (see 6.3.1.1).

6.2.2.3 *The owner's state of mind*

Having considered what is required of the squatter by way of intention and knowledge, it may be helpful to deal here briefly with the owner's state of mind. There is no requirement that he should know about the adverse possession; use must be open, so that he has the opportunity of finding out about it, but the fact that he does not do so is no bar to the squatter's claim (*Powell* v *McFarlane* (1979) 38 P&CR 452). Nor does the owner even have to be aware that he owns the land: adverse possession can operate against an owner who believes that the land already belongs to the squatter (see Gray and Gray, at p. 268).

6.2.3 **Possession must be adverse**

There is no statutory definition of 'adverse', but it may be understood as meaning possession which is inconsistent with the rights of the owner, (although it is clear that it does not have to be in any way hostile or aggressive). In consequence, anyone taking possession with the consent of the owner, for example under a licence, will not be in *adverse* possession, and so cannot acquire rights under the Limitation Act. When a licence comes to an end or is withdrawn, time will, of course, start to run against the owner if the licensee remains on the land without acknowledging his title.

6.2.3.1 *Possession by tenants*

Similarly it is not possible for a tenant to lay claim to the freehold title because clearly he occupies the land with the permission of the estate owner and in accordance with the terms of his lease. In the case of a lease for a fixed term, or a periodic tenancy granted in writing, time only starts to run against the former landlord if the tenant remains on the land at the end of the term or period, not paying rent or acknowledging the owner's title in some way.

A tenant who holds the land under a periodic tenancy where there is no lease in writing is, however, in a special position. In the case of such oral tenancies the limitation period will run against the landlord as soon as the first period of the tenancy ends. However, should the tenant pay rent after this date the period will restart from the date that the rent was paid (Limitation Act 1980, Sch. 1, para. 5). Thus if a periodic tenant with an oral lease fails to pay rent he may be able to obtain title to the leased property (*Moses* v *Lovegrove* [1952] 2 QB 533), and should a landlord in such a position wish to excuse his tenant from paying rent, he should require that the tenant give a regular written acknowledgement that the landlord is the true owner of the property.

The risk to a landlord who fails to do this can be seen from the facts of *Smith* v *Lawson* [1997] 75 P&CR 466. In this case, the defendant, now an elderly woman, had lived for many years in a house owned by her brother, paying him a small weekly rent. On the brother's death in 1978, the property passed to his son, the plaintiff in this action, who told his aunt that she could continue to live there for the rest of her life and that he would not in future bother to collect the rent. Some 13 years later, the defendant made a statutory declaration that she had become the freehold owner of the property and then sold it to a purchaser, who in fact later retransferred it to her. The plaintiff sought a declaration that he was the freehold owner of the property.

At first instance, it was held that time had started to run against the plaintiff at the date when the payment of rent stopped and that, accordingly, his title had been extinguished. The Court of Appeal reversed this decision, holding that the aunt had never been in adverse possession. The plaintiff's statement that he would not collect any more rent amounted to a promise which the defendant had acted upon and this gave rise to a promissory estoppel within the rule in *Central London Property Trust Ltd* v *High Trees House Ltd* [1947] 1 KB 130. In the words of Sir John Balcombe:

> If the plaintiff had sought to obtain possession of the property for non-payment of rent . . . he would have been unable to do so because of what he had said . . . and the defendant's subsequent reliance on that representation (p. 470).

In other words, the plaintiff had no cause of action against the defendant in respect of her continuing occupation of the property. In consequence, she could not be said to be in adverse possession, time did not run against the plaintiff, and as a result his title had not been extinguished.

Although in the end the plaintiff here had a lucky escape, the facts of the case do show very clearly that in a similar situation it would be sensible to require written acknowledgement from the occupier.

6.2.4 Land reserved by owner for specific purpose

Before leaving the topic of possession, we must mention briefly a problem which could arise in cases where the the owner is not currently using the land, but has some specific purpose planned for it in the future. A classic example of this is to be found in the facts of *Leigh* v *Jack* (1879) 5 Ex. D 264.

In this case, the owner of some land had intended to use it to build a highway but no action had been taken to start the construction of the road. From 1854 onwards a neighbouring landowner had used the property to store materials used in his factory and in 1865 and 1872 he had erected fences on the land. The court held that none of these actions amounted to adverse possession of the disputed property, because the prior owner of the property had no intention to build upon or cultivate the land and therefore the actions of the neighbouring owner were not inconsistent with the intentions of the prior owner. In the words of Bramwell LJ (at p. 273):

in order to defeat a title by dispossessing the former owner, acts must be done which are inconsistent with his enjoyment of the soil for the purposes for which he intended to use it: that is not the case here, where the intention of the plaintiff . . . was not either to build upon or cultivate the land, but to devote it at some future time to public purposes.

In later cases, this statement was treated as giving rise to the rule that an owner who was keeping land dormant for some particular purpose in the future was not dispossessed by a squatter who made use of it in the meantime. This approach came to be supported by the idea that a person who occupied land for which the owner had no immediate use did so under an implied licence from the owner. Such possession, being by licence, was not adverse, and therefore time did not run against the owner (*Wallis's Caytown Bay Holiday Camp Ltd* v *Shell-Mex and BP Ltd* [1975] QB 94).

The theory of an implied licence was, however, regarded as doubtful (Nourse LJ later describing it in *Buckinghamshire County Council* v *Moran* [1990] Ch 623 at p. 646 as 'an original heresy of [Lord Denning's] own'), and Sch. 1, para. 8(4) of the Limitation Act 1980 now specifically provides that the existence of such a licence shall not be assumed merely because the squatter's occupation is not inconsistent with the owner's present or future enjoyment of the land.

Further, the Court of Appeal in *Buckinghamshire County Council* v *Moran* [1990] Ch 623, on facts very similar to those of *Leigh* v *Jack*, cast doubt on the existence of the special rule supposedly derived from that decision. In this case the council had acquired a plot of land in 1955, for the purpose of constructing a road diversion. It was known that the roadworks would not be carried out for many years and so the council merely fenced the plot from the road (but not from the neighbouring properties) and initially sent council workmen to cut the grass and keep the plot in order. From the late 1960s the owners of one of the neighbouring properties, to the knowledge of the council, began to cut the grass on the council's plot and keep it tidy. From that time on the council ceased to send its workmen to the plot. The neighbouring property changed hands several times and was bought by Mr Moran in 1971. Mr Moran knew that the title to the empty plot was vested in the council, but the plot appeared to form part of the garden of the property which he had bought and was always maintained as such. As we have noted above (at 6.2.2.2), he erected a fence and a gate, which was secured with a lock and chain. In 1976 the council wrote a letter disputing his rights to use the plot but thereafter took no action to recover it for at least nine years. Thus by the time that the action was brought Mr Moran and his predecessors in title had been using the plot as a garden for well over 12 years in total. The council argued, however, that as it had not had any use for the plot, other than to let it lie fallow until the road scheme could go ahead, the possession of Mr Moran and his predecessors had not been adverse to the council's rights. The Court of Appeal held, however, that Mr Moran had established a good claim to title by adverse possession over the plot of land. The court doubted the existence of any special rule applicable to these circumstances, and distinguished *Leigh* v *Jack* on the ground that the squatter in that case had not satisfied the court of his intention to exclude the owner.

6.2.5 **Pye v Graham**

The requirements for establishing adverse possession which we have outlined above have recently been considered and affirmed by the House of Lords in *J. A. Pye (Oxford) Ltd* v *Graham* [2003] 1 AC 419. In this case Pye, a property development company, owned fields adjoining the Grahams' farm. Pye hoped to obtain planning permission to build on the fields, but meanwhile permitted the Grahams to make limited use of them, at first under a written grazing licence for a period in 1983 and then by permission to cut hay in 1984. Further licences were requested in 1984 and 1985; these requests were not answered but the Grahams continued to use the land from 1986 to 1999. In 1997 Michael Graham, the current owner of the farm, registered a caution against Pye's registered title (see 5.8.1.3) on the basis that he had acquired title by adverse possession. Pye sought to 'warn off' this caution (i.e. have it removed from the register) and in 1999 commenced proceedings for possession.

Although Neuberger J at first instance ([2000] Ch 676) held that adverse possession had been established, the Court of Appeal ([2001] Ch 804) considered that Graham's evidence showed that he did not have the necessary intention to possess the property to the exclusion of the owner. His evidence made it clear that he intended to carry on using the land in the hope that Pye would subsequently renew the grazing licence, and that he would have been willing to pay for the use of the land if asked to do so. In these circumstances, the court held that the intention to possess had not been established; there was thus no dispossession of Pye and time had not started to run against it under the Limitation Act.

On appeal, the House of Lords reversed the Court of Appeal decision, holding that the Grahams had been in adverse possession of the property and that time had run in their favour ([2003] 1 AC 419). In explaining this decision, Lord Browne-Wilkinson, with whom the others concurred, considered and approved the principles stated by Slade J in *Powell* v *McFarlane* (1977) 38 P&CR 452 (see 6.2.2). Lord Browne-Wilkinson emphasised the need for both the fact of possession, and the intention to possess, which he defined as involving respectively 'a sufficient degree of physical custody and control' and 'an intention to exercise such custody and control on one's own behalf and for one's own benefit' (p. 435). This second element, the intention to possess, was an essential ingredient in establishing adverse possession. The fact that physical control by itself was not enough could be illustrated by the hypothetical situation in which a person in occupation of a house in the owner's absence might be, depending on his intention, a friend of the owner who was looking after it for him, a temporary trespasser seeking only a night's lodging, or a squatter who intended to remain in the property. In order to establish adverse possession the occupier must show an intention to use the property for his own benefit, but he did not have to intend to acquire ownership of it (*Buckinghamshire County Council* v *Moran* [1990] Ch 623 was approved on this point), and most significantly in the present case, a willingness to pay for the use of the land did not indicate an absence of intention to possess. As Lord Browne-Wilkinson put it (at p. 438):

Once it is accepted that the necessary intent is an intent to possess not to own and an intention to exclude the paper owner only so far as is reasonably possible, there is no inconsistency between a squatter being willing to pay the paper owner if asked and his being in the meantime in possession. An admission of title by the squatter is not inconsistent with the squatter being in possession in the meantime.

Support for this view was to be found in the observations of Lord Diplock in the Privy Council decision in *Ocean Estates Ltd* v *Pinder* [1969] 2 AC 19, which it appeared had not been given sufficient weight by the Court of Appeal in the present case (p. 438).

In their Lordships' view, both the elements necessary for adverse possession were present in the Grahams' use of the land belonging to Pye. They had physical control of the property (the fields being surrounded by hedges and accessible only through gates which they controlled), and they had the necessary intention to use the land for their own purposes, maintaining and using it as though it was part of their farm. The Grahams were thus entitled to be registered as owners, but it should be noted that several of their Lordships expressed concerns about the apparent injustice of this result (see further 6.6).

As we said earlier, the requirements for establishing adverse possession are the same, regardless of whether title to the land in question is registered or unregistered. However, from this point onwards the rules relevant to each system of title diverge, and accordingly we will deal with them in separate sections.

6.3 Adverse possession of unregistered land

6.3.1 Time

A squatter on unregistered land, who satisfies the requirements for adverse possession which we have noted above, must then remain in possession for the period prescribed by the Limitation Act ('the limitation period') in order to bar the owner's right to recover the land from him. Possession must be continuous; if the squatter gives up possession and then retakes it at a later date, the owner will have a new claim. Time will start to run afresh, and the squatter will have to complete the full limitation period after his second entry.

The period generally required to bar the owner's claim is 12 years (Limitation Act 1980, s. 15), but we need to look in a little more detail at the circumstances in which time starts to run, and at a few cases in which the Act gives the owner extra time to bring his claim. We will also consider how the owner can stop time running against him.

6.3.1.1 *When does time start to run?*

Time will start to run against a prior owner only once he has been dispossessed or has discontinued possession (Limitation Act 1980, Sch. 1, para. 1) *and* when adverse possession has been taken by another person (para. 8). This requires that the true owner has either been forced out of possession or has abandoned possession. In the case of 4 Trant Way it would appear that at some date more than 15 years ago Oscar Oregano abandoned the use of the property. However the limitation period did not start to run against Mr Oregano, or his successors, until a third party (Mr Sorrell) took possession of the property 15 years ago.

Postponement of limitation period

In the case of claims based on fraud or for relief from the consequences of a mistake, and in any case where a fact relevant to the claimant's claim has been deliberately concealed from him by the defendant, time does not start to run under the Act until the claimant has discovered the relevant matter, or could have done so with reasonable diligence (Limitation Act 1980, s. 32). These are general provisions, applicable to all claims covered by the Act, and it is not easy to find examples of their application to claims against squatters. You may like to note the view expressed in Smith at p. 76 that 'few adverse possession cases will fall within this rule; it is certainly not enough that it is difficult to discover the adverse possession or that there is a false assertion of title'.

6.3.1.2 *Extension of time within which owner may bring claim*

If the prior owner is subject to a disability then the time period is *either* 12 years from the date of the dispossession or six years from the date at which the disability ends, *whichever is greater*, with a maximum available period of 30 years. If a person dies whilst still under a disability, then his estate will have a period of 12 years from the date of dispossession or six years from the date of the death, with a maximum of 30 years. For these rules to apply the disability must have existed at the date at which the claim arose. If the disability arises even a day later the ordinary 12-year period will apply. These rules are to be found in s. 28 of the Limitation Act 1980.

The states which amount to a disability for the purposes of s. 28 are (a) that the estate owner is an infant (i.e., a person under the age of 18 years, now more usually called a 'minor'), and (b) that the estate owner is a patient under the Mental Health Act 1983.

6.3.1.3 *Running of time against persons with future interests in the land*

The usual rules are further modified in favour of persons who have future interests in land. If land is held upon trust for A for life and then for B, A has an immediate interest in the property and B has a future interest. If A was dispossessed by S in 1970 the usual rule applies to the running of the period against A and in 1982 his rights would be time-barred. However, the rights of B are further protected by s. 15(2) of the Limitation Act 1980. In the case of B the time period within which he must sue is either 12 years from the date of the adverse possession commencing or six years from the date at which he obtains an interest in possession in the property, *whichever is the greater*. B's interest will become an interest in possession when A dies and so, if A died in 1984, B's interest would only become time-barred in 1990, which is 20 years after S first obtained possession.

6.3.1.4 *How can the owner stop time running?*

The most obvious way to do this is to start proceedings to recover the land within the time allowed by the Limitation Act. However, as *Markfield Investments Ltd* v *Evans* [2001] 1 WLR 1321 shows, the proceedings once begun must be continued to judgment; merely issuing the writ does not stop time running if the action is subsequently dismissed for want of prosecution or otherwise discontinued. If, on the other hand, the owner is content for the possession to continue, but wants to avoid losing his rights to the land, he should ensure that the occupier provides written acknowledgement of his title.

An interesting decision of the Court of Appeal suggests that the owner may also be able to stop time running by simply giving permission for the squatter to remain. In *BP Properties Ltd* v *Buckler* (1987) 55 P&CR 337, the appellant's parents had been in adverse possession of a farmhouse, holding on after the tenancy of the farm expired. The owner of the property had made several attempts to recover it but this caused local hostility, and as a result the owner gave up the attempt, informing the occupier by letter that she would be allowed to stay in the house rent-free for the rest of her life. At her death, the owner sought possession, and the appellant, who had been living in the property with his mother, claimed title by adverse possession. The Court of Appeal held that the permission to remain given by the owner had stopped time running against it; from that time the mother was in possession as a licensee of the owner (i.e., under a 'lawful title'); in consequence her possession was no longer adverse, and accordingly the owner's right of action was not time-barred under the Limitation Act.

This decision has been criticised as allowing owners to prevent time running against them by a unilateral act of giving permission, without having to incur the expense or publicity of court proceedings. However, it should be noted that the court left open the question of the effect which any rejection of the licence might have (there having been, in this case, no express acceptance or rejection of the owner's letters). Accordingly, it remains to be seen whether there is any way in which the squatter could counteract the effect of such a unilateral licence. (For comment on this decision see Wallace [1994] Conv 196.)

6.3.2 **Rights of squatter during the limitation period**

6.3.2.1 *The squatter's estate in the land*

The adverse possessor of unregistered land is regarded as having an estate in fee simple from the moment when he first takes possession (*Leach* v *Jay* (1878) 9 ChD

42 at p. 45), although until the limitation period has been completed, his title is always liable to be defeated by the owner. Thus even before the period is completed, the squatter has the rights and powers of an owner, against everyone except the person he has dispossessed. This means that he can sue for torts against the land (such as trespass and nuisance), and can recover the land if he himself is dispossessed by a third party.

6.3.2.2 *Completion of period by another person*

The squatter's rights in the property are capable of being transferred to another, by gift or sale during his life, or by succession at his death. If the recipient takes possession of the property, time will continue to run in his favour, and he can complete the limitation period by adding his time to that of his predecessor.

Similarly, if the original squatter is himself dispossessed by another, the later dispossessor may complete the limitation period so as to bar the original owner (although he will have to hold for the full 12-year period in order to bar the first squatter's right to recover the land from him).

6.3.3 **Effect of completing the limitation period**

In describing the effect of completing the limitation period against the owner of a fee simple, we need to consider the position of three people: the dispossessed owner, the adverse possessor and any third party who has rights over the land. Where the adverse possession has been against a tenant, a fourth person, his landlord, will also be involved.

6.3.3.1 *The dispossessed owner*

Completion of the limitation period not only bars the owner's right to recover the land, but also extinguishes his title to it (Limitation Act 1980, s. 17).

6.3.3.2 *The adverse possessor*

It used to be thought that at the end of the limitation period the Limitation Acts vested the previous owner's estate in the squatter. This is what is meant by references you may see in reported cases to 'a parliamentary conveyance'. It was however held in *Tichbourne* v *Weir* (1892) 67 LT 735 that the Acts did not have this effect. Instead, the previous owner's title is extinguished (as provided now by the Limitation Act, 1980 s. 17), and the squatter holds his own estate in the land under a new title.

The estate held by the squatter is regarded as a fee simple, irrespective of whether his adverse possession has been against the fee simple owner or only against a tenant (see Megarry and Wade, p. 1332; Smith, p. 82). As we shall see, where possession has been against a tenant, the squatter's estate is liable to be defeated if the landlord re-enters when he is entitled to do so at the end of the lease, but until that happens the squatter has a freehold estate. He does not take over the leasehold estate which was held by the dispossessed tenant, and so does not enter into any relationship with the landlord and is not liable as a tenant on the covenants in the lease.

6.3.3.3 *Third party with rights over the land*

The squatter takes the land subject to all the rights which affect it, such as, for example, easements or restrictive covenants benefiting neighbouring landowners. His title to the land is acquired by operation of law, not by any transfer or conveyance to him. Consequently, he is not a 'purchaser' in the technical sense (see 1.7.3.2), and so cannot take advantage of the rules which invalidate certain third-party rights against purchasers. As a result, he is bound by such rights despite the fact that he has no notice of them or that they have not been protected by registration on the Land Charges Register.

6.3.3.4 *The landlord of the dispossessed tenant*

Completion of the limitation period against a tenant will bar that tenant's rights against the squatter, but does not affect the position of his landlord, who has no right to physical possession of the land (and therefore no claim against the squatter) until the lease comes to an end. Thus, the squatter may complete the limitation period against the tenant and be able to stay on the land for the duration of the lease, but once it comes to an end, the landlord will be able to recover possession from him. It is only if the squatter remains on the land for a further limitation period after the lease has ended that he will be able to bar the landlord's rights and extinguish *his* estate.

When you come to study leases in more detail you will find that one of the ways in which a lease can end is by the tenant surrendering it, that is, giving it up, to his landlord (for a more detailed explanation of this, see 8.5.2.3). On several occasions, a tenant whose right to recover the land from the squatter has been barred under s. 17 has purported to surrender his lease to the landlord, thus bringing forward the landlord's right to seek possession from the squatter. It was however questioned whether such a surrender was valid: if the tenant's estate had been extinguished at the end of the limitation period (in accordance with s. 17), what did he have left to surrender?

This question was considered by the House of Lords in *Fairweather v St Marylebone Property Co. Ltd* [1963] AC 510. A lease had been granted in 1894 for 99 years; the tenant's rights were barred by adverse possession, and he purported to surrender the lease to his landlord in 1959, when it still had a considerable period to run. If the surrender was effective, the landlord could seek possession immediately; if it was not, the squatter would be able to retain the land for another 34 years.

The House of Lords held that the surrender was effective. The tenant's rights and title which were extinguished by the Limitation Act were those which he had against the squatter; the rights and duties which existed between himself and his landlord were unaffected, and he therefore retained an estate which he could surrender. In other words, the tenant's estate was somehow divisible into two portions, only one of which was extinguished by the squatter's adverse possession.

Although the decision of the House of Lords in this case has received a fair amount of criticism (see, for example, Wade [1962] 78 LQR 541), it is generally accepted as representing the current law where the title to the lease is unregistered.

6.3.4 **4 Trant Way**

From what we have said so far, you will have realised that there are a number of factors to be taken into account when deciding whether a claim to recover unregistered land is time-barred. These include: the need for possession to be adverse; the possibility that the person who has been dispossessed is a tenant or is under a disability; and the chance that there are persons entitled to future interests in the land. It should not, therefore, be too readily assumed that occupation of another's land for a simple period of 12 years will necessarily allow one to obtain good title as against any prior owners.

However, unless Nicholas Oregano can show that his uncle was a mental health patient when Sidney Sorrell moved into 4 Trant Way, it would seem that he has little chance of recovering the property. Mr Sorrell's actions seem to be clear evidence of adverse possession commencing 15 years ago. Moving into a house, renovating it and going to the lengths of paying the rates are all actions which are inconsistent with the title of the prior owner.

Mr Sorrell may wish to consider making a voluntary registration of his title. If this is done he will be able in time to improve the registration into a registration with absolute title (see 5.5.3.3(1)) and it will facilitate the conveyancing process should he ever wish to sell the land. Further, as we shall see in the next section, registering his title will reduce very considerably the risk of any future squatter being able to acquire title to the property by adverse possession.

6.4 Adverse possession of registered land under LRA 1925

6.4.1 Application of existing rules to registered land

In Chapter 5 we mentioned that registration of title, when first introduced, was regarded as being part of the conveyancing process and was not expected to affect the underlying substantive law governing the ownership of land (see 5.2.2). In fact of course, the new process introduced the concept of absolute title into a system which until then was based on the relativity of title (6.1.3), and over the years it became clear that there are indeed substantive differences between registered and unregistered land.

These differences became particularly apparent in cases concerning adverse possession, but at the outset the intention was to apply the existing rules to registered land with as little alteration as possible. Thus time ran against the registered proprietor in exactly the same way as it did against the owner of unregistered land, and his right of action against the dispossessor was barred under the Limitation Act 1980 s. 15 at the end of 12 years. It was recognised at the outset that some variation of the existing rules was needed at the end of the limitation period, to take account of the fact that the registered proprietor remained owner of the estate until someone else was registered in his place. Accordingly, LRA 1925 s. 75(1) provided that the proprietor's title was not extinguished at the end of the limitation period (as it would be in unregistered land), but would be held by him in trust for the squatter, who could then apply for registration in his place (s. 75(2)).

Although the possibility of losing title to an adverse possessor undermined the security of a registered title, the device of imposing a trust on the time-barred proprietor seemed for a time to be a reasonable way of adapting the old law of adverse possession to the new system. However, it gradually became obvious that the very real difference between registered and unregistered title required different rules about adverse possession, and this was particularly evident in cases of adverse possession against a tenant.

Since this is now old law, it is sufficient to illustrate the point with one example: the question of whether a time-barred tenant could defeat the adverse possessor by surrendering his lease to the landlord. You will remember that in *Fairweather* v *St Marylebone Property Co. Ltd* [1963] AC 510, a case involving unregistered land, the House of Lords held that a tenant whose title to the lease had been extinguished under the Limitation Act 1980 s. 17 nevertheless retained an estate which he could surrender to the landlord, who could then recover the land from the squatter. In *Central London Commercial Estates Ltd* v *Kato Kagaku Co. Ltd* [1998] 4 All ER 948, a case involving registered land, the limitation period had been completed, but the squatter had not applied to be registered as leasehold proprietor. The dispossessed tenant surrendered its lease to the landlord, and in consequence the Land Registry closed the register of title for the lease. The landlord then sought possession from the squatter, and the court had to decide whether the surrender had brought the lease to an end—as it would have done in the case of unregistered land.

The court held that the surrender, although effective, did not give the landlord the right to possession of the property. It applied the provisions of LRA 1925, s. 75(1), under which the dispossessed owner holds the estate on trust for the squatter. When the tenant surrendered that estate to his landlord:

the trusteeship passed to the freeholder. [The squatter's] beneficial interest [under the trust] was an overriding interest under s. 70 (1)(f) or (g) or both [of the LRA 1925] (at p. 960)

and accordingly bound the landlord.

The judgment of Sedley J emphasised the considerable difference between registered and unregistered land in this context. The effect of s. 75(1) was that the lease was not extinguished, and the squatter was registered as owner of *that* lease, not of his own independently acquired interest:

This is to all appearances a statutory conveyance of the entire leasehold interest (at p. 959).

The squatter took over the benefits and burdens of the lease, and was placed in a landlord–tenant relationship with the freeholder, who, unusually, could not refuse to accept this new tenant. In the judge's view, the House of Lords' analysis in *Fairweather*, which splits the leasehold estate into two tranches, was inapplicable to registered land, in view of the clear provisions of s. 75.

The divergence in this and other decisions in the application of adverse possession rules to registered and unregistered land was an important factor in proposals for change.

6.4.2 Proposals for reform

We have already seen in Chapter 5 that a Joint Working Party of the Law Commission and the Land Registry made major proposals for the reform of the registered title system, most of which have been enacted in LRA 2002. The Consultative Document (*Land Registration for the Twenty-First Century A Consultative Document*, 1998, Law Com No. 254) identified a number of problems in relation to adverse possession of registered land, most of which we have already noted in this chapter.

In outline, the adverse possession rules were developed by reference to unregistered land, where title is relative, and were inappropriate in a system where title is absolute and depends on registration. Adjustments had been made to the basic rules in their application to registered land (most notably in the imposition of the statutory trust by LRA 1925, s. 75(1)), but these were not thoroughly thought through, and appeared inadequate to deal with the sort of questions raised in recent litigation.

Most serious of all, perhaps, was the fact that the very possibility of adverse possession undermined the effectiveness of registered title. The registered proprietor ought to be able to rely on registration as safeguarding his title, but he could in fact lose it to a squatter in substantially the same way as if it were not registered. The fact of registration did nothing to preserve his title for him.

The possibility of adverse possession also affected the purchaser from the registered proprietor. He should be able to buy relying on the state of the register and his own inspection of the land. However, the overriding interests of the squatter under LRA 1925, s. 70(1)(f) could constitute a trap for him, since once the squatter had completed the limitation period, he could leave the land while still retaining his title to it (see 5.5.5.1 and 5.9.2.4(1)). In such a case, the purchaser would have no chance of finding out about the squatter, but would still take subject to his rights, and in fact would find himself holding the property on trust for the squatter.

The working party considered that there was a role for adverse possession in respect of registered land, most notably to facilitate dealings with land which had been abandoned by its owner, and should not be allowed to become derelict and unmarketable.

In addition, three exceptional cases were identified in which the working party considered it would be fair to allow an adverse possessor to acquire title against the wishes of the registered proprietor. These were: where he had acted to his detriment in reliance on some representation by the proprietor that he was entitled to the land (i.e., in an estoppel situation); where he could show some independent right to the land which entitled him to be registered; and where he had entered on the land under some reasonable mistake, as for example about the line of a boundary.

The working party proposed a number of changes to the system then in operation. It recognised that these would increase the differences between the rules for registered and unregistered land, but considered that this was inevitable and that it was time to accept that the two systems involve differences in substantive law as well as in conveyancing procedures. Accordingly the Consultative Document recommended the introduction of

a wholly new substantive system of adverse possession that would apply only to registered land, and [would be] consistent with the principles of title registration (para. 10.2).

This new system is now contained in LRA 2002.

6.5 Adverse possession of registered land under LRA 2002

LRA 2002 introduces a completely new scheme for dealing with adverse possession of registered land, which is set out in ss. 96–98 and Sch. 6 of the Act. Apart from the transitional arrangements (see 6.5.5), the old rules cease to apply: time does not run against the registered proprietor under the Limitation Act 1980, and the provisions for imposing a statutory trust are abolished with the repeal of LRA 1925. However, it is important to remember that, under Sch. 6, para.11, the rules about what constitutes adverse possession (which we considered in 6.2) will continue to apply and it will still be possible for the required period of adverse possession to be begun by one person and completed by another (see Sch. 6, para. 11(2)).

Under the new arrangements, an adverse possessor who is entitled to be registered as proprietor of an estate can obtain that registration either by applying for it or on a court order following his successful defence of a court action.

6.5.1 First application by adverse possessor for registration

Under Sch. 6, the squatter may apply to the registrar to be registered as proprietor of a registered estate if he has been in adverse possession of that estate for ten years (para. 1). In general, he must be able to show possession up to the date of application, but para. 1(2) and (3) permit an application where the applicant has completed the ten-year period and then has been evicted by the owner, subject to a number of conditions which include that the eviction was not in consequence of a court order and that the application is made within six months of the eviction.

On receiving the application, the Registrar must give notice of it to the registered proprietor, and to a number of other people with interests in the property, including the proprietor of any registered charge and, where the estate in question is leasehold, the proprietor of any superior registered estate (i.e., the freehold owner and any intervening landlords). LRR 2003 rr. 194 and 198 provide for the notification of such interests to the registrar, together with contact information.

Where such notice is given and the recipients either do not respond or do not oppose the application, the applicant may be registered as proprietor of the estate (para. 4). Thus in such cases, which will usually arise where the property has been abandoned, the period for acquiring title by adverse possession is reduced from 12 to 10 years.

Where the proprietor or some other recipient of the notice does respond and opposes the application, it will in general be rejected. There are, however, three special cases in which, despite opposition, the adverse possessor may succeed in achieving registration. These cases are set out in Sch. 6, para. 5, and may be summarised as involving: estoppel; some other right to the land; and reasonable mistake as to boundaries. We will consider these in more detail below, but must mention here that it is hoped that claims based on these three matters will be settled by agreement between the parties, and in some cases possibly on terms which include a payment by the applicant or his assumption of some obligation (under an easement or covenant) in respect of the land he acquires (see Consultative Document, para. 10.55). However, if agreement is not possible, the application for registration must be referred to the Adjudicator, an official appointed under the Act (see s. 107 and Sch. 9), who will exercise judicial functions in respect of various applications under the Act, including those by adverse possessors under Sch. 6.

6.5.1.1 *Three special cases*

We will now consider in a little more detail the three situations set out in para. 5 of Sch. 6, which the Joint Working Party described as being circumstances in which it considered that 'the balance of fairness plainly lies with the squatter and he or she should prevail' (Consultative Document 14.3.6).

(1) *Estoppel*

Under para. 5(2) the applicant is entitled to be registered:

> where it would be unconscionable because of an equity by estoppel for the registered proprietor to seek to dispossess the applicant and the circumstances are such that the applicant ought to be registered as proprietor.

As we explained in 1.6.5, an estoppel may arise where one person has made a representation to another (by words or conduct) and the other has acted in reliance on that representation to his detriment (for example, where an owner allows another to build on his land in the mistaken belief that it belongs to him). In such circumstances, the representor is estopped from going back on his representation and the situation is said to give rise to an equity in the claimant (i.e., the right to some relief). It is for the court to decide how that equity is to be satisfied. In the case of applications under Sch. 6, the relief may take the form of registering the applicant as owner of the land in question, but s. 110(4) provides that if the circumstances are not such that he should be registered, the Adjudicator must decide how else the equity is to be satisfied (with, if necessary, an appeal to the High Court—s. 111).

It may seem strange to talk of adverse possession in this context, but the working party explained that if a person with such rights is in possession of the land, it will be easier and cheaper for him to apply for registration under Sch. 6 than it would be to seek to enforce his rights through the courts (*Land Registration for the Twenty-First Century A Conveyancing Revolution*, 2001, Law Com No. 271, para. 14.37—'the Report'). The same considerations apply to the next ground for registration (applicant has some other right to the property).

(2) *Some other right to the land*

Paragraph 5(3) provides for registration:

> where the applicant is for some other reason entitled to be registered as the proprietor of the estate.

This category is intended to cover situations in which the adverse possessor does in fact have some right to the land. The examples given by the working party include situations where he is entitled to the land under the will or intestacy of the deceased proprietor or where a prospective purchaser of the estate is entitled to it under a bare trust, which has arisen because he has paid the full purchase price to the vendor but has not taken a transfer of the legal estate. (the Report, para. 14.43.)

(3) *Reasonable mistake as to boundaries*

Paragraph 5(4) provides for registration of the applicant where the land in question is adjacent to his own, the exact line of the boundary between the two has not been determined and during at least ten years of adverse possession he has reasonably believed that the land belongs to him.

Thus, under the new scheme, a squatter who has been in possession for just ten years will be able to acquire title to the estate by registration if he can make out his claim under one of the three categories noted above.

If those with interests in the property oppose the application, and it is held not to fall within one of the three special cases described above, it will be rejected. This will be so even if the squatter has been in adverse possession for considerably longer than the minimum period of 10 years needed to make the application. The registered proprietor and other interested persons have been alerted to the presence of a squatter on their land and they now have an opportunity to recover possession by legal proceedings.

6.5.2 Further application by adverse possessor for registration

Where an applicant has been unsuccessful under Sch. 6, para. 5 one would expect the registered proprietor or other interested person to take steps to recover the property from him. However, if they do not do so and the applicant remains in possession for a further two years from the date of his application, he may then make a further application under para. 6 for registration. Paragraph 7 provides that in such a case he is entitled to be entered in the register as the new proprietor.

Thus a minimum period of 12 years adverse possession continues to give title to the property, by entitling the possessor to be registered as proprietor, but in circumstances in which the proprietor has been informed of the squatter's presence and given an opportunity to safeguard his title.

6.5.3 Defence to proceedings for possession

So far we have been considering the situation in which the adverse possessor takes the initiative and applies for registration. However, the question of his entitlement to the estate may be raised in a very different way, by the registered proprietor bringing proceedings against him to recover possession. In general terms, s. 98 allows the adverse possessor to raise in his defence those matters on which he could rely in making an application for registration under Sch. 6, and s. 98(5) provides that if he is successful in establishing his defence, the court must order the registrar to register him as proprietor of the estate in question.

6.5.4 What does an adverse possessor obtain on registration?

Under Sch. 6, a successful applicant will be registered as proprietor of the estate of which he has been in adverse possession (paras. 5.1.4.5 and 7). This means that if he has dispossessed a leasehold owner, he will be registered as proprietor of that leasehold estate. Presumably, registration as proprietor of either a freehold or leasehold estate will give the class of title with which the dispossessed proprietor was registered.

6.5.5 **Adverse possessors and purchasers**

We have already considered in Chapter 5 the extent to which the rights acquired or being acquired by adverse possessors can bind the purchaser of registered land under the new Act (see 5.9.2.4(1)). All we will do here is to remind you briefly that under the old system these rights were a separate category of overriding interests (LRA 1925, s. 70(1)(f)) and did not depend on actual occupation. Thus, if the squatter completed the limitation period and then went out of occupation, a purchaser would still be bound by his rights, although he might have no way of discovering them.

Under the new Act, a squatter's rights will have overriding effect on the sale of the registered estate only if he is in actual occupation and can claim that his rights are overriding under Sch. 3, para. 2. The same is true on first registration (Sch. 1, para. 2), but with the additional provision in s. 11(4)(c) that the first registered proprietor will also be subject to any interests acquired under the Limitation Act of which he has notice.

In keeping with the general scheme of the Act, existing rights are preserved by the transitional arrangements, although in some cases for a limited period only (Sch. 12, paras. 7, 11 and 18).

6.6 **Adverse possession and HRA 1998**

As we mentioned earlier (6.1.6), acquisition of title by adverse possession could be said to be incompatible with the provisions of the Human Rights Act 1998. In the case of unregistered land, completion of the necessary period extinguishes the owner's title to the land, without any reference to a court (Limitation Act 1980, s. 17). The owner is deprived of his property without compensation, arguably in breach of both Art. 1 of the First Protocol (protection of property) and Art. 6 (right to a fair trial). In dealing with a case of adverse possession, the court is applying statutory rules, and so under ss. 3 and 4 of HRA 1998 is required to give effect to them in a way which is compatible with Convention rights. If it is unable to do so, the court may make a declaration of incompatibility under s. 4. As a result, it seems that dispossessed owners may seek to rely on the Act even where no public authority is involved in the case.

Human rights issues were raised in *J. A. Pye (Oxford) Ltd* v *Graham*, which we have already considered earlier in this chapter. They were dealt with fairly briefly in the House of Lords ([2003] 1 AC 419), where it was conceded that HRA 1998 had no retrospective effect and so did not apply to this case. The paper owner, Pye, submitted that under common law principles of construction which pre-date the Act the court should seek to apply the law so as to make it compatible with the European Convention, but this principle applies only in cases of ambiguity and uncertainty, and their lordships considered that there was no ambiguity in the relevant provisions of the Limitation Act 1980.

Although the substance of the human rights argument was not considered by the House of Lords, it had been addressed by the Court of Appeal ([2001] Ch 804), which considered the case at a time when there was still some uncertainty about the possible retrospective effect of the 1998 Act. Although the court's judgment is of course overruled by the House of Lords decision, it may be of interest to note the views of the lower court on this aspect of the case.

The Court of Appeal dealt relatively briefly with the points raised on HRA 1998, refusing to express an opinion on the argument put to it that s. 6, which makes it unlawful for public authorities including courts to act in a way incompatible with a Convention right, required the court to give effect of such rights in proceedings between private individuals (the 'horizontal effect' argument—see 1.10). However, the court *was* willing to express views on the argument based on s. 3 (interpretation of legislation in a way which is compatible with Convention rights), although the remarks made were only *obiter dicta* (since as we saw at 6.2.5 the court's decision in favour of Pye was based on its finding that the Grahams had not established the necessary intention to possess). The court considered that Art.1 of the First Protocol did not impinge on the provisions of the Limitation Act. In the words of Mummery LJ (at p. 821), those provisions:

deprive a person of his right of access to the courts for the purpose of recovering property if he has delayed the institution of his legal proceedings for 12 years . . . The extinction of the title of the [owner] in those circumstances is not a deprivation of possessions or a confiscatory measure for which payment of compensation would be appropriate: it is simply a logical and pragmatic consequence of the barring of his right to bring an action after the expiration of the limitation period.

Further, even if Art. 1 did impinge on the relevant provisions of the Act, the judge considered that the provisions were:

conditions provided for by law and . . . 'in the public interest' within the meaning of Art. 1. Such conditions are reasonably required to avoid the real risk of injustice in the adjudication of stale claims, to ensure certainty of title and to promote social stability by the protection of the established and peaceable possession of property from the resurrection of old claims. The conditions provided in the 1980 Act are not disproportionate; the period allowed for the bringing of proceedings is reasonable; the conditions are not discriminatory; and they are not impossible or so excessively difficult to comply with as to render ineffective the exercise of the legal right of a person who is entitled to the peaceful enjoyment of his possessions to recover them from another person who is alleged to have wrongfully deprived him of them (p. 822).

Agreeing with Mummery LJ, Keane LJ commented that decisions of the European Court of Human Rights show that limitation periods on the bringing of legal proceedings are not in principle incompatible with the Convention, and that there are even limitation provisions for bringing cases before that court.

Thus it seems that the Court of Appeal had little doubt that the principles of adverse possession were 'Convention-proof'. However a different view of the matter is to be found in the words of Neuberger J, who at first instance in this case ([2000] Ch 676 at 710) described the supposed justification for adverse possession in no uncertain terms:

A frequent justification for limitation periods generally is that people should not be able to sit on their rights indefinitely . . . However, if as in the present case the owner of land has no immediate use for it and is content to let another person trespass on the land for the time being, it is hard to see what principle of justice entitles the trespasser to acquire the land for nothing from the owner simply because he has been permitted to remain there for 12 years. To say that in such circumstances the owner who has sat on his rights should therefore be deprived of his land appears to me to be illogical and disproportionate. Illogical because the only reason that the owner can be said to have sat on his rights is because of the existence of the 12-year limitation period in the first place; if no limitation period existed he would be entitled to claim possession whenever he actually wanted the land ... disproportionate because, particularly in a climate of increasing awareness of human rights including the right to enjoy one's own property, it does seem draconian to the owner and a windfall to the squatter that, just because the owner has taken no steps to evict a squatter for 12 years, the owner should lose ... land to the squatter with no compensation whatsoever.

It seems that these views, rather than those of the Court of Appeal, were shared by at least some members of the House of Lords [2003] 1 AC 419, Lord Bingham saying (at 426) that he would echo the misgivings expressed by Neuberger J, and Lord Hope speaking of the 'apparent injustice of the result' (at p. 445). Their Lordships welcomed the changes which LRA 2002 makes to the adverse possession of registered land (with warnings being given to those interested in the property, provision for decision by a judicial process and the possible payment of compensation), and it may be that these improvements will be sufficient to withstand any challenge under HRA 1998. Nevertheless the old rules will continue to operate in respect of unregistered land, and later courts may find it difficult to agree with the Court of Appeal that such rules are not incompatible with the Convention. However, it is interesting to see that the Court of Appeal's view is shared by at least one Law Lord: see *Harrow LBC* v *Qazi* [2003] 3 WLR 792 (a case not involving adverse possession) in which Lord Scott observed (at p. 831) that under HRA 1998:

[t]he divesting operation of the statutes of limitation would be justifiable as being in the public interest . . . .

FURTHER READING

Dockray, 'Why Do We Need Adverse Possession?' [1985] Conv 273.

Gray and Gray, *Elements of Land Law*, 3rd edn., Butterworths, 2001, pp. 241–5 (the rationale of acquisition by adverse possession).

Megarry and Wade, *The Law of Real Property*, 6th edn., Sweet & Maxwell, 2000, pp. 86–94 (ownership, possession and title).

Wade, *Landlord, Tenant and Squatter* (1962) 78 LQR 541.

Proposals for reform

Land Registration for the Twenty-First Century A Consultative Document, 1998, Law Com No. 254, Part X (in particular, 10.1–10.19, and 10.43–10.64).

Land Registration for the Twenty-First Century A Conveyancing Revolution, 2001, Law Com No. 271, Part XIV (in particular, 14.1–14.8—summary of changes).

Human Rights implications

Dixon, 'Bringing Home Another's Rights' [2001] 65 Conv 276.

Rook, *Property Law and Human Rights*, Blackstone Press, 2001, pp. 205–8.

PART III

Legal estates

Introduction

Having considered the general background to the modern law relating to land, we will examine in this Part the nature of the two legal estates.

You will recall that, under the provisions of LPA 1925, s. 1(1), there are two legal estates in land:

(a) the fee simple absolute in possession—the freehold estate;

(b) the term of years absolute—the leasehold estate.

The fee simple estate, or freehold, is the larger of the two estates, being capable of lasting indefinitely, and it underpins everything else that we deal with in this book. Leasehold estates, for example, are created out of the freehold (or out of a superior lease which is itself derived directly or indirectly from the freehold) and thus derive their validity from the existence of the fee simple.

In view of the importance of the freehold estate, you may find it rather strange that our chapter on it (Chapter 7) is relatively short, but you should remember that other aspects of the estate are dealt with throughout the book—for example in relation to trusts and co-ownership. Further material on the nature of the estate will be found in Chapter 25, where we outline the rights which a freehold owner has over his land.

By contrast with the freehold estate, you will find that, because of the additional complexities involved in the landlord and tenant relationship, we have to explain rather more detailed rules in relation to the leasehold estate, and so are devoting three chapters to this topic. In Chapter 8 we consider the nature and characteristics of a lease, and the ways in which it is created and brought to an end. In Chapter 9 we deal with the rights and duties of the landlord and tenant who are the parties to the lease and in Chapter 10 discuss the remedies available to one party when the other is in breach of duty.

In Chapter 11 we will tell you about the new form of landholding, called 'commonhold', which is introduced by the Commonhold and Leasehold Reform Act 2002.

7

The freehold estate

7.1 Introduction

7.1.1 **5 Trant Way**

The estate in fee simple in 5 Trant Way (i.e., the freehold) is owned by David Derby. He has decided to give the estate to one of his three nephews and is considering the following three possible dispositions:

(a) giving the estate to his nephew Eric 'on condition that he does not marry';
(b) giving the estate to his nephew Frank 'until he finds full-time employment' (Frank is at present a student);
(c) giving the estate to his friend George for life and then to his nephew Hal for life, 'provided that Hal marries before George dies'.

It is necessary to consider whether each of these three possible gifts would vest in the nephew or friend concerned a legal fee simple absolute in possession, or whether the gift would create an interest in land which is less than a legal estate.

As we mentioned briefly in Chapter 1, the phrase 'fee simple absolute in possession' imposes a series of requirements, all of which must be satisfied if the estate is to qualify as a legal one. We will now look at these requirements in more detail, and consider whether David's proposed gifts would satisfy them.

7.2 **Fee simple**

We have already explained (at 1.2.1) that a fee simple used to be an estate in land which was inheritable by the heirs general of its owner. This distinguished the fee simple from the life estate (which was not inheritable) and the fee tail (which was inheritable only by a restricted class of heirs, e.g., 'heirs of the body male'). When the rules of intestate succession were changed in 1925, the concept of 'the heir' became in the main obsolete, and it was no longer correct to define the fee simple as being inherited by the general heirs. It is, however, still true that the fee simple is an estate which lasts indefinitely, so long as there is anyone entitled to take the property under the will or on the intestacy of the previous owner.

The other two freehold estates which used to exist (the life estate and the fee tail) do not come within the definition of legal estates in LPA 1925, s. 1(1), and, since they are not on the list of legal interests in s. 1(2), they therefore took effect after 1925 as equitable interests under s. 1(3). This meant that the legal fee simple had to be held on trust to give effect to such interests. As we have already mentioned (1.2.4.1), it is no longer possible to create a new entailed interest.

7.3 Absolute

The word 'absolute' in s. 1(1) indicates that there must be no provision in the grant of the fee simple whereby it might end prematurely while there is still someone qualified to take it. Fees which are subject to such provisions are known as 'modified' fees, and can arise in two forms: (a) conditional interests, and (b) determinable interests. The disposition of 5 Trant Way to Eric Derby 'on condition that he does not marry' would be a conditional interest, whilst a disposition of the property to Frank Derby 'until he finds full-time employment' would be a determinable interest.

7.3.1 Conditional interests

A conditional interest arises where a fee simple is granted subject to a limitation which provides that the grantor will be able to re-enter the property at some date in the future on the occurrence (or non-occurrence) of specified events. In such a case the grantor appears initially to be giving a fee simple absolute, but then reserves the right to recover the land (right of re-entry). This type of arrangement is said to be an interest subject to a condition subsequent. Such interests do not comply with the requirements of LPA 1925, s. 1(1), and so, under the terms of that statute, could not amount to legal estates.

However, this rule gave rise to immediate problems when the 1925 legislation came into force, because many estates were subject to rentcharges, which usually provided that the owner of the rentcharge would be entitled to re-enter the land if the payments secured by the rentcharge were not made. In certain parts of the country (e.g., Bristol and Manchester) most of the fee simple estates were then subject to rentcharges, and the effect of s. 1(1) was to turn all these estates into equitable interests, since they were all subject to a right of re-entry on occurrence of a specified condition. As a result, the Law of Property (Amendment) Act 1926 was passed, and the Schedule to that Act amended LPA 1925, s. 7(1), to read:

[A] fee simple subject to a legal or equitable right of entry or re-entry is for the purposes of this Act a fee simple absolute.

This wording was, however, wider than was necessary to deal solely with the problem caused by rentcharges and produced the result that all fees simple subject to a right of re-entry became legal estates. Thus a conditional fee simple will be a legal estate within the meaning of LPA 1925, s. 1(1). Therefore, if 5 Trant Way is given to Eric Derby in fee simple on condition that 'he does not marry', Eric will receive a legal estate. The form of words used may, however, give rise to objections on the grounds of public policy, and in addition could possibly be said to infringe Eric's right to respect for private and family life under the Human Rights Act 1998 (see 7.5.1).

7.3.2 **Determinable interests**

A determinable fee is one which according to its terms will last only until a specified event occurs, or does not occur. Thus a grant of the fee simple in 5 Trant Way to Frank Derby 'until he finds full-time employment' is a determinable fee. The fee lasts only until Frank gets a job. The fee would still be determinable even if it is very unlikely that the specified event will ever occur, because from the outset the period of the interest has been cut down. Such interests are not within LPA 1925, s. 1(1), and are not saved by s. 7(1) as amended. Since they are not included in the list of legal interests in s. 1(2), they take effect as equitable interests under s. 1(3). The grantor retains an interest in the land, known as the 'possibility of reverter', and when the determining event occurs the property reverts automatically to him.

7.3.3 **Differences between conditional and determinable fees**

Whether a grant creates a conditional fee or a determinable fee may well be an accident of wording, and the grantor may not intend to create one rather than the other. The same arrangement can often be expressed in either way. Thus a grant 'to A on condition that he does not become a lawyer' is a conditional fee and creates a legal estate, subject to a right of re-entry; whilst a grant 'to A until he becomes a lawyer' is a determinable fee, which can only be an equitable interest. Because of this many students (and even courts, see *Re Moore* (1888) 39 ChD 116) find it difficult to distinguish between the two classes of right. The following lists of expressions which have been categorised as creating either conditional or determinable fees may help in identifying the nature of a particular grant:

CONDITIONAL	DETERMINABLE
'on condition that . . .'	'until . . .'
'providing that . . .'	'as long as . . .'
'but if . . .'	'for the duration of . . .'
	'while'

However, although the distinction between the two types of fee appears to be a matter of form, rather than of substance, the difference can be of considerable importance to the grantee. We have already seen that a conditional fee takes effect as a legal estate, while a determinable fee can exist only as an equitable interest. A further difference will be experienced if the specified event occurs, for in the case of the determinable fee the interest will immediately come to an end and the grantee has no further right to the land. By contrast, the fee on condition subsequent will in fact continue until the grantor or his successor exercises his right of re-entry, and so the grantor could find himself entitled to remain on the land almost indefinitely.

Thus a distinction which might seem to the grantor to be little more than a matter of style can have far-reaching consequences for the grantee and, as Parker

MR said in *Re King's Trusts* (1892) 29 LR Ir 401 at 410, the difference between the two produces a rule which is 'little short of disgraceful to our jurisprudence'.

7.3.4 **Reverter to transferor on failure to apply for first registration**

We saw in 5.4.1.3 that where a transfer triggers a requirement of first registration, the estate will revert to the transferor if the transferee fails to apply for registration within the prescribed period. Where the estate in question is a fee simple, the possibility that this might happen could give rise to doubts as to whether it is a fee simple *absolute*, and accordingly LRA 2002, s. 7 (4) provides that the possibility of such reverter is to be disregarded for the purposes of determining whether a fee simple is a fee simple absolute.

7.4 **In possession**

7.4.1 **Future interests**

Land owners may wish to create future interests in their property, that is, interests which will come into existence on the happening of some future event such as the performance of a condition precedent (i.e., a condition which has to be ful-filled before the grantee can enjoy the property). An illustration of such a condi-tion is provided by the grant of 5 Trant Way to David Derby's friend George 'for life', and then to his nephew Hal for life, 'provided that Hal marries before George dies'.

If the gift was made in these terms, Hal would, at the outset, have no interest in the property, but merely a chance of acquiring one in the future. Rather confus-ingly, he is said to have a 'contingent', or 'conditional', interest, but in fact no interest in the land will arise until the condition is met. Should Hal marry before George's death, he will have satisfied the condition and will then have a future interest in the property; that is, an interest entitling him to possession of the house at some time in the future. For two reasons, this interest would not be capable of being a legal estate: not only is it for life, but it also takes effect in the future, and so does not satisfy the requirement of LPA 1925, s. 1(1), that to be legal an estate must take effect in possession. Thus, under the Act, a future interest, even in fee simple, cannot be legal and takes effect only in equity.

7.4.2 **Remainders and reversions**

We must now mention two technical terms used to describe future interests: 'remainders' and 'reversions'.

A 'reversion' arises where a grantor gives away an estate, or series of estates, which will last for a shorter time than his own estate. The gifts to George and Hal are an example of this, for David Derby has a fee simple, which is capable of lasting for ever, and he would have given away, at the most, only two life interests. When they came to an end, the property would *revert* to Mr Derby, or, if he was dead, would form part of his estate and devolve according to the terms of his will, or by the rules of intestate succession. The grantor therefore has a future right to the property from the date of the gift, and that future right is called a 'reversion'.

If, however, the grantor were to give away his full estate to a series of people, he will have kept no reversion in the property and the future interests he has created will be called 'remainders'. Thus, if Mr Derby were to provide that, after George and Hal have died, the property should belong in fee simple to Ian, the grantor will have no reversion, and Hal and Ian would both be said to have remainders. George would have an interest in possession, and would be entitled to enjoy the property immediately the gift took effect.

We have seen that the full fee simple absolute in possession is the only freehold estate which can exist in law, and that all the other dispositions which David Derby wants to make (such as a life interest, a determinable fee simple and a future interest) can take effect only in equity. In order to give effect to his wishes, therefore, it would be necessary to make use of a trust, so that the legal fee simple would be held by trustees and Mr Derby's nephews and friend would be entitled to equitable interests for the period and on the conditions stated in the grant (see further Part IV).

7.5 Intervention of public policy

It should not be thought from what has gone before that an estate owner is entitled to grant estates or interests subject to any limitations that he wishes. It is clear that the courts will intervene in cases in which a limitation is considered to be contrary to public policy. Thus in general a grant of an estate 'on condition that A does not marry' will be regarded as being contrary to public policy and the grant will take effect absolutely and free of the objectionable condition (*Kelly* v *Monck* (1795) 3 Ridg Parl Rep 205). It is permissible, however, to make a provision the purpose of which is simply to provide for someone until he or she marries, rather than to prevent marriage (*Jones* v *Jones* (1876) 1 QBD 279). Thus normally an estate which is determinable on marriage is not so objectionable. David Derby, therefore, would be well-advised to reconsider the proposed grant to his nephew Eric, for the present wording could result in a fee simple absolute free from condition.

It should also be noted that there are other cases in which public policy will intervene, e.g., where a disposition might have the effect of discouraging the religious education of a child (*Re Borwick* [1933] Ch 657) or preventing an adult taking public office or being employed in the armed services (*Re Edgar* [1939] 1 All ER 635; *Re Beard* [1908] 1 Ch 383). Obviously, however, the views expressed by the courts on such clauses are likely to vary with the times.

One class of conditions or determining events to which the courts have always taken strong exception consists of provisions by which the grantor tries to restrict the power of the recipient to dispose of the property freely. Ever since the statute *Quia Emptores* in 1290 it has been a principle of the law that generally an estate owner should have a free and unfettered power to alienate his property. Across the centuries the courts have continued to enforce this principle. Thus in *Hood* v *Oglander* (1865) 34 Beav 513 at p. 522 it was said that a condition preventing alienation at any time would be void. The courts will, however, tolerate some restrictions on disposal of an estate which fall short of an absolute bar and indeed in some cases have been remarkably tolerant in dealing with restrictions which prevent disposal outside a particular family. Thus in *Re Macleay* (1875) LR 20 Eq 186 a disposition to someone 'on condition that he never sells it out of the family' was upheld. One cannot guarantee, however, that modern courts would be so generous and in any event this decision was rather more limited in its scope than may first appear: the recipient alone was bound by the condition, it did not bind anyone to whom he transferred the estate, and it only prevented a *sale* outside the family, the recipient could *give* the property to anyone. Despite this limited approval given to such a restriction upon disposal, it is best to avoid such arrangements for fear that they may be struck down, leaving the estate owner with a free power to alienate the property. However, as we shall see in Part IV, it may be possible under the Trusts of Land and Appointment of Trustees Act 1996 to create a trust for the specific purpose of retaining land, and it is certainly possible to provide that trust property cannot be alienated without the consent of specified persons.

7.5.1 Implications of Human Rights Act 1998

It is suggested in robust terms in Gray and Gray at p. 296 that the Human Rights Act may be effective in striking down objectionable limitations:

Although, like the determinable fee simple, the conditional fee has spawned a rich case law, much of the common law elaboration of this form of estate ownership has now been rendered embarrassingly redundant by the advent of the Human Rights Act 1998. The capacity for invidious discrimination so freely offered to the eccentric testator is certain, in many instances, to fall foul of the horizontal effect likely to be accorded to various Convention-based guarantees of individual freedom.

It is certainly possible to imagine limitations which might infringe the prohibition of discrimination (Art. 14) or violate rights such as those to respect for private and family life (Art. 8) or to freedom of conscience and religion (Art. 9), but as we noted in Chapter 1 it still remains to be seen whether the courts will interpret the Act as having horizontal effect.

FURTHER READING

Megarry and Wade, *The Law of Real Property*, 6th edn., Sweet & Maxwell, 2000, pp. 64–72 (types of fee simple).

Smith, *Property Law*, 4th edn., Longman, 2003, pp. 35–43 (freehold estates).

8

The leasehold estate

8.1 Introduction

8.1.1 2 Trant Way

You will recall, from Chapter 1, that 2 Trant Way is for sale 'leasehold'. The current fee simple owner of No. 2 is Fingall Forest, who is a widower and who has no children. He has lived there for many years, and title to the property is still unregistered. Mr Forest has decided that the house is too large for his needs and he has had it divided into three sections: a flat, consisting of the second floor of the property, in which he lives; the ground and first-floor maisonette, which is now for sale 'leasehold' (a 99-year lease); and the basement which Mr Forest has let on a weekly tenancy to an old friend, Gerald Gruyère, at a rent of £100 a week. Mr Forest's estate agent has now found a prospective purchaser for the maisonette, Harry Harding.

These two transactions, the sale of the maisonette on a 99-year lease, and the letting of the basement on a weekly tenancy seem at first glance to have very little in common. However, we shall see that although these rights to use property appear very different from each other, they both fall into the category of leases (or tenancies); that is to say, both are 'terms of years absolute'. We should mention here that in modern use the terms 'lease' and 'tenancy' are interchangeable, although there is a tendency to use the word 'tenancies' when speaking of periodic (weekly or monthly) arrangements.

8.1.2 Fixed-term and periodic tenancies

The lease of the maisonette for 99 years is an example of a lease for a *fixed term*, that is, for one period which can last for weeks, months or years, as the parties agree. At the end of the agreed period, the lease ends automatically, without either side having to give the other notice. By contrast, the letting of the basement on a weekly tenancy is an example of a *periodic tenancy*. It is not granted for a fixed number of weeks, but runs on indefinitely, from week to week, until one of the parties does not want to continue the arrangement, and therefore gives notice to the other. In a similar way, tenancies can run on from month to month, quarter to quarter or year to year, being known as monthly, quarterly or yearly tenancies respectively.

Leases for a fixed term and periodic tenancies are the types of lease most frequently encountered. We will concentrate on these at first in this chapter, and will leave until later any consideration of other forms, such as tenancies at will and at sufferance, tenancies by estoppel and concurrent leases (for all of which, see 8.10).

8.1.3 Term of years absolute

In general, a legal lease creates a legal estate, which itself is called a 'lease' or, more technically, a 'term of years absolute'. It appears, however, from the House of Lords' decision in *Bruton* v *London & Quadrant Housing Association* [2001] 1 AC 406 that it is possible for a lease to create the contractual relationship of land-lord and tenant between the parties, without giving an estate in land to the tenant. The House of Lords held that this had happened in the special circumstances of *Bruton*, and we will consider this decision and its consequences in more detail later (see 19.2.4.4). We must emphasise here though that the situation in *Bruton* was unusual, and that, in general, a tenant taking under a legal lease will hold a legal estate.

As we have already mentioned, the technical name for this estate is 'term of years absolute'. This may seem less strange at first sight than that used to describe the freehold estate (fee simple absolute in possession), but nonetheless it is necessary to consider carefully the terminology used.

8.1.3.1 *The 'term'*

The Law of Property Act 1925 requires that the leasehold estate should be for 'a term', that is, for a fixed period rather than for an indefinite one. Thus in *Lace* v *Chantler* [1944] KB 368, it was held that a lease 'for the duration of the war' was not a legal estate because it was not for a fixed term, since at the time that the lease was granted the exact period for which it would continue to exist could not be known until it had ended. A lease 'for 99 years', or other specified period, is clearly 'a term' which satisfies the requirements of LPA 1925, s. 1(1); but is this true of a periodic tenancy? One would imagine that a periodic tenancy which runs on indefinitely from one period to another could not be an estate in land, because when it commences one does not know how long it will last. However, the law does regard such a tenancy as satisfying the requirement of a fixed term, because it is regarded as being a lease for a period (fixed term), followed by another lease for that period, and so on until the lease is correctly terminated. As Lord Templeman explained in *Prudential Assurance Co. Ltd* v *London Residuary Body* [1992] 2 AC 386 at p. 394:

A tenancy from year to year is saved from being uncertain because each party has power by notice to determine at the end of any year. The term continues until determined as if both parties made a new agreement at the end of each year for a new term for the ensuing year.

Therefore, even the tenant with a periodic tenancy does have a lease for a fixed term, which is thus capable of being a legal estate.

8.1.3.2 *'Of years'*

It is clear also that a 99-year lease is a term *of years* but a periodic tenancy will be for a period of a year, or frequently less than a year. Nonetheless the periodic tenancy will still qualify as a legal estate, as would a lease for, say, a fixed period of three months, because LPA 1925, s. 205(1)(xxvii), provides that 'the expression "term of years" includes a term for less than a year, or for a year or years and a fraction of a year or from year to year'. Therefore, all that is necessary is a fixed period, and accordingly it is possible to grant a lease for a very short period (e.g., two days) even though this is not likely to be common.

In *Smallwood* v *Sheppards* [1895] 2 QB 627 it was held that a legal lease could be created for a period of three successive bank holidays, that is, for three separate days. More recently, it has been accepted that a time-sharing arrangement, giving the right to use a holiday cottage for one week a year over an 80-year period, can amount to a legal lease for 'a single discontinuous period' (*Cottage Holiday Associates Ltd* v *Customs and Excise Commissioners* [1983] 1 QB 735).

8.1.3.3 *'Absolute'*

The inclusion of this word in the definition of the leasehold estate causes some difficulty. When used to describe the fee simple it means, as we have seen in Chapter 7, that the estate is not liable to end prematurely, before the full period is up. However, leases often provide for determination before the term has run its full course; for example, as we shall see, it is common practice to provide that the landlord may forfeit the lease for any breach of covenant by the tenant. Indeed some long leases even contain provisions allowing either the landlord or tenant, or both, the right to terminate the lease early on notice. Such clauses are often called 'break clauses'. However, there has never been any suggestion that such a provision prevents the lease taking effect as a legal estate, even though that lease cannot be described as absolute in the same sense as the fee simple. It is in fact difficult to explain the use of the word 'absolute' in this context, and it may be instructive to note the view expressed by Megarry and Wade at p. 114, that, 'This word is here used in no intelligible sense'.

8.1.3.4 *No requirement for the leasehold estate to be 'in possession'*

One further difference between the statutory definitions of the two legal estates may be noted here. We have seen already in Chapter 7 that, in order to be legal, a fee simple absolute must take effect 'in possession', and that a future interest cannot be a legal estate. There is no similar provision in LPA 1925, s. 1(1) with regard to leases and accordingly leases may be granted to take effect in the future and still have the status of legal estates.

Leases to start in the future

A lease granting a term which does not start immediately but at some time in the future is called a 'reversionary lease'. In order to prevent the creation of such interests very far into the future, LPA 1925, s. 149(3), provides that any lease expressed to commence more than 21 years from the date of the instrument which creates it is to be void. This rule does not apply to agreements which were made before 1926.

Similarly, a contract to grant a lease, which, when granted, will take effect more than 21 years from the date of the grant, is also void. On this latter point, it is important to note that the time-limit specified in s. 149(3) still relates to the period between the grant of the lease and the commencement of the term; the section does not impose any restriction on the length of time which may elapse between entering into the contract to grant a lease and actually making the grant. Thus it is possible, and, indeed, standard practice, for a landlord to covenant that he will, if the tenant wishes, grant him a further term when the present lease ends (*option for renewal*). Any such option can be enforced at the end of the lease, however long the original term may be. It should be noted, however, that a contract to renew a lease for over 60 years after the termination of a current lease is void if the agreement was made after 1925 (Law of Property Act 1922, Sch. 15, para. 7).

8.2 Basic requirements for a lease

8.2.1 Definition of a lease

The lease has been defined (see *Woodfall's Law of Landlord and Tenant*, Sweet & Maxwell, Release 48, April 2001, para. 1.003) as, 'the grant of a right to the exclusive possession of land for a determinate term less than that which the grantor has himself in the land'. This definition identifies three essential elements:

(a) exclusive possession,

(b) determinate term,

(c) term less than that of the grantor.

8.2.2 Exclusive possession

Exclusive possession is an essential ingredient of a lease; without exclusive possession there can be no lease. Exclusive possession is the right to use premises to the exclusion of all others, including the landlord himself. In the words of Lord Templeman in *Street* v *Mountford* [1985] AC 809 at p. 816:

The tenant possessing exclusive possession is able to exercise the rights of an owner of land, which is in the real sense his land albeit temporarily and subject to certain restrictions. A tenant armed with exclusive possession can keep out strangers and keep out the landlord.

If the occupier has no right to exclusive possession of the premises then his right to use the premises cannot amount to a lease, but may be some lesser right, such as a licence or possibly an easement. However, the fact that a person has been given exclusive possession is not conclusive proof that he has a lease, for it is also possible to have a licence, or certain other rights in land, with exclusive possession. This point is also emphasised by Lord Templeman in *Street* v *Mountford* (at p. 818):

There can be no tenancy unless the occupier enjoys exclusive possession; but an occupier who enjoys exclusive possession is not necessarily a tenant. He may be owner in fee simple, a trespasser, a mortgagee in possession, an object of charity or a service occupier. To constitute a tenancy the occupier must be granted exclusive possession for a fixed or periodic term certain in consideration of a premium or periodical payments.

However, this case also emphasises that, normally, where there is exclusive possession, the courts will regard the arrangement as a lease.

It should be noted that although exclusive possession normally gives the tenant the right to exclude everyone else, including the landlord, from the premises, the lease may reserve the right for the landlord to enter the premises on certain occasions (e.g., to inspect the state of repair of the property). Such a right must be exercised at reasonable hours and in a reasonable manner and does not prevent the tenant having exclusive possession, though a right for the landlord to come and go as he pleased without the tenant's permission would have this effect. Thus in *Appah* v *Parncliffe Investments Ltd* [1964] 1 WLR 1064, in which the 'landlord' had reserved the right to come into the premises as and when he chose in order to empty meters and change linen, the arrangement was held to be a licence, since the occupier did not have exclusive possession.

These points may be summarised by saying that, for a lease to exist, the tenant must have exclusive possession, but exclusive possession is not in itself conclusive evidence of the existence of a lease. We shall return to this point in Chapter 19, when we look in more detail at the distinction between leases and licences.

8.2.3 **Determinate term**

We have already seen that a lease must be granted for a fixed period, and that both fixed-term and periodic tenancies satisfy this test. In addition the commencement of the period must also be certain. Normally, if no mention is made in the agreement, it will be deemed to start immediately (*Furness* v *Bond* (1888) 4 TLR 457). If, however, one has only an agreement for a future lease, it will be void unless it is clear at what date the lease is to start, either from an express term in the contract or by inference (*Harvey* v *Pratt* [1965] 1 WLR 1025).

8.2.3.1 *Attempts to avoid requirement of a fixed period*

It is not infrequently the case that a landlord will nonetheless wish to permit the use of his property for an uncertain period. This was the position with wartime lettings, where leases were made 'for the duration of the war', but were held to be invalid because they did not create a term for a certain period (*Lace* v *Chantler* [1944] KB 368). More recent cases have involved owners who intend to redevelop their land at some future date, and so want to avoid creating leases for fixed periods which might delay them when they are ready to start work. For a time it was thought that this could be achieved by creating a periodic tenancy with a provision that the landlord would not give notice to quit until he was ready to redevelop the land. This gave the tenant some measure of security, but enabled the landlord to regain possession when needed.

Such a restriction on the landlord's right to give notice was however held to be invalid by the House of Lords in *Prudential Assurance Co. Ltd* v *London Residuary Body* [1992] 2 AC 386. In Lord Templeman's words (at p. 394):

A [periodic] tenancy . . . is saved from being uncertain because each person has power by notice to determine at the end of any [period].

On this view, restrictions on the power to give notice result in uncertainty as to how long the periodic tenancy will continue and thus fall foul of the rule in *Lace* v *Chantler*. The Court of Appeal, in earlier decisions upholding restrictions on the power to give notice (*Re Midland Railway Co.'s Agreement* [1971] 1 Ch 725, and *Ashburn Anstalt* v *Arnold* [1989] 1 Ch 1) had taken the view that *Lace* v *Chantler* did not apply to periodic tenancies, but the House of Lords in *Prudential Assurance* overruled these decisions and emphasised that the principle of *Lace v Chantler* applies to all leases and tenancy agreements. (For a further consideration of the House of Lords' decision, see 8.5.2.2(4)).

There are, nevertheless, other ways of satisfying the parties' wish to avoid being held to a fixed period. A lease may be granted for a certain term but with a provision for earlier determination on the occurrence of a certain event. Thus during the war a lease could have been granted for 10 years with a provision for determination if the war ended earlier, and this would satisfy the rule in *Lace v Chantler*. It is also acceptable for a periodic tenancy to restrict the landlord's right to give notice, unless for a specified purpose, during a prescribed period (*Breams Property Investment Co. v Stroulger* [1948] 2 KB 1: quarterly tenancy in which the landlords agreed not to give notice for three years, unless premises were required for their own occupation and use). Other ways of giving possession for an indefinite period are by the creation of an express tenancy at will as in *Manfield & Sons Ltd v Botchin* [1970] 2 QB 612, or by the use of a contractual licence, which we will explain in Chapter 19.

8.2.3.2 *Lease for life or until marriage*

The requirement that the maximum duration of the lease must be certain means that the grant of a lease 'for T's life' or 'until T marries' would not under the general rules be capable of amounting to a legal estate. However, it used to be not uncommon for such leases to be granted and therefore the draftsmen of the property legislation provided a saving provision for such cases. Accordingly, by virtue of LPA 1925, s. 149(6), a lease for life, or until marriage, which has been granted at a rent or in consideration of a fine (premium) will be converted automatically into a fixed term of 90 years determinable on the tenant's death, or marriage. Such a fixed term is, of course, a legal estate within the meaning of s. 1(1). *Skipton Building Society v Clayton* (1993) 66 P&CR 223 provides an example of the effects of s. 149(6). The section applies to such leases even if they were created before 1926. The term, it should be noted, does not terminate automatically on the death or marriage of the tenant. It terminates if thereafter either party to the agreement (including the tenant's personal representatives in the case of death) serves on the other one month's notice, expiring on a quarter day.

A lease comes within the section even if it is granted 'to T for the lifetime of X', so the life specified need not be that of the tenant but might be that of a third party, or of the landlord himself. The section applies to all cases of leases determinable on marriage or death (provided they are granted for value), so even if L, in an attempt to 'get it right', grants T a lease for '100 years determinable on T's earlier death' this will also be converted into a term of 90 years determinable on death. Similarly, a lease for '25 years if T remains a spinster' will also be converted into a lease for 90 years determinable on T's earlier marriage.

Where a lease for life or until marriage is granted without rent or fine, the lease takes effect only in equity. In the case of such leases granted before 1 January 1997 (the commencement date of the Trusts of Land and Appointment of Trustees Act 1996), the tenant may have special powers under the Settled Land Act 1925; if granted after that date, the lease will take effect under a trust of land, as explained in Chapter 13.

8.2.4 **Term less than that of the grantor**

An owner in fee simple is able to grant a lease of his property for any term because the fee simple is itself effectively perpetual. Thus there is nothing to prevent a fee simple owner granting a lease to a tenant for 9,000, or even 90,000 years. In fact 99-year leases are common and 999-year leases, though hardly frequent, are to be found in practice.

8.2.4.1 *Underleases and subleases*

However, whilst there can only be one fee simple estate in one piece of land, there can be more than one term of years. A tenant may himself grant a lease of the premises (a *sublease*) to a subtenant, as long as this sublease will last for a shorter period than the original lease (the *head lease*). The subtenant may also grant a further lease of the same premises (an *underlease*) to an undertenant, as long as the underlease is for a shorter period than the sublease. Thus if L, the fee simple owner, grants T a 99-year lease of a property on 1 January 1980, T may grant a sublease to S for any shorter period (e.g., 25 years) and S may grant an underlease to U for any period shorter than the sublease (e.g., a monthly tenancy). This can be expressed diagrammatically as follows:

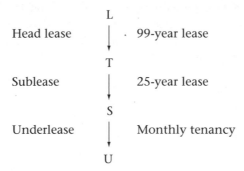

In our diagram, L is a landlord, T and S are both tenants and landlords, and U is a tenant only. Each of these four people has a legal estate in the property concerned. S may recover the property by bringing U's tenancy to an end (this can be done by serving notice, but today this right to terminate such a lease may be affected by statutory provisions which give security of tenure to certain tenants; see 8.5.1). T will recover the use of the property when S's 25-year term expires. Thus S and T both have a right that the property will revert to them on the expiration of the terms which they have carved out of their own. This right is called a *'reversion'*, and since S and T are owners of leasehold estates they are each said to have a *'leasehold reversion'*. Once T's 99-year lease expires, L (or his successors) will recover the property and thus L has a *'freehold reversion'*. Finally, we should mention that although the terminology of 'sublease' and 'underlease' given above is in common usage, it is not used consistently by all lawyers and you may find cases of what we call 'underleases' being called 'subleases'.

The process of creating further terms out of a leasehold estate may continue almost indefinitely, so long as each subsequent lease will end before the end of the term belonging to the person who grants it. However, if the grantor attempts to create a lease as long or longer than his own term, no new lease will be created and instead the grant will operate as an *assignment* of the grantor's own lease (see 8.4.3.2).

8.2.5 Is payment of rent an essential requirement?

We have now discussed the three essential elements identified in Woodfall's definition of a lease (see 8.2.1). You may have noticed that that definition makes no mention of the payment of rent or premium as being an essential characteristic of a lease. It is true that leases are usually commercial arrangements, in which the tenant pays for his use of the land, either by regular instalments throughout the lease (rent, technically called '*rent-service*') or by a lump sum at the start of the lease (called a '*premium*' or '*fine*'), or by a combination of both. In the case of a periodic tenancy, the tenant is likely to pay rent which is based on a commercial estimation of the rental value of the property in the open market, and is payable weekly, monthly, quarterly or, more rarely, annually. With a long lease for a fixed period (e.g., a 99-year lease), it is more usual for the tenant to pay a premium or fine, at the start of the lease, and then to pay a smaller, sometimes almost nominal, rent, usually called '*ground rent*', on a yearly or half-yearly basis. Alternatively, it is possible, although very uncommon, to have a lease in consideration of one initial payment of a lump sum, rather than in consideration of the periodical payment of rent (*Hill* v *Booth* [1930] 1 KB 381). In general, therefore, a tenant will pay some rent to his landlord, although in the case of ground rent it may be a trivial sum of money.

However, it is clear that the payment of rent, although usual, is not an essential characteristic of a lease; LPA 1925, for example, defines a term of years absolute as 'a term of years . . . (whether or not at a rent)' (s. 205(1)(xxvii)). The limitation of other provisions in that Act to leases at a rent or premium (for example, s. 149(3) and (6)) implies that a valid lease can exist where there is no provision for payment in either form. Such leases are likely to be found as a part of family settlements, or as conveyancing devices, for instance, in connection with mortgages.

There was, therefore, some surprise when Lord Templeman in *Street* v *Mountford* [1985] AC 809 appeared to suggest (in the passage quoted at 8.2.2) that the payment of a premium or rent was necessary to constitute a tenancy. However, in *Ashburn Anstalt* v *Arnold* [1989] 1 Ch 1 the Court of Appeal confirmed that rent is not an essential characteristic of a lease and said that the remarks in *Street* v *Mountford* were not to be read as introducing such a requirement. In *Ashburn Anstalt* v *Arnold* a vendor of a leasehold estate had been given by the purchaser the right to exclusive possession of the premises rent-free until a specified date, the agreement to continue thereafter until terminated by a quarter's notice. This arrangement was held to be a lease and Fox LJ said, at p. 10:

. . . the reservation of rent is not necessary for the creation of a tenancy.

This case was overruled on other grounds by the House of Lords in *Prudential Assurance Co. Ltd* v *London Residuary Body* [1992] 2 AC 386. However, the long-established principle that it is possible to have a lease without payment of rent has been affirmed by the Court of Appeal in *Skipton Building Society* v *Clayton* (1993) 66 P&CR 223.

Finally, it should be noted that although rent and premiums usually take the form of money payments, it is possible for payment to be made in kind or through the performance of services.

8.3 Creation of leases

8.3.1 Grant of a legal lease

8.3.1.1 *Express grant*

Subject to certain exceptions, which we explain below, the requirements for express grant can be summarised as follows:

- leases for not more than three years may be created orally or in writing;
- leases for longer than three years but not more than seven years must be created by deed;
- leases for more than seven years must be created by deed and registered in accordance with LRA 2002.

We will now look at these requirements in more detail.

(1) *leases for not more than three years* As we noted in Chapter 1 (1.6.2.3), the general rule imposed by LRA 1925 s. 52(1) is that a deed must be used to create or transfer a legal estate.

This rule is, however, inconvenient when one is dealing with a short lease or a periodic tenancy, and accordingly the harshness of s. 52(1) is mitigated in the case of certain short leases by s. 54(2), which provides that s. 52(1) shall not:

affect the creation by parol of leases taking effect in possession for a term not exceeding three years (whether or not the lessee is given power to extend the term) at the best rent which can reasonably be obtained without taking a fine.

Thus, a lease for not more than three years (which includes periodic tenancies— *Hammond* v *Farrow* [1904] 2 KB 332 at 335) may be created by a simple oral or written agreement, as long as it is granted at the best rent which can be obtained (without a premium) and takes effect in possession. This last requirement means that the lease must begin at the date of grant, not at some time in the future, and as a result a reversionary (future) lease, even one for not more than three years, must always be granted by deed. (For an application of this rule, see *Long* v *Tower Hamlets LBC* [1998] Ch 197.)

However, most short leases do take effect in possession and accordingly are granted without a deed, in simple written form or by word of mouth. Thus many tenants have no written lease, though weekly tenants should normally have a rent book recording the basic agreement if the premises are residential in nature (Landlord and Tenant Act 1985, s. 4). It is most unlikely that Mr Gruyère, the weekly tenant of the basement flat at 2 Trant Way, has a deed setting out his lease. Indeed, as he is a friend of the landlord, Mr Forest, he may well have no written document at all. Nonetheless, Mr Gruyère will have a legal lease, a legal estate, if his rent of £100 a week satisfies the 'best rent' test.

Where a periodic tenancy is expressly granted, the grant will usually indicate the type of tenancy being created (i.e., yearly, quarterly, monthly or weekly).

Finally we should remind you that there are a few special leases which may require registration under LRA 2002 irrespective of their length (see 5.3.1.2). This means that, for example, a lease providing for discontinuous possession may have to be completed by registration even if the overall period is for not more than three years.

(2) *leases for longer than three years but not more than seven years*   Leases which are for more than three years or for other reasons do not fall within the exception provided by LPA 1925 s. 54(2) are subject to the general rule set out in s. 52(1) of that Act, which states that a grant is not effective to create a legal estate 'unless made by deed'. This means that such a lease should be signed, witnessed and delivered in accordance with the requirements of the Law of Property (Miscellaneous Provisions) Act 1989 s. 1.

Leases in this category are not subject to the registration requirements of LRA 2002 unless they are of the type which require registration irrespective of length (see (1) above).

(3) *leases for more than seven years*   Such leases must be granted by deed in accordance with LPA 1925 s.52(1), and in addition must be registered as required by LRA 2002 (see 5.6).

Unregistered land   Where a lease for more than seven years is granted by the owner of an estate which is itself not yet registered, the grant of the lease creates a legal estate and the new tenant must then apply for registration of his title to that estate. If he does not make the application in the prescribed time, his legal estate ceases to exist and the grant operates as a contract to grant the lease (LRA 2002 ss. 4(1)(c) and 7(2)(b)).

In accordance with these rules, the proposed grant of the 99-year lease of the maisonette at 2 Trant Way should be made by deed and followed by an application for registration.

Registered land   Where the owner of a registered estate grants out of it a lease for more than seven years, the grant is a disposition which must be completed by registration, and does not operate at law until this has been done (LRA 2002 s. 27(1) and (2)).

8.3.1.2 *Implied grant*

Because a lease for not more than three years may be created without any formalities, it is possible for certain leases to arise by implication, from the actions of the parties. Where it could be shown that a person was in possession of land with the owner's consent and that rent calculated on a periodic basis was paid and accepted, the common law would presume the existence of a periodic tenancy (*Martin v Smith* (1874) LR 9 Ex 50). This presumption could, of course, be rebutted by showing a contrary intention but, in the absence of any evidence about what the parties had intended, common law would fill the gap by inferring the creation of a periodic tenancy.

In more recent times, however, the introduction of various forms of statutory protection for tenants meant that it was no longer safe to presume the intention to create a tenancy, and the courts now emphasise the importance of discovering the real intentions of the parties (see *Cardiothoracic Institute* v *Shrewdcrest Ltd* [1986] 1 WLR 368). Thus, as emphasised by Nicholls LJ in *Javad* v *Mohammed Aqil* [1991] 1 WLR 1007, at p. 1012:

> the inference sensibly and reasonably to be drawn will depend upon a fair consideration of all the circumstances, of which payment of rent on a periodical basis is only one, albeit a very important one.

In this case, the occupier had gone into possession in the course of negotiations for a fixed term lease, and had paid a quarterly sum described as 'rent'. When the negotiations broke down, and the owner sought to recover possession, the occupier claimed that a quarterly tenancy had arisen from the payment and receipt of rent. The Court of Appeal, having regard to all the circumstances, including the continuing negotiations, refused to infer an intention to create a periodic tenancy, and held the occupier to be a tenant at will only (see 8.10.3). Other decisions in which the courts have refused to infer an implied grant include *Manfield & Sons Ltd* v *Botchin* [1970] 2 QB 612 (express grant of a tenancy at will), and *Tickner* v *Buzzacott* [1965] Ch 426 (landlord was unaware that the person paying rent was not the person he had in contemplation). (See further Bridge [1991] CLJ p. 232.)

In many cases, however, it may well be found that the parties' intentions are consistent with the grant of a periodic tenancy. The occupier may have gone into possession under a contract to grant a fixed-term lease, which is never performed, or under a defective grant (e.g., a lease for more than three years not made by deed), or on the other hand may 'hold on' in the property after a previous lease has come to an end. In these circumstances, if rent is paid and accepted on a periodic basis, a periodic tenancy may arise by implied grant.

The type of periodic tenancy arising by implication will in general depend upon the period for which the rent is said to be due rather than upon that for which it is paid. For example, a yearly tenancy will arise by implication if the tenant is in possession of the land and is paying a rent which is stated as an annual sum, even if payments are actually made in monthly instalments (*Ladies' Hosiery and Underwear Ltd* v *Parker* [1930] 1 Ch 304). However, this is only the general rule, and it is possible for the period of the tenancy to be determined by other terms of the agreement which indicate a particular period (e.g., reference to provisions for notice), or by local or business custom. Leases arising by implied grant will be legal because such periodic tenancies may be created informally within the provisions of LPA 1925, s. 54(2).

8.3.2 **Non-compliance with requirements for legal grant: position in law and equity**

We can identify two situations in which parties do not comply with the requirements for the grant of a legal term of years absolute. It may be that the parties simply make an agreement for a lease, but never proceed to the formal grant. Alternatively, they may attempt to make the grant but fail to do it properly. For example, the grantor may purport to grant a lease for more than three years but uses only a written document, not a deed; or alternatively a deed is used, but the registration requirements are not observed. In both situations, the parties have not created the legal lease they intended. It is true that a legal periodic tenancy may arise by implied grant if the tenant, relying on the contract or the defective grant, goes into possession, and rent is paid and accepted (8.3.1.2), but this will probably fall far short of the term which the parties originally intended to create.

Where there is *an agreement to grant a lease*, both law and equity may be able to assist one of the parties with remedies for breach of contract. Moreover both systems may treat a *defective lease* as a contract to grant a lease and give relief accordingly. Of course, these contractual remedies will be available only if the parties have complied with the statutory requirements for contracts relating to land in force at the time when the agreement or the defective grant was made. The rules for the form of such contracts are dealt with in detail in Chapter 3, but it may be helpful to summarise them here.

8.3.2.1 *Formal requirements for contracts relating to land*

Contracts made on or after 27 September 1989 must be made in writing, and must contain all the terms agreed by the parties and be signed by both of them (Law of Property (Miscellaneous Provisions) Act 1989). Leases for not more than three years are exempted from the general requirements of the 1989 Act as to the form of the contract (LP(MP)A 1989, s. 2(5)(a)).

By contrast, contracts made before 27 September 1989 could be made orally, but were not enforceable unless evidenced in writing, or, for the purposes of equity, by part performance (LPA 1925, s. 40).

Where the parties attempted to grant a lease but failed to do it properly, the defective grant might, before 27 September 1989, constitute sufficient written evidence for the transaction to be treated as a contract to grant a lease. Alternatively, if the tenant had been allowed to enter into possession of the property and had paid rent, these actions amounted to sufficient acts of part performance by both parties and the contract would be enforceable in equity (see, e.g., *Wills* v *Stradling* (1797) 3 Ves Jr 378).

Since the 1989 Act came into force, the position of defective grants is less clear. As we have seen (3.4), it is generally acccepted that the doctrine of part performance can no longer apply, although there may be cases in which equity will assist by means of proprietary estoppel or the constructive trust. There is also some doubt as to whether a defective grant is likely to meet the new statutory requirements for a written contract (see Howell [1990] Conv 441), but this would of course have to depend on the exact nature of the documents in any particular case.

8.3.2.2 *Remedies for breach of contract*

Assuming that a party to an agreement for a lease or a defective lease can satisfy the relevant statutory requirements, he can seek the common law remedy of damages for breach of contract. However, it is the relief available from equity, in the form of an order for specific performance of the contract, that may well prove of greater value to him, and we consider this in the next section.

8.3.3 **Leases in equity: the doctrine in *Walsh* v *Lonsdale***

Provided the requirements as to the form of the contract are satisfied, either party may seek an order for specific performance of the contract which, if awarded, would result in the proper execution of a legal lease. As we explained in Chapter 1, the equitable maxim that equity regards as done that which ought to be done will apply in this situation. In consequence, equity regards the relationship between the parties as it would be if the order for specific performance had been made and the lease executed, and the parties are treated as having a lease in equity from the date of the contract. Exactly the same approach is adopted where a defective grant is treated by equity as a contract for a lease (*Parker* v *Taswell* (1858) 2 De G & J 559).

The existence of an equitable lease depends, however, on the availability of specific performance, and it is important to remember that this is an equitable remedy and subject to the usual equitable rules. Thus the party seeking to enforce the contract must not delay unduly and must 'come to equity with clean hands'. Accordingly, he must not himself be in breach of any of the terms of the agreement. Although the court in *Parker* v. *Taswell* (1858) 2 De G & J 559 said that equity would not usually refuse its help unless the applicant's breaches are 'gross and wilful' (at p. 573), there are several cases where relief has been refused because of the applicant's behaviour. In *Coatsworth* v *Johnson* (1886) 55 LJ QB 220, in which the tenant of a farm was in continuing breach of an obligation to cultivate the land in a proper manner, the tenant was refused an order for specific performance. A similar position arose in *Cornish* v *Brook Green Laundry Ltd* [1959] 1 QB 394, in which the performance of certain works by the plaintiff was a condition precedent to the grant of lease and those works had not been performed. However, you may like to note the view expressed in Gray and Gray at p. 578 that 'the courts tend not to refuse equitable assistance in circumstances where relief against forfeiture would normally be granted under a legal lease' (as to which, see 10.3.2.4).

There may, of course, be reasons other than the applicant's behaviour which make the court unwilling to grant specific performance, as, for example, in *Warmington* v *Miller* [1973] QB 877, where the effect of granting the order would have been to procure the breach of a term in a superior lease.

In cases where, for one reason or another, specific performance is not available, the parties are not subject to an equitable lease, and the only remaining possibility for redress would be to seek damages at law for breach of contract.

8.3.3.1 *Application of legal and equitable rules*

The interaction of common law and equitable rules and of the provisions of the Supreme Court of Judicature Act 1873, s. 25(11) (now Supreme Court Act 1981, s. 49(1)), is clearly illustrated by the leading case of *Walsh* v *Lonsdale* (1882) 21 ChD 9. In this case, the landlord and tenant had entered into a written agreement (not under seal and so not a deed) under which a mill was to be let to the tenant for seven years. The rent was to vary according to the productivity of the mill and it was agreed that the tenant would pay the rent annually, in advance, if the landlord so demanded. The tenant thereupon took possession of the mill and paid rent at six-monthly intervals, in arrears, for a year and a half. At this point the landlord demanded the next year's rent in advance, in accordance with the written agreement. The tenant refused to pay rent in advance and the landlord accordingly distrained for it (a 'self-help' remedy—see 10.3.1). The tenant thereupon sued, claiming that the distraint was unlawful, and applied for an interim injunction to restrain the landlord.

It is clear from the rules set out above that the relationship between the landlord and tenant in this case differs depending upon whether one applies the legal rules or the equitable rules. At law, the tenant had an implied legal lease arising from his possession of the property and the payment of rent. Payment of rent at six-monthly intervals gives rise to an annual tenancy and, since rent had been paid and accepted in arrears, law would presume that it was a term of the legal lease that rent should be paid in this manner. In equity, however, the act of entering the property and paying rent merely supports the written agreement, which is an agreement for a lease of seven years with rent payable annually in advance. Provided that the party seeking to enforce had done nothing wrong, this contract would be enforced by equity with an order for specific performance (finally producing the lease originally intended). In the meantime, since 'Equity regards as done that which ought to be done', the parties would be regarded by equity as already having a seven-year lease.

Which lease then prevailed: the annual legal lease or the seven-year equitable lease? Only if the equitable lease prevailed would the landlord's action in distraining be proper. The Supreme Court of Judicature Acts 1873 and 1875 required that, where the rules of law and equity conflict, the equitable rule should prevail (see now Supreme Court Act 1981, s. 49(1)). The court applied this provision, and accordingly held that the equitable lease prevailed and that therefore the landlord's actions were lawful.

For a modern application of these principles, see *R* v *Tower Hamlets LBC, ex parte Von Goetz* [1999] QB 1019. Here the Court of Appeal held that a written lease for 10 years created an equitable estate which was a sufficient 'term of years' to entitle the applicant to a renovation grant under the Local Government and Housing Act 1989. The council had refused the grant because it regarded the equitable interest as too precarious, but in Mummery LJ's view:

There may be circumstances in which an equitable lease is overridden, but in most cases a person with an equitable lease is in the same position as a person who has had a legal estate vested in him by deed.

8.3.4 Is an equitable lease as good as a legal lease?

Since normally an equitable lease can be converted into a legal lease by obtaining an order for specific performance, and since in the meantime equity will uphold the rights of the parties as though the legal lease had already been granted, it has often been said that, 'A contract for a lease is as good as a lease' (see *Re Maughan* (1885) 14 QBD 956). However, this is not necessarily true, as an equitable right is invariably more precarious than a legal right. We have already seen that the force of a contract for a lease depends upon the availability of an order for specific performance. Whereas a legal remedy (e.g., damages) will be available without reference to the behaviour of the claimant, an equitable remedy is not available where the claimant has 'dirty hands'. Thus a contract for a lease is only 'as good as a lease' if the circumstances are such that an order for specific performance can be obtained.

8.3.4.1 *Enforcement against third parties*

Furthermore there are other difficulties when the position of third parties is involved. Let us assume that L1 agrees to give T a five-year lease of property and that this agreement is specifically enforceable. T will have an equitable lease of the property. If later L1 sells the fee simple of the property to L2, L2 may not necessarily be bound by T's lease because it is only an equitable interest in the property. In the case of unregistered land the contract for a lease will be an estate contract, a C(iv) land charge, under LCA 1972, s. 2(4) and will bind L2 only if it was registered as a land charge before the date of the conveyance to him (LCA 1972, s. 4(6)). Even if L2 knew of the agreement, he is not bound by it, as notice is irrelevant in the case of registrable but unregistered land charges (see 4.4.5.3).

If title to the land is registered, L2, as a person taking the estate for valuable consideration, will take free of T's equitable lease unless it has been protected by a notice on the register of title to that estate, or is capable of taking effect as an interest that overrides a registered disposition (LRA 2002 s. 29 and Sch. 3). We have already mentioned that it is very unlikely that an equitable lease will be treated as an overriding interest under Sch. 3, para. 1, which is likely to be limited to *legal* leases (5.9.2.3(1)). However, if at the time of the transfer to L2, T was occupying the property and could satisfy the other requirements of Sch. 3, para. 2, he could claim that his equitable lease was overriding as the interest of a person in actual occupation. Nevertheless, as *Strand Securities Ltd* v *Caswell* [1965] Ch 958 shows, there are circumstances in which a tenant may not be in actual occupation at the relevant time, and a tenant with an equitable lease would therefore be well advised to protect his position by making an entry on the register.

Thus, while a legal lease will bind any purchaser, an equitable lease will only be binding in certain circumstances. Since such equitable leases usually only arise in cases in which the parties are unaware of the legal formalities for the creation of a lease, it is most unlikely that the tenant will know that he has to take further steps to protect his interest.

Where an equitable lease is not protected in the appropriate way, and so cannot be enforced against the purchaser of the legal estate for value, it is worth remembering that the tenant may also have a legal periodic tenancy, arising from his going into possession and the payment and receipt of rent. *Walsh* v *Lonsdale* (1882) 21 ChD 9 shows that where both legal and equitable rights are available, the equitable right prevails, and indeed the tenant may often prefer to rely on an equitable lease which gives him a longer term. However, if for some reason the equitable right cannot be enforced, either party may fall back on the protection of the legal lease.

8.3.4.2 *Do the covenants run?*

A further defect of the contract for a lease arises in relation to the covenants in the lease. Each party to the lease will usually undertake certain duties, such as to pay rent or to keep the property in repair, by entering into covenants set out in the lease. Such covenants are not only enforceable between the original parties to the lease, but, provided the lease is legal, will normally run to bind and benefit both a purchaser from the landlord and a purchaser from the tenant. However, this has always depended on the purchaser acquiring an estate in the property; in the case of a purely equitable lease there is no legal estate in existence, and so the benefits and burdens of the covenants do not pass automatically if the tenant assigns his interest, although they probably do so on an assignment by the landlord. As we shall see, the Landlord and Tenant (Covenants) Act 1995 substantially alters the rules governing this matter in respect of leases granted on or after 1 January 1996

(s. 1(3)) and we will look further at the old and new rules relating to equitable leases in the next chapter (9.6.1.6(2) and 9.6.2.2).

8.3.4.3 *Contract is not a conveyance*

A further disadvantage of an equitable lease is that, whilst a legal lease comes within the definition of a 'conveyance' for the purposes of LPA 1925, s. 62, and so carries with it automatically certain rights enjoyed in connection with the land, a contract for a lease does not fall within s. 62 and so does not carry with it such benefits. We will explain this more fully in Chapter 22.

8.3.4.4 *Other differences*

There are other ways in which an equitable lease is not the equivalent of a legal lease. Thus whilst certain 'usual covenants' (a term of art explained at 9.3.3) are implied into a contract for a lease, they are not implied into a full legal lease and the parties are bound by the stated terms only. In this case, the contract for a lease seems to have an advantage over a poorly drafted legal lease.

A further difference, which is a disadvantage to the tenant, is that a purchaser of an equitable lease is not the purchaser of a legal estate and so will be bound by certain earlier equitable interests in the property. Where title to the land is unregistered, he cannot claim to be a 'bona fide purchaser of a legal estate for value' in respect of earlier rights to which the notice rules apply, nor can he claim the benefit of LCA 1972, s. 4(6), and so will be bound by unregistered class C(iv) and D land charges. He will of course be a purchaser within s. 4(5) and (8) of the Act and will take the property free of unregistered class C(i)–(iii) and F land charges (see Chapter 4).

Where title to the land is registered, he will be bound by earlier equitable interests (see 5.15).

From all this it can be seen that it is certainly not the case that a contract for a lease is as good as a lease. These rules provide a strong incentive for ensuring that leases are correctly granted but, unfortunately, are not understood by many landlords and tenants. Accordingly, it is fortunate that the most common types of informal leases (periodic tenancies) are saved from this unsatisfactory position under the provisions of LPA 1925, s. 54(2).

8.4 **Disposition of leases and reversions**

8.4.1 **Power of disposition**

Both landlord and tenant have legal estates which may pass to others on sale, by way of gift or under the rules of testate or intestate succession. In what follows, we are primarily concerned with disposition on sale, but it must be remembered that there are other occasions besides sale on which leases and reversions may pass to new owners.

8.4.2 **Sale of the freehold reversion**

It is always possible for the owner of the reversion in fee simple (the freehold landlord) to sell his estate in the land. This will be done in the normal manner by conveyance, in the case of unregistered land (see Chapter 4), and by transfer and registration, in the case of registered land (see Chapter 5).

8.4.2.1 *Unregistered land*

In the case of unregistered land, the purchaser will acquire the fee simple subject to any legal lease which exists, regardless of whether he knew of its existence, for 'Legal rights are good against the world' (4.5.1). Thus the purchaser of the fee simple becomes the tenant's new landlord and, as we shall see later, takes over most if not all of the original landlord's rights and duties under the lease.

8.4.2.2 *Registered land*

Where the title to the fee simple is registered the position varies according to the length of the lease.

Where the lease is granted for not more than seven years it will be an overriding interest under LRA 2002 Sch. 3, para. 1, and so will bind the purchaser of the fee simple even if he did not know of it (see 5.9.2.3(1)).

If the lease is for more than seven years (or is one of the few leases requiring registration irrespective of length) it must have been registered in order for it to take effect as a legal lease. When this is done the lease will also be noted on the charges register of the landlord's title, and anyone who takes the landlord's estate for valuable consideration will take subject to the lease (LRA 2002 s. 29; see 5.6).

8.4.3 **Sale of the lease by the tenant**

A sale of his leasehold estate by the tenant is also possible (subject to any covenants in the lease restricting this right). The disposition of a lease is usually called an '*assignment*'.

8.4.3.1 *Express assignment*

Since the assignment of a lease is the conveyance or transfer of a legal estate it should be made by deed (LPA 1925, s. 52(1)). This rule applies even to leases for not more than three years, because s. 54(2) provides an exception only for the original grant of such leases and does not apply to assignments (see *Crago* v *Julian* [1992] 1 WLR 372).

However, a defective assignment will be regarded in equity as a contract to assign, provided that it satisfies the formalities for a contract relating to land. Where such a contract arises, either party may then apply for an order for specific performance in order to effect a full legal assignment.

8.4.3.2 *Assignment by operation of law*

An exception to the requirement for a deed arises in cases in which the assignment takes effect due to operation of law. This can be important in cases in which a tenant purports to grant a sublease of the property but grants a term which is equivalent to, or greater than, the unexpired portion of his own lease. As we have already seen (8.2.4.1) such a disposition takes effect as an assignment of the lease rather than as the creation of a sublease. The reason for this is that a sublease can only be created if the tenant retains some interest in the property when he grants the sublease: he must be in such a position that he will recover the property at some point. In other words he must retain the leasehold reversion. If he parts with the property for the *whole* of the remainder of his head lease there is no leasehold reversion and the transaction can only take effect as an assignment of the head lease and not as a sublease (*Beardman* v *Wilson* (1868) LR 4 CP 57).

If the purported sublease is for not more than three years it is likely that the parties will not have concluded their agreement by deed (relying on s. 54(2)). If the effect of the agreement is to transfer the whole remaining term of the head lease to the 'sublessee' (in fact, the assignee) the result appears to be a valid legal assignment without the need for a deed. Lord Greene MR seems to have accepted this reasoning in the case of *Milmo* v *Carreras* [1946] KB 306 at p. 312, on the ground that such an assignment arose by operation of a rule of law and this approach has recently been followed in *Parc (Battersea) Ltd v Hutchinson* [1999] 2 EGLR 33.

8.4.4 Sale of a leasehold reversion

We have already seen that the owner of a leasehold reversion performs two roles, being at the same time both the tenant of the head lease and the landlord of the sublease. Thus the sale of his estate must involve a consideration of the rules relating to both a lease and a reversion; the assignment of his lease must take the form described above, while the question of whether his purchaser takes subject to the sublease depends on principles similar to those relevant to the sale of the freehold reversion.

8.5 Determining a lease

8.5.1 Statutory protection for tenants

Leases can be brought to an end in a very large number of ways. Some of these methods of determining a lease have a reduced effect today, however, due to the provisions of various statutory codes, relating respectively to residential accommodation (Rent Act 1977 and Housing Acts 1988 and 1996, in respect of leases at or above a prescribed minimum rent, and Leasehold Reform Act 1967, Leasehold Reform, Housing and Urban Development Act 1993 and Commonhold and Leasehold Reform Act 2002 in respect of longer leases usually granted for a premium and a low ground rent); business premises (Landlord and Tenant Act 1954, Part II); and agricultural holdings (Agricultural Holdings Act 1986 and Agricultural Tenancies Act 1995). In a variety of ways these statutory provisions enable the tenant to remain on the property even after the tenancy has been terminated in accordance with contractual rules.

Additionally, individual tenants or, in some cases, a group of tenants of residential property may have a statutory right to buy the landlord's freehold reversion, so as to become the fee simple owners of their homes, instead of holding them merely as tenants (Leasehold Reform Act 1967, Leasehold Reform, Housing and Urban Development Act 1993, and Housing Act 1980).

For these various statutory provisions, which are in general outside the scope of this book, reference may be made to Megarry and Wade, or Cheshire and Burn, or to a suitable specialist text on the law relating to landlord and tenant.

8.5.1.1 *Some general points about statutory protection*

There are three general points which it may be helpful to mention here:

(i) In general, the introduction of new forms of statutory protection does not supersede the earlier rules, which continue to apply to tenancies already created under them. Thus, in respect of residential accommodation, the Rent Act 1977 continues to govern those tenancies within its terms which were granted before 15 January 1989, when the Housing Act 1988 came into operation.

(ii) The Acts employ a wide variety of technical terms, including, for example: 'protected tenancy', 'statutory tenancy', 'restricted contract', 'protected shorthold tenancy', 'assured tenancy' and 'assured shorthold tenancy'. We mention these terms here simply because you may come across references to some of them, either elsewhere in this book or in reports of cases. For the purposes of this book, you do not need to know anything more about these terms beyond the fact that they are created and defined by the relevant statutory codes, but if you should want further information it is to be found in the Acts themselves or in the books referred to above.

(iii) The protection given to tenants by some of these codes is very considerable. For example, security of tenure under the Rent Act 1977 could pass on the tenant's death to any member of his family who was living with him at that time, and there could be a further similar transmission on the death of that second tenant. The landlord's inability to recover possession, coupled with the fact that the rent he could charge was subject to statutory control, forms the background to many of the decisions about residential licences which we shall consider in Chapter 19, and explains why landlords were so anxious to avoid the statutory provisions by granting licences rather than leases.

8.5.2 **Common law rules for determining leases**

Despite the statutory provisions discussed above, the older common law rules governing the determination of a lease are still of great importance, because in general the statutory rules which protect the tenant at the end of his lease do not come into effect until after the contractual tenancy has been terminated. Accordingly, a landlord who wishes to end a tenancy may first have to terminate the contractual tenancy and then take further action in order to bring to an end the tenant's statutory protection.

At common law a lease may be determined in any of the following ways:

(a) expiry;
(b) notice to quit;
(c) surrender;

(d) merger;

(e) enlargement;

(f) disclaimer;

(g) forfeiture.

In addition, there are modern decisions which suggest that the contractual doctrines of frustration and repudiation by fundamental breach may apply to leases, and we will discuss these after the other methods of determining a lease have been considered (see 8.6).

Statutory extinction of lease

A new statutory way of ending a lease will be created when Part 1 of the Commonhold and Leasehold Reform Act 2002 takes effect. The Act provides that certain leases of commonhold land will be extinguished when a commonhold scheme comes into operation. We consider the new commonhold system in Chapter 11 and will explain then the circumstances in which leases may be extinguished (see 11.3.3).

8.5.2.1 *Expiry*

A fixed-term lease gives rise to few problems, since it will expire automatically once the specified term comes to an end. In such cases it is not necessary for either party to the lease to take any action in order to terminate the lease.

In addition, if a lease is granted for a fixed term but is subject to termination on the occurrence of a specified event, then the lease terminates automatically when the event occurs (see *Doe d Lockwood* v *Clarke* (1807) 8 East 185 and *Great Northern Railway Co.* v *Arnold* (1916) 33 TLR 114). As we have already seen, leases determining on death or marriage are affected by statutory provisions requiring notice and do not terminate automatically.

Break clauses

Some fixed-term leases contain clauses ('break clauses') allowing one party, or both, to determine the lease on notice before the term expires. The break clause may be exercisable on the occurrence of certain events (for example, if the landlord wants to redevelop the property), or at specified intervals throughout the term (e.g., at the end of the 7th or 14th year in a 21-year lease). Such a lease will usually provide for notice to be given before the break clause is exercised. In the past, problems have arisen over the need for complete accuracy in the giving of such notice, but recently a more relaxed attitude has been adopted by the courts (see 8.5.2.2(3)).

8.5.2.2 *Notice to quit*

Periodic tenancies run on indefinitely, from one period to the next, until one party gives notice to the other that he does not wish the arrangement to continue. In this context it is important to remember the basic principle underlying the periodic tenancy, namely that:

continuation beyond the end of each [period] depends on the will of the parties that it should continue . . . and the tenancy continues no further than the parties have already impliedly agreed upon by their omission to serve notice to quit . . . it is by his omission to give notice of termination that each party signifies the necessary positive assent to the extension of the term for a further period. (*Hammersmith LBC* v *Monk* [1992] 1 AC 478 at p. 490.)

It was always open to the parties to make any agreement they pleased about the form and period of notice required. In the absence of such agreement, however, the common law would apply standard rules, and more recently the statutory codes designed to protect tenants have created a number of requirements which cannot be varied by agreement.

(1) *Form*   In general there appears to be no requirement at common law that notice must be given in writing, at least in the case of tenancies created orally (*Timmins* v *Rowlinson* (1765) 3 Burr 1603). However, under s. 5(1) of the Protection from Eviction Act 1977, notice to quit in respect of premises let as a dwelling must be given in writing. In addition any such notice must be given in a statutory form which draws to the attention of the tenant the fact that he may be entitled to security of tenure under statutory provisions. The provisions of Part I of the Housing Act 1988 thereafter generally prevent the landlord from recovering possession of such premises without a court order. Most business tenancies must also be terminated by written notice, in the statutory form, under the provisions of the Landlord and Tenant Act 1954.

(2) *Period*   The correct period for notice will vary according to the type of lease or tenancy involved and these are considered separately below. However, there are certain statutory amendments to these rules which apply to leases of dwellings, business premises, and agricultural holdings, and to long tenancies at low rent. These rules are more appropriately dealt with in a detailed text on landlord and tenant law, but we must mention here that any notice to quit premises let as a dwelling must be given not less than four weeks before the date on which it is to take effect (Protection from Eviction Act 1977, s. 5(1)) unless the lease falls within one of the excluded categories set out in s. 3A. The exempt categories cover the sort of situation where the tenant has something more of the character of a 'lodger', rather than that of a normal tenant.

In the absence of any express agreement between the parties (which must not, of course, exclude the statutory provisions), common law will govern the length of notice required. Save in the case of a yearly tenancy, the correct period for notice is a full period under the lease. Thus, for a quarterly tenancy one gives a quarter's notice, for a monthly tenancy a month's notice, and for a weekly tenancy a week's notice. The notice should expire at the end of one period of the lease. A yearly tenancy can be terminated by half a year's notice, expiring at the end of a year (*Doe d Shore* v *Porter* (1789) 3 TR 13).

(3) *Calculation of notice period*   It seems that parties to a lease can experience difficulty in calculating the exact period of notice required either to end a periodic tenancy or to exercise a break clause in respect of a fixed term. A particular concern has been whether the notice to quit should refer to the last day of the period or to the anniversary of the commencement date. For example, in the case of a yearly tenancy beginning on 19 May, should the notice refer to 18 May (the last day of the term) or to 19 May (the anniversary of the term's commencement)? It used to be thought that complete accuracy in the giving of notice, whether under a break clause or to determine a periodic tenancy, was essential and that any error in the date, even by one day, would invalidate the notice.

A more liberal approach however, was adopted by the House of Lords in *Mannai*

Investment Co. Ltd v *Eagle Star Life Assurance Co. Ltd* [1997] AC 749. Here the tenant company sought to exercise its rights under a break clause which permitted it to end the lease by giving six months' notice to expire on the third anniversary of the commencement date. By mistake the notice specified 12 January as the date on which the lease should end, rather than 13 January, which was the correct date. In the Court of Appeal, the error was held to be fatal, and the notice was in consequence completely ineffective. This decision was reversed by the House of Lords, which applied what it described as the objective test of how a reasonable recipient would understand the notice. A reasonable landlord would be aware of the 'contextual setting', that is, the terms of the break clause and the date on which notice should take effect. The question for the court was: 'Does the notice construed against its contextual setting unambiguously inform a reasonable recipient how and when the notice is to operate under the right reserved?' On the facts of the case before it, the House of Lords considered that it would have been obvious to a reasonable recipient that the notice contained a minor error and that the tenant wished to end the lease on the third anniversary of its commencement. In the words of Lord Steyn (at p. 768),

Prima facie one would expect that if a notice unambiguously conveys a decision to determine a court may nowadays ignore immaterial errors which would not have misled a reasonable recipient.

The approach indicated by the House of Lords was followed shortly afterwards by the Court of Appeal in *Garston* v *Scottish Widows Fund and Life Assurance Society* [1998] 1 WLR 1583. A notice to exercise rights under a break clause was held to be valid, although the tenant had wrongly specified the date for determination as 9 July 1995 instead of 23 June 1995. Nourse LJ noted that the 'reasonable recipient' had now joined the company of 'the man on the Clapham omnibus, the officious bystander and the man skilled in the art', and described him as a 'formidable addition to the imagery of the law' (at pp. 1585–6). More seriously, he commented (at p. 1587) that the use of the new approach is likely to cause greater difficulty in some cases than did the application of the old test, although there was no such difficulty in the case currently before the court. (Note, however, the Court of Appeal's recent decision that complete accuracy is still essential in a statutory notice: *Fernandez* v *McDonald* [2004] 1 WLR 1027.)

(4) *Excluding the right to give notice*   It is clear from *Breams Property Investment Co. Ltd* v *Stroulger* [1948] 2 KB 1 that the landlord's right to give notice does not have to be identical with that of the tenant, and the decision also shows that one party's right to give notice may be restricted for a defined period. However, as we have already seen (8.2.3.1), it is not possible to exclude the right to give notice for an indefinite period, because this has the effect of making the periodic tenancy uncertain, and therefore void under the rule in *Lace* v *Chantler* [1944] KB 368. This was the basis of the House of Lords' decision in *Prudential Assurance Co. Ltd* v *London Residuary Body* [1992] 2 AC 386. In *Prudential* the original 'lease' was held to be void as not creating a term of years because the period of the supposed grant was 'until the . . . land is required by the Council for the purposes of widening of Walworth Road . . .' and was accordingly for an indeterminate term. However, the tenants had gone into possession and paid rent and sought to establish that they had a legal periodic tenancy (which was accepted) and that it could not be terminated by the

landlord until the land was needed for the specified purpose. Since it appeared that the road alteration would not now take place (the lease having continued already for some 60 years and the current landlords having no road-making powers), the incorporation of such a term into the periodic tenancy would have given the tenant a lease, at a 1930 rent, which the landlord could never terminate. The House of Lords concluded that the landlord's right could not be excluded in this manner: a periodic tenancy is saved from being an indeterminate term because each party has power to terminate on notice expiring at the end of each period. Accordingly in *Prudential* the landlord could terminate the periodic tenancy by giving the appropriate notice (six months' notice in this instance). Therefore, any term which seeks to exclude the right to give notice, or to restrict it so that it cannot be used, will be disregarded and either party may give notice according to the usual rules.

8.5.2.3 *Surrender*

A surrender is the means whereby a tenant relinquishes his estate to his landlord, the reversioner, with the agreement of the landlord. A surrender releases the tenant from any future liability under the lease but does not release him from liability for past actions (e.g., past breaches of covenant) (*Richmond v Savill* [1926] 2 KB 530). Accordingly, the landlord would still be able to seek compensation for any past losses arising from such breach. It should be noted, however, that the circumstances of the surrender may be such that the landlord will be taken to have waived his right to compensation for past breaches (*Dalton v Pickard* [1926] 2 KB 545).

(1) *Express surrender*   Since a surrender is a dealing with a legal estate in land, it should be done expressly and by deed. This is true even where one wishes to surrender a short lease, for the exemption in LPA 1925, s. 54(2), applies only to the grant of such leases and not to their surrender. A defective surrender (e.g., a surrender which, due to mistake, is unwitnessed) may operate in equity as a contract to surrender the lease, under the usual principles.

(2) *Surrender by operation of law*   No deed is required, however, in cases in which the lease is surrendered by operation of law (LPA 1925, s. 52(2)(c)). In practice this is quite common, since often the surrender is evidenced by the actions of the parties who would thereafter be estopped from denying the fact of the surrender (*Foster v Robinson* [1951] 1 KB 149). Such surrenders commonly arise when a landlord accepts back possession of the property and agrees that the tenant will be under no further liability. Thus in *Phené v Popplewell* (1862) 12 CB NS 334 a surrender was held to have been made without formalities when the landlord accepted back the premises, painted out the name of the former tenant on a signboard and put up a board advertising the property as being available to let. Since a surrender requires the agreement of both parties, no such surrender will arise from a purely unilateral act (e.g., the tenant returning the key without the landlord's assent, *Cannan v Grimley* (1850) 9 CB 634), and the other party to the lease may insist on the continued performance of the lease.

Surrender by operation of law may also occur in situations where landlord and tenant have agreed variations to the terms of the current lease, which are so significant that they can take effect only through the creation of a new lease. Such a new lease could not be granted except on the basis that the old one had been surrendered, and the law will achieve the result sought by the parties by implying both a surrender of the old lease and a grant of a new one. In *Friends' Provident Life Office* v *British Railways Board* [1996] 1 All ER 336 the Court of Appeal emphasised that such implied 'surrender and regrant' will occur only in exceptional circumstances, where the changes agreed are such as 'would change the legal estate' (for example, by purporting to add additional land to the lease or to extend the period for which it is granted).

8.5.2.4 *Merger*

A merger arises when the tenant acquires the immediate reversion to his lease or a third party acquires both the lease and the immediate reversion. In such an event the tenant would, in theory, become his own landlord, or the third party would become both landlord and tenant. This is ridiculous, unless there is some specific reason for wishing the lease and the reversion to remain separate, and so normally the lease will merge into the reversionary estate when they come into the hands of the same owner. However, this only occurs where it is the intention of the owner that the estates should merge, and LPA 1925, s. 185, preserves the equitable rule to this effect.

Since a merger involves the acquisition of the superior estate, the events which give rise to it can usually only be effected by deed (LPA 1925, s. 52(1)).

8.5.2.5 *Enlargement*

In practice, this is very rare, because under the provisions of LPA 1925, s. 153, it can only be done in the case of a lease originally granted for 300 years or more and upon which no rent of any money value is payable. Where the numerous conditions of s. 153 are satisfied, the tenant may execute a deed of enlargement, which has the effect of increasing his interest to that of an estate in fee simple, and thereby extinguishing the title of the previous fee simple owner.

8.5.2.6 *Disclaimer*

A right to disclaim a lease normally arises by statute. The most common examples are the rights of trustees in bankruptcy and liquidators of companies to disclaim certain property under the provisions of the Insolvency Act 1986. A disclaimer releases the tenant from future liabilities under the lease.

8.5.2.7 *Forfeiture*

In certain circumstances it is possible for a landlord to forfeit a lease for breach, by the tenant, of one of the terms of the agreement. This method of determining a lease is considered in detail in the section dealing with remedies for breach of covenant in Chapter 10.

8.6 Determination by discharge of contract

Historically, the relationship between a landlord and his tenant was viewed as no more than a contractual one, so that the tenant's rights under the arrangement were enforceable only against his landlord. At a later stage, the tenant was able to assert his rights to possession of the land against anyone who dispossessed him. He thus came to be regarded as having an estate in the land, which was enforceable against the whole world. In consequence, it is generally possible to view the lease as operating on two levels, being both a contract between the landlord and the tenant and a conveyance creating an estate in the land. In most of this chapter so far, we have been focusing on the lease-as-conveyance, and have been describing the special rules governing the estate which it creates. However, there are circumstances in which parties to the lease may wish to emphasise the contractual nature of the arrangements between them. We will look at this dual aspect of leases in a little more detail in 8.8, but need to note here the way in which two methods of discharging *contracts* have been applied to *leases*.

If you have already studied the law of contract, you may remember that there are a number of ways in which contracts may be discharged so that parties no longer have any obligations under them. Two forms of discharge, frustration and repudiatory breach, have been held by the courts to be applicable to leases, and therefore constitute two further ways in which a lease may be brought to an end.

8.6.1 **Frustration**

In general, the doctrine of frustration applies in cases in which external factors prevent the parties to an agreement performing their obligations under the contract. As explained by Lord Simon in *National Carriers Ltd* v *Panalpina (Northern) Ltd* [1981] AC 675, at p. 700:

Frustration of a contract takes place when there supervenes an event (without default of either party and for which the contract makes no significant provision) which so significantly changes the nature (not merely the expense or onerousness) of the outstanding contractual rights and/or obligations from what the parties could reasonably have contemplated at the time of its execution that it would be unjust to hold them to the literal sense of its stipulations in the new circumstances; in such case the law declares both parties to be discharged from further performance.

It may well happen that property let to a tenant becomes unusable, through no fault of his own or the landlord's, and the tenant may claim that as a result his lease is frustrated. It used to be thought that he would not succeed, for he had an estate in the land and his duties under the lease would continue. Thus, if the house on the property was destroyed by fire, the tenant was still obliged to pay any rent due under the lease, for he still had an estate in the land (*Matthey* v *Curling* [1922] 2 AC 180). In the famous old case of *Paradine* v *Jane* (1647) Al 26, a tenant was evicted from the property by the King's army during the Civil War. The tenant was held to be liable to pay the rent on the property, for the risk of such interference was that of the current legal occupier of the land. This rule is generally in the best interests of others who have an interest in the land which is based on that of the tenant (e.g., a mortgagee who has taken a mortgage of the tenant's estate), who would otherwise be deprived of their interest or security.

At the date of *Paradine* v *Jane*, the doctrine of frustration of contract had not been developed. Even after it had emerged in the nineteenth century, there was for many years considerable uncertainty whether the doctrine could ever apply to a term of years. The issue appears to have been settled, at long last, by the House of Lords in *National Carriers Ltd* v *Panalpina (Northern) Ltd* [1981] AC 675. In that case the lease was of a warehouse. For some 20 months during the lease the street giving access to the premises was closed by the local authority, because a neighbouring derelict property was in a dangerous condition. The tenants were thus prevented from using the warehouse for that period. They failed to pay rent and defended an action for its recovery by claiming that the lease had been frustrated. The House of Lords considered that in the circumstances the lease had not been frustrated because the interruption of 20 months (in a 10-year lease) did not destroy the entire contract. Their Lordships did, however, accept the principle that in exceptional circumstances the doctrine of frustration could apply to a lease. Lord Wilberforce said (at p. 697):

[T]hough such cases may be rare, the doctrine of frustration is capable of application to leases of land. It must be so applied with proper regard to the fact that a lease, that is, a grant of a legal estate, is involved. The court must consider whether any term is to be implied which would determine the lease in the event which has happened and/or ascertain the foundation of the agreement and decide whether this still exists in the light of the terms of the lease, the surrounding circumstances and any special rules which apply to leases or to the particular lease in question.

In reaching this conclusion, their Lordships considered in some detail the argument that a lease is more than a contract, because it creates an estate in land. They were not, however, persuaded that this was any reason for refusing to apply the doctrine of frustration, if justice required its use. Frustration would have the effect of ending the estate prematurely, but, as we have seen, a leasehold estate is already capable of ending prematurely, for example on the occurrence of some prescribed event, or on forfeiture for breach of covenant. The argument that termination of the estate could prejudicially affect third parties (such as mortgagees) who have taken an interest in it, was noted, but was not regarded as a sufficient reason for excluding the doctrine. In dealing with the questions raised by this case, several members of the House of Lords found support from developments in the United States and in Canada, in which the doctrine of frustration has been applied to leases. It was accepted that in reality the question is one of where the risk should fall: upon the tenant or upon the landlord.

The circumstances in which a lease may be frustrated remain to be seen, but would almost certainly include the destruction of the land itself (by cliff-fall, rising sea levels or other natural occurrence), and possibly the total destruction of buildings (by analogy with *Taylor v Caldwell* (1863) 3 B & S 826, in which a contract granting a licence for use of buildings was held to be frustrated when the premises were destroyed by fire). Views expressed in the House of Lords suggest that frustration may also apply where property is let for a specific use which then becomes illegal (as for example during the Prohibition era in the United States when tenants were discharged from their obligations to pay rent for premises which they had taken for the specific purpose of using as liquor saloons).

However, the House of Lords emphasised that frustration of a lease is likely to occur only very rarely, or, to paraphrase a Gilbert and Sullivan operetta: 'not "never" but "hardly ever"'!

8.6.2 **Repudiatory breach**

This method of discharging a contract involves a breach by one party of an obligation under the contract which is so fundamental that its breach is tantamount to his repudiating or rejecting the contract as a whole. In such a situation, the innocent party may accept the repudiation and treat it as terminating the contract, or may choose to ignore it and treat the agreement as continuing.

In *Hussein* v *Mehlman* [1992] 2 EGLR 87 the question arose of whether repudiatory breach could apply to a three-year residential lease (described throughout by the court as 'a contract of letting'). Under covenants implied by the Landlord and Tenant Act 1985, s. 11, the landlord was under a duty to keep in repair the structure and exterior of the house, and the installations for the supply of water, gas and electricity and for space and water heating. He was in serious breach of these covenants, and the court found that he had no intention of performing them. In the view of the judge 'the tenants suffered real hardship as a result of the breach and were deprived of an essential part of what they had contracted for ... the breach vitiated the central purpose of the contract of letting' (at p. 91). After 15 months, the tenants handed back the keys and vacated the property, claiming that the landlord's behaviour constituted repudiatory conduct which they accepted, thus ending the lease and their obligations under it.

In the County Court, Assistant Recorder Sedley QC considered whether a repudiatory breach of a contract of letting was legally possible, and held that it was. An earlier opinion that repudiation was not applicable to leases (*Total Oil Great Britain Ltd* v *Thompson Garages (Biggin Hill) Ltd* [1972] 1 QB 318 at p. 324) was based on the view that a lease is essentially different from other contracts, and derived support from the then-accepted principle that the doctrine of frustration did not apply to leases. However, as we have already seen, the House of Lords in *National Carriers Ltd* v *Panalpina (Northern) Ltd* [1981] AC 675 has more recently emphasised the contractual aspects of the lease and specifically accepted that in exceptional circumstances a lease can be frustrated. This enabled the court in *Hussein* v *Mehlman* to conclude that *Total Oil* had ceased to be an authority for the proposition that a lease cannot be repudiated. Support for the view that a lease could be repudiated was to be found in a number of nineteenth-century cases in which it was treated as 'axiomatic that a contract of letting could be terminated by an innocent party without notice if the other party failed to fulfil a fundamental term of the contract' (at p. 89). Thus the judge held that a lease can be ended on repudiation by the other party and that, on the facts before him, the landlord's behaviour constituted repudiatory conduct, which had been accepted by the tenants. The lease had come to an end, and both parties were released from their obligations under it.

It is important to note that the concept of repudiatory breach could be used against the tenant as well as against the landlord.

If the obligation to pay rent is as fundamental as the obligation to keep the house habitable, it will follow that a default in rent payments is a repudiatory act on the tenants's part (at p. 90).

Such breaches of covenant by the tenant are at present dealt with by the remedy of forfeiture which, as we shall see (at 10.3.2), is subject to statutory controls protecting the tenant and giving him every opportunity to remedy the breach and avoid losing his lease. Assistant Recorder Sedley QC suggested that the landlord's right to terminate on repudiatory breach by his tenant may in some way be modified by provisions in the lease relating to forfeiture, but it remains to be seen whether this approach will be adopted by the courts.

Although the decision in *Hussein* v *Mehlman* is only at first-instance and in the County Court, it has received considerable attention, and is recognised as a significant development (see Harpum [1993] CLJ 212). Its effect at present is to introduce into English land law another method of terminating a lease, which is already recognised in other jurisdictions.

Some five years after the decision in *Hussein* v *Mehlman*, repudiation of a lease was accepted by the Court of Appeal apparently without question in *Chartered Trust plc* v *Davies* (1997) 76 P&CR 397. In this case, the tenant of a unit in a shopping mall withheld rent because the business carried on in the premises was adversely affected by the landlord's failure to control the activities of other tenants in the mall. The tenant claimed that the landlord had broken his covenant not to derogate from his grant (see 9.2.1.2), and that this was so serious that it amounted to a repudiatory breach. This claim was accepted at first instance and the decision was upheld by the Court of Appeal. The judgment, given by Henry LJ, deals in some detail with derogation from grant, but does not discuss repudiation, merely saying at the end that that the trial judge's finding of repudiation was one which he was entitled to make (at p. 409). Despite its brevity, and the fact that no mention is made of *Hussein* v *Mehlman*, this would seem to support the view that a lease can now be treated as repudiated. The matter has been further considered by the High Court in *Nynehead Developments Ltd* v *RH Fibreboard Containers Ltd* [1999] 1 EGLR 7, in which the judge accepted that a lease could be terminated by acceptance of repudiatory breach, but found in the case before him that the breaches were not sufficiently serious to amount to repudiation.

Finally, you may like to note the view expressed in Megarry and Wade at p. 858:

Clearly both the length and the terms of the lease will be relevant to whether there has been a breach that will justify treating it as terminated. The longer the lease, the more artificial it is to regard it as other than an estate in land. It is therefore only in relation to shorter lettings that an allegation of discharge by breach is normally likely to be successful.

8.7 Determination by joint tenants

As you will see in Chapter 16, it is possible for a legal estate (either freehold or leasehold) to be owned by several people together, in the form of co-ownership known as 'joint tenancy'. In general, the rules about leases which we have considered so far apply to joint tenants of the estate in exactly the same way as to a sole tenant, but we do need to mention briefly here the special principles governing the termination of a lease which is jointly owned.

As Lord Bridge explained in *Hammersmith LBC* v *Monk* [1992] 1 AC 478 at p. 490:

... all positive dealings with a joint tenancy require the concurrence of all joint tenants if they are to be effective. Thus a single joint tenant cannot exercise a break clause in a lease, surrender the term, make a disclaimer, exercise the option to renew the tenancy or apply for relief from forfeiture.

This requirement that all joint tenants should agree to all dealings with the estate has a somewhat unexpected result when applied to the ending of a periodic tenancy. You may remember (from 8.5.2.2) that the theory underlying periodic tenancies is that their running on from one period to another depends on the will of the landlord and tenant that they should continue in this way. The notice to quit is an indication by one side to the other that he does not want to continue, i.e., does not want the lease to be renewed for another period.

In the context of a jointly owned tenancy, this means that all the joint tenants must want the tenancy to continue by being renewed for another period. If one of the tenants does not want to continue, the necessary agreement for renewal is not present and accordingly the periodic tenancy will come to an end. This means that, as the House of Lords held in *Hammersmith LBC* v *Monk* [1992] 1 AC 478, a notice to quit given by one joint tenant, without the concurrence of the other(s), is effective to determine a periodic tenancy.

The facts of *Monk*'s case were that a cohabiting couple held a joint periodic tenancy of a council flat, which was terminable on four weeks' notice. After some time, the woman left her partner and moved out of the flat. The local authority agreed to re-house her if she ended the periodic tenancy she already held from them, and she therefore gave the appropriate notice to quit without her co-tenant's knowledge or consent. The House of Lords held that this was a valid notice to quit which brought the periodic tenancy to an end, and the council was entitled to recover possession of the flat and evict the other joint tenant. Members of the House of Lords agreed that at first sight it seems amazing that one co-owner, acting unilaterally, can terminate the other owner's rights in his home. However, their decision was based both on the nature of periodic tenancies (as we have explained above), and also on general contractual principles:

If A and B contract with C on terms that are to continue in operation for one year in the first place and thereafter from year to year unless determined by notice at the end of the first or any subsequent year, neither A nor B has bound himself contractually for longer than one year ... the agreement is intended to continue beyond the initial term only if and so long as all parties to the agreement are willing that it should do so (at p. 483).

8.8 'Contractualisation' of leases

In the previous two sections we have noted some recent developments which emphasise the contractual nature of the lease and play down its proprietary aspects. In *Panalpina* the House of Lords applied the contractual doctrine of frustration to leases, while in *Monk* it was guided by general contractual principles in considering the effect of notice given by one of two joint tenants. Again, the Court of Appeal in *Chartered Trust* has apparently accepted that leases can be determined by acceptance of repudiatory breach.

These examples all relate to the process of ending a lease. The trend is also apparent in other cases, however, for example in *C. H. Bailey Ltd* v *Memorial Enterprises Ltd* [1974] 1 WLR 728 (on retrospective increases in rent following a rent review). Here Lord Denning rejected the suggestion that the matter was to be governed by considerations derived from feudal conceptions about the landlord–tenant relationship, saying:

It is time to get away from the medieval concept of rent ... in modern law, rent is not conceived of as a thing, but rather as a payment which a tenant is bound by his contract to make to his landlord for the use of the land.

The importance of the contractual relationship was also emphasised by Lord Browne-Wilkinson in *Prudential Assurance Co. Ltd* v *London Residuary Body* [1992] 2 AC 386 as he queried the justification for the ancient rule which requires leases to be certain, a rule which he described as operating to 'defeat contractually agreed arrangements between the parties'.

By contrast, Morritt LJ in his dissenting judgment in *Ingram* v *IRC* [1997] 4 All ER 395 at p. 422 considered that:

It is easy to make too much of the contractual nature of the relationship. The feature of a tenancy which distinguishes it from a licence or merely contractual right of occupation is the lessee's right to exclusive possession. But this right is a consequence of the ownership of the legal estate; it is not merely a contractual right, or it could not be the feature which distinguishes a lease from a licence.

It seems that this approach was favoured by the House of Lords, which reversed the decision of the Court of Appeal ([2001] 1 AC 293), Lord Hoffmann saying that in the particular circumstances of the case 'the contractual nature of the lease seems to me a matter of conveyancing theory rather than substance' (at p. 304).

Nevertheless, despite *Ingram*, it remains true that recent developments reveal a tendency by the courts to view the lease, at least initially, primarily as a contract. The development is summed up by one writer as follows:

when determining leasehold issues the courts will start from the premise that their foundation is in contract, instead of being reluctant to apply more general contractual principles to leases because of the fact that as property interests they are somehow special and sheltered from the rigours of contract (see Bright [1993] Conv 71).

The development we have noted in this section has been, so far, one of emphasis. As we explained in 8.6, the lease has been seen traditionally as operating on two levels, being both contractual and proprietary, and the shift in recent decisions has simply shown reliance on one aspect rather than another. *Bruton* v *London & Quadrant Housing Trust* [2000] 1 AC 406, however, introduced what seems to some commentators to be a new explanation of the nature of leases. It appears now that it is possible to have a contractual or non-proprietary lease, which gives rise to a landlord and tenant relationship but does not create an estate in the property. We will consider this analysis in more detail later (19.2.4.4), but it is worth noting here that some leases, albeit perhaps only a few, seem to have now come full circle, and returned to their purely contractual origins.

8.9 Effect on subtenant of determination of head lease

As we have seen (8.2.4.1), a tenant may himself grant a lease of the premises, giving his subtenant an estate for a shorter period, which he has carved out of his own estate. The resulting position can be portrayed diagrammatically:

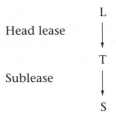

Head lease

Sublease

In this situation, S's term clearly depends upon the continuance of the head lease, and the general rule is that it comes to an end automatically if the head lease expires, or is determined by L's giving notice to quit or forfeiting the lease for breach of covenant.

8.9.1 Effect of surrender or merger

The general rule described above does not, however, apply. in the cases of surrender or merger, which are recognised as exceptions to it.

Thus, in the situation illustrated above, a surrender of the head lease by T will not end the sublease granted to S. In the words of Cockburn CJ in *Mellor* v *Watkins* (1874) LR 9 QB 400 at p. 404:

... when a person vountarily surrenders his lease, he cannot by so doing put an end to an undertenancy created by himself ...

S will become a tenant of L, on the terms and conditions of the sublease. In other words, the surrender has no real effect on the subtenant; it merely alters the person to whom he is to pay his rent and to whom he owes a duty to observe the covenants in the sublease (LPA 1925, s. 150). Similarly, if T's head lease and L's reversion merge, either in T or in some third party, the new owner of the combined estate will hold it subject to the sublease, and S's position will be in all respects the same as we have described in relation to surrender. In both cases, there is no hardship in the head landlord, or his successor, being bound by the sublease, because he has consented to the arrangement which has produced this situation.

8.9.2 Head lease ended on tenant's initiative

Although the effect on the subtenant of the determination of the head lease is in general well-established, there was, until recently, some uncertainty about his position in cases where the head lease was brought to an end on the initiative of the tenant, through operating a break clause or by giving notice to quit to his landlord (sometimes called an 'upwards notice'). Despite various *obiter dicta* on this matter, and one unreported first-instance decision (*Brown* v *Wilson* (1949)), it emerged in *Pennell* v *Payne* [1995] QB 192 that there was no authority on this point binding on the Court of Appeal. The court was therefore required to decide as a matter of policy between the competing interests of a hypothetical subtenant and a head landlord ('hypothetical' because no sublease had been granted in this case). If the sublease were to survive the determination of the head lease, the tenant would impose his subtenant on the landlord against the landlord's will; if, on the other hand, the sublease were to end, the tenant, by ending his own lease, would destroy the interest he had created, thus derogating from his grant. Faced with this choice, the Court of Appeal took the view that 'the considerations against allowing a tenant unilaterally to foist his subtenant upon the landlord are in total compelling' (at p. 270), and the court held that if the tenant terminated his lease by an upwards notice, the landlord would be entitled to regain the land from the subtenant. This decision was subsequently approved by the House of Lords in *Barrett* v *Morgan* [2000] 2 AC 264.

In such a case, it is likely that the tenant would be liable to his subtenant for breach of his covenant for quiet enjoyment (as to which, see 9.2.1.1) and Lord Millett, in *Barrett* v *Morgan*, suggests that a subtenant, if forewarned, could seek an injunction to restrain his landlord from serving the upwards notice.

8.9.3 Head lease ended by landlord with tenant's consent

Finally, we should note that the fact that the landlord's notice to quit is served by pre-arrangement with the tenant who does not oppose it, because he wants to determine the sublease, does not prevent that sublease from ending along with the head lease. In *Barrett* v *Morgan* ([1999] 1 WLR 1109), the Court of Appeal had held that in such circumstances, where the landlord and tenant had agreed on a course of action, the notice was consensual rather than unilateral. The termination of the lease by notice in this way was indistinguishable from surrender, and accordingly the sublease survived the determination of the head lease. This decision was, however, reversed on appeal by the House of Lords (*Barrett* v *Morgan* [2000] 2 AC 264), Lord Millett (at p. 274) describing the lower court's decision as having 'the extraordinary result that the parties to a tenancy cannot achieve together by agreement what either can achieve alone without it'. To the House of Lords the essential distinction was not between consensual and unilateral acts, but between agreements made by the parties to the head lease before and after the grant of the sublease. A subtenant takes his interest subject to the terms of the head lease agreed *before* his tenancy was created, and his title cannot survive the termination of the head lease in accordance with those terms. By contrast, his title cannot be prejudiced by any agreement (such as for surrender) between the parties to the head lease which is made *after* the creation of his sublease.

8.10 Some more types of lease

8.10.1 Special forms of tenancy

So far in this chapter we have concentrated on leases for a fixed term and on periodic tenancies, but it is now time to mention three more types of lease: tenancies at sufferance, tenancies at will and tenancies by estoppel. We will also consider concurrent leases, which arise where a landlord grants two or more leases, taking effect at the same time, in respect of the same piece of land.

8.10.2 **Tenancies at sufferance**

Tenancies at sufferance are rather peculiar in that they arise purely by operation of law and entirely without any form of agreement between the landlord and the tenant. They arise in cases in which the tenant originally had a valid tenancy but continues to occupy the property after the expiration of that term. This occupation must be without the landlord's consent, for if the tenant remains with the land-lord's assent he holds as a tenant at will rather than at sufferance, while if the landlord dissents the former tenant is in the position of a trespasser.

Thus, in *Remon* v *City of London Real Property Co. Ltd* [1921] 1 KB 49 in which a tenant remained in possession of the premises after a valid notice to quit had expired, the tenant was held not to be a tenant at sufferance since his landlords had taken action to endeavour to remove him from the premises. Scrutton LJ said (at p. 58):

[T]enants by sufferance seem to have been confined to persons who held over without the assent or dissent of their landlords, and not to have included persons who held over wrongfully in spite of the active objection of their landlords.

In such a case there is no real tenancy, despite the name 'tenancy at sufferance' and no real relationship of landlord and tenant. The landlord cannot sue for rent (but may claim recompense for the use of the land—called 'mesne profits'). Should the landlord accept rent then this will normally give rise to a fresh periodic tenancy (*Mann* v *Lovejoy* (1826) Ry & M 355 and *Doe d Clarke* v *Smaridge* (1845) 7 QB 957). At common law the tenant at sufferance was in a very precarious position, because the landlord was able to recover possession of the premises, even by force. However, the landlord's rights are now subject to ss. 6 and 12(3) of the Criminal Law Act 1977 and s. 3 of the Protection from Eviction Act 1977.

8.10.3 **Tenancies at will**

The tenancy at will may arise in any case in which the tenant occupies the land with the permission of the landlord on the terms that the tenancy may be terminated by either party at any time. Parke B once described the tenancy at will as being the lowest estate known to the law (*Doe d Gray* v *Stanion* (1836) 1 M & W 700), although at an earlier date Littleton had said that a tenant at will 'hath no certain nor sure estate'. Unlike the tenancy at sufferance it does give rise to a real relation-ship of landlord and tenant and rent may be payable (*Anderson* v *Midland Railway Co.* (1861) 3 El & El 614), although this is unusual. However, it must be noted that a tenancy at will, being for an uncertain period, appears to fall outside the definition of 'term of years' provided by the 1925 legislation, and thus be incapable of amounting to a legal estate. As a result, it used to be suggested that the tenancy would take effect in equity, but this of course involves the notion of a trust, which seems remarkably cumbersome in the usual circumstances of a tenancy at will. Megarry and Wade (at p. 794) now suggests that:

probably the best analysis of [the tenancy at will] is that it is a form of tenure but one that confers no estate. Although an estate cannot exist without tenure, there seems no reason why tenure should not exist without any estate. A may hold land of B, but for no fixed period and merely for so long as B may allow.

8.10.3.1 *Creation*

The tenancy at will may be expressly granted (as in *Manfield & Sons Ltd* v *Botchin* [1970] 2 QB 612—a case in which rent was payable) or may arise by implication from the act of the parties. Thus a tenancy at will may be inferred where a former tenant continues to occupy the property with his landlord's consent after his lease has expired (as in *Dean and Chapter of the Cathedral and Metropolitan Church of Christ Canterbury* v *Whitbread* (1995) 72 P&CR 9). It may also arise where the purchaser of a freehold or leasehold estate is allowed into possession of the property before the conveyance or transfer, or grant of the lease, has been concluded, and we have already seen an example of this in *Javad* v *Mohammed Aqil* [1991] 1 WLR 1007 (8.3.1.2). Again, an owner may allow friends or members of his family to occupy his property for an indefinite period, and this arrangement may give rise to a tenancy at will. However, recent case law suggests that today the courts will be more inclined to regard some of these arrangements as licences, rather than as tenancies at will (*Heslop* v *Burns* [1974] 1 WLR 1241; *Street* v *Mountford* [1985] AC 809), and this is considered further in Chapter 19.

8.10.3.2 *Determination*

A tenancy at will may be brought to an end in a number of ways. On the one hand, it may be converted into an implied periodic tenancy, if rent is paid and accepted on a regular basis; while on the other hand, the whole arrangement may be determined at will by either side, without any period of notice. Moreover, the relationship is a personal one, so that it ends if either party dies, or assigns his interest to another.

8.10.4 **Tenancies by estoppel**

8.10.4.1 *Circumstances in which tenancies by estoppel arise*

So far, we have assumed that the leases we are considering have been created by a landlord who has a right to grant an estate or interest in the property, either by virtue of being a fee simple owner or having a valid, superior lease. It may be, however, that the person purporting to grant the lease proves to have a defective title himself. In earlier cases, he may be a mortgagor who under pre-1926 law has conveyed his full estate to the mortgagee as security for a loan. In more recent times, he may have only an equitable lease (as in *Industrial Properties (Barton Hill) Ltd* v *Associated Electrical Industries Ltd* [1977] 1 QB 580), or may be in the process of buying the property, but not yet have completed the purchase (*Church of England Building Society* v *Piskor* [1954] Ch 553). Yet again, as in *Bruton* v *London & Quadrant Housing Trust* [2000] 1 AC 406, he may be only a licensee.

Before the amendment of LPA 1925 s. 44 by LRA 2002, a prospective tenant had no right to investigate his landlord's title, unless provision for this was made in the preliminary contract. (For details of this amendment and the circumstances in which a tenant still has no right to investigate title, see 5.5.3.2.(1).) Thus a tenant might well take a lease in good faith and only later discover the truth. In such cases the tenant is not, however, able to repudiate his obligations under the lease, relying on the landlord's defective title, nor is the landlord able to deny the existence of the tenant's lease. In other words both parties are estopped from later denying one another's title (see *Industrial Properties (Barton Hill) Ltd* v *Associated Electrical Industries Ltd* [1977] QB 580). In this situation, there is said to be a tenancy 'by estoppel'.

We should mention briefly here that since the decision of the House of Lords in *Bruton* v *London & Quadrant Housing Trust* [2000] 1 AC 406 it appears that the parties are also bound by a contractual lease, which creates a landlord and tenant relationship between them, despite the fact that no leasehold estate has been created. A full account of this decision and its implications can be found in Chapter 19 (see 19.2.4.4).

8.10.4.2 *Estoppel by representation and estoppel by grant*

There are two ways in which a tenancy by estoppel may arise. The prospective landlord may make a specific *representation* about his title, for example reciting in the document granting the lease that he is the fee simple owner of the property. He is then estopped by this representation from denying the title. However, even if he does not make such a statement, the fact that he purported to *grant* the lease is considered sufficient to create an estoppel by virtue of the common law principle that a grantor is precluded from disputing the validity and effect of his grant (see *First National Bank* v *Thompson* [1996] Ch 231 at 237, a decision which, though dealing with a mortgage by estoppel, states the general principles which apply equally to tenancies). Estoppel by grant is often described as '*estoppel by deed*', but it applies to all cases of purported grant, in whatever form they are made.

Historically, both these forms of estoppel are common law developments. We mention this in case you should be tempted to explain tenancy by estoppel by reference to the principles of *equitable* proprietary estoppel (i.e., representation, reliance and detriment), which are discussed at various other points in this book. It is important to realise that the forms of estoppel we are considering here are quite distinct, being derived from different authorities and operating on different principles.

Although both forms of estoppel may prevent denial of the landlord's title, there are some differences between the way in which they operate. Estoppel by grant arises only where the grantor has no legal estate at all in the land at the date at which the purported grant was made. If he had some legal estate, less in extent than that which he purported to grant, the whole estate would pass to the grantee and no tenancy by estoppel would arise. Thus, if the landlord had, for example, a leasehold estate for five years and attempted to grant a sublease for a longer period than his own lease (e.g., for 25 years) the purported grant of the sublease would not create a lease by estoppel but would operate as an assignment of the existing five-year term (see 8.2.4.1).

By contrast, where the estoppel arises from a specific representation by the grantor about his title, he is estopped from denying that he has the particular estate which he claimed to hold. The fact that he has some lesser estate does not prevent the estoppel operating, so that a tenancy by estoppel for the full period which he purported to give will come into existence.

8.10.4.3 *Rights and duties under a tenancy by estoppel*

As between themselves, the parties have all the rights and duties of a landlord and tenant. Moreover, such a tenancy can be assigned and in general binds the grantor's successors, although the rules on this vary depending on whether the estoppel arises by grant or by representation (see further Megarry and Wade, p. 801). The tenancy is also regarded as a lease for the purpose of various statutory codes protecting the tenant (e.g., the Rent Acts).

Thus, unless an owner with superior title intervenes, a tenancy by estoppel is generally as effective and binding as any other lease (*Gouldsworth v Knights* (1843) 11 M & W 337). If, however, at any time the superior owner does assert his claim to the property, then the tenant may become liable to the superior owner, to compensate him for the use of the land. In such a case, or if evicted by a superior owner, the tenant may then dispute his landlord's title and resist successfully a claim for rent. In the *Industrial Properties* case [1977] 1 QB 580 Lord Denning MR said (at p. 596):

> Short of eviction by title paramount, or its equivalent, . . . the tenant is estopped from denying the title of the landlord. It is no good his saying: 'The property does not belong to you but to a third person' unless that third person actually comes forward and successfully makes an adverse claim . . . If the third person . . . makes no adverse claim or is debarred from making it, the tenant remains estopped from denying the landlord's title.

8.10.4.4 *Feeding the estoppel*

If at any time during the continuance of the lease by estoppel the landlord obtains a full legal title to the land, this acquisition of title is said to 'feed' the lease by estoppel, which thereupon becomes a full legal lease (*Rawlin's Case* (1587) Jenk 254). Thus, if a purchaser, before taking a conveyance of the fee simple estate, should purport to grant a lease of the property, that lease will take effect only as a lease by estoppel, but will become a full legal lease as soon as the fee simple is conveyed to the purchaser.

This can cause problems when the purchaser obtains a mortgage in order to finance the purchase of the estate but later fails to keep up his mortgage repayments. Both the lease and mortgage must have been created after title to the estate vested in the purchaser but in which order? If the first thing that happens is the feeding of the estoppel, the property over which the mortgage was granted was the estate subject to the lease and thus the mortgagee (the lender) is bound by the pre-existing legal lease. If however the mortgage is made before the legal lease is created, the result is different: the mortgage gets priority and the mortgagee could sell the mortgaged estate free of the lease. It used to be thought that, even if all the documents were prepared and signed in advance, there must be a moment ('a scintilla of time') between the vesting of the legal estate in the purchaser and the creation of the mortgage during which the estoppel could be fed (see *Church of England Building Society v Piskor* [1954] Ch 553). The defendants in *Abbey National Building Society v Cann* [1991] 1 AC 56 (see 5.10.4.2) relied upon this argument (although not in relation to tenancy by estoppel), claiming that there had been a scintilla of time between the transfer to Cann and his grant of the mortgage to the building society, and that in this brief moment their beneficial interests took effect and became overriding interests under LRA 1925, s. 70(1)(g). The House of Lords rejected this argument, holding that the transfer and the grant of the mortgage, both of which occurred on the same day, were to be regarded as happening together, and overruling *Church of England Building Society v Piskor*. Since this decision it seems, therefore, that although a tenancy by estoppel may be fed by the acquisition of the legal estate it cannot gain priority over a mortgage created at the same time.

8.10.5 **Concurrent leases**

Finally, a brief mention must be made of concurrent leases, or 'leases of the reversion' (not to be confused with reversionary or future leases, which we described earlier in 8.1.3.4). When L has granted a lease to T, it is possible for L to grant another lease to A in respect of the same piece of land. A cannot take physical possession of the property, because T is already entitled to that, so the lease to A is regarded as a lease of L's reversion on T's lease. If the lease to A is longer than that to T, A will eventually be able to take physical possession of the property, but if it is for the same period, or a shorter one, he will never be able to enter, and he acts simply as T's landlord, collecting any rent due and enforcing covenants in the lease.

In the past, concurrent leases were not granted very often, except as the conveyancing device which permitted the creation of successive mortgages of the same estate (see Chapter 21). However, under the Landlord and Tenant (Covenants) Act 1995, a landlord may, in certain circumstances, be required to grant a lease of the reversion (described by the Act as 'an overriding lease'), and as a result concurrent leases may become more common. We shall explain how the 'overriding lease' works later in the next chapter (see 9.5.3.1(3)), when describing the changes introduced by the Act.

FURTHER READING

Certainty of term
Bright, 'Uncertainty in Leases—Is it a Vice?' (1993) 13 LS 38.
Smith, 'What is Wrong With Certainty in Leases?' [1993] Conv 461.
Smith, 'An Uncertain Shift' [1998] Conv 326.

Repudiation
Bright, 'Repudiating a Lease—Contract Rules' [1993] Conv 71.
Harpum, 'Leases as Contracts' [1993] CLJ 212.
Pawlowski and Brown, 'Repudiatory Breach in the Leasehold Context' [1999] 63 Conv 150.

9

Obligations of landlord and tenant

9.1 Introduction

9.1.1 Obligations of landlord and tenant

Every lease, even the most informal, contains provisions which define the obligations of the landlord and tenant under the lease. In a formally granted long lease it is likely that these obligations will be detailed and complex, and will be embodied in a long document. In the case of an informal periodic tenancy the obligations will be few, and will, in the main, be implied into the agreement by operation of law. The effect of these obligations is crucial to the operation of leases and gives rise to two main issues:

(a) the nature of the obligations placed upon the original contracting parties (the original landlord and tenant); and

(b) the effect of those original obligations on those who later acquire the lease or the reversion.

9.1.2 Covenants and conditions

Obligations in a lease may be imposed in one of two ways: by covenants or by conditions. A 'covenant' is a promise made by one party (the '*covenantor*') for the benefit of another party (the '*covenantee*') which is contained in a deed. As all leases for more than three years should be made by deed (LPA 1925, s. 52), normally the promises made in the lease will be covenants. However, there is a problem in the case of shorter leases, which can be created informally (s. 54(2)) and which therefore will not require a deed. It appears, however, that the promises in such leases are still to be regarded as enforceable covenants and may even pass to bind successive owners of the property (see *Boyer* v *Warbey* [1953] 1 QB 234 which involved a written lease for three years, at 9.6.1.6(1), and *Weg Motors Ltd* v *Hales* [1962] Ch 49).

Covenants must be distinguished from 'conditions', which may also impose obligations on a tenant. If a tenant breaks a condition in the lease the landlord will have an automatic right to bring the term to an end, whilst the landlord does not automatically have such a right for breach of covenant and must make express provision for it in the lease. The question of whether a particular term in a lease is a covenant or a condition is a matter which is decided by reference to the intention of the parties. A condition arises in cases in which it is clear that the continuance of the term is conditional upon the fulfilment by the tenant of his obligations.

Generally, the courts presume that the terms of the lease are covenants, unless clear words are used to show that the obligation is intended to be a condition. Thus, in *Doe d Henniker* v *Watt* (1828) 8 B & C 308 it was held that a term in which the tenant 'stipulated and conditioned' that he would not assign or sublet the property, was a condition rather than a covenant. In fact most obligations, even the most fundamental (e.g., to pay rent) will be covenants rather than conditions.

9.1.3 Types of covenant

Every lease, however simple, contains some covenants, because certain basic covenants by both landlord and tenant are implied into every lease. (It should always be remembered that a lease is a reciprocal arrangement which accordingly imposes obligations on the landlord, as well as upon the tenant.) Some leases, typically long leases, contain in addition to (or in substitution for) the *implied covenants* a very large number of *express covenants*. It is not possible to include here a list of all possible covenants because there are huge variations in such matters depending on the circumstances. We will accordingly deal only with the common express covenants and with implied covenants. In addition there is a list of covenants, called the *usual covenants*, which are important in cases in which the grant of a lease is preceded by a contract to grant the lease (as is normal conveyancing procedure in the case of long leases). In such cases it is an implied term of the contract that the lease, once granted, will contain at least the 'usual covenants' and thus the parties can be obliged to include those covenants when the lease is granted. In the following sections we look first at express covenants, and then at implied and usual covenants, but before doing so will first consider some practical examples of the formats used for various leases.

9.1.4 Some examples of leases

9.1.4.1 *2 Trant Way: basement flat*

You will recall from the last chapter that the basement flat at 2 Trant Way has been let by Fingall Forest, the fee simple owner, to his friend Gerald Gruyère at a rent of £100 per week. This agreement was made orally and no further terms were specified. Mr Gruyère has been in possession of the flat for some time and pays his rent regularly.

9.1.4.2 *2 Trant Way: maisonette*

The ground and first-floor maisonette of 2 Trant Way is to be let by Fingall Forest to Harry Harding. The lease term is to be 99 years and Mr Harding is to pay a premium of £160,000 and a ground rent of £100 per annum, for the first 10 years, with a provision for regular increases thereafter. The draft lease, which has been prepared by Mr Forest's solicitor for approval by Mr Harding's legal adviser, is a very detailed document, which is over 40 pages long. In this lease, which will be made by deed, the tenant will undertake a long list of obligations, ranging from a promise not to keep pets to covenants not to assign etc. without the landlord's consent and to contribute to the cost of maintaining the structure of the premises. The landlord will also enter into a number of covenants, including a covenant to keep the building insured (though the tenant will pay a share of the insurance premium).

9.1.4.3 *6 Trant Way*

The fee simple in 6 Trant Way was owned by Irene Ivy. On 25 March 1979 Mrs Ivy granted a 40-year lease of the property to John Jarlsberg. The lease was made by deed and is in the following form:

THIS LEASE made the 25th day of March 1979 between IRENE IVY of 15 Proudie Street, Grantchester in Stilton (hereinafter called 'the landlord') of the one part and JOHN JARLSBERG of 63 Upper Terrace, Mousehole in Stilton (hereinafter called 'the tenant') of the other part WITNESSETH as follows:

1. The landlord hereby demises unto the tenant ALL THAT messuage or dwelling-house, together with the garden, offices and outbuilding thereto belonging, known at 6 Trant Way, Mousehole in the County of Stilton, which premises for the purposes of identification only are outlined in red on the plan attached hereto, TO HOLD the same unto the tenant from the 25th day of March 1979 for the term of 40 years YIELDING AND PAYING therefore the yearly rent agreed or determined in accordance with the provisions of clause 2 hereof by equal quarterly instalments in advance on the usual quarter-days (the first payment to be made on the date hereof).

2. (a) The rent shall be £3,000 per annum for the first five years of the said term.

   (b) [Rent review clause for later portion of term.]

3. The tenant hereby COVENANTS with the landlord as follows:

   (a) To pay the rent hereby reserved on the days and in the manner aforesaid without any deductions whatsoever.

   (b) To pay all rates, taxes and outgoings of an annual or recurring nature in respect of the demised premises.

   (c) Not to use or permit the use of the demised premises or any part thereof otherwise than as a private dwelling-house.

   (d) Not without the prior written consent of the landlord to assign, sublet or part with possession of the whole or part of the demised premises.

   [Further covenants by the tenant.]

4. The landlord hereby COVENANTS with the tenant as follows:

   (a) That the tenant paying the rent hereby reserved and observing and performing the covenants on his part herein contained shall peaceably and quietly hold and enjoy the premises hereby demised during the said term without any interruption or disturbance by the landlord or any person claiming under or in trust for the landlord.

   (b) That if at any time during the continuance of the term hereby created the tenant shall desire to purchase the fee simple reversion in the demised premises the landlord on receipt of six months' notice in writing from the tenant shall assure the demised premises unto the tenant in fee simple in consideration of a sum equal to 95 per cent of the market value of the premises, such value to be assessed as at the date upon which such notice shall expire.

   [Further covenants by the landlord, including one 'to keep in repair the structure and exterior of the premises'.]

5. PROVIDED ALWAYS and it is hereby expressly agreed and declared as follows:

   (a) That if at any time the rent hereby reserved or any part thereof is 21 days in arrears (whether formally demanded or not) or if the tenant has failed to observe or perform any of the tenant's covenants herein contained, the landlord may re-enter upon the demised premises or any part thereof in the name of the whole and thereupon the term hereby granted shall absolutely determine but without prejudice to any claim by the landlord against the tenant for any antecedent breach of the covenants herein contained.

. . .
IN WITNESS whereof the hand and seal of the landlord and of the tenant have been hereunto set the day and year first above-written.
SIGNED SEALED AND DELIVERED
by the said landlord   [Signature of Irene Ivy] SEAL
in the presence of:
[Signed by witness]
SIGNED SEALED AND DELIVERED
by the said tenant   [Signature of John Jarlsberg] SEAL
in the presence of:
[Signed by witness]
[There follows a plan of the property.]

(Note that this lease was made before the Law of Property (Miscellaneous Provisions) Act 1989 came into force and thus it complies with the old formalities for a deed and was signed, sealed and delivered.)

9.2 Express covenants

There is a very wide range of express covenants which can be made by landlord or tenant, and, as we have already said, all we can do here is to mention the most important express covenants and discuss general matters of construction. One point which can be made about all express covenants is that usually they will be construed strictly against the landlord, since it is he who was responsible for the form of the lease.

9.2.1 Express covenants by the landlord

9.2.1.1 Landlord's covenant to allow tenant quiet enjoyment
The effect of this covenant is that the landlord must let the tenant into possession of the premises and that the landlord will be liable if the tenant's enjoyment of the property is substantially disturbed by any action of the landlord or by the action of someone deriving an interest in the property from the landlord. The landlord is not responsible for the actions of unrelated third parties.

It should be noted that the covenant for 'quiet enjoyment' is not about noise made by the landlord. It is a wider concept involving any acts which prevent the tenant from using the demised premises. The creation of considerable amounts of noise might, of course, have this effect (as was accepted by the House of Lords in *Southwark LBC* v *Tanner* [2001] 1 AC 1—see below), but the word 'quiet' in this context means 'uninterrupted', rather than 'noiseless', enjoyment of the property, and most of the cases involve something other than noise.

(1) *Examples of breach*   An obvious example of the breach of this covenant is the case of *Perera* v *Vandiyar* [1953] 1 WLR 672 in which the landlord tried to force the tenant out of the premises by continual harrassment of a serious nature, including having the gas and electricity supplies to the property cut off. Such severe breach of

a landlord's basic obligations can also amount to a criminal offence under s. 1(3) or 1(3A) of the Protection from Eviction Act 1977 if the landlord's intention is to force the tenant to leave the premises (see 10.2.1).

It has also been held to be a breach of the covenant to erect scaffolding which prevents the tenant gaining access to the premises (*Owen* v *Gadd* [1956] 2 QB 99). Other examples of breach of this covenant include: removing the windows and doors (*Lavender* v *Betts* [1942] 2 All ER 72); persistently threatening the tenant in an attempt to force him to leave (*Kenny* v *Preen* [1963] 1 QB 499); and causing the land to subside by carrying out mining activities beneath the surface (*Markham* v *Paget* [1908] 1 Ch 697).

It should be noted, however, that acts which merely inconvenience the tenant do not amount to a breach of the covenant, particularly if the act complained of occurs outside the demised area. Thus, in *Browne* v *Flower* [1911] 1 Ch 219 a landlord who erected an external staircase, outside the demised premises, was held not to have broken the covenant even though persons using the new staircase were able to look in through the windows of the demised premises and the tenant was thereby deprived of his privacy.

(2) *Condition of property*   It should also be noted that the covenant for quiet enjoyment does not impose on the landlord any liability in respect of the condition of the property at the start of the lease. In *Southwark LBC* v *Tanner* [2001] 1 AC 1 the tenants of a block of flats complained that noise from each other's flats seriously affected their quality of life, and claimed that their landlord was in breach of its covenant of quiet enjoyment. It was generally agreed that the neighbouring tenants were using their flats in a normal manner, and that the disturbance they caused to each other was attributable to the lack of soundproofing between the flats, which were old and not constructed to modern standards.

The House of Lords accepted in principle that excessive noise may constitute a substantial interference with the tenant's enjoyment of his property, and could amount to a breach of the covenant for quiet enjoyment. However, this covenant is prospective, that is to say, it is a covenant that the tenant's enjoyment will not be disturbed by any act of the landlord or those claiming under him *after* the tenancy has begun. It does not apply to things done *before* the grant of the tenancy, even though these may have continuing consequences for the tenant. Here, the cause of the problem was the lack of soundproofing, which existed before the premises were let and before the landlord had given its covenant for quiet enjoyment.

The House also drew attention to the fact that in general (with a minor statutory exception—see 9.3.1.3) there is no implied warranty by the landlord as to the condition or fitness of the premises; it is understood that the risk is on the tenant, who takes the property as he finds it ('caveat lessee'). In Lord Hoffmann's words (at p. 12):

It would be entirely inconsistent with this common understanding if the covenant for quiet enjoyment were interpreted to create liability for disturbance or inconvenience or any other damage attributable to the condition of the premises.

Whether such a liability should be created, with its resulting financial burdens on private and public landlords, was a question for Parliament not for the judges.

(3) *Acts of persons claiming under landlord*   A landlord may be liable under this covenant even if the act amounting to a breach is committed by a third party. He

will only be liable, however, for the lawful actions of those deriving their title under him, or for the actions of his servants or agents within the scope of their authority. The landlord is not liable for actions committed by persons deriving their title from him who are acting in excess of their own legal rights. In *Sanderson* v *Berwick-upon-Tweed Corporation* (1884) 13 QBD 547, a tenant complained that he was unable to use the demised premises (a farm) in a normal way because of flooding caused by drains on two neighbouring farms which were also owned by the landlord. Both the neighbouring farms were also let to tenants. On one farm the drains were in good order but the flooding was caused by the excessive use of them by the tenant: here the tenant was acting in excess of his lawful rights. On the second farm the tenant was using the drains perfectly properly, but flooding was being caused by a defect in the drain: here the tenant was acting within his lawful rights. The landlord was held not to be liable for the damage caused by the actions of the first tenant, but was liable for damage caused by the actions of the second.

(4) *Acts of persons with superior title*   The landlord is not responsible for acts committed by a person with a title which is superior to (rather than derived from) the landlord's title. Such a superior title is described as a 'title paramount'. This rule creates a substantial danger for the tenant, as is demonstrated by the case of *Jones* v *Lavington* [1903] 1 KB 253. In that case a tenant, who had only 8½ years left to run on his own lease, purported to grant a sublease of the property for 10½ years. (As we have already seen (8.2.4.1), this in fact operates as an assignment of the lease.) In due course the freehold owner recovered the property from the 'subtenant' two years before the 'sublease' should have ended. The 'subtenant' could not resist the claim of the freehold owner because the original tenant had no power to give more than he had got (*nemo dat quod non habet*) and could only give an 8½-year term. An action by the 'subtenant' against the tenant also failed because the tenant was not liable for actions by someone with title paramount (the freehold owner). However, we have already noted (at 8.9.2) the Court of Appeal's view that a subtenant would have a claim for breach of this covenant if his landlord determined the head lease by giving notice to quit to his own landlord (or possibly by operating the provisions of a break clause), thus automatically destroying the sublease (*Pennell* v *Payne* [1995] QB 192).

9.2.1.2 *Covenant that landlord will not derogate from his grant*

It is a general principle of law that you must not take away with one hand what you have given with the other, because to do so is to derogate from your grant (*Palmer* v *Fletcher* (1663) 1 Lev 122). To a certain extent this covenant overlaps with the covenant for quiet enjoyment but since this covenant not to derogate from the grant can be broken without there being a physical interference with the use of the premises, it is still worth considering it separately.

(1) *Examples of breach*   A good illustration of the point is provided by *Aldin* v *Latimer Clark, Muirhead & Co.* [1894] 2 Ch 437, in which premises had been let to a tenant subject to a covenant that the tenant would use the property to run the business of a timber merchant. The demised premises included a wood-drying shed which depended on a natural flow of air passing on to the demised premises from neighbouring property, which also belonged to the landlord. Buildings were

erected on the neighbouring property which prevented the free flow of air to the drying shed and thereby rendered it useless. This did not amount to a breach of the covenant for quiet enjoyment because there was no physical interference with the demised premises. These facts did, however, amount to a breach of the obligation placed on the landlord not to derogate from his grant, because the action complained of prevented the very use for which the demised premises had been let.

Another example is provided by *Harmer v Jumbil (Nigeria) Tin Areas Ltd* [1921] 1 Ch 200, in which land was let to store explosives. In order to store such items the tenant had to obtain a licence and it was a condition of the licence that there should be no other buildings within a specified distance. Accordingly the tenant was entitled to prevent the landlord from building on neighbouring land, which he also owned, because this would lead to the loss of the tenant's licence and prevent him from using the premises for the purpose for which they were let.

The tenant who relies on this principle must have made it clear to the landlord at the time of the grant what use he has in mind for the land (*Robinson v Kilvert* (1889) 41 ChD 88). Also the act complained of must actually interfere with the contemplated use and it is not sufficient to say that the landlord's actions have made the use more expensive or less profitable. Thus, permitting a competing business to be run from a neighbouring property has been held not to be derogation from grant (*Port v Griffith* [1938] 1 All ER 295—a decision recently considered and applied in *Romulus Trading Co. Ltd v Comet Properties Ltd* [1996] 2 EGLR 70).

(2) *Acts of persons claiming under landlord* Once again the landlord is liable also for the actions of persons deriving title from him (*Aldin v Latimer Clark, Muirhead & Co.*). A recent illustration is provided by *Chartered Trust plc v Davies* (1997) 76 P&-CR 396. A tenant of a unit in a shopping mall complained that trade was adversely affected by the activities of neighbouring shopkeepers (such as blocking access to the shop), which were held at first instance to constitute nuisance. The common landlord had the power to stop the activities complained of, but did not do so. He was held by the Court of Appeal to have continued or adopted the nuisance committed by his other tenants, and thus to have derogated from his grant.

9.2.1.3 *Landlord's covenant to grant a further term (option for renewal)*

It is quite common to include a covenant giving the tenant a right to renew the lease for a further period on the expiration of the first term. The tenant is free to choose whether or not to exercise this option; if he does so, the landlord is bound to grant the further term. The option is enforceable against the landlord's successor or assignee but, perhaps rather surprisingly in the landlord–tenant context, such an option in a lease of unregistered land has to be registered as a class C(iv) land charge if it is to be enforced against a purchaser of the legal estate for money or money's worth (*Beesly v Hallwood Estates Ltd* [1960] 1 WLR 549).

Perpetually renewable leases

A covenant to grant a further term can give rise to problems if it is badly drafted. In *Northchurch Estates Ltd v Daniels* [1947] Ch 117, a lease for a year contained a clause which gave the tenant a right to renew the lease at the end of the year 'on identical terms and conditions'. Unfortunately this clause, if interpreted literally, means that the second term will include an identical provision allowing the tenant to call for a third term, the third term a clause providing for a fourth, and so on. As a result, the tenant would have a right to renew the lease perpetually. This caused considerable difficulties for the landlord, who would be able to terminate this perpetual lease only if the tenant broke a term of the agreement or forgot to give notice of his wish to renew.

Such perpetually renewable leases are subject to s. 145 and Sch. 15 of the Law of Property Act 1922 (which applies to all leases created after 1925). These provisions convert the affected lease into a fixed term of 2,000 years, subject to a right of the tenant to terminate the lease on 10 days' notice in writing on any occasion on which the original lease would have expired if it had not been renewed. The landlord has no similar right to terminate.

These rules produce a result in which a landlord is heavily penalised for the careless drafting of the original lease. Usually it is quite clear that the original intention of the parties was that the tenant should have the right to renew the lease for a second term, with a further right to a third and final term at his choice. In *Northchurch Estates Ltd* v *Daniels* the real intention of the parties was that the tenant should have a lease for one year with a right to renew the lease twice if he so chose. The unfairness of transforming such an agreement into a 2,000-year term, when three years were intended, is obvious. Accordingly, in more recent decisions the courts have reversed their earlier tendency to apply a literal interpretation of such leases and have adopted a more liberal approach, in order to prevent tenants obtaining an unjustified windfall through poor drafting (see, e.g., *Marjorie Burnett Ltd* v *Barclay* [1981] 1 EGLR 41).

9.2.1.4 *Landlord's covenant to sell the reversion to the tenant (option to purchase)*

In appropriate cases, a covenant of this sort may be included. We have given an example in the lease of 6 Trant Way (see 9.1.4.3), and will consider questions about the enforcement of such an option later, at 9.7.1.3.

9.2.2 Express covenants by the tenant

9.2.2.1 *Tenant's covenant to pay rent*

Very few leases are concluded without there being an express agreement between the parties about the payment of rent. It is a general rule that the rent must be certain (a court cannot enforce an uncertain agreement) but this rule may be satisfied by providing a means whereby the rent is to be determined (e.g., rent to be set by a surveyor chosen by a named body). It is also common to include a clause whereby the rent is to be reviewed (usually with a view to increasing it) at intervals during the lease: see cl. 2(b) in the lease at 9.1.4.3. A great deal of case law on the interpretation of such rent-review clauses exists, but this is beyond the scope of this book. For further information you should consult a specialist text on landlord and tenant law.

9.2.2.2 *Tenant's covenants not to assign, sublet or part with possession*

A tenant is the owner of a legal estate in land and it is a basic principle of English law that an estate in land is freely alienable. However, the right to sell, or otherwise dispose of, an estate can be limited if the estate owner enters into a covenant to that effect. Most landlords take great care when selecting tenants (e.g., to ensure that they are of good character and can pay the rent) and, quite reasonably, will wish to ensure that the premises do not come into the hands of some less desirable person through assignment or subletting. Accordingly it is common to include in a lease a covenant which restricts the tenant's right to assign, sublet or otherwise part with possession of the demised premises.

(1) *Absolute and qualified covenants*   Covenants against assigning, subletting or parting with possession come in two forms:

   (a) an absolute covenant, i.e., not to assign, etc.;

   (b) a qualified covenant, i.e., not to assign, etc., without the landlord's consent.

In the case of the absolute covenant, it is, of course, open to the tenant to ask the landlord if he will allow a particular disposition, but the landlord is under no obligation to agree to this, even if he is acting quite unreasonably in refusing. By contrast, if the covenant is in the qualified form that the tenant may not assign etc. *without consent*, the position is affected by s. 19(1)(a) of the Landlord and Tenant Act 1927, which implies into such a covenant the proviso that 'consent is not to be unreasonably withheld'.

(2) *When is refusal of consent unreasonable?*   Although the Landlord and Tenant Act 1927 implies the proviso that 'consent shall not be unreasonably withheld', it gives no guidance on what would constitute reasonable grounds for refusal. The only statutory provisions on the matter are to be found in anti-discrimination legislation, which provides that it is unlawful to refuse consent on the grounds of race, nationality, ethnicity, gender or disability, unless the landlord or his relatives share facilities with the tenant (Race Relations Act 1976, s. 24; Sex Discrimination Act 1975, s. 31; and Disability Discrimination Act 1995, ss. 22(4) and 23).

Turning to case law, the nearest approach to a general principle is to be found in the statement of the Court of Appeal in *Houlder Bros* v *Gibbs* [1925] 1 Ch 575: to be an acceptable reason for refusal of consent, an objection must relate to the personality of the intended assignee or to the use which he is likely to make of the property. (As summarised more recently by Aldous LJ in *Jaison Property Development Co. Ltd* v *Roux Restaurants Ltd* (1996) 74 P&CR 357 at p. 359, the landlord is entitled to require 'acceptable use and acceptable assignees'.) This can be a helpful guide, but it does have the effect of excluding a number of reasons which, to the landlord at least, may well seem good. Thus, in *Houlder Bros* v *Gibbs* the assignment was opposed because the proposed assignee already occupied other property belonging to the landlord, who feared that if the assignment was permitted, the assignee would give up that other property, which would be difficult to relet. This quite understandable reason was rejected by the Court of Appeal, which took the view that a refusal was not reasonable where 'the reason given is independent of the relationship between the lessor and the lessee, and on the grounds which are entirely personal to the lessor and wholly extraneous to the lessee' (at p. 583) or, as the Court of Appeal put it in *International Drilling Fluids Ltd* v *Louisville Investments (Uxbridge) Ltd* [1986] Ch 513, 'where the refusal was designed to achieve a collateral purpose unconnected with the terms of the lease' (at p. 520).

The approach in *Houlder Bros* v *Gibbs* was criticised by the House of Lords in *Tredegar* v *Harwood* [1929] AC 72. However, although their Lordships were again considering what constitutes unreasonable refusal, they were not dealing with a proposed assignment or subletting, but with a request by the tenant for permission to insure the property with an insurer other than the one prescribed by the terms of his lease. The landlord refused consent on the grounds that it was more convenient for the management of his properties to have them all covered by the same insurer. The House of Lords regarded this as reasonable grounds for refusal, and their Lordships indicated that they considered the approach in *Houlder Bros.* v *Gibbs* to be too narrow. Nevertheless, the views expressed by their Lordships, although always referred to with respect, were no more than *obiter dicta*, and the Court of Appeal continued to refer with approval to its earlier decision (see, for example, *Bickel* v *Duke of Westminster* [1977] QB 517).

This approach has now been confirmed by the House of Lords in *Ashworth Frazer Ltd* v *Gloucester CC* [2001] 1 WLR 2180, which, perhaps surprisingly, makes only a brief reference to *Tredegar* v *Harwood*, and does not refer to the criticism voiced there of *Houlder Bros* v *Gibbs*. On the contrary, their Lordships expressly approved the restatement of the *Houlder Bros* v *Gibbs* formula in the *International Drilling* case ([1986] Ch 513 at 520):

a landlord is not entitled to refuse his consent to an assignment on grounds which have nothing to do with the relationship of landlord and tenant in regard to the subject matter of the lease.

In the view of Lord Bingham (at p. 2183): 'while difficult borderline questions are bound to arise, the principle to be applied is clear'.

It is important to realise that satisfying the *Houlder Bros* v *Gibbs* test is only the first step in the process of deciding whether the landlord's refusal is reasonable. His reason for refusing may well relate to the nature of the assignee or his proposed use of the property, and yet still be regarded by the court as unreasonable. The House of Lords in *Ashworth Frazer* emphasised that the question of whether the landlord's conduct is reasonable is always a question of fact, to be decided on the circumstances of each particular case. Previous decisions on similar reasons for refusal may be referred to for guidance, but they should not be regarded as laying down legal rules as to what is or is not reasonable. Their Lordships referred with approval to the earlier expression of this approach by Lord Denning in *Bickel* v *Duke of Westminster* [1977] QB 517 at p. 524:

Seeing that the circumstances are infinitely various, it is impossible to formulate strict rules as to how a landlord should exercise his power of refusal. The utmost that the courts can do is to give guidance to those who have to consider the problem. As one decision follows another, people will get to know the likely result in any given set of circumstances. But no one decision will be a binding precedent as a strict rule of law. The reasons given by the judges are to be treated as propositions of good sense—in relation to the particular case—rather than propositions of law applicable to all cases.

The House of Lords was particularly concerned to emphasise this approach because, in the case before it, the Court of Appeal had held itself bound by an earlier decision that particular grounds for refusal were unreasonable. In *Ashworth Frazer*, the landlord, Gloucester CC, had refused consent to an assignment because it considered that the assignees' proposed use of the property would be in breach of a covenant in the lease. (We should mention briefly that there was considerable doubt about the meaning of this covenant, and that major parts of the speeches in the House of

Lords are devoted to its interpretation, a majority holding that it did not impose restrictions on the use of the premises. This, however, does not detract from the significance of the House of Lords' judgment on the consent issue, which is dealt with by Lord Bingham and, at greater length, by Lord Rodger.) At first instance, the landlord's refusal had been held not to be unreasonable, but on appeal by the tenant the Court of Appeal considered itself bound by its earlier decision in *Killick* v *Second Covent Garden Property Co. Ltd* [1973] 1 WLR 658. In that case, the Court of Appeal had held that the landlord's belief that the assignee would use the premises in breach of the user covenant was not an acceptable ground for refusing consent to assign. If assignment took place, the landlord would still be able to enforce the covenant, and would be in no worse position than if the assignor himself had proposed to break it. The Court of Appeal in *Ashworth Frazer* treated the *Killick* decision as establishing a rule that consent could not reasonably be refused in such circumstances, and accordingly held that the landlord's refusal in the case before them was unreasonable.

In reversing the Court of Appeal's decision on this point, the House of Lords overruled *Killick*. In Lord Rodger's words (at p. 2203):

> . . . it cannot be said as a matter of law, that the belief of a landlord, however reasonable, that the proposed assignee intends to use the demised premises for a purpose which would give rise to a breach of a user covenant, cannot, of itself, be a reasonable ground for witholding consent to assignment.

The correct approach would be to ask what the reasonable landlord would do when asked to consent in these circumstances. While it was true, as *Killick* had said, that the landlord would have the same ability to enforce the covenant against the assignee as he would have had against the assignor, a reasonable landlord might well consider that his position would be significantly altered by the assignment. After the assignment, he could find himself involved in the trouble and expense of enforcing the covenant, whereas he had previously had a tenant who was prepared to comply with it. The probability that the assignee might break the covenant could be enough to justify the withholding of consent:

> In deciding whether to withhold consent to an assignment reasonable landlords need not confine their consideration to what will necessarily happen; like everyone else taking an important decision, they may have regard to what will probably happen (p. 2202).

Whether refusal on such grounds was reasonable must, however, be decided as a question of fact on the circumstances of each case. Lord Rodger was at pains to emphasise that, in overruling *Killick*, the House of Lords were not substituting a contrary rule of law that it would always be reasonable to refuse consent on these grounds; there could be circumstances where refusal of consent for such a reason would be unreasonable. Accordingly, the case was remitted to the Chancery Division, for consideration of whether in the particular circumstances of the case the landlord's refusal was reasonable.

While bearing in mind the House of Lords' warning that previous decisions on refusal of consent must be regarded as illustrative only and not taken as laying down rules of law, it is still often helpful to consider previous decisions on specific grounds of refusal. For example, it has been held unreasonable to refuse consent on the ground that a proposed tenant has diplomatic immunity (*Parker* v *Boggon*

[1947] KB 346) or because the landlord wants to recover possession for himself (*Bates* v *Donaldson* [1896] 2 QB 241).

Examples of acceptable reasons for refusal include: the unsatisfactory nature of the assignee's references (*Shanly* v *Ward* (1913) 29 TLR 714); the fact that the proposed assignment would interfere with the future development of the property (*Pimms Ltd* v *Tallow Chandlers Co.* [1964] 2 QB 547); and the fact that assignment back to the original tenant would enable him to operate a break-clause and bring the lease to an end (*Olympia & York Canary Wharf Ltd* v *Oil Property Investments Ltd* [1994] 2 EGLR 48).

Finally, you may like to note that *International Drilling Fluids Ltd* v *Louisville Investments (Uxbridge) Ltd* [1986] Ch 513 provides an answer to a question on which there had been some divergence of authority: could the landlord be said to be acting unreasonably in refusing consent if he did not take into account the effect that this would have on the tenant? In the view of the court, 'there may be cases where there is such a disproportion between the benefit to the landlord and the detriment to the tenant if the landlord withholds his consent ... that it is unreasonable for the landlord to refuse consent' (at p. 521). The court considered that the case before it was of this type, and accordingly held that the landlord's refusal was unreasonable.

(3) *Landlord and Tenant Act 1988*   The 1988 Act introduced a number of changes to assist the tenant who seeks permission to assign, etc. Before the Act, the landlord could cause the tenant inconvenience and even financial loss, by delay in dealing with this request. The Act requires the landlord to respond to the tenant 'within a reasonable time' (as to which, see *Go West Ltd.* v *Spigarolo* [2002] 2 WLR 987), and to give written notice of his decision, including, in the case of refusal, the reasons for withholding consent (s. 1(3)). In the past, there has been uncertainty as to whether a landlord who has to justify his decision in subsequent court proceedings may rely on reasons for refusal which he did not give to the tenant at the time. In interpreting the new provisions of the Act, it has now been held that the landlord cannot subsequently rely on reasons which are not given in his written response (*Footwear Corp. Ltd* v *Amplight Properties Ltd* [1998] 3 All ER 52, a first instance decision described as 'rightly decided' by the Court of Appeal in *Spigarolo* at p. 992).

A further significant change introduced by the Act relates to the burden of proof. It used to be the case that the tenant had to prove that the landlord's refusal was unreasonable. Under s. 1(6), the burden has now shifted to the landlord, who is required to prove that his decision was reasonable.

(4) *Agreement in advance of request*   While the provisions of the 1927 and 1988 Acts have the effect of improving the tenant's position, a more recent amendment to s. 19(1) of the 1927 Act, introduced by the Landlord and Tenant (Covenants) Act 1995, s. 22, is designed to assist the landlord. It applies only to 'new tenancies' as defined by the Act (in outline, those created on or after 1 January 1996—see further at 9.4.3), and, moreover, residential leases are specifically excluded. In the case of leases within the provisions, s. 22 provides that the landlord and tenant may enter into an agreement specifying the circumstances in which the landlord may in the future withhold his consent to any assignment etc. and the conditions subject to which any consent may be given. If the landlord subsequently withholds consent on the ground that such circumstances exist or attaches such conditions to the

granting of consent, he shall not be regarded as acting unreasonably. Where the agreement in fact requires the landlord to exercise discretion in applying the pre-scribed circumstances or conditions to the facts of a particular application, the agreement must provide either that the discretion must be exercised reasonably or that the tenant has a right to an independent review of the decision. The agreement need not be contained in the lease, and can be made at any time before the tenant seeks consent. Undoubtedly this new provision will strengthen the landlord's position in commercial leases, enabling him, for example, to impose conditions about future guarantees, and criteria for assessing the creditworthiness of any proposed assignee, without having to justify them by reference to the financial standing of any specific assignee in respect of whom the tenant later seeks his consent.

(5) *What should tenant do if landlord refuses consent?* Where a lease contains a covenant not to assign etc. without consent the tenant who wishes to assign should, of course, ensure that he does ask the landlord for permission. However, if the tenant asks for permission and it is refused there are three courses of action open to him:

(a) He may seek a declaration from the court that the landlord's refusal is unreasonable and that he is therefore entitled to assign, sublet or part with possession.

(b) He may seek a remedy (damages or an injunction) for the landlord's breach of statutory duty under the Landlord and Tenant Act 1988, s. 4.

(c) He may take the risk and make the disposition, which will be effective even if it is in breach of covenant (*Parker* v *Jones* [1910] 2 KB 32: subletting; *Old Grovebury Manor Farm* v *W. Seymour Plant Sales* [1979] 3 All ER 504: assignment). If the tenant takes this third course it is then open to the landlord to take action against him for breach of covenant. The tenant will have a defence to the action if he can show that the landlord's refusal was unreasonable (*Ideal Film Renting Co.* v *Nielson* [1921] 1 Ch 575). It should be remembered, however, that the proposed assignee or subtenant may well refuse to proceed unless the landlord's consent has been obtained, as to do otherwise could well cause him problems in the future (see *Southern Depot Co. Ltd* v *British Railways Board* [1990] 2 EGLR 39).

(6) *Strict interpretation of covenant* It should be noted that covenants of this type are strictly interpreted. Accordingly a covenant forbidding 'assigning' does not prevent the creation of a subtenancy or a licence; similarly a covenant against 'subletting' does not prevent an assignment or the creation of a licence. Attention should therefore be given to the exact wording of the covenant in question (*Sweet & Maxwell Ltd* v *Universal News Services Ltd* [1964] 2 QB 699; *Re Doyle and O'Hara's Contract* [1899] IR 113). Similarly a tenant should take care when applying for a licence under such a provision, for should he obtain a licence to sublet the premises he will nonetheless be in breach of the covenant if thereafter he mistakenly assigns the property.

9.2.2.3 *Other covenants by the tenant*

The covenants mentioned above are only examples of the more common covenants. There are many other covenants in use, e.g., covenants about noise levels, keeping animals, not erecting signs or other external additions (e.g., window-boxes) and many others. One common covenant is a covenant restricting the use of the premises, for example, to use as 'a private dwelling only' or for a particular type of business. In leases of premises such as public houses or petrol stations, there could be a tie or solus agreement, by which the tenant agrees to take all his supplies (beer or petrol, as the case may be) from the brewery or petrol company which is letting the premises to him (although note that in certain circumstances such a provision might now be void under Art. 85(1) (now Art. 81) of the EC Treaty; see *Passmore* v *Morland* [1999] 1 EGLR 51.

9.2.3 Express covenants by landlord or tenant

9.2.3.1 *Covenants concerning repairs*

Most leases for any period other than the shortest will contain detailed covenants obliging the landlord or the tenant to effect certain repairs. These covenants vary considerably with the circumstances, but in the case of a long lease (e.g., 99 years) it is quite normal for the tenant to be obliged to undertake all necessary repairs, including structural repairs to buildings. In shorter leases the burden may well be shared, with the tenant undertaking to decorate and to carry out internal repairs, whilst the landlord agrees to maintain the structure. The landlord will have an implied right to enter the premises in order to inspect, but this right must be exercised reasonably.

A covenant 'to repair' involves not only the maintenance of the existing property but will include replacement of parts which are irreparable (*Lurcott* v *Wakeley* [1911] 1 KB 905) and even complete rebuilding if the structure is destroyed, for example, by fire (*Bullock* v *Dommitt* (1796) 2 Chit 608). Obviously it is wise to insure against such risks.

9.2.3.2 *Covenants to insure*

In some cases the landlord will covenant to insure premises (though the tenant may have to agree to pay some, or all, of the premium), whilst in others the tenant will undertake this obligation. Such covenants will be broken if the property is uninsured for any period, however short, and even if no damage occurs during that time (*Penniall* v *Harborne* (1848) 11 QB 368).

9.3 Implied and usual covenants

In many leases, the parties will not need to rely on the implied covenants because they will have regulated all necessary matters by express covenants in the lease. If, however, a lease contains express covenants but is silent on certain issues (e.g., contains no covenant referring to quiet enjoyment), implied terms will be added to the express terms in the lease.

In the absence of express provision, the following covenants are regarded as being of such fundamental importance and so much part of the landlord and tenant relationship that they are implied into every lease. They will all be implied

into the oral lease of the basement flat at 2 Trant Way, made between Fingall Forest
and Gerald Gruyère (see 9.1.4.1).

9.3.1 Implied covenants by the landlord

9.3.1.1 *Landlord's covenant to allow tenant quiet enjoyment*

(See 9.2.1.1) A covenant by the landlord that the tenant is to be allowed quiet
enjoyment is implied into every lease which does not expressly provide for this
(*Markham* v *Paget* [1908] 1 Ch 697).

9.3.1.2 *Covenant that landlord will not derogate from his grant*

See 9.2.1.2.

9.3.1.3 *Landlord's covenants that the premises are fit for the purpose for which they are
let or are habitable*

Subject to the obligations imposed by the two previous implied covenants, there is
in general no implied covenant that the premises will be fit for any particular
purpose.

This is true even where the premises are domestic in character and yet prove to be
unfit for human habitation (*Lane* v *Cox* [1897] 1 QB 415). This general rule arises
because of the application of the principle of *caveat emptor*; it is for the prospective
tenant to examine the property and decide whether it is fit for his purpose. However, the general rule is modified in the case of furnished houses and houses let at a
low rent.

(1) *Where a house is let furnished*   It is clear from a number of authorities that if a
house is let furnished then it must be fit for human habitation at the start of the
term (*Smith* v *Marrable* (1843) 11 M & W 5). It should be noted that this implied
condition relates only to the state of the premises at the commencement of the
term, and the landlord is not liable under this heading if the premises become unfit
during the lease term (*Harrison* v *Malet* (1886) 3 TLR 58; *Sarson* v *Roberts* [1895]
2 QB 395).

(2) *Where a house is let at a low rent*   A covenant by the landlord that the premises
are fit for human habitation is implied into certain leases at a low rent by the
Landlord and Tenant Act 1985, s. 8. The levels of rent prescribed are, however,
so low (e.g., maximum of £80 a year in London) that today very few premises
come within the provisions of the Act, and accordingly we will say no more about
them.

9.3.1.4 *Landlord's covenants to repair: short leases*

In general there is no implied obligation on the landlord to maintain or repair
the property, but under ss. 11–14 of the Landlord and Tenant Act 1985, certain
covenants by the landlord are implied into all leases of dwellings for a term of less
than seven years. The covenants implied are:

(a) to keep the structure and exterior in repair; and
(b) to keep in repair and working order the facilities for the supply of water, gas,
     electricity, sanitation, space heating and water heating.

9.3.1.5 *General duty of care*

Where a landlord is under a duty to repair, s. 4 of the Defective Premises Act 1972 imposes on him a duty in tort, to see that all persons who might reasonably be expected to be affected by defects in the state of the premises are reasonably safe from injury or damage to their property caused by such defect. Under the Act the landlord will also be liable to any person who acquires an interest in a dwelling which was built by the landlord, or where the landlord has done any work in connection with its provision.

It appears that there has been some doubt as to whether this duty extends to the tenant himself. However, it has been held recently by the Court of Appeal in *Sykes* v *Harry* [2001] QB 1014 that the tenant is included in the category of 'persons who might reasonably be expected to be affected', and the landlord in that case was held liable for physical injury caused to his tenant by a defective gas fire.

9.3.2 **Implied covenants by the tenant**

9.3.2.1 *Tenant's covenant to pay rent*

As we have already explained (at 8.2.5), it is perfectly possible to have a lease without an obligation to pay rent. Accordingly a covenant to pay rent will not be implied automatically into every lease. However, the payment of rent is usual and it will normally be the intention of the parties that it should be paid.

9.3.2.2 *Tenant's covenant to pay rates and other taxes on the premises*

The tenant is under an implied obligation to pay all the rates and taxes for which the landlord is not made expressly liable, either by the terms of the lease or under a rule of law. Because tenants are impliedly liable for the rates and similar obligations, such as council tax, on a property, they should take care to ascertain whether their rent is inclusive or exclusive before they enter into the agreement, as fairly large sums can be involved.

9.3.2.3 *Tenant's liability for damage or disrepair*

A tenant's implied duties in respect of damage or disrepair are usually said to arise from his liability for 'waste'. Waste may be defined as an act or omission which alters the state of the land, and it can even include changes which *improve* the land ('ameliorating waste'). We are concerned here, however, with the sort of behaviour which may damage the property and it is usual to divide such waste into two categories: 'voluntary waste', which consists of doing something which should not be done (e.g., knocking down a wall), and 'permissive waste', which consists of leaving undone something which ought to be done (e.g., allowing a wall to fall down). The distinction is therefore between causing damage and failing to repair damage which occurs without the tenant doing anything. The extent of liability for waste depends on the type of lease involved and so we will consider the various leases separately.

(1) *Weekly tenancies*   Generally the rule is that a weekly tenant is liable for voluntary waste but not for permissive waste: in other words he may not knock a wall down but he can let it fall down (*Mint* v *Good* [1951] 1 KB 517). The duty is increased beyond this point, however, by the further rule that he must use the

premises in a 'tenant-like manner' (*Warren* v *Keen* [1954] 1 QB 15). This means that the tenant must clean the premises, mend the electric light if it is fused, unstop blocked sinks and generally 'do the little jobs about the place which a reasonable tenant would do'. The exact duties of the tenant under this heading are not entirely clear, however, and each case must be judged on its facts.

(2) *Monthly and quarterly tenancies*   The rules here seem to be the same as for a weekly tenancy.

(3) *Yearly tenancies*   The position here is similar to that of other periodic tenancies save that additionally a yearly tenant is deemed to be obliged to keep the premises wind and water-tight (*Wedd* v *Porter* [1916] 2 KB 91). This obligation is, however, rather watered down by the further rule that the tenant is not liable for 'fair wear and tear' (*Warren* v *Keen* [1954] 1 QB 15). This means that he is not responsible for the gradual deterioration caused by normal use or by the normal action of the elements (*Haskell* v *Marlow* [1928] 2 KB 45), so that he does not have to replace stone steps which are worn down by use or tiles which are blown off the roof by the wind.

(4) *Fixed-term tenancies*   A tenant with a fixed term of years is certainly liable for voluntary waste. The position with regard to permissive waste was less clear, and an earlier edition of Woodfall expressed the view that there was 'considerable doubt whether a tenant for years would be found liable for permissive waste if the matter were thoroughly tested at the present day' (*Woodfall's Law of Landlord and Tenant*, Sweet & Maxwell, Release 41, para. 13.124). However, after a very thorough review of case law and juristic writing, the High Court in *Dayani* v *Bromley LBC* [1999] 3 EGLR 144 has now held that a tenant for years can be liable for permissive waste. Thus, if a lease for a fixed term makes no express provision about repairs, there will be an implied term that such a tenant should maintain the premises in the condition in which he received them at the start of the term.

9.3.2.4 *Tenant's obligation to allow landlord entry*

In general, as the tenant has exclusive possession, he may exclude the landlord from the premises. However, a term will be implied that the landlord is to be allowed to enter the premises if the landlord is under a duty to repair (*Saner* v *Bilton* (1876) 7 ChD 815). This will give the landlord a right, to be exercised reasonably, to enter and inspect and carry out necessary repairs. A similar implied term is also included where statutory provisions require a landlord to repair.

9.3.3 **Usual covenants**

We cannot end our general discussion of covenants in leases without mentioning the class of such agreements which is normally described as 'the usual covenants'. In any instance in which the grant of a lease is preceded by a contractual agreement, it is an implied term of that contract that the lease, when granted, will contain the usual covenants (*Propert* v *Parker* (1832) 3 My & K 280) and the lease may therefore be rectified if these are not included when it is granted. The class of usual covenants is not entirely fixed and will vary depending on the area in which the property stands or because of the nature of a trade run on the premises. In *Flexman* v *Corbett* [1930] 1 Ch 672, it was suggested that a covenant must be regarded as 'usual' if nine out of ten leases of the same kind would include the term. It was also pointed out that 'what is normal in Mayfair or Bayswater is not usual . . . in Whitechapel' (per Maugham J at p. 678). The following covenants are, however, always regarded as 'usual':

(a) that the tenant will pay rent;

(b) that the tenant will pay rates and taxes (other than those which must, by statutory provision, be borne by the landlord);

(c) that the tenant will keep the premises in repair;

(d) that, if the landlord has expressly covenanted to repair, he will be allowed reasonable access to view and repair the premises;

(e) that the landlord will allow the tenant quiet enjoyment and that he will not derogate from his grant; and

(f) that the landlord will have a right to re-enter should the tenant fail to pay his rent (but not in the case of the breach of other covenants).

A more recent decision, *Chester* v *Buckingham Travel Ltd* [1981] 1 WLR 96, provides an example of the court accepting a wider range of covenants as being 'usual' in a modern commercial lease, including both restrictions on the use or alteration of the buildings, and a right of re-entry for the landlord for breach of any covenant in the lease.

9.4 Enforcement of covenants

Having identified the covenants which are in common use we need now to consider the question of the effect these covenants have on the original parties to the lease, their successors in title and persons, such as subtenants, who derive their title under such persons.

9.4.1 Enforcement between the original parties to the lease

There is little problem when one is dealing with either of the original parties to a covenant contained in a lease, because between the original landlord and tenant there will be privity of contract, with the result that either party can enforce an obligation against the other, as is normal in the case of any contractual promise.

9.4.2 Enforcement after the lease or the reversion has passed to new owners

We have seen in Chapter 8 that both landlord and tenant have legal estates in the property which may pass to other owners by sale, as gifts or by succession on death (see 8.4). In such circumstances two questions arise:

(i) do the original parties to the lease retain any rights or duties under the covenants once they have parted with their estates?

(ii) are the covenants in the lease enforceable by or against the new owners of the lease and the reversion?

The Landlord and Tenant (Covenants) Act 1995 (which we will refer to in future as 'the 1995 Act') makes major changes in this regard, but these changes are not retrospective, despite the Law Commission's recommendation that they should be (*Landlord and Tenant Law: Privity of Contract and Estate* (Law Com No. 174)). As a result, there are now two very different sets of rules in operation, the choice of which to apply depending, in general, on whether the lease was created on or after 1 January 1996 (the date on which the Act took effect), or before that date. Leases can, of course, be granted for very long periods, and in consequence the older law, relating to covenants in leases created before 1996, will continue in operation for many years to come—certainly for much of this century and possibly even beyond.

9.4.3 New and old leases

New leases   Most of the provisions of the 1995 Act apply only to '*new tenancies*', which the Act defines in s. 1(3) as tenancies granted on or after the date on which the Act came into force (i.e., 1 January 1996).

Old leases   Leases which do not fall within the definition of 'new tenancies' are described by the Act as '*other tenancies*', but we will refer to them in the rest of this chapter as 'old leases'. As you would expect, this category of leases consists mainly of tenancies granted before 1 January 1996. However, under s. 1 it also includes leases granted after that date if they are made under an agreement (which includes an option or right of first refusal) or a court order which was in existence before the Act came into force. In consequence of this, it is likely that the effect of the old law will be further prolonged by the exercise of options to renew contained in long leases.

Finally, we should mention that there are a few provisions in the 1995 Act which apply to both new and old leases, and we will note these briefly in 9.5.3.

In the next two sections we will look first at the effect of the covenants in the lease on the position of the original parties when they no longer have estates in the land (9.5), and will then consider the enforcement of the covenants between the new landlord and tenant (9.6). In each case, we will deal with old leases first, and then consider the changes made by the 1995 Act in respect of new leases. We will then see how these various rules may be applied to the Trant Way tenancies in 9.7, and finally will discuss the position of subtenants in 9.8.

9.5 Position of original parties after transfer of lease and/or reversion

9.5.1 The old law, which governs old leases

9.5.1.1 *Continuing liability of the original tenant*

The contractual obligation arising from the covenant will usually continue even if the covenanting party has disposed of his interest in the property, for generally covenants are so phrased that they relate not only to the covenantor's acts and omissions but also to those of his successors in title and persons deriving title under him. Even if the covenantor does not covenant expressly in these terms, they will be implied into the covenant by LPA 1925, s. 79, unless clearly excluded by the wording of the covenant. Accordingly, in leases granted before 1996, an original tenant will usually have covenanted not only about his own conduct, but also about that of his assignees ('successors in title') and subtenants ('persons deriving title under him'). Thus, if a tenant has covenanted that he will not do a specified act, he can still be sued by the landlord even after he has disposed of his whole estate and despite the fact that the act complained of is that of his assignee, for he is in breach of his covenant that neither he nor his successors will do that act (*Thursby v Plant* (1690) 1 Saund 230).

In this way, the original tenant will remain liable throughout the whole term of the lease for any breach of covenant by his successors in title. As we shall see later, the burden of most covenants in a lease will pass on the assignment of the lease or the reversion, so that the new estate owner will become personally liable for any breach. This means that the covenantee often has a choice between suing the present estate owner, who has caused the breach, or proceeding against the original covenantor. It is usually more convenient to proceed against the present owner, if only because it is easier to find him, but if he should disappear, or be not worth suing, it may be better to try to recover from the original covenantor.

9.5.1.2 *Hardship caused by continuing liability*

The fact that the original tenant remained liable for any breach of covenant by his successors throughout the whole term of the lease had always been capable of producing apparently unfair results, largely because the original tenant was often unaware of the provisions of LPA 1925, s. 79, and did not appreciate fully the obligations he was assuming. However, economic difficulties during the 1980s intensified the hardship experienced by original tenants. Many found themselves being held liable for breaches of covenant committed by current tenants, who were in financial difficulties and could not afford to pay rent or perform other covenants. The lease had often passed through a series of assignments, and it might well be that the original tenant knew nothing of the current holder, and certainly had no control over him. It was these difficulties which led to pressure for change.

9.5.1.3 *Continuing liability of original landlord*

So far, we have concentrated on the position of the original tenant, but it is important to note that the same general principles apply to the landlord, who will be presumed to have covenanted for himself and his successors in title, in accordance with LPA 1925, s. 79. He will thus remain liable on his covenants after assigning the reversion, and so could find himself being sued by the tenant for breaches of covenant committed by the assignee (the tenant's current landlord).

9.5.1.4 *Possible indemnity for original covenantor held liable for breach*

If the original covenantor (whether tenant or landlord) does have to compensate for breach of covenant, he will naturally want to recoup his losses and may do so in one of two ways. To illustrate this, we will assume a series of assignments of a lease, which may be shown diagrammatically as follows:

L

| Lease

▼

T   Assignment A1 Assignment A2 Assignment A3
────────────▶   ────────────▶   ────────────▶

L has recovered damages from T in respect of a breach of covenant by A3, and two courses of action are now open to T. He may seek to recover directly from A3, relying on the rule in *Moule* v *Garrett* (1872) LR 7 Ex 101 that 'where one person is compelled to pay damages by the legal default of another, he is entitled to recover from [that person] the sum so paid'. However, the fact that L preferred to sue T may suggest to T that it will not be worthwhile to proceed against A3 and so he may prefer the second choice, of going against his own assignee, A1. He is able to do this because, by virtue of LPA 1925, s. 77 or, in the case of *registered land*, LRA 2002 s. 134 and Sch. 12, para. 20 (replacing the earlier provision contained in LRA 1925 s. 24), any assignment of a lease includes an implied covenant by the assignee to indemnify the assignor for any breach of covenant in the lease.

Thus, T may sue A1, because A1 covenanted to indemnify T against such claims. Thereafter, A1 may sue A2 and A2 may sue A3, also on the basis of the indemnity covenant which is implied into every assignment.

It is, of course, important to realise that in the situations we have just been considering, where a claimant has a choice of whom to sue, he can recover only one set of damages, and there is no question of his gaining double compensation by proceeding against two different defendants in respect of the same breach of covenant.

9.5.2 The new law, which governs new leases

In contrast with the rule for old leases, under which the original covenantor remains liable on his covenants despite assigning his estate, the 1995 Act provides release from their covenants for both tenant and landlord (save for personal covenants—for which, see 9.5.2.3). For the tenant, release is automatic, subject to certain exceptions which we note below. For the landlord, release is obtained with the consent of the tenant or on a court order.

9.5.2.1 *Release of the original tenant*

Where a tenant assigns his lease, s. 5 of the 1995 Act provides that, from the assignment, he is released from the burden of his covenants and ceases to be entitled to the benefit of the landlord's covenants. The section relates to any assigning tenant, and therefore applies to an assignee who himself assigns, as well as to the original tenant under the lease. However, assignees have always been freed from future liability on the covenants in the lease when they in turn assign (*City of London Corporation* v *Fell* [1994] 1 AC 458 at p. 465), and the principal beneficiary from this provision will undoubtedly be the original tenant and covenantor, who is thus freed from the continuing liability on his covenants. To accord with this major change in the law, the Act includes two consequential provisions:

(a) Section 30(4)(a) provides that LPA 1925, s. 79 (by which a covenantor is deemed to covenant on behalf of himself, his successors in title and the persons deriving title under him), shall not apply to new tenancies.

(b) With reference to new tenancies only, s. 30(2)–(3) repeals those parts of LPA 1925, s. 77, and LRA 1925, s. 24, which insert the implied covenant for indemnity into an assignment of a lease (see 9.5.1.4). Nevertheless, as we shall see, there may be occasions where the assigning tenant is not released from his liability under the covenants, and it might therefore be wise for the tenant to include an express covenant for indemnity in the assignment, since he can no longer rely on the implied one.

It is important to note that there are certain circumstances in which the tenant will not be freed from his continuing liability. He continues to be liable in the case of 'excluded assignments', which are defined in s. 11(1) as:

(a) assignments in breach of a covenant in the tenancy, i.e., assignments of the lease by a tenant in breach of an absolute or qualified covenant against assignment; and

(b) assignments by operation of law, for example, on death, where the estate vests in the deceased's personal representatives, or on bankruptcy, where the estate vests in the trustee in bankruptcy.

Where the tenant (or his estates) remains bound by his covenants after assignment, he will be freed by the next assignment of the lease which is not an excluded one (s. 11(2)(b)).

Authorised guarantee agreement

Although the tenant may be freed automatically from continuing liability on his covenants, it should be noted that the landlord may require him to enter into an 'authorised guarantee agreement', by which he guarantees the assignee's performance of the covenants in the lease (s. 16). The landlord is permitted to do this only when:

(1) his consent to the assignment is required under the lease; and

(2) he makes the giving of the guarantee a condition of his consenting to the assignment.

The guarantee is to last only while the assignee is liable under the covenants of the lease and must end when his liability ceases, i.e., the tenant giving the guarantee cannot be required to guarantee performance by successive assignees. Thus although it may look at first sight as though the Act is taking away with one hand what it has just given with the other, the tenant's position is in reality still considerably better than it would be under the old rules, where his liability as original covenantor would normally continue throughout the full period of the lease.

9.5.2.2 *Release of the original landlord*

The 1995 Act provides for the release of the landlord from his covenants on the assignment of the reversion (s. 6), but this release does not take place automatically on the assignment as it does for the tenant. Instead, the Act creates a procedure under which the landlord is required to give notice to the tenant, informing him of the proposed or actual assignment of the reversion, and requesting release from the covenants. The landlord will be released if the tenant consents, or does not respond within the prescribed period; if the tenant refuses consent the landlord may apply to the court, which may either uphold the tenant's objection or declare that it is reasonable for the covenant to be released. Details of the procedure (content of notice, time limits, etc.) are to be found in s. 8 of the Act.

The provisions of s. 11 relating to excluded assignments (which we have noted above in connection with the release of the tenant) apply also to assignments by the landlord, with the result that assignment by operation of law does not end the continuing liability of the original landlord.

Where a landlord has not been released from liability (for example, because the assignment is an excluded one, or because the tenant successfully opposes the landlord's application), he may apply for release on any future assignment of the reversion (ss. 7 and 11(3)(b)).

The provisions of the Act in relation to the landlord may appear to be less favourable than those applying to the tenant, but it must be remembered that the tenant has no say in the landlord's choice of an assignee (despite the fact that the assignee will become the tenant's new landlord), whereas very often the requirement of the landlord's consent to any assignment of the lease gives him an adequate opportunity to 'vet' any prospective new tenant (although the original tenant will still be released from continuing liability even where the landlord's consent to assignment is not required). The creditworthiness of a new landlord is very relevant to a tenant where, for example, the landlord has repairing obligations under the lease, and if there is any doubt about the financial standing of the assignee the tenant may well want the current landlord's liability to continue, and so oppose the application for release.

9.5.2.3 *No release from personal covenants on assignment*

As we shall see later when we consider the position after transfer of the lease and the reversion, most covenants in a lease will be enforceable between the new landlord and tenant (see 9.6). However, any covenant which normally would pass in this way may be worded so as to make it clear that it is intended to be a *personal covenant*, benefiting or binding only the original tenant or landlord. In *BHP Petroleum Ltd* v *Chesterfield Ltd* [2002] Ch 194 the question arose of whether a covenantor who assigns his estate is able to free himself from liability on his personal covenants.

In this case, the original landlord had undertaken to carry out certain remedial work to the property and it was clear from the agreement that this was to be a personal obligation which would not be enforceable against the landlord's successors (see pp. 199–200). On assigning the reversion, the landlord served a notice on the tenant seeking release from its covenants and the tenant did not respond. Subsequently, the tenant sought to enforce the obligation to remedy certain defects against the original landlord, and the defendant claimed that it had been released from the obligation by its assignment of the reversion and the tenant's failure to serve a counter-notice. The Court of Appeal rejected this claim, holding that the provisions of the Act concerning release applied only to a 'landlord covenant' (see 9.6.2.1) which, relying on the definition of 'landlord' in s. 28(1) of the Act, the court defined (at p. 212) as:

an obligation falling to be complied with by the person who may from time to time be entitled to the reversion on the tenancy.

By contrast, an obligation under a personal covenant by the landlord does not bind successors; it, therefore, falls outside the definition of a 'landlord covenant', and so does not come within the statutory provisions for release from 'landlord covenants'. Thus, the original landlord may secure release from burdens which will pass to his assignees, but cannot free himself from a personal covenant. The court considered that this interpretation accorded with the basic principle underlying the statutory provisions for release which was, in the words of Lightman J at first instance (quoted with approval by the Court of Appeal at p. 205):

> that the release of a landlord or tenant from a covenant was intended to be sequential upon, and only sequential upon, a parting by the landlord or tenant with his interest in the property let and the successor taking his predecessor's place as the party responsible for complying with that covenant.

Accordingly, the original landlord remained liable on his personal covenant and was obliged to remedy the defects which had become apparent.

9.5.2.4 *Loss of benefit*

We have concentrated so far on the release of the assignor from the burden of the covenants, but it must be noted that when this occurs he also ceases to be entitled to the benefit of the other party's covenants under the lease (ss. 5(2)(b) and 6(2)(b)). However, s. 24(4) specifically provides that this loss of benefit does not affect any rights arising from an earlier breach of covenant. One result of this provision appears to be to change the rule that a landlord who assigns his reversion loses the right to sue for a previous breach of the tenant's covenants (see 9.6.1.4), so that a landlord who is released under the Act from his covenants will in future retain a right of action against his former tenant in respect of pre-existing breaches.

9.5.3 **Provisions of 1995 Act which apply to both old and new leases**

Sections 17–20 of the Act provide further help for former tenants who may have continuing liabilities in respect of leases even after they have been assigned. These sections apply to 'both new and other tenancies' (s. 1(2)), and so will apply to leases granted before 1 January 1996, which in general continue to be governed by the older law, as we have already described. This part of the Act will be of particular relevance to original tenants under these pre-1996 leases, who remain liable on their covenants for the whole period of the lease, but they will also be of benefit to tenants under new leases who have been required by their landlords to enter into authorised guarantee agreements under s. 16 (see above), or who for some reason have not been released from their covenants on assignment.

Guarantors

These provisions of the Act also apply to guarantors of the former tenant. So far, we have not referred to the practice of landlords requiring a tenant or assignee of a lease to provide guarantors or sureties for his performance of the covenants in the lease. In general, such matters are beyond the scope of this book, but the practice is a common one, and guarantors can be seriously affected in times of recession by the inability of tenants to meet their commitments. The protection given to the tenant by these sections is accordingly extended to his guarantor, and references to the former tenant in the following accounts of ss. 17–21 should be read as including any guarantors, even though we do not specifically mention them.

9.5.3.1 *Three forms of help*

The Act assists the tenant in three ways: by restricting the arrears that can be recovered; by ensuring that the tenant is not made subject to increased liability by variation of the terms of the lease; and by giving him an opportunity to acquire a landlord's rights over the current tenant.

(1) *Restriction of liability for rent or service charge*   Section 17 provides that a landlord cannot recover from a former tenant arrears of rent or other fixed payments (such as service charges), unless within six months of the money becoming due the landlord has notified the former tenant of the amount due and of the fact that he intends to recover the money. The purpose of this provision is to put an end to a practice of some landlords, who allowed arrears to accumulate, sometimes over a period of years, before having recourse to the former tenant, who meanwhile had no knowledge that the current tenant was in breach of covenant.

(2) *Restriction of liability where tenancy is subsequently varied*   Section 18 is designed to deal with the supposed rule in *Centrovincial Estates plc* v *Bulk Storage Ltd* (1983) 46 P&CR 393 by which the liabilities of the original tenant could be increased by a subsequent variation of the lease agreed between an assignee and the landlord, without the former tenant's knowledge or consent. However, after this provision had been included in the statute, it became apparent from the Court of Appeal decision in *Friends' Provident Life Office* v *British Railways Board* [1996] 1 All ER 336 that the decision in *Centrovincial* was based on a misinterpretation of an earlier decision, so that in fact there may have been no need for legislation on this matter. In any event the 1995 Act now provides that the former tenant shall not be liable to pay any amount referable to any relevant variation of the tenant covenants effected after the assignment (s. 18(2) and (3)).

It is a different matter, however, if the original lease itself provided for some future variation of the tenant's obligations (for example, by a rent review clause), in which case the original tenant might well be bound by the enhanced obligation.

(3) *Right to an overriding lease*   A former tenant who remains liable on his covenants may be described as having responsibility without power, since he is liable for breach of covenants committed by assignees of the lease, without having any control over them. It is true that he is responsible for the choice of his own assignee, but he has no say in the making of any subsequent assignment (unless he makes special contractual arrangements for this). He may very well be unaware of breaches of covenant by an assignee, and even if he knew of them has no way of compelling the landlord to take action.

A solution to these difficulties is offered by s. 19 which gives the former tenant the right to require the landlord to grant him an 'overriding lease'. This will take effect as a concurrent lease, or a lease of the reversion (see 8.10.5), and its effect is to make the former tenant the immediate landlord of the defaulting current tenant.

This means that he has the landlord's power to enforce the covenants in the lease against the tenant and, if there are further breaches, can take action to remedy them, if necessary by forfeiting the lease. In this way, he can prevent further liability accruing to himself. It remains to be seen how effective this device will be, or how popular with former tenants, especially if there is no realistic prospect, for economic reasons, of being able to relet the property if the current lease is forfeited. It is nevertheless an attempt to assist the former tenant in a difficult situation.

9.6 Position of new landlord and/or tenant after transfer of lease and/or reversion

9.6.1 The old law, which governs old leases

Although, as we have seen, the original covenantor in an old lease remains liable for breach of covenant, most covenantees would in general find it more convenient to proceed against the person who has actually caused the breach. Accordingly, it is often essential to know whether an assignee of a covenanting tenant, or a purchaser of a reversion from a covenanting landlord, can be made directly liable for breaches of covenant. Similarly such an assignee may well wish to know whether he has a right to enforce the original covenants in the lease. The problem here is that such a person is a later arrival on the scene, and is not a party to the contract between the original landlord and tenant. As it is a basic principle of contract law that a contract cannot be enforced against someone who is not privy to the contract, one might foresee difficulties arising. In the words of Lord Templeman in *City of London Corporation* v *Fell* [1994] 1 AC 458 at p. 464:

... common law, and statute following the common law, were faced with the problem of rendering effective the obligations under a lease which might endure for a period of 999 years or more beyond the control of any covenantor.

In consequence, a second doctrine, that of 'privity of estate', has developed alongside the doctrine of privity of contract.

9.6.1.1 *Privity of estate*

There is said to be privity of estate when two persons have a relationship of tenure with each other. In other words privity of estate arises when there is a relationship of landlord and tenant between the parties. If the following situation exists:

then there is both privity of contract and privity of estate between L and T. If T later assigns his lease to A there will be privity of contract between L and T but privity of estate between L and A. After the assignment L becomes A's landlord and A becomes L's tenant:

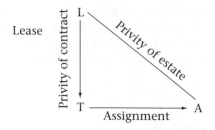

Similarly, if the landlord, L, sells the reversion to P, a purchaser, there will continue to be privity of contract between L and T but there will be privity of estate between T and P:

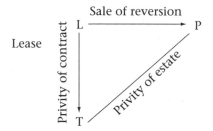

If the landlord sells the reversion and the tenant assigns the lease the situation illustrated below will arise:

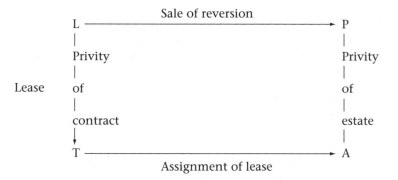

Thus, there will be privity of estate between the purchaser of the reversion, P, and the assignee of the lease, A; they are, respectively, the new landlord and the new tenant.

This pattern of privity of estate is important because, as we shall see below, certain covenants are enforceable between parties who are linked by privity of estate, as well as between parties linked by privity of contract. The position was summarised by Nourse LJ, in a judgment which the House of Lords later described as impeccable, as follows:

A lease of land, because it originates in a contract, gives rise to obligations enforceable between the original landlord and the original tenant in contract. But because it also gives the tenant an estate in the land assignable, like the reversion, to others, the obligations, so far as they touch and concern the land, assume a wider influence, becoming, as it were, imprinted on the term or the reversion [as the case may be, or] . . . enforceable between the owners thereof for the time being as conditions of the enjoyment of their respective estates. (*City of London Corporation* v *Fell* [1993] QB 589 at p. 603; approved by the House of Lords [1994] 1 AC 459 at p. 465.)

In general, covenants in leases can be enforced only between parties who are linked by privity of contract and/or privity of estate. Some possible exceptions to this principle will be considered later (see 9.6.1.5 and 9.8).

We must now consider which covenants can be enforced only between the original parties to the lease on the basis of privity of contract and which covenants will pass on assignment so that they will be enforced between the new landlord and tenant on the basis of privity of estate. It is convenient to deal with the assignment of the lease and the assignment of the reversion separately, as the rules which apply to each are slightly different. In both cases, however, the rules we describe relate only to legal leases granted by deed; for the position of leases not made by deed, both legal and equitable, see 9.6.1.6.

9.6.1.2 *Running of covenants on assignment of an old lease*

The rule which applies when a tenant assigns a lease granted before 1 January 1996 is that the assignee will acquire the burden and the benefit of all covenants in the lease which 'touch and concern' the demised premises. This rule is derived from *Spencer's Case* (1583) 5 Co Rep 16a, in which it was held that a covenant made by a tenant to build a brick wall on the premises could be enforced against an assignee of the tenant. For a third party to be affected by a covenant in a lease two things have to be established:

(a) that there is a privity of estate between the third party and the person seeking to enforce, or against whom enforcement is sought; and

(b) that the relevant covenant 'touches and concerns' the demised premises.

Thus, it was said in *Spencer's Case* that if the tenant covenants to build a wall on other property belonging to the landlord, that covenant will not bind an assignee of the tenant because it does not 'touch and concern' the demised premises. In addition at the date of *Spencer's Case*, one had to establish that the original covenantor had covenanted on behalf of his assigns and successors in title, as well as for himself. This requirement is now presumed by virtue of LPA 1925, s. 79, but may be excluded by clear words to the contrary. If for some reason (e.g., the covenant does not 'touch and concern' the demised property) the covenant cannot be enforced against the assignee, it can still be enforced, as we have seen, against the original covenantor.

Under the rule in *Spencer's Case*, the assignee acquires not only the burden of certain covenants in the lease, but may also receive the right to enforce such of the landlord's covenants as 'touch and concern' the land.

Meaning of 'touching and concerning'

Unfortunately it is almost impossible to construct a simple test for covenants which will satisfy the *Spencer's Case* requirement of 'touching and concerning' the land. In *Breams Property Investment Co. Ltd* v *Stroulger* [1948] 2 KB 1 it was said that covenants fall into this class if they affect the landlord qua (as) landlord and the tenant qua tenant. It may be thought that this only substitutes one formula for another, and is not particularly helpful in practice. It does, however, draw attention to *Woodall* v *Clifton* [1905] 2 Ch 257, in which it was held that an agreement by the landlord giving the tenant an option to purchase the premises did not come within the rule in *Spencer's Case*, because the covenant does not affect the parties as landlord and tenant but as vendor and purchaser. A further and perhaps more helpful explanation of the phrase is to be found in *P & A Swift Investments* v *Combined English Stores Group plc* [1989] AC 632 at p. 642 (which is considered in more detail in 23.4.1.1).

Thus, not all covenants which appear to concern the land which is the subject of the lease will fall within the rule and pass on assignment. Non-competition clauses (*Congleton Corporation* v *Pattison* (1808) 10 East 130; *Thomas* v *Hayward* (1869) LR 4 Ex 311), covenants to keep other premises in repair (*Dewar* v *Goodman* [1909] AC 72), and covenants to repair chattels which are not fixed to the land (*Williams* v *Earle* (1868) LR 3 QB 739; *Gorton* v *Gregory* (1862) 3 B & S 90) are all covenants which have been held not to touch and concern the land, and to be merely 'collateral covenants'. It would be impossible to compile a complete list of all covenants which do satisfy the rule in *Spencer's Case* but all the implied and common covenants which are set out in the earlier part of this chapter will do so.

Personal covenants
It is important to realise that any covenant which would normally be regarded as touching and concerning the land, and therefore running on an assignment of the lease, may be worded so as to make it clear that it is intended to be a personal covenant, benefiting or binding only the original tenant or landlord, and in that case will not run with the lease on assignment.

9.6.1.3 *Running of covenants on assignment of reversion of an old lease*
The rules which apply to a purchaser of the reversion from the landlord are similar to those which apply to the tenant's assignee, but are covered by statutory rules under LPA 1925, ss. 141 and 142. The rule here is that covenants run to bind and benefit a purchaser where the covenant 'has reference to the subject-matter of the lease'. The statutory phrase 'having reference to the subject-matter of the lease' seems to be identical to the common law test of covenants 'touching and concerning the land' and the remarks made above on that test will also apply here, as also will the exclusion of personal covenants.

9.6.1.4 *Who can sue in respect of breaches occurring before assignment?*
So far in this section we have been considering how the assignee of the lease or the reversion can deal with breaches of covenant which occur *after* he takes his estate. However, it may be that the other party to the lease was already in breach at the time of the assignment, and the question then arises of who is entitled to sue for this: the assignor, who was the estate owner at the time of the breach, or the assignee who is the current estate owner? The answer to this question depends on whether it is the reversion or the lease which has been assigned, because different rules apply in each case.

Assignment of reversion   Where the original landlord assigns his reversion on an old lease, he loses his right to sue the original tenant. At one time he could have sued the tenant, even though he had ceased to have any interest in the property, because there was still a contractual obligation between them. However, due to LPA 1925, s. 141, it now appears that on the assignment of the reversion the original landlord divests himself of all rights to enforce the covenant (*Re King* [1963] Ch 459). It seems that this rule is now changed by the Landlord and Tenant (Covenants) Act 1995, s. 24(4), but this is only in respect of leases to which that Act applies (see 9.5.2.4).

Assignment of lease By contrast, where the lease is assigned, the former tenant may sue the landlord in respect of breaches occurring during the currency of his lease, even after he has assigned it. This right may be valuable if he has spent money remedying a breach for which the landlord was responsible, and which had to be remedied before the assignee would agree to take the lease (see, for example, *City and Metropolitan Properties Ltd* v *Greycroft Ltd* [1987] 1 WLR 1085).

9.6.1.5 *Enforcement by assignee against original covenantor*

There is one final point we want to mention here, because students sometimes find it confusing. The continuing liability of the original tenant, even after he has assigned his lease, combined with the fact that the right to enforce certain covenants in the lease runs to the assignee of the reversion means that covenants can be enforced by the current landlord against the original tenant, even though there has never been any privity of estate between them. This does seems surprising, in view of the general rule that covenants can be enforced only where there is privity of contract or privity of estate. It is, however, clear from decided cases that the assignee of the reversion does have the right to enforce against the original covenantor in this way (see for example, *Parker* v *Webb* (1693) 3 Salk 5 (91 ER 656) and *Milverton Group Ltd* v *Warner World Ltd* [1995] 2 EGLR 28). It seems that the right to enforce the contract passes to the new landlord automatically under the relevant statutory provisions (now LPA 1925, s. 141), without its having to be expressly assigned. It is suggested that in a similar way the assignee of the lease might enforce against the original landlord, again without any privity of estate between them, but there is no decision on this point. (See further, Megarry and Wade, pp. 945–6.)

9.6.1.6 *Leases not made by deed*

(1) *Legal parol leases* These are leases made orally or in writing. The old rule expressed in *Elliott* v *Johnson* (1866) LR 2 QB 120 was that covenants did not run on the assignment of a parol lease: the principles in *Spencer's Case* applied only to legal leases made by deed. However, it was held in *Boyer* v *Warbey* [1953] 1 QB 234 that the rule in *Spencer's Case* could also apply to a written lease for not more than three years which created a legal estate by virtue of LPA 1925, s. 54(2). Accordingly, a covenant made by the tenant to pay £40 towards repairs at the end of the term ran to bind an assignee of the written lease. It seems probable that the same approach would be adopted in the case of oral leases within the s. 54(2) exception, but no mention was made of this in *Boyer* v *Warbey*, so the position remains uncertain.

(2) *Equitable leases* The rule that covenants in a legal lease will run to benefit or burden an assignee of the lease or reversion depends upon the assignee's acquiring an estate in the property. In the case of an equitable lease, the tenant has no

estate, merely an equitable right to specific performance of the agreement for a lease, and therefore the benefits and burdens of the terms of the agreement do not pass automatically to the new tenant.

The right to enforce a contract may, however, be assigned, subject to the usual rules governing assignment of choses in action, and so if the landlord were to make some promise in the original agreement (e.g., to repair the structure) the benefit of that promise could be assigned to a purchaser from the tenant. The new tenant would be able to sue the landlord to enforce the landlord's part of the contract.

By contrast, whilst the *benefit* of a chose in action may be assigned, the *burden* is not transferable. If the tenant under an equitable lease agrees to decorate the interior of the property, the burden of this agreement cannot be transferred to a person buying the lease from the tenant. The original tenant will remain contractually liable for any breach of the agreement, but the landlord will not be able to take action against the new tenant (*Purchase* v *Lichfield Brewery Co.* [1915] 1 KB 184).

In *Boyer* v *Warbey* [1953] 1 QB 234, Denning LJ suggested that the position we have just described had changed as a result of the Judicature Acts 1873–5:

... since the fusion of law and equity, the position is different ... There is no valid reason nowadays why the doctrine of covenants running with the land—or with the reversion— should not apply equally to agreements under hand as to covenants under seal; and I think we should so hold, not only in the case of agreements for more than three years which need the intervention of equity to perfect them, but also in the case of agreements for three years or less which do not.

As we have noted above, *Boyer* v *Warbey* was dealing with a written legal lease for three years. Remarks about equitable leases were therefore merely *obiter dicta*; and although they pointed the way to a solution of this problem, they have not been taken up in any later decision. (See further Smith [1978] CLJ 98.)

So far, we have been considering what happens if the *tenant* under an equitable lease assigns his interest. The passage quoted above from *Boyer* v *Warbey* implies that similar difficulties arise if the *landlord* transfers his interest in the land, i.e., assigns his reversion on the equitable lease.

In fact there are a number of earlier decisions which hold that equitable leases are covered by the statutory provision that the benefit of the lessee's covenants runs with the reversion (see, for example, *Rickett* v *Green* [1910] 1 KB 253, interpreting s. 10 of the Conveyancing Act 1881, the forerunner of LPA 1925, s. 141).

There has as yet been no decision on whether the burden of the landlord's covenants runs to the assignee under LPA 1925, s. 142, but the reasoning of the decisions on the running of the benefit would seem equally applicable to the running of the burden (see Megarry and Wade, p. 966).

The various difficulties and uncertainties about the running of covenants in equitable leases provide a further reason for saying that an equitable lease is not as 'good as' a legal lease (see 8.3.4). These problems are now resolved in the case of new tenancies by the provisions of the 1995 Act (see 9.6.2.2), but old leases, of course, are still subject to them.

9.6.2 **The new law, which governs new leases**

9.6.2.1 *Landlord covenants and tenant covenants*

The 1995 Act makes very considerable changes to the rules relating to the running of covenants on the assignment of the lease or the reversion. In doing so, it introduces two new technical terms: 'landlord covenants' and 'tenant covenants'. These are defined in s. 28(1) as the covenants to be performed by the landlord and tenant respectively; in other words, the classification of the covenant is determined by considering who is to bear its burden. For an interpretation of the statutory definition of these terms, see *BHP Petroleum Ltd* v *Chesterfield Ltd* [2002] Ch 194, in which, as we noted in 9.5.2.3, the Court of Appeal held that 'landlord covenants' are those which fall to be complied with by the person who may from time to time be entitled to the reversion (i.e., the current landlord), and do not include personal covenants by the original landlord. Although the court in this case was concerned only with landlord covenants, it seems most likely that a similar approach would be adopted in defining 'tenant covenants'.

9.6.2.2 *Transmission of benefit and burden of covenants and rights of re-entry in a new lease*

Section 3 of the Act provides that the benefit and burden of all landlord and tenant covenants in the tenancy shall be annexed to the whole and each and every part of the demised premises and of the reversion in them, and shall pass on the assignment of the whole or any part of the premises or of the reversion. Section 4 makes a similar provision in respect of the landlord's right of re-entry. Section 23(3) adds that such a right of re-entry may be exercised by the new landlord in respect of breaches of covenant by the tenant which occurred *before* the assignment of the reversion.

Thus, in general, all the covenants in the lease (with the exception of personal covenants, which are specifically excluded by s. 3(6)(a)) will run on the assignment of the lease or the reversion, and there will be no need to consider whether covenants 'touch and concern the land' or 'have reference to the subject matter of the lease' (*Spencer's Case* (1585) 5 Co Rep 16a and LPA 1925, ss. 141 and 142—see 9.6.1.2 and 9.6.1.3). The Act specifically states that its provisions apply to a landlord covenant or a tenant covenant 'whether or not the covenant has reference to the subject matter of the tenancy' (s. 2(1)(a)), and the Act further provides that nothing in LPA 1925, ss. 141 and 142 shall apply in relation to new tenancies (s. 30(4)(b)). It seems therefore that covenants which under the old law will be classified as 'collateral covenants', and accordingly will not pass on assignment, will under the Act run to benefit and burden assignees of new tenancies and their reversions. Examples of some of these collateral covenants can be found at 9.6.1.2.

Equitable leases   A further welcome change is that by virtue of s. 28(1), which defines 'tenancy' as including an 'agreement for a tenancy', the new rules about the running of covenants apply to equitable leases just as they do to legal ones, thus freeing the parties to new agreements from the problems we have noted above at 9.6.1.6(2).

Requirement for registration   Section 3(6)(b) (as amended by LRA 2002) specifically provides that it shall not operate to make enforceable against any person any covenant which would otherwise be unenforceable against him by reason of its not having been registered under the LRA 2002 or the LCA 1925. Thus options to renew the lease, or to purchase the reversion will still continue to require protection by entry on the register of title or by registration as a class C(iv) land charge.

9.7 Enforcement of covenants in the Trant Way tenancies

Now that we have outlined the rules relating to the enforcement of covenants in a lease between both the original parties and their successors, it may be helpful to consider how these apply to some of the inhabitants of Trant Way.

9.7.1 6 Trant Way

As we have seen (at 9.1.4.3), 6 Trant Way was held by John Jarlsberg on a 40-year lease, granted in 1979, i.e., well before the operative date of the Landlord and Tenant (Covenants) Act 1995. Some time ago, Jarlsberg moved away to a different part of the country to take up a new job, and, with the consent of his landlord, Irene Ivy, he sold his lease to Keith Kale. Later, Irene Ivy sold the fee simple estate in 6 Trant Way to Liam Lyle, who was registered as proprietor of the estate, i.e., he bought using the unregistered conveyancing procedure and thereafter applied for first registration of title. Keith Kale has now decided that he would like to take advantage of the option to purchase which was given to the original tenant by the original lease made between Mrs Ivy and Mr Jarlsberg (cl. 4(b), see p. 184). Mr Kale has served written notice on Mr Lyle of his intentions. He has also been having some problems lately with the tile cladding on part of the exterior wall of the house and wants Mr Lyle to sort this out, under the landlord's repairing covenant in the lease, before the purchase of the property goes ahead.

In this situation we must consider:

(a) which of the terms in the original lease bind or benefit Mr Kale, the tenant's assignee; and

(b) which of the terms bind or benefit Mr Lyle, the purchaser of the freehold reversion.

The situation may be expressed diagrammatically as follows:

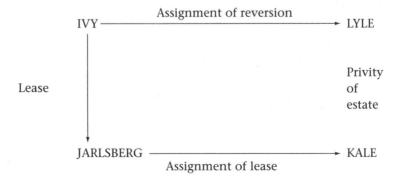

9.7.1.1 *Enforcement of covenants between assignees of lease and reversion*

As a result of the transactions which have occurred, Mr Lyle is now Mr Kale's landlord. There is privity of estate between them. Mr Lyle will be bound by any of the landlord's covenants (LPA 1925, s. 142) and will benefit from any of the tenant's covenants (s. 141) in the original lease which have 'reference to the subject-matter thereof'. Similarly, Mr Kale will automatically receive both the benefit and the burden of any covenants in the original lease which 'touch and concern' the land (*Spencer's Case* (1583) 5 Co Rep 16a).

This means that Mr Kale is bound by Mr Jarlsberg's covenants, and so is obliged to pay rent, to obtain the landlord's consent before assigning or subletting, and not to use the premises otherwise than as a dwelling. Mr Lyle has the right to enforce these covenants against him. In his turn, Mr Lyle is bound by Mrs Ivy's covenants for quiet enjoyment and for the repair of the exterior, and Mr Kale has the right to enforce these against him. It follows from this that Mr Kale should be able to require his landlord to remedy the problems he is experiencing with the exterior wall.

9.7.1.2 *Continuing liability of original landlord and tenant*

Although they probably do not realise it, both Mrs Ivy and Mr Jarlsberg remain liable on their covenants, even although both of them have given up all connection with the property. This means that if, for any reason, Mr Lyle fails to carry out the necessary repairs, Mr Kale could seek compensation from Mrs Ivy. In reality, though, this is only likely to happen if Mr Lyle is unable to meet his obligations for financial reasons.

9.7.1.3 *Option to purchase the reversion*

The question of whether Mr Kale has the right to enforce the option to purchase against his landlord is more complicated. It has been held that this covenant does not touch and concern the land: the option does not affect the parties qua landlord and tenant but qua vendor and purchaser (*Woodall* v *Clifton* [1905] 2 Ch 257). Accordingly, this right does not automatically benefit or burden Mr Kale and Mr Lyle. The option did, however, give the original tenant, Mr Jarlsberg, an equitable interest in the fee simple estate. The benefit of that right could have been assigned to Mr Kale, as can the benefit of any chose in action, but a clear assignment of the right will be required if Mr Kale is to establish a claim to it.

Even if Mr Kale can prove that the benefit of the right has been assigned to him, he must still establish that the option is binding on Mr Lyle, who has bought the legal estate in fee simple. Mr Lyle will be bound by the equitable interest only if it had been protected as a C(iv) land charge before he purchased the fee simple (see *Phillips* v *Mobil Oil Co. Ltd* [1989] 1 WLR 888). If the option had not been registered it will not bind Mr Lyle and cannot be enforced against him.

Finally, it may be helpful to mention that at one time the Rule against Perpetuities (see Chapter 15) would have prevented the enforcement of the option by Mr Kale against Mr Lyle (*Woodall* v *Clifton* [1905] 2 Ch 257), but this obstacle has now been removed by s. 9 of the Perpetuities and Accumulations Act 1964.

9.7.2 **2 Trant Way: maisonette**

By contrast with the lease of 6 Trant Way, the lease of the ground and first-floor maisonette at 2 Trant Way (see 9.1.4.2), which Harry Harding is to take from Fingall Forest, will, when granted, fall within the main provisions of the Landlord and Tenant (Covenants) Act 1995.

9.7.2.1 *Release of original covenantor*

Harry is taking on a number of obligations under the lease, but he can be assured that, if he assigns the lease in the future, he will be released from any continuing liability on the tenant covenants (provided he is not so foolish as to assign the lease without his landlord's consent, thus making an 'excluded assignment'). By contrast, assigning the reversion would not relieve Fingall Forest automatically from his liability on the landlord covenants, but he could seek release from his current tenant or, in case of refusal, from the court. If for any reason he was not released, he could make a further application on any occasion in the future when the reversion was assigned again.

9.7.2.2 *Enforcement of covenants between assignees of lease and reversion*

Assignees from the original landlord and tenant will take the reversion and the lease with the relevant benefits and burdens of the tenant and landlord covenants (with the exception of any which are expressed to be personal to the original parties). There will be no need to ask whether the covenants touch and concern the land (*Spencer's Case*) or have reference to the subject matter of the lease (LPA 1925, ss. 141 and 142); all that will be needed is a reference to the terms of s. 2 of the 1995 Act, which provides that the benefit and burden of all landlord covenants and tenant covenants are annexed to the premises and to the reversion, and pass on assignment.

9.8 **Effect on a subtenant of covenants in the head lease**

9.8.1 **Covenant in head lease not enforceable against subtenant**

We have seen that when a tenant assigns his lease, certain covenants in the lease are enforceable between the landlord and the assignee. If, however, the tenant, T, instead of assigning his lease, creates a sublease, we get a different situation. In such a case the subtenant, S, is the tenant of T and has no landlord and tenant relationship with L, the head landlord. Accordingly, there is neither privity of contract nor privity of estate between L and S, but there is both privity of contract and privity of estate between T and S. This can be expressed in diagrammatic form as follows:

	L	
Head lease	↓	Privity of contract *and* estate between L and T
	T	
Sublease	↓	Privity of contract *and* estate between T and S
	S	

As a result, covenants in the head lease are not usually enforceable against a sub-tenant. However, since the tenant usually could be held liable for the actions of persons who derive their title from him he would normally take the precaution of including in the sublease the same set of covenants which he himself had entered into in the head lease. If T has done this, it would allow him to take action against S for breach of any covenant and thereby to protect himself against any liability to L.

9.8.1.1 *Exceptions in respect of restrictive covenants*

The only covenants in the head lease which could be enforced by L against S are those which restrict the use of the property. It has always been possible to enforce these against a subtenant if they satisfy the rules relating to restrictive covenants derived from *Tulk* v *Moxhay* (1848) 2 Ph 774 (which are dealt with in Chapter 23). A recent example is provided by *Hemingway Securities Ltd* v *Dunraven Ltd* [1995] 1 EGLR 61, in which it was held that a covenant not to assign or sublet without the landlord's consent was a restrictive covenant within the doctrine of *Tulk* v *Moxhay*, and could be enforced by the head landlord directly against the subtenant.

In addition, s. 3(5) of the Landlord and Tenant (Covenants) Act 1995 now provides in respect of 'new tenancies' (in general, those granted on or after 1 January 1996) that:

Any landlord or tenant covenant of a tenancy which is restrictive of the user of land shall, as well as being capable of enforcement against an assignee, be capable of being enforced against any other person who is the owner or occupier of any demised premises to which the covenant relates, even though there is no express provision in the tenancy to that effect.

The full effect of this provision remains to be seen, as does its relationship to the rule in *Tulk* v *Moxhay*, but it is certainly clear that it will enable the head landlord to enforce such covenants directly against the subtenant without reference to the equitable rules about restrictive covenants.

A suggestion that s. 3(5) would also enable a tenant to enforce the covenants his landlord had made with him against other tenants holding from the same landlord was rejected in *Oceanic Village Ltd* v *United Attractions Ltd* [2000] Ch 234. In this case, the landlord of a large building in central London, which was being developed as a tourist attraction, leased one part of it to Oceanic Village for use as a gift shop. In the lease the landlord undertook that it would not permit any other gift shop to be operated in the building. Later, the landlord granted a lease of another part of the building to United Attractions, but did not impose any restriction against use as a gift shop. Oceanic Village sought to restrain its fellow tenant from operating such a shop. In doing so, Oceanic Village relied both on s. 3(5) and on the rule in *Tulk* v *Moxhay*.

In seeking to enforce under s. 3(5), Oceanic Village claimed that the phrase 'any demised premises' used in the subsection referred to any premises demised by the landlord, and so enabled a tenant to enforce a landlord covenant in his lease against anyone occupying other premises leased by the same landlord. Neuberger J rejected this argument, holding that the section referred only to premises demised by the lease which contained the covenant. In his view, this more limited interpretation accorded with the meaning to be attributed to the phrase as used in other parts of s. 3. It also avoided the difficulty inherent in the wider interpretation, which would raise, for example, the question of whether the section was limited to land owned by the landlord at the date of the covenant, or would extend to cover land which he subsequently acquired and let to tenants.

The judge accepted that the narrower interpretation was not entirely without problems. If the section is limited in this way to activities on the demised property it is difficult to see how these could amount to a breach of a landlord covenant, since one assumes that the property will be occupied by the tenant or by someone claiming through him. Neuberger J accept counsel's suggestions that there could be circumstances in which a landlord might be in a position to carry out activities on the premises in breach of his covenant. He might, for example, be on the premises to carry out repairs. Again, the property might have been sub-divided by the tenant, and an assignee of part might have surrendered or forfeited his lease to the landlord, so that the landlord could be in occupation of part of the demised premises. In conclusion on this point, the judge emphasised (at p. 247) that s. 3(5) is also concerned with the enforcement of tenant covenants:

The legislature may well have concluded that it would be safer and fairer to apply section 3(5) to both types of covenant, even though it would have been obvious that it would be far more frequently appropriate to tenant covenants, and it may have been hard to envisage that it would often apply to landlord covenants.

For a short but helpful note on this decision, see Bridge [2002] CLJ 450.

9.8.1.2 *Assignment of sublease or reversion on head lease*

The same principles will apply if S assigns his sublease to SA and if L assigns his reversion on the head lease to P:

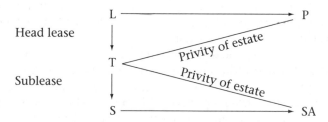

P becomes T's landlord, and, according to the date on which the head lease was granted, covenants in it may be enforced between them under either LPA 1925, ss. 141 and 142, or the Landlord and Tenant (Covenants) Act 1995. SA becomes T's tenant, and, again depending on the date of the lease, covenants in the sublease will be enforceable between them under either the rule in *Spencer's Case* (1583) 5 Co Rep 16a or the 1995 Act. There is, however, no relationship of any kind between P and SA, and no covenants (except those within either the *Tulk* v *Moxhay* rule or s. 3(5) of the 1995 Act) can be enforced between them.

9.8.2 **Attempts by head landlord or subtenant to enforce covenants in leases to which they are not parties**

So far, we have been considering the extent to which the head landlord might be able to enforce covenants in the *head lease* against the subtenant. However, the question also arises of whether he has any standing to enforce covenants in the *sublease* (to which he is not a party) against the subtenant. An example of an occasion on which a head landlord tried to do this is to be found in *Amsprop Trading Ltd* v *Harris Distribution Ltd* [1997] 1 WLR 1025. In this case the subtenant had covenanted with *his* landlord that he would repair the property, and that if he did not do so the head landlord might enter and do the repairs, at the expense of the subtenant. The head landlord sought to enforce this covenant directly against the subtenant, relying on LPA 1925, s. 56, which provides that:

a person may take . . . the benefit of any . . . covenant . . . respecting land, although he may not be named as a party to the conveyance [in which the covenant is made].

The landlord's claim was rejected because the covenant did not purport to be with him (i.e., did not name him as a covenantee), a requirement which has been developed by the courts in their interpretation of s. 56. Had this requirement been met, it seems that the head landlord could have relied on the section and enforced the covenant against the subtenant.

There may well be similar situations in which a subtenant wishes that he could enforce a covenant in the head lease against the head landlord. The head landlord may, for example, be in breach of his repairing obligations, and it would help the subtenant, who suffers the effects of disrepair, if he could proceed directly against him, instead of having to leave it to his own landlord to take action. It is possible that a tenant under an 'old' lease (i.e., one granted before 1 January 1996) could do this by relying on LPA 1925, s. 78, as interpreted in *Smith and Snipes Hall Farm Ltd* v *River Douglas Catchment Board* [1949] 2 KB 500 (see 23.4.1.4), but even if this were so it would not help a tenant under a new lease (granted after 1995), to which s. 78 no longer applies (Landlord and Tenant (Covenants) Act 1995, s. 30(4)).

Where the lease in question is made on or after 11 May 2000, it seems very likely that both head landlord and subtenant may be able to rely on the provisions of the Contracts (Rights of Third Parties) Act 1999, which came into force on that date. In outline, the Act provides that a person who is not a party to a contract (a 'third party') may enforce a term of the contract if either the contract expressly provides that he may do so, or if the term purports to confer a benefit on him, and the parties have not excluded the statutory provisions. As yet, there has not been any reported attempt to rely on the Act in this context, but it certainly seems that it could be used by head landlords and subtenants in the situations we have outlined above. (See further Law Commission Report, 1996, No. 242, para. 2.11, and Elias *Third Party Benefits* [1999] 13 EG 117.)

9.8.3 **7 Trant Way**

An example of the working of these rules is to be found at 7 Trant Way which is owned in fee simple by Martin Mount. The property is divided into two parts: the ground floor (7A) being adapted for use as a shop, while the upstairs (7B) provides office accommodation. The entire property was let to Nigel Norman in 1982 for 99 years. The lease was made by deed and included a number of covenants on the part of Mr Norman, including covenants to pay rent, at present £1,500 per month, to keep the property in good repair and not to keep any animals on the property. Immediately after completion of the lease, Mr Norman sublet 7A to Olav Orion, who uses it as a showroom for his antiques business, and 7B to Paula Primrose, who carries on a small employment agency from the premises. The two subtenants both have monthly tenancies, which were granted in writing and which contain covenants identical in form to those in the headlease.

This situation can be expressed diagrammatically:

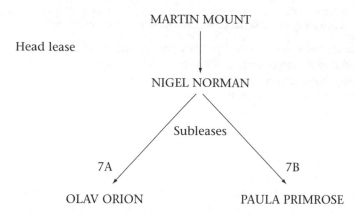

In this situation, Mr Mount can enforce the tenant's covenants in the head lease against Mr Norman, because there is privity of contract between them. There is, however, neither privity of contract nor privity of estate between Mr Mount and Mr Orion, or between Mr Mount and Miss Primrose, and so Mr Mount cannot take any action against either of the subtenants for breach of the covenants in the head lease (subject to the special rules in *Tulk* v *Moxhay* (1848) 2 Ph 774). Accordingly, should Mr Orion or Miss Primrose break a covenant, Mr Mount may sue only Mr Norman, who in the absence of any provisions excluding the operation of LPA 1925, s. 79 is responsible for the actions of persons deriving title under him, and Mr Norman should then take action against Mr Orion or Miss Primrose.

FURTHER READING

'Touching and concerning'
Smith, *Property Law*, 4th edn., Longman, 2003, pp. 435–42.

1995 Act
Davey, 'Privity of Contract and Leases—Reform at Last' (1996) 59 MLR 78.
Walter, 'The Landlord and Tenant (Covenants) Act 1995: A Legislative Folly' [1996] Conv 432.

10

Remedies for breach of leasehold covenants

In the previous chapter we considered the typical covenants which may be contained in a lease, and how the rights and duties arising from them may pass to assignees of the lease and the reversion. We must now go on to see what happens if some of these covenants are broken and what remedies are available to the other party. We will deal first with general contractual remedies which are, of course, available in respect of breach of covenant. We will then go on to consider in more detail some special remedies which are peculiar to leases, and in particular the landlord's power to forfeit the lease, i.e., to bring it to an end and to evict the tenant.

10.1 General contractual remedies

Where a party to a lease is in breach of covenant, the usual battery of contractual remedies is available to the other party. Thus, for example, in appropriate cases either landlord or tenant may seek specific performance of a covenant by the other party to repair. Similarly, if a tenant uses the premises to run a business, contrary to a covenant to use the premises only as a dwelling, the landlord could seek an injunction to restrain the breach. Further, either party might decide to claim damages for breach of contract as an alternative or additional remedy. Finally, since *Hussein* v *Mehlman* [1992] 2 EGLR 87 (see 8.6.2), the possibility of acceptance of repudiatory breach as a discharge of the contract should also be borne in mind as a possible response to a breach of covenant by either landlord or tenant.

If you feel that you need it, further information on contractual remedies is available in any standard textbook on the law of contract. However, there have recently been some important decisions on the specific enforcement of certain covenants in leases, and we need to consider these here.

10.1.1 'Keep-open' covenants

If you think of your local shopping precinct, you may see that one store, perhaps a grocery supermarket, is clearly a major attraction, bringing customers to the area and thus providing passing trade for other smaller shops in the precinct. In recognition of this fact, the landlords of such shopping areas may require the tenants of the major store to enter into a 'keep-open' covenant, i.e., to covenant that they will continue to trade in the premises leased to them for the period of their lease, or, if they no longer wish to carry on business there, until they have assigned or sublet the property with their landlord's consent.

It had always been thought that such covenants were not enforceable by an order for specific performance. This was because such an order, compelling the tenant to carry on business, would involve the court in supervising the way in which he did so, a role which the court is not willing to undertake. However, to everyone's surprise, an order of specific performance of such a covenant was granted by the Court of Appeal in *Co-operative Insurance Society Ltd* v *Argyll Stores (Holdings) Ltd* [1996] Ch 286. Thus Argyll Stores, who had closed their Safeways store in Hillsborough shopping centre in breach of their keep-open covenant, were required to continue to trade there until the end of the lease in 2014, or until they could assign or sublet the premises with their landlord's consent.

The Court of Appeal's decision was, however, reversed by the House of Lords in *Co-operative Insurance Society Ltd* v *Argyll Stores (Holdings) Ltd* [1998] AC 1. Lord Hoffmann, in a speech adopted by the other Law Lords, gave a number of reasons for holding that it was inappropriate to compel a defendant to carry on a business; while none of the reasons would necessarily be sufficient on its own, he said (at p. 16), that the cumulative effect seemed to show that the settled practice of refusing to order specific performance of such an obligation is based upon sound sense. Those reasons included: the difficulty of defining precisely what the defendant was required to do; the hardship caused to him by requiring him to carry on a loss-making business; and the perpetuation of conflict between the parties who were required to continue in a hostile relationship.

In terms of the principles governing the grant of specific performance, possibly the most significant of the reasons discussed by Lord Hoffmann relates to the need for continuing supervision. The suggestion that performance will require supervision by the court has often been given as a reason for refusing the order, because the court has no mechanisms by which it can ensure such supervision. Lord Hoffman's speech helpfully clarifies what is meant by 'continued supervision': not that the judge or some court official actually supervises ongoing performance, but that any failure to perform entitles the aggrieved party to return to court seeking the defendant's committal for contempt. An order to carry on an activity, such as a business, over an extended period of time, would give rise to the possibility of repeated applications to the court, alleging incidents of non-compliance. It would thus be expensive both to the parties and to the resources of the judicial system. A clean break, with the payment of damages for breach, would be a far better solution. By contrast, an order to achieve a result, such as to repair property, does not involve the court in ongoing supervision. Provided the required outcome could be defined sufficiently precisely when the order was made, the court would, at most, have to decide on one further application whether the work had been done to a satisfactory standard, i.e., whether the desired result had been achieved. As we shall see (10.1.2(2)), this distinction between carrying on an activity and achieving a required result has been relied upon in a later decision dealing with specific performance of repairing covenants, and the House of Lords decision in the *Argyll* case is not only relevant to the enforcement of keep-open covenants, but has a wider significance for the general principles underlying the award of specific performance.

For a case note which sets the *Argyll* decision in its commercial context, see

Luxton [1998] Conv 396; and for a critical comment on the House of Lords' decision, see Tettenborn [1998] Conv 23.

10.1.2 **Repairing covenants**

Although we have not dealt in any detail with repairing covenants, you should be aware that either party to the lease may be subject to an obligation to repair, either by express agreement or under certain covenants implied by common law or statute (see 9.3). In considering remedies for breach of such covenants, we need to note first some special statutory provisions which protect the tenant, and then recent case law developments which have made the remedy of specific performance available against both landlord and tenant.

10.1.2.1 *Leasehold Property (Repairs) Act 1938*

The background to this Act is to be found in the activities of property speculators, who would buy tenanted property in a poor state of repair at a low price, with a view to enforcing the tenants' repairing covenants and evicting them (by forfeiture proceedings) if they were unable to carry out the repairs. The Act applies to leases of not less than seven years, with at least three years left to run, and provides that proceedings to recover damages or to forfeit the lease for failure to repair may be brought only with leave of the court. Such leave is to be given only on specified grounds, which in general involve satisfying the court that the landlord has a valid reason for requiring repairs to be done immediately rather than at the end of the lease (e.g., that lack of repair is injurious to other occupiers of the property, or that leaving the repairs until later will substantially increase their cost).

10.1.2.2 *Specific performance of repairing covenants*

It used to be thought, on the supposed authority of *Hill* v *Barclay* (1810) 16 Ves Jun 402, that specific performance of a covenant to repair was not available against either a landlord or a tenant. Several reasons were suggested for this rule, including the problem of continued supervision by the court, discussed above in connection with the *Argyll* case.

Where the landlord was in breach of a repairing obligation, the tenant's only remedy therefore was to do the repairs himself, and then seek to recover the cost from the landlord, either by withholding rent (*Lee Parker* v *Izzet* [1971] 1 WLR 1688) or by suing for damages for breach of covenant. More recently, as we have seen (8.6.2), if the breach is sufficiently serious the tenant may regard it as repudiatory and treat the contract as discharged, freeing himself from further obligation but at the same time retaining the right to seek damages for breach.

Where it was the tenant who was in breach, the landlord could seek damages or forfeiture, subject of course to the provisions of the Leasehold Property (Repairs) Act 1938, noted above.

The first change to the old approach is to be found in *Jeune* v *Queen's Cross Properties Ltd* [1974] Ch 97, where a landlord who had covenanted to maintain and repair the structure of a block of flats was ordered to reconstruct an exterior balcony which had collapsed. The balcony did not form part of the property leased to any of the plaintiff tenants, and since they did not have possession of it they would have had difficulty in following the usual route of doing the repairs and recovering the cost from the landlord. The court reviewed the supposed authority of *Hill* v *Barclay* (1810) 16 Ves Jun 402, and considered that it did not preclude the grant of an order of specific performance against a landlord. Statutory power to order specific performance of a landlord's repairing covenants is now to be found in the Landlord and Tenant Act 1985, s. 17, replacing the Housing Act 1974, s. 125.

In *Jeune* v *Queen's Cross Properties Ltd*, *Hill* v *Barclay* was said in *obiter dicta* to be an authority for the proposition that specific performance of a repairing covenant could not be awarded against a *tenant*. However, this has now been done in a recent first-instance decision: *Rainbow Estates Ltd* v *Tokenhold Ltd* [1999] Ch 64. The facts of the case were unusual, in that the original landlord who granted the lease was a company controlled by the individuals to whom the lease was granted, and, possibly in consequence of this, there was no provision either for forfeiture for breach of covenant or for the landlord to enter and do repairs if the tenant failed to do so. The property was a listed building, in a serious state of disrepair; if the current landlords were not able to obtain specific performance of the tenants' repairing covenant there was no way in which they could effect repairs until the lease ended in some six years' time. In these circumstances the judge considered it appropriate to grant an order against the tenants for specific performance of their repairing obligations.

In doing so, he reviewed the reasons which used to be given for refusing specific performance to either landlord or tenant, and concluded that today 'there is little or no life in these reasons' (at p. 69). In particular, the supposed need for continued supervision by the court was no longer seen as a problem. An order to repair was an order to achieve a specified result, rather than to carry on an activity, and so, on the distinction drawn in the *Argyll* case (see 10.1.1), need not involve repeated applications to the court.

A further point which the judge had to consider was that the remedy of specific performance does not fall within the provisions of the Leasehold Property (Repairs) Act 1938. In consequence, a landlord would not need to obtain leave from the court before seeking this remedy (as he would have to do if seeking damages or forfeiture), and applications for specific performance could therefore be used to harass or oppress a tenant. In the judge's view, it would not be right to extend the Act by judicial interpretation to cover applications for specific performance, but the court would take care to ensure that such applications were not used to bring about the mischief which the Act was designed to remedy. An order for specific performance against a tenant was likely to be appropriate only in rare cases, but:

subject to the overriding need to avoid injustice or oppression, the remedy should be available when damages are not an adequate remedy (at p. 73).

10.2 Tenant's remedies against a defaulting landlord

As we have seen above, the tenant has all the usual contractual remedies against his landlord in case of breach. In addition, there are various statutory provisions which may give the tenant additional protection against harassment or eviction, or may offer alternative ways of ensuring that the landlord complies with his repairing obligations.

10.2.1 **Harassment or eviction**

Treatment which is calculated to drive the tenant out of the premises, whilst being a breach of the covenant of quiet enjoyment, may also amount to the criminal offence of harassment. This offence is committed where acts are done which are likely to interfere with the tenant's peace or comfort or where services, reasonably required for occupation of the premises as a residence, are withdrawn (Protection from Eviction Act 1977, s. 1(3) and 1(3A)). Only the local authority may institute proceedings for this offence, and the original provisions gave no real assistance to the tenant who wished to obtain a remedy in civil proceedings. However, the Housing Act 1988, s. 27, also provides a tenant who is a residential occupier with a statutory cause of action should he be evicted by his landlord. The ingredients of this tort are the same as those of the criminal offence under the Protection from Eviction Act 1977 but it is not necessary for a criminal conviction to have been obtained before the tenant brings his action. In addition to this statutory right the tenant may also be able to found an action upon trespass, nuisance or even, if appropriate, assault, as well of course as on breach of contract.

For an interesting article based on research into the effectiveness of the provisions of the Protection from Eviction Act, see Cowan [2001] 65 Conv 249.

10.2.2 **Landlord's failure to repair**

We have already considered the tenant's contractual remedies for the landlord's breach of his covenant to repair, but it may be that a tenant wants to avoid a direct confrontation in the courts with his landlord (possibly because the tenant cannot afford the legal costs) and yet wants to ensure that repairs to the property are made. You should therefore be aware that failure to repair can, in some circumstances, be dealt with by the local authority, under statutory powers contained in the Housing Act 1985, Pt VI, and thus in some cases a tenant may be able to seek the assistance of the local authority. It should, however, be noted that the statutory provisions concerning repair are only of assistance when the defects are serious in nature.

10.3 **Landlord's remedies against a defaulting tenant**

In addition to his contractual remedies for breach of contract, the landlord has a special remedy for non-payment of rent (distress), and subject to various safeguards may be able to forfeit the lease so as to rid himself entirely of a tenant who has proved to be unreliable.

10.3.1 **Distress**

Distraint is an ancient remedy for non-payment of rent. It involves direct action by way of self-help. Put simply, the landlord will enter the demised premises and take possession of the tenant's belongings, up to the value of the unpaid rent. The goods are held for five days (usually they are left in place, the landlord taking what is called 'walking possession') and then may be sold if the rent is not paid. Certain goods are protected against distraint (e.g., clothing and the tools of the tenant's trade). The action must be taken by the landlord in person or by a certificated bailiff: he cannot 'send round the heavies' (Law of Distress Amendment Act 1888, s. 7).

The remedy of distress, although ancient, is still in use in this country. Frequently it can have serious consequences for the tenant since enforced sales of tenants' property rarely produce a high price for the goods sold. As we note below, there have been several proposals for reform in the past, and increased impetus for change is likely to be provided by the Human Rights Act 1998. There are concerns that distress, along with other self-help remedies such as peaceful re-entry without a court order by a landlord (10.3.2.3(1)) or by a mortgagee (21.7.2), may prove to be in breach of rights such as those to a fair trial (Art. 6), to respect for private and family life and the home (Art. 8), and to the peaceful enjoyment of possessions (Art. 1 of first protocol). On this, see Karas and Maurici [1999] 17 EG 126.

As we have seen (1.10), the question of the possible horizontal effect of the Act is still open, with the result that it is not yet possible to say whether the use of distress by private landlords will be directly affected by the Act. However, many local authority landlords rely on the remedy against tenants of their public sector housing, and such landlords are undoubtedly subject to the provisions of s. 6 of the Act, which make it unlawful for a public authority to act in a way incompatible with a Convention right.

In *Fuller* v *Happy Shopper Markets Ltd* [2001] 2 EGLR 32 at 36 Lightman J warned all landlords (not just those who are public authorities) of the dangers involved in levying distress:

The ancient (and perhaps anachronistic) self-help remedy of distress involves a serious interference with the right of the tenant, under Article 8 of the European Convention on Human Rights, to respect for his privacy and home, and, under Article 1 of the First Protocol, to the peaceful enjoyment of his possessions. The human rights implications of levying distress must be in the forefront of the mind of the landlord before he takes this step, and he must fully satisfy himself that taking this action is in accordance with the law.

Concerns about the remedy of distress had been voiced for some time in the past, long before the advent of the Human Rights Act. Its abolition had been recommended by the Law Commission in 1966, and by the Payne Committee on the Enforcement of Judgment Debts in 1969. A similar recommendation was made by the Law Commission again in 1991 (*Landlord & Tenant. Distress for Rent*, 1991, Law Com No. 194), but with the proviso that abolition should be postponed until the procedure for recovery of arrears of rent through court action could be improved. This proposal met with considerable opposition from landlords, who continue to regard distress as a valuable remedy. As a result, a more recent consultation paper issued by the Lord Chancellor's Department in May 2001 (*Enforcement Review Consultation Paper No. 5: Distress for Rent*), while supporting the abolition of distress for residential leases, proposes that it should be retained for commercial property, subject to certain safeguards designed to secure compliance with the Human Rights Act 1998. Thus, among other reforms, the landlord would be required to give notice to the tenant before seizing the goods and again before selling them, and the tenant would have the right to apply to the court to challenge the debt and to seek an injunction restraining distress. The proposals aim to give the tenant sufficient access to the courts to ensure compliance with Art. 6, and to bring interference with rights under Art. 8 and Art. 1 of the First Protocol within the limits permitted by those articles.

10.3.2 **Forfeiture**

Where a tenant has broken a covenant in a lease the landlord may wish to rid himself of the defaulter altogether, although he will have to take into account, of course, his possible loss of income if he is unable to relet the property. However, a landlord does not have an automatic right to forfeit the lease for breach of a covenant (though, as we mentioned earlier in 9.1.2, there is such a right in the case of breach of a condition). Before a landlord can seek to forfeit the lease he must show that the lease contained a clause permitting him to re-enter for breach of covenant. An example of a typical clause is given in cl. 5(a) on p. 184. In the absence of such a clause the landlord will have no right to forfeit the lease and must fall back on his contractual remedies (*Doe d Wilson* v *Phillips* (1824) 2 Bing 13).

Avoiding waiver   Even where the lease contains a provision which gives the land-lord a right of re-entry for breach, the landlord will be prevented from forfeiting the lease if he can be shown to have waived the breach. Waiver may be express (e.g., if the landlord states that he will ignore a breach) or may be implied.

It is implied waiver which may cause difficulties to a landlord, since he may be taken to have waived a breach when he did not intend to do so. For an implied waiver to arise the landlord must first know that a breach has occurred and thereafter have acted in such a way that he has treated the lease as still continu-ing. The most common way of waiving a breach is found where the landlord claims or accepts rent from the tenant when he knows that a breach has occurred (*Segal Securities Ltd* v *Thoseby* [1963] 1 QB 887). However, any act which treats the lease as continuing will do (*Ward* v *Day* (1864) 5 B & S 359), although Slade LJ in *Expert Clothing Service and Sales Ltd* v *Hillgate House* [1986] 1 Ch 340 at p. 360 emphasised that where some act other than the acceptance of rent is in question:

the court is . . . free to look at *all* the circumstances of the case to consider whether the act . . . relied on [as constituting waiver is] so unequivocal that, when considered objectively, it could only be regarded as having been done consistently with the continued operation of a tenancy . . .

If the breach is continuing in nature (e.g., breach of the covenant to repair), the waiver will not extend beyond the time during which the landlord knew that the breach would continue (*Segal Securities Ltd* v *Thoseby*). Nor does a waiver cover further breaches committed after the waiver was made (*Cooper* v *Henderson* (1982) 263 EG 592).

The rules relating to waiver may cause problems for the landlord who, on discovering a breach of covenant, first ensures that he collects the rent before seeking to take further action against his tenant. This is particularly a problem because the landlord is also bound by the actions or knowledge of his servants or agents. Thus, should the landlord's agent accept rent at a date at which the land-lord knew of a breach, this would amount to waiver. Of course, where the breach of covenant in question is a failure to pay rent, making the formal demand which may be a necessary step in forfeiture proceedings (see 10.3.2.1 below) will not constitute waiver. However, as shown in *Re A Debtor* (No. 13A-10–1995) [1995] 1 WLR 1127, a demand for a later quarter's rent indicates that the landlord regards the lease as continuing into that quarter and so waives his right to forfeit in respect of an earlier quarter's non-payment.

There are formal requirements which a landlord must observe before forfeiting a lease, and these differ depending on whether the landlord seeks to forfeit for breach of the covenant to pay rent, or for breach of some other covenant.

10.3.2.1 *Forfeiture for non-payment of rent*

Theoretically, the first thing that the landlord must do, before he attempts to forfeit the lease for non-payment of rent, is to make a *formal demand* for the rent. The formal demand must be made by the landlord, or his agent, at the demised premises between the hours of sunrise and sunset on the day on which payment is due (see *Duppa* v *Mayo* (1669) Saund 282 at p. 287 n 16). However, this performance is usually rendered unnecessary by a clause in the lease which specifies that the landlord may forfeit for non-payment of rent 'whether formally demanded or not' (see lease clause 5(a), p. 184). In any event, s. 210 of the Common Law Procedure Act 1852 dispenses with the need for a formal demand in cases where the rent is at least half a year in arrears and there are insufficient goods on the premises to satisfy the debt should distress be levied.

10.3.2.2 *Forfeiture for breach of covenants other than that to pay rent: the s. 146 notice*

Forfeiture of a lease for breach of covenants other than that to pay rent is governed by LPA 1925, s. 146. The aim of the procedure required by s. 146 is to allow the tenant a chance to remedy his fault before the ultimate sanction of forfeiture is imposed. Accordingly the section imposes a requirement upon the landlord to serve notice in the prescribed form. The s. 146 notice must:

(a) specify the breach;

(b) require that the breach be remedied, if it is remediable; and

(c) require the tenant to pay financial compensation for the breach.

Item (a) must be contained in all notices; item (c) need not be included if the landlord does not require financial compensation (*Lock* v *Pearce* [1893] 2 Ch 271). It is item (b) which has given rise to the most problems, however, since it requires that the tenant be called upon to remedy the breach *if it is remediable*. If the breach is irremediable the notice need only specify the breach and the landlord may then proceed to forfeit the lease. It is therefore necessary to know whether a breach of covenant is remediable.

(1) *Is the breach of covenant remediable?* Since the mid-1980s there has been a very marked change in the courts' approach to the question of whether a breach of covenant is 'capable of remedy' within the terms of LPA 1925, s. 146(1). In earlier decisions attention focused on the fact of a breach by the tenant, rather than on the harm which such breach might cause to the landlord. As Harman J commented in *Hoffmann* v *Fineberg* [1949] Ch 245 at p. 253:

in one sense, no breach can ever be remedied because there must always . . . be a time in which there has not been compliance with the covenant.

However, s. 146 clearly contemplated that some breaches *were* remediable, and, in deciding which these were, the courts found it helpful to distinguish between positive and negative covenants, and between continuing breaches and once-and-for-all breaches.

An early suggestion, to be found at first instance in *Rugby School (Governors)* v *Tannahill* [1934] 1 KB 695 at p. 701, was that breach of a positive covenant could be remedied, but breach of a negative one could not:

A promise to do a thing, if broken, can be remedied by the thing being done. But breach of a promise not to do a thing cannot in any true sense be remedied; that which was done cannot be undone.

Obiter dicta in the Court of Appeal's judgment in this case ([1935] 1 KB 87 at pp. 90–1) cast some doubt on the general test proposed by MacKinnon J at first instance, and suggest that in some cases (although not in the one before the court) breaches of a negative covenant might be remedied by immediately ceasing the activity prohibited by the covenant and giving an undertaking against further breach.

Thus, it appeared from statements in *Rugby School (Governors)* v *Tannahill* that some breaches of both positive and negative covenants might be remediable, but the question remained: which ones? In answer, the courts distinguished between continuing breaches, which could be remedied, and once-and-for-all breaches, which could not. Thus a continuing breach of a positive covenant, such as a continuing failure to repair, could be remedied by undertaking the repairs, for the performance of the covenant, even if later than it should be, would fulfil the obligation. Similarly, a continuing breach of a negative covenant, such as using the premises for the purposes of trade, could, as the Court of Appeal suggested in *Rugby School (Governors)* v *Tannahill*, be remedied by ceasing the use. However, some covenants were broken once and for all on the occurrence of some event. A positive covenant to make alterations to a building by a prescribed date was broken once and for all when the work was not done by that date; a negative covenant against making alterations to the property without the landlord's consent was broken once and for all when the alterations were done without that consent. In the courts' view, such breaches could not be remedied; the breach had occurred on a given event in the past, and there was no way in which the tenant could re-write history to make it appear that it had not.

This rather literal approach to the question may have been logically correct, but must have been somewhat baffling to the tenant, who, for instance, might have been willing to undo the alterations he had made without consent, and could not see why this would not amount to 'remedying' the breach. It also led to a result which, although again logically correct, seemed somewhat strange: if the tenant had already ceased the activity complained of, the breach was, in the court's view, irremediable, because there was no longer any continuing breach which could be put right (a view taken by the Court of Appeal in *Scala House & District Property Co. Ltd* v *Forbes* [1974] QB 575, and subsequently described by O'Connor LJ in *Expert Clothing Service and Sales Ltd* v *Hillgate House Ltd* [1986] 1 Ch 340 at p. 364 as 'unsatisfactory').

The view that certain once-and-for-all breaches were irremediable may seem unduly harsh, but you should bear in mind that tenants in such a position were able to apply for relief from forfeiture (see 10.3.2.4), and that the courts did grant such relief even though the breach could not, technically, be remedied. An example is to found in *Scala House & District Property Co. Ltd* v *Forbes*, where subletting without the landlord's consent was held to be an irremediable breach, but relief from forfeiture was granted. In deciding to give relief, the court took a number of reasons into account, including the fact that the sublease had been created through an error by the tenant's solicitor, and that the tenant had already procured the surrender of the sublease, so that the subtenant was no longer in possession.

Thus, tenants who had committed irremediable breaches could be saved from losing their leases, but nevertheless were involved in the uncertainty and expense of seeking relief from the court, while had the breach been treated by the landlord as remediable, it could have been remedied on a s. 146 notice without reference to the court.

A major change in the courts' approach to the question of remediable breach is to be found in the Court of Appeal decision in *Expert Clothing Service & Sales Ltd* v *Hillgate House Ltd* [1986] 1 Ch 340. In this case both the covenants in question were positive: (a) to give notice to the landlord of any charge created over the property and (b) to reconstruct the premises for occupation by a stated date, or as soon as possible thereafter. The tenant charged the premises without giving notice, and allowed the specified date to pass without making the reconstruction. The landlord served a notice under LPA 1925, s. 146, which complained of the two breaches but did not require them to be remedied, and in subsequent court proceedings was granted an order for possession. On appeal, the Court of Appeal held that both of these breaches were remediable; accordingly the landlord's notice was invalid, and he was not entitled to possession.

In giving judgment, Slade LJ emphasised (at p. 358) that the principal object of s. 146 procedure is to give the tenant the opportunity to remedy the breach:

An important purpose of the s. 146 procedure is to give even tenants who have hitherto lacked the will or the means to comply with their obligations one last chance . . . before the landlord re-enters.

In considering whether a breach was remediable, the court should focus on the harm which had been done to the landlord and on whether that harm could be remedied. The test was said to be whether compliance with the covenant (albeit late) together with financial compensation would 'have effectively remedied the harm which the lessors had suffered or were likely to suffer from the breach'. In other words, emphasis shifts from attempting to remedy the *breach* (by 'undoing' it or trying to put the clock back) to remedying the *harm* which that breach has caused.

In certain cases compliance plus compensation would not be enough, and in these cases the breach would be irremediable. However, in the case before the court, any damage to the landlord by breach of the positive covenants was capable of being remedied by the late performance coupled if necessary with compensation. In *obiter dicta*, the court suggested that even negative covenants are very often capable of remedy by compliance, by ceasing to do the act complained of, so that if, for instance, a covenant has been broken by the erection of window-boxes, it may be remedied by removing the boxes and paying for the repair of any damage done.

Some 10 years later, this approach to the question of remediability was applied by the Court of Appeal to the once-and-for-all breach of negative covenants in *Savva v Hussein* (1997) 73 P&CR 150. Here the landlord had treated the breach of negative covenants (not to put up signs or alter the premises without the land-lord's consent) as being irremediable. The court referred with approval to the approach adopted in *Expert Clothing Service & Sales Ltd v Hillgate House Ltd*, stating that the question posed there in relation to positive covenants was equally rele-vant in considering negative covenants. There was nothing in the statute or in logic which required the courts to differentiate between these two forms of coven-ant. The court accepted that it was established law that breach of a covenant not to assign without the landlord's consent could not be remedied, but was of the opinion that failure to seek consent for other actions did not, by itself, make the breach irremediable. There was a remedy if the mischief caused by the breach could be removed. In the present case the breaches could have been remedied by removing the signs or restoring the property to its original condition, and the landlord's failure to require the tenant to remedy his breaches made the s. 146 notice invalid.

Following these two modern decisions of the Court of Appeal, it now appears that most breaches of covenant will be regarded as remediable. Nevertheless the possi-bility of irremediable breach remains in cases where the harm done to the landlord is held to be incapable of being remedied. There is also one particular breach (of a covenant against assigning, etc.), which the Court of Appeal holds itself bound by precedent to treat as irremediable.

(2) *Irremediable breach*

(a) *Irremediable harm to landlord*   A number of earlier decisions regarded the use of premises for immoral purposes (*Rugby School (Governors) v Tannahill* [1935] 1 KB 87) or for gambling (*Hoffmann v Fineberg* [1949] Ch 245) as irremediable breaches of covenant, because the improper use would cast a stigma on the premises, which could not be removed by merely ceasing the use. (Note, how-ever, that in *Glass v Kencakes Ltd* [1966] 1 QB 611 the tenant was held to have remedied his breach when he forfeited the sublease of his subtenant, who had used the premises for immoral purposes.) In more recent cases, breach has been held to be irremediable where the premises were used for the sale of porno-graphic material (*Dunraven Securities v Holloway* (1982) 264 EG 709), or for activ-ities in breach of the Official Secrets Act (*Van Haarlem v Kasner* (1992) 64 P&CR 214).

Although it is important to remember that changes in society's view of morality may make some activities less injurious to the property than they might have been formerly, it seems clear that breaches which in modern times would be seen as casting a stigma on the property would not satisfy the *Expert Clothing* test, and would therefore still be regarded as irremediable.

Other examples of irremediable harm to the landlord may be found in hypo-thetical cases of irremediable breach considered by the Court of Appeal in *Expert*

Clothing. They include: breach of covenant to insure against fire, which would be irremediable after the property had burned down; and failure to alter or repair property where there is insufficient time to complete the work required before the end of the lease.

(b) *Breach of covenant against assigning, etc.*   In *Scala House & District Property Co. Ltd* v *Forbes* [1974] QB 575, the Court of Appeal held that a breach of covenant against assigning, subletting or parting with possession without the landlord's consent could not be remedied. Such a breach has consequently been accepted by the Court of Appeal as irremediable in both *Expert Clothing Service and Sales* v *Hillgate House* (1986] 1 Ch 340 at p. 363, and *Savva* v *Hussein* (1997) 73 P&CR 150 at p. 154.

In conclusion we would emphasise that failure to include a request for remedy in a s. 146 notice will invalidate that notice if the court considers that the breach is remediable. If in doubt therefore it is wise to include a specific request for the breach to be remedied 'if it is capable of remedy'.

(3) *Giving tenant time to remedy breach*   Once a notice requiring remedy has been served, the landlord must thereafter give the tenant a reasonable time in which to remedy the breach (LPA 1925, s. 146(1)). Obviously some breaches may be swiftly remedied (e.g., removing a window-box) whilst others, such as the building works in *Expert Clothing*, may take some time. Once a reasonable time has elapsed without remedial action by the tenant the landlord may then proceed to forfeit the lease.

10.3.2.3 *Forfeiting the lease*

Traditionally there were two ways in which the landlord could end the lease and regain possession of the property—by self-help or by seeking a court order for possession—and both methods were available irrespective of the reason for forfeiture.

(1) *self-help*   It used to be open to the landlord simply to take possession of the premises, bringing the lease to an end by this physical re-entry. Today this right is considerably restricted. Under the Protection from Eviction Act, 1977, s. 2, it cannot be used at all where the premises, or any part of them, are used as a residence by any person (subject to certain exceptions in the case of those whose position is that of, or akin to, lodgers). In cases where self-help is available, such as in leases of commercial property, the landlord must ensure that any such entry is peaceable and without force (Criminal Law Act, 1977, s. 6, as amended by Criminal Justice and Public Order Act 1994, s. 72).

In *Billson* v *Residential Apartments Ltd* [1992] 1 AC 494 the House of Lords was critical of this self-help remedy, referring to the actions of the landlord as 'a dawn raid' (p. 540) and describing physical re-entry as a 'dubious and dangerous method of determining the lease' (p. 536), although it still accepted that it was open to the landlord to use this method. In addition, as we noted earlier (10.3.1), there are now concerns that this process may infringe rights under the Human Rights Act 1998. As long ago as 1985, the abolition of physical re-entry was recommended by the Law Commission, as part of an overall reform of the law relating to forfeiture. More recently, however, following consultation, this proposal has been amended to allow for the retention of physical re-entry subject to certain safeguards. (See further, 10.3.2.9.)

(2) *Seeking an order for possession*   The alternative and more acceptable method (and indeed the only method in respect of residential property today) is to obtain a court order for possession.

It is important to note that even where the landlord chooses to regain possession by court order, the lease is regarded as being forfeited at the outset, by the commencement of court proceedings. Although the former tenant may in fact remain on the land for some considerable time, pending the court action and enforcement of any resulting order, he is no longer a tenant and the landlord cannot enforce any of the obligations in the lease against him. A sum of money for use of the land during this period can be recovered, but technically this is not rent, but the 'mesne profits' payable by a trespasser on the land.

10.3.2.4 *Relief from forfeiture*

Even when the landlord has taken steps to forfeit the lease, the tenant may avoid forfeiture by seeking relief. In case of failure to pay rent, the tenant can generally obtain relief (i.e., be allowed to keep his lease) provided he pays the arrears of rent and any costs incurred by the landlord.

Relief is also available in the case of breach of covenants other than that to pay rent. It is governed by LPA 1925, s. 146(2), which allows the tenant to apply for relief at any time up until the landlord has actually re-entered. Relief may be granted because the tenant is at last willing, or able, to remedy the breach, but as we have already seen from the decision in *Scala House & District Property Co. Ltd* v *Forbes* [1974] QB 575 relief can also be available where the breach is technically irremediable. In such cases the court may need to weigh the harm caused to the landlord by the breach against the advantage which he will gain by recovering the property. Thus, in *Van Haarlam* v *Kasner* (1992) 64 P&CR 214 the court considered that the value to the landlord of forfeiting a lease with some 80 years left to run was out of all proportion to the damage caused by the tenant's irremediable breach, and indicated that it would have been willing to grant relief had the question arisen.

If relief is granted, the lease will continue as though proceedings had never been started, though it is open to the court to impose such terms as it thinks fit before granting relief (*Duke of Westminster* v *Swinton* [1948] 1 KB 524). Relief is not available in certain cases specified in LPA 1925, s. 149(8) and (9), nor in the case of a breach which denies the landlord's title (*Warner* v *Sampson* [1958] 1 QB 404, reversed on other grounds [1959] 1 QB 297), although *obiter dicta* in *British Telecommunications plc* v *Department of the Environment* [1996] NPC 148 suggest that even in such a case the court now might grant relief from forfeiture.

Although relief will not be available after a landlord has re-entered the property on a court order, it appears that it will be available if the landlord has effected a peaceable re-entry after service of a notice under s. 146 without obtaining and enforcing a judgment (*Billson* v *Residential Apartments Ltd* [1992] 1 AC 494). Accordingly, the safest course for the landlord appears to be to seek possession through the courts, although, if he does this, the tenant may of course seek relief in the course of the proceedings.

10.3.2.5 *Protection for subtenants when the head lease is forfeited*

A subtenant may be very badly affected if the head lease is forfeited for a breach of covenant by the tenant, for the destruction of the head lease also destroys the sublease which is derived from it. This can be unfair to an innocent subtenant who has paid his rent and complied with the covenants in his lease. Today this situation is governed by LPA 1925, s. 146(4), which applies wherever a landlord seeks to enforce a right of re-entry or forfeiture, even in those situations in which the tenant himself has no right to relief. Under this provision the subtenant may apply to the court for relief if the head lease from which he derives his title is forfeited. If relief is granted, the subtenant will become an immediate tenant of the head landlord, but for the period of the sublease, not for that of the head lease. The court may impose any conditions it sees fit upon the subtenant (e.g., compliance with covenants in the original head lease or payment of a higher rent).

A similar provision in the County Courts Act 1984 (s. 138(9A)) enables the subtenant to seek relief where the forfeiture is for non-payment of rent.

10.3.2.6 *Protection for mortgagees where the lease is forfeited*

Relief from forfeiture may also be sought under the provisions relating to subtenants by a mortgagee who has lent money to a tenant on the security of his lease. If the lease is forfeited by the landlord for breach of covenant, the mortgagee will lose his security and could suffer considerable financial loss. As we shall see in Chapter 21, a mortgage of leasehold property is made by giving the mortgagee a sublease of the property, or a charge over the property which gives him the same rights as if the mortgage had been made by sublease. Accordingly, the mortgagee may seek relief from forfeiture in the same way as any other subtenant, and, if successful, will hold a lease directly from the landlord which will continue to provide security for the loan. (Note however that although a mortgagee may seek relief from forfeiture in this way, it has been held by the Court of Appeal in *Smith* v *Spaul* [2003] QB 983 that he is not entitled to receive the s. 146 notice of breach of covenant, even though he may be in possession of the property.)

10.3.2.7 *Statutory restrictions on forfeiture*

Although the statutory protection of tenants is in general too detailed for this book (see 8.5.1), we must mention briefly that there are a number of provisions which regulate the operation of forfeiture procedures in relation to particular types of tenancies. A recent example, in respect of long leases of residential property, is to be found in ss. 168–9 of the Commonhold and Leasehold Reform Act 2002, which provides that a notice under s. 146 may not be served by the landlord, unless the tenant has admitted a breach of covenant or the fact that a breach has occurred has been determined by a leasehold valuation tribunal or in other court or arbitration proceedings. In addition, s. 168 of the Act prevents a landlord from forfeiting such a lease for failure to pay rent or other specified charges where the sum owed is less than a prescribed amount or has been due for less than a prescribed period.

10.3.2.8 *Application of the forfeiture and relief rules to tenancies at 7 Trant Way*

You will recall from 9.8.3 that the current situation with regard to 7 Trant Way is as follows:

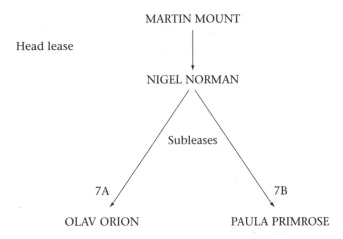

You will also recall that the head lease and both subleases contain covenants (a) against keeping animals on the property and (b) to keep the premises in good repair. Nigel Norman is also bound by a covenant to pay rent of £900 per month. For the last five months, Mr Norman has not paid his rent to Mr Mount, even though both the subtenants, Mr Orion and Miss Primrose, have been paying their rent regularly to Mr Norman. In addition, for the last three months Mr Orion has been stabling his daughter's pony in a shed at the back of the property. What can Mr Mount do to enforce the covenants which have been broken?

(1) *Enforcement of covenant against keeping animals* As we have seen already, there is no privity of contract or estate between a head landlord and a subtenant, and generally one cannot take action directly against the other. However, the covenant against keeping animals is a negative one, restricting the use of the property, and therefore Mr Mount could proceed directly against Mr Orion, seeking an injunction to restrain the breach, under the *Tulk* v *Moxhay* doctrine described in Chapter 23. Mr Mount could not rely on s. 3(5) of the Landlord and Tenant (Covenants) Act 1995 (9.8.1.1) because that Act, in general, applies only to leases granted on or after 1 January 1996, but this section could be used if a similar situation arose in respect of a lease which falls within the Act's provisions.

Alternatively, or additionally, Mr Mount may wish to take action against his tenant, Mr Norman. Provided the operation of LPA 1925, s. 79, was not expressly excluded in the lease, Mr Norman will have covenanted on behalf of 'persons deriving title under him', and so will be liable for the breach, even though it has been caused by his subtenant. Accordingly, Mr Mount should serve a s. 146 notice on Mr Norman. It is likely that this breach will be regarded as remediable (see *Savva* v *Hussein* (1997) 73 P&CR 150) and so the notice should ask that the situation be remedied. After service of the notice, Mr Mount must allow Mr Norman a reasonable period in which to remedy the breach. On receipt of the s. 146 notice Mr Norman would be advised to serve a similar notice on Mr Orion, who is himself in breach of a covenant in the sublease of 7A. The result will be, either that Mr Orion ceases to keep the pony on the premises, or that the sublease will be forfeited for the breach. Either result will have the effect of remedying the breach of the covenant in the head lease.

(2) *Forfeiture for non-payment of rent* The head lease contains the usual clause

which exempts the landlord from making a formal demand for the rent and also contains a clause allowing him to re-enter the premises if any covenant is broken. Accordingly, unless Mr Mount has in some manner waived the breach complained of, he may start proceedings against Mr Norman to forfeit the lease for the non-payment of the rent. At or before the hearing Mr Norman may ask for relief from forfeiture, and this will normally be granted as long as he pays the back rent and the costs of the action. In practice any offer of payment, as long as it is reasonable (e.g., by instalments over a prescribed period) will be accepted by the court. If, however, Mr Norman cannot make a reasonable offer, the lease will be forfeited for breach of the covenant to pay rent.

(3) *Relief of subtenant*   If, for any reason, the head lease is forfeited, Miss Primrose is placed in a difficult position. Although she has behaved perfectly properly, she is in danger of losing her own lease because it is dependent upon the head lease from which it is derived. Accordingly Miss Primrose should apply for relief under LPA 1925, s. 146(4). As she is wholly innocent, it is very likely that if the head lease is forfeited, Miss Primrose will be protected by the court. If this happens she will become a direct tenant of Mr Mount, for the period and upon the terms of her sublease but subject to any altered terms imposed by the court. If, however, Mr Norman manages to avoid the forfeiture of the head lease, Miss Primrose has nothing to fear. As long as the head lease is valid the sublease will be safe, provided, of course, that Miss Primrose continues to observe the covenants in her own sublease.

10.3.2.9 *Forfeiture: proposals for reform*

As we have already mentioned, the Law Commission proposed far-reaching changes in its *Report on Forfeiture of Tenancies,* 1985, Law Com No. 142. The report described many defects in the current law, which the Law Commission has characterised as complex and confused, and as giving rise to a number of un-certainties, anomalies and injustices (see the summary in Appendix C of the Law Commission's later report: *Landlord and Tenant Law: Termination of Tenancies Bill,* 1994, Law Com No. 221).

The problems identified with the present system include:

(a) the difficulties which arise from the termination of the lease by re-entry or the start of court proceedings, followed by a 'twilight' period during which the lease may be revived by the grant of relief;

(b) the unnecessary complication caused by having separate rules for the failure to pay rent and for breach of other covenants;

(c) the dangers of inadvertent waiver by the landlord; and

(d) the lack of adequate protection for those with derivative interests in the lease, such as subtenants and mortgagees.

The Law Commission proposed a complete overhaul of the system to address these and many other problems. Forfeiture by physical re-entry was regarded as particularly objectionable, and it was to be abolished and replaced by a scheme of Termination Orders, so that leases could be ended only through court proceedings.

Several consultation processes followed the publication of the draft Bill in 1994, and it became apparent that landlords were particularly unwilling to lose the right of physical re-entry, which, although recognised as a harsh remedy, was seen as both effective and justifiable in cases of persistent breach. As a result, the Law Commission issued a further consultation paper in January 2004: Termination of Tenancies for Tenant Default, 2004, Law Com No. 174. The results of this consultation are not yet known.

FURTHER READING

Distress

Walton, 'Landlord's Distress—Past Its Sell By Date?' [2000] 64 Conv 508.

Defects of current law of forfeiture

Landlord & Tenant Law: *Termination of Tenancies Bill*, 1994, Law Com No. 221—Appendix C.

Termination of Tenancies for Tenant Default: A Consultation Paper, 2004, Law Com Consultation Paper No. 174.

11

Commonhold

11.1 Introduction

11.1.1 The Grange, Trant Way

Richard and Helen are getting married in a few weeks time and are house-hunting in the Stilton area. They currently own a leasehold flat, which they bought together two years ago, but it is already too small for their needs, and they are looking for something larger. They saw a newspaper article the other day which said that a new form of land-holding, called commonhold, is just coming in and that this is supposed to be a better way of owning a flat than their current leasehold arrangement. An old country house called The Grange, which lies at the far end of Trant Way, is going to be developed and sold off in flats and Richard and Helen wondered whether this might be an opportunity to acquire a commonhold property. So they went to see the local agents who are dealing with the development of The Grange to find out if there were going to be any commonhold flats—and if so, what the advantages would be.

They found that the agents seemed to know very little about commonhold—which perhaps is not surprising, since it is being introduced by Part 1 of the Commonhold and Leasehold Reform Act 2002, most of which is not yet in force. As we shall see, the Act sets out the bare bones of the new system and leaves a great deal of detail to be filled in by regulations. The sections of the Act which provide for rule-making powers in relation to commonhold are already in force, and it is hoped that the rest of Part 1 and the regulations made under it will come into force before the end of 2004. This means not only that at this stage there are still a number of unanswered questions about what is involved, but also that it will be some time yet before the scheme is up and running, and even longer, one imagines, before the first commonhold properties come on the market. It is, therefore, unlikely that the developer of The Grange will be intending to use the new system for his property, although, as we shall see, it would be possible for the flats to be sold on long leases and later converted to commonhold.

11.1.2 Why do we need commonhold?

Commonhold is designed to meet the needs of flat owners and of those who own other types of property which are said to be 'interdependent', such as homes in a retirement village or units on an industrial estate or business park. Although these sound like very different types of property—some residential and some commercial—they have several similarities. For a start, there are likely to be 'common parts' in all these developments; that is, areas which do not belong to any individual unit but are used by all unit holders. In a block of urban flats, the common parts probably will consist of the entrance hall, stairs, passages, lifts, parking areas and perhaps a small communal garden, while in a country-house development (like The Grange) there may well be extensive grounds and perhaps even a swimming pool. Any scheme of development for property of this sort will need to provide for the ownership and upkeep of these common parts.

The other similarity between all these forms of property is that, in the interests of all the owners, there need to be regulations controlling the use of individual units, and requiring each to be kept in a proper state of repair. If a flat in a block is allowed to deteriorate it can have an adverse effect on those above and below it, and obviously excessive noise or other anti-social behaviour will be of immediate concern to the neighbours. What is needed is a web of mutually enforceable covenants under which each unit holder takes on certain duties with the understanding that he also has the right to enforce the same obligations against other owners in the development. This could easily be achieved at the outset by requiring each purchaser to enter into a mix of positive and negative covenants, the positive ones requiring him or her to keep the unit in repair and perhaps to contribute to the cost of maintaining the common parts, and the negative ones restraining certain activities, such as the keeping of pets. However, over the years the units are likely to change hands, and it is essential that the original covenants should run to bind and benefit the new owners. We have already seen that the burden of restrictive covenants made between freehold owners runs with the land (1.6.2.4 and 9.8.1.1; see further, Chapter 23); but unfortunately, the same is not true of positive covenants (23.4.2.2(1)), and as a result, there is no easy way to provide for the enforcement of positive obligations against successors of the original freehold owners.

This is a major difficulty associated with freehold ownership and so far it has not been overcome, despite repeated proposals for reform (see 23.8). By contrast, we have seen in Chapter 9 that when a leasehold estate is assigned, covenants in the lease will run to bind (and benefit) the new tenant, irrespective of whether they impose positive or negative obligations. For this reason, flats and other interdependent properties are almost invariably sold on long leases, and the owner of a unit does not acquire the fee simple estate in his property, however much he may have paid for it.

Using leases in this way overcomes the problems about ownership of the common parts and the imposition of positive obligations on successive owners, but at the same time it raises a number of other problems. Most important of all, perhaps, is the fact that the leasehold estate is essentially of limited duration and is, therefore, a 'wasting asset', which, unlike freehold property, becomes progressively less valuable as time goes by. In consequence banks and building societies these days are often unwilling to lend money on the security of leases with less than 60 years left to run, and as a result some leasehold properties become difficult to sell, because prospective buyers cannot arrange to finance their purchase. Leaseholders can also find that they have problems with their landlord, who may either fail to do repairs for which he is responsible or, where leaseholders are obliged to contribute to the cost of repairs, may insist on doing much more than they consider to be necessary. In addition, there is always the possibility that a relatively minor breach of covenant may lead to forfeiture of the lease, resulting in loss of home and capital investment for the leaseholder and in some cases considerable financial gain for the landlord (although on the possibility of the court granting relief in such circumstances, see *Van Haarlam* v *Kasner* (1992) 64 P&CR 214; and see also 10.3.2.7 for new statutory provisions designed to help those with long leases of residential property).

Over the years, a number of statutory reforms have improved the position of the long leaseholder of residential property, and we will return to these later (11.7.3). However, these improvements are seen by some as only 'tinkering' with the problem, and, since 1984, there have been proposals for a more thorough-going reform, which would allow freehold ownership of flats and other similar units. Now that there is statutory provision for commonhold schemes there is no need to consider the various proposals for reform in any detail. In outline, the idea was first mooted in the Law Commission Report, *Transfer of Land—The Law of Positive and Restrictive Covenants*, 1984, Law Com No. 127, and was developed by the Aldridge Working Group, which reported in 1987 (*Commonhold: Freehold Flats and Freehold Ownership of Other Interdependent Buildings* Cm 179—often referred to as 'the Aldridge Report'). A draft Bill was circulated in 1990 (*Commonhold—A Consultation Paper*, 1990, Cmnd 1345), and a second consultation process was launched in November 1998 (*Residential Leasehold Reform in England and Wales*), which eventually led to the introduction of the Commonhold and Leasehold Reform Bill in June 2001. The only reason for noting these various stages along the road to commonhold is to remind you that, over a period of nearly 20 years, proposals have necessarily developed and changed, so that any articles you find which comment on suggestions about commonhold may well relate to an earlier scheme which could differ quite significantly from that which is finally being introduced.

In the same way, it is important to realise that the exact details of the system are still being developed. The Lord Chancellor's Department (now the Department of Constitutional Affairs) issued a consultation paper on the draft regulations in October 2002, and has indicated that it may well make significant amendments in the light of comments received (see Commonhold A Response Paper CP (R) 11/02, August 2003, (referred to in the rest of this chapter as the 'DCA's Response Paper') available on **www.dca.gov.uk**). This means that certain defects identified in journal articles (for example, the length of leases to be permitted in residential commonhold—see 11.5.1.1) may well prove to have been cured when we see the final regulations.

11.2 The commonhold scheme

In this section, references to statutory provisions are to sections of the Commonhold and Leasehold Reform Act 2002 (CLRA 2002).

11.2.1 Outline

Where the new commonhold system is to be used, the property concerned (for example, a block of flats or a business park) will be registered at the Land Registry as 'commonhold land'. The owner of each individual unit (the 'unit holder') will be registered as its freehold owner, and will be a member of the 'commonhold association'. This association will be a company limited by guarantee, with membership limited to unit holders, and it will be registered as the freehold owner of the common parts. The rights and duties of all unit holders will be prescribed by the 'commonhold community statement', and the Act ensures that these rights and duties will benefit and bind successive owners of the unit.

A commonhold scheme thus overcomes the difficulties we noted in 11.1.2: it makes provision for the ownership and maintenance of the common parts; it allows each individual owner to own the freehold estate in his or her unit; and it enables positive and negative obligations to be enforced between unit holders.

We will now look at each element of the scheme in a little more detail.

11.2.2 **Commonhold land (ss. 1–4)**

The Act opens with a definition of commonhold land. Section 1 provides that land is commonhold land if three conditions are satisfied:

— the freehold estate must be registered as 'a freehold estate in commonhold land';
— the land must be specified in the memorandum of a commonhold association as land in relation to which the association is to exercise functions; and
— there must be a commonhold community statement which makes provisions for the rights and duties of the association and of the unit holders.

Under s. 2 the application for registration as commonhold land is to be made by the registered proprietor of the freehold estate with absolute title or a person who has applied for such registration (i.e., someone who holds the fee simple in unregistered land and is now either compulsorily or voluntarily seeking first registration).

Section 3 provides that an application for registration as commonhold land cannot be made without the consent of certain people who may have interests in the land. They include: the registered proprietor of a leasehold estate granted for more than 21 years; the registered proprietor of a charge over the land; and 'any other class of person which may be prescribed' (by regulations made under the Act). The DCA's Response Paper (see 11.1.2) indicates that the requirement for consent may be extended to include *unregistered* proprietors of charges and of leases for more than 21 years, and persons with interests protected by entries on the register of title or under LCA 1972. The details of the provisions relating to consent are to be filled in by regulations, and in particular provision may be made for deeming consent to have been given and for dispensing with the need for consent on a court order.

Section 4 and Sch. 2 provide that an application to register land as commonhold may not be made in respect of certain types of land. The only exclusion we need to note here is that contained in Sch. 2, para. 1: land above ground level cannot be registered as commonhold unless the property below it is part of the same scheme. In other words, it will not be possible to register the top floors of a block of flats unless the intervening floors down to ground level are similarly registered. There can be no 'flying freeholds' (see rubric to Sch. 2, para. 1).

11.2.3 **Unit holders (s. 12)**

A unit holder is the person who is registered, or entitled to be registered, as the proprietor of the freehold estate in a unit (s. 12). The estate may, of course, be vested in more than one person (for a general account of co-ownership, see Chapter 16), and the Act contains elaborate provisions for its application in cases of co-ownership.

Each unit holder is entitled, and indeed required, to be a member of the commonhold association (see below). The Explanatory Notes which accompanied the Act on its passage through Parliament comment that:

> this means that all unit-holders will have two interests in the property of the commonhold: a direct interest in the unit they own and membership of the commonhold association which owns the common parts (Exp. Notes, para 8).

11.2.4 **Commonhold association (ss. 33–5)**

Section 34 provides that the commonhold association will be incorporated as a private company limited by guarantee (see Companies Act 1985, s. 1(2)(b)). Documents known as the memorandum and articles of association are required for the incorporation of companies registered under the Companies Act 1985, s. 1, and special forms of these documents for use in incorporating a commonhold association will be prescribed by regulation (s. 33 and Sch. 3). As we shall see, using the device of a registered company in this way will enable unit holders to control the operation of the commonhold scheme through established procedures, while at the same time it provides a separate legal entity, distinct from its members, which can be registered as owner of the common parts.

Membership of the association will be limited to the holders of commonhold units within the scheme (s. 34(2) and Sch. 3, paras. 7, 10 and 12). In the case of any company limited by guarantee, the liability of the members for the debts of the company is limited to the amount they are said to guarantee, and s. 34(1) provides that the memorandum of association for commonhold associations will specify £1 as the amount to be guaranteed by each unit holder.

The commonhold association will be registered as owner of the common parts of the property (defined in s. 25(1)), and will be responsible for all aspects of managing the property. In practice, the work of management will be carried on by the directors of the association, and funding for all necessary activities will be obtained from the unit holders, under arrangements to be specified in the commonhold community statement (see below).

11.2.5 **Commonhold community statement (ss. 31–3)**

The commonhold community statement ('CCS') will combine the functions of describing the physical attributes of the development and containing the rules and regulations by which a specific commonhold system will be conducted (Exp. Notes, para. 79). The form and content of the statement must be as prescribed by the Act and by regulations made under it (s. 32). It will include a plan of the property, showing the individual units. It must make provision regulating the use of commonhold units and must impose duties in respect of insurance, repair and maintenance of each unit; such duties may be imposed on either the commonhold association or the unit holder (s. 14). Subject to the provisions of the Act and the terms of the memorandum and articles, the statement will make provision for the rights and duties of both the commonhold association and the unit holders, and may also regulate the way in which decisions about any matter concerning the commonhold are taken (s. 31(3) and (4)).

Thus, it is the CCS which will regulate the behaviour of the unit holders, imposing on them the sort of obligations—both positive and negative—which we have already noted as being necessary for communal living. The Act provides that the statement may include restrictions on the use of units, and may require owners to refrain from causing nuisance and annoyance and from other types of behaviour which may be specified (s. 31(5)). The statement may also impose a duty to pay money (s. 31(5)(a)), and it is by this means that the commonhold association will raise money both to provide a reserve fund (s. 39), and to meet the expenses of running the property as a whole. This would include all those matters which, in leasehold properties, are covered by service charges: repairs and maintenance; the provision of central services (such as heating, if this is centrally provided); and the employment of staff, like cleaners, security men, and gardeners. Under s. 38 the CCS must require the directors to make an annual estimate of the income needed to meet all expenses. It must also specify the percentage of the assessment to be attributed to each unit, and impose on each unit the obligation to pay that amount. In addition the statement may authorise the directors to raise money in addition to the annual assessment, if this proves necessary (s. 38(1)(b)).

From a land law point of view, a particularly interesting provision relating to the CCS is to be found in s. 31(7):

A duty conferred by a commonhold community statement on a commonhold association or a unit holder shall not require any other formality.

Thus, there will be no need for the purchasers of units to enter into covenants in the deed of transfer, and it appears from the Explanatory Notes (para. 80) that inclusion in the statement will also be sufficient to create easements over both individual units and the common parts, which again, save for the commonhold scheme, would normally require formal grant or reservation by deed. We do not know yet what formalities will be required for the creation of the CCS, but there is no indication yet of any intention that it should be made by deed, and it appears at the moment that writing will suffice. If that is correct, then it seems that s. 31(7) will create an exception to the general rule that the grant of a legal interest must be made by deed (LPA 1925, s. 52(1)). There is no reference in CLRA 2002 to amending this provision of the 1925 Act, so it remains to be seen whether s. 31(7) will have the effect of creating legal easements without a deed, and exactly how this will operate.

We have now described the various elements in a commonhold scheme, and noted several statutory definitions. You may have noticed, however, that we have not attempted to define 'commonhold' itself, and that is because there is no definition to be found in the Act. Section 1(2) explains that:

a reference to a commonhold is a reference to land in relation to which a commonhold association exercises functions

but this merely takes us back to commonhold land, and does not help to define the concept of 'commonhold'. We make this point because, as we noted in Chapter 1, some writers speak of commonhold as a new form of tenure, but this is not a notion which one finds in the Act itself, which bases the structure of commonhold schemes on the existing system of freehold tenure. Thus each unit holder will own the fee simple estate in his unit, while the commonhold association will hold a similar estate in the common parts. The rights and duties of the various parties will be regulated by terms imposed by the CCS and by the relevant provisions of company law, but the land itself, although registered as 'commonhold land', will still be held on socage tenure from the Crown and it does not appear that any other tenurial relationship will be created. On this point, you may like to see a note by Riddall ([2003] 67 Conv 358), in which he records a message from the Lord Chancellor's Department:

Commonhold is a new way of holding freehold land, not a new form of tenure.

11.3 Creating commonhold

A commonhold scheme may be created at the time of a new development, when for example a block of flats is being built or, as in the case of The Grange, an existing building is being remodelled and converted to a new use. However, commonhold can also be introduced in respect of an existing block of flats (or any other property with interdependent units), which is currently operated on a leasehold basis but in which everyone concerned agrees to convert to commonhold.

11.3.1 New development with no existing unit holders (ss. 7 and 8)

A developer will presumably decide at an early stage that he intends to market the property as commonhold and will set up the scheme before selling off any of the units. To do this he will need to incorporate the commonhold association and prepare the commonhold community statement. He will then apply for registration of the land as commonhold, supporting his application with the documents needed for incorporation (i.e., memorandum and articles of association), and the CCS. As we have seen, such an application can be made only by the registered proprietor of the freehold estate or the person entitled to be registered, but we assume that the developer will fall into one or other of these categories. If he does not, the application will, of course, have to be made by whoever is entitled to the freehold estate. The application must also be accompanied by any necessary consents (s. 3).

Following registration of the development site as commonhold land, there will be a transitional period, during which the development is carried out. At this stage, the commonhold scheme is not yet functioning, and it is still possible for the developer to change his mind and seek cancellation of the registration (s. 8).

The scheme becomes operative with the sale of the first unit. The purchaser is entitled to be registered as proprietor of the freehold estate in the unit he has bought and automatically becomes a member of the commonhold association; the commonhold association will be registered as proprietor of the freehold estate in the common parts (this will be done by the registrar automatically without the need for any application by the association); and the rights and duties created by the CCS come into operation (s. 7(3)). The developer continues as registered proprietor of the freehold estate in the remaining units until each is sold.

11.3.2 **Conversion of property with existing unit holders (s. 9)**

Section 9 of the Act applies the registration procedure already described to property in which there are already existing unit holders, thus enabling property in which the units are already owned by long leaseholders to be converted to commonhold.

The application for registration will be made by the freeholder in accordance with the procedure we have outlined above, but in this case must be accompanied by a list of the commonhold units and the proposed initial unit holders. Where the property is already fully occupied, as for example where an established block of leasehold flats is being converted to commonhold, the 'proposed initial unit holders' will be the current long leaseholders. However, in the case of a new development in which some units have been sold but others remain unsold, the developer, or his nominees, would be named as the initial unit holder of any unsold units. (It seems unlikely that this situation will arise often in practice since developers wishing to create a commonhold scheme will presumably do so at the outset under the provisions we outlined above.)

Where property with existing unit holders is registered as commonhold land, the scheme will come into operation immediately (without the transitional period which applies under s. 8). The registrar will, without requiring separate applications, register the various unit holders as proprietors of the freehold estates in their respective units and the commonhold association as freehold owner of the common parts.

Although the desirability of converting properties with long leasehold units into commonhold was a driving force behind the introduction of the new system, it appears unlikely that such conversions will be straightforward or even frequent occurrences. The difficulty arises from the requirement for consents set out in s. 3 of the Act. We have already mentioned this briefly, but need to emphasise its importance here. Under that section, an application for registration as commonhold land can be made only with the consent of a number of people who may have interests in the property. These include the registered proprietor of the freehold estate (who as we have seen has to make the application), and all registered owners of leases granted for more than 21 years. This means that a block of flats cannot convert to commonhold without the agreement of the freeholder and of registered leaseholders. In the course of the Bill's passage through Parliament repeated efforts were made to amend this provision, so as to enable conversions to be made with the consent of a smaller proportion of leaseholders (80 per cent being suggested as a suitable figure). In the view of the Government, however, this would lead to an undesirable mix of commonhold and leasehold units in the same property (because the unwilling leaseholders could not be compelled to convert their interests into commonhold and so would continue as leaseholders, with the commonhold association as their landlord), and it was therefore essential to insist on the requirement that all should consent. Opponents of this requirement consider that it rules out all possibility of conversion of existing properties, and that commonhold will be used only for new developments. Only time will tell whether they are right about this, and meanwhile there remains the theoretical possibility for Helen and Richard that, if they buy a leasehold flat in The Grange, the property could convert to commonhold at some future date.

11.3.3 Extinction of existing leases

One final point which we must note is that the Act provides that when a commonhold scheme comes into operation:

any lease of the whole or part of the commonhold land shall be extinguished by virtue of this section (ss. 7(3)(d) and 9(3)(f)).

As we noted briefly in Chapter 8, the Act thus creates a new way in which leases may come to an end: extinction on conversion to commonhold. This should cause no difficulty where the lease is for more than 21 years, since the consent of the leaseholder will have been required under s. 3 (or by regulations made under that section), and in the case of new developments the developer presumably will have bought out any tenants holding under shorter leases. The real effect of the provision, therefore, is likely to be felt only by tenants holding on short subleases from long leaseholders in an existing block. The implications for any such sub-tenants whose rights may be protected under a statutory code (most notably the Rent Acts, but also, in respect of business premises, the Landlord and Tenant Act 1954, Pt II) is not addressed in the Act nor in the Explanatory Notes which accompanied the Bill. Given that conversion to commonhold now appears relatively unlikely, the problem may be more apparent than real, but the provisions still raise interesting questions about the interaction between the new system and the statutory protection of certain tenants. For more detail on this point, see Clarke [2002] 66 Conv 349 at 354–8; but note that some of the concerns identified in this article may be addressed in the final version of the regulations (see 11.1.2).

If any tenants do lose their leases in this way, s. 10 provides that they are entitled to compensation, which in general will be payable by their immediate landlord, that is, the long leaseholder who consents to the conversion to commonhold. This may, of course, be a further reason why some leaseholders will refuse consent to conversion, thus in effect preventing it from taking place.

11.4 Managing a commonhold property

The commonhold association is the registered proprietor of the common parts of the property, and has overall responsibility for all aspects of managing the development, including an ability to bring the whole scheme to an end through the process of voluntary winding-up (see 11.6.1). Since only unit holders are permitted to be members of the association this means that they are in effect solely responsible for the conduct of commonhold affairs, and through their votes can control the operation of the scheme.

For practical reasons, however, it is necessary for day-to-day management to be carried on by a few individuals, and the Act gives responsibility for this to the directors of the association. In addition to the general duties to which they are subject as directors of a company limited by guarantee, the directors of a commonhold association will have specific duties imposed on them under the Act. We have already seen that it is their duty to take the necessary financial decisions (11.2.5) and under s. 35(1), they are charged with the general duty of using their powers to facilitate the unit holders' enjoyment of their rights and property. Conversely, the directors are also responsible for ensuring that individual unit holders act in compliance with commonhold rules. General regulations, to be made under s. 37, will provide for the enforcement of rights and duties under commonhold schemes, and s. 35(2) requires the directors to use all available means to secure compliance by unit holders. In doing so, however, they are to be mindful of the desirability of using alternative dispute resolution methods wherever possible, and interestingly the Act provides (s. 35(3)(a)) that the directors:

need not take action if they reasonably think that inaction is in the best interests of establishing or maintaining harmonious relationships between all the unit-holders, and that it will not cause any unit-holder (other than the defaulter) significant loss or . . . disadvantage.

When considering the enforcement of unit holders' duties, you should note that one sanction for breach which is available to landlords of leasehold properties is specifically excluded from commonhold schemes. Section 31(8) provides that:

a commonhold community statement may not provide for the transfer or loss of an interest in land on the occurrence or non-occurrence of a specified event.

In other words, there can be no provision for a unit holder to forfeit his estate, however serious or repeated his breaches of duty may be.

11.5 Nature of a unit holder's interest

We have already noted that unit holders will be registered as the freehold owners of their units, and this is, of course, the principal advantage of a commonhold scheme. In addition, unit holders have the right to use the common parts of the development, although under s. 25(2) a CCS may provide that certain common parts may be reserved for the use of specified unit holders (as for example if separate parking areas are designated for use by particular units).

Unit holders also have the benefit and burden of the various obligations imposed by the CCS: they will have to contribute their prescribed share to the annual budget and meet any additional financial demands; they will almost certainly have some obligations about the repair and maintenance of their individual properties; and they will be subject to restrictions on the use of their units and their behaviour in them. But all their neighbours will be subject to similar obligations, and unit holders who are affected by breaches of duty, whether by another unit holder or by the commonhold association, should be able to take appropriate action (under regulations to be made under s. 37(2)).

When a unit is transferred to another holder (as for example when a current owner sells his flat), s. 16 provides that the new owner takes subject to all existing rights and duties, and that the previous owner shall not incur any liabilities or acquire any rights in respect of the property after the transfer. This latter provision cannot be disapplied or varied by agreement, so there should be no way of providing for any continuing liability on the part of the out-going owner—nor indeed any way in which he could stipulate for some continuing right under the scheme.

11.5.1 Restrictions on dealing with the freehold estate

While in general the unit holder has the usual powers of a freehold owner, it is important to note that there are some unusual restrictions on what he may do with his property. We noted in Chapter 7 the general principle that an estate owner should have a free and unfettered power to alienate his property (7.5), and we have seen that tenants of leasehold property can assign or sublet the property with legal effect even though in breach of covenant (9.2.2.2(5)). Section 15(2) maintains this principle in so far as a complete transfer of the property is concerned:

a commonhold community statement may not prevent or restrict the transfer of a commonhold unit

but ss. 17–20 impose considerable restrictions on other dealings with the freehold estate.

11.5.1.1 *Restrictions on leasing*

A major restriction relating to *residential* commonhold is to be found in s. 17, which provides:

(1) It shall not be possible to create a term of years absolute in a residential commonhold unit unless the term satisfies certain prescribed conditions.

(2) The conditions may relate to—

(a) length;

(b) the circumstances in which the term is granted;

(c) any other matter.

The notes accompanying the Bill explained that:

It is Government policy that residential commonhold units should not be let for long unbroken periods ... to avoid the possibility of repeating the difficulties which exist in leasehold blocks now. (Exp. Notes, para. 65).

Thus, the provision is designed to guard against the situation in which flats are held by non-resident owners who regard the property as an investment but have no direct personal interest in it, while the actual occupiers, who are immediately affected by the condition of the development, have no say in its management.

In support of this policy, s. 17(3) provides that an attempt to create a term which contravenes the prescribed conditions will be 'of no effect'. Under s. 17(4) a party to such a void transaction may seek appropriate relief from the court, which may include an order that the transaction shall take effect as if 'it provided for the creation of a term of years of a specified length' (presumably a term complying with the required conditions).

The conditions required for such a lease are to be prescribed by regulations made under the Act, and it was originally intended to limit the length of the lease to a maximum period of seven years, and to provide that no premium should be payable. However, many commentators have suggested that such restrictions might make the commonhold system less attractive to purchasers and detract significantly from the benefits of freehold ownership of the unit. Following the consultation process on the draft regulations, the DCA has said that it is considering increasing the prescribed maximum length to 21 years and is reviewing the proposal that no premium should be charged, although it is unlikely that such leases will be permitted to contain options for renewal (DCA's Response Paper, p. 95).

Leases of units in a *non-residential* commonhold scheme, are to take effect subject to any provisions of the CCS (s. 18), and it remains to be seen whether the prescribed form for these statements will include any significant restrictions on leasing, or whether the matter will be left to be regulated by the needs of individual schemes.

11.5.1.2 *Restrictions on other transactions*

Section 20 regulates the creation of other interests by the freehold owner. The section opens with the very general provision that:

A commonhold community statement may not prevent or restrict the creation, grant or transfer by a unit-holder of—

(a) an interest in the whole or part of his unit

(b) a charge over his unit.

However, s. 20(3) then cuts this freedom down by providing that:

It shall not be possible to create an interest of a prescribed kind in a commonhold unit unless the commonhold association—

(a) is a party to the creation of the interest, or

(b) consents in writing to the creation of the interest.

Any attempt to create an interest in contravention of this requirement shall be 'of no effect'. At first glance, you might think, therefore, that a unit holder cannot even mortgage his property without securing a resolution of the commonhold association, but at the very end of the section (s. 20(6)), we are told that the 'interest' referred to throughout does not include a charge—so at the end of the day, it appears that the unit holder may mortgage his estate without in effect having to ask for his neighbours' permission.

We shall have to wait for the regulations to discover which interests will be 'prescribed', and therefore capable of being created only with the participation or consent of the commonhold association, but it is thought that they may very well include easements, profits and rentcharges (see Clarke [2002] 66 Conv 349 at 375–6).

11.6 Ending commonhold

The Act provides for the commonhold scheme to be brought to an end either voluntarily, with the consent of the unit holders, or compulsorily in the event of the association's being unable to meet its debts.

11.6.1 Termination by voluntary winding-up (ss. 43–9)

In certain circumstances, the unit holders may agree that it is desirable to bring the commonhold to an end. It could be, for example, that the building is old and nearing the end of its useful life, and that the members wish to sell out to a developer and divide the proceeds between themselves.

In order to do this, the consent of at least 80 per cent of the members of the association is required (s. 43(1)(c)), voting in favour of resolutions to wind-up the association and appoint a liquidator. They must also agree the terms of a statement (the 'termination statement'), which sets out the association's proposals for dealing with the land and for distributing the association's assets (which, of course, would include the purchase money to be obtained on the sale of the property).

Section 44 provides that where 100 per cent of the members vote in favour, the liquidator may make an application for the land to cease to be commonhold land (a 'termination application') directly to the registrar. If the vote is not unanimous but does satisfy the minimum requirement of 80 per cent, s. 45 requires that the liquidator must apply to the court to determine the terms on which a termination application may be made and the content of the termination statement. This process is, of course, designed to protect the interests of the dissenting minority.

Once the necessary procedures have been followed, the association is entitled to be registered as the proprietor of the freehold estate in each commonhold unit (i.e., the individual unit holders are divested of their titles), and the property can then be dealt with as proposed in the termination statement.

11.6.2 Termination by winding-up by the court (ss. 50–4)

This method is used where the association is unable to meet its debts and a creditor presents a petition for winding-up under the Insolvency Act 1986, s. 124. This is obviously a very serious matter for the unit holders, since the role of the commonhold association in owning the common parts and managing the whole property is crucial to the operation of any commonhold scheme.

Accordingly, where the court makes a winding-up order, s. 51 empowers it to make a further order as well, a 'succession order', which gives recognition to a new association ('the successor commonhold association') which will take over responsibility for running the commonhold and will be registered as proprietor of the common parts. The circumstances in which this will be done are not specified, the Act merely providing in s. 51(4) that:

The court shall grant an application [for a succession order] unless it thinks that the circumstances of the insolvent commonhold association make a succession order inappropriate.

It seems likely that such an order would be granted in circumstances in which the debts of the association can be met, presumably from the reserve fund (see s. 39) with, if necessary, additional funds raised by the members. The Explanatory Notes describe the arrangements for a succcessor commonhold association as being designed to ensure that:

those members of the association who have paid all their liabilities to the creditors of the insolvent association may continue to live in a stable commonhold development (para. 102).

If a succession order is not made, the winding-up goes ahead and s. 54(4) provides that once it is completed the registrar is required to take such action as will result in the land no longer being registered as commonhold land and to give effect to the liquidator's determination.

11.7 Evaluation

It may seem a little premature to try to evaluate a scheme which is not yet in operation, but in fact it is already possible to identify some advantages and disadvantages of the new system, and these may be of interest to Helen and Richard who, as you may remember from the start of this chapter, are wondering about the possibility of buying a commonhold flat. It is also tempting to speculate whether commonhold, which has been awaited for so long, will at last prove to be an acceptable alternative to long leaseholds.

11.7.1 Advantages of commonhold

We have already noted the principal advantages of the new system. The unit holder is enabled to hold the freehold title to his property and can benefit from the positive and negative obligations which bind his neighbours. The problem of ownership of the common parts is solved by vesting it in the commonhold association, and management of the property and enforcement of obligations can be undertaken by the association on behalf of its members instead of by a landlord acting in his own interests.

Another advantage which we have not mentioned yet, is that the form and content of commonhold community statements are required to follow a standard pattern (to be prescribed by regulations—ss. 31(2) and 32(1)), and it is thought that this will simplify the process of dealing with individual units, both on their original purchase and on subsequent sale. By contrast, there is no common form for the grant of a lease, and a good deal of time can be spent on negotiating terms at the outset and then scrutinising them when the property comes to be sold.

11.7.2 Disadvantages of commonhold

There are several aspects of the new scheme which may prove unattractive to purchasers, although some of them may appear less worrying when the regulations to be made under the Act are published, and it is possible to see more clearly how commonhold will work.

11.7.2.1 Restrictions on the power of the unit holder to deal with his freehold estate

We have already noted these restrictions (11.5.1). The most serious one appears to be the limitation on the length of leases which may be created in respect of a residential commonhold unit. It remains to be seen whether the maximum permitted term will be extended from seven years to 21 years (see 11.5.1.1) and, if this is done, whether such a change will be sufficient to remove any possible disincentive to prospective purchasers.

11.7.2.2 No provisions for forfeiture for breach of obligations

One would not expect there to be provisions for forfeiture of a freehold estate, and indeed many will see the absence of forfeiture as giving commonhold a positive advantage over long leaseholds. Nevertheless, it does mean that there is no ultimate sanction for persistent breach of obligation, and no way in which unit holders of the association can rid themselves of 'nuisance' neighbours. From this standpoint, it may be that leasehold property will come to be seen as having some advantages in comparison with commonhold.

11.7.2.3 Problem of insolvency

It is difficult to assess the effect of the Act's provisions on winding-up until we see the circumstances in which the court will recognise a successor association, but obviously there would major difficulties for unit holders if the original association were to be wound-up without a replacement.

Earlier proposals for the introduction of commonhold contained very detailed provisions about what would happen in cases of insolvency. By contrast, the Act goes to the opposite extreme and really tells us very little about what will happen if the association cannot meet its debts. The possibility of insolvency is of concern not only to prospective purchasers but also to their lenders, and it must be remembered that if commonhold is to succeed it has to be attractive to the lending institutions. In the last resort the whole property, units and common parts, could be sold to meet the association's debts. By contrast, in the case of long leases, the leaseholders (and their mortgagees) would not be directly affected by the insolvency of their landlord; the freehold might be sold and a new landlord take over, but this would not affect the continuing existence of the leasehold interests in the property. The possible danger to commonhold owners may, however, be more apparent than real, since it seems that 'experience in other countries, including the United States, suggests that it is very rare for a commonhold association to be wound up on the grounds of insolvency' (Driscoll [2000] *Solicitor's Journal* 849 at p. 852).

11.7.2.4 Lack of any regulatory body or specialist tribunal

The process of setting up a commonhold scheme depends solely on producing the right documents to the Land Registry and securing registration of the property as commonhold land. It does not appear that there will be any process for scrutinising the original proposals nor for monitoring the management process when the scheme is in operation. Further, it appears that disputes between unit holders or with the association will be dealt with through the existing court system, although experience in other jurisdictions with similar schemes suggests that it would be better for such matters to come before a separate body or tribunal which could build up specialist expertise (see Charlesbois [1997] 61 Conv 169, and Kenny [2001] 65 Conv 1).

One of the draft regulations (made under s. 41 of CLRA 2002) provides that a commonhold association must be a member of an approved ombudsman scheme. It appears from comments on this proposal that the ombudsman would deal with disputes between unit holders and the commonhold association, but not with disputes between individual unit holders, but as yet there are no further details of how the scheme would work (DCA's Response Paper, pp. 135–6).

11.7.3 How will commonhold compare with long leaseholds?

In assessing the likely response to the introduction of commonhold, it is necessary to bear in mind that the position of long leaseholders of residential property has been very considerably improved in recent years. Early in this chapter, we outlined the disadvantages of leasehold ownership, drawing your attention to the nature of the lease as a 'wasting asset' and the fact that landlords, naturally enough, tend to manage property in their own interests, rather than in those of their tenants. The details of the statutory protection of long leaseholders is outside the scope of this book, but you should be aware in general terms that their position has been significantly improved by a series of reforms which began in 1967 with the Leasehold Reform Act. Thus individual leaseholders now have the right to require the grant of new leases when their old ones expires and, through a process known as 'leasehold enfranchisement', also have the right to buy out their landlord, thus acquiring the freehold estate in the property. In the case of flats, the difficulties we have already noted about the running of covenants and the ownership of the common parts prevent owners acquiring the freehold of individual flats, but the leaseholders as a group may buy the freehold of the whole property, vesting it in a company formed for the purpose.

Part 2 of the CLRA 2002 makes further improvements to the position of long leaseholders of residential property. We have already noted the restrictions it imposes on the use of forfeiture (10.3.2.7). More generally, the Act facilitates both the acquisition of a new lease and the purchase of the reversion, and also gives leaseholders a new right to take over the management of the property without having to show fault on the part of the landlord.

These statutory reforms go a long way towards making leasehold property a more attractive option than it was in the past, and it may well be that, for a time at least, purchasers and lenders will consider that leasehold property offers more security than is to be found in the untried system of commonhold.

11.8 Updating this chapter

Throughout this chapter we have referred to various matters which are to be clarified by regulations made under Part 1 of the CLRA 2002. It seems likely that these regulations will take effect during the lifetime of this edition of the book. If this is the case, we will outline the relevant provisions on the companion web site at **www.oup.com/uk/booksites/law/land**.

FURTHER READING

Aldridge Report—'*Commonhold: Freehold Flats and Freehold Ownership of Other Interdependent Buildings*', 1987 Cm 179 Part 1—Introduction.

Charlesbois, 'Commonhold: Lest We Forget' [1997] 61 Conv 169 (includes some account of similar systems in other jurisdictions).

Clarke, 'The Enactment of Commonhold—Problems, Principles and Perspectives' [2002] 66 Conv 349.

Crabb, 'The Commonhold Association—As You Like It?' [1998] 62 Conv 285 (considers earlier proposals—but still of interest).

Jones, 'All Very Well In Theory', *Estates Gazette*, 7th April 2001 (Issue 14), p. 144.

Kenny, 'Commonhold—At Last?' [2001] 65 Conv 1.

PART IV

···

Trusts and proprietary estoppel

Introduction

In this part of the book we move on to consider more complex forms of ownership, in which ownership at law and ownership in equity are separated. This is the area of trusts, with which you may have some general familiarity from your other reading. If, however, you have never previously had occasion to consider the law of trusts, you may find it helpful to read an introductory book on trusts and equity before going on to consider the special rules relating to trusts which have an estate or interest in land as the trust property.

We start in Chapter 12 with a brief outline of certain matters relating to trusts, and an explanation of the two forms of settlement which existed before the Trusts of Land and Appointment of Trustees Act 1996 introduced the new trust of land in 1997. We then deal with the new trust in Chapter 13, and in Chapter 14 go on to consider the other form of trust that still exists in relation to land: the SLA settlement.

In Chapter 15, we look at the 'perpetuities and accumulations' rules. These are rules which can govern the validity of a trust but which, as you will see, in modern law often only have effect in practice to regulate the period for which a trust can continue. Having considered the basic trusts rules, we go on in Chapter 16 to consider in detail the rules relating to co-ownership of land. As you will see, these are included in this Part because all co-owned estates become subject to the statutory imposition of a trust, really in order to make it easier to deal with the land while protecting properly the rights of all the co-owners. (Note also that we look further at family property in Chapter 24.)

Finally, we look in some detail at resulting and constructive trusts in Chapter 17 and in Chapter 18 consider the doctrine of proprietary estoppel.

12

Trusts: an introduction

12.1 Nature and creation of trusts

In this introductory chapter we try to provide a brief outline of certain matters relating to trusts, but we would emphasise that what follows is a highly selective account, aimed simply at giving you the information we think you need for land law purposes.

12.1.1 Separation of title and enjoyment

We explained briefly in Chapter 1 (1.6.2.1) that the essential characteristic of the trust is the separation of title to property from the right to use and enjoy it. The trustee is the owner of the property, but he holds it not for himself but for the beneficiary, who is protected by equity and accordingly has an equitable interest in that property. In general, the trustee will have the *legal* title (in a trust of land, he will usually hold the legal estate). However, it must be realised that it is also possible to create a trust of an equitable interest; for example, a beneficiary under a trust may transfer his equitable interest to some other person and direct him to hold it on trust for some third party. Thus, the interest of the beneficiary under a trust is always equitable, but that of the trustee may be legal or equitable, according to the nature of the property which is subject to the trust.

12.1.2 Express and implied trusts

In Chapter 1 we also noted that trusts may be created expressly or may arise without express creation through recognition by the courts. It is convenient to describe this second category of trusts, those which are not expressly created, as 'implied trusts'; this terminology was adopted by the court in *Cowcher* v *Cowcher* [1972] 1 WLR 425 at p. 430, and is used by Gray and Gray as a main sub-division of private trusts (see Gray and Gray at p. 635).

12.1.3 Creation of trusts

Express trusts

While a trust may be created simply by the settlor manifesting an intention to do so, a trust of land will not be *enforceable* unless there is some written evidence of that intention. LPA 1925, s. 53(1)(b) provides:

a declaration of trust respecting any land or any interest therein must be manifested and proved by some writing signed by some person who is able to declare such a trust or by his will.

Thus, while a trust of land may be created orally, a beneficiary will not be able to enforce his interest under it unless the trust is evidenced in writing. The trust will be valid, but unenforceable.

Implied (non-express) trusts

By contrast, writing is not required for the creation or enforcement of non-express trusts. LPA 1925, s. 53(2) provides that the earlier part of the section (which imposes the requirement for evidence in writing which we have noted above):

does not affect the creation or operation of resulting, implied or constructive trusts.

We deal with these trusts in more detail in Chapter 17 but all you need to note at this stage is that these types of trust are enforceable without any written evidence.

Statutory trusts

In certain circumstances statutes provide that property is to be held on trust. Thus, for example, statutory trusts operate in all cases of co-ownership of land (see further, Chapter 16), and similar trusts are applied to property where the owner has died without making a will (Administration of Estates Act 1925, s. 33(1)).

12.1.4 Circumstances in which a trust may be created

It is always possible to have property held by trustees on trust for one adult beneficiary who is solely entitled to it (a 'bare' trust), but more usually a trust is created because the beneficiary is still a minor or because the property is to be enjoyed by several people in succession.

Where successive interests are created by a disposition the traditional name for the arrangement was a '*settlement*'. To give an example of such an arrangement involving successive interests, a settlement would exist if land were given 'to A for life and then to B'. As we have already mentioned, trusts are also imposed by statute in all cases of co-ownership i.e., where two or more people are entitled to enjoy the property at the same time.

12.1.5 Settlements

Before 1997 there were two forms of trust used to create settlements relating to land:

the *strict settlement* (giving rise to what is usually called 'settled land'), the ancient form of trust, governed largely after 1925 by the Settled Land Act 1925 (SLA 1925).

the *trust for sale*, which was slightly the more modern form and governed largely after 1925 by the LPA 1925.

A brief explanation of these two types of settlement is given below. Although we usually prefer to avoid excursions into historical matters, we feel that you need a very short explanation of these two forms and how they developed. Settled Land Act settlements are still in existence today, and we want to set the scene here for the further account we will give in Chapter 14. It is true that trusts for sale no longer exist, but we shall be referring to them fairly frequently in describing the new trust of land which replaces them (see Chapter 13). We think that having an outline knowledge of the effect of trusts for sale and how they were created will help you to understand the significance of this new trust.

12.2 A short historical background

12.2.1 Strict settlements (or 'Settled Land Act settlements')

We must begin by emphasising that we are describing a process which began in the Middle Ages, and that, as far as the history of the settlement is concerned, we are talking about people who owned large amounts of land. The landowner who made the sort of strict settlement we will describe probably owned at least several large country estates, and at a later period may also have had a London town house, a 'hunting-box' in the shires and a grouse moor in Scotland. The settlement in its developed form is designed to meet the needs of large landowners, like the Victorian Trollope's Duke of Omnium, rather than those of small modern owner-occupiers.

The purpose of making a strict settlement was in the main to ensure that the family estates remained in the family, passing intact to the heir, and that at the same time provision was made from the income of the estate for wives, widows and younger children. In a typical marriage settlement, made by a fee simple owner on his marriage, the settlor would deprive himself of his absolute title to the estate and create a mere life estate for himself, followed by a fee tail in favour of his eldest (probably yet unborn) son (see 1.2.4.1). He would also make a provision for the payment of a personal allowance to his wife ('pin-money') during the marriage, and a larger sum to support her during her widowhood, if she survived him, as well as providing 'portions' for the daughters and younger sons to support them in later life. The settlor had thus split the legal fee simple into several smaller estates (a life estate, a fee tail and a reversion in favour of his general heirs—see 7.4.2), which was possible at law before 1926.

An alternative way of making the same provision was to give the full fee simple to trustees, directing them to hold on trust for the family on similar terms, so that the settlor and his heir took equitable interests under the trust equivalent to the life estate and the fee tail, and money payments were provided for the rest of the family.

Whichever form was adopted, the result was the same, for, although the land could be sold or mortgaged if all those entitled under the settlement were of full age and agreed to act together, there was no one person who by himself could dispose of the whole legal and beneficial interest. Thus the chances of the property being lost to the family were greatly reduced.

There was one danger which threatened to interfere with the settlor's plans, for from the Middle Ages the common law had permitted a tenant in tail to 'bar' the fee tail and convert his limited estate into the full fee simple. We cannot give any details of this procedure here, but if you are interested (and it is a fascinating example of the use of legal fictions) you will find an account in Megarry and Wade at pp. 72–5.

This danger was, however, traditionally overcome by the settlor persuading his eldest son to bar the entail as soon as he came of age and to resettle the resulting fee simple, giving himself a life estate and creating an entail in favour of his eldest son. This seems to have worked satisfactorily in most cases, and a process of barring the entail and resettling would go on for one generation after another, so that the current owners of the property never had more than a life estate. However, we can see from Jane Austen's *Pride and Prejudice* (which was, in part, based on the author's personal experiences) the type of trouble that could arise were no son to arrive to enable the entail to be barred.

Settling property in this way certainly had the desired effect of keeping land in the family, but preventing alienation had its own disadvantages.

Some settlements did permit limited sale and mortgaging, so that money could be raised to improve the rest of the estate, but if such powers were not expressly provided, the current owner of the estate might well find himself unable to raise money for much-needed repairs and improvements, and as a result the property would deteriorate. A series of nineteenth-century Acts, culminating in the Settled Land Act 1882, gave the current beneficiary (the 'tenant for life') powers to deal with settled land and even to sell it, despite the settlor's intentions. We shall return to this point in more detail when we come to look at the powers of the tenant for life under SLA 1925 (see 14.6).

12.2.2 Trusts for sale

As we have seen, the strict settlement was designed for landowners with a senti-mental attachment to land which had probably been owned by their families for hundreds of years. It was not, however, particularly appropriate in the case of land which had been bought relatively recently, and as an investment rather than for occupation. Land on which housing estates or factories were built was of no senti-mental value to its owners, and they usually intended to hold it as long as the yield was satisfactory but to sell and reinvest the proceeds when better bargains were available. Yet, all the same, such landowners might want to make settlements, in order to keep their capital intact for later generations and to provide for the present members of their families. Their needs were met by the use of the trust for sale.

Title would be vested in trustees, who would be under a duty to sell and reinvest, but who could postpone sale until the time was right. The income until sale, and the resulting capital, could be held in trust for a series of beneficiaries, as defined in the trust instrument, and so the settlor could provide an income for family members without dividing his capital between them. The major defining factor in these trusts was that they imposed upon the trustees an *obligation* to sell the trust property but usually also included a power to postpone the sale, so that the trustees could choose the best moment at which to realise the trust investment in the property.

However, the fact that the trustees were under a *duty* to sell brought into operation an equitable doctrine known as 'conversion'.

12.2.2.1 *Doctrine of conversion*

In any case where there is a specifically enforceable obligation to convert land into money, or money into land, the maxim that equity regards as done that which ought to be done leads equity to treat the property as notionally converted from the moment the obligation arises. This notional conversion operates when any contract to buy or sell land is made (see 3.5.3), and also applied to all trusts for sale. The trustees for sale could be compelled to perform their duty to sell the trust property and so such property was treated by equity as though it had been sold already, and the beneficiaries were regarded as having interests in money rather than in the land. This may appear somewhat strange today, but seemed appropriate when the trust for sale was first developed as a commercial alternative to the strict settlement.

12.2.3 Need for reform

In origin, as we have seen, each type of settlement had its own specific purpose, the strict settlement being used where particular land was to remain in the family, and the trust for sale being employed where the land was an investment which changed from time to time. Both forms were retained in the 1925 property legislation, but in more recent years a number of problems became apparent.

12.2.3.1 *SLA settlements*

The machinery for dealing with a settlement under the Settled Land Act 1925, although intended to facilitate the sale of the land, often appeared cumbersome and expensive. Over the years clever draftsmen had managed to construct trusts for sale which had most of the benefits of the SLA settlement, while retaining the advantages provided by the greater flexibility of the trust for sale. True SLA settlements were increasingly rare (though they were still sometimes used for very large estates or where there was a tax advantage) and some forms (notably the entail) were regarded as inappropriate in the modern world, as they imposed the restraint of a 'dead hand' over the land for many years to come, sometimes with undesirable results.

However, great care had to be taken in drafting the trust for sale, because unless it could be described as 'an immediate binding trust for sale' (SLA 1925, s. 1(7) and LPA 1925, s. 205(1)(xxix)) it would be treated as a SLA settlement. In particular the word 'binding' was taken to have a technical meaning requiring the trust to have effect in relation to all interests and for there to be no interests with priority to the trust. For examples of some of the difficulties of the old law, which arose from this definition, see *In re Leigh's Settled Estates* [1926] Ch 852, *In re Parker's Settled Estates* [1928] Ch 247, *In re Norton* [1929] 1 Ch 84, and the article by Lewis in (1938) 54 LQR 576. The penalty for getting it wrong and creating a SLA settlement was to have imposed upon the trust the more cumbersome format which applied under that Act. In recent years, very few settlors would intentionally create such a settlement, but the possibility of doing so constituted a trap for the unwary, particularly for the makers of 'home-made' wills.

12.2.3.2 *Trusts for sale*

The principal source of difficulty and dissatisfaction with trusts for sale rose from the fact that they were imposed automatically on most cases of co-ownership by the 1925 legislation (see 16.3.5). This meant that most co-owners held the legal estate upon trust for sale for themselves as beneficiaries and, under the doctrine of conversion, were regarded as having beneficial interests in money not in land. This was intended to facilitate the sale of the land at a time when co-ownership was relatively unusual, and does not seem to have caused any particular problems at the outset. In the course of the twentieth century, however, a rise in home ownership, combined with the change in the status of women, meant that co-ownership of residential property became increasingly common. Couples who acquired a house or flat generally regarded it as a family home, which they intended to keep; even though there was usually an implied power to postpone sale, the imposition of a statutory duty to sell began to seem inappropriate.

The rule in Re Mayo
A particular difficulty was caused by the decision in *Re Mayo* [1943] Ch 302, which derived from the fact that, under a trust for sale, there was a *duty* for the trustees to sell and only a *power* to postpone sale. If the trustees disagreed about what was to happen, the property had to be sold, because the mere power (to postpone sale) had, like all powers, to be exercised unanimously; when unanimity as to its exercise no longer existed, the duty to sell had to have priority. This rule was particularly unhelpful where couples had bought houses intending to provide a home for themselves and their children, but on the breakdown of the relationship one partner left the house and demanded that it be sold (perhaps leaving the children and remaining partner homeless). Accordingly, over the years, the courts were forced to develop a principle that the obligation to sell could be in some way tempered by the intention of the parties when they bought. They were thus able to allow sale to be delayed, and even to give one party the right to live in the premises until sale (as for example in *Bull* v *Bull* [1955] 1 QB 234; see further 13.7.3). This development was essential in practice but was somewhat at odds with the theory that the person whom the court was recognising as having a right to reside on the land had in equity only an interest in money.

12.2.4. Law Commission proposals for reform

The problems we have been discussing, and many others, were identified by the Law Commission in 1989 in *Transfer of Land: Trusts of Land* (Law Com No. 181). This report provided a useful summary of the difficulties caused by the old system and set out proposals for major changes, which paved the way for the reforms introduced by the Trusts of Land and Appointment of Trustees Act 1996.

12.3 Trusts of Land and Appointment of Trustees Act 1996

The Trusts of Land and Appointment of Trustees Act 1996 (TOLATA 1996) came into force on 1 January 1997. It introduced the new 'trust of land', which is defined so as to include all types of trust, however created. Any trusts for sale in existence when the Act came into operation were converted into these new trusts, and any attempts in future to create trusts for sale will take effect as trusts of land. Rather confusingly, the Act continues to use the term 'trust for sale' to identify any trust which imposes a duty to sell (even if created after the commencement of the Act), but it makes it clear that such trusts take effect as trusts of land and specifically provides that the doctrine of conversion is not to operate in such circumstances.

Trusts imposed by statute (for example in cases of co-ownership) now take effect as trusts of land, not as trusts for sale.

The Act also provides that no new SLA 1925 settlements may be created (again, attempts to do so would give rise to trusts of land), but it exempts any existing settlements of this type, which continue to operate under the old rules.

The result of the Act, therefore, is that today there are still two forms of trust:

(a) *trusts of land* governed by TOLATA 1996; and

(b) *the strict settlement*, governed by the SLA 1925,

but new examples of the second class cannot now be created. Since use of the SLA settlement was becoming reasonably uncommon, and due to rules which limit the period for which property may be settled (see Chapter 15), SLA settlements will become increasingly rare and will eventually disappear altogether. However, for some time to come it will remain necessary to be able to spot a pre-1997 SLA settlement and to know the differences between the TOLATA 1996 rules which we consider in detail in the next chapter, and the older SLA procedures described in Chapter 14.

FURTHER READING

Clements, 'The Changing Face of Trusts' [1998] MLR 56.

Transfer of Land: Trusts of Land, 1989, Law Com No. 181 (in particular, Part I on problems of existing law and Part II on proposals for reform).

13

Trusts of land

13.1 Introduction

In this chapter, we begin by looking in some detail at the rules relating to the new trust of land, which was introduced by TOLATA 1996, and will explain them by reference to an *express trust* which a settlor might create after the Act came into force. Having done this, we will consider trusts of land which arise other than by express creation (13.10) and, in particular, will deal with those trusts which formerly would have taken effect as trusts for sale or SLA settlements. Finally, we will draw some comparisons between the old law and the rules which are currently in operation (13.11).

13.1.1 **20 Trant Way**

The fee simple estate of 20 Trant Way is owned by John Brown, who lives there with his wife, Janet. John has not yet made a will, although his wife keeps urging him to do so. John has no doubt about what he wants to happen to the house and his investments when he dies: he wants them all to go to his wife, if she survives him, and then at her death to pass on to his two married daughters. He is, however, very uncertain about how to achieve this. He remembers reading a newspaper article some time ago, which said that all this could be done with a trust, but warned that there were several different types of trust and that it was important to choose the right one. Apparently, it was possible to make the wrong one by mistake, and this worries John, and has deterred him from doing anything.

13.1.1.1 *Creating a settlement*

In legal terms, what John is wanting to do is to create a settlement, giving successive interests to members of his family: a life estate to his widow and a remainder in fee simple to his daughters. Since 1925, neither of these interests can exist as a legal estate, and they will, therefore, have to take effect behind a trust (see Chapter 7).

13.1.1.2 *Trusts of Land and Appointment of Trustees Act 1996*

As you will know from the previous chapter, there used to be two ways of creating a settlement of land: under the Settled Land Act 1925 or by means of trust for sale. The article which John read was probably warning against the dangers of inadvertently creating SLA settlements, which would be quite inappropriate for small properties, and advising that the mechanism of a trust for sale should be used. However, if John consults a legal adviser (as we hope he will), he will learn that, since 1 January 1997, any trust of No. 20 which he might make would take effect as a trust of land under the Trusts of Land and Appointment of Trustees Act 1996 (TOLATA 1996). It is no longer important, as it was in the past, to worry about the words used to create a settlement. If there is a trust and the trust contains land, the trust will be a trust of land.

We imagine that John will probably have a number of questions to ask about this new trust. Will it apply to his investments as well as to the house, or will he have to do something different with them? Who should he appoint as trustees, and what is their role? Who will own the house? Will his wife be able to do what she wants with the property? In particular, will she be able to sell the house if she wants to move to something smaller, and will his daughters have any say in this? Will the fact that the house is subject to a trust make it more difficult to sell if she does want to move? Any settlor is likely to ask questions such as these, and we will try to provide some answers to them in the following sections. Before doing so, however, we need to look at another property in Trant Way, which is already subject to a trust.

13.1.2 **9 Trant Way**

Janice and Gianni Thorne are looking for a house in Mousehole and they have been to view 9 Trant Way, which is for sale. It is occupied by Mrs Green, who is an elderly widow. Mrs Green tells the Thornes that her husband left her the house in his will but that she is now finding it too large and too far from the shops and that her trustees have agreed to sell the house and buy her a flat closer to the centre of the town. The Thornes are rather concerned about the mention of trustees and cannot understand why trustees are involved if Mrs Green was left the house by her husband. Wisely, they ask their conveyancing adviser to check the situation and to give them an explanation of whether it will be safe for them to negotiate a price for the property with Mrs Green.

13.1.2.1 *Edward Green's will*

Their adviser learns that the will of Mrs Green's husband did indeed give rise to a trust and that Mrs Green's interest in the property will only last for her lifetime and that afterwards her nephew William will be entitled to the house. Mr and Mrs Thorne will need to be advised whether it would be safe to go ahead with the purchase or whether there is a risk that William Green may later make a claim to the property. The will of Mrs Green's husband (Edward Green, who died in 1995) contained the following provision:

I give all my real and personal property . . . (hereinafter called 'my residuary estate') to my trustees upon trust to sell, call in and convert the same into money at such time or times and in such manner as my trustees shall think fit. . . .

My trustees shall stand possessed of my residuary estate upon trust to pay the income thereof to my wife, Margaret Jane Green, during her life.

After the death of my wife, and in the meantime subject to her interest, my trustees shall hold my residuary estate and the income thereof in trust for my nephew William Francis Green.

> I direct that the house in which my wife and I shall be residing at the date of my death . . .
> shall not be sold during the lifetime of my wife without her consent in writing and that until
> the sale thereof my trustees shall permit my wife to occupy the same rent-free so long as she
> shall desire.
>
> At the request of my wife my trustees shall sell this house (or any house purchased in lieu
> thereof in pursuance of a previous request) and apply the whole or any part of the net
> proceeds of sale in the purchase of another house selected by her . . . and shall hold the same
> upon the trusts declared by this my will.

As you can see, this will specifically referred to the land being held 'upon trust to
sell . . .'. Mr Green died in 1995 and thus at his death the old rules treated his will as
creating a trust for sale governed in the main by the LPA 1925 rules. On 1 January
1997 this trust was therefore converted into a trust of land under TOLATA 1996 (see
further 13.10.2.2).

13.2 Definition of a trust of land

13.2.1 Statutory definition

The new trust of land is defined by TOLATA 1996, s. 1(1)(a):

'trust of land' means any trust of property which consists of or includes land.

Section 1(2)(a) expressly provides that the reference in s. 1(1) to a trust includes all
descriptions of trust, including express, implied and resulting trusts, trusts for sale
and bare trusts. (A bare trust is one in which property is held on trust for one adult
absolutely.)

13.2.2 Mixed trusts

In order to constitute a trust of land, it is sufficient that the trust property 'includes
land' (s. 1(1)(a)). Thus, mixed trusts, containing both land and personalty, will also
be subject to the rules in TOLATA 1996. This is a useful rule because it allows a
house and its contents, or, indeed, all the settlor's property, to be held under a
single trust. As a result, John Brown will be able to create one trust which will
apply to both his house and his investments.

13.2.3 Conversion of existing trusts for sale

Existing trusts for sale were converted into trusts of land as a consequence of s. 1(2)
(b), which makes it quite clear that the statute catches trusts created or arising
before the commencement of TOLATA 1996. Thus, at the first moment of 1 January
1997 all existing trusts for sale (including Mrs Green's) were converted into trusts
of land, including, as we will see in Chapter 16, those relating to every piece of
co-owned land.

13.2.4 **What happens if a settlor tries to create a trust for sale?**

As we explained in the previous chapter (12.3), TOLATA 1996 continues to use the term 'trust for sale' to describe any trust which imposes a duty to sell, but there are no longer special rules governing such a trust and under s. 1(2)(a) it would simply take effect as a trust of land. Although the settlor has imposed a duty to sell on the trustees, the Act gives them a power to postpone sale (see 13.4.2.3), and also provides that, despite that duty to sell, there is no longer any notional conversion of the property (13.10.2.1).

13.2.5 **SLA settlements**

TOLATA 1996, s. 2(1), prevents the creation of any new SLA settlement after 1 January 1997, and any attempt to create such a settlement will take effect as a trust of land. Section 2(6) and Sch. 1 deal with certain specific circumstances which formerly would have given rise to a settlement under the 1925 Act; these require more detailed explanation and we will deal with them in 13.10.1.

SLA settlements which were in existence at 1 January 1997 continue to exist in their original form and are not converted into trusts of land. We consider these settlements in Chapter 14.

13.3 **Appointment of trustees**

Once it is clear that a trust of land exists, it will be necessary to establish who will be the trustees of that trust. Here the rules are to be found partly in the Trustee Act 1925 and partly in TOLATA 1996.

13.3.1 **Number of trustees**

It is usual to have a minimum of two trustees because the 'overreaching' provisions which are designed to protect purchasers, will lead anyone dealing with the trust to demand signatures from at least two trustees on any receipt for capital money.

It is not possible to have more than four owners of a legal estate in land (and thus four trustees of a legal estate) because where there is an attempt to appoint more than four, the Trustee Act (TA 1925), s. 34(2) will vest the legal estate in the first four of full age (that is the first four listed but omitting anyone who is named but who is under 18 when the disposition takes effect).

13.3.2 **Who appoints trustees?**

In the case of an express trust, it is normal for the disposition creating the trust to specify who are to be the trustees. Thus, if John Brown decides to create a trust in his will, he will most probably name the trustees, who could be family members or friends, but could also be drawn from his professional advisers, such as his solicitors or bank.

If the settlor does not nominate trustees, or for any reason replacement or additional trustees are needed, the rules on appointing trustees are to be found in TA 1925, s. 36. The essential rule is that where a new trustee is needed, either as a replacement for an existing trustee (s. 36(1)) or because an additional trustee would be beneficial (up to the maximum of four) (s. 36(6)), that new trustee should be appointed:

(a) first, by any person named in the instrument which created the trust as a person who is to have a power to appoint trustees (there can be more than one appointor named, if so desired); or

(b) secondly, if no appointor is named or the person named cannot or will not act, then by any existing trustees.

The appointment of the trustee must be made in writing and should be made by deed because a deed is needed in order to ensure that the legal estate in the land which is the trust property vests in the new trustee (TA 1925, s. 40).

You will realise that there may be cases in which the rules in s. 36 will not provide someone to appoint a trustee. This will happen if no person is specified to appoint trustees (possible, in any event, only in an express trust) and if there are no current trustees capable of appointing. If, however, there has been a trustee but he has died, the personal representatives of the last surviving trustee may make the appointment (TA 1925, s. 36(1) and (6)). In other cases where there is no one under these rules capable of appointing, it will be necessary to apply to the court for the court to appoint a trustee under the power in s. 41. This power to appoint is very wide and allows the court also to act where an appointment under the s. 36 rules is theoretically possible but in practice difficult (for example if the existing trustees cannot agree). The s. 41 power applies:

whenever it is expedient to appoint a new trustee or new trustees, and it is found inexpedient, difficult or impracticable to do so without the assistance of the court.

The court may also, where necessary, follow such an appointment by an order vesting the trust property in the new trustee or trustees (TA 1925, s. 44).

13.3.3 Retirement and discharge of trustees

We have already seen that s. 36 allows trustees to be replaced. The circumstances which permit the replacement of a trustee are: where a trustee dies; is out of the United Kingdom for more than 12 months; wishes to retire from the trust; refuses or is unfit to act (this would cover dishonesty or bankruptcy amongst other things); is incapable of acting (illness or mental incapacity); or is an infant (under 18).

A trustee may also retire, without a fresh appointment being made to replace him, under TA 1925, s. 39, but only if there remain at least two trustees or the remaining trustee is a trust corporation. Trust corporations are defined in s. 68(18) and include the Public Trustee and certain other corporations.

13.3.4 Control by beneficiaries of appointment and retirement

The impact of TA 1925, s. 36, is now modified by TOLATA 1996, ss. 19–21, which give extensive powers to the beneficiaries to direct the person with the right to appoint under TA 1925, s. 36, so that the choice of new trustee is in fact no longer always controlled by the person who actually appoints. In addition TOLATA 1996, s. 19, allows beneficiaries to require trustees to resign from the trust. The combination of these powers means that in many cases beneficiaries will be in a position to replace the trustees entirely should they disagree with them or replace particular trustees to whom they object. You should note, however, that the beneficiaries are not given the actual power to make the appointment but just the power to select the person(s) to be appointed. Where the new powers operate, the beneficiaries can choose the new trustees, but the appointment is still made by the person(s) with power to appoint under s. 36. Thus, were there to be two trustees, T1 and T2, and two beneficiaries who have TOLATA 1996 powers, the beneficiaries could, if they wished, direct T1 and T2 to appoint a new trustee (T3) of the beneficiaries' choice and then direct TI to retire.

You should also note that the beneficiaries' new powers do not apply to every trust. They do not apply if the settlor has in the trust instrument specified a person for the purpose of appointment of new trustees: in such a case the express wishes of the settlor take precedence and the beneficiaries have no power to direct the appointment of trustees of their choice (TOLATA 1996, s. 19(1)(a)).

The new power also only applies where the beneficiaries are all of full age and capacity and (taken together) are absolutely entitled to the trust property (TOLATA 1996, s. 19(1)(b)). Those are the conditions which would have to be satisfied in order to allow the beneficiaries to elect to end the trust under the rule in *Saunders* v *Vautier* (1841) 4 Beav 115 and to vest the trust property in themselves absolutely *or* to re-settle on new trusts with fresh trustees (which was the only way that, in the past, the beneficiaries could control the choice of trustee). Thus, TOLATA 1996 simply allows the beneficiaries to control the appointment of new trustees without the expense and possible adverse tax consequences of ending the old trust and creating a new one.

In order to exercise their powers under s. 19(2), the beneficiaries must be unanimous; they must all agree on the new appointment (or retirement) and must give a direction (or matching directions if several documents are used) in writing (TOLATA 1996, ss. 21(1) and 19(2)). If the beneficiaries cannot agree, they cannot exercise the new power to give directions and as far as appointments are concerned the choice of the new trustee(s) remains with the person who has power to appoint under TA 1925, s. 36. Similarly, the provisions of TA 1925, s. 36 continue to govern the appointment of trustees in the case of trusts which do not satisfy the requirements of TOLATA 1996, s. 19(1).

Finally, we should note that powers in TOLATA 1996, ss. 19–21, apply to *all* trusts and not just to the new trusts of land. Thus they apply also to SLA settlements and to trusts of pure personalty. It would be a mistake to think that TOLATA 1996 relates solely to trusts of land: the provisions of Part II of the Act are general in their application.

13.4 Powers of trustees of a trust of land

Under the older legislation relating to trusts there were considerable restrictions on the powers of trustees in relation to trust property. These were originally designed to protect the beneficiaries but in time had come to be regarded as simply putting a brake on quite reasonable choices for trustees. Accordingly, it has long been customary for well-drafted settlements of both of the old types to widen the powers of trustees (and of tenants for life who, as we will see in Chapter 14, have management powers in the case of strict settlements).

TOLATA 1996 recognises that the old restrictions on the powers of trustees are redundant and inconvenient in the cases to which they apply (usually cases where trusts arise by operation of some statutory provision or due to a mistake). The new powers for trustees are set out in ss. 6 and 7 of TOLATA 1996 and are very wide. Any of the powers in ss. 6 and 7 can be excluded or restricted by the settlor when creating the trust (s. 8(1)). The effect of the new rules will be to reverse the old position, so that wide powers will be available unless excluded.

13.4.1 Trustees hold the legal estate

If John Brown's will does create a trust of land in respect of No. 20 Trant Way, the legal estate in the property would be transferred after his death to the trustees, who would hold it for the duration of the trust.

13.4.2 Trustees' statutory powers

13.4.2.1 *Powers of an absolute owner*

Under s. 6(1) of TOLATA 1996, the trustees of land 'have in relation to the land subject to the trust all the powers of an absolute owner'. This means that John's trustees would be able to manage the property as they thought fit, since the 'powers of an absolute owner' include the ability to sell the land, to mortgage it, to grant leases and to create other rights over it, such as easements or options.

This approach is the opposite of that which applied to SLA settlements and the old trusts for sale, where the trustees were given a limited range of powers by the statutes and the settlor was free to increase these powers if he or she saw fit. In the case of the trust of land the trustees are given automatically the power to do anything which an absolute beneficial owner could do. This is important because it is quite common for trusts to arise accidentally or without the parties being fully aware of the position (for example, where trusts are imposed by legislation). In those cases, because the settlor was unaware that a trust was being created or because it was created unintentionally, no thought was given to the widening of the limited powers of the trustees and the result was that dealings with many pieces of trust land could be hampered, often to the detriment of the interests of the beneficiaries. In properly drafted express trusts, on the other hand, a great deal of thought was usually given to the issue of how far the powers of the trustees should be widened in order to give them a chance to manage the trust property effectively. In the vast majority of cases the decision which was taken was to give all the powers of a beneficial (an absolute) owner. Accordingly, the new rules for trusts of land adopt this far more generous approach to trustees' powers and produce the effect which was usual in the past in most well-drafted express trusts.

In addition to these very general powers given by s. 6(1), the Act makes specific provision for four particular powers:

to buy land;
to postpone sale;
to partition the trust land between the beneficiaries; and
to compel the beneficiaries to accept a conveyance of the trust land to themselves.

13.4.2.2 *Power to buy land*

Section 6(3), as amended by the Trustee Act 2000, s. 40 and Sch. 2, para. 45(1) provides that:

the trustees of land have power to purchase freehold or leasehold land in the United Kingdom.

Before the amendment, this power was restricted to the purchase of land 'in England and Wales' (a restriction which had also applied under the pre-TOLATA rules), so that if a settlor wished to permit purchase of other land—even in other parts of the United Kingdom—express provision for this had to be included in the trust instrument.

Section 6(4) makes it clear that the trustees' power to purchase land may be used to acquire land as an investment, or for occupation by a beneficiary or 'for any other reason'.

13.4.2.3 *Power to postpone sale*

Section 4(1) of TOLATA 1996 gives trustees of a trust for sale an implied power to postpone sale, which cannot be excluded by the settlor. This marks a change from the old law, since the power to postpone which was formerly implied under LPA 1925, s. 25(1) could be excluded by the settlor's expressing 'a contrary intention'.

13.4.2.4 *Power to partition*

Section 7 of TOLATA 1996 gives the trustees power to partition the land between the beneficiaries, where the beneficiaries are all of full age and absolutely entitled. While of little use in the majority of cases, this power may assist where it is intended to divide a large estate between beneficiaries or even where a large house can effectively be partitioned into smaller lots. Partition requires the consent of the beneficiaries (s. 7(3)).

13.4.2.5 *Power to compel beneficiaries to take conveyance*

A new power for the trustees is contained in TOLATA 1996, s. 6(2), which only applies where all the beneficiaries are of full age and absolutely entitled. This is a power which is designed to permit the trustees to force the beneficiaries to take a conveyance of the trust land, effectively making the beneficiaries themselves the trustees. This will enable the trustees, if they wish, to discharge themselves from the obligations under a settlement where it is no longer necessary for them to be involved.

It appears from the wording of this section, that this power applies only where there are two or more beneficiaries. Where there is one beneficiary solely entitled to the trust property, the trustees may bring the trust to an end by conveying the property to him or her, and do not need specific statutory authority to do so (see further Megarry and Wade, pp. 447–8).

13.5 Limitation of trustees' powers

As we have seen in the previous section, trustees have very wide powers under TOLATA 1996. Settlors like John Brown may be worried by the extent of those powers, fearing that they may be used to override the wishes of the beneficiaries and, indeed, sometimes misused in the trustees' own interests. It may reassure John to know that there are a number of provisions in the Act which can have the effect of considerably limiting the trustees' powers.

13.5.1 Exclusion and restriction of powers

The Act recognises that the wide powers it confers on trustees may not always be appropriate. Accordingly, s. 8(1) allows the settlor to exclude the powers contained in ss. 6 and 7 by making express provision in the disposition which creates the trust. This will still give the settlor who is creating an elaborately drafted express trust the chance to select the precise powers which the trustees should have in order to carry out the settlor's intentions, but means that in the badly prepared, accidentally created or statutorily imposed trusts the trustees will have the wide powers which will allow them the best chance to produce a good result for the trust.

13.5.1.1 *One power which cannot be restricted or excluded*

As we have already noted above, the implied power to postpone sale, given to trustees for sale by s. 4(1) of TOLATA 1996, cannot be restricted or excluded by the settlor. The power is implied:

in the case of every trust for sale of land created by a disposition . . . despite any provision to the contrary made by the disposition. . . .

This provision applies to all trusts for sale of land, even those which were already in existence before the Act came into force, and which, therefore, might have contained an express exclusion of the power implied by LPA 1925, s. 25(1).

13.5.1.2 *Situation where trustees disagree about postponing sale*

Although TOLATA 1996 makes it impossible for the settlor to exclude the power to postpone, there is no provision in the Act which prevents a minority of trustees refusing to postpone and insisting on sale, in reliance on the rule in *Re Mayo* [1943] Ch 302 (see above, 12.2.3.2). There must be unanimous agreement among the trustees to exercise their implied power to postpone sale; if even only one of them disagrees, they must perform their duty of selling the property.

Thus if the trust is expressed to contain an obligation to sell, should one trustee no longer wish to postpone sale, the property will have to be sold even against the wishes of the majority of the trustees. In such a case, if the beneficiaries disagree with the one trustee, they may be able to prevent the sale by exercising their power under TOLATA 1996, s. 19, to require that trustee to retire (if that power applies on the facts of the case). This may require fast action on the part of the beneficiaries, however, and they will have to agree about requiring the trustee's retirement. If this is not possible, another way of seeking to stop the sale could be an application to the court under TOLATA 1996, s. 14 (see 13.8.1).

13.5.2 Requirements for consents and consultation

If the settlor wishes, he can require the trustees to obtain the consent of named individuals before exercising some or all of their powers. In addition, there are statutory provisions requiring the trustees to consult the beneficiaries, so that even if the settlor does not impose the need for consents, the beneficiaries will still have some say in what is to be done by the trustees.

13.5.2.1 Consents

TOLATA 1996 retains the possibility that existed under the old rules of a settlor imposing upon trustees the requirement to obtain a consent or consents before any power is exercised (as was done in the will of Edward Green—13.1.2.1). Section 8(2) says that where this is done, '. . . the power may not be exercised without the consent'. This means that if the trustees act without all the prescribed consents (should the need for more than one be specified) their act will constitute a breach of trust, and the beneficiaries could seek an injunction to restrain the breach, or could claim compensation if it had already occurred.

The persons chosen by the settlor as persons whose consent should be obtained do not have to be beneficiaries or even persons who are in any way connected with the trust, but usually there will be some form of connection. Thus, John Brown, for example, could provide that his trustees must not exercise their power to sell 20 Trant Way without the consent of his widow and his two daughters.

As we shall see later (13.9), the Act tries to hold the balance between protecting the interests of the beneficiaries and ensuring that purchasers can buy trust property without having to make unduly burdensome enquiries. Checking that a large number of consents has been obtained could be expensive and time-consuming, and so TOLATA 1996 retains the rule (formerly contained in LPA 1925, s. 26(1)) that a purchaser need only check that at least two consents of those required have been obtained. Section 10(1) of TOLATA 1996 provides:

If a disposition creating a trust of land requires the consent of more than two persons to the exercise by the trustees of any function relating to the land, the consent of any two of them to the exercise of the function is sufficient in favour of a purchaser.

Note, however, that this only provides protection for the purchaser. Should a trustee fail to ensure that all the consents are obtained, that trustee would be in breach of trust.

Should it prove impossible to obtain the consent of a person specified in the trust instrument, it will be necessary for the trustees to protect themselves by making an application to the court under TOLATA 1996, s. 14, which expressly mentions the possibility of the court making an order relieving the trustees of an obligation to obtain any consent or to consult any person, before exercising a power.

Section 10(3) of TOLATA 1996 also contains provisions to deal with cases in which the person whose consent is required is a minor (under 18) at the time at which the need for consent arises. In this case the consent of the minor is not required as far as any purchaser is concerned, but the trustees will be in breach of trust unless they obtain the consent of a person who has parental responsibility for the minor.

The consents rules will permit settlors will seek to tie the hands of their trustees by requiring that they obtain consent from someone who will be guaranteed to refuse. Although the trust of land no longer carries with it the obligation to sell which was a feature of the trust for sale, the power to sell is always available to the trustees under s. 6(1) of TOLATA 1996 which, as we have seen, provides that the trustees are to have 'all the powers of an absolute owner'. It is true that the power of sale could be excluded by the settlor under s. 8(1) of the Act, but if he does not want to do this he could instead use the requirement of consent to prevent the sale.

An old case that illustrates what can be done in this regard is *Re Inns* [1947] Ch 576, in which the settlor had left a large house by his will to his widow during her lifetime and thereafter to the district council, for use as a hospital. The trust instrument also provided that should the council use the property as a hospital, it would receive an additional gift of £10,000 to pay for equipment. It was provided that the property could not be sold without the consent of both the widow and the council. The widow wished to sell the property because it was too large and expensive for her to maintain but the council was forced to refuse its consent because if it gave consent it would lose its interest in remainder in the trust property and the additional £10,000 (because there would be no house to use as a hospital). The court held that these provisions in the trust instrument were valid and both consents were required in order to sell, even though the effect of enforcing them was to ensure that the property would never be sold because the council could never give its consent since, whatever its sympathies for the widow, it was constrained to act in the interests of its ratepayers.

13.5.2.2 *Consultation*

You will realise that provision for consents will only be capable of being used in an express (and properly drafted) trust, because it is necessary to insert consent provisions into the trust instrument if they are to work. Accordingly, there has long been provision in trusts legislation in order to require some degree of consultation of beneficiaries by trustees before the trustees exercised their powers. In the case of the trust for sale some provision for consultation appeared in LPA 1925, s. 26(3). The advantage of these rules was that they applied automatically to a trust which arose by operation of law where the settlor might not really have been aware that a trust was being created and so would not, or could not, have provided for consents. The old requirements did not, however, work in an entirely satisfactory manner because they did not apply to expressly created trusts unless specifically included by the settlor.

Accordingly, the old requirements are adapted and extended in TOLATA 1996, s. 11(1), which provides:

The trustees of land shall in the exercise of any function relating to land subject to the trust—

(a) so far as practicable, consult the beneficiaries of full age and beneficially entitled to an interest in possession in the land, and

(b) so far as consistent with the general interest of the trust, give effect to the wishes of those beneficiaries, or (in the case of dispute) of the majority (according to the value of their combined interests).

The mandatory requirement to consult and to 'give effect to the wishes' of the majority means that the wishes of the beneficiaries take priority over even an obligation to sell (where the settlor has imposed this); but you should note generally that the requirement to follow the wishes of the beneficiaries applies only 'so far as consistent with the general interest of the trust'.

If the trustees do not consult as required by s. 11(1), or ignore the results of consultation, the beneficiaries may seek an injunction to restrain any intended breach of trust by the trustees, or may claim compensation should the objectionable transaction have been completed. However, as part of the protection offered to a purchaser, the Act provides that a purchaser of land held on the trust is not required to ensure that the trustees have in fact complied with the consultation procedure. As long as the overreaching provisions are satisfied, the purchaser gets a good title free of the beneficial interests, even if the beneficiaries have not been consulted (TOLATA 1996, s. 16(1)). The trustees would, of course, be liable to the beneficiaries for breach of trust.

Cases where there is no duty to consult
The duty to consult can be expressly excluded by the settlor in the disposition by which the trust was created (TOLATA 1996, s. 11(2)(a)), and the wording of the statutory provision suggests that the exclusion could be either total or in part (for example, excluding the need to consult a particular beneficiary). This rule reverses the old position under which trustees of an express trust were under a duty to consult only if this was expressly provided; a requirement to consult is now implied unless expressly excluded.

Another case in which the duty to consult will not apply is where the trustees are using the power under TOLATA 1996, s. 6(2), to force the beneficiaries to take a conveyance of the trust property. In that case consultation is obviously pointless because this power would not be being used unless there were disagreement and the aim of s. 6(2) is to allow the trustees to free themselves of their trust obligations without the agreement of the beneficiaries.

TOLATA 1996, s. 11 also provides that the implied duty to consult does not apply to trusts which were created by wills or dispositions which had effect before I January 1997 (s. 11(2)(b)). However, where the settlor of an old trust is living, he or she can make a deed applying the new rule to the old trust (s. 11(3)). As Mrs Green's trust was created by a will which took effect before TOLATA 1996 came into force (see 13.1.2.1), the new duty will not apply. This may not matter very much because her husband's will contained an express requirement that the house should not be sold without her consent but it does mean that the trustees will have no duty to consult her under s. 11 before exercising their other powers.

13.5.3 **Trustees' fiduciary duties**

Even if the settlor does not exclude or restrict the trustees' very wide powers or impose requirements for consent, the trustees are not free to do exactly what they want with the trust property. They are, of course, subject to all the general equitable rules about how trustees must conduct themselves. Thus, in all their dealings, the trustees must act in the interests of the trust as a whole and not, for example, for any personal advantage, for that would constitute a breach of trust.

The Act seeks to reinforce the general duties of trustees by a number of statutory provisions. Section 6(1) gives the trustees all the powers of an absolute owner 'for the purpose of exercising their functions as trustees', which could be interpreted as meaning that they could not exercise these powers for an improper purpose. Section 6(6) requires that the powers 'shall not be exercised in contravention of . . . any other enactment or any rule of law or equity'. Thus, for example, powers of investment must still be exercised in accordance with the requirements of the Trustee Act 2000. A further restriction is contained in s. 6(5), which says that in exercising their powers the trustees shall have regard to the rights of the beneficiaries. This part of the Act has given rise to some critical comment, which suggests that these duties are inherent in the role of trustee and do not need express statutory provision. There is also uncertainty about the possible effect of s. 6, and we will come back to this later (see 13.11.8).

13.6 **Delegation of trustees' functions**

13.6.1 **Power to delegate**

TOLATA 1996, s. 9 will allow trustees in appropriate cases to delegate any of their functions as trustees which relate to the land. Although elsewhere (in the main) TOLATA 1996 follows and adapts the old trust for sale system, in this respect it draws on the SLA settlement as a model, where, as we shall see in the next chapter, powers of management are in the hands of the tenant for life (generally the beneficiary currently entitled to enjoy the property).

The functions which may be delegated are those 'which relate to the land' (s. 9(1)) and in consequence the trustees cannot for example delegate their power of choosing investments for any capital money which may arise from dealing with the land. The Act specifically provides (s. 9(7)) that beneficiaries to whom trustee functions have been delegated shall not be regarded as trustees for other purposes—in particular, for the receipt of capital money.

It appears that the trustees' power of delegation cannot be excluded by the settlor. There is no provision in s. 9 for the expression of 'a contrary intent' and the power is not included in the general provisions for exclusion or restriction contained in s. 8(1).

13.6.2 **To whom may trustees delegate?**

Section 9(1) authorises delegation to:

any beneficiary or beneficiaries of full age and beneficially entitled to an interest in possession in land subject to the trust.

It is important to emphasise that in order to be eligible under this provision, the beneficiary or beneficiaries must be 'entitled to an interest in possession'. Where a trust is designed to benefit several individuals in succession (as, for example, it would be if John Brown leaves his property to his wife for life and then after her death to his two daughters), the beneficiary entitled to actual enjoyment of the property (in this example, Mrs Brown) is said to have an interest 'in possession', while the later beneficiaries merely have 'future interests'—although in due course they too will have 'interests in possession'. We will explain this further in Chapter 15, when we deal with the rules about perpetuities and accumulations, but for the moment all you need to note is that the trustees may delegate only to the beneficiary or beneficiaries who are currently entitled to enjoy the property. Thus, if John Brown's trustees were to delegate their powers, they could do so only to Mrs Brown and not to her daughters.

Because the people to whom the trustees may delegate are strictly defined in the Act, third parties dealing with a delegate (for example, buying the trust land from him) might have concerns as to whether he was a person to whom the trustees could properly delegate their powers. This is yet another case in which the Act makes specific provisions to protect the purchaser of trust land: s. 9(2) provides that in such circumstances it is to be presumed that the delegation is to a person in whose favour the power to delegate could have been exercised, unless the purchaser 'has knowledge at the time of the transfer that he was not such a person'.

Where more than one beneficiary is entitled 'in possession' the trustees may delegate to one or more of them. A delegation to several beneficiaries can be expressed to be 'joint', in which case all the delegates must agree to any exercise of power, or 'separate', in which case decisions could be taken by one delegate alone. It is also possible to delegate on terms that the power may be exercise 'jointly or separately'.

13.6.3 **Form of delegation, and its duration and revocation**

Section 9 regulates various matters relating to the delegation. It must be made by all the trustees jointly, by power of attorney, that is by an authority given by deed to act as agent. The delegation may be for any period or indefinitely, and may be expressly revoked by one or more of the trustees. Further, it is automatically revoked by the appointment of a new trustee (so that the new trustee can consider whether he wishes to delegate his functions), and also by the delegate ceasing to be a beneficiary under the trust.

13.6.4 **Liability of delegates and trustees**

As we have seen, the trustees have the powers of an absolute owner for the purpose of exercising their functions (s. 6(1)), and it is, therefore, possible for a delegate of those functions to enter into major transactions affecting the property. When we come to look at Settled Land Act settlements (Chapter 14) you will see that a beneficiary, as tenant for life, has similar wide powers of managing the trust property, but in general he has to give notice to the trustees when he proposes to exercise those powers, and in some cases actually has to obtain the trustees' consent. There are no similar requirements in respect of beneficiaries to whom powers are delegated under TOLATA 1996, s. 9 and it is, therefore, possible that delegates may act unwisely and in some way cause loss to the other beneficiaries. If something like this happens, who will be liable?

Section 9(7) of the Act provides that beneficiaries to whom functions have been delegated:

are, in relation to the exercise of the functions, in the same position as trustees (with the same duties and liabilities). . . .

This means that they would be liable for any behaviour which would constitute a breach of trust, and this potential liability may help to ensure that they act responsibly. If they fail to do so, however, and do not have the means to compensate the other beneficiaries for resulting loss, questions may well arise about the liability of the trustees, who made the delegation and thus enabled the beneficiaries to engage in these transactions.

In such a situation, the liability of the trustees was, under the original terms of the Act, surprisingly limited. Section 9(8) provided that:

where any function has been delegated to a beneficiary or beneficiaries under [s. 9(1)], the trustees are jointly and severally liable for any act or default of the beneficiary, or any of the beneficiaries, in the exercise of the function if, and only if, the trustees did not exercise reasonable care in deciding to delegate the function to the beneficiary or beneficiaries.

Thus, provided that care was exercised at the time at which the delegation was made, the trustees would not be obliged to monitor the performance of the delegate, because liability arose only for lack of reasonable care when deciding to delegate.

Section 9(8) has now been repealed and replaced by the Trustee Act 2000, which inserted a new s. 9A, dealing with both the decision to delegate and supervision after delegation. Under s. 9A(1), trustees considering delegation are subject to a duty of care, defined by the Trustee Act 2000, s. 1, as the duty of each trustee 'to exercise such care and skill as is reasonable in the circumstances', having regard to any special knowledge or experience that the trustee has (or, if a professional trustee, might be expected to have). Section 9A(2) imposes a duty on trustees who make a revocable delegation to keep that delegation under review, and if necessary to intervene by, for example, giving directions to the delegate or revoking the delegation. Section 9A(6) provides that a trustee is not liable for any act or default of the delegate, unless the trustee has failed to comply with the duty of care in making or reviewing the delegation.

13.7 **The rights of beneficiaries**

In this section we will consider only those rights which are conferred on a beneficiary by TOLATA 1996, and you will need to refer to a textbook on Trusts for a more general discussion of the rights which a beneficiary enjoys under any trust.

We have already noted the right of a beneficiary under s. 11 of the Act to be consulted by the trustees (13.5.2.2), and the privilege enjoyed under s. 9 of exercising such functions of the trustees as they may choose to delegate to beneficiaries (13.6). In addition, beneficiaries enjoy an important new statutory right, created by TOLATA 1996: the right to occupy the trust property.

13.7.1 **The right to occupy**

TOLATA 1996, s. 12(1) provides:

A beneficiary who is beneficially entitled to an interest in possession in land subject to a trust of land is entitled by reason of his interest to occupy the land at any time if at the time—

(a) the purposes of the trust include making the land available for his occupation (or for the occupation of beneficiaries of a class of which he is a member or of beneficiaries in general), or

(b) the land is held by the trustees so as to be so available.

You will note that by using the phrase 'entitled to an interest in possession' the Act limits this right to those beneficiaries who are entitled to actual enjoyment of the property and excludes those who currently have only a future interest (see 13.6.2). Thus, under the proposed trust of No. 20, only Mrs Brown would have the right to occupy the property during her lifetime, although at her death her daughters would acquire 'interests in possession' and consequently have a right to occupation.

The wording of s.12(1) gives rise to some uncertainty. As Gray and Gray put it, 'the essence of a trust "purpose" is left perilously undefined' (Gray and Gray, p. 899), and as yet there has been no judicial consideration of this provision. It may be that the phrase is intended to refer simply to the purposes expressed in the trust instrument, but, as we shall see later (13.8.4), there is a considerable body of old case law in which the courts have tried to deduce the 'purpose of the trust' from surrounding circumstances, and it could be that the words of s. 12 will be open to similar interpretation.

Meanwhile, in an express trust it will be best to state expressly whether occupation is, or is not, one of the purposes of the trust. However, even in the absence of such a provision or, it seems, even if this is said not to be a purpose, s. 12(1)(b) will allow a claim to exercise the right where the property is in fact available for occupation. Thus, if a domestic property is let to a tenant, it will not be available and the beneficiaries could not seek to occupy, but if it is empty and there is no intention to sell (for which vacant possession will be needed) or otherwise use for trust purposes, the beneficiaries will have a right to occupy. Indeed, s. 12(2) says that no right is conferred where the land is unavailable or unsuitable for occupation by the beneficiary seeking to exercise the right, which seems to recognise that in some cases the property will be suitable for use by some and not for others. An example of this situation might perhaps arise were the beneficiaries to be two couples and the property to be small (a one-bedroom flat). The premises might be suitable for couple A who have no children but not suitable for couple B, who have three small children. However, we will have to wait to see whether the courts take this practical approach or whether they would regard the problem of overcrowding as being a matter for the personal choice of the beneficiary (in some cases over-crowded premises may be better than no premises at all).

13.7.2 Exclusion or restriction of right to occupy

Section 13 of TOLATA authorises the trustees to choose which beneficiaries are to occupy the property and to impose conditions on those who do so.

13.7.2.1 *Selection by trustees*

Section 13(1) provides that where two or more beneficiaries are entitled under s. 12 to occupy the property, the trustees may select which beneficiaries shall occupy, as long as they act reasonably in making their selection (see s. 13(1) and (2)). In practice this may be the way in which the issue identified above is solved: the trustees might reasonably decide that the flat should be occupied by couple A but in order to show that they have acted reasonably in making their choice, they would probably be well advised to ensure that they consider the relative needs of the beneficiaries (as well as any other relevant factors) before making their choice.

13.7.2.2 *Imposition of restrictions*

In addition the trustees may impose reasonable restrictions on occupying beneficiaries (s. 13(3)). This will tend to mean that a set of terms for occupation will have to be drawn up and these may well draw on the sort of terms usually included in leases as a pattern. In a domestic case, one might expect conditions as to keeping the premises clean and in reasonable order, requirements to decorate from time to time, obligations not to use the premises for certain purposes, obligations to pay outgoings (see s. 13(5)) and other such terms. Trustees will have to give considerable thought to the imposition of appropriate terms, as they may be liable to other beneficiaries if they take insufficient care and there is loss to the trust as a result (for example, if the property deteriorates as a consequence).

13.7.2.3 *Compensation payments*

Section 13(6) also permits the trustees to require any occupying beneficiary to make compensation payments to other beneficiaries who are not allowed to occupy, or to forgo other payments under the trust to which they would be entitled. This allows the imposition of something resembling a partial rent for the property, in order to ensure that other parties are not disadvantaged. Of course, this provision applies only where several beneficiaries are simultaneously 'entitled in possession' and, therefore, have a right to occupy the property. John Brown can be assured that it does not mean that his widow will have to pay rent to her daughters in order to be allowed to occupy the family home!

13.7.2.4 *Protection for beneficiaries already in occupation*

There is protection for any beneficiaries who are already in occupation of the trust property, either before the trust started or because they have been allowed to occupy under the s. 12 right. Section 13(7) says that the powers of the trustees under s. 13 (including the powers to impose terms and require payments) may not be exercised so as to prevent any beneficiary from continuing to occupy or in a manner which makes it likely that he or she will cease to occupy. This protection does not apply if the occupying beneficiary consents or if the court so orders. Accordingly, it will normally be necessary to obtain a court order in order to oust a beneficiary who is already in occupation. However, note that an existing occupant cannot use his occupation to block the exercise of the trustees' other powers, including the power of sale. If he wishes to prevent sale, the consents or consultation provisions under ss. 10 and 11 may be relevant and, if need be, the powers of the court under TOLATA 1996, s. 14.

13.7.3 Significance of the statutory right of occupation

The creation of the beneficiaries' right to occupy the trust property constitutes a major change in the law. Before 1997, the only beneficiaries under settlements who had an automatic right to occupy the land were tenants for life under SLA settlements (see Chapter 14). Beneficiaries under a trust for sale had no right of occupation, unless this was expressly created by the settlor. The reason for this was that, as we have seen in Chapter 12, the doctrine of conversion operated on all trusts for sale, and in consequence the beneficiaries were regarded as having interests in the proceeds of sale, not in the land itself. It was, therefore, difficult to argue that they had any right to occupy the land and, as a result, settlors who wanted their beneficiaries to have this right had to make express provision for it when setting up the trust (as was done by Edward Green—see 13.1.2.1).

Where trusts arose by implication or were imposed by statute there was no opportunity to provide for a right of occupation and this led to particular difficulties in cases of co-ownership where statutory trusts were imposed. Where a house or flat was acquired by a couple as a family home the effect of the statutory trust was that neither of them had a right to occupy the property, and this became highly significant if the relationship broke down and one partner wanted the other to leave.

Eventually, when it became obvious that in some cases the doctrine of conversion would in effect defeat the whole point of the trust in question, the courts began to develop a new principle, that in some cases the obligation to sell could be tempered, if the property had been acquired for a purpose which required its retention and also started to accept some kinds of rights to use the property while it was unsold: see, for example, *Bull v Bull* [1955] 1 QB 234. In *Bull v Bull* the beneficiaries under a trust for sale were a mother and son, who were the co-owners of the equitable (beneficial) interest in the property. On his marriage, the son sought to prevent his mother living in the property. The court held that, while the trustees remained under an obligation to sell, until sale each beneficiary was equally entitled to occupy the premises. In this way the courts started to recognise the real position, that in truth beneficiaries were concerned in many cases with something other than the money that would result on any sale. This approach was adopted in many later cases (see further 13.8.4).

Despite these developments, the position of beneficiaries remained unsatisfactory, since the right of any particular beneficiary to occupy trust property depended entirely on the court's view of the purpose for which that property had been acquired. There was clearly a need for reform here, and several provisions of TOLATA 1996 combine to bring it about. As we shall see in Chapter 16, the trusts imposed in cases of co-ownership will in future be trusts of land, not trusts for sale, and all existing trusts for sale were converted into trusts of land on 1 January 1997. Further, s. 4(1) provides that even where a settlor expressly imposes a duty to sell on the trustees, the doctrine of conversion no longer applies, so that the trust property will continue to be regarded as land not as money.

As a result of these changes, beneficiaries under all trusts of land, however created, can be said to have interests in land. This meets the difficulty we noted earlier of how beneficiaries could seek rights in relation to the land, for example to live on it, when their interests were only in the proceeds of sale. However, the fact that a beneficiary now had an interest in land was not the end of the story; that interest was not in itself sufficient to give the beneficiary the right to occupy the property, since usually trust property should be regarded as an investment for the trust as a whole and not as something for the personal use of one or more beneficiaries. Accordingly, specific provision is made for the right to occupy by s. 12, and at last beneficiaries can look forward to the possibility of being able to occupy the trust property.

13.8 Powers of the court

In the last three sections, we have considered the trustees' duties to consult and where necessary to obtain consent, and their powers to delegate their functions and to permit beneficiaries to occupy the trust property. All this means that there could be several people involved in decisions about the management and disposal of the property, who may each have different views about what ought to be done with it.

In any case in which the trustees cannot agree or in which there is a dispute which cannot be resolved between beneficiaries or between beneficiaries and the trustees, the powers of the court under TOLATA 1996, ss. 14 and 15 may become of key importance.

13.8.1 TOLATA 1996, s. 14

Section 14(1) provides:

Any person who is a trustee of land or has an interest in property subject to a trust of land may make an application to the court for an order under this section.

Thus, applications under this section may be made not only by trustees and beneficiaries, but also by anyone else with an interest in the property, such as a mortgagee or a trustee in bankruptcy.

On an application, the court may make an order relating to the exercise by the trustees of any of their functions (including an order relieving them of the requirement to obtain consent or to consult) or declaring the nature and extent of a person's interest in the property (s. 14(2)). These are similar but wider powers than those given to the court under LPA 1925, s. 30. Under s. 14 the court could be asked to order the sale of the property or conversely to prevent its being sold, and applications could also raise questions about whether or not the trustees should delegate their powers or allow the occupation of the property by beneficiaries.

13.8.2 **TOLATA 1996, s. 15**

Section 15 provides guidance for the court on matters it must consider when determining an application. Section 15(1) reads:

The matters to which the court is to have regard in determining an application for an order under section 14 include—

(a) the intention of the person or persons (if any) who created the trust,

(b) the purposes for which the property subject to the trust is held,

(c) the welfare of any minor who occupies or might reasonably be expected to occupy any land subject to the trust as his home, and

(d) the interests of any secured creditor of any beneficiary.

This provision gives statutory force to various criteria developed by the courts in dealing with applications for sale under LPA 1925, s. 30 (see 13.8.4).

You will see that paragraphs (a) and (b) emphasise the increased importance of indicating any underlying intention or purpose when an express trust is created, since this will have an important effect should an order under s. 14 be sought.

Section 15(1)(c) is a recognition of the importance of having regard to the needs of children, who may be the persons who are most affected by any exercise of the trustees' powers but who may themselves have no interest in the trust property. The inclusion of this provision is a recognition of the increased importance of trusts relating to land in modern family circumstances.

Section 15(1)(d) recognises the needs of creditors, in order to ensure that they also are properly considered when any decision is made (frequently sale of property is sought by mortgagees who have not been paid).

You should note that while the court is required to have regard to the matters specified in s. 15(1), it may also take other relevant matters into account (for example, the health of one of the parties—*Bank of Ireland Home Mortgages Ltd* v *Bell* [2001] 2 FLR 809), and also that s. 15(1) gives no guidance on the relative weight to be given to each of the factors mentioned. These issues will be for the court to determine in each case and an example of this is to be found in *Mortgage Corporation* v *Shaire* [2001] Ch 743, which we consider below.

As well as considering the matters mentioned in s. 14(1), the court is required to consider the needs and preferences of the beneficiaries. Where an application relates to the exercise of the powers under s. 13 (the exclusion or restriction of the right to occupy), the court is required by s. 15(2) to have regard to the circumstances and wishes of each of the beneficiaries who would be entitled to occupy the land under s. 12, including any who would be entitled to occupy were it not for a previous decision to allow another beneficiary to occupy.

In the case of the exercise of powers other than the s. 13 powers, however, the relevant provision (in addition to s. 15(1)) is s. 15(3), which requires the court to have regard to the wishes of any beneficiary who is of full age and who is entitled to an interest in possession or, where the beneficiaries disagree, to the wishes of the majority of the beneficiaries by value. This requirement in s. 15(3) mirrors the duty placed upon the trustees to consult beneficiaries and have regard to their wishes (s. 11).

Application by a trustee in bankruptcy ss. 14 and 15 do not apply in cases in which application is made by a trustee in bankruptcy. In those cases the approach is governed by the rules under the Insolvency Act 1986, s. 335A, which is a new provision inserted by TOLATA 1996, Sch. 3, para. 23. This reflects the other provisions of the Insolvency Act 1986, which are designed to provide some short-term protection for the spouse and children of a bankrupt but nonetheless to ensure that creditors are able to realise the bankrupt's assets within a reasonable period, in order to have their debts paid. Accordingly, the new s. 335A requires the court to have regard to the conduct of a spouse (or former spouse) in relation to the bankruptcy (essentially, whether the spouse was a party to any fault), the needs of a spouse (or former spouse) and the needs of any children, alongside the interests of the creditors. However, after one year, unless the circumstances are exceptional, the court is instructed to assume that the interests of the creditors are paramount.

13.8.3 How will these new provisions work in practice?

The brief explanation of the rules in ss. 14 and 15 given above cannot really indicate the likely approach of the courts to applying their new wider powers. A further unanswered question relates to the extent to which the courts are likely to be guided by decisions interpreting the earlier provisions contained in LPA 1925, s. 30. So far, there are just two decisions which throw some light on the matter: *Mortgage Corporation* v *Shaire* [2001] Ch 743, and *Bank of Ireland Home Mortgages Ltd* v *Bell* [2001] 2 FLR 809.

13.8.3.1 Mortgage Corporation *v* Shaire *[2001] Ch 743*

Taken as a whole, the facts in this case are complicated, but the particular point with which we are concerned can be dealt with separately and the facts which it involves are relatively simple. Mrs Shaire and her unmarried partner were the legal owners of their house, which they held on the statutory trusts imposed in cases of co-ownership (originally a trust for sale, converted into a trust of land by TOLATA 1996 on 1 January 1997). For reasons we need not explain, Mrs Shaire was held to be entitled to 75 per cent of the value of the property, while her partner was entitled to the remaining 25 per cent. After his death, it was discovered that he had mortgaged the property to secure a large loan, having forged Mrs Shaire's signature on the documents creating a charge by way of legal mortgage. The mortgage repayments were in arrears and in order to enforce its security the chargee sought an order for sale under TOLATA 1996, s. 14.

The court accepted that Mrs Shaire was not responsible for what had happened, and in consequence her share in the property was held not to be subject to the mortgage. The chargee was, however, entitled to the 25 per cent share in the property which had belonged to the deceased, and it could recover this only if the property was sold. However, Mrs Shaire wanted to remain in the property, in which she had lived since 1976, and so opposed the application for an order for sale.

In dealing with the question of whether to order sale, Neuberger J began by considering the position on the old law before the Act. There was clear authority (*Re Citro* [1991] Ch 142) that, save in exceptional cases, sale would be ordered on any application by a trustee in bankruptcy and that a similar approach was adopted in dealing with applications by mortgagees or chargees ((*Lloyds Bank plc v Byrne & Byrne* [1993] 1 FLR 369). As we have seen, this approach in cases of bankruptcy is now given statutory force by the new s. 335A added to the Insolvency Act 1986 by TOLATA 1996. Should applications by chargees continue to be treated in the same way, or had the 1996 Act changed the law?

In the view of Neuberger J, the law on this point has been changed by s. 15 and it was no longer necessary to apply the same approach to applications by chargees as one would to those by trustees in bankruptcy. Among the reasons given for this view was the fact that 'the interests of the secured creditor' is just one of four factors to be taken into account under s. 15(1) and there is no suggestion that it is to be given any more importance than the interests of the children living in the house (p. 758). Further (at p. 760) the judge thought it not unlikely that:

the legislature intended to relax the fetters on the way in which the court exercised its discretion . . . so as to tip the balance somewhat more in favour of families and against banks and other chargees. Although the law under s. 30 was clear following *Citro* and *Byrne*, there were indications of judicial dissatisfaction with the state of the law at that time.

In the judge's opinion, s. 15 had changed the law and the court now had greater flexibility in dealing with applications of this sort. In doing so it must take account of the factors set out in s. 15(1) and the circumstances and wishes of the beneficiaries under s. 15(3). In addition, there might be other factors in a particular case which the court could or should take into account. Once the relevant factors to be taken into account had been identified, it was a matter for the court as to what weight to give to each factor in a particular case.

The decision in *Shaire* can be seen as an authority on the very specific point of the relative positions of a chargee and a trustee on bankruptcy on applications under s. 15(1). There were, however, a number of more general observations in the judgment which we ought to note. In particular, the judge commented (at p. 758) on the change of emphasis resulting from the replacement of the statutory trust for sale by the trust of land:

. . . the very name 'trust for sale' and the law as it has been developed by the courts suggests that under the old law, in the absence of a strong reason to the contrary, the court should order sale. Nothing in the language of the new code as found in the 1996 Act supports that approach.

The judge also considered the extent to which the case law which grew up around s. 30, LPA 1925, may be relevant in interpreting ss. 14 and 15 of the new Act. An earlier County Court decision, *TSB Bank plc v Marshall* [1998] 3 EGLR 100 considered that the old case law remained relevant in interpreting the new provisions (thus confirming the view advanced by the Law Commission when the legislation was prepared). However, this led the judge, on facts very similar to those in *Shaire*, to apply the old rules in *Citro* and *Byrne*—which as we have just seen, were thought in the later case to be no longer applicable to chargees. Neuberger J accordingly disagreed with the conclusions reached in *TSB Bank v Marshall*, and (at p. 761) expressed a more measured view on the extent to which old authorities would be of assistance in interpreting the new Act:

On the one hand, to throw over all the wealth of learning and thought given by so many eminent judges to the problem. . . . seems somewhat arrogant and possibly rash. On the other hand, where one has concluded that the law has changed in a significant respect so that the court's discretion is significantly less fettered than it was, there are obvious dangers in relying on authorities which proceeded on the basis that the court's discretion was more fettered than it now is. I think it would be wrong to throw over all the earlier cases without paying them any regard. However, they have to be treated with caution, in light of the change in the law, and in many cases they are unlikely to be of great, let alone decisive, assistance.

In case you are wondering what happened to Mrs Shaire, we will mention the outcome of the case briefly, although the way in which the judge exercised his discretion on the particular facts is of less general interest than the earlier part of his judgment. Having taken into account the various factors noted above, he concluded that the interest of the chargee in realising his security outweighed Mrs Shaire's wish to remain in her home, particularly given her ability to buy another house with her share of the proceeds. He indicated, therefore, that he was minded to order sale, unless Mrs Shaire found herself able to take on the amount owed to the chargee as an additional loan on which she would pay interest. He, therefore, postponed making an order so as to give the parties time to consider their positions—and the report is silent as to what happened next.

While the decision between the parties in *Shaire* gave adequate protection to the mortgagee's interest, Neuberger J's view of the radical changes introduced by ss. 14 and 15 were seen by some commentators as likely to cause anxiety and concern among professional lenders. As Pascoe put it ([2000] 64 Conv 315 at 327):

Neuberger J's approach is not one of consolidation and rationalisation; rather he is wiping the slate clean and starting afresh with secured creditors the likely casualties of the new approach. It will be a welcome change in the law for spouses, partners and children living in the property, but an inexpedient, prejudicial and financially detrimental development if one is a secured creditor.

However, a somewhat more conservative approach has more recently been adopted by the Court of Appeal in *Bank of Ireland Home Mortgages Ltd* v *Bell* [2001] 2 FLR 809.

13.8.3.2 Bank of Ireland Home Mortgages Ltd *v* Bell *[2001] 2 FLR 809*

In outline, the facts of this case were similar to those in *Shaire*. Mr and Mrs Bell were the legal owners of a house bought with a loan secured by a mortgage of the property, on which repayments were in arrears, the marriage having broken down. On an application by the mortgagees for an order for sale under s. 14, the trial judge accepted the wife's claim that her husband had forged her signature on the relevant mortgage documents, and in consequence held that the mortgage operated only as an equitable charge over his beneficial interest in the property. Although the wife's interest in the property was relatively small (10 per cent at most), the judge refused to order sale. In doing so, he took into account the fact that the property was purchased as a family home and was currently occupied by Mrs Bell and her son, who at that stage was still under age. He also took into account the fact that Mrs Bell was in poor health.

On appeal by the lender, the Court of Appeal reversed the decision below and ordered sale, holding that the trial judge had erred in exercising his discretion under s. 15. The matters to which he had given weight in reaching his decision should either not have been regarded or deserved only slight consideration. The acquisition of the property as a family home and its continued occupation by the wife, on which the trial judge had relied, had ceased to be relevant considerations under s. 15(1)(a) and (b) with the departure of the husband on the break-down of the marriage. The occupation by the son might be relevant under s. 15(1)(c), but at the time of the trial he was not far from the age of majority, and his welfare 'should only have been a very slight consideration' (*per* Peter Gibson LJ at p. 816). The court agreed that the judge could properly have regard to the wife's poor health, but considered that this would be a reason for postponing sale rather than for refusing to order it.

By contrast, the trial judge had not mentioned the matter which the Court of Appeal regarded as most significant: that the debt had now grown to more than £300,000, more than the value of the house, and was increasing daily. Peter Gibson LJ commented (at p. 816) that before 1996 the creditors' interest would prevail over the spouse and family of the debtor save in exceptional circumstances, and went on to say:

The 1996 Act, by requiring the court to have regard to the particular matters specified in s. 15, appears to me to have given scope for some change in the court's practice. Nevertheless, a powerful consideration is and ought to be whether the creditor is receiving proper recompense for being kept out of his money, repayment of which is overdue.

By refusing to order sale the judge had condemned the bank to go on waiting for its money with no prospect of recovery from the Bells, and that seemed to the judge to be very unfair to the bank. The other two members of the Court of Appeal agreed with this approach, and sale of the property was ordered.

As far as the actual outcome for the parties is concerned, there is no significant difference between the decisions in *Shaire* and in *Bell*, the respective courts being willing to order sale in both cases. However, as we have seen, there is a considerable difference in the views expressed about the overall effect of s. 15, Neuberger J treating it as producing a significant change in the law, and Peter Gibson LJ seeing it as giving 'some scope for change in the court's practice'. The Court of Appeal made only a brief reference to *Shaire* (see p. 816), citing it as an example of the importance of giving due weight to the interests of the creditor, but it certainly appears from the judgments that Neuberger J's radical approach is not shared by the higher court.

13.8.4 Doctrine of continuing purpose

Before leaving our consideration of s. 15(1), we must consider the provision of s. 15(1)(b) that the matters to which the court is to have regard include—

the purposes for which the property subject to the trust is held.

This is reminiscent of a case law development associated with LPA 1925, s. 30 which came to be known as 'the doctrine of continuing purpose'. It seems to have developed as a way of circumventing the duty to sell imposed by the trust for sale, and was of particular importance in co-ownership cases where land was held on the statutory trust for sale and one owner wanted to sell while the other did not.

An early illustration of its use is to be found in *Re Buchanan-Wollaston's Conveyance* [1939] Ch 738. There a group of neighbours had jointly bought a piece of land adjoining their properties with the intention of keeping it as an open space and thereby preventing further building. Later one neighbour sold his house and wished also to realise the money he had tied up in the open land. His application for an order for sale of the co-owned property was rejected on the ground that the land had been bought for a particular purpose and that purpose was still being satisfied by the retention of the property.

Other examples of the idea of the continuing purpose were found in cases about the matrimonial home. In *Jones* v *Challenger* [1961] 1 QB 176, a husband and wife jointly acquired leasehold premises as a matrimonial home. After divorce proceedings the wife sought an order for sale. The court granted the order because the purpose for which the property was bought had ended on divorce. The outcome could, however, be different in a case where there were children, and a home was still being provided for one partner and the children. In *Rawlings* v *Rawlings* [1964] P 398 Salmon LJ indicated that in such cases an order for sale should be delayed until the children 'are grown up'. Today such disputes in the case of married couples would normally be resolved by the courts as part of divorce proceedings but similar considerations could still arise in the case of other co-owners, such as unmarried couples or family members.

We shall have to wait and see the extent to which decisions on 'continuing purpose' will be relied upon by the courts in applying s. 15(1)(b), but the inclusion of this reference to purpose certainly emphasises the importance of indicating any underlying intention or purpose when an express trust is created.

13.9 Protection of purchasers

13.9.1 Introduction

As we saw in 13.1.2, the Thornes are thinking of buying 9 Trant Way which, under the will of Edward Green, is held by trustees for his widow for life and then for his nephew. The Thornes find this arrangement rather worrying. They do not know the details of the trust, but are just concerned that in some way buying from trustees may have some hidden pitfalls.

It is certainly true that many years ago, there were considerable dangers in buying trust property. We explained earlier (1.7.2) the general principle that if trustees sold property which was subject to a trust the purchaser would take the property subject to the rights of the beneficiaries if he knew (or ought to have known) of them. The purchaser in such a case, on acquiring the property, became no more than a trustee and held the property for the beneficiaries. However, during the nineteenth century, as land ownership became less and less static and as trust land became subject to sale rather more frequently (even land held subject to strict settlements) it became necessary to change this approach in some way, as otherwise no purchaser would ever have been prepared to purchase trust property unless all the beneficiaries had expressly agreed to release their rights. Accordingly, a series of statutes, culminating in the 1925 legislation, established a process of 'overreaching' the rights of beneficiaries, where a transaction is conducted in a manner that provides sufficient safeguards for their interests.

We have already explained how overreaching works (4.5.2.1) and you will remember that it is a process by which, provided the proper procedures are followed, the beneficiaries' interests are lifted from the existing trust property and attached instead to the money paid by the purchaser, and in due course to any property in which the trustees may invest that money. Where overreaching operates, the purchaser will acquire the property free of the interests of the beneficiaries, even if he knows of those interests. We will consider the overreaching process in more detail below, but before doing so must note various provisions in TOLATA 1996 which are designed to protect the purchaser.

13.9.2 Protection of purchaser by TOLATA 1996

We have already mentioned that TOLATA 1996 continues the provisions of LPA 1925 designed to ensure that the purchaser can buy trust property without having to make lengthy enquiries as to whether the trustees have secured consents, consulted the beneficiaries and exercised their powers of delegation appropriately. Section 16 contains a range of provisions which save the purchaser from having to make these enquiries, and also protect him from the consequences of any breach of duty by the trustees, such as failing to act in the interests of the beneficiaries or making dispositions which contravene restrictions on their powers.

Section 16 applies only to purchasers of unregistered land (see s. 16(7)), because it is assumed that a purchaser of registered land will discover from the register any restrictions in relation to dispositions of the land and thus be warned of the need to comply with them. Normally, where there is a trust of registered land, a restriction will have been entered on the register requiring any capital moneys to be paid to two trustees before any disposition can be registered. There has been some academic debate about the consequences of excluding registered land from the protection given by s. 16, and we will return to this point later (13.11.8).

13.9.3 Operation of overreaching

13.9.3.1 *Statutory rules*

The statutory provisions which govern overreaching in relation to a trust of land are contained in LPA 1925, s. 2(1)(ii) and s. 27, as amended by TOLATA 1996, Sch. 3, para. 4(1). The provisions apply to both registered and unregistered land. In order to be protected, the purchaser must ensure that the capital money (purchase price or other capital sum arising on the transaction, such as a mortgage advance or the premium paid on the grant of a lease) is paid to not fewer than two trustees or to a trust corporation. The money must not be paid to the beneficiaries (unless they also happen to be the trustees and even then it will be usual to require a receipt from them in their capacity as trustees). It is for this reason that TA 1925 s. 39 seeks to ensure that there are never fewer than two trustees unless the trustee is a trust corporation. If a trust has, for some reason, only one trustee for the time being, a purchaser should insist on the appointment of a second trustee before he pays over any purchase money.

The importance of the second trustee is well illustrated by the two cases of *Williams & Glyn's Bank Ltd* v *Boland* [1981] AC 487 and *City of London Building Society* v *Flegg* [1988] AC 54, which we have already discussed in the context of registered land (see 5.10.4.4 and 5.10.4.5(1)). In the *Boland* case, capital money (in the form of a secured loan from the bank) was paid to the sole registered proprietor, with the result that Mrs Boland's equitable rights were not overreached, so that the mortgagee took subject to her interest in the property. By contrast, in *Flegg* the mortgage advance was made to the two registered proprietors, who held as trustees for themselves and the Fleggs, and in consequence the Fleggs' interest was overreached. As a result, they no longer had an interest in the land which could be asserted against the mortgagee, but only an interest in the purchase money in the hands of the trustees. Theoretically, beneficiaries in this situation are protected by their rights against the capital money, but in practice, of course, this may be illusory. In *Flegg*, the money had been applied for the trustees' own purposes, and although they might be liable to the beneficiaries for breach of trust any judgment against them would be worthless if they did not have the financial means to meet it.

We must emphasise that the position would have been different if the trustees had actually exceeded their powers, for it appears that ultra vires transactions (i.e., transactions outside the trustees' powers) do not overreach the beneficiaries' interests (*State Bank of India* v *Sood* 1997 Ch 276 at p. 281). However, in *Flegg* the House of Lords took the view that the transaction in question was within the powers of the trustees, even if it was in breach of trust.

13.9.3.2 *Effect of non-compliance with requirements for overreaching*

The Law of Property Act 1925 does not say what the position would be were a purchaser not to comply with s. 27. Accordingly, one must in such a case consider the ordinary rules which determine whether a purchaser is bound by an equitable interest in land. Normally, he will take free of such interests in unregistered land where he is a bona fide purchaser for value without notice. Therefore it is possible to obtain a legal estate free of the beneficial interests, even where capital money is not paid to two trustees (*Caunce* v *Caunce* [1969] 1 WLR 286) although only if the purchaser can avoid the rigours of actual, constructive and imputed notice (see 1.7.3).

In registered land normally the purchaser will be aware of the trust and the rights of the beneficiaries because a restriction will have been entered on the register. Accordingly, the purchaser would be warned to insist on the appointment of a second trustee for his own protection. Under LRA 1925 interests of the beneficiaries which had not been protected by such an entry might nevertheless be protected under s. 70(1)(g), if those entitled were in actual occupation of the land, as was the case in *Williams & Glyn's Bank Ltd* v *Boland* [1981] AC 487. Under LRA 2002 such interests would also override a registered disposition, provided they satisfied the more restrictive requirements of Sch. 3, para. 2. However, if money is paid to *two* legal owners, the overreaching provisions operate to overreach even an overriding interest as happened in *City of London Building Society* v *Flegg* [1988] AC 54, and more recently in *Birmingham Midshires Mortgage Services Ltd* v *Sabherwal* (2000) 80 P&CR 256 (considered further in 13.11.8 and 18.6).

13.9.3.3 *Overreaching outside the Act?*

Interestingly, a slightly different problem arose in *State Bank of India* v *Sood* [1997] Ch 276, in which the issue was whether overreaching can only take place under

s. 27 or whether there are other occasions upon which beneficial interests can be overreached. The issue arose in this case because there had been no payment of capital moneys at the time of the disposition in question. The case involved a dwelling that was registered in the names of the first and second defendants but which was held on trust by them for themselves and for the third to seventh defendants. All seven defendants occupied the premises and thus the beneficial interests under the trust were overriding interests under LRA 1925, s.70(1)(g) in relation to later dispositions. The disposition in question was a mortgage of the premises to the bank. Normally, a mortgage will give rise to a mortgage advance and that advance would constitute capital money (that was the case in *Flegg*) but in this instance the trustees mortgaged the property as security for the discharge of their existing debts and the existing debts of a company with which they were concerned and for any future indebtedness of the trustees or the company. No actual moneys were advanced at the time the mortgage was granted. Later, one of the trustees was made bankrupt and the bank tried to enforce its security, relying on the principle set out in *Flegg* that where overreaching occurred it was irrelevant that the beneficial interests were overriding interests under the LRA 1925, s. 70. The problem was that the bank could not rely on LPA 1925, s. 27 because no capital money had been paid. Nonetheless, the Court of Appeal held that in this case the interests of the beneficiaries had been overreached, saying that s. 27(2) was relevant only where capital money actually arose and that it did not mean that there could be no overreaching without capital money. In reaching this conclusion Peter Gibson LJ adopted the analysis of the position set out in Charles Harpum's article 'Overreaching trustees' powers and the reform of the 1925 legislation' [1990] CLJ 277 that

the exercise *intra vires* of a power of disposition which does not give rise to any capital money, such as an exchange of land, overreaches just as much as a transaction which does.

The case clearly establishes that the courts will consider whether other overreaching events have arisen. You may like to note that Peter Gibson LJ's judgment also provides a useful analysis of the overreaching provisions in the LPA 1925. (Also see Oldham, 'Overreaching where no capital monies arise' [1997] CLJ 494.)

13.9.4 **Need for a deed of discharge**

To complete our consideration of the ways in which a purchaser is protected, we must also consider what a prospective purchaser should do if the vendor tells him that the trust of land has already come to an end and he does not, therefore, need to pay the purchase price to two trustees. In this case the purchaser should still insist on paying to two trustees, because under TOLATA 1996, s. 17, any trust will continue to apply to the proceeds of sale, *unless* a deed of discharge vesting the property in a beneficiary can be produced (see TOLATA 1996, s. 16(4) and (5)).

13.9.5 **Trusts of the proceeds of sale of land**

Finally, though it does not concern the purchaser, you may be wondering what happens to the proceeds of sale when they have been paid to the trustees and the rights of the beneficiaries have been overreached. This depends on the terms of the trust. It may be that the capital money is to be paid over to a sole beneficiary or divided between several beneficiaries. On the other hand, if the trust is to continue, the trustees could invest in any authorised investments, and their power to do so would include the purchase of any estate in land for any purpose (ss. 17(1) and 6(3), TOLATA 1996). Of course, where this power is exercised the trustees will again hold land and this will give rise to a fresh trust of land. These rules do not, however, apply to the proceeds of sale of settled land (s. 17(5)): such moneys remain subject to the SLA 1925 rules. Obviously, as new strict settlements will in future only arise in very restricted circumstances, this rule will decline in importance over the years as settlements come to an end.

13.10 When will a trust of land arise?

In this chapter so far, we have been describing the main provisions of Part I of TOLATA 1996, setting them where necessary in the context of the *express trust* which John Brown may wish to create in his will. However, as we noted in Chapter 12, trusts may not only be expressly created but may arise by implication in certain circumstances (resulting and constructive trusts) and also may be imposed by statute, as for example in cases of co-ownership of land.

With the exception of existing Settled Land Act settlements, all trusts consisting of or including land now take effect as trusts of land, and are subject to the provisions of TOLATA 1996. In this section, we will look at:

(i)   the way in which the Act replaces Settled Land Act settlements for the future;

(ii) the position of those trusts for sale which were in existence when TOLATA 1996 took effect and were converted by it into trusts of land; and

(iii) a situation in which a trust will *not* arise, despite the intentions of the grantor.

13.10.1 Trusts of land in place of new Settled Land Act settlements

Settled Land Act settlements in existence at 1 January 1997 continue in operation (subject to an exception in respect of land held on charitable, ecclesiastical or public trusts—s. 2(5)), and are considered in detail in the next chapter. Section 2(1) of the 1996 Act provides that after the commencement of the Act, no new SLA settlement may be created.

Dispositions which would have created such settlements will in future take effect as trusts of land, and we must now consider how the Act accomplishes this.

13.10.1.1 *Successive interests in land*

TOLATA 1996 contains no specific provisions as to how dispositions creating successive interests (for example, 'to A for life, and then to B'), which would have created a SLA settlement, are to take effect as trusts of land, but leaves this to be deduced from general principles. You may remember from Chapter 7 that as a result of LPA 1925, s. 1(1) a disposition creating successive interests in land can take effect only in equity. As a result, such a disposition can operate only through the mechanism of a trust, and under s. 1(1) of TOLATA 1996 any such trust will now take effect as a trust of land.

13.10.1.2 *Imposition of a trust in certain cases which would formerly give rise to a SLA settlement*

Section 2(6) and Sch. 1 of TOLATA 1996 make provision for several cases which in the past would have fallen within SLA 1925, s. 1 (see further, 14.2). Specific provision is needed in these circumstances because in themselves they do not give rise to trusts. By imposing a trust in each case, Sch. 1 brings them within the ambit of TOLATA, s. 1(1), so that in future they will take effect as trusts of land.

(1) *Conveyance to a minor or minors (that is, to a person or persons aged under 18)* The 1925 legislation introduced the rule that a minor cannot hold a legal estate in land. Attempts to convey such an estate to a minor operated as a contract to create a SLA settlement, and until this was done the person making the conveyance held the estate on trust for the minor. Where a conveyance was made to an adult and a minor, the adult held the legal estate on a trust for sale for himself and the minor.

The relevant provisions of the 1925 legislation are repealed by TOLATA 1996 and replaced by Sch. 1, para. 1. Para. 1(1) provides that a purported conveyance (and this will include LRA transfers) to a minor or a group of minors operates instead as a declaration of trust. Thus, in such a case, a minor can only become a beneficial (equitable) owner. The legal estate will have to be vested in an adult or adults as trustee(s).

Where a legal estate is conveyed to a minor or minors *and* an adult or adults, para. 1(2) provides that that estate will vest in the adult(s) upon trust for the minor(s) and the adults in question.

Paragraph 2 provides a 'catch all' provision, that ensures that any other event which would otherwise vest a legal estate in a minor is to take effect as a trust in favour of the minor.

(2) *Charges 'by way of family arrangement'* We mentioned in Chapter 12, when explaining some of the background history to trusts, that sometimes in the past a large landowner would use a trust (usually but not always a SLA settlement) to ensure that a single heir inherited but that the estate was charged with payments to a widow or other children. Although less common today, this practice does still continue in some cases and this sort of arrangement is now caught by para. 3 of Sch. 1 to TOLATA 1996. This covers charges 'by way of family arrangement' of an estate with the payment of rentcharges or other capital, periodic or other sums. In such a case the land becomes subject to a trust of land and is held on trust for the purpose of giving effect to the charge. Thus, were F to vest his legal estate in S (F's eldest son) but subject to the payment by S of periodic payments to S's mother and his younger brothers and sisters, this arrangement would create a trust of land. Usually such arrangements would be created by will but there is nothing to stop the disposition being made in F's lifetime and, either way, the disposition would have the same effect.

(3) *Attempt to create an entailed interest* As we saw in 1.2.4.1, an entailed interest (formerly known as a fee tail) was created by a disposition in favour of 'the heirs of the body' of a specified person. If the holder of such an interest had no lineal

descendants, the interest came to an end at his death and the property reverted to the donor or his successors, who were said to have a 'reversion' in it. In modern times, this succession of interests took effect as a SLA settlement (see further 12.2.1 and 14.2.2).

This form of settlement was regarded as inappropriate in modern law and under TOLATA 1996 it is no longer possible to create an entailed interest. Schedule 1, para. 5(1) provides that a purported grant of an entailed interest does not create that interest but instead takes effect as a declaration that the property is held in trust absolutely for the intended grantee. If a settlor purports to create an entailed interest in himself, the whole disposition is ineffective (para. 5(2)). Thus, it is that no new entailed interests can be created. They were already quite rare and in time any existing interests of this sort will die out.

(4) *Charitable, ecclesiastical and public trusts*   Paragraph 4 of Sch. 1 covers certain charitable, ecclesiastical and public trusts and ensures that they also operate as trusts of land.

(5) *Property held on settlement which has ceased to exist*   Paragraph 6 deals with property which becomes subject to a SLA settlement after the SLA settlement in question has already ceased to exist because there remained no relevant property subject to the trust. If new land is later acquired by the trust, this will not revive the SLA settlement: the new land will be held instead on a trust of land under the TOLATA 1996 provisions.

13.10.2 Trusts for sale take effect as trusts of land

13.10.2.1 *Trusts for sale created on or after 1 January 1997*

Section 1(2)(a) of TOLATA 1996 specifically provides that trusts of sale are included within the statutory definition of the new trust of land as 'any trust of property which consists of or includes land'. Thus, although a settlor may still create a trust for sale, in the sense that he imposes a duty on the trustees to sell the property, the trust will be categorised as 'a trust of land' and will operate within the framework provided by TOLATA 1996. In particular, the trustees will automatically have the implied power to postpone sale which is given by s. 4(1) and, as we have already seen, that power cannot be excluded by the settlor.

Further, s. 3(1) provides that:

Where land is held by trustees subject to a trust for sale, the land is not to be regarded as personal property . . .

In other words, the land is not to be regarded as converted into money (a type of personal property—see 1.9), and this means that the doctrine of conversion is no longer brought into operation by the trustees' duty to sell the trust property. You should note, however, that despite the marginal note to s. 3 ('Abolition of doctrine of conversion') notional conversion continues to apply in other circumstances where there is a specifically enforceable obligation to convert land into money, or vice versa—as for example under a contract to buy or sell land.

13.10.2.2 *Trusts for sale created before 1 January 1997*

Existing trusts for sale were converted into trusts of land as a consequence of

s. 1(2)(b), which makes it quite clear that the statute catches trusts created or arising before the commencement of TOLATA 1996. Thus, at the first moment of 1 January 1997, the trust for sale which Edward Green created in respect of 9 Trant Way was converted into a trust of land, as were many thousands of other trusts throughout England and Wales, including all those relating to co-owned land (see Chapter 16).

In general, these existing trusts became subject to the statutory rules applicable to trusts of land, so that for example trustees acquired the power to delegate to beneficiaries and to postpone sale (even where that power had been excluded expressly by the settlor), while beneficiaries acquired the right to occupy the property. Moreover, the doctrine of conversion ceased to apply to some of these trusts for sale.

There were, however, a few changes which the Act did not apply to existing trusts for sale. In particular, as we have already noted (13.5.2.2), the trustees' duty to consult the beneficiaries does not apply to trusts created by wills or dispositions which had effect before 1 January 1997 (s. 11(2)(b)), and so does not apply to Mrs Green's trust. In addition, the doctrine of conversion continues to apply to trusts created by will where the testator had died before the Act came into force, and thus continues to apply to the trust of 9 Trant Way.

In general, however, trusts for sale in existence when TOLATA came into force operate completely as trusts of land and are subject to all the standard rules. Nevertheless, it is worth remembering that many of the changes introduced by the Act are based on provisions which, in practice, were often expressly incorporated in trust instruments, so that in many trusts for sale there was no significant change overnight in the position of individual trustees and beneficiaries. An example of this is to be found in the trust created over 9 Trant Way. If you look back at the will of Edward Green (13.1.2.1), you will see that it included express requirements for the trustees to allow Mrs Green to reside in the house which formed part of the trust property, to sell the land on her request, to apply the proceeds in purchasing a new house 'selected by her' and to hold the new house on the same trusts as the old. These provisions had the effect (among other things) of making it clear that a house could be purchased otherwise than simply as an investment, something which, without express provision, was not within the trustees' powers at that time. There is, of course, now specific provision for this in TOLATA 1996 (s. 6(4)(b)), along with the beneficiary's right to occupy the trust property.

13.10.3 **Statutory trusts become trusts of land**

Section 5(1) and Sch. 2 of TOLATA 1996 amend the various statutory provisions which impose trusts in certain circumstances, so as to provide that the trust imposed is a trust of land and not, as formerly, a trust for sale. Existing statutory trusts for sale, which had been imposed in, for example, cases of co-ownership and on intestacy, were converted into trusts of land on 1 January 1997 by s. 1 of the Act.

13.10.4 **A situation in which a trust will not arise**

SLA settlements tended in more recent years to arise most frequently when created by accident; a common cause being badly drafted (often 'home-made') wills. An example might be a disposition worded, 'to my wife and after she dies to be divided between the children'. Accordingly, a limited amendment to the law was made by s. 22 of the Administration of Justice Act 1982. The effect of this provision would be to transform the example given above into an *absolute* gift to the widow, thus avoiding the expense and complexity of a SLA settlement. This deprives the children of any interest but this may not matter too greatly, as normally they will obtain an interest in the property on their mother's death, unless she has exhausted the property or left it by will to others. Because s. 22 creates an absolute gift to the spouse, whatever the form of trust the testator attempts to create, the provision continues to be relevant even after the reforms made by TOLATA 1996.

Section 22 is very limited in effect, however, and only applies where the testator first purports to give an absolute gift to his or her spouse but later, by the same instrument, purports to give an interest in the property to his or her issue. Thus the provision does not apply to an *inter vivos* gift nor to gifts to persons other than the testator's spouse. Nor will s. 22 apply if the gift in remainder is to someone who does not fall into the class of the testator's issue. Due to these restrictions of s. 22 the following dispositions in the past still created SLA settlements and would now create a trust of land:

(a) a disposition *inter vivos* 'to my wife and then on her death to our children';

(b) a devise (disposition by will) 'to my sister and then when she dies to my children';

(c) a devise 'to my husband and then on his death to my friend X'; and

(d) a devise: 'I give my wife my house for her lifetime but when she dies it is to be divided between our children'. (This is not a devise in terms which would give the widow an absolute interest were the children not mentioned.)

Accordingly, s. 22 reduces the cases in which trusts can be created accidentally but does not prevent such cases altogether.

13.11 Comparison of old and new law

In this section, we will try to compare the rules about the new trust of land introduced by TOLATA 1996 with the two different sets of rules which used to apply to trusts for sale and settlements under the SLA 1925. We will take this opportunity to tell you a little more about the rules which governed trusts for sale: although such rules no longer apply, you still need some knowledge of them in order to understand old reported decisions and the drafting of old trusts. In future you may also need to check that any trust which existed as a trust for sale prior to 1997 was correctly created and managed under the old law, since its validity as a trust of land today and the effect of past transactions with the trust property may depend on this. The SLA 1925 rules are, of course, still in operation, governing existing settlements, and we will deal with these in more detail in Chapter 14.

As you have probably noticed already when reading this chapter, some of the changes introduced by TOLATA 1996 are completely new, while others are based on past good practice in drafting express trusts. Thus, certain provisions which in the past had to be specifically included by the settlor are now implied into every trust of land, unless expressly excluded.

13.11.1 **All trusts relating to land take effect as trusts of land and are subject to the same rules**

With the exception of SLA settlements created before 1 January 1997, all trusts relating to land now operate as trusts of land, subject to the rules of TOLATA 1996. The new trust includes:

— all expressly created trusts, whether they be for one beneficiary (a bare trust) or for several beneficiaries in succession (creating a settlement) or concurrently, and whether or not they impose a duty to sell on the trustees;
— all implied trusts, whether resulting or constructive; and
— all trusts imposed by statute—as in cases of co-ownership or on intestacy.

This contrasts with the position before the Act, when a variety of rules governed trusts involving land, and in a few cases (such as a bare trust) there was some uncertainty about which rules applied.

13.11.2 **Only one way of making a settlement**

Where a land owner wishes to create a settlement, he no longer has to worry about the choice between trusts for sale and SLA settlements: if he wishes to create successive interests in land, the only way now in which this can be done is by means of a trust of land. It is true that existing SLA settlements remain in existence, but they will gradually come to an end with process of time, and no new ones may be created.

13.11.3 **Formalities for creation**

Creation of a *SLA settlement* is dealt with in Chapter 14, but we need to mention here that two instruments were required (a vesting deed and a trust instrument) and that difficulties in dealing with the trust property might arise if these requirements were not met.

For a settlor who did not wish to create the somewhat cumbersome SLA 1925 settlement the only alternative was the *trust for sale*. A key concept in the trust for sale was that there had to be an obligation to sell the trust property; that is, the trustees had to be under a duty to sell rather than simply having a power to sell the property. This arose from the definition of trust for sale in LPA 1925, s. 205(1)(xxix) as:

an immediate binding trust for sale, whether or not exercisable at the request or with the consent of any person, and with or without a power at discretion to postpone the sale.

Some problems which might have arisen from unhelpful wording in certain trusts were solved and the trusts in question converted into trusts for sale by specific provisions in the legislation. Thus, trusts 'to sell or retain' became trusts to sell by virtue of LPA 1925, s. 25(4).

Nevertheless, even where the duty to sell was satisfactorily created, the settlor had to ensure that the trust he created was also 'immediate' and 'binding' if it was to come within the exception provided by SLA 1925, s. 1(7) and escape the provisions of that Act. As we saw in 12.2.3.1, these words as interpreted by the courts had a highly technical meaning and could give rise to considerable difficulty.

Providing the settlor's arrangements did constitute an immediate binding trust for sale, the creation of the trust for sale generally required no greater formality than the creation of other trusts, save that LPA 1925, s. 53(1) generally required writing for any disposition of land to be effective. Thus, the creation of the trust for sale did not require the use of two documents as did the SLA settlement, though those who preferred to do so could choose to use two documents.

Similarly, the new *trust of land* requires only one document, although again there is nothing to prevent the use of an additional document containing information about the nature of the beneficial interests which the settlor might wish to keep confidential. However, it must be remembered that purchasers will want to see all relevant information, so care would be needed in allocating information in an appropriate way between the two documents.

13.11.4 **Position of trustees**

13.11.4.1 *Trustees hold the legal estate*

Under a trust of land, the legal estate will be vested in the trustees, as it was in the case of trusts for sale. In SLA settlements, however, the legal estate was held by the current beneficiary as tenant for life (see Chapter 14).

13.11.4.2 *Trustees' powers*

Trustees of a *trust of land* have 'all the powers of an absolute owner' of the property. Although one might think that these very wide words of s. 6(1) needed no additions, the Act includes a number of specific powers. One which may represent a change from the previous law is the provision contained in s. 6(4)(b) that the trustees may buy land 'for occupation by any beneficiary'—a matter which was by no means certain under the earlier law.

In the case of *SLA settlements*, the main powers of management were vested in the tenant for life, although some were exercisable only if he gave notice to the trustees, or, in a few cases, obtained their consent.

The powers of trustees of a *trust for sale* were conferred on them by LPA 1925, s. 28, which gave them 'all the powers of a tenant for life and the trustees of a settlement under the Settled Land Act 1925', including the powers conferred by SLA 1925, s. 102, to manage the property during a minority.

It was always possible for the settlor to confer additional powers upon the trustees and this was usually done where the trust was created expressly. This illustrates the difference in approach between the old and new law. Under the old rules, trustees were given more limited powers, which could be expressly extended, whereas under the new law, trustees are given wide powers, which can be expressly reduced.

13.11.5 **Trustees' duties**

Trustees of a trust of land are subject to all the general duties imposed by their fiduciary role and, in addition, have some further statutory obligations imposed on them by various provisions in TOLATA 1996, s. 6.

13.11.5.1 *Duty to sell*

A major change in the area of trustees' duties relates to the duty to sell the trust property. Under the old law relating to *trusts for sale*, this would be imposed expressly by the settlor in order to create an 'immediate binding trust for sale' so as to take his settlement outside the ambit of the SLA 1925. A duty to sell would also be imposed on trustees under any statutory trust, most notably those which operated in cases of co-ownership, because the relevant statutes provided that the statutory trusts were to be trusts for sale (see for example LPA 1925, s. 35). Section 25(1) provided that a power to postpone sale should be implied in every trust for sale of land, but this could be excluded by the settlor in the case of expressly created trusts.

By contrast, under TOLATA 1996, trusts imposed by statute operate as trusts of land, not as trusts for sale, and so no duty to sell is imposed in such cases. Where an express trust is created, the settlor may impose a duty to sell, but the statutory power to postpone will be implied in all cases, and cannot be excluded by the settlor.

13.11.5.2 *Duty to consult the beneficiaries*

Under a *SLA settlement*, the powers of management, including decisions about selling the property, were in the hands of the tenant for life, rather than with the trustees, and so no question arose of the trustees consulting him about the performance of their functions.

In the case of a *trust for sale*, the LPA 1925, s. 26(3) imposed on the trustees a duty to consult the beneficiaries in terms very similar to that of s. 11(1) of TOLATA 1996. However, although the 1925 provisions applied automatically to trusts imposed by statute, they applied to express trusts only if specifically incorporated by the settlor.

As with a number of other provisions, TOLATA 1996 reverses this process, and the beneficiaries' right to be consulted applies in all *trusts of land*, unless specifically excluded.

13.11.6 **Position of beneficiaries**

13.11.6.1 *Nature of beneficiaries' Interests under trust of land*

While beneficiaries under a *SLA settlement* had an interest in the land itself, the equitable doctrine of conversion which applied to all *trusts for sale* had the result that beneficiaries under such a trust were regarded as having an interest in the proceeds of sale rather than in the land. By contrast, beneficiaries under a *trust of land* have an interest in the land itself, and the Act provides that even where the settlor has imposed a duty to sell, notional conversion will not take place.

13.11.6.2 *Control of appointment and retirement of trustees*

As we have seen, TOLATA gives certain beneficiaries control over the choice of new trustees and the ability to require their resignation. However, this merely enables them to do within the trust what they could previously have done by bringing the trust to an end and creating a new one, and so does not amount to a very significant change in the law.

13.11.6.3 *Delegated powers*

The tenant for life under a *SLA settlement* possessed major powers of management under the Act, and did not depend on any delegation by the trustees.

Under a *trust for sale*, the trustees had a very limited right to delegate their powers to lease or manage the land to any person of full age who was beneficially entitled in possession to the rents and profits of the land.

By contrast, trustees of a *trust of land* may delegate all or any of their powers to one or more of the beneficiaries. Thus, a beneficiary could come to exercise powers which were close to those of a tenant for life under the SLA 1925, or, in the case of complete delegation, actually exceeded them.

13.11.6.4 *Right to be consulted by the trustees*

We have already considered this right in connection with trustees' duties—see 13.11.5.2.

13.11.6.5 *Right to occupy trust land*

Under a *SLA settlement* the tenant for life holds the legal estate and accordingly has the right to occupy the property. As we have seen, beneficiaries under a *trust for sale* had no right of occupation, unless expressly conferred by the terms of the trust. Under *a trust of land*, beneficiaries have a right of occupation, subject to the trustees' discretion to choose who shall occupy when several are entitled to do so.

13.11.7 **Powers of settlor**

An interesting consequence of the changes introduced by TOLATA 1996 is that the settlor appears to have greater power over future dealings with the trust property than he did in the case of either SLA settlements or trusts for sale.

Under a *SLA settlement*, the tenant for life holds the legal estate in the land and has the power to sell it. We have seen (Chapter 12) that although the original purpose of the settlement was to keep land in the family, it came to be realised that this could be disadvantageous, and a major aim of the nineteenth-century reforms—followed through in the 1925 legislation—was to free the land from the 'dead hand' of the settlor and make it freely marketable. For this reason, the SLA 1925 provided that the power of the tenant for life to sell the property could not be excluded, and invalidated any terms in the settlement which attempted to deter him from exercising this power (for example, by providing that his interests under the settlement would end if the property were sold—see 14.7.3).

Under a *trust for sale*, the trustee was under a duty to sell and in consequence a settlement made in this form would not seem to be an appropriate device for keeping the land in the family. However, the trustees' implied power to postpone sale, combined with the possibility of requiring a number of consents before the property could be sold, meant that trusts for sale could be used to retain the land for a considerable time, and with greater certainty that it would remain unsold than under a SLA settlement. We have seen that an example of the use of a trust for sale for this purpose is to be found in *Re Inns* [1947] Ch 576 (see 13.5.2.1). The circumstances in this case were, however, relatively unusual, and although a settlor might be able to postpone sale for some time in this way, he was not able to tie the property up in the way that had been possible before the nineteenth century.

By contrast, it appears that a *trust of land* could be created with the express purpose of retaining land. This by itself would not be sufficient to prevent the property being sold, because the trustees would have the power of sale as part of their overall powers of 'an absolute owner'. However, it would also be open to the settlor to exclude this particular power and if that were done it would seem that the land could be kept unsold for the duration of the trust. This possibility could be seen as an undesirable return to control by the 'dead hand' of the settlor; for possible ways of escaping its grip, see Watt [1997] 61 Conv 263.

13.11.8 Protection of purchaser

As we have seen, the provisions of LPA 1925 which were designed to save the purchaser from having to make lengthy checks on the performance by the trustees of various statutory duties have been carried forward into TOLATA 1996. The purchaser's main protection, the process of overreaching, also appears to continue to operate under the new Act, which indeed amends the relevant provisions of LPA 1925 to bring them in line with the terminology used in the later Act. The wide scope of the definition of 'trust of land' also means that it clearly includes bare trusts, with the result that the interests of a beneficiary under such a trust are now capable of being overreached (previously this had been in doubt—see Megarry and Wade, pp. 441–2).

Yet although it seems certain that Parliament intended the overreaching provisions to continue in operation, it has been suggested that TOLATA 1996 has made a fundamental, although unintentional, change to the application of this process to registered land (see Ferris and Battersby [1998] 62 Conv 168). The arguments for this view are complex and difficult to summarise briefly, but in outline are as follows.

As we noted above (13.9.3.1), beneficial interests are not overreached by ultra vires transactions. Section 6 of TOLATA 1996 gives the trustees increased powers but limits them by providing in s. 6(6) that these powers:

shall not be exercised in contravention of . . . any other enactment or any rule of law or equity.

If the trustees act in breach of trust, they are acting in contravention of general equitable principles and accordingly any apparent exercise of their powers is unauthorised and ultra vires. Section 16 of TOLATA provides that a purchaser shall not be affected by the trustees' breach of various duties under the Act, but this protection applies only to purchasers of unregistered land (s. 16(7)). It follows from this that the purchaser of registered land who takes as a result of the trustees' breach of duty may be said to be taking under an ultra vires transaction. He is not protected by TOLATA, s. 16 and so cannot rely on the overreaching process. Indeed it is suggested that if the events in *City of London Building Society* v *Flegg* [1988] AC 54 had occurred after TOLATA 1996 came into force, the trustees' actions would have been ultra vires and the beneficiaries' interests would not have been overreached.

So far, there has not been any judicial consideration of this argument. In *Birmingham Midshires Mortgage Services Ltd* v *Sabherwal* (2000) 80 P&CR 256, on facts very similar to *Flegg*, it was argued on behalf of the beneficiary that TOLATA 1996 *had* changed the law on overreaching, but it does not appear from the report that the court's attention was drawn to the Ferris and Battersby article. The Court of

Appeal approved the view of the trial judge that the Act had not changed the law on this point, referring among other reasons to the fact that the amendment of the overreaching provisions in LPA 1925 by TOLATA does in effect confirm them. However, the views of the Court of Appeal on this point are at best *obiter dicta*, since the transaction before the court had taken place some six years before the Act came into force. Thus, the question of the Act's effect on overreaching in relation to registered land must be regarded as still open. (For a note on the decision in *Sabherwal* and an alternative view of the whole question, see Dixon [2000] 64 Conv 267; and for a reply to that note, see Ferris and Battersby [2001] 65 Conv 221.)

If TOLATA 1996 does in fact have the unfortunate effect that is suggested, it may be countered by the terms of LRA 2002 s. 26, which relate to the protection of disponees (i.e., those who take under a disposition of registered land). Section 26 provides that subject to an exception for limitations protected by an entry on the register or imposed by the Act:

a person's right to exercise owner's powers in relation to a registered estate or charge is to be taken to be free from any limitation affecting the validity of a disposition.

Section 26(3) adds that this provision has effect:

only for the purpose of preventing the title of a disponee being questioned (and so does not affect the lawfulness of a disposition).

The effect of this provision may well be that a purchaser who takes registered land under an ultra vires transaction will be protected, while the beneficiaries will retain their rights against the trustees for any breach of trust.

13.11.9 Powers of court

The new provisions of TOLATA 1996, ss. 14 and 15 build upon the old trusts for sale rules in LPA 1925, s. 30, but remove some constraints on the old powers and clarify various points. If you look at s. 30, you will realise that it is not entirely clear whether a trustee who had no beneficial interest in the property, but who wished to enforce compliance with the trust by the other trustees, could have made use of the section. Also, it did not appear to cover cases in which beneficiaries wished to avoid sale rather than compel it (though that may be understandable when one allows for the primary purpose of the trust for sale). Section 14 avoids these difficulties by making it clear that any trustee or person having an interest in the property can apply and that the application can relate to any of the functions of the trustees.

Further, s. 15 adopts a more modern approach to legislating, by providing a list of matters which the court is to consider in determining disputes brought before it under s. 14 although as we have seen (13.8.3) judicial opinions differ as to the significance of this change.

13.12 **The future**

There has as yet been relatively little judicial consideration of TOLATA 1996. We have indicated in this chapter several areas in which commentators can foresee problems, and others may be revealed as more cases come before the courts. Nevertheless it seems that the new provisions are a considerable improvement upon the rules embodied in the 1925 legislation (although that legislation was in itself a very considerable achievement), and in general it can be said that they are more flexible and better suited to the role played by trusts of land in modern society.

FURTHER READING

Clements, 'The Changing Face of Trusts' [1998] MLR 56.

Hopkins, 'The Trusts of Land and Appointment of Trustees Act 1996' [1996] Conv 411 (and see Sydenham [1997] Conv 242).

Martyn, 'Co-Owners and Their Entitlement to Occupy Their Land Before and After the Trusts of Land and Appointment of Trustees Act 1996: Theoretical Doubts Are Replaced by Practical Difficulties' [1997] Conv 254.

Smith, 'Trusts of Land Reform' [1990] Conv 12.

TOLATA 1996 s. 15

Pascoe, 'Section 15 of the Trusts of Land and Appointment of Trustees Act 1996—A Change in the Law?' [2000] 64 Conv 315.

Probert, 'Creditors and Section 15 of the Trusts of Land and Appointment of Trustees Act 1996: first among equals?' [2002] 66 Conv 61.

14

Settled Land Act settlements

14.1 Introduction

14.1.1 Existing settlements

A Settled Land Act settlement under SLA 1925 is the second form of trust that can exist in relation to land after 1996. In general, it is true to say that no new SLA settlements can be created due to TOLATA 1996 but that any settlement under the SLA 1925 that existed when TOLATA 1996 came into force will remain a SLA settlement (TOLATA 1996, 2(1)). However, there are very limited exceptions to both parts of this statement, which we will explain briefly in the following paragraph and in 14.5.5.

The exception to the rule that old SLA settlements remain as they are is contained in TOLATA 1996, s. 2(5), which provides that land which is held on charitable, ecclesiastical or public trusts shall not be or be deemed to be settled land after the commencement of TOLATA 1996. Such land became subject to the new trusts of land rules with the result that the trustees of such trusts now have wider investment powers.

14.1.2 10 Trant Way

When the Thornes were looking for a property to buy (see 13.1.2) they also viewed 10 Trant Way, which was also occupied by a widow, Mrs Silver. Mrs Silver mentioned when talking to the Thornes that No. 10 was subject to a trust and that she had a life interest in the property but that on her death it was to pass to her brother-in-law, Henry Silver. In fact, the will of Mrs Silver's husband contained the following provision:

I give the house in which my wife Sylvia Silver and I shall be residing at the date of my death ... to my trustees upon trust for my said wife during her lifetime and on her death for my brother Henry Silver absolutely.

When told this the Thornes were quite surprised to be told by Mrs Silver that she believed that, nonetheless, 10 Trant Way had been registered in her name and they were worried that this was in some way wrong as there were trustees involved. The arrangements seemed to them to be very different to those of Mrs Green at No. 9 although the family arrangements involved seemed almost identical. They are also worried that Henry Silver might have views about the sale of the house or that the trustees might intervene.

14.1.3 **The two types of trust**

The differences between the arrangements at 9 and 10 Trant Way lie, of course, in the fact that while Mrs Green's trust was created as a trust for sale and converted into a trust of land by TOLATA 1996, the will of Mrs Silver's husband created a SLA settlement. The rules relating to the two types of trust often produce very different results, even in very similar circumstances.

14.1.4 **Basic form of a settlement**

Before dealing with SLA settlements in detail it is as well to have a simple idea of their form. Under her husband's will Mrs Silver has only a life interest in the property which, on her death, will pass to her brother-in-law, Henry Silver. Mrs Silver will therefore not be able to leave 10 Trant Way to anyone in her will: her interest in the property is limited and will die with her. As we already know (1.2.4), a life interest cannot be a legal estate or interest in land under the provisions of LPA 1925, s. 1, and Mrs Silver's interest in the land can therefore only amount to an equitable interest. On her death, Henry Silver will be entitled to the full fee simple and can expect to become the legal owner of No. 10. However, at the moment he has no right to immediate possession of the property, only a right to possession in the future, and so for the time being his interest does not satisfy LPA 1925, s. 1(1), and he too has only an equitable interest.

It is, however, a basic rule that land cannot be left without a legal owner, some-one to hold the land 'of' the Crown. (The technical phrase which expresses this is that 'there can be no abeyance of seisin'.) Accordingly, someone must hold the legal estate upon trust for Mrs Silver and Henry Silver as beneficiaries. One might expect that the trustees appointed by the settlor would perform this function as would be the case were the property to be held on a trust of land, but SLA 1925 does not adopt this method. Instead it provides that the person with the current interest (Mrs Silver) should hold the land as a trustee upon trust for herself and the other beneficiary. Mrs Silver is described as the 'tenant for life' and she not only holds the legal estate but also has a wide range of statutory powers to deal with the land, including the power to sell it. The trustees of the settlements do not hold the legal estate but they do have a number of functions, including the obligation to receive and invest the proceeds of any sale of the land. This explains why Mrs Silver is the registered owner of 10 Trant Way and why she has power to sell the property. Even after the implementation of TOLATA 1996 Mrs Silver's trust continues to operate under these SLA 1925 rules.

We will now look at the various types of arrangement which could give rise to a settlement under the Act, and consider the rules which govern its administration.

14.2 **Types of settlement**

The definition of a settlement is provided by SLA 1925, s. 1, which sets out the types of arrangement which make property settled land and subject to a trust governed by the provisions of that statute. The section provides that 'Any deed, will, agreement . . . or other instrument' under which land stands limited in certain ways will give rise to a settlement. We will consider each of the types of limitation in turn.

14.2.1 **SLA 1925, s. 1(1)(i): limited in trust for any persons by way of succession**

This covers the position of Mrs Silver, for her husband has by his will created an arrangement under which she is to have a limited interest (for life) and will be succeeded in possession by his brother. This is the simplest, the classical, form of settlement and it arises whenever property is granted 'To A for life and then to B'. This paragraph of s. 1(1) of the Act is very widely drawn and in fact the wording is wide enough to include several of the other specific arrangements set out in the later paragraphs.

14.2.2 **SLA 1925, s. 1(1)(ii): limited in trust for any person in possession**

a) for an entailed interest whether or not capable of being barred or defeated
Entails have been very rare for a long time, though in the past they had some popularity with the great landed families. An entail arose in a case in which land was granted to 'A and the heirs of his body'. This phrase meant that only a particular class of heirs could inherit A's interest. Accordingly it could not be a fee simple estate and it did not come within LPA 1925, s. 1. Under such a provision A's interest passed only to his lineal descendants. In fact, the provision was often made in the form 'heirs of the body male' in order to exclude inheritance by lineal female heirs as well. Thus, if A died childless, the land did not pass to those more remote members of his family (e.g., his brother or his father) who would be entitled to take if he had held a fee simple. In such a case the entail ceased and the property reverted to the settlor, or to his successors, who accordingly were said to have a 'reversion' in the property.

In modern times the entail has not been so much of a problem because it could be brought to an end ('barred') fairly easily and also because the current holder has considerable powers to deal with the property under SLA 1925.

The long and fascinating history of the entail largely came to an end with the implementation of TOLATA 1996 because, while existing entails will continue, any attempt to create a fresh entailed interest will, as a consequence of para. 5 of Sch. 1 to the Act, become instead a declaration that the property is held in trust for the person who otherwise would have had the entailed interest, which in many cases will make that person absolutely beneficially entitled to the property (see 13.10.1.1(3)).

b) for [a] . . . fee simple or . . . term of years . . . subject to an executory limitation, gift, or disposition over

This type of settlement is best explained by an example. It would arise if a grant were made 'to A in fee simple but to B when B is admitted as a solicitor'. In this situation A may lose his interest in the property if B ever manages to qualify as a solicitor; only if B predeceases A, without so qualifying, will A get an unconditional right to the land. Accordingly one is again faced with the possibility of a succession of interests and this created a settlement.

c) for a base or determinable fee or any corresponding interest in leasehold land

The nature of the determinable fee has already been discussed (see 7.3.2). The base fee is now extremely rare and a modern lawyer is most unlikely ever to encounter one. It is an interest which would arise if someone with an entailed interest sold that interest. He could not give the purchaser a greater interest than he himself had, and so the purchaser would acquire an interest which could be inherited by any of his own heirs, but which would last only as long as the heirs of the body of the original entailed owner exist. These base fees are rare because entails themselves are now relatively uncommon and also because it is usually possible for the holder of an entailed interest to bar the entail completely and to convey a full fee simple to a purchaser under the provisions of the Fines and Recoveries Act 1833. In these circumstances, it would be rare for a purchaser ever to settle for a base fee. As mentioned above, TOLATA 1996 will soon render base fees even more rare because no new entails can be created.

d) being an infant [now known as a 'minor'], for an estate in fee simple or for a term of years absolute

Any person under the age of 18 years is legally a 'minor' and is incapable of owning a legal estate. Obviously, a minor might well be entitled to such an estate (e.g., under a will) and accordingly the land will be held by trustees upon trust for the minor, who will have an equitable interest in the property. Such trusts can be brought to an end when the minor reaches 18 and is capable of holding the legal estate for himself. Until 1997 a simple conveyance to a minor created a SLA settlement, but now it will operate as a declaration that the land is held as a trust of land upon trust for the minor (and if there are adult beneficiaries, for them) by virtue of TOLATA 1996, Sch. 1, para. 1 (13.10.1.2(1)).

14.2.3 SLA 1925, s. 1(1)(iii): limited in trust for any person for an estate in fee simple or for a term of years absolute contingently on the happening of any event

Such contingent interests arise when an ascertained person will obtain a legal estate at some point in the future if a specified event occurs. For example, parents, fearing youthful indiscretions, might provide that a young person is not to take property until he reaches an age greater than the age of majority, e.g., 21 or 25 years. Until that age, the beneficiary has only a contingent interest and this must be held behind a trust. If and when he reaches the prescribed age he will obtain a fully vested legal estate in the property. These contingent interests are often described as 'springing interests', because they will 'spring up' in the future, rather than following some earlier interest. After 1996 any new arrangements of this type have simply taken effect as trusts of land (TOLATA 1996, s. 1).

14.2.4 **SLA 1925, s. 1(1)(iv)**

This paragraph was repealed in 1949.

14.2.5 **SLA 1925, s. 1(1)(v): charged . . . with the payment of any rentcharge for the life of any person, or any less period, or of any capital, annual, or periodical sums for the portions, advancement, maintenance, or otherwise for the benefit of any persons . . .**

This paragraph covered arrangements of a family nature, where a settlor attempted to give one person a legal estate but at the same time charged the property with the payment of sums of money for the maintenance of other persons (e.g., younger children). It was intended that these sums should be paid from the income of the estate, which in general goes to the tenant for life. It should be noted that not all land subject to a rentcharge thereby became settled land; the paragraph only covers payments for portions, advancement and maintenance of another person. Accordingly land subject, for example, to a rentcharge to pay for the maintenance of a road would *not* fall within this provision, and so the existence of estate rentcharges (see 23.5.2.3) did not make the property into settled land.

Moreover, even where the rentcharges do fall within this paragraph, it remained possible to deal with the land without using SLA 1925 machinery. This is because it was realised, after the Act was passed, that a number of purchasers had in the past bought land subject to such rentcharges, on the vendors' undertaking to indemnify them against the charges. These owners now found themselves subject to SLA 1925 provisions, requiring complicated documents and the appointment of trustees. The Law of Property (Amendment) Act 1926, s. 1, therefore provided that such land could still be dealt with as if it were not settled land, and thus its owner now has a choice. He may sell the land without going through the SLA 1925 formalities, provided the land is sold *subject to* the charges (probably with a provision for the vendor to indemnify the purchaser). However, if the purchaser wishes to buy the land *free of* the charges, the SLA 1925 overreaching machinery must be adopted: a vesting deed will be required and trustees must be appointed to receive the purchase money. The purchaser will then take the land free of the charges, which will attach instead to the purchase money. The reduction of the number of rentcharges by the Rentcharges Act 1977 makes these situations more unusual. After 1996 new arrangements of this kind will operate as trusts of land (see 13.10.1.2(2)).

These then are the types of arrangement which have in the past given rise to a settlement. It was, however, possible to create similar interests but behind a trust for sale. Such arrangements were exempt from the provisions of the SLA 1925 (s. 1(7)) provided they satisfied the strict rules defining 'an immediate binding trust for sale' (see 12.2.3.1). From 1997 onwards any attempts to create a trust containing provisions of the types listed in SLA 1925, s. 1 (other than the entail, which can no longer be created) will, however, all be handled by use of the trust of land by virtue of TOLATA 1996, whether previously they would have constituted SLA settlements or trust for sale. Only pre-1997 SLA settlements of this type will continue.

14.3 **Tenant for life**

The SLA 1925 gives day-to-day control of settled land to the tenant for life, and it is accordingly essential to identify this person. Section 19 of the Act says that the tenant for life is, 'The person of full age who is for the time being beneficially entitled under a settlement to possession of settled land for his life'. Thus in the case of 10 Trant Way, Mrs Silver, who has a life interest in possession (i.e. not a future life interest), will be the tenant for life.

Obviously in a number of the forms of settlement no one has a life interest in the property. For example, the owner of an entailed interest has an inheritable interest and not one which will last for his lifetime only. Accordingly s. 20 of the Act provides that other 'limited' owners should have the powers of a tenant for life. The effect of s. 20 is to give the person who is currently entitled to an estate or interest in possession the powers of the tenant for life, as long as that person is of full age (18 or more). This will include a person who is entitled only to the income of the property for his life, or for the lifetime of another (s. 20(1)(viii)), even though such a person appears to have only an interest in money rather than in the land. It also includes a tenant under a lease for life, provided he is not holding at a rent (s. 20(1)(iv) to (vi)), so that such a tenant, whose lease is not converted into a fixed term by LPA 1925, s. 149(6), can exercise the powers of a tenant for life.

Sometimes there is no person who qualifies as tenant for life, either under s. 19 or s. 20. This is most commonly the case when the person currently entitled to the land is a minor (see s. 26). In such cases the powers of the tenant for life will be exercised by the 'statutory owner' (see definition of this phrase in SLA 1925, s. 117(1)(xxvi)). The statutory owner will be:

(a) any person upon whom the settlement confers the powers of the tenant for life; or

(b) in any other case, the trustees of the settlement.

Thus the settlor may make an express appointment of the statutory owner under (a); but if he does not do so, the trustees will assume that role.

14.4 **Trustees**

14.4.1 **Identifying the first trustees**

Although the tenant for life deals with the day-to-day management of the property, the trustees of a settlement are still extremely important, as we will see in due course. It is accordingly also important to be able to identify the trustees correctly. For this purpose reference should be made to SLA 1925, s. 30, which lists the possibilities in order of preference.

If there are no trustees, or in any case in which it is expedient, the court can appoint trustees under SLA 1925, s. 34 on the application of any beneficiary under the settlement (or, in the case of a beneficiary who is a minor, his guardian or next friend). A settlement should not be left without trustees, as they have important duties and powers in relation to the settled land and this provision ensures that, whatever the difficulties, trustees can be appointed.

14.4.2 New, or additional, trustees

It is essential that the settlement should have the services of the correct number of trustees throughout its existence. The Trustee Act 1925, s. 34, provides that the number of trustees should never be increased above four. The same Act, by s. 39, provides that no trustee may retire so as to reduce the number of trustees below two, unless the remaining trustee is a 'trust corporation' (defined in SLA, s. 117(1)(xxx), as including 'the Public Trustee or a corporation . . . appointed by the court in any particular case to be a trustee' and including other bodies recognised under the Public Trustee Rules 1912 or s. 37, Law of Property (Amendment) Act 1926).

Where it is necessary to appoint a new trustee, this must be done under the provisions of s. 36 of the TA 1925 which we have already considered in detail in Chapter 13 (see 13.3).

However, as we have already explained above (13.3.4) the impact of TA 1925, s. 36, is now modified by TOLATA 1996, ss. 19–21, which give extensive powers to the beneficiaries to direct the person with the right to appoint under TA 1925, s. 36, so that the choice of new trustee is in fact no longer really controlled by the person who actually appoints. In this respect the TOLATA 1996 provisions apply to SLA settlements as well as to trusts of land. This will provide a degree of control for the beneficiaries where the new rules can be used. However, you should bear in mind that if the beneficiaries cannot agree they cannot exercise the new power to give directions and the choice of the new trustee(s) will remain with the person who has power to appoint under TA 1925, s. 36.

14.5 Creating a settlement

14.5.1 Settlements created *inter vivos*

The basic procedure for the creation of a settlement *inter vivos* was in the past governed by SLA 1925, s. 4. Of course, no new SLA settlements can be created now, but it is still important to understand what formalities were required, so as to be able to check whether any existing SLA settlement has been properly created. SLA 1925, s. 4 required that the settlement should be effected by two deeds:

(a) a trust instrument; and

(b) a vesting deed.

14.5.1.1 *Trust instrument*

The trust instrument is the document which sets out in detail the intentions of the settlor. Under SLA 1925, s. 4(3), it should contain the following information:

(a) a declaration of the trusts affecting the land;

(b) the appointment of trustees;

(c) a statement of who is to have the power to appoint new trustees (if any); and

(d) any extra powers to be given to the tenant for life or trustees, in addition to those conferred by the Act.

It can be seen from this that the trust instrument could have been a very long document, particularly if the settler chose to extend the statutory powers, and that it included all the personal details of the trust, including the names (or descriptions) of all the beneficiaries and the nature of their interests in the property. Some of this information may well be of a private nature and be such that the beneficiaries would not wish it revealed to an outsider, such as an intending purchaser of the settled land.

14.5.1.2 *Vesting deed*

Contents   It is the second document, the vesting deed, which provides all the necessary public information about the trust. The contents of the vesting deed are set out in SLA 1925, s. 5(1):

(a) a description of the settled land (e.g., its address; or, if necessary, a description by reference to a plan; or, in registered land, the title number);

(b) a declaration that the land is vested in the person to whom it is conveyed, or in whom it is declared to be vested, upon the trusts affecting the land;

(c) the names of the trustees;

(d) any powers, additional to the statutory powers, conferred by the settlement; and

(e) the name of any person who is entitled to appoint new trustees.

The details contained in this document provide all the information that a purchaser of the settled land needs to know. It is not necessary for him to know anything of the details of the beneficial interests in the settlement and so this information does not appear in the vesting deed.

Unregistered land   Section 4(2) requires that settled land should be legally vested in the tenant for life or statutory owner, and it is the vesting deed which performs this function in the case of unregistered land. The wording of s. 5(1)(b) on this point may seem a little confusing and in order to understand it one has to realise that it is designed to cover two possible situations. In the first, the settlor gave himself an interest under the settlement, for instance keeping a life interest for himself and providing that other interests should take effect on his death. In such a case, he is the first tenant for life and so should hold the legal estate. In fact, that estate was already vested in him, for he owned the legal estate absolutely before making the settlement. The vesting deed therefore merely declared that he held the legal estate, for it was not necessary to convey it to him. In the other possible situation, the settlor divested himself of all interest in the property and the first tenant for life was therefore someone other than the settlor. In this case, the legal estate was actually conveyed to the tenant for life by the vesting deed.

The vesting deed should have been executed by the settlor at the same time as the trust instrument. If this was not done the trust was only partially constituted and the tenant for life or statutory owner had a right, under SLA 1925, s. 9(2), to demand that the trustees of the settlement execute the necessary vesting deed.

Should they refuse to do so, the court might make an order which operates as a vesting deed (s. 9(2)).

Registered land   Where title to the land was registered, the procedure for creating a settlement followed the same pattern, except that a prescribed form of vesting transfer had to be used in place of the vesting deed (Land Registration Rules 1925, r. 99) and, most importantly, the legal estate did not vest in the tenant for life until the transaction was completed by registration. The tenant for life was registered as the sole proprietor, and the interests of the beneficiaries should be protected by the entry of a restriction, which in general terms would provide that no future dealing with the land was to be registered unless any capital money arising from the transaction was paid to two named persons (the trustees of the settlement). This serves the purpose of alerting intending purchasers to the fact that this is settled land, and also should ensure compliance with the overreaching procedure. If for any reason the Registrar was unaware of the need to enter the restriction, a beneficiary might protect his or her interest by means of a caution. This might, for example, be necessary where the tenant for life, being also the settlor, was registered as proprietor before he made the settlement and then did not apply for entry of the restriction.

Even if the beneficiary is in occupation of the land, it is still important that his rights are protected by an entry on the register. The Law Commission had recommended that such rights should be overriding by virtue of actual occupation, as are interests under other trusts, but this recommendation was not supported on consultation (see *Land Registration for the Twenty-First Century A Conveyancing Revolution*, 2001, Law Com No. 271, para. 8.17). Accordingly, LRA 2002 specifically excludes interests under SLA settlements from taking effect as overriding interests (Sch. 1, para. 2(1) and Sch. 3, para. 2(1)(a)—see further 5.10.2.1).

14.5.2 Settlements created by will

Where a settlement was created by will, SLA 1925, s. 6, provides that the will itself should fulfil the functions of the trust instrument. The estate did of course pass on a grant of probate or letters of administration to the personal representatives of the settlor. In such cases, the trust was completed by the execution by the personal representatives of a 'vesting assent' in favour of the tenant for life or statutory owners. In the case of registered land, the transfer should have been completed by registration, as explained above.

14.5.3 The curtain principle

We have seen that the vesting deed (or transfer or assent, as the case may be) should contain all the information required by a prospective purchaser, without revealing to him any confidential or unnecessary information contained in the trust instrument. SLA 1925, s. 110(2), provides that, subject to certain exceptions, the purchaser is neither entitled nor bound to see the trust instrument but may rely on information contained in the vesting deed. This rule is commonly described as 'the curtain principle', for the trust instrument and the information it contains is concealed from the purchaser by the 'curtain' of the vesting deed.

However, in certain cases set out in the proviso to s. 110(2), the purchaser is required to satisfy himself of certain matters, including the fact that the person in whom the settled land is vested by the vesting deed is the person in whom it ought to be vested. In other words, the purchaser should check that the apparent tenant for life is really entitled under the settlement, and this will involve lifting the curtain and looking at the trust instrument. Reference should be made to the proviso for the circumstances under which this is necessary, but they may be summarised very generally by saying that they are all cases in which the vesting deed has been made after, rather than contemporaneously with, the trust instrument. Thus where a settlement was made as prescribed by the Act, the curtain should remain intact.

14.5.4 **The paralysing section**

In order to ensure that the structure required by SLA 1925 was adopted, s. 13 contains a provision which paralyses certain transactions until the trust is fully constituted. The section provides that once a tenant for life or statutory owner has become entitled to the execution of a vesting deed in his favour and until such a deed is executed, any purported disposition of the settled land by the tenant for life or statutory owner is void. Thus, any attempt by the tenant for life to convey the land to a purchaser would be ineffective to pass the legal estate. Such a transaction, however, operates as a contract to transfer the estate once the necessary vesting instrument has been made.

Since this provision might unfairly disadvantage an innocent purchaser, s. 13 does provide protection for a 'purchaser of a legal estate without notice of such tenant for life or statutory owner having become . . . entitled . . .' to the execution of a vesting deed. Thus the paralysing provision does not operate where an innocent purchaser acquires the legal estate.

The provisions of s. 13 were most likely to be relevant in those settlements where the tenant for life was also the settlor, for, in other cases, the tenant for life would normally be unable to prove his title to the land until the legal estate has been vested in him by the vesting deed.

Finally, it should be noted that it is unnecessary to execute a vesting deed in the rare situation in which the settlement comes to an end before the deed has been made (*Re Alefounder's Will Trusts* [1927] 1 Ch 360) and in such a case the owner can dispose of the land without being affected by s. 13.

14.5.5 **One SLA settlement which can be created after 1996**

We said at the beginning of this chapter that there is one very limited exception to the rule that no new SLA settlements can be created after TOLATA 1996 came into force. This exception is provided by s. 2(2), which allows a new SLA settlement to be created if it is a derivative settlement of an existing SLA settlement. The reason for this exception is to prevent the inconvenience of the trust having to operate under two different systems should there be a re-settlement of part of the trust property or should fresh property be added to the settlement (even if not on identical trusts). However, a derivative settlement will only be effective as an SLA settlement under s. 2(2) (as opposed to becoming a trust of land) if an express provision to this effect is included in the instrument creating the derivative trust (TOLATA 1996, s. 2(3)). Accordingly, when altering an existing SLA settlement it will be necessary to decide whether to take advantage of s. 2(2) or, perhaps, to elect to re-settle the entire trust as a trust of land (though there may be tax disadvantages in doing this). It is also possible, if one wishes, to make the new derivative settlement a TOLATA 1996 settlement, while leaving the parent settlement to operate under SLA 1925.

14.6 Powers of a tenant for life

One of the main purposes of the Victorian reforms of the law on settled land was to ensure that such land could be dealt with when necessary. This is an advantage to the tenant for life who might otherwise find himself burdened with land which he could not afford to maintain but which he could not mortgage or sell. Accordingly, SLA 1925 gives a tenant for life or statutory owner extensive rights to deal with the land, which may allow him to act in a way completely contrary to the wishes of the settlor. In particular, the tenant for life has the power to sell the land, despite the fact that the settlor's main purpose in making the settlement may well have been to keep the land in the family.

We will look at these powers in detail later on but first we must explain how the SLA 1925 rules on overreaching operate for the SLA settlement.

14.6.1 Overreaching under SLA 1925

In the case of land settled under SLA 1925, the overreaching provisions will operate provided the transaction is carried out correctly and in accordance with the Act: that is, if the transaction is within the powers of the tenant for life and any capital money is paid to two trustees or a trust corporation (s. 18(1)). If these requirements are met, the overreaching provisions in s. 72 will apply. Under this section, with certain exceptions, an authorised transaction is effective to pass the estate or interest 'discharged from all the limitations, powers, and provisions of the settlement, and from all estates, interests, and charges subsisting or to arise thereunder' (s. 72(2)). Accordingly, should Mr and Mrs Thorne decide to buy 10 Trant Way from Mrs Silver, they will obtain a fee simple estate free of the equitable interests of Mrs Silver and of her brother-in-law, Henry Silver, *as long as* the formalities required by the Act are observed. In particular, they must pay the purchase money to the trustees. The interests of Mrs Silver and Henry Silver will become interests in the purchase price, which will be in the hands of the trustees of the settlement. Mrs Silver, as tenant for life, will have the power to direct how the money is to be invested, and will enjoy the income from it for the rest of her life. When she dies, Henry Silver will become absolutely entitled to the property in which the money has been invested.

14.6.1.1 *Interests not overreached*

Finally, it should be noted that s. 72(2) sets out a list of interests which are *not* overreached on a dealing by the tenant for life. The position may be summarised briefly by saying that the overreaching provisions do not affect estates or interests which were created before the settlement was made, nor those created during the settlement in exercise of the tenant for life's powers. All these bind the purchaser according to the usual principles of registered or unregistered title, as the case may be. Thus, if Mr Silver had mortgaged 10 Trant Way before his death, the settlement made by his will would be subject to the prior interest of the mortgagee. If Mrs Silver sells the property to the Thornes, the conveyance would not overreach the mortgage and the Thornes would take the house subject to it unless, as will undoubtedly be the case, they insist that she repays the debt and redeems the mortgage before passing the property to them. Similarly, if Mrs Silver has let part of the house in exercise of her powers as tenant for life, the Thornes will take the property subject to that lease, in the same way as a purchaser from an absolute owner would take subject to any legal lease.

It is now time to look in detail at the powers of the tenant for life.

14.6.2 **Power to sell**

The most important of the rights of the tenant for life is the right to sell the settled land or to sell any easement or other right over the land. This right is granted by SLA 1925, s. 38, which also allows the settled land to be exchanged for other land or rights (though exchanging is rare). The tenant for life is under no obligation to sell the property (and this used to be the major difference between the SLA settlement and the trust for sale, where the trustees were under a duty to sell); the section merely gives him the right should he choose to exercise it. Any sale made under s. 38 must be made in accordance with s. 39: most importantly the sale must be 'made for the best consideration in money that can reasonably be obtained'. The sale may be by auction or by private contract, as the tenant for life wishes. The conveyance will be executed by the tenant for life, since the legal estate in the land is vested in him. However, in order to prevent the tenant for life selling the land and then making off with the proceeds of sale (a fraud on the other beneficiaries) the proceeds of sale ('capital money') must be paid to two trustees or into court under s. 18(1)(b) in order to trigger the overreaching provisions.

14.6.3 **Power to lease**

The power of the tenant for life to grant leases arises under SLA 1925, s. 41. Leases so granted may continue after the death of the tenant for life, and fetter those next entitled under the settlement, and so the period for which a tenant for life may grant leases is limited. Normally, they may be granted for any period not exceeding 50 years, with special provisions for mining leases (100 years) and building or forestry leases (999 years). These rules have, of course, been abandoned in the trust of land.

Any lease granted under SLA 1925, s. 41, must comply with the requirements of s. 42, as to the way in which it is made, the date on which it takes effect and the rent to be charged. The tenant must covenant to pay rent, and there must be a provision for forfeiture if he fails to do so.

14.6.4 **Power to grant options**

The tenant for life has power to grant options to purchase, to take a lease or to take any other interest in the settled land under SLA 1925, s. 51. Such options must be exercisable within an agreed period not exceeding 10 years (s. 51(2)).

14.6.5 **Power to mortgage**

SLA 1925, s. 71, gives a tenant for life the power to mortgage the settled land but only in order to raise money for specified purposes. These purposes are set out in s. 71(2) and include the right to mortgage in order to pay for those improvements which are authorised by the Act. The authorised improvements are set out in Sch. 3 to the Act and fall into three categories, divided according to who is to meet the costs. In all cases, the settled land may be mortgaged to provide the money needed for the work but the tenant for life must repay the cost of improvements listed in Part III of the Schedule (for example, the installation of central heating) and may be required to pay for those in Part II (such as structural alterations of buildings). Part I, however, contains long-term improvements (including drainage, irrigation and the provision of labourers' cottages) which benefit the remainderman as much as the present tenant for life. Such improvements should be paid for out of capital, and the trustees cannot require the tenant for life to meet such costs.

It should be noted that these provisions cover improvements and not *repairs*. Normally, with some exceptions relating to agricultural land, repairs to the settled land must be paid for by the tenant for life at his own expense.

The powers to mortgage are, accordingly, very limited and will normally be expressly extended by the settlor. Contrast with these statutory powers the very wide powers of trustees under a TOLATA 1996 trust of land (13.4.2).

14.6.6 **Other statutory powers**

In addition to the major statutory powers mentioned above, SLA 1925, ss. 52 to 70, include a number of other rights which are not used so commonly. In addition s. 64 confers a general power for the tenant for life to effect any transaction under an order of the court. In *Hambro* v *Duke of Marlborough* [1994] Ch 158 it was held that under s. 64 it was possible to authorise a dealing which would alter the beneficial interest of an adult beneficiary. The aim of the Duke (the current tenant for life) was to prevent his son, the Marquess of Blandford, from living in or managing Blenheim Palace and the surrounding estates, which had been settled on the Dukes of Marlborough since 1706. The use of s. 64 for this purpose was approved, provided that the effect was for the benefit of the settled land or all the beneficiaries under the settlement. In the particular circumstances of the case, the proposal was accepted as being in the interests of the trust.

14.6.7 **Extra powers conferred by the settlor**

The settlor was free to grant any extra powers which are not included in SLA 1925 and this was commonly done. Obviously such powers would vary from trust to trust, but in many cases the tenant for life would be given the same rights 'as a beneficial owner'. In such cases the discretion of the tenant for life was only restricted by his duties towards the other beneficiaries and the trust as a whole, and any grant of wide additional powers would in practice have produced a result very similar to the powers conferred on trustees of a trust of land under TOLATA 1996. The limited powers under SLA 1925 will accordingly be relevant only in a limited range of cases (often where a SLA settlement arose by mistake).

14.7 Giving notice and obtaining consent

14.7.1 Giving notice

In a number of cases the tenant for life is not entitled to exercise his powers unless he gives notice of his intentions to the trustees. This does not mean that the tenant for life must obtain the consent of the trustees, and normally they will have no right to prevent the tenant for life entering into the proposed transaction. The purpose of these provisions is to keep the trustees informed about the property and also to warn them of occasions on which they will be required to receive capital money. SLA 1925, s. 101, requires the tenant for life to give notice to the trustees when he intends 'to make a sale, exchange, lease, mortgage, or charge or to grant an option'. A person dealing in good faith with the tenant for life is not, however, required to ensure that proper notice has been given (s. 101(5)). Whilst notice is generally required for the grant of a lease, one for not more than 21 years which otherwise complies with the Act may be granted without notice being given (s. 42(5)).

14.7.2 Obtaining consent

In general it was not possible for a settlor to provide that the tenant for life might exercise a statutory power only with the consent of some other person (e.g., the trustees or another beneficiary), since such a provision would amount to an attempt to restrict or fetter the tenant for life's powers (see below). Contrast this position with that which used to apply to the trust for sale and which now applies to trusts of land (13.5.2.1). There are, however, certain limited exceptions to this rule:

(a) The settlor might provide that the tenant for life must not make any disposition in relation to the principal mansion house on the settled land without the consent of trustees (or an order of the court dispensing with such consent) (SLA 1925, s. 65). This rule would apply relatively infrequently, for a 'principal mansion house' is a house, where the grounds and lands normally enjoyed with the house exceed 25 acres and which is not a farmhouse (s. 65(2)).

(b) SLA 1925, s. 66(1), provides that in certain restricted cases, the consent of the trustees or a court order is required to cut and sell timber (for this is an act which decreases the capital value of the property).

(c) The compromise of claims and settling of disputes by the tenant for life is subject to the consent of the trustees (SLA 1925, s. 58(1)), as is the power to release, waive or modify rights (s. 58(2)).

Apart from these specific cases the tenant for life does not require consent before he exercises his powers. You will see that the very nature of the restrictions indicates that the SLA machinery was really only designed to operate for substantial trusts involving large estates.

14.7.3 Attempts to fetter or restrict the powers of the tenant for life

Whilst it was open to the settlor to extend the power of the tenant for life, he had no right to cut down the statutory powers. SLA 1925, s. 106, says that any provision which forbids the exercise of a statutory power or which attempts or tends to prevent the exercise of any such power is void. This section is very wide and renders void any provision in the trust which discourages the use by the tenant for life of his powers. Thus, in *Re Ames* [1893] 2 Ch 479, a provision that the tenant for life lost the right to a monetary benefit should the land be sold was held to be void since it discouraged sale.

A common restriction, which has given rise to much judicial consideration, is a provision that the tenant for life should lose his interest in the property should he cease to reside in it, or alternatively, that the interest is given to him while he lives there. This restriction, if fully operative, would discourage the exercise of the powers to sell or let the property, because on selling or letting the tenant for life would be required to leave the property and would thereupon forfeit his interest. As a result of SLA 1925, s. 106, the courts have held that should the tenant for life in such a case leave the property in furtherance of the exercise of his statutory powers he will *not* lose his interest in the estate (*Re Acklom* [1929] 1 Ch 195), for such a forfeiture is void under the section. Should, however, the tenant for life leave the premises for some other reason (e.g., his own convenience) then the forfeiture clause is valid (see *Re Haynes* (1887) 37 ChD 306 and *Re Trenchard* [1902] 1 Ch 378). Accordingly it should be regarded as a question of fact in each case whether the provision to which objection is taken does in fact amount to a fetter under s. 106. By contrast, the wide power given to trustees of a trust of land can be restricted or excluded by the settlor (TOLATA 1996, s. 8(1)—see 13.5.1).

SLA 1925, s. 104(1), provides that the powers given to the tenant for life are not assignable by him. Thus, even though the tenant for life is free to sell his equitable life interest to another person, he is not able to vest his statutory powers in that purchaser. In addition any contract by which a tenant for life agrees not to exercise any of his statutory powers is completely void (s. 104(2)).

14.8 A tenant for life is trustee of his powers

A tenant for life is in a rather unusual position because, although he has the legal estate of the settled land vested in him, he only has a partial beneficial interest in the property. Accordingly the tenant for life holds the legal estate as trustee upon trust for himself and the other beneficiaries. In addition, by virtue of SLA 1925,

s. 107, the tenant for life is a trustee of all the powers granted to him by the Act, and when exercising them must 'have regard to the interests of all parties entitled under the settlement'. The result is that, to some extent, the other beneficiaries are protected against an abuse of power by the tenant for life.

It appears, however, that the court will not force a tenant for life to exercise any of his powers, such as to improve the settled property or to sell it (*Re 90 Thornhill Road* [1970] Ch 261), for these are powers, rather than duties. It is also clear that the court will not intervene if the proposed transaction is for a fair price and is otherwise proper, even though the tenant for life has decided to enter into the transaction for some malicious purpose. Thus, in *Wheelwright* v *Walker* (1883) 23 ChD 752, the court refused to intervene when a tenant for life proposed to sell settled land in order to prevent the remainderman, whom he disliked, from ever residing in the property. Since the sale was at a fair price and complied with the Act the court would not prevent it, even though the tenant for life's motivation for sale was malice towards the remainderman.

The court will, however, intervene where the tenant for life seeks to use his powers in a way which would be prejudicial towards other beneficiaries (*Hampden* v *Earl of Buckinghamshire* [1893] 2 Ch 531). An exercise of a power in an attempt to evade the terms of the settlement will also be objectionable. In *Middlemas* v *Stevens* [1901] 1 Ch 574 the tenant for life was the widow of the settlor, and according to the terms of the settlement had an interest terminating on her death or remarriage. The tenant for life wished to remarry and, in order to ensure that she could continue to live on the settled land after her remarriage, granted a 21-year lease of the property to her future husband. The court held that the lease had been granted in bad faith and, since the grantee was aware of the circumstances, the lease was void. This does not mean, however, that any grant of a lease to a spouse of the tenant for life is necessarily bad; there must be something further in the circumstances to suggest *mala fides* (bad faith) (*Gilbey* v *Rush* [1906] 1 Ch 11).

14.9 Defective dispositions

14.9.1 Dispositions in excess of powers

Although the powers of the tenant for life or statutory owner are considerable, they are by no means unlimited. Accordingly it is necessary to consider the position should these powers be exceeded. What, for example, would happen if Mrs Silver purported to grant a 99-year lease of 10 Trant Way (contrary to SLA 1925, s. 41) or mortgaged the property to buy a new car for herself (contrary to s. 71)? Here we are assuming that Mr Silver's will did not confer wider powers on the tenant for life.

Defective or improper dispositions are covered primarily by SLA 1925, s. 18(1), which provides that any disposition by a tenant for life or statutory owner in excess of his powers shall be void. The disposition may, however, have effect against the tenant for life's own equitable interest. Thus, an improper mortgage would not bind the legal estate or the interests of the other beneficiaries but could bind the tenant for life's own equitable interest in the property.

14.9.2 **Protection of recipients**

It is necessary to protect the interests of those who, in good faith, are the recipients of an estate or interest granted in excess of powers. This protection is provided by s. 110(1), which provides that on any disposition the purchaser (which includes tenants, mortgagees, etc.: s. 117) shall 'be conclusively taken to have given the best price, consideration, or rent . . . that could reasonably be obtained . . . and to have complied with all the requisitions of . . .' the Act, provided that the purchaser was 'dealing in good faith with a tenant for life or statutory owner'.

14.9.2.1 *Purchaser under an authorised transaction*

This provision can be of considerable help to a purchaser under an authorised transaction, if the trustees or remainderman later suggest that the price paid was inadequate. An example of this is found in *Hurrell* v *Littlejohn* [1904] 1 Ch 689. In this case, a purchaser had bought settled land from the tenant for life at £2,000 and immediately resold it for £3,000. In an action brought against him by the remainderman, the purchaser relied successfully on s. 110(1), and was held to have given the best price reasonably obtainable.

14.9.2.2 *Unauthorised transactions*

The section is, however, perhaps of less use in the case of unauthorised trans-actions, because before entering into a transaction the purchaser will investigate the title to the property and discover that the land is settled. Once this discovery is made, the purchaser cannot 'in good faith' rely on a transaction which is in breach of the Act. The problem may arise, however, if the transaction is one for which no proof of title is normally required (e.g., some leases, particularly periodic tenancies such as weekly or monthly tenancies—which in practice can endure for a long period and thus might affect the trust property for some time) or where the tenant for life has some means of establishing his title which conceals the existence of the trust. This can occur when the settlor is also the first tenant for life under the settlement and has retained the original conveyance to himself as absolute owner of unregistered land. This will enable him to conceal the settlement and represent himself as absolute owner to a purchaser, who would then deal with him in good faith.

An illustration of how this can occur is found in the rather unusual facts of *Weston* v *Henshaw* [1950] Ch 510. Here, a father conveyed land to his son as absolute owner in 1921. In 1927 the son reconveyed the property to his father, and the father later settled the estate upon his son as tenant for life. The legal estate was conveyed to the son by a vesting deed but he also retained the 1921 deed of con-veyance and later used this as evidence of his title when mortgaging the settled land to raise money for purposes not authorised by the Act. On the death of the son the truth was discovered and the remainderman claimed that the mortgage was void under SLA 1925, s. 18, and did not bind him as beneficiary under the trust. The mortgagee, however, claimed to be a bona fide purchaser and therefore protected by s. 110(1). One would imagine that this is a clear example of a case in which s. 110 should apply but the court held that it did not, because the mortgagee did not *know* that he was dealing with a tenant for life. The court therefore decided in favour of the remainderman and against the mortgagee. This decision has been heavily criticised, for it seems to deprive the purchaser of any protection in the case of unauthorised transactions. We have already seen that he is not protected if he knows he is dealing with the tenant for life, because he is taken to know too that the transaction is outside the SLA provisions; and *Weston* v *Henshaw* then excludes him in just those situations where he does appear to be acting in good faith. Accordingly, in *Re Morgan's Lease* [1972] Ch 1 the court held that s. 110(1) applied even where a purchaser was not aware that he was dealing with a tenant for life. Both cases were heard at first instance only and are accordingly only persuasive authority. Generally *Re Morgan's Lease* is regarded as being the better authority, particularly as the court there was able to base its decision on an earlier case (*Mogridge* v *Clapp* [1892] 3 Ch 382) which was not considered by the court in *Weston* v *Henshaw*.

Even if s. 110(1) applies where the purchaser acts in good faith not knowing that he is dealing with a tenant for life, there may still be difficulties. The section says that the purchaser is deemed to have complied with the 'requisitions' of the Act. Obviously this protects a purchaser who has failed to comply with, for example, the requirement that capital money be paid to the trustees. However, what of the 'purchaser' who has been granted a 99-year lease? Under the Act normally only 50-year leases can be granted. The requirement that longer leases be not granted is a requirement placed on the tenant for life and not on the purchaser (as, too, is the requirement that mortgages should be made for authorised purposes only). It could be argued that unauthorised transactions lie outside the scope of s. 110(1), not because of the state of the purchaser's knowledge but because the subsection is concerned with the purchaser's conduct and is not phrased in such a way as to protect him against bad faith on the part of the tenant for life. This might have been a better reason for the decision in *Weston* v *Henshaw* but it is not a point which has received much consideration. In any event, it seems that there is, thus far, no decision on the position of a lease granted for more than the prescribed period and now perhaps there never will be.

14.9.2.3 *Registered land*

Finally, we must mention that none of these problems about unauthorised dispositions should arise in the case of registered land (and so are unlikely to trouble any purchaser of No. 10 Trant Way). The restriction or caution should make it clear to any prospective purchaser that he is dealing with settled land and, indeed, the standard form of restriction directs that no disposition is to be registered unless authorised by SLA 1925. If no restriction or caution is entered, the purchaser should be protected in his dealings with the registered proprietor and it is thought that SLA 1925, s. 18, and *Weston* v *Henshaw* could not prevail over the general provisions of relating to registered land.

14.10 Role of trustees of settlements

We have already mentioned that, although the tenant for life holds the legal estate and has wide powers of management, the trustees of the settlement are extremely important. It is now time to look at their duties and functions; some of these have already been described, and we will refer to them only briefly, but others require more detailed consideration here.

14.10.1 Duties where settlement defectively created

Where a settlement was created before 1997 but no vesting deed has been executed, the trustees should perfect the settlement by themselves executing a vesting deed.

14.10.2 Functions where there is no tenant for life, or where the tenant for life has ceased to have a substantial interest in the property

We have already seen that where the person currently entitled under a SLA settlement is a minor, the trustees will be required, in the absence of any express provisions by the settlor, to exercise the tenant for life's powers as statutory owners.

The trustees also act as statutory owners in any other case where there is no tenant for life (SLA 1925, s. 23). This situation would arise, for example, in the sort of settlement envisaged by SLA 1925, s. 1(1)(iii), where an interest is to 'spring up' in the future, with no preceding earlier interest. Until the interest arises, there is no tenant for life, and the legal estate will be held and the powers exercised by the trustees as statutory owners.

The trustees may also be called upon to exercise the statutory powers if the tenant for life has ceased to have a substantial interest in the property (e.g., because he has sold his equitable interest or has become bankrupt) *and* has unreasonably refused to exercise his powers *or* has consented to the change (SLA 1925, s. 24). However, before the powers can be transferred to the trustees in this way, a court order must be obtained.

14.10.3 Functions in connection with dispositions of settled land

As we saw earlier, the trustees must be given notice before a tenant for life or statutory owner makes certain dispositions of settled land. In certain cases, moreover, the consent of the trustees may be required.

The major function of the trustees is, however, to receive any capital money which arises from the transaction, since under SLA 1925, s. 18(1)(b), the over-reaching provisions can only operate where capital money is paid either to the trustees of the settlement or into court (see also s. 75). Accordingly no disposition which gives rise to capital money can be completed where the trust lacks trustees.

Should the tenant for life wish to acquire the estate for himself, the trustees take on a special importance. The tenant for life is himself a trustee and as such, under general equitable rules, would be unable to acquire the settled land or any interest in it for his own benefit (*Keech* v *Sandford* (1726) Sel Cas T King 61). SLA 1925, s. 68, however, makes such transactions possible by temporarily (and only for the purpose of the particular disposition) transferring the powers of the tenant for life to the trustees. This avoids the tenant for life being placed in a position in which his interests as purchaser and trustee conflict.

14.10.4 **Powers of investment**

Since one of the main functions of trustees is to receive capital money, they are given statutory powers in relation to the investment of that money (SLA 1925, s. 75(1)). Some capital money, for example, a mortgage advance will, of course, simply be applied for the purpose for which it was raised, but in general capital money must be invested and the income obtained paid to the tenant for life.

The statutory powers of investment are set out in SLA 1925, s. 73.

Section 73(1)(i), as amended by the Trustee Act 2000 (TA 2000), Sch. 2, para. 9 gives the trustees power to invest in securities either under the general power of investment in TA 2000, s. 3 or under powers conferred on them by the settlement. Under s. 73(1)(xi) the trustees may purchase land in England and Wales, but this territorial restriction remains in force for settlements under SLA (see TA 2000, s. 10(1)(a)), despite the relaxation we noted at 13.4.2.2, which permits capital money arising under a *trust of land* to be invested in land anywhere in the United Kingdom.

Under s. 75(2) the tenant for life had the right to choose the investments to be made, and to direct the trustees accordingly, although if he did not do so the trustees were to exercise their own discretion. However, TA 2000, Sch. 4, para. 10(1) amends this subsection so as to provide that investments shall be made according to the discretion of the trustees, but subject to any consent required or direction given by the settlement. Section 75(4) as amended now provides that:

The trustees, in exercising their power to invest or apply capital money, shall—

(a) so far as practicable, consult the tenant for life; and

(b) so far as consistent with the general interest of the settlement, give effect to his wishes.

14.10.5 **Duties when the interest of the tenant for life comes to an end**

Depending on the terms of the settlement, the interest of a tenant for life may come to an end during his lifetime, or at his death. For example, an interest given to a widow 'until remarriage' will end during her lifetime if she remarries (see *Middlemas v Stevens* [1901] 1 Ch 574, above 14.8); but if she does not remarry, or if the interest given to her is simply for life, with no restriction, the interest will end at her death.

Where the interest ends during the tenant's life, it is the responsibility of the tenant to convey the legal estate to the person next entitled under the settlement, and the trustees are not concerned with the matter. If the land continues to be settled, so that the person next entitled takes only a limited interest, the transfer should be made by vesting deed (SLA 1925, ss. 7(4) and 8(4)), which will contain all the information needed by a prospective purchaser. This would be appropriate where, for instance, the widow's interest is followed under the settlement by an entailed interest. However, where the settlement in fact comes to an end, and the person receiving the estate is absolutely entitled, the estate should be passed to him by an ordinary conveyance and not one containing all the details prescribed for a vesting deed (SLA 1925, s. 7(5)). If, in either case, the tenant for life fails to execute the required deed, the court may make a vesting order (SLA 1925, s. 12).

Where the tenant for life's interest comes to an end with his death, the trustees may have a role to play. If the land remains settled (as above), the estate does not vest in the deceased's ordinary personal representatives, but instead vests in the trustees as special personal representatives (Administration of Estates Act 1925, s. 22(1), in the case of a will; Supreme Court Act 1981, s. 116, in the case of intestacy). The trustees are then required to convey the estate to the next tenant for life by a vesting deed or vesting assent, which again will contain all the information a purchaser would need to know.

If, however, the settlement has come to an end, the estate vests in the deceased tenant for life's ordinary personal representatives, and they will transfer it to the person who is absolutely entitled by an ordinary conveyance or assent (*Re Bridgett & Hayes's Contract* [1928] Ch 163).

14.10.6 **Functions when settlement ends**

Normally, the trustees' functions end when the settlement ends but, in certain cases in which it would not be clear to an intending purchaser that the trust has ended, the final function of the trustees will be to execute a deed of discharge which declares that the trust has come to an end (SLA 1925, s. 17).

A practical example may serve to explain this further. A settlor settles land 'upon A for life and then to B absolutely'. The land is vested in A as tenant for life. Thereafter A buys B's equitable interest in the property. A thus becomes solely entitled to the property but must ask the trustees to execute a deed of discharge so that he can prove to any intending purchaser that the trust has indeed ended.

The purpose of the deed of discharge is thus to cancel the effect of the earlier vesting deed, which told a prospective purchaser that the land is subject to a settlement. If no vesting deed has been executed before the settlement ends (as in *Re Alefounder's Will Trusts* [1927] 1 Ch 360), no deed of discharge is required to neutralise it, and similarly such a deed will not be needed if there are other documents in the title which show that the settlement has come to an end. Thus, the ordinary conveyance by a tenant for life or his ordinary personal representatives to the person absolutely entitled (see below) is sufficient evidence that the settlement has come to an end, and there is no need for a deed of discharge.

14.10.7 **General functions of trustees**

As well as exercising their specific powers, trustees must also have regard to their general fiduciary relationship to the trust. Accordingly the trustees should keep a general 'watching brief' over the trust and ensure that all is proceeding properly. In *Re Boston's Will Trusts* [1956] Ch 395 at p. 405, Vaisey J said that the general duty of the trustees is to 'conserve the settled property'. Accordingly the trustees should intervene should it come to their attention that the tenant for life intends to act in excess of his powers. Also the trustees must be parties to any legal action brought in respect of the land. Therefore, Mrs Silver's trustees cannot prevent her selling 10 Trant Way but could intervene if it became clear, for example, that she intended to sell the property at a gross undervalue.

14.11 **End of a settlement**

SLA 1925 s. 3 provides that a settlement lasts as long as:

(a) any limitation, charge, or power of charging under the settlement subsists or is capable of being exercised; or

(b) . . . the person who would otherwise be owner of the legal estate is an infant.

Thus, if a grant is made 'to A for life and then to B absolutely', the settlement will end on A's death unless, at that date, B is under 18, in which case it will end on B's 18th birthday. If the settlement is, 'to C for life and then to D in tail male', the settlement will end when there are no more lineal male heirs of D. At that point the estate will revert to the settlor or his heirs.

In Mrs Silver's case the settlement will end upon her death, and Henry Silver will then be entitled to have the fee simple of 10 Trant Way vested in him. On Mrs Silver's death the estate will pass first to her ordinary personal representatives who will then be obliged to vest the estate in Henry Silver (i.e., it does not pass to him automatically). Should Mrs Silver have sold 10 Trant Way, the capital money would have been paid to her trustees and on her death Henry Silver would be absolutely entitled to all the capital money (probably represented by investments) held by the trustees and he can call for this to be placed in his own hands.

Finally, we should mention that under TOLATA 1996, s. 2(4), a SLA settlement will also come to an end when there remains no relevant property subject to the trust (as presumably would happen if the whole of the settled land was sold and the capital money invested in property other than land). If, subsequently, new land is acquired by the trustees, Sch. 1(6) provides that this does not revive the SLA settlement: the new land will be held instead on a trust of land under the provisions of TOLATA 1996.

FURTHER READING

Cheshire & Burn's Modern Law of Real Property, 16th edn., Butterworths, 2000, Chapter 9, pp. 187–215 (the Strict Settlement).

15

Perpetuities and accumulations

15.1 Introduction

Before we leave the subject of trusts, we must give a brief account of the rules which govern the kind of future interests which can be created under them, and so this chapter will be concerned with the 'rule against perpetuities'.

Common law has always disliked uncertainty in relation to future interests in land, for such uncertainty tends to make the property inalienable for some time, and common law has always opposed any arrangement which restricts free alienation. For example, should a settlor, who as yet has no children, wish to settle land upon 'the first of my great-grandchildren to obtain a law degree', it could easily be 70 or 80 years before the great-grandchild who is to take the gift can be ascertained. For that period of time there would be no one absolutely entitled to the property and, certainly under the older trusts rules, no one with a power to dispose of it. As a result, the courts developed rules ('against perpetuities') which invalidated certain objectionable future interests. Unfortunately, the rigid application of these rules frequently led to ridiculous results (as we will see below), and finally statutory amendments were made by the Law of Property Act 1925 (to a limited extent) and the Perpetuities and Accumulations Act 1964. As the changes are only modifications of the earlier rules, it is still necessary to understand those rules and accordingly we will consider them first. For convenience, we will call them the 'common law rules', but throughout this section that phrase denotes the rules applied in both law and equity, in contrast to the later amendments made by statute.

15.2 The common law rules

15.2.1 Contingent and vested interests

The common law rules against perpetuities are concerned only with *contingent* (or conditional) future interests. Such an interest is a gift under a trust which is to take effect in the future but is conditional, either because the person who is to take it has not yet been identified or because some other requirement has to be fulfilled before he is entitled to the interest. Thus, in the example of a gift over on a specified event (for example, the death of a specified person) 'to the first of my great-grandchildren to obtain a law degree', there is no way of knowing who, if anyone, will eventually qualify for the gift. Even when several great-grandchildren have been born, the interest will remain contingent until one of them is awarded the necessary degree. When the person who is to take the future interest has been identified and all necessary conditions fulfilled, he will be said to have a future interest which is 'vested in interest'. He now has an interest in the property, an immediate right to future possession, and he can sell or mortgage that right (Victorian novels are full of characters who waste their future interests in this way), and pass it to his successors on his death. By contrast, a contingent future interest, though called an 'interest', does not give any right to the property: even if the person who may be entitled can be identified, he has nothing more than a hope or chance of acquiring an interest if the condition is fulfilled.

In the trusts we have considered in Chapters 13 and 14, both Henry Silver (No. 10) and William Green (No. 9) have future interests which are vested in interest, for each is identified and does not have to perform any condition before taking his interest. All each has to do is to wait for the end of the previous interest (which will occur on the deaths of Mrs Silver and Mrs Green respectively). When that happens, the interest of each will be said to be 'vested in possession', and each one will at last be entitled to the actual enjoyment of the property.

Some further examples may help to clarify the point. If a settlor grants land *inter vivos:*

to A for life, then to A's first child to reach 21 for life, then to B absolutely

the interests of A and B are not covered by the rule, for they both have interests which have vested. Their interests are vested, because the person who is to obtain an interest is *ascertained* and no condition which has yet to be fulfilled is attached to the gift. A's interest is vested in possession, entitling him to immediate enjoyment of the property, and B has a future right, vested in interest. However, the gift to A's child has not vested, unless A already has a child who is aged 21 or more. Even if A has a younger child (e.g., aged 5) the gift is still contingent upon that child reaching 21. It is quite possible that this child may yet die, and that another child of A will be the first to reach 21, or, a further possibility, that no child will ever qualify. If a grant is made:

to C but if C ever becomes a doctor then to D,

C has a vested interest but D has a contingent interest, because he will get the property only if C becomes a doctor.

15.2.2 **The rule**

As we have said, the rule against perpetuities is concerned with contingent interests and with the period of time within which they vest in interest. The rule is sometimes described as a rule against remoteness of vesting, for it prescribes a limited period within which a contingent interest must vest (in interest, not in possession) and invalidates any interest which may vest outside that time. It should be noted that the rule is not about the length of time that a trust can last, but the operation of the rule can sometimes look as though this is the case. In *In re Peel's Release* [1921] 2 Ch 218, a charitable gift of land was made to a school 'for ever thereafter', but the document creating the trust also provided for what was to happen should the purposes of the charitable trust ever fail. This part of the document said that, in such a case, the land should revert to the person making the grant and his heirs. You will realise that a charitable trust could continue for a very long time. It was also theoretically possible that the charitable trust would never fail. Thus, it was possible that the heirs of the grantor who were intended to take the property could be born many years in the future (perhaps hundreds of years). Accordingly, the provisions about the reversion were contrary to the rules against perpetuities because the gift over to the successors might take effect outside the permitted period (which we cover in more detail below). As a result the gift over (the provision for reverter) was void.

The rule is that: *a contingent interest is void unless it must vest in interest, if it vests at all, within the perpetuity period*. The period consists of the lifetime of a life or lives in being at the date at which the disposition takes effect, plus 21 years (plus any necessary period of gestation).

When applying the rule, you will need to know when the disposition you are considering took effect. Settlements made *inter vivos* (during the lifetime of the settlor) take effect from the date of the grant, and those made by will take effect from the death of the testator (*not* from the date when he made the will).

15.2.3 **The period**

The rule against perpetuities operates by invalidating contingent future interests which may fail to vest in interest within a prescribed period. This period is expressed by the formula: 'a life in being plus 21 years'. The 21-year requirement is quite straightforward, and has its origin in the days when one reached majority at that age and accordingly became capable of holding a legal estate in land. It has not been amended even though the age of majority has for many years been reduced to 18. It is the first portion of the formula, the 'life in being', which tends to cause difficulties.

15.2.3.1 *A life in being*

The 'life in being' may be that of any human being who is alive at the date at which the grant becomes effective. The use of the lives of animals has been ruled out (*Re Dean* (1889) 41 ChD 552; *Re Kelly* [1932] IR 255), which is eminently sensible when one considers the great age which some beasts (e.g., tortoises) can attain. Because it is impossible to ascertain the names and dates of death of all human beings who were alive on a particular date, the common law rule requires that the persons who are to be regarded as the relevant 'lives in being' should be identifiable from the grant. They may be identified expressly, or by implication. Thus, should I make a gift to:

the first child of my son A to reach the age of 21,

A would be a relevant life in being. A settlor might, however, choose to identify a particular group of people (preferably those who are expected to be long-lived and easy to identify), solely to serve as lives in being. Such people need not have any connection with the trust. Thus, often a 'royal lives clause' has been used which (today) might identify as the class of lives in being 'all the lineal descendants of George V' who are living at the date of the grant. Such clauses provide a large group of persons to act as lives in being, who are sufficiently in the public eye to be readily identified (see *Re Leverhulme (No. 2)* [1943] 2 All ER 274; also, on 'descendants of Queen Victoria', *Re Villar* [1928] Ch 471).

Some examples of the rules on lives in being may illustrate:

To A for life and thereafter to the first child of A to reach 21.

In this example A is a relevant life in being. The perpetuities rule is satisfied, for the gift to A's child must vest, if it vests at all, within 21 years of the death of A.

To B (who is not married) and then to any widow of B.

In this case B is a relevant life in being and the gift to his widow will be valid, for it must vest, if it vests at all, within 21 years of B's death because it vests on his death.

A gift by will to such of the settlor's grandchildren who reach 21.

In this case the settlor's children will be relevant lives in being, for even if he had no children when he made the will, any child he may have in the future must have been born by the date of his death, which is when the gift takes effect. The grant is valid if the gift must vest within 21 years of the death of the settlor's last living child (which it must).

15.2.3.2 *Addition of a period of gestation*

It may have occurred to you that in the last example it is not quite true to say that all the settlor's children must be lives in being at his death, for it is possible that the settlor's wife was pregnant at his death and gave birth to his last child after his death. Similarly, the last of the settlor's children to die might be a son who dies leaving a pregnant wife. The child thus born would reach the age of 21 more than 21 years after his father's death. As a result of such possibilities, the common law has always accepted that any relevant gestation period should be included in the perpetuity period. Thus, the settlor's posthumous child is regarded as a life in being, and the last grandchild also is regarded as receiving a vested gift in time, because his period of gestation is added to the 21-year period. Any foetus in this position of being between its conception and birth at a relevant time is commonly referred to as being *en ventre sa mère* (in his mother's womb).

It is perhaps worth mentioning that the development of methods of freezing semen, ova and embryos could cause considerable difficulties for the law in the realm of perpetuities. Thus far, no case has been brought which depends on the possibility of a 'test-tube baby' forming a relevant life in being, but one can imagine the problems that might result. (Sections 27–30 of the Human Fertilisation and Embryology Act 1990 illustrate the problems of defining 'father' and 'mother' today and there have been instances in which children have been born several years after their father's death, as the result of the use of frozen sperm or embryos).

15.2.3.3 *A rule about possibilities not probabilities*

The common law rule renders void any gift which *might* vest outside the period, however unlikely it is that this will occur. An example may illustrate the problem: assume a gift to:

the first child of X to become an accountant.

In this example X is a life in being. The gift is invalid, because it is possible that X may have a child born after the date of settlement (and who is not therefore himself a life in being) and who qualifies as an accountant more than 21 years after the death of X. It is not relevant that, at the date of the grant, X has a son Y, who is due to qualify as an accountant in a year's time. The common law will not wait and see whether the gift does in fact vest within the perpetuity period. It insists on considering the position at the date of the grant. If at that date there is *any possibility*, however remote, that the gift could vest outside the period, it will be void. It is possible (even if not probable) that Y might die before qualifying as an accountant, that X might then have a further child, Z, who would not be a life in being, and that Z might become an accountant more than 21 years after X's death. Thus, there is a remote possibility that this gift may vest outside the perpetuity period, and accordingly *the grant will be void*. The rule is about possibilities not probabilities.

A favourite illustration of this difficulty is that of the 'unborn widow', which arises in the following grant:

to A for life and then to any widow of A for life and thereafter to the eldest of A's children then living.

If A is unmarried at the date of the grant, it is fairly easy to see what difficulties might arise, because there is a possibility that he might not marry for some time and might then marry a woman who was not born when the gift took effect. For example, if A were 25 at the date of the grant and 20 years later, at the age of 45, married a woman of 18, Mrs A would obviously not have been a life in being at the date of the grant. The grant to A's widow would, however, still be valid, because it must vest within 21 years of the death of A, the life in being. The problem arises with regard to the gift to the eldest of A's children living at the date of the death of A's widow. Imagine that Mr and Mrs A have a child, B, two years after their marriage and that one year later A dies. At the date of A's death, Mrs A will be 21 and B will be 1. If Mrs A lives until she is 43 (22 years after A's death) the gift to B will vest more than 21 years after A's death. (The gift cannot vest in interest before Mrs A's death, because B might die before his mother and therefore would not qualify as the eldest child of A 'then living'.) Accordingly, because events *might* fall out this way, the remainder to A's eldest child is void.

It might be thought that the position would be different if A were married at the date of the grant, for Mrs A would then be a life in being. In fact, this would make no difference at all, for it is still possible for Mrs A to die before her husband, and for him to remarry, taking as his second wife a woman who was not born at the date of the gift. The difficulties we have considered above, on the assumption that A is a bachelor, would then arise in relation to the second Mrs A. Therefore, the gift to the eldest child is void at the outset, even if A had a wife at the time of the grant.

All these 'but what if' forecasts may seem very far-fetched but the common law regards the unlikelihood of the events occurring as irrelevant. The remotest possibility of the gift vesting outside the perpetuity period will render it invalid.

15.2.3.4 *Fertile infants and ancients at common law*

The nightmarish and nonsensical quality of the common law rules on perpetuities is exacerbated by a number of decisions, which establish that, at common law, a person is deemed to be fertile however young or old he or she may be. Thus, in

Re Dawson (1888) 39 ChD 155, Chitty J insisted that a woman aged 60 years and 3 months was to be regarded as still being capable of bearing children (see also *Jee* v *Audley* (1787) 1 Cox 324 and *Re Sayer's Trusts* (1868) LR 6 Eq 319), though in the light of recent developments in the field of *in vitro* fertilisation this attitude now seems more reasonable than it did in 1888. In recent years some women have, with medical assistance, given birth at what once would have been regarded as very advanced years in terms of fertility. In *Re Gaite's Will Trusts* [1949] 1 All ER 459 a gift was held to be valid, not because a five-year-old could be presumed incapable of bearing a child but because a five-year-old could not marry and therefore could not bear a *legitimate* child. For dispositions after 1 January 1970 illegitimate children are included in the term 'children' but before that date were not: Family Law Reform Act 1969, s. 15. Thus, if the parents of the child in question have not married, you must check the date of the settlement. A similar change was made in relation to adopted children by s. 42 of the Adoption Act 1976, which led, in *In re Levy Estate Trust* [2000] CLY 5263, to the court having to grapple with the question of whether a lady aged 68 years and 11 months could be expected to adopt (this was a modern case and thus, under the statutory rules explained below, the question was whether everyone was obliged to wait to see whether this in fact happened).

15.2.4 Class gifts

It is quite common for settlors to make gifts to groups or classes of people rather than to a single person: e.g., to A's daughters. These class gifts can give rise to particular problems, for in their case there is a further requirement for vesting, namely, that the share to be taken by each person must be identified. This of course cannot be done until it is known how many people there are in the class, and in the example given above one cannot know with any certainty how many daughters A will have until he is dead. In this particular case, there should be no danger of the gift being void for remoteness, for A will be a life in being and so his daughters' interests must all vest within the perpetuity period. However, difficulties could be caused by the following gift:

to A for life and then to B's grandchildren.

Here the gift in remainder is to a class of people, B's grandchildren. The problem in this case is that, for the gift to B's grandchildren to be valid, it must be shown that the interest of each grandchild must vest, if it vests at all, within the perpetuity period. If the interest of any one grandchild could vest outside the period, the gift to the whole class is void because it is impossible to determine within the perpetuity period how much each member should take. Obviously it is quite possible that one of B's grandchildren may be born more than 21 years after the deaths of A and B (lives in being). Therefore, this gift gives rise to difficulties and one might think that the whole gift to the grandchildren will be void.

In such cases the gift may, however, be rescued by the 'class closing rule'. This rule was not invented to save gifts that might be void for perpetuity but rather to solve the problem of the size of share each member of a class is to receive. In our example it may be that on A's death there are living two children of B, one of whom has two children. Accordingly, there are in existence two members of the class, 'B's grandchildren', but it is possible that more may be born later. If the gift is otherwise valid, B's two existing grandchildren are entitled to demand their shares immediately A dies. However, *if all* B's future grandchildren are to share in the gift, it is not possible to calculate at A's death the amount which each should take. This would prevent any distribution being made until B's children had both died, for until then there is still a possibility of further grandchildren being born. This is so even if B's children are both daughters and both clearly past the age of child-bearing (see above).

15.2.4.1 *The class closing rule*

Common law recognised the undesirability of this position, and accordingly, in *Andrews v Partington* (1791) 3 Bro CC 401, introduced a rule by which the list of possible members of a class is closed when the first member of the class is able to claim his interest in possession. In our example, B's two existing grand-children will take interests in possession on A's death. Accordingly, the rule in *Andrews* v *Partington* closes the class of 'B's grandchildren' at A's death, and B's two existing grandchildren will each receive a half share in the property. Any later grandchildren are excluded from the gift and receive nothing.

If a gift is contingent on members of the class reaching a certain age,

to such of B's grandchildren as reach 21,

the class closes when the first of B's grandchildren reaches that age. Any other grandchildren existing at that date are presumed to be potential members of the class and a share should be allocated for them but they only receive that share when they reach 21. If any one of them should die before reaching that age, his or her notional share will be distributed between those members of the class who do reach the qualifying age. Thus *Andrews* v *Partington* enables a distribution of a minimum share to be made as each one qualifies, with a possibility that the size of the share may increase in future.

Any grandchildren who are born after the date on which the first grandchild reached 21 are excluded from the class by the rule in *Andrews* v *Partington*.

15.2.4.2 *Effect of class closing*

The operation of the class closing rules is very important because it can save a gift which might otherwise have offended the perpetuity rule. In the case of the gift:

to C for life and then to D's grandchildren,

the class will close when C dies, if at that date D has at least one grandchild. You will recall that, unfortunately, common law will never wait to see what happens and so here it is not possible to wait until C dies in order to see whether the class closing rule will save the gift. The issue must be decided finally at the date of the grant. However, if at the date of the grant D already has a grandchild, E, it is clear that on C's death the class of 'D's grandchildren' will close immediately and that the interests of those grandchildren alive at C's death will vest in possession. This *must* be within the perpetuity period (C's life plus 21 years), and so in this case the class closing rule saves a grant which would otherwise be void.

The rule still works even if E dies before C, because E's successors will be entitled to E's share on C's death. This is because E has a future right which vested in interest as soon as he was born, and this is property which can pass under E's will or on intestacy. His position is different from that of B's grandchildren in the previous example, who have only contingent interests until they qualify by reaching 21. Although a notional share is allocated to them as soon as they are born, their interests do not vest in interest until they reach the specified age. Until then, they have no right to the property and therefore, if they die before meeting the condition, they have nothing to pass to their successors and their notional share enhances the amount taken by those who do qualify.

If, however, D has no grandchild at the date of the grant, one cannot be sure that such a child will be born before C's death so as to enable the class closing rule to operate. Thus in such a situation the grant will be void under the perpetuity rule. By the same principle if the gift is:

to F for life and then to such of G's grandchildren as reach the age of 21,

then the gift will be saved if G already has a grandchild who is aged 21 at the date of the grant. Otherwise the entire gift to G's grandchildren is void.

15.3 Reforms made in 1925

The 1925 property legislation introduced limited reforms in relation to grants made in an instrument executed on or after 1 January 1926, or contained in the will of a testator who died on or after that date (LPA 1925, s. 163(2)). The reform introduced was aimed at the following kind of disposition:

to A for life and then to the first of A's children to reach the age of 25.

If A has no child aged 25 at the date of the grant, this disposition would be void at common law because A might die leaving a child aged 2 who would not reach the age of 25 until 23 years after A's death and outside the perpetuity period (A's life plus 21 years).

The alteration made by s. 163 is that where a limitation is void because of an excess in the age of a beneficiary, or class of beneficiaries, then one may reduce the stipulated age to 21. Accordingly, the gift given above will be saved, because the age requirement will be reduced to 21 and obviously any child of A must reach 21 within 21 years (plus any gestation period) after A's death. Not only does this validate an otherwise invalid gift, it also will give A's child an interest vested in possession four years earlier than the settlor intended, so that the child will begin to enjoy the property at that earlier date.

The statutory amendment does not alter a disposition which was valid under the common law rules. Thus, a gift to:

the first child of B to reach 25

produces different results depending on whether B is dead or alive at the date of the grant. If B was dead at the date of the grant, all his children are identifiable and can themselves operate as lives in being. In such a case the disposition would be valid at common law, since it must vest, if at all, during the lifetime of a life in being, and so would vest in possession in the first child to reach 25.

However, if B is still alive at the date of the gift, there is a possibility that all his existing children might die and that B would then produce a further child, who would not be a life in being and who would reach 25 more than 21 years after his father's death. The gift would therefore be void at common law, and s. 163 accordingly reduces the specified age to 21.

15.4 Perpetuities and Accumulations Act 1964

The perpetuities rules were given a rather more thorough overhaul by the Perpetuities and Accumulations Act 1964, which applies to dispositions which came into effect after 15 July 1964. However, the Act amends rather than replaces the old rules and so the common law rules are still of importance to anyone drafting a modern settlement. We will consider the principal changes introduced by the Act.

15.4.1 Power to specify fixed perpetuity period

One of the problems of the common law rules is that one has a variable (and therefore unpredictable) perpetuity period, since calculation of the length of time involved will depend upon the imponderable question of how long the 'lives in being' will live. Accordingly s. 1 of the 1964 Act gives the settlor the alternative of stating a fixed period, which must not be more than 80 years, as the perpetuity period for his settlement. This fixed period is generally used as a substitute for the old 'royal lives' clauses. Such clauses may still be used if the settlor so chooses but the fixed period provides a neater and more convenient alternative.

15.4.2 Introduction of a 'wait and see' rule

As we have seen already, one of the major problems with the common law rule is that one is obliged to judge the issue of perpetuities at the outset and this leads to a consideration of every possibility, however far-fetched. This unsatisfactory position is altered by s. 3(1) of the 1964 Act. This section provides that where a disposition is void under the common law rule, it should be treated as though it was not subject to that rule, until such time as it becomes clear that it will vest, if at all, outside the perpetuity period. In other words, one can wait through the perpetuity period to see what really happens, rather than basing the decision on what *might* happen. Accordingly, the only type of disposition which is void *ab initio* is one which clearly *must* vest outside the perpetuity period and cannot possibly vest within it. If we consider again the grant:

to the first child of X to become an accountant,

we will see that under the 1964 rule all we have to do is to wait and see whether any child of X does ever become an accountant within the perpetuity period. Similarly, in the case of the grant:

to A for life and then to any widow of A for life and thereafter to the eldest of A's children then living, we simply wait to see what happens. If A dies, leaving a widow who was alive at the date of the gift, she does constitute a life in being and it becomes clear that the eldest child's interest will vest, if at all, during the perpetuity period. If, however, A has married the 'unborn widow' (someone who was not alive at the date of the gift) then one waits again to see whether she dies within 21 years of A's death, leaving a child in whom the property can vest. If she outlives A by 21 years it then becomes clear that the gift must vest outside the perpetuity period. No more can be done to save the gift under the 'wait and see' provisions but all is not lost, for there are special statutory provisions designed to rescue such a disposition which we shall describe later.

It is important to note that s. 3(1) applies only where the disposition would be void at common law. Therefore, when dealing with perpetuity problems, one must first apply the common law rule, and explain why it invalidates the gift, before going on to apply the provisions of the section: it is not enough to adopt a general approach of 'wait and see' with regard to all contingent interests.

If the 'wait and see' principle does not save a gift, it may nonetheless be saved by one of the other amendments made by the Act, as we will see below.

15.4.3 Introduction of statutory 'lives in being'

A further amendment to the common law rules is that when we 'wait and see' we do not apply the same test for 'lives in being' as under the earlier rules. Thus, the 'wait and see' perpetuity period is calculated by reference to the lives that are prescribed by the statute for this purpose. These rules are contained in s. 3(4) and (5) of the 1964 Act. They provide that one calculates the period by reference to any of the following who are in being and ascertainable at the *start* of the perpetuity period:

(a) the person making the disposition (settlor);

(b) a person in whose favour the disposition is made (in the case of class gifts this includes all members and potential members of the class);

(c) the parents or grandparents of any person in whose favour a disposition is made (basically any parent or grandparent of someone who falls into category (b)); or

(d) any person on the failure of whose prior interest the disposition is limited to take effect.

It was thought that by increasing the categories of people who can be lives in being, a greater chance is given of the interest vesting in time.

No other persons may be used as lives in being for the 'wait and see' provisions. If there are no persons falling into this category at the date at which the disposition takes effect, then a fixed period of 21 years is imposed (s. 3(4)(b)).

15.4.4 Reduction of age

The 1964 Act repealed s. 163 of the LPA 1925 (but only in respect of dispositions made after 15 July 1964) and provided new age reduction rules, which apply where 'a disposition is limited by reference to the attainment by any person or persons of a specified age exceeding 21 years' (s. 4). These new rules apply only where the interest would be void at common law, and one should not apply them until one has waited (under s. 3(1)) to see whether the interest will vest within the period. Thus, if we take a disposition made after 1964 to:

the first child of B to reach 25,

the first reaction must be to wait and see whether the gift vests within the common law period (B's life plus 21 years). If B dies leaving one child, C, aged 2, it will be clear that C can never hope to reach the age of 25 within 21 years of B's death. At this point we know that the 'wait and see' provisions have not helped. The next step will therefore be to apply s. 4, which requires that an age reduction should be applied in order to attempt to save the disposition. However, we do not simply reduce the qualifying age to 21 (as was the case under the 1925 Act). Instead we have to apply a two-stage process:

(a) we decide whether the gift would be valid were the qualifying age 21 and if the answer is yes, then

(b) we reduce the age 'to the age nearest to that age which would, if specified instead, have prevented the disposition from being . . . void'.

If we apply this rule to our example we will see that the disposition would have been valid had the age limit been 21. C will reach 21 within 21 years of B's death. However, since C was 2 at his father's death, it is not necessary to reduce the qualifying age to 21 in order to ensure that the disposition vests in the period, for C will become 21 only 19 years after his father's death. The effect of s. 4 is therefore to reduce the qualifying age to 23, because that is the age closest to the specified age of 25 which is capable of satisfying the perpetuity rule. Accordingly, if C lives until he is 23 he will obtain an interest vested in possession under the 1964 Act.

15.4.5 **Introduction of presumptions about fertility**

As well as allowing us to 'wait and see', the 1964 Act introduced certain presumptions about fertility, which help to remove some of the more ridiculous problems caused by the common law rules. Under s. 2 of the Act the following presumptions apply:

(a) a male cannot be a father if he is aged under 14; and

(b) a female cannot be a mother if she is aged under 12 or over 55.

There is no upper age limit presumed in respect of a man's fertility. It is obvious that these presumptions are not an entirely accurate reflection of physical possibilities, particularly as far as the lower age limits are concerned. As a result, s. 2(2) allows the court to make such order as it thinks fit to readjust the position should it later be discovered that a birth has in fact occurred outside the presumed fertility periods. In addition to making use of the statutory presumptions described above, it is also open to the court to receive evidence that a particular male over 14 or female aged 12–55 is in fact infertile (s. 2(1)(b)). This is most likely to be of assistance in the cases of women who have undergone hysterectomies. More care would have to be taken in the case of evidence relating to sterilisation operations (e.g., vasectomy) as these can sometimes be reversed, rendering the individual fertile once more.

15.4.6 Amendment of rules on the 'unborn widow'

You will recall from 15.2.3.3 that a disposition:

to A for life and then to any widow of A for life and thereafter to the eldest of A's children then living,

gives rise to considerable problems at common law, because of the possibility that the future Mrs A might not have been born at the date of the disposition and so is not a life in being. We have seen above how, under the 1964 Act, it is possible to 'wait and see' whether Mrs A is a life in being and, if she is not, whether she does in fact die within 21 years of A's death, leaving a child of A in whom the gift can vest. However 'wait and see' will not help in that case if Mrs A survives her husband by more than 21 years. Accordingly, in such cases, s. 5 of the 1964 Act provides that the disposition 'to the eldest of A's children' shall be treated 'as if it had instead been limited by reference to the time immediately before the end of [the perpetuity] period'. Thus, in our example, if Mrs A is not a life in being and outlives her husband by more than 21 years, the eldest child of A who is living at the end of the period (A's life plus 21 years) will obtain a vested interest at that date. If A dies leaving two children, B and C (B being the elder) and a widow who outlives him by 21 years, B will obtain a vested interest 21 years after his father's death. Should B then die *before* the widow, B's estate will retain a vested interest and C will *not* obtain any interest in the property, even though this is contrary to the express wishes of the settlor. Although the result is to alter the intended outcome slightly, this rule does have the merit that it prevents the gift over to A's eldest child being wholly void.

15.5 Summary of common law rules and legislation

In conclusion, we must remind you that most of the statutory provisions are designed to rescue dispositions which are invalidated by the rule against perpetuities and do not, apart from the statutory 80-year period, provide any alternatives to it. This means that, when drafting a trust, regard must be had to the common law rules. No modern trust should ever be drafted in such a way as to be void under those rules. However, mistakes will no doubt continue to be made and discovered and accordingly you may find the following summary useful:

(a) *Dispositions coming in to effect before 1 January 1926.* Apply common law rules only.

(b) *Dispositions coming into effect between 1 January 1926 and 15 July 1964.* Apply common law rules but with the modification of the age reductions provided by LPA 1925, s. 163.

(c) *Dispositions coming into effect on or after 16 July 1964.* Apply common law rules, but with the modifications imposed by the Perpetuities and Accumulations Act 1964, and in particular:

    (i) in drafting a trust, take into account the availability of an 80-year fixed period;

   (ii) in interpreting a document creating a trust, take into account:

       (1) 'wait and see' (including statutory lives in being);

       (2) age reductions under s. 4;

       (3) presumptions about fertility in s. 2; and

       (4) special 'unborn widow' rules in s. 5.

15.6 To which other situations do the perpetuities rules apply?

Thus far in this chapter we have been concentrating on the application of the perpetuities rules in relation to trusts. However, the rules apply not only to trusts but also to many other arrangements and interests. The rules originated in relation to wills and family settlements but over time they were extended to other property rights, some of which are now primarily regarded as commercial interests and in relation to which the rules can seem unusual. In some cases the rules apply in full, whereas in other cases the rules apply only to a limited extent.

15.6.1 Powers

Before going on to discuss other interests it is worth mentioning first the position in relation to the powers of trustees under the rules. The discussion earlier in this chapter has been largely about the *creation* of a trust; however, the exercise by trustees of their powers can in themselves give rise to issues in relation to perpetuities. Section 8(1) of the Perpetuities and Accumulations Act 1964 excludes from the perpetuities rules the *exercise of the administrative powers* of trustees and this provision has retrospective effect (ss. 8(2) and 15(5)). This prevents problems in relation to powers such as the power of investment or the power of sale, which are regarded as being 'administrative' in character. These are powers which do not affect the position in relation to the beneficial interests under the trust and the application of the rule is not really necessary because the period during which the powers will be available will be controlled by the perpetuity period for the trust itself. However, the 1964 Act did not exempt what are generally called 'dispositive' powers: that is, powers that do have an effect on the interests under the trust. The major powers that fall into this category are those of appointment and advancement, since their exercise will control what beneficiaries actually receive. Such powers are subject to the perpetuity rules and the power may be void if it could be exercised at too remote a time. In addition, the actual exercise of a valid power is in itself subject to the perpetuity rules (so that, if the trustees appoint in favour of someone, that disposition must itself take effect within the perpetuity period). To make matters worse, in relation to powers of appointment, the calculation of the period starts at a different time depending on whether the power is a 'general' or a 'special' power of appointment. A general power of appointment permits the trustees to appoint in favour of anyone they choose (including the settlor). In this case the perpetuity period in relation to that power starts when the power is exercised. However, in the case of a special power of appointment (which allows appointment in favour of persons other than the settlor), the period runs from the date of the instrument that conferred the power to appoint.

15.6.2 Options and rights of pre-emption

The perpetuities rules do apply to options to acquire or create interests in land. At one time an option could not be void for perpetuity as between the contracting parties but only as against third parties or successors (see *Borland's Trustee* v *Steel Bros & Co. Ltd* [1901] 1 Ch 279 at p. 289). However, s. 10 of the Perpetuities and Accumulations Act 1964 abolished this rule and thus widened the scope of the perpetuities rules. Nevertheless, some options are still excluded. At common law, the rules do not apply to a tenant's option to renew his existing lease (*Muller* v *Trafford* [1901] 1 Ch 54 at p. 61). Also, s. 9(1) of the 1964 Act provides that the rules do not apply to an option to acquire for valuable consideration an interest reversionary on the term of a lease, if it is exercisable before the expiration of one year after the end of the lease and if the option is exercisable by the lessee or his successors in title. Section 9(2) provides a perpetuity period of 21 years for options to which the rules apply, where they are granted for valuable consideration; this is a 'wait and see' period. (Note that s. 9(2) does not apply in some cases in relation to land used for religious purposes.) However, one cannot use, in relation to an option, the fixed period of 80 years which applies to other cases under the 1964 Act.

Rights of pre-emption are in effect rights of 'first refusal'. They are in one sense a form of option but at common law it was never quite clear whether the options rules did apply. However, s. 9(2) of the 1964 Act contains an express exclusion for one type of right of pre-emption and this suggests that s. 9 must be intended to apply to any other cases. It appears that this was the view taken when the Act was debated by Parliament (*Hansard* (HL), 19 March 1964, vol. 256, col. 979 onwards).

A recent case, which illustrates the problems that can be caused due to unfamiliarity with the perpetuities rules and particularly s. 9, is *Wilson* v *Truelove* [2003] 23 EG 136. Truelove Ltd sold a farm to Mr and Mrs Wilson and their son David in 1974 but included in the contract a term that the Trueloves (who owned the company) had a right to re-purchase for £20,000 on the death of the second of David's parents to die. It was clear from surrounding evidence that the intention was that this right should not be limited in terms of time, one reason for the slightly strange agreement being that the parties were related by marriage. When the case came to court in 2003 it was held that the right to purchase was an interest in land, which arose at the date of the agreement in 1974. It was accordingly subject to the time limit imposed by s. 9(2) and since more than 21 years had passed since the date on which the interest was created (here the 'wait and see' rule was being applied), it was void. The court further held that no estoppel arose. This case therefore illustrates that the perpetuities rules can still be a source of problems in modern law and may well have the effect of giving someone much greater rights to property than he or she might reasonably have expected.

15.6.3 **Easements and restrictive covenants**

The grant of an easement to arise at some time in the future is subject to the perpetuity rules. Thus, if A tries to grant B rights to use any road that may be constructed over a field, that grant can be void for remoteness because the road may be constructed outside the perpetuity period (a right of way is a well-recognised easement, see 22.2.2.1)—see *Dunn* v *Blackdown Properties Ltd* [1961] Ch 433, which related to future drains. This can prove difficult when one is building an estate in parts over time but often the problem is solved in practice by the operation of the 'wait and see' rule.

Restrictive covenants to take effect at some time in the future can give rise to the same difficulties as future easements.

15.6.4 **Other applications of the rules**

You should note that there are other circumstances to which the perpetuities and accumulations rules apply but which are outside the scope of this book. The main example in practice arises in relation to pension schemes.

Interests that are not caught by the rules include the rights of re-entry by a landlord on a tenant's breach of covenant (see 10.3.2), by a mortgagee for default on a mortgage (21.7.2) for non-payment of a rentcharge (see LPA 1925, s. 121(6)), the purely administrative powers of trustees (see 15.6.1) and a joint tenant's right of survivorship (this is about co-ownership, not leases—see 16.3.1.3).

15.7 **Accumulations**

15.7.1 **Restrictions on the accumulation of income**

The rules we have set out above are about the creation of estates and interests and their validity. There is, however, a related set of rules which relate to the accumulation of income in trust. In essence the issue addressed in this rule is the case in which the trustees, rather than expending income as it arises in favour of the beneficiaries, accumulate that income and add it to the capital investment. The rules prevent such an accumulation for periods in excess of those prescribed by statute. This rule has always been statutory and does not arise from either common law or equity. In *Thelluson* v *Woodford* (1799) 4 Ves 227 it was held that at common law the trustees could be directed by the settlor to accumulate for the whole period for which the trust could exist (the perpetuity period in relation to the trust itself). The aim of the settlor in this case seems to have been to attempt to amass the largest possible sum with a view to the considerable enrichment of only a few of his descendants (three were specified). In fact, it appears that bad investment wrecked this grand plan but the approach was held to be acceptable at law. However, the case produced considerable concerns, it being believed (apparently) that such a power to accumulate could produce trusts with greater financial power than the State itself. Accordingly, in 1880 the first Accumulations Act was passed.

15.7.1.1 *The present rule*

The present law on accumulations is to be found in s. 164 of the LPA 1925 and s. 13 of the Perpetuities and Accumulations Act 1964. The rules apply to powers to accumulate whether they are express or implied. Section 164(1) says:

No person may by any instrument or otherwise settle or dispose of any property in such a manner that the income thereof shall, save as hereinafter mentioned, be wholly or partially accumulated for any longer period than one of the following, namely:

(a) the life of the grantor or settlor;

(b) a term of twenty-one years from the death of the grantor, settlor or testator; or

(c) the duration of the minority or respective minorities of any person or persons living or *en ventre sa mère* at the death of the grantor, settlor or testator; or

(d) the duration of the minority or respective minorities only of any person or persons who under the limitations of the instrument directing the accumulations would, for the time being, if of full age, be entitled to the income directed to be accumulated.

Section 13(1) of the 1964 Act adds two more periods to those in s. 164. The 1964 Act provision permits accumulation for:

(a) a term of 21 years from the date of the making of the disposition, and

(b) the duration of the minority or respective minorities of any person or persons in being at that date.

The creator of the settlement that authorises the accumulation can pick any of the periods set out above but in *Re Cattell* [1914] 1 Ch 177 at p. 186 it was said that one cannot choose to select two or more as alternatives (or cumulatively). If the accumulation is to be solely for the purpose of purchasing land, the sole permissible choice is period (d) under s. 164 (see s. 166). If the settlor does not actually select a period, in any case other than accumulation for the purpose of acquiring land, the court has to go through a very artificial exercise of working out which of the statutory periods appears to have been impliedly selected, by looking at the other provisions in the instrument (see *Re Ransome* [1957] Ch 348 at p. 361 for a comment on how realistic this approach is).

15.7.1.2 *Permitted extensions*

As well as the period selected under the rules set out above, the period permitted for accumulation may be extended if at the end of the statutory period a minor (person under 18) is entitled to a vested or contingent interest (LPA 1925, s. 165). In such a case the accumulation can continue until that person reaches 18. Thus if the 21-year period were selected but the beneficiary were to be aged 8 at the end of that period, the accumulation would in fact continue for 31 years.

15.7.2 **Excessive periods**

If a disposition breaks the perpetuities rule as well as the accumulations rule, that provision will be void, as explained above in relation to the perpetuities rule. However, if the accumulation provision is acceptable under the perpetuities rule but a period is selected that breaks the accumulations rule, the accumulation provision has effect for the permissible statutory period but is void in so far as it exceeds that period: *Eyre* v *Marsden* (1838) 2 Keen 564 at p. 574. It is not clear whether the 'wait and see' rule can apply (see Megarry and Wade, p. 366). After the authorised period expires, the trustees must pay the income to the person or persons who would have been entitled to it in the absence of the accumulation provision.

Note that s. 14 of the 1964 Act applies the presumptions as to fertility to accumulations and this may assist in determining when an accumulation will end.

15.7.3 Exceptions

The accumulations rule does not apply (s. 164(2)) to provisions: for the payment of anyone's debts; to raise 'portions' for the settlor's issue or the issue of a beneficiary under the settlement (for example to provide a dowry for a granddaughter); or for the accumulation of the produce of timber or wood. Note also that the rule does not bar the type of arrangement under which trustees simply adjust the application of income from year to year to iron out peaks and troughs: this is sometimes called 'administrative retention'. In the modern case of *Re Earl of Berkeley* [1968] Ch 744 the law on this point was considered and said to be acceptable as being simply an administrative precaution against future deficiencies.

Finally, we must mention that, in relation to both perpetuities and accumulations, we have concentrated on stating the general principle and giving a few examples of its application. Those who want information about the authorities from which the principle is derived, or the many other detailed rules which we have not mentioned, should refer to the materials listed in the Further Reading section at the end of this chapter.

15.8 Reform of the law

By now you will almost certainly be thinking that the rules on perpetuities are horribly complex and that it is not apparent that in all cases they serve a useful purpose. If that is how you feel, you are in good company: in the Executive Summary at the start of its Report on *The Rules Against Perpetuities and Excessive Accumulations* (Law Com No. 251 of March 1998), the Law Commission has said:

The law applicable to the operation of both rules is needlessly complicated and can only be understood by specialists. In a number of situations it is uncertain whether or how it applies.

The rule against perpetuities was originally devised to deal with interests arising under wills and family settlements, but it now applies to many other types of property rights, including those which often arise in commercial transactions such as options, rights of first refusal and grants of future easements. In these other situations the justification for it is absent. The application of the rule creates considerable practical difficulties in commercial property transactions.

In most situations, there is very little reason for the rule against excessive accumulations. It creates many practical difficulties for those who have to draft wills and trusts. In many other jurisdictions it has either been abolished or was never introduced in the first place.

15.8.1 **Rationale for old rules**

The basic reason for the application of the rules originally was that family trusts could impose the will of a dead hand (the settlor) on many successive generations and the result was the tendency to sterilise land. However, with modern changes in society in which land is no longer concentrated in the hands of a few and where even large landowners tend to deal with their property fairly readily, the whole underlying idea behind the rules may have become redundant. However, the Law Commission concluded that the rules should not be abolished in their entirety but that they should be modified to make them simpler to understand and to apply and that their ambit should be restricted to a narrower field.

15.8.2 **Aims of proposed reforms**

The aims behind the Law Commission's proposals were accordingly: to facilitate dealings with land by allowing reasonable arrangements that at present are void under the rules; to allow greater flexibility in land dealings and in trusts; to make the law easier to understand; to simplify and shorten drafting of legal documents; and, as a consequence of all these reforms, to reduce legal costs for those involved.

15.8.3 **The proposed reforms**

The proposals for reform start with a conclusion that in future the perpetuities and accumulations rules should not apply at all in the following cases:

(a) future easements;
(b) future restrictive covenants;
(c) options;
(d) rights of pre-emption; and
(e) pension schemes.

It is proposed that in future there should be a statutory rule on perpetuities that applies only to specified interests, which are essentially only those arising under wills and trusts. It is also proposed that the rule should continue to apply to powers of appointment.

Where the perpetuity rule does apply the Law Commission advise that there should be one statutory period of 125 years and that no other period should be permitted. This removes the 'life in being plus 21 years' rule and the possibility of use of Royal lives clauses or the existing elective statutory period of 80 years. The new period would apply whatever the instrument creating the trust or interest might say but would, in general, apply only to new instruments taking effect after the reforms 'bite'. This means, of course, that we would still all have to learn the old rules alongside the new rules for many years to come! It is, however, suggested that in certain circumstances trustees of existing settlements should have a power to opt into the new period. The proposal is that the new period, where it applies, will take effect from the date of the instrument which creates the interest or estate in question. In relation to powers of appointment the period should start at the date of the instrument which granted the power (and not from the date on which the power is exercised).

In all cases in which the perpetuities rule applies, it is proposed that the wait and see principle should be applied. Thus, no interest would become void for perpetuity until it became clear that it *must* vest outside the 125-year period.

In relation to the rule against excessive accumulations, it is proposed that the rule should be entirely abolished save in relation to charitable trusts. It is recommended that accumulations in charitable trusts should be restricted to a period of 21 years and that no other period should be permitted.

These proposed reforms are interesting and would do a great deal to simplify the law in what is a dreadfully complex area of law which, at present, although in some ways fascinating due to its arcane nature, frequently amounts only to a trap for the unwary and a source of work for those who are experts. The Report of the Law Commission provides a useful summary of the existing rules and the main difficulties with them and is well worth study.

Whether legislation will indeed be brought forward to amend this area of the law is a matter only for conjecture. However, it should be noted that a number of other Law Commission proposals in relation to land law have been abandoned (see *Hansard* (HL) 19 March 1998, col. 213) or have taken a long time to come to fruition (e.g., commonhold). For the time being we must all continue to wrestle with the current rules.

FURTHER READING

Cheshire & Burn's Modern Law of Real Property, 16th edn., Butterworths, 2000, Chapter 14 (Future Interests).

Lawson and Rudden, *The Law of Property*, 3rd edn., Oxford University Press, 2002, Chapter 13 (The Control of Endowment).

Megarry and Wade, *The Law of Real Property*, 6th edn., Sweet & Maxwell, 2000, Chapter 7 (Perpetuities and Accumulations).

Maudsley, *The Modern Law of Perpetuities*, Butterworths, 1979.

16

Co-ownership

16.1 Background

At one time the normal pattern of land ownership in Britain was that the estate in land, unless it was a large property subject to a complex settlement, was vested in one person as sole beneficial owner. The family home tended to be vested in the man who was regarded as head of the household (whether it was held freehold or leasehold). Changes in social conditions and in particular the alteration in the status of women, have meant that today sole ownership has become far more rare and that it is normal for domestic property to be the subject of co-ownership. This co-ownership may arise deliberately because the property is conveyed to two or more persons as co-owners, or by operation of law (e.g., as the product of a resulting trust—see Chapter 17). It can arise in relation to either of the legal estates (a fee simple or a lease) or any interest in land.

16.2 Introduction

Mr and Mrs Armstrong have now completed the purchase of the fee simple estate in **1 Trant Way**. The property was transferred 'to Arnold Armstrong and Arriety Armstrong' and they have now been registered as proprietors at the Land Registry.

12 Trant Way was bought in 2003 by six friends who are all studying Outer Mongolian history on a four-year course at Mousehole University. The friends each contributed one-sixth of the purchase price and, because they were short of money, one of their number did the conveyancing himself. The property was conveyed to all six: i.e., to Alice, Brian, Colin, David, Eric and Fanny. At the date of the conveyance Alice was 17 and all the others were 18. The intention was that the house was to be kept until all six graduated and that it should then be sold.

13 Trant Way belongs to a firm of chartered surveyors. The partners in the firm are Sidney Search and Frederick Find and the legal estate, a 99-year lease, has been conveyed into the names of the two partners.

16.3 **Two types of co-ownership**

In modern law there are two main types of co-ownership: (a) the *joint tenancy*, and
(b) the *tenancy in common*. It is essential to be able to distinguish between the two
and so we will first look at the characteristics of each, before going on to consider
how they arise. You should, however, note that in very rare cases it is possible to
come across a third form of co-ownership, called *coparcenary*. This is a form of
co-ownership which cannot be created after 1925 but a few pre-1926 cases may still
continue in operation today. The most common case in which coparcenary arose
was where an estate owner died intestate leaving only female heirs: in such a case
the eldest child did not inherit, instead all the women entitled took the estate as
coparcenors. Coparcenary usually involves the four unities that, as we will see below,
are a mark of the joint tenancy but in other ways resembled the tenancy in
common, because the coparcenors were treated as having individual shares in the
property.

Prior to the 1925 legislation coming into force on 1 January 1926, it was also
possible to have a form of co-ownership called *tenancy by entireties*, which applied
only to co-ownership by a husband and wife and was based on the ancient concept
that a husband and wife should in law be treated as one unit: all property held by
married couples was held automatically in this way. This idea as an automatic
concept is sufficiently repugnant to modern thought that the Married Women's
Property Act 1882, ss. 1 and 5 prevented the creation of any new tenancies by
entireties and thus permitted married women to have their own interests in marital
property. Any remaining tenancies by entirety were laid to rest by LPA 1925, Sch. 1,
Part IV, which converted them into joint tenancies.

From this it will already be obvious that the law of co-ownership is strongly
related to family law. However, co-ownership does not only arise within families:
the students at 12 Trant Way and the surveyors at 13 Trant Way provide examples
of co-ownership outside family relationships. Bearing this in mind, we now look at
joint tenancies and tenancies in common.

16.3.1 **Joint tenancy**

16.3.1.1 *The 'four unities'*

The joint tenancy is, in a way, the more perfect of the two types of co-ownership. It
is a method of ownership in which the co-owners are *not* regarded as having 'shares'
in the land but as together owning the whole estate. It is as though the co-owners
are not really treated as separate owners but as an inseparable group owner. Thus,
if Arnold and Arriety Armstrong are joint tenants in respect of 1 Trant Way, we
cannot say that Arnold owns half and that Arriety owns half. We must say that
Arnold and Arriety *together* own the whole estate. In the notation used in this
chapter we will place joint tenants inside brackets,

(Arnold and Arriety)

to indicate this relationship.

For this 'perfect' relationship to exist one must establish first that what are traditionally called the 'four unities' exist. These unities are essential to the joint nature of the ownership, in which no co-owner has a share distinguishable from that of the other co-owners. The unities are:

(a) time;

(b) title;

(c) interest; and

(d) possession.

(a) *Time*   This unity requires that the interests of all the co-owners should vest at the same time. Thus in a disposition, 'to A for life and then to B and C', B and C have the unity of time because the interest of each vests on the death of A. In the case of Mr and Mrs Armstrong this unity exists because the interest of each vested when 1 Trant Way was transferred to them as co-owners.

(b) *Title*   This requires that the co-owners should all have acquired their title by the same means, e.g., all from the same document. In the case of Mr and Mrs Armstrong they both derive their title from the transfer that, on registration, vested the legal estate in them. This unity would also be satisfied if two or more persons together took land by adverse possession. In this case, title is derived from the action of taking possession of the land and if this action is taken by persons acting jointly the unity of title would be present (*Ward* v *Ward* (1871) LR 6 Ch App 789).

(c) *Interest*   For a joint tenancy to exist, the interests of all the co-owners must also be identical. Each interest must be of the same duration and of the same nature and extent. Thus, if one co-owner has a life interest and the other an interest in fee simple, they cannot be joint tenants because this unity is not present.

(d) *Possession*   Finally, the co-owners must be equally entitled to the possession of the whole land (see *Bull* v *Bull* [1955] 1 QB 234). If one could point to a portion of the land and say, 'That portion is mine alone', then there would be no co-ownership. In such a case each would be a sole owner of a smaller part of the land. This would arise, for example, if two people were to divide one parcel of land between themselves and each took a different portion.

16.3.1.2 *Words of severance*

Even where all four unities are present it is still possible for the arrangement not to satisfy the requirements for a joint tenancy. This will happen where it is clear that the parties are to be regarded as having separate *shares* in the property (even though they may not wish to partition the land). Any words suggesting that the co-owners are to be regarded as owners of shares, rather than as a kind of group sole owner, will prevent the ownership being a joint tenancy. This will happen in particular if the conveyance or transfer to the co-owners contains 'words of severance'. These are words such as 'in equal shares' (*Payne* v *Webb* (1874) LR 19 Eq 26), which show that the co-owners do not have the indivisible relationship which is necessary for the joint tenancy. Other words that have been held to produce this result include:

'equally' (*Lewen* v *Dodd* (1595) Cro Eliz 443);

'share and share alike' (*Heathe* v *Heathe* (1740) 2 Atk 121);

'to be divided between' (*Peat* v *Chapman* (1750) 1 Ves Sen 542); and 'between' (*Lashbrook* v *Cock* (1816) 2 Mer 70).

16.3.1.3 *Right of survivorship*

One crucial aspect of joint tenancy is the 'right of survivorship' or *jus accrescendi*. Since a joint tenant is not regarded as having a distinct share in the co-owned land, he or she is not able to dispose of his or her interest by will on death, nor will it pass on intestacy if no will is made. Instead, on the death of one joint tenant, the remaining joint tenants obtain the interest of the deceased. This is the natural result of regarding joint tenants as a kind of unified and indivisible group. The last survivor of the group will of course become a sole beneficial owner and will be able to dispose of the property as he or she pleases on death. With the joint tenancy it pays to be long-lived! This rule may prove to be a nuisance in some types of co-ownership and may encourage the choice of the tenancy in common instead. However, in some cases, for instance, between husband and wife, it may be very convenient and avoid unnecessary dispositions on the death of one co-owner.

16.3.2 **Tenancy in common**

The tenancy in common is not such a 'perfect' relationship of co-ownership. For such a tenancy to exist, only one unity is required, that of possession. This unity is essential for, as we have already seen, if it did not exist there would be no co-ownership but merely individual ownership of separate portions of land. The tenant in common, unlike the joint tenant, is entitled to a notional share of the property (e.g., a half or a quarter), which he or she can dispose of during life or at death, but this is an 'undivided share' and, until partition or sale occurs, all the tenants in common are entitled to possession of the whole. Thus, provided unity of possession is present, a tenancy in common will arise in any case of co-ownership where the other unities are absent, and the arrangement cannot therefore give rise to a joint tenancy.

However, it must be remembered that often all four unities may be present, but there will still be only a tenancy in common because of the clear intention of the parties that they should hold in this way, or because of the presence of words of severance in the document creating their interests. Further, even where such intention or words are *not* present, there are some very important cases in which equity will presume that a tenancy in common has been created.

Thus, if the co-owners have contributed in unequal portions to the purchase price, equity considered it unfair to impose upon them the equality of the joint tenancy and the effects of the right of survivorship, for it might be that the tenant who had contributed least might prove to be the longest lived, and thus become the sole owner of the whole property. Accordingly, in such cases equity has always presumed that unequal contributors hold the property as tenants in common, each co-owner having a share in the property proportional to his contribution to the purchase price (*Lake* v *Gibson* (1729) 1 Eq Rep 290; and, in modern law, *Bull* v *Bull* [1955] 1 QB 234). This presumption could of course be rebutted by clear evidence of an intention to the contrary: either that the parties should, after all, hold as joint tenants, or that as tenants in common the size of their shares should not correspond to the amount of their respective contributions. Again, where the co-ownership is of a commercial character, the right of survivorship appears to equity to be inappropriate. Thus, in the case of partnership property, equity also leans in favour of the tenancy in common, and so would assume that the type of co-ownership applicable to 13 Trant Way (owned by the chartered surveyors) is the tenancy in common (*Re Fuller's Contract* [1933] Ch 652). Another example of this principle is found where two people lend money on mortgage (joint mortgagees): they are presumed to hold the estate which they receive by way of security as tenants in common (*Morley* v *Bird* (1798) 3 Ves Jr 628). See also *Malayan Credit Ltd* v *Jack Chia-MPH Ltd* [1986] AC 549, PC.

16.3.3 Different positions in law and equity

Whilst equity has always preferred the tenancy in common, law leaned in favour of the joint tenancy. The reason for this was that with the joint tenancy the number of co-owners always decreases (because of the right of survivorship). This facilitates dealings with the legal estate, by concentrating the title to it into fewer hands, rather than by increasing the number of owners, as can happen when the share of a tenant in common passes on his death to several people. Thus, it has always been true that, whilst equity might regard a set of co-owners as tenants in common, law might regard the same persons as joint tenants. It is useful therefore always to think of co-owners under two separate headings thus:

13 Trant Way

LAW	EQUITY
(Search and Find)	Search and Find
Joint tenancy	*Tenancy in common*

In this example Search and Find are legal joint tenants but are tenants in common in equity. To put it another way, they hold the legal estate as joint tenants but the beneficial interest (the equitable interest) as tenants in common. We will adopt this standard diagrammatic form hereafter and you will note that joint tenants appear together in brackets, whereas tenants in common appear without brackets.

It may be thought that considerable difficulties would be caused if law and equity regarded one arrangement as giving rise to different forms of co-ownership. Are the owners to be regarded as joint tenants, subject to the right of survivorship, or as tenants in common? The difficulty may be illustrated by considering the position of A and B, who hold the legal estate as joint tenants but who, because of unequal contributions, are regarded by equity as tenants in common. During their lifetime, this may cause no great difficulty but what happens when B dies, having made a will by which he leaves his interest in the property to C? At law, A will become solely entitled to the property and C will take nothing. In equity B's share under his tenancy in common passes under his will and C is, therefore, entitled to that share. What will happen? Fortunately, the apparent difficulty has always been resolved by the use of the trust. From the outset, equity accepted that at law A and B were joint tenants, but required that they should hold the estate in trust for themselves as tenants in common in equity (or, in other words, as tenants in common of the beneficial interest). When B dies, A is left holding the legal estate, not for himself alone but in trust for himself and C, again as tenants in common.

LAW	EQUITY
(A and B)	A and B
A	A and C

16.3.4 **No legal tenancies in common**

A further occasion for a divergence between law and equity came with the modern rule, introduced by the 1925 legislation, that there cannot be a tenancy in common of the legal estate. This change was one of many designed to facilitate conveyancing; as we have already seen, the joint tenancy offers considerable advantages in this regard.

This rule is to be found in LPA 1925, s. 34(1): 'An undivided share in land shall not be capable of being created except as provided by the Settled Land Act 1925 or as hereinafter mentioned'.

This does not prevent the creation of tenancies in common in equity because the later subsections of s. 34 (as amended by TOLATA 1996, Sch. 2, para. 3) go on to permit the creation of an undivided share in land behind a trust (which will, save in old SLA 1925 cases or new sub-trusts of old SLA cases, be trusts of land). Nowadays, therefore, if a conveyance of a legal estate is made 'to A and B as tenants in common', or if words of severance are used ('to A and B in equal shares'), this will not affect the legal estate, which will pass to A and B as joint tenants. However, effect will be given to the intention by treating them as tenants in common in equity.

16.3.5 **Imposition of statutory trusts**

We have seen already that when law and equity differed over the nature of the tenancy created, any apparent conflict was resolved by the use of a trust. The 1925 property legislation went further than this and imposed statutory trusts on most forms of co-ownership (see LPA 1925, s. 34(2) (tenancies in common) and s. 36(1) (joint tenancies)). The 'statutory trusts' were defined in LPA 1925, s. 35 and until 1997 consisted of a trust for sale. Thus the co-owners held the legal estate upon trust for sale for themselves as beneficiaries. As we have seen (12.2.2.1), the operation of the doctrine of conversion meant that the equitable interests of the co-owners were interests in money and not in land, and this seemed particularly inappropriate in relation to a family home. The statutory trusts now take effect as trusts of land and there is no longer any problem about the notional conversion of the property. TOLATA 1996 has amended both s. 34 and s. 36 of LPA 1925 so that each provision imposes a trust in the relevant cases of co-ownership, that trust necessarily being a trust of land (TOLATA 1996, Sch. 2, paras. 3 and 4), and s. 35 has been repealed (TOLATA 1996, Sch. 4).

This imposition of the trust must be related to the overall policy of the 1925 legislation (which has been reinforced by recent reforms): to simplify conveyancing and to make it easier for a purchaser to buy land. The fact that any property subject to co-ownership was made subject to a trust enables the purchaser to take advantage of the overreaching machinery (which we have explained in 13.9): provided the purchase money is paid to two trustees, the purchaser takes free of the beneficial interests and need not worry about questions of who is entitled in equity and whether they agreed to the sale (e.g., *City of London Building Society* v *Flegg* [1988] AC 54—see 5.10.4.5(1)). The purchaser is concerned only with title to the legal estate.

So far, we have spoken as though the 1925 legislation imposed a trust for sale in all cases of co-ownership but we must mention briefly that there used to be certain gaps not covered by the provisions of LPA 1925, ss. 34 to 36. One example will suffice: the wording of s. 34 did not apply to tenancies in common which arose otherwise than expressly (e.g., on a resulting trust). However, this gap was filled by the court in the case of *Bull* v *Bull* [1955] 1 QB 234, in which the trust for sale was imposed in these circumstances. However, these problems do not now arise because the wording of TOLATA 1996, s. 1 ensures that wherever a trust arises, if part of the trust property is land, that trust will necessarily be a trust of land. This will even cover the cases in which there are several joint tenants of the legal estate holding as trustees for a sole beneficiary.

16.3.6 Maximum of four trustees

In order to prevent a trust having an inordinate number of trustees, the Trustee Act 1925, s. 34(2), limits the number of trustees to a maximum of four. Where more than four are named, the property vests in the first four who are of full age. Where land is simply conveyed to a group of persons as tenants in common, LPA 1925, s. 34(2), provides that the first four of full age will take the legal estate as joint tenants and hold it upon trust for the whole group as tenants in common in equity. As a result, the conveyance of 12 Trant Way to the six students will have vested the legal estate in the first four who are over 18 (Brian, Colin, David and Eric) and these four should have been registered as proprietors on first registration. Alice, who was only 17 at the date of the conveyance, and Fanny will be owners in equity only. The legal estate must be held by the trustees as joint tenants but the nature of the equitable ownership will depend on the presence or absence of the four unities and words of severance. We know that all six contributed equally to the purchase price, so there is no question of equity presuming a tenancy in common. Assuming that there are no words of severance, the result is as follows:

LAW	EQUITY
(B, C, D and E)	(A, B, C, D, E and F)

There is a joint tenancy in both law and equity but with six equitable owners and only four (the maximum) at law. The trust will necessarily be a TOLATA 1996 'trust of land': s. 1. Following the conveyance or transfer the students will have had to apply for registration of the title. The Land Registrar will have ensured that Brian, Colin, David and Eric were registered as joint proprietors of the legal estate and will have entered a restriction, warning that purchase moneys must be paid to two trustees. (See LRA 2002, s. 44(1) for the rule on restrictions.)

16.4 **Severance of a joint tenancy**

A relationship which begins as a joint tenancy need not remain so, for, in certain circumstances, it is possible for a joint tenant to sever his or her interest and thereby to convert it into a tenancy in common. A primary reason for severance may be to avoid the effects of the right of survivorship. This is why the Married Women's Property Act 1882 regarded a joint tenancy as preferable to tenancy by entireties: in the case of a joint tenancy a married women could establish a right to a separate share in the property by severing her interest, if she so chose. Of course, it is *never* possible these days to sever a joint tenancy of the legal estate, for to do this would be to create a legal tenancy in common, which is prohibited by LPA 1925, s. 34(1). Accordingly LPA 1925, s. 36(2) provides that: 'No severance of a joint tenancy of a legal estate, so as to create a tenancy in common in land, shall be permissible'.

Severance of an *equitable joint* tenancy is, however, still possible (and frequent in practice) and may be effected in a number of ways, which are set out in the proviso to s. 36(2) (as amended by TOLATA 1996, Sch. 2, para. 4(3)):

Provided that, where a legal estate (not being settled land) is vested in joint tenants beneficially, and any tenant desires to sever the joint tenancy in equity, he shall give to the other joint tenants a notice in writing of such desire or do such other acts or things as would, in the case of personal estate, have been effectual to sever the tenancy in equity, and thereupon the land shall be held in trust on terms which would have been requisite for giving effect to the beneficial interest if there had been an actual severance.

When the equitable joint tenancy is severed, the joint tenant severing will take an equal portion of the interest as a tenant in common. Thus, if the property was expressly conveyed to two persons as joint tenants, on severance each will acquire a half share as tenants in common (*Goodman* v *Gallant* [1986] Fam 106).

We will now look in detail at those methods of severing.

16.4.1 **Notice in writing**

This is probably the simplest way today of severing a joint tenancy. The notice, if posted, should be served on all the other joint tenants, in a registered or recorded delivery letter, at their last known place of abode or business (LPA 1925, s. 196(4)). Provided that this method of service is adopted, it is irrelevant that the co-owner does not in fact receive knowledge of the notice. In *Re 88 Berkeley Road NW9* [1971] Ch 648 the two joint tenants both occupied the premises. One co-owner served notice of severance on the other joint tenant by registered post to the property. It later became clear that, when the letter was delivered, it was received and signed for by the person who had sent it and that it was never handed to the addressee. This was held nonetheless to amount to good service and the joint tenancy had accordingly been severed. (Although s. 196(4) only refers to registered post, recorded delivery is also acceptable: Recorded Delivery Service Act 1962, s. 1 and Sch. 1, para. 1.) Instead of posting the notice it will also be enough to address it to the other joint tenants and leave it at, or affix it to, their last known abode or place of business (LPA 1925, s. 196(3)).

Lest you should think that *Re 88 Berkeley Road* was an isolated case, something very similar happened in *Kinch* v *Bullard* [1999] 1 WLR 423. Here a husband and wife were beneficial joint tenants of the matrimonial home. In 1995 the wife issued divorce proceedings and, being aware that she was terminally ill, also instructed her solicitors to serve notice of severance on her husband because she wished to ensure that the right of survivorship would not have effect. The solicitor sent such a letter by ordinary first-class post on 3 August. Over the weekend of 5–6 August the husband had a heart attack. The evidence was that the postman had delivered the letter by putting it though the letter-box at the property either on 5 or 7 August and it came into the hands of the wife, who had changed her mind by that point about wanting to sever and destroyed the letter without showing it to her husband. The husband died on 15 August 1995 and the wife on 6 January 1996. If the letter of severance was effective, the husband's share passed on his death to his executors but, if it were not effective, on his death the right of survivorship operated and the wife's estate could claim the entire property. Neuberger J held that the notice had been served effectively and the husband's estate was entitled to his share.

A first issue was that the letter had been sent by ordinary post. This was not relevant, however, because s. 196(3) says that, 'Any notice . . . shall be sufficiently served if it is left at the last-known place of abode . . . of the . . . person to be served . . .'. In this case in fact evidence was produced that the postman had left the letter at the husband's abode, by putting it through the letter-box. Accordingly, it was not necessary to go on and rely on the postal rule in s. 146(4), which provides simply an additional mode of service. (Note, however, that you might be dependant on the memory of the postman if you use something other than recorded or registered post and would run the risk of ineffective service should the letter not be delivered. If you use the normal postal services, s. 7 of the Interpretation Act 1978 may assist.) Second, the fact the husband had not received the letter personally was not relevant because service was effected when the letter was 'left' at the premises and not when the person being served actually read the letter. Third, the wife's change of mind was irrelevant because she could not withdraw the letter once it had been served: the severance took effect at the time of service, when the letter was left at the premises. It was accepted, however, that it may be possible to withdraw a notice if the sending co-owner said to the other *before* the letter was served, 'I have sent a notice but I have changed my mind'. However, this view is *obiter* and tentatively expressed. Presumably, it cannot work if the notice is sent by registered or recorded post because in that case the notice appears to be served when the letter is sent (see the wording of s. 36(4)). However, Neuberger J seems also to have taken the view that had the wife wished to argue that her notice had the effect of severing her interest, then she would not have been entitled to do so because she had taken positive steps to ensure that the letter did not ever come to her husband's attention. The judge was of the view that to permit this would be to permit the statute 'to be used as an engine of fraud' and this is contrary to long-standing equitable principles. It would therefore, in such a case, be open to the recipient to raise the deliberate intervention as a defence in order to allege that, despite delivery ('leaving'), the notice was not effective. Presumably this principle would apply whether the letter was sent registered or recorded delivery, or simply 'left' because in both cases the statutory rule has operated by the time the intervention occurs: it would be the later deliberate act of the sender that would prevent reliance on the statutory effect that would otherwise apply. This case is well worth reading as an interesting illustration of how legal and equitable rules can interact and as an example of statutory interpretation, as well as an illustration of the severance rules in practice.

A recent interesting case on severance is *Grindal* v *Hooper* [1999] EGCS 150 (and see the article on the case at [2000] Conv 461). Here, in the conveyance to them-selves, joint tenants had agreed that any notice purporting to sever their joint tenancy would not be effective unless it had been annexed to the conveyance to them. This term takes one step further a usual conveyancing practice, under which notice of severance is noted on the title deeds as a warning to later acquirers. However, here the parties had tried to ensure that the notice itself was not effective unless annexed to the conveyance. One joint tenant did serve a notice that com-plied with s. 36(2) but which was not annexed to the conveyance. That joint tenant subsequently died and the survivor claimed that there had been no valid severance in this instance. The court held that the agreement between the joint tenants could not displace the effect of the statutory rule that a notice complying with s. 36(2) did effect severance and thus the parties had been tenants in common in equity from the point at which notice was validly given. (There is a second issue in this case about protection of a subsequent acquirer, on which see 16.6.2.)

16.4.2 'Such other acts or things as would, in the case of personal estate, sever the tenancy in equity'

It may seem strange that methods of severing appropriate to personal property are prescribed here but you will remember that the old statutory trust for sale had the effect of notionally converting the beneficiaries' interest into an interest in money (i.e., personal property). Although this conversion will no longer occur, due to TOLATA 1996, s. 3, this rule is not altered.

Next, one has to consider what 'acts or things' bring about severance in equity. The classic statement, to which later decisions usually refer with approval, is that of Sir William Page Wood V-C in *Williams* v *Hensman* (1861) 1 John & H 546 at p. 557:

A joint tenancy may be severed in three ways: in the first place, an act of any one of the persons interested operating upon his own share may create a severance as to that share . . . Each one is at liberty to dispose of his own interest in such manner as to sever it from the joint fund losing, of course, at the same time, his own right of survivorship. Secondly, a joint tenancy may be severed by mutual agreement. And, in the third place, there may be a severance by any course of dealing sufficient to intimate that the interests of all were mutually treated as constituting a tenancy in common.

We will look at each of these three methods in turn.

16.4.2.1 'An act . . . operating upon his own share'

The example given of this method is that of disposing of one's own interest in such a way as to sever it from the joint property—for example, on sale. This creates severance because it has the effect of destroying one of the unities essential to the joint tenancy: that of title. The purchaser does not share the unity of title with the other co-owners, for he takes under a different document and so cannot be a joint tenant with them. In law, severance would occur when the estate was conveyed to the purchaser. In equity, it takes place as soon as there is a specifically enforceable contract to sell. It will be remembered that equity recognises the purchaser as owner from the date of the contract, and the change of equitable ownership is enough to destroy the unities.

Where severance is effected by sale of the beneficial interest, the joint tenant cannot transfer his interest in the *legal* estate to the purchaser, for to do so would amount to severance of the legal joint tenancy, which is forbidden (LPA 1925, s. 36(2)). So, even after he has disposed of his beneficial interest, he continues to hold the legal estate as a trustee, and can only cease to be a trustee by releasing his interest to his fellow joint tenants or by retiring from the trust (Trustee Act 1925, s. 39) or, if the other trustees agree (even if all the beneficiaries do not) by making, with the other trustees, a forced conveyance in favour of the beneficiaries under TOLATA 1996, s. 6(2).

Another way of disrupting the unities and therefore of severing a legal joint tenancy before 1926 occurred when one joint tenant acquired a greater interest than his fellows and thereby destroyed the unity of interest. Thus, if A, B and C were equitable joint tenants for life and A acquired the interest in remainder, this would transform A's interest into a tenancy in common. Although not specifically mentioned in *Williams* v *Hensman*, it could perhaps be described as an act which operates on one's own share, and therefore may come within this first category.

An example which falls within this category (although this may at first seem odd) arises if one of the joint tenants is declared bankrupt. This is an involuntary effect of the law relating to bankruptcy which transfers the bankrupt's interest to his trustee in bankruptcy when a bankruptcy order is made. Thus, while not really an act of the bankrupt co-owner, it nonetheless does create a separate share in the property by means of a transferring disposition. However, on this point see the comments of Russell LJ in *Bedson* v *Bedson* [1965] 2 QB 666 at p. 690 and see Insolvency Act 1986, s. 306 (which is not construed as overriding LPA 1925, s. 36(2) and so does not vest the legal estate in the trustee, just the beneficial interest) and s. 283A of the Insolvency Act 1986 (inserted by s. 261 of the Enterprise Act 2002), which now provides for the interest to re-vest in the bankrupt unless the trustee's powers are exercised within three years. See also s. 313A of the Insolvency Act 1986 (also inserted by s. 261 of the Enterprise Act 2002) which prevents the trustee in bankruptcy from obtaining sale, possession or a charge over a dwelling-house that is the sole or principal residence of the bankrupt or his or her spouse or former spouse, if the value of the bankrupt's interest in the property is of low value.

Another example of alienation arises when one joint tenant charges (mortgages) his interest in the property. Acting alone, the joint tenant can only affect his or her own interest (the equitable interest) and can only charge it if it constitutes a share separate from that of the other co-owner. Thus, charging your own interest severs the joint tenancy (the legal owners would have to act together as trustees to charge the legal estate). In *First National Securities* v *Hegarty* [1984] 1 All ER 139, Bingham J held that the same effect occurred where a husband purported to mortgage the legal estate by resorting to the forgery of his wife's signature. The result was a charge operating only on the husband's interest and which severed the joint tenancy in equity.

16.4.2.2 *Mutual agreement*

Severance can be effected by the agreement of all the joint tenants. The agreement may, of course, be express, but can also be inferred from the conduct of the parties. The leading modern case which illustrates this method of severance is *Burgess* v *Rawnsley* [1975] 1 Ch 429. Here it was held that an oral agreement by one joint tenant to purchase the share of the other had effected a severance (because the parties were thinking in terms of 'shares'), even though such an agreement would not be legally enforceable because there was no written memorandum or part performance to satisfy LPA 1925, s. 40 (the predecessor to the Law of Property (Miscellaneous) Provisions Act 1989, s. 2). We have seen that a contract must be specifically enforceable if it is to constitute severance under the first rule in *Williams* v *Hensman*; but the Court of Appeal emphasised that this requirement 'only applies where the suggestion is that the joint tenancy has been severed by an alienation by one joint tenant to a third party and does not apply to severance by agreement between the joint tenants' (per Browne LJ [1975] Ch 429 at p. 444). The principle that an unenforceable agreement can serve as evidence of a common intention to sever was confirmed in *Hunter* v *Babbage* [1994] EGCS 8, in which a divorcing couple's unenforceable agreement was held to sever when the husband died before the agreement could be formalised. Another example of severance by agreement is to be found in *Re Woolnough* [2002] WTLR 595. Here, the joint tenants were brother and sister and they went to their solicitor together and both made wills, each leaving his or her interest in their property to the other but with a remainder to their niece. After the sister's death the brother changed his will and it became essential to know whether after the making of the earlier wills the joint tenancy had been severed. The court held that it had. This is because for each to make a will leaving a share to the other, there must have been an intention on the part of both to treat themselves as each having a share. If they agreed that each had a share they must both have regarded themselves as having interests in common (rather than joint) because joint interests do not give rise to share that can be disposed of by a will.

16.4.2.3 *'Any course of dealing [which shows] that the interests of all were mutually treated as constituting a tenancy in common'*

In *Burgess* v *Rawnsley*, members of the Court of Appeal expressed views on this third category, although they emphasised that as the decision was based on the second ground (mutual agreement), these views were necessarily *obiter dicta*. Thus, Sir John Pennycuick explained that it includes 'negotiations which, although not otherwise resulting in any agreement, indicate a common intention that the joint tenancy should be regarded as severed' (at p. 447). It should be noted that Lord Denning MR gave a slightly wider interpretation (at p. 439), which seems to cover a unilateral declaration by the party wishing to sever:

It is sufficient if there is a course of dealing in which one party makes clear to the other that he desires that their shares should no longer be held jointly but be held in common.

This does not seem to fit too well with the requirement of *mutual* behaviour stated in *Williams* v *Hensman*, and it should be noted that Sir John Pennycuick expressly states that in his view 'a mere verbal notice' by one party to the other cannot operate as severance (p. 448). Written notice is validated by the statutory rules in LPA 1925, s. 36(3) and (4).

16.4.2.4 *Forfeiture*

One final method of severance, not covered by LPA 1925, s. 36(2) or *Williams* v *Hensman* (1861) 1 John & H 546 must be noted briefly. Should one joint tenant kill the other (which is not altogether unknown), it seems that the right of survivorship cannot operate because this would allow the homicide to benefit from his or her criminal act. The general principle that this is not permitted is to be found in *In the Estate of Hall* [1914] P 1, and some recent decisions in Australia and New Zealand have applied this to cases of joint tenancy, although it seems there is as yet no English decision directly on the point. However, you should see the Forfeiture Act 1982 and the judgments in the Court of Appeal in *Dunbar* v *Plant* [1998] FLR 157, which suggest that the same result would apply in English law. On the impact of the forfeiture rule, see also *T.W.G.S.* v *J.M.G.* [2000] 3 WLR 1910. For a detailed analysis of the overseas authorities on this point and the jurisprudence, see Gray and Gray, at pp. 871–6.

16.4.2.5 *Example of the operation of the severance rules*

Let us take the position at 12 Trant Way (the six students) and assume that the following events occur:

(a) A serves notice of severance on B, C, D, E and F;

(b) B sells his interest to X; and

(c) C dies.

This produces the following devolution of title to the legal estate and the equitable interest:

EVENT	LAW	EQUITY	EXPLANATION
	(B, C, D and E)	(A, B, C, D, E and F)	At start all are joint tenants.
(a)	(B, C, D and E)	A (B, C, D, E and F)	Position at law not affected. A becomes tenant in common in equity with a one-sixth share, but others remain joint tenants *inter se* ('between themselves').
(b)	(B, C, D and E)	A, X (C, D, E and F)	Position at law not affected. In equity, severance by destruction of unities. X becomes tenant in common with a one-sixth share. C, D, E and F remain joint tenants *inter se* of four-sixths.
(c)	(B, D and E)	A, X (D, E and F)	Right of survivorship operates in law and equity. D, E and F now jointly own four-sixths of equitable interest. A and X each own a one-sixth share.

16.5 **Relationship between co-owners**

It is not uncommon for co-owners of property to have differences of opinion about the management of their property and accordingly we now consider the legal position in relation to the common areas of dispute.

16.5.1 **Selling**

Because all co-owned property is subject to a trust of land, disputes about whether the estate should be retained or sold need careful consideration. We have already considered many of the rules that will be applied in such a dispute in the earlier chapter on trusts of land, and you will need to refer back to Chapter 13 for the relevant provisions of TOLATA 1996. Of these, the most important requirement is that of consultation (13.5.2.2). This is contained in s. 11(1) of the Act, which provides:

The trustees of land shall in the exercise of any function relating to land subject to the trust—

(a) so far as practicable, consult the beneficiaries of full age and beneficially entitled to an interest in possession in the land, and

(b) so far as consistent with the general interest of the trust, give effect to the wishes of those beneficiaries, or (in case of dispute) of the majority (according to the value of their combined interests).

The mandatory requirement to consult and to 'give effect to the wishes' of the majority means that the wishes of the beneficiaries take priority over even an obligation to sell.

The Act also provides that the trustees have an implied power to postpone sale, which cannot be excluded even by a specific term in an expressly created trust (13.4.2.3). However, as we have seen, it appears that the trustees must be unanimous if they are to exercise this power and apparently one dissenting trustee can still compel sale under the rule in *Re Mayo* [1943] Ch 302 (13.5.1.2).

In general, the trust which operates in the case of co-ownership is the statutory one imposed automatically under LPA 1925, but should you be considering an express trust with two or more beneficiaries entitled concurrently, there are the additional possibilities that the trust deed: (1) imposed requirements for consent (13.5.2.1); (2) indicated the purpose of the trust; or (3) gave one or more of the beneficiaries the right to live in the property.

16.5.1.1 *Applying the principles in practice*

The requirement for consultation imposed by TOLATA 1996, s. 11(1) makes it sound as though deciding whether or not to sell is relatively simple, the decision being taken by a majority of the beneficiaries who will direct the trustees what to do. In real life, however, it is likely to be a much more complicated matter, because usually in cases of co-ownership the same people are acting as both trustees and beneficiaries, they are very often connected by marriage or family relationship, and the property in question is their only home. The majority decision to sell may deprive the minority of a home and the proposal to sell may be only part of a larger dispute about the parties' future together. It therefore must not be assumed that having 'consulted the beneficiaries', the 'trustees' can always readily give effect to the wishes of the majority, and a particular problem arises where the minority refuses to move out so that the house can be offered for sale with vacant possession.

It was this problem which was considered by the Court of Appeal in *Bull v Bull* [1955] 1 QB 234. Here a financial contribution by the mother to the purchase price of a house conveyed to her son created a resulting trust, in which the son held the legal estate in trust for himself and his mother as tenants in common. The house was bought to provide a home for both of them but after his marriage the son wanted his mother to move out, and finally sought a possession order against her. The Court of Appeal held that such an application against a fellow tenant in common was completely inappropriate: as we have seen, each tenant in common has a right to possession of the whole of the property (unity of possession) and in principle one should not be able to evict another.

Thus, it appeared that, before 1997, *Re Mayo* was displaced by the consultation rule (in the limited cases to which it then applied under LPA 1925, s. 26(3)—see 13.11.5.2) and was then further overlaid by the decision in *Bull v Bull*. Where the minority was in occupation and could not be reconciled to the decision, it seemed that the trustees could not simply disregard the minority's wishes and give effect to those of the majority but had to obtain a court order before they could sell the property.

16.5.1.2 *Court order to sell*

The power of a court to order the sale of the property arose under LPA 1925, s. 30. That provision has now been replaced by TOLATA 1996, s. 14 (see 13.8.1), which has two important features:

(a) it is drafted to ensure that it applies to a wider range of cases than LPA 1925, s. 30; and

(b) it is subject to TOLATA 1996, s. 15, which imposes a list of matters to which the court is to have regard when making any order.

The s. 15 factors are an important advance and to a certain extent they both codify and improve upon principles developed by the courts over the years in an attempt to deal with the many difficult cases which came before them under LPA 1925, s. 30. You will recall that one important principle which developed was that the courts would not normally make an order for sale where land had been bought with a particular purpose in mind and that purpose was still continuing. This idea seems to be reflected in TOLATA 1996, s. 15(1)(a) and (b), which refer to the intentions of the persons creating the trust and the purposes for which the land is held. The courts are already developing new law on this issue in the light of ss. 14 and 15 and the authorities are discussed above at para. 13.8.3.1. Thus far there have been few such cases reported but it is perhaps worth recalling the remarks of Neuberger J in *Mortgage Corporation Ltd v Shaire* [2001] Ch 743 (see above at para. 13.8.3.1) and *TSB Bank plc v Marshall* [1998] 2 FLR 769, in which the court indicated that where the intention had been to provide a home for a mother and children until the children were of full age, they were not prepared to delay sale after the youngest child reached 18, even where the child was still in full time education. This suggests purpose may have some mileage left in it as an argument but that the courts will tend to move to sale as soon as the agreed intention is fulfilled.

16.5.1.3 *Other matters to be considered under s. 15*

Today, as well as express reference to the intentions of those who created the trust and the purposes for which the property is held, TOLATA 1996, s. 15(1), also requires the court to have regard to the welfare of minors who are or might be expected to occupy the premises and to the interests of secured creditors. However, no guidance is given on how to balance competing interests as between, for example, children needing a home and creditors needing to realise their security. Nor is the list in s. 15(1) exclusive and the court will be perfectly entitled to take into account any other relevant matters which may be brought to its attention (for example, the particular needs of a disabled adult might be an additional relevant factor in an appropriate case).

At this point it is worth noting the decision in *Bank of Baroda* v *Dhillon* [1998] 1 FLR 524. In that case a wife, who had contributed to the cost of acquiring the matrimonial home, claimed an interest in the property, which had been registered in the husband's sole name. Thus, the house was held upon trust by the husband for himself and his wife. The problem arose because the husband had, without the knowledge of the wife, charged the house in favour of the bank. On the husband's bankruptcy the bank sought to enforce its charge and sought an order for sale under (then) LPA 1925, s. 30. Note that the wording of s. 30 was, and now of s. 14 is, wide enough to permit this because the bank in such circumstances has an interest in the property. The wife resisted the order for sale on the basis that her interest in the property was an overriding interest under LRA 1925, s. 70(1)(g) because she had an interest in the property and had been in actual occupation of the premises when the charge was granted. The Court of Appeal accepted that Mrs Dhillon did have rights in the property and that those rights were an overriding interest in relation to the bank but nonetheless held that the court had power to order sale under LPA 1925, s. 30. On the facts of the case an order for sale was acceptable because the children of the family were adults and after sale Mrs Dhillon would have sufficient money left from the sale to re-accommodate herself. The court took note of the fact that unless an order for sale were made the bank would have no realistic means of enforcing its security and that, had Mr Dhillon's trustee in bankruptcy applied for an order for sale in order to pay Mr Dhillon's debts, s. 335A(3) of the Insolvency Act 1986 would have led to an order being made one year after the bankruptcy. Although decided under the earlier law, the case is a good illustration of the way in which a court may have to decide between competing interests on such an application. It also reminds us that the existence of an overriding interest, of a type which can be overreached on sale, will not prevent the court from granting an order for sale. In *Bank of Ireland Home Mortgages Ltd* v *Bell* [2001] 2 FLR 809 the Court of Appeal also was of the view that, where a mortgagee applied for sale, this was appropriate in a case in which otherwise the mortgagee would have no prospect of recovering its money and the debt would continue to increase. See also *Mortgage Corporation* v *Shaire* [2001] Ch 743 and note that the same approach was also applied in *First National Bank plc* v *Achampong* (2003) (unrep.).

16.5.2 **Right to occupy the land**

Before 1997, because of the imposition of the statutory trust for sale and the doctrine of conversion, the interest of a co-owner was theoretically in money and not land. Accordingly, it was not entirely clear that a co-owner could claim any rights in relationship to the land itself. However, as we have seen, the Court of Appeal in *Bull* v *Bull* [1955] 1 QB 234 held that one tenant in common could not evict another, because each had the same right to possession of the land. Over the years the courts appeared increasingly willing to concern themselves with the needs of the co-owners and did not press the concept of the statutory trust to its logical conclusion.

With TOLATA 1996 the old illogicalities have disappeared and now, not only are the interests of the co-owners interests in land, but also the various beneficial owners will have a statutory right to occupy the premises (s. 12). Where the interests of competing co-owners are concerned, the trustees have powers to balance their interests under the provisions of s. 13. Of course, where the competing beneficiaries are also the trustees this may simply lead to continued conflict. The solution in such a case is to apply to the court under s. 14.

Section 12 confers a right to occupy where the purposes of the trust include making the property available for such occupation or where the land is held by the trustees so as to be so available. No right arises where the land is unavailable or unsuitable for occupation by the beneficiary (it might, for example, be let to a tenant and thus be unavailable). Where two or more beneficiaries have a right to occupy, the trustees may exclude or restrict the entitlement of any (but not all) of them as long as the trustees act reasonably in doing so. The trustees are also given power to impose reasonable conditions on the occupying beneficiary or beneficiaries. This might presumably be used in order to protect the trust land from improper usage by the beneficiary which might damage its value and also to regulate the relationships between co-occupying beneficiaries. Section 13(5) expressly allows trustees to require the occupant to pay expenses or outgoings on the property or to assume any obligation in relation to the land or any activity to be carried on on the land.

In exercising their powers to exclude, restrict or impose restrictions the trustees are, by reason of s. 13(4), to have regard to the intentions of the person who created the trust, the purposes for which the land is held and the wishes of all the beneficiaries who would be entitled to occupy. (On the effects of ss. 12 and 13 on the right to occupy see Barnsley, 'Co-owners' rights to occupy trust land' [1998] CLJ 123.)

The use of TOLATA 1996, s. 13 was considered by the court in *Rodway* v *Landy* [2001] Ch 703. There the parties were in partnership as medical practitioners. Eventually the partnership was wound up and a dispute arose as to what should happen to the property that the parties co-owned for their business purposes. Dr Rodway sought an order that the property be sold. Dr Landy defended the action and counter-claimed for the property to be partitioned, or for an order that the trustees be required to exercise the powers under s. 13 to give each doctor exclusive access to part of the property (which was a medical centre). Here the option of one party buying the other's share and thus staying in the premises would not work in practice because of special rules relating to the disposal of premises used by medical practitioners (which prevent the sale of the goodwill of a practice).

Section 13(1) reads:

> Where two or more beneficiaries are (or apart from this subsection would be) entitled under section 12 to occupy the land, the trustees of land may exclude or restrict the entitlement of any one or more (but not all) of them.

On s. 13, the argument related to the proper construction to be placed on the words 'but not all'; the question being whether the provision could in fact be used to produce a partition in effect, though not in law. The Court of Appeal held that the correct answer, on the particular facts of the case, was to require the trustees to use their powers, so that each beneficiary had access only to part of the premises and to the exclusion of the other. Furthermore, it was possible to use s. 13(3) to require a beneficiary to pay any costs needed to make the physical separation possible. Peter Gibson LJ said (at para. 41):

> On any footing section 13 allows the trustees to divide a building subject to a trust of land between two out of three or more beneficiaries entitled to occupy, and also, if I am right, between the only beneficiaries entitled to occupy. It would be surprising if the cost of adapting the building to make each part suitable for the separate occupation of the beneficiary could not be imposed on the beneficiary . . . In my judgment a condition requiring a beneficiary to contribute to the cost of adapting the property to make it suitable for his occupation falls within the statutory wording.

16.5.3 Liability for rent to other co-owners

Before the implementation of TOLATA 1996 the general rule was that co-owners were not liable to one another for an occupation rent, for there was no right to exclude the other co-owner, who might still, if he so chose, exercise his rights in relation to the premises (*Henderson* v *Eason* (1851) 17 QB 701). In rare circumstances, however, rent was payable. Thus in *Dennis* v *McDonald* [1982] Fam 63, in which one tenant in common, by his violence towards the other owner, prevented her from occupying the premises, it was held that rent was payable. The sum payable was assessed at half the fair rent which would be payable in respect of the property, were it subject to a protected tenancy under the Rent Acts.

The problem of the right to the equivalent to rent is specifically addressed by TOLATA 1996, s. 13(6), which gives power to the trustees to require an occupying beneficiary to make appropriate compensation payments to other beneficiaries. This power only applies in favour of a beneficiary who has been excluded from occupation or whose right to occupy has been restricted in some way. The power is not so worded as to permit a beneficiary who simply decides not to occupy to claim payments from occupying beneficiaries. However, in *In re Byford* [2004] 1 FLR 56, it was held that the court could order payment of an occupation rent not just where one party had ousted the other but also in any case in which it was necessary in order to do broad justice or equity between co-owners. Here the co-owners were Mrs Byford and Mr Byford's trustee in bankruptcy. Since the bankruptcy in 1991, Mrs Byford had made the mortgage repayments and the court agreed that on sale (which was ordered in 2002) she was entitled to credit for these but the trustee was entitled to a set-off for an occupation rent. By way of contrast, in *Wright* v *Johnson*

[2002] 2 P&CR 15, the payment of an occupation rent was refused by the Court of Appeal because the applicant for the rent had earlier sought a possession order against others but not against the person from whom rent was now sought and this was taken as acceptance of the occupation.

16.5.4 Partitioning

Where the land is sufficiently extensive it may prove convenient for the co-owners to decide to partition the premises between themselves. In this way each becomes a sole beneficial owner of a portion of the land. Such partition can always be effected by agreement between all the co-owners. Under TOLATA 1996, s. 7(1), trustees may partition the land and convey the portions thus created to the co-owners. Before exercising this power the trustees are required to obtain the consent of each beneficiary to whom a conveyance of a portion of the land is to be made (s. 7(3)). This is a true partition, not just a partition as to use of the sort mentioned in para. 16.5.2.

16.6 Position of a purchaser

A primary purpose of the 1925 property legislation was to simplify conveyancing. The rules of land law were accordingly altered in order to facilitate this process. The main aim in the case of co-ownership was to ease the burden placed upon the intending purchaser, by making the investigation of title simpler, and enabling him to take the property free of the beneficial interests. Investigation of title has been simplified by the abolition of legal tenancies in common, and the imposition of the trust for sale enables the purchaser to take advantage of the overreaching provisions. This means that the purchaser need not concern himself with the position in equity. There may be 20 co-owners in equity and considerable disagreement between them about what should be done with the land. This need not trouble the purchaser at all. He will have a maximum of four legal owners with whom he must deal and need not concern himself with the opinions of the other co-owners, nor with whether the statutory duty of consultation, imposed by TOLATA 1996, s. 11(1), has been performed (TOLATA 1996, s. 16(1)).

16.6.1 Sale by a sole surviving joint tenant

There used to be, however, one problem which the purchaser might encounter in the case of unregistered title, and this arose when property held originally by joint tenants in law and equity finally vested in one sole surviving tenant. In such a case, the documents showing title would inform the purchaser that the land had been held by joint tenants, and accordingly he would know that the property had been subject to a trust. Was it safe for him to accept a conveyance from the sole survivor or should he demand the appointment of a second trustee? On the face of it, the survivor, through the right of survivorship, was solely entitled in law and equity and could dispose of the whole legal and beneficial interest. However, there was the danger that one of the deceased tenants might have severed his joint tenancy during his lifetime, creating a tenancy in common and thus having a share in the property which at his death would vest in someone other than the remaining original co-owner. Usually, when severance is made, a note (a 'memorandum of severance') is endorsed on the original conveyance to the joint tenants, so that any later purchaser will know that a tenancy in common has been created. Nevertheless, the severance is valid even if this is not done, and so its absence is no guarantee to the purchaser that severance has not occurred. Thus, the apparent 'sole survivor in law and equity' might really be holding in trust for himself and another, and if the purchaser did not pay the purchase money to two trustees the overreaching provisions would not operate and he would take the land subject to the right of any beneficiary of whom he could be said to have notice. To guard against this danger, purchasers would insist on the appointment of a second trustee, even when in fact this was not necessary.

16.6.2 **Statutory resolution of problem**

The matter was finally resolved by the Law of Property (Joint Tenants) Act 1964. This statute, as amended by the Law of Property (Miscellaneous Provisions) Act 1994, ensures that where a sole surviving joint tenant sells, the purchaser will obtain good title free of any equitable interests and need not concern himself about the possibility of an earlier severance unless a memorandum of severance has been endorsed on or annexed to the conveyance which vested the property in the joint tenants. Accordingly, if a joint tenant does sever and wishes to avoid the possibility of the 1964 Act being used by a sole survivor of the original co-owners he should ensure that a memorandum of severance is so endorsed. You may recall that in *Grindal* v *Hooper* [1999] EGCS 150 (see 16.4.1) the joint tenants had provided that no notice of severance of their joint tenancy would be effective unless it was annexed to the conveyance but that the court had held that a notice complying with LPA 1925, s. 36(2) would suffice. However, there was a second point in that case because, after the death of the co-owner who had served the notice, the survivor had purported to sell the estate in reliance on the 1964 Act. However, the sale was to the survivor's brother, who knew that notice of severance had been served. Despite the wording of the 1964 Act (which suggests that a purchaser is only bound if a memorandum of severance has been recorded on the conveyance to the co-owners), the court concluded that LPA 1925, s. 205 applied and that, accordingly, a purchaser could only take the benefit of the 1964 Act if he was a purchaser in good faith and for value. In this case, due to the relationship between the vendor and purchaser and the purchaser's knowledge of the earlier events, he was unable to claim the protection of the Act.

It should be noted that the 1964 Act does not apply at all to registered land (s. 3). In this case, there will be no restriction on the register requiring payment to two trustees, if when registering the estate it was made clear to the registrar that the co-owners were equitable joint tenants (a restriction will be entered in other cases of co-ownership). The name of the deceased joint proprietor of an estate (or a charge where there are joint mortgagees) will be removed from the register if an application is made that is 'accompanied by evidence of his death' (Land Registration Rules 2003, r. 164). Usually, the simplest method of providing such evidence will be to produce a death certificate. The register will then be changed to show the surviving joint tenant as sole proprietor.

FURTHER READING

Crown, 'Severance of Joint Tenancy of Land by Partial Alienation' (2001) 117 LQR 477.

Hayton, 'Joint Tenancies—Severance' (note on *Burgess* v *Rawnsley* and *Nielson-Jones* v *Fedden*) [1976] CLJ 20.

Percival, 'Severance By Written Notice—A Matter of Delivery?' (note on *Kinch* v *Bullard*) [1999] Conv 61.

Tee, 'Severance Revisited' [1995] Conv 105.

Thompson, 'Beneficial Joint Tenancies: A Case For Abolition?' [1987] Conv 29; Pritchard, 'Beneficial Joint Tenancies: A Riposte' [1987] Conv 273; Thompson, 'A Reply to Professor Pritchard' [1987] Conv 275.

Wells, 'Sale of the Matrimonial Home—*Bank of Baroda* v *Dhillon*' (1998) 29 Fam Law 208.

TOLATA 1996 s. 15

Pascoe, 'Section 15 of the Trusts of Land and Appointment of Trustees Act 1996—A Change in the Law?' [2000] 64 Conv 315.

Probert, 'Creditors and Section 15 of the Trusts of Land and Appointment of Trustees Act 1996: first among equals?' [2002] 66 Conv 61.

17

Resulting and constructive trusts

17.1 Introduction

As we explained in Chapter 12, trusts may be created expressly or may arise without express creation through recognition by the courts. Under LPA 1925, s. 53(1)(b), an express trust is unenforceable unless evidenced in writing, but s. 53(2) provides that this requirement does not affect the creation or operation of resulting, implied or constructive trusts.

You will notice that s. 53(2) contemplates the existence of three types of trust for which writing is not required: resulting, implied and constructive. As you will see from the rest of this chapter, there is no shortage of material about resulting and constructive trusts, but it is not easy to say exactly what is meant by the term 'implied trust'. Hanbury and Martin, *Modern Equity*, 16th edn., at p. 67, briefly outlines some suggestions as to what this category may include, but concludes that the classification of implied trusts 'serves little purpose, and the examples commonly given might preferably be regarded as express, resulting or constructive trusts, as the case may be'. None of the possible types of implied trust, in the narrower sense, has any immediate relevance to your study of land law, and so we will say no more about them, but will go on to deal in more detail with resulting and constructive trusts.

17.1.1 11 Trant Way

The fee simple in 11 Trant Way is vested in Mark Mould, who bought the property in 1989. The house is also occupied by Sally Mould, Mark's wife, and their two children. Mrs Mould has not worked outside the home during the marriage, but has been engaged full time in bringing up the children.

17.2 Resulting trusts

There are several recognised situations in which a resulting trust arises, i.e., in which the court finds that a particular transaction has given rise to a trust, although there has been no express declaration.

17.2.1 **Examples of resulting trusts**

In some of these situations, the existing owner of property has transferred it to another person, in circumstances in which the beneficial interest returns or 'results' to the transferor. One example is to be found in the creation of an express trust, where the settlor directs the trustees to hold on trusts which do not dispose fully of the beneficial interest in the property. In these circumstances, the trustees will hold the property on a resulting trust for the settlor in respect of that remaining part of the beneficial interest.

Similarly, where an owner conveys property to a 'volunteer' (someone who does not give value for it), the new owner will hold on a resulting trust for the transferor—provided of course that he is not able to show that the property was given to him as a gift. A good example of a trust arising in these circumstances is to be found in *Hodgson* v *Marks* [1971] Ch 892.

Another typical situation in which a resulting trust may arise (and, for our purposes, one of the most important) is to be found where property is bought with money belonging wholly or in part to another. In these circumstances, the purchaser, who becomes the legal owner, holds the property on a resulting trust. Where he has made some contribution to the purchase price, he will have a share in the beneficial interest and will hold the property in trust for himself and the other person (*Dewar* v *Dewar* [1975] 1 WLR 1532); where he has made no contribution, he will hold the whole property for the other's benefit (*Dyer* v *Dyer* (1788) 2 Cox 92). We have already seen an example of such a trust arising in the case of the matrimonial home in *Kingsnorth Finance Co. Ltd* v *Tizard* [1986] 1 WLR 783 (see 4.5.2.3) and will look in more detail at trusts arising from contribution at 17.4.

17.2.2 **Presumption of intention, and ways of rebutting that presumption**

In the various situations we have mentioned, the courts' recognition of the resulting trust appears to be based on the presumed intention of the person who has conveyed the property or provided the purchase money. This presumption is, however, rebuttable, and can be displaced by evidence of a contrary intention, for example to make a gift or a loan. It can also be displaced by another presumption: the presumption of advancement. This arises in certain relationships (such as that of father and child), where the donor is under an obligation to support or provide for the recipient (*Stock* v *McAvoy* (1872) LR 15 Eq 55). Thus, if a father buys a flat which is conveyed into his daughter's name, the presumption that she holds the property on trust for him could be displaced by the presumption of advancement; i.e., it would be presumed that the father intended to provide for his daughter by giving her the beneficial interest in the property. It is of course possible again for this presumption itself to be rebutted by proof that the father did not intend to make a gift, in which case a resulting trust would arise in the usual way.

17.3 **Constructive trusts**

17.3.1 **Nature of constructive trusts**

Constructive trusts arise by operation of law. They are imposed upon the owner of property by the court, in general as a result of his conduct, so that instead of enjoying his property as beneficial owner, he is required to hold it, in whole or in part, for the benefit of some other person. (We have already seen an example of this in *Yaxley* v *Gotts* [2000] Ch 162—see 3.4.2.) Unfortunately it is almost impossible to give a simple explanation of what constitutes a constructive trust or to explain when it will arise. In *Carl-Zeiss Stiftung* v *Herbert Smith & Co. (No. 2)* [1969] 2 Ch 276, Edmund Davies LJ said, at p. 300:

English law provides no clear and all-embracing definition of a constructive trust. Its boundaries have been left perhaps deliberately vague, so as not to restrict the court by technicalities in deciding what the justice of a particular case may demand.

This statement may point to a major reason for the difficulty of discerning an entirely logical pattern in decisions involving constructive trusts; namely that the courts make use of this area of law as a means of evading the strictures of other more rigid rules or principles, thus giving themselves some freedom to provide a just solution in a difficult case. The best approach, possibly, to understanding the cases is to concentrate upon the circumstances in which a constructive trust has so far been imposed by the courts. These are summarised by Oakley in *Constructive Trusts*, 3rd edn., at pp. 30–1 as follows:

(a) where a person has obtained an advantage by acting fraudulently or unconscionably or (perhaps) inequitably;

(b) where a fiduciary has obtained an advantage as a result of a breach of his duty or loyalty; and

(c) where there has been a disposition of trust property in breach of trust.

If you are able to do so, you might find it helpful to spend a little time looking at Oakley (at the contents pages if at nothing more!), to give yourself some idea of the very wide range of circumstances in which constructive trusts have been imposed. All we can do here is to deal with a few examples, in circumstances which are particularly relevant to land law. The examples we have chosen may all be described in Oakley's terms as being imposed as a result of fraudulent, unconscionable or, possibly, inequitable conduct. It is important, however, to remember that these are not the only circumstances which could lead the court to impose a constructive trust.

17.3.2 **Trusts imposed as a result of fraudulent or unconscionable behaviour**

We have already noted in this book a number of statutory provisions requiring some form of writing for transactions involving land (e.g., LPA 1925, ss. 40, 52(1) and 53(1)(b); Law of Property (Miscellaneous Provisons) Act 1989, s. 2). Many of these provisions are derived from earlier statutory rules, in some cases dating back to the Statute of Frauds in 1677. At a fairly early stage, the courts of equity became concerned at the use which was being made of the statutory provisions. Estate owners who had acquired property subject to some oral understanding or agreement (perhaps to hold it on trust for the transferor) were using the lack of writing to avoid their undertakings and to claim absolute ownership of the property. In equityís eyes, such conduct was fraudulent, and in such circumstances the transferee would be compelled by the court to hold the property on trust (see, for example, *Rochefoucauld* v *Boustead* [1897] 1 Ch 196).

17.3.2.1 Bannister *v* Bannister

The approach in *Rochefoucauld* v *Boustead* [1897] 1 Ch 196 was applied by the Court of Appeal in the modern decision of *Bannister* v *Bannister* [1948] 2 All ER 133. In this case a purchaser had bought a cottage from his sister-in-law, on the understanding that she would be allowed to live in it rent-free for the rest of her life. The understanding between the parties was not recorded in any document. When the purchaser went back on his agreement and tried to obtain possession of the cottage, the defendant claimed that the oral agreement amounted to an informal declaration of trust, i.e., that the purchaser would hold the property upon trust for her for her lifetime. As we have seen, such a declaration of trust would normally require writing under LPA 1925, s. 53(1)(b), but because of the unconscionable conduct of the purchaser in seeking to avoid his undertaking the court imposed a constructive trust upon him.

In its judgment, the Court of Appeal referred to *Rochefoucauld* v *Boustead* and relied upon what it described (at p. 136) as:

the equitable principle on which a constructive trust is raised against a person who insists on the absolute character of a conveyance to himself for the purpose of defeating a bene cial interest which, according to the true bargain, was to belong to another.

The court held, therefore, that the purchaser must honour his undertaking, despite the lack of written evidence. He had promised his sister-in-law that she would have a life interest in the property and, consequently, held the property on trust to give effect to that interest.

A further point to note is that the agreement was held to have created a SLA 1925 settlement, under which the woman became the tenant for life, and had the power to call for the estate to be conveyed to her and the power to sell it (see Chapter 14).

17.3.2.2 Binions *v* Evans

The approach adopted in *Bannister* v *Bannister* was followed by the Court of Appeal in *Binions* v *Evans* [1972] Ch 359. Here a widow had been given the right to live in a cottage for her lifetime. According to the express terms of the agreement, she was to be a tenant at will, and she agreed to take care of the premises while she had the use of them. The property was then sold to purchasers, who agreed with the vendor that they would allow the widow to remain, and accordingly paid a reduced price for the cottage. Later, they sought to eject her, and the court had to consider the nature of her rights and whether they bound the purchasers for value. The Court of Appeal held unanimously that, although the agreement described the widow as a tenant at will, its terms were inconsistent with such a tenancy. The majority of the court (Megaw and Stephenson LJJ), applied *Bannister* v *Bannister*, holding that the agreement had given the widow a life interest, and accordingly had made her a tenant for life under a SLA 1925 settlement. In their view, the purchasers took with express notice 'of the agreement which constitutes or gives rise to, the trust' (at p. 370), and were accordingly bound by it.

By contrast, Lord Denning MR considered that the agreement gave rise to a contractual licence. We shall see in Chapter 20 that there are considerable difficulties in seeking to enforce such a licence against a purchaser from the original licensor. Here, however, Lord Denning considered that the circumstances justified the imposition of a constructive trust on the purchasers. The contract of sale had stipulated that the purchasers were to take subject to the widow's rights, and they paid a reduced price because of this. In Lord Denning's view (at p. 368):

In these circumstances this court will impose on the [purchasers] a constructive trust for [the widow's] benefit: for the simple reason that it would be utterly inequitable for [them] to turn [her] out contrary to the stipulation subject to which they took the premises.

For a further decision in which the court recognised a life interest under a constructive trust as giving rise to a SLA 1925 settlement, see *Ungurian* v *Lesnoff* [1990] Ch 206.

17.3.3 Trusts imposed as a result of inequitable conduct

The examples of constructive trusts which we have considered so far were imposed because of the fraudulent or unconscionable conduct of the estate owner. In the 1970s, the Court of Appeal, under the influence of Lord Denning MR, began to impose constructive trusts more widely, in cases where the conduct of the estate owner was regarded as 'inequitable', although not sufficiently blameworthy to be described as 'fraudulent or unconscionable'. For Lord Denning, the authority for this development was to be found in the speech of Lord Diplock in *Gissing* v *Gissing* [1971] AC 886 at p. 905, which referred to the imposition of a trust:

wherever the trustee has so conducted himself that it would be inequitable to allow him to deny to the [beneficiary] a beneficial interest in the land acquired.

We will look at this speech in more detail later on (see 17.5.1), when you will see that this apparently wide statement is in fact subject to considerable limitation. However, taken out of context, it enabled Lord Denning to talk about 'a constructive trust of a new model', of which he said in *Eves* v *Eves* [1975] 1 WLR 1338 at p. 1341:

Lord Diplock brought it into the world and we have nourished it.

In the view of the Master of the Rolls, such a trust could be imposed to do justice between the parties wherever the result would otherwise have been inequitable, and he used it widely to provide equitable solutions to property disputes between spouses and co-habitants. Some of these decisions relate to contractual licences, and we will look at them in Chapter 20, although they are in general now discredited. Others form the background to the current law on common-intention constructive trusts, and are considered in the next section (17.4) on trusts arising from contribution.

Section E -f

17.4 **Trusts arising from contribution**

17.4.1 **Introduction**

You might think that we have already covered this topic in our earlier section on resulting trusts (17.2). There we noted the traditional view that financial contribution by one person to the cost of acquiring property which is vested in another, may give the contributor a share in the beneficial interest under a resulting trust (unless of course the contributor was making a gift or a loan). From the 1970s onwards, however, the courts were asked to consider claims based on less direct forms of contribution: payment of household expenses, DIY improvements, and the performance of general domestic duties, such as taking care of a spouse or partner and bringing up children. In general, these claims related to the family home, when the relationship between spouses or cohabitants had come to an end, and the legal title to the house was vested in only one of the partners (usually, but not inevitably, the man). In such cases, unless the other partner could establish a share arising under a trust, that partner would have to leave the house, and would have no right to a share of the proceeds if it was sold.

You may remember that the pattern of home ownership we have just described, with the legal estate vested in one spouse, applies to No. 11 Trant Way, where Mark Mould alone holds the title to the family house. The Moulds' marriage appears to be a happy and successful one and they have no money worries, but if things did go wrong, either with their relationship or their finances, the considerations we are going to discuss could be very relevant.

17.4.1.1 *Property adjustment orders on divorce*

These days, when marriage ends in divorce, the court has wide powers, under Part II of the Matrimonial Causes Act 1973 (as amended by the Family Law Act 1996), to make property adjustment orders, which require the transfer of property from one party to the other. In exercising these powers, the court is authorised to take into account a range of matters, which include: the financial resources and commitments of each party; their age; the duration of the marriage; and the contribution which each has made or is likely to make to the welfare of the family by looking after the home or caring for the family (Matrimonial Causes Act 1973 s. 25(2)). These provisions were not introduced, however, until 1970 (under the Matrimonial Proceedings and Property Act 1970) and before then the only way of obtaining a share in the former matrimonial home was by establishing entitlement under a trust.

17.4.1.2 *Claims involving cohabitants*

The provisions relating to property adjustment orders do not apply when a relationship between unmarried partners comes to an end, and any claim to a share in the family home has to be decided according to the rules of property law, rather than by any consideration of what each party needs or deserves. As Millet J put it in *Windeler* v *Whitehall* [1990] 1 FLR 505 at p. 506, when considering a claim by a woman to a share in her former partner's property:

It is not enough for her to persuade me that she deserves to have such a share. She must satisfy me that she already has it.

17.4.1.3 *Claims involving mortgagees*

Further, you should note that a number of cases in this area arise when couples, whether married or not, find themselves in financial difficulties and their mortgagees seek possession of the property. When this happens, one partner may claim to have a share in the house, which takes priority over the mortgage, so that the mortgagee cannot enforce his rights against that share. This is, of course, the background to *Kingsnorth Finance Co. Ltd* v *Tizard* [1986] 1 WLR 783, with which you are already familiar. Thus, if the Moulds were to find themselves in financial difficulties, Sally Mould might want to claim that she was entitled to a share in the family home, despite the fact that the legal title is in her husband's name.

In such a case, where the dispute is not between the family partners themselves but between one of the partners and the mortgagee, the existence and size of any share in the beneficial interest will have to be decided in accordance with basic trust principles.

In dealing with these family home cases, the courts have developed a new type of constructive trust, which is sometimes called a *'common-intention'* trust. We are going to look in some detail at this development, but before considering the major decisions, we need to note some confusion in the terminology used by the courts.

17.4.1.4 *Terminology*

In our account of implied trusts so far, we have tried to draw a clear distinction between resulting trusts and constructive trusts. Unfortunately, the courts have not always been so careful to make this distinction. Lord Diplock in *Gissing* v *Gissing* [1971] AC 886 at p. 905, in referring to resulting, implied and constructive trusts, said:

It is unnecessary for present purposes to distinguish between these three classes of trust.

This statement may be acceptable when taken in context, but it led other judges to use the phrases almost interchangeably. Thus, Lord Denning MR in *Hussey* v *Palmer* [1972] 1 WLR 1286 at p. 1289 said that although the plaintiff alleged that there was a resulting trust:

I should have thought that the trust in this case . . . was more in the nature of a constructive trust: but this is more a matter of words than anything else. The two run together.

As a result of this approach being adopted over a number of years, it is often unclear which type of trust is involved in a particular decision, and as a result it is difficult to give a clear account of the circumstances in which each of these trusts operates.

This somewhat cavalier approach by the courts might suggest to you that the distinction is unimportant, and that you too could say: 'It doesn't matter which it is!'. However, a very different approach was taken by the Court of Appeal in *Drake* v *Whipp* (1995) 28 HLR 531. Peter Gibson LJ described the earlier judicial statements as 'a potent source of confusion' (at p. 533), and made it clear that the distinction was of crucial importance in deciding the size of the claimant's share (see 17.6.2). Today, therefore, it is very important to try to distinguish between these two types of trust, but if you find the topic confusing it may help to remember that there is a genuine lack of clarity in many of the cases.

In considering claims to a share in the family home (and indeed in any other property as well), the court has to deal with two questions. The first is whether the claimant is entitled to a share in the beneficial interest, i.e., does the legal owner hold the property on trust for himself and the claimant? If the answer to that question is 'Yes', the court then has to deal with the second question: what is the size of the claimant's share? We will now look in detail at how the court goes about dealing with each question.

17.5 Establishing the claim to a share in the beneficial interest

17.5.1 *Gissing* v *Gissing*

In the early 1970s, just before property adjustment orders were introduced, the House of Lords had to consider two cases in which the claim of a divorced spouse to a share in the family home was based not on direct financial contribution but on, in the one case, work done on the house and in the other, on relatively minor contributions to household expenses. In *Pettit* v *Pettit* [1970] AC 777, the house was owned by the wife. Her divorced husband's claim to a share in the proceeds of sale was based on redecorations and improvements to the property which he had carried out, and which he claimed had increased its value. In *Gissing* v *Gissing* [1971] AC 886 a wife, whose marriage had ended in divorce after some 30 years, sought to establish a claim to a share in the family home which was owned by her husband, relying on financial contributions she had made over the years in buying items of furniture and equipment, and paying for some improvements to the garden.

In each of these cases, the Court of Appeal had considered that the applicant was entitled to a share in the property, but the House of Lords did not share this view, and in both cases held that the claimants had no share in the beneficial interest. While the speeches in both decisions are of interest, it is Lord Diplock's speech in *Gissing* v *Gissing* which has received the most attention, as setting out the requirements for the modern common-intention constructive trust. The relevant passage runs as follows:

A resulting, implied or constructive trust—and it is unnecessary for present purposes to distinguish between these three classes of trust—is created by a transaction between the trustee and the [beneficiary] in connection with the acquisition by the trustee of a legal estate in land, whenever the trustee has so conducted himself that it would be inequitable to allow him to deny to the [beneficiary] a beneficial interest in the land acquired. And he will be held so to have conducted himself if by his words or conduct he has induced the [beneficiary] to act to his own detriment in the reasonable belief that by so acting he was acquiring a beneficial interest in the land.

This is why it has been repeatedly said in the context of disputes between spouses as to their respective beneficial interests in the matrimonial home that if at the time of its acquisition . . . an express agreement has been made between them as to the way in which the beneficial interest shall be held, the court will give effect to it—notwithstanding the absence of any written declaration of trust. Strictly speaking this states the principle too widely for if the agreement did not provide for anything to be done by the spouse in whom the legal estate was not to be vested, it would be a merely voluntary declaration of trust and unenforceable for want of writing. But in the express oral agreements contemplated by these *dicta* it has been assumed . . . that they provide for the spouse in whom the legal estate . . . is not vested to do something to facilitate its acquisition. . . . What the court gives effect to is the trust resulting or implied from the common intention expressed in the oral agreement between the spouses that if each acts in the manner provided for in the agreement the beneficial interest in the matrimonial home shall be held as they have agreed.

But parties to a transaction in connection with the acquisition of land may well have formed a common intention that the beneficial interest in the land shall be vested in them jointly without having used express words to communicate this intention to one another. . . . In such a case . . . it may be possible to infer their common intention from their conduct.

Thus, it appears that there are two stages in establishing a common intention trust of this sort: an agreement, and some detrimental act in reliance on it.

17.5.1.1 *The agreement*

There must be an agreement between the parties at the time the property is acquired (or, exceptionally, at a later stage—see *Burns* v *Burns* [1984] 1 Ch 317 at p. 327) that the partner without the legal estate is to have a beneficial interest in the land.

Such an agreement or undertaking may have been made expressly—either orally or in writing. Even if there is no express agreement, however, the court may be able to infer one from the conduct of the parties. After the passage we have quoted, Lord Diplock went on to outline the type of conduct from which such an intention could be inferred. All the examples he gave involved reasonably direct contributions to the cost of acquiring the property, i.e., contributions to the outright payment of the price, or to the deposit and legal charges, or to the mortgage instalments. Indirect contributions to the mortgage repayments would also be acceptable if, for example, the claimant paid other outgoings so as to enable the estate owner to use his funds to pay off the mortgage debt. Such contributions, however, must be clearly referable to the acquisition of the property (i.e., it must appear that the contributor was meeting those expenses in order to facilitate mortgage repayments). In the absence of such evidence, mere contributions to household expenses by itself would not be enough.

We have noted that the express agreement could be made orally or in writing. If in writing, the agreement would constitute a declaration of trust for the purposes of LPA 1925, s. 53(1)(b), and could be enforced as an express trust. If the agreement was oral, or had to be inferred from conduct, it would be unenforceable for lack of writing, unless the court could find an implied, resulting or constructive trust. This, therefore, brings us to Lord Diplock's second requirement: that the claimant has been induced to act to his detriment in the belief that he is acquiring an interest. For the owner to go back on the agreement after this has happened would be inequitable, and it is this that justifies the recognition of some sort of implied trust.

17.5.1.2 *Action by claimant to his detriment in reliance on agreement*

Lord Diplock's speech in *Gissing* v *Gissing* suggests that the sort of acts required here are very much the same as those noted above from which an agreement may be inferred: contributions direct or indirect to the cost of acquisition. However, he did not exclude the possibility that other acts might be sufficient and in later decisions the courts have accepted a wider range of activities which do not involve financial contribution.

17.5.1.3 *How were these principles applied to the facts of* Gissing *v* Gissing?

The House of Lords considered that there was no evidence of any express agreement between the parties at the time the house was bought. Nor were the contributions by the wife sufficient to support the inference of a common intention. The contributions she made were not sufficiently referable to the acquisition of the property and, in consequence, the wife's claim to a share in the house belonging to her husband was rejected.

17.5.2 **Lord Denning's interpretation of *Gissing* v *Gissing***

The immediate result of the decision in *Gissing* v *Gissing*, at least at Court of Appeal level, was an increased use of non-express trusts to achieve a fair result between the parties when a strict application of legal rules would appear inequitable. This development was very much associated with the Master of the Rolls who, as we have noted (17.3.3), read Lord Diplock's words as authorising the use of the new model constructive trust wherever it was equitable to do so. At the time, these decisions aroused considerable interest and comment, but in view of the more restrictive approach adopted by the Court of Appeal from the mid-1980s onwards (see 17.5.3) it now seems improbable that Lord Denning's broad approach will have very much influence today. Accordingly we will give only a brief account of four of his more outstanding decisions.

The first three of these cases all involved unmarried couples, and on each occasion the Court of Appeal upheld the woman's claim to a share in the house owned by her partner.

(1) *Cooke* v *Head* [1972] 1 WLR 518   Here the woman had contributed to the mortgage repayments and had also done hard physical work on improving the property. On resulting trust principles, her financial contribution would have entitled her to a one-twelfth share in the property, but the Court of Appeal considered that she was entitled to more and awarded her one-third.

(2) *Eves* v *Eves* [1975] 1 WLR 1338   In this case, the woman had made no financial contribution, but again had done a good deal of manual work in restoring the house and garden, and had looked after her partner and cared for their children. In Lord Denning's view, it would in these circumstances have been inequitable for her partner to deny her a share in the house; equity would impose a constructive trust under which she would receive a quarter share.

(3) *Hall* v *Hall* [1982] 3 FLR 379   The parties in this case had lived together for seven years. The woman had made no direct payments towards the cost of acquisition, but had paid for furnishings, bought a car and contributed to housekeeping

expenses. The Court of Appeal considered that these contributions gave rise to a trust in her favour, Lord Denning saying (at p. 381):

It depends on the circumstances and how much she had contributed—not merely in money—but also in keeping up the house; and if there are children, in looking after them.

(4) *Hussey* v *Palmer* [1972] 1 WLR 1286 The dispute here did not involve unmarried partners, but was concerned with a family arrangement between a man and his mother-in-law. The plaintiff was an elderly widow who was invited to live with her daughter's family in the house belonging to her son-in-law. She paid for the cost of building a small extension to the house, for her own occupation. Family difficulties developed, and the plaintiff moved out and later tried to recover the money she had spent. There were suggestions that the money had been provided as a gift or a loan, and there was certainly no evidence of any agreement, express or implied, that she should have a share in the house. Nevertheless, the Court of Appeal considered that this was an appropriate case in which to recognise a resulting or constructive trust. In one of his more sweeping statements (at p. 1290), Lord Denning referred to:

a trust imposed by law whenever justice and good conscience require it. It is a liberal process, founded upon large principles of equity, to be applied in cases where the legal owner cannot conscientiously keep the property for himself alone, but ought to allow another to have the property or the benefit of it or a share in it. . . . It is an equitable remedy by which the court can enable an aggrieved party to obtain restitution.

In consequence, the court held that the claimant was entitled to a share in the house proportionate to the amount of money she had expended (in other words, if the value of the house increased, she would be entitled to more than she had put in). However, rather strangely in view of this, Lord Denning added that alternatively her claim could be satisfied by the repayment of the amount she had spent.

17.5.3 **A change of approach**

By contrast with the decisions we have been considering, the mid-1980s saw a change in the Court of Appeal's approach, and a more careful application of the principles in *Gissing* v *Gissing*. The new approach can be seen most clearly in *Burns* v *Burns* [1984] 1 Ch 317, which concerned an unmarried couple who had been living together for 19 years. The man was the legal owner of the house in which they lived and had provided the initial deposit and paid the mortgage instalments. For some time the woman stayed at home and cared for the children of the relationship. Later she undertook paid work and used her salary to pay some domestic bills and to buy furniture and equipment for the house and clothes for the children. She also redecorated the interior of the house.

On the approach adopted by Lord Denning, one would have expected these facts to support the recognition of some form of implied trust. On this occasion, however, the Court of Appeal followed very closely the principles laid down by Lord Diplock in *Gissing*, emphasising the need for some agreement, express or inferred from conduct. The conduct from which an agreement could be inferred was summarised in *Gissing* terms, as essentially involving some money payment referable to the acquisition of the property. A substantial contribution to housekeeping expenses would be sufficient if its intended effect was to enable the other partner to pay the mortgage instalments but such contributions by themselves without such an intention were not enough.

Mrs Burns' financial contributions were small and could not be said to be referable to the acquisition of the house and were no evidence of a common intention that she was to have a share. The decorating work she had carried out was of no assistance, the court following the view expressed on this by the House of Lords in *Pettit* v *Pettit* [1970] AC 777. Finally, the court had to consider the claim that the performance of domestic duties (running the household and looking after her partner and the children) was a sufficient contribution to entitle Mrs Burns to a share. We have seen that in *Hall* v *Hall* Lord Denning considered that such a contribution could be taken into account. The court in *Burns* v *Burns* was of the opinion that his view was not supported by precedent, nor was it consistent with principle; or, as May LJ put it more bluntly (at p. 342), Lord Denning's *dictum* 'was wrong'.

A useful summary of the court's position is to be found towards the end of the judgment of May LJ, and you may in particular like to note his concluding words:

> When the house is taken in the man's name alone, if the woman makes no 'real' or 'substantial' financial contribution towards either the purchase price, deposit or mortgage instalments by the means of which the family home was acquired, then she is not entitled to any share in the beneficial interest in that home even though over a very substantial number of years she may have worked just as hard as the man in maintaining the family in the sense of keeping the house, giving birth to and looking after and helping to bring up the children of the union.

Thus, today, as we have already noted, there is a very major difference between the position of unmarried and married couples, when their relationships come to an end (for a further consideration of this, see Chapter 24).

17.5.4 **The present position**

The most recent attempt to restate the law in this area is to be found in *Lloyds Bank* v *Rosset* [1991] 1 AC 107. Here property was purchased with money provided by the husband's family trust. On the insistence of the trustees the property was registered in the sole name of the husband. The house required a great deal of alteration and the necessary building work was paid for by the husband, with money obtained on an overdraft from his bank, secured by a charge on the property. Mrs Rosset made no financial contribution to the cost of the property, but was heavily involved in its renovation, giving instructions to the builders and later doing much of the decoration of the premises herself. The marriage broke down, with the husband moving out and failing to repay the loan, and the bank sought possession of the house. The wife claimed that she had a beneficial interest in the property under a constructive trust and that this took effect as an overriding interest binding on the bank under LRA 1925, s. 70(1)(g). Thus, this case came to the courts as a dispute between the claimant and her spouse's mortgagees and her claim, therefore, had to be decided on basic trust principles, rather than on the statutory provisions which would have had applied if she had been asserting it against her husband in divorce proceedings.

Mrs Rosset's interest was said to derive from an express agreement reached in conversations with her husband, in reliance on which she had made a significant contribution to the acquisition of the property by the work she had done on its renovation. The judge at first instance rejected the claim of an express agreement but was prepared to infer a common intention from the wife's conduct in undertaking the work of renovation. This finding was, however, rejected by the House of Lords. The monetary value of the work done was trifling when compared with the cost of the property as a whole, and their Lordships doubted whether it would even have been enough to constitute detrimental reliance in the case of an express intention, let alone sufficient to support an inferred agreement. In Lord Bridge's view, the work done by Mrs Rosset was the sort of work which any wife might do to prepare a new home for occupation; it could not be said to be the sort of work which she would not have undertaken if she had not been expecting to acquire an interest in the house.

Lord Bridge, in a speech adopted by his brethren, decided against Mrs Rosset's claim on the simple basis that she had not established any agreement with her husband, express or inferred, that she was to have a share in his property. This was, in essence, a decision on the facts, and Lord Bridge doubted whether any further analysis of the relevant law would be helpful. He went on, however, to draw attention to what he described as 'one critical distinction', and in doing so may have created further confusion in this already complicated and difficult area.

The passage in question (at p. 132) reads:

The first and fundamental question which must always be resolved is whether, independently of any inference to be drawn from the conduct of the parties in the course of sharing the house as their home and managing their joint affairs, there has at any time prior to acquisition, or exceptionally at some later date, been any agreement, . . . reached between them that the property is to be shared beneficially. The finding of an agreement . . . to share in this sense can only, I think, be based on evidence of express discussions between the partners, however imperfectly remembered and however imprecise their terms may have been. Once a finding to this effect is made it will only be necessary for the partner asserting a claim . . . to show that he or she has acted to his or her detriment or significantly altered his or her position in reliance on the agreement in order to give rise to a constructive trust or a proprietary estoppel.

In sharp contrast with this situation is the very different one where there is no evidence to support a finding of an agreement . . . to share, however reasonable it might have been for the parties to reach such an arrangement if they had applied their minds to the question, and where the court must rely entirely on the conduct of the parties both as the basis from which to infer a common intention to share the property beneficially and as the conduct relied on to give rise to a constructive trust. In this situation direct contributions to the purchase price by the partner who is not the legal owner, whether initially or by payment of mortgage instalments, will readily justify the inference necessary to the creation of a constructive trust. But, as I read the authorities, it is at least extremely doubtful whether anything less will do.

This passage may well have been intended as a restatement or summary of the rules in *Gissing* v *Gissing*, but the reference in the second paragraph to the need for *direct* contribution seems to limit the scope of the principles as so far understood, and to rule out the indirect contribution to mortgage repayments by meeting household expenses which was accepted as sufficient in both *Gissing* v *Gissing* and *Burns* v *Burns*. In addition, some writers take the view that what is described in the second paragraph is really a *resulting* trust (see Thompson [1990] Conv 314; Hanbury and Martin, *Modern Equity*, 16th edn., p. 267 n. 59; and Gray and Gray, p. 669 n. 19). If this view is correct, one is left wondering what has become of the inferred common intention constructive trust which formed the second limb of the *Gissing* v *Gissing* rule.

Thus, Lord Bridge's words contributed to the process, which we have already noted (17.4.1.4), of blurring the distinction between resulting and constructive trusts. However, as we shall soon see, the distinction between these two types of trust was reasserted in no uncertain terms by the Court of Appeal in *Drake* v *Whipp* (1995) 28 HLR 531.

A further cause for concern to which we shall return later (see 18.7) is to be found in Lord Bridge's reference to proprietary estoppel as an alternative to a constructive trust. There are differences, as well as similarities, between these two equitable concepts, and referring to them as though they are almost synonymous is unhappily reminiscent of the courts' earlier lack of precision in the use of the resulting and constructive trust labels.

17.6 Quantifying the share

If the claimant can establish entitlement to a share in the beneficial interest—whether under a resulting or a constructive trust—the court will then have to quantify the share, i.e., decide the proportion of the beneficial interest to which the claimant is entitled.

17.6.1 Resulting trusts

In the case of a resulting trust, the share should be proportionate to the amount contributed to the cost of acquisition. In other words, if the contribution amounted to one-quarter of the purchase price, the claimant is entitled to a quarter of the value of the property, and this applies regardless of whether the value of the property falls or rises.

17.6.2 Constructive trusts

In the case of a constructive trust, the process of determining the parties' shares may be more complicated, as Lord Diplock explained in *Gissing* v *Gissing* [1971] AC 886 at p. 908 onwards. There may be an express agreement on the matter and, if so, this is conclusive (as in *Killey* v *Clough* [1996] NPC 38, where the Court of Appeal accepted that there had been an express common intention that the property would be shared 'fifty-fifty'). It is, however, much more likely that there is no express agreement, and in that case the court will try to see if it can draw any inference from the parties' conduct as to what was intended. In doing so, it may take into account any contributions made by the claimant—not only at the outset, but during the course of the relationship as well. If no inference as to intention could be drawn, the court would apply the maxim 'equality is equity' and regard each party as being entitled to a half-share (at p. 908), although several of their Lordships indicated that in their view this was very much a last resort (see pp. 897 and 903).

In a number of constructive trust cases, however, the court seems to have adopted a different more flexible approach. This is typical of the decisions in which Lord Denning played a part, examples being *Cooke* v *Head* [1972] 1 WLR 518, in which the claimant's financial contribution would have entitled her to one-twelfth, but the court awarded her one-third; and *Eves* v *Eves* [1975] 1 WLR 1338 at pp. 1342 and 1346, in which the court was of the opinion that a half share would be too much, but a quarter would be about right (with no indication of how it arrived at this figure).

Two recent decisions of the Court of Appeal give further examples of how shares under a constructive trust may be assessed.

In *Midland Bank plc* v *Cooke* [1995] 4 All ER 562, the Court of Appeal was satisfied that the wife had made a direct contribution, albeit a small one, to the purchase price of the matrimonial home owned by her husband, and apparently accepted that there had been sufficient agreement between husband and wife to give rise to a constructive trust under which the wife took a beneficial interest in the property. At first instance, the size of her interest was quantified by reference to the size of her contribution to the purchase price, and in consequence she was held to have a 6.47 per cent share in the house. On the wife's appeal, it was argued against her that this mathematical approach must be adopted in the absence of any express agreement between the parties as to their relative shares. The Court of Appeal, however (at p. 574), considered that in deciding such a case the court should:

undertake a survey of the whole course of dealing between the parties relevant to their ownership and occupation of the property and their sharing of its burdens and advantages [and should] take into consideration all conduct which throws light on the question of what shares were intended.

Accordingly, the Court of Appeal held that it was not bound to deal with the matter on the strict basis of the trust resulting from the cash contribution to the purchase price, and was free to attribute to the parties an intention to share the beneficial interest in some different proportion—in this case, in equal shares.

In *Drake* v *Whipp* (1995) 28 HLR 531 an unmarried couple bought a barn for conversion into a house, the property being conveyed to the man alone. The woman made a substantial contribution to the purchase price, but the costs of conversion, which were considerably greater than the purchase price, were largely borne by the man. When the couple separated, the woman claimed a share in the beneficial interest proportionate to her contribution of 40 per cent of the purchase price, while her former partner claimed that her share should be determined by reference to her contribution of just under 20 per cent to the overall cost of purchase and conversion.

The Court of Appeal considered that the distinction between resulting trusts and constructive trusts was crucial in deciding whether the parties' shares should be determined by reference to the purchase price alone, or to the combined cost of purchase and conversion. In the case of a resulting trust, the size of share must be quantified by reference to the cost of acquisition, and the cost of subsequent enhancement is irrelevant. In constructive trust cases, however, the court could adopt 'a broad brush approach' (p. 536) to determining the parties' respective shares, and could thus take into account their relative contributions to the overall cost of the property.

In consequence, it was necessary for the court to decide whether the arrangement between the parties gave rise to a constructive or a resulting trust. As we have already noted, modern decisions have tended to blur the distinction between these two concepts, but the Court of Appeal emphasised its importance. The distinguishing feature between the two forms of trust was to be found in the intention of the parties. In the case of a constructive trust,

all that was required . . . was that there should be a common intention that the party who was not the legal owner should have a beneficial interest and that that party should act to his or her detriment in reliance thereon (at p. 536).

By contrast, a resulting trust operates

as a presumed intention of the contributing party in the absence of rebutting evidence of actual intention (at p. 535).

Here there was undisputed evidence of a common understanding between the parties that they were to share beneficially, and in consequence, this gave rise to a constructive, not a resulting, trust.

In the court's view, the woman was not limited to the 20 per cent share she would receive under strict resulting trust rules. The court 'would approach the matter more broadly, looking at the parties' entire course of conduct together' (at p. 537). Matters to be taken into account included direct financial contributions, the work each party did to improve the property, the joint bank account fed mainly by the man's earnings, and the fact that the woman paid for food and some other household expenses and took care of the housekeeping for them both. In all these circumstances the court considered that the woman's 'fair share' should be one-third.

Although you should not concern yourself too much with detail, a quick look at the sums of money involved in this decision is illuminating. On the first instance decision, the woman would have received just over £43,000; her claim to 40 per cent amounted to £90,000; and the Court of Appeal award of a one-third share gave her £75,000. We mention these figures only to illustrate the very considerable difference which the distinction between resulting and constructive trusts may now make to the parties' financial position: it is clearly no longer safe to say that there is no significant difference between these two forms of implied trust.

FURTHER READING

Clarke, 'The Family Home: Intention and Agreement' (1992) 22 Fam Law 72.

Dunn, 'Whipping up Resulting and Constructive Trusts' [1997] Conv 467.

Eekelaar, 'A Woman's Place—A Conflict between Law and Social Values' [1987] Conv 93.

Gardner, 'Fin de siècle chez *Gissing* v *Gissing*' (1996) 112 LQR 378.

18

Proprietary estoppel

18.1 Introduction

In this chapter we want to tell you some more about proprietary estoppel, which we have already discussed in Chapter 3 as a possible substitute for the doctrine of part performance. We preface this account, however, by saying that estoppel as a whole is an area of law which is still very much in the developmental stage. Judges and academic writers are by no means sure yet how the various bits of the jig-saw fit together, and there is a good deal of debate on issues which in the main relate to classification. We mention this only in order to warn you not to be too confused by variations in the labels attached to apparently similar forms of estoppel. The only classification point we want to draw to your attention is that proprietary estoppel differs from other forms of estoppel in that it can be used to ground a legal claim, rather than simply being relied on as a defence against another's claim. It is usual to say that estoppel can be used as a shield but not as a sword; proprietary estoppel, as you will see from cases such as *Crabb* v *Arun DC* [1976] 1 Ch 179 can very definitely be used as a sword. (See also the observations of Cumming-Bruce LJ in *Pascoe* v *Turner* [1979] 1 WLR 431 at p. 436.)

18.2 Nature of proprietary estoppel

Proprietary estoppel is usually said to be one of the two forms of equitable estoppel, the other being promissory estoppel.

The basis of equitable estoppel is explained by Lord Denning MR in *Crabb* v *Arun DC* [1976] 1 Ch 179 at p. 187 as follows:

Equity comes in . . . to mitigate the rigours of strict law . . . it will prevent a person insisting on his strict legal rights . . . when it would be inequitable for him to do so having regard to the dealings which have taken place between the parties.

Thus, if one party promised not to enforce his legal rights and the other party acted upon this, equity would not allow the promisor to go back on his promise, even though it might not be enforceable against him on a contractual basis. This aspect of equitable estoppel (promissory estoppel) may be familiar to you from the law of contract, and you probably remember the decision in *Central London Property Trust Ltd* v *High Trees House Ltd* [1947] KB 130.

By contrast, proprietary estoppel arises from an owner's encouragement of or acquiescence in another's mistaken belief about his present or future rights in the owner's property: in other words, the owner represents in some way that the belief is correct. A simple example is to be found in the hypothetical case discussed by Lord Cranworth in *Ramsden* v *Dyson* [1866] LR 1 HL 129 at pp. 140–1:

> If a stranger begins to build on my land, supposing it to be his own and I, perceiving his mistake, abstain from setting him right and leave him to persevere in his error, a court of equity will not allow me afterwards to assert my title to the land on which he had expended money on the supposition that the land was his own.

This sort of situation, in which the estoppel arises from the true owner's acquiescing in another's mistaken belief as to his own legal rights, has led to the suggestion that the estoppel arises only where the person seeking to rely on it (whom we will call 'the claimant') believes that he has an existing right in the property (see *Willmott* v *Barber* (1880) 15 ChD 96 below at 18.3). However, in modern decisions, the doctrine has been extended to cover situations in which the claimant is led to believe, possibly by a promise, that he will have some right to the property in the future.

It is the aspect of proprietary estoppel which relates to expectations about future rights which is of particular interest in cases involving family arrangements. It provides an alternative route for spouses or partners who believed that they were to receive a share in the family home but cannot show the common intention necessary for a constructive trust. It may also be helpful when a person has been led to believe that he can continue to live in the house, but later has this permission withdrawn. We consider this second situation in more detail in Chapter 20, in connection with licences.

18.2.1 Expectation as to future rights

In *Crabb* v *Arun District Council* [1976] Ch 179 the plaintiff had a right of access to his land through a gate leading from a road owned by the Council over which he had a right of way. He wanted to sell the part of his land which adjoined the gate, but intended to retain the rest of it, which lay further along the road. The Council agreed informally to grant him a right of way along the further stretch of road and to permit him to gain access to his property by a new gate. Relying on this understanding, the plaintiff completed the sale without reserving any right of way to the existing gate, but the Council did not grant the extended right of way, and indeed fenced the road so that the plot retained by the plaintiff became landlocked.

The Court of Appeal held that the Council had led the plaintiff to believe that he would be granted the right of way, and thus had encouraged him to act to his detriment in selling part of his land without reserving an easement over it. This gave rise to an equity in the plaintiff's favour which the court would satisfy by requiring the Council to grant the necessary right of way and right of access.

In a number of decisions since *Crabb* v *Arun DC* the courts have recognised that the encouragement of expectations relating to future rights (including an expectation of inheriting property) may give rise to an estoppel, with the result that the representor (or his personal representatives) may be required to give effect to this expectation. Thus, in *Re Basham* [1986] 1 WLR 1498, the court was satisfied that the plaintiff's stepfather had led her to believe that he would leave his property to her in his will. There was evidence that she and her husband had acted to their detriment in reliance on this belief, and the judge held that this gave rise to an equity in the plaintiff's favour, which would be satisfied by declaring that the deceased's personal representatives held his estate in trust for her.

In the course of his judgment, Mr Edward Nugee QC stated the principles of proprietary estoppel in the following terms:

> where one person [A] has acted to his detriment on the faith of a belief which was known to and encouraged by another person [B] that he either has or is going to be given a right in or over B's property, B cannot insist on his strict legal rights if to do so would be inconsistent with A's belief.

Although this statement was criticised in *Taylor* v *Dickens* [1998] 1 FLR 806 at p. 821, it has been referred to with approval by the Court of Appeal in a number of decisions including *Wayling* v *Jones* (1993) 69 P&CR 170, and most recently *Gillett* v *Holt* [2001] Ch 210.

In *Gillett* v *Holt* the claimant, Gillett, had been persuaded by Holt, a wealthy local landowner, to give up his plans for further education and leave school at an early age in order to work for Holt on his farm. Over the years Gillett was treated almost as a member of his employer's family, took on increasing responsibilities for the management of the property and was led to believe that, in due course, he and his family would inherit the whole property and the farming business carried on upon it. There was evidence that on several occasions when Gillett expressed concerns about his position, he received assurances that his future was secure and that the whole property would be left to him in Holt's will. Unfortunately, after some 40 years of a close working relationship, the two men fell out, the claimant was summarily dismissed and Holt made a new will, leaving his property elsewhere. In the resulting action, Gillet claimed that Holt was under an obligation founded on proprietary estoppel to bequeath to him substantially the whole of his estate.

At first instance, this claim was rejected, Carnwath J holding that the claimant had failed to establish that there was an irrevocable promise that Gillett would inherit. It seems that on this point the judge was influenced by the first instance decision in *Taylor* v *Dickens* [1998] 1 FLR 806. In that case, a claim by a gardener who had worked without payment for an old lady in reliance on her assurance that she would make her will in his favour was rejected on the grounds that the promise was only to make a will in his favour and did not contain the further promise that she would not revoke the will subsequently (as in fact she did). The gardener was taken to know that a will once made could be revoked and was, therefore, not able to establish the necessary assurance required to establish an estoppel. This decision had attracted some criticism (see, for example, Thompson [1998] Conv 210), but was apparently relied upon by the trial judge in *Gillett* v *Holt*, who considered that in order to ground an estoppel in such circumstances there had to be a specific undertaking not to revoke the promise. The judge also found against Gillett on the further ground that he failed to establish that he had suffered detriment as a result of relying on Holt's assurance.

The Court of Appeal reversed this decision, holding that there was no need for an express assurance that the promise would not be revoked ('it is the other party's reliance on the promise which makes it irrevocable' (p. 229)), and expressing the view that the criticisms of *Taylor* v *Dickens* were well founded (p. 227). The court was also of the opinion that there was clear evidence that Gillett had suffered detriment through relying on the assurances about Holt's testamentary intentions which he had received over a prolonged period of time.

Since *Gillett* v *Holt*, there have been two further Court of Appeal decisions on inheritance expectations: see *Campbell* v *Griffin* [2001] EWCA Civ 990 [2001] W & TLR 981, and *Jennings* v *Rice* [2003] 1 P&CR 8, p.100, which are considered further at 18.3.1.2 and 18.4.

18.3 Criteria for proprietary estoppel

An early statement of the criteria for establishing proprietary estoppel is to found in *Willmott* v *Barber* (1880) 15 ChD 96 at pp. 105–6, in the form of five propositions. Two relate to the person seeking to raise the estoppel: he must have made a mistake as to his legal rights, and must have expended money or done some other act in reliance on his mistaken belief. The other three relate to the person who is said to be estopped: he must know that he himself has some right inconsistent with the other party's mistaken belief; he must be aware of the mistake; and he must have encouraged the other party to act in reliance on the belief, either directly or by refraining from asserting his own right.

Some cases have applied these five criteria very strictly, but a more relaxed approach was adopted by Oliver J in *Taylors Fashions Ltd* v *Liverpool Victoria Trustees Co. Ltd* [1982] 1 QB 133. In this case, both parties to a lease were unaware of the true legal position, namely, that the tenant's option to renew the lease required registration as a land charge, and was in consequence void against the new landlord for non-registration. The tenant who was seeking to establish an estoppel therefore failed to satisfy the strict requirements of *Willmott* v *Barber*, but, in the judge's view (at p. 151), proprietary estoppel required a broader approach

which is directed rather at ascertaining whether . . . it would be unconscionable for a party to be permitted to deny that which, knowingly or unknowingly, he has allowed or encouraged another to assume to his detriment.

This more relaxed formulation has been followed in a number of later cases, most recently being quoted with apparent approval in *Gillett* v *Holt* (although note the rather surprising return to the strict *Willmott* v *Barber* tests in *Matharu* v *Matharu* (1994) 68 P&CR 93).

18.3.1 Essential elements

Even on the more relaxed approach adopted in *Taylors Fashions Ltd* v *Liverpool Trustees Co.*, there are certain essential elements which must be shown to exist before an estoppel can be said to arise. There must be a representation; the representation must be relied on by the claimant; and reliance on the representation must lead the claimant to act to his detriment. However, although it is helpful to consider these elements separately, it must be remembered that, in the words of Robert Walker LJ in *Gillett* v *Holt* [2001] Ch 210 at 225:

It is important to note that the doctrine of proprietary estoppel cannot be treated as sub-divided into ... watertight compartments ... the quality of the relevant assurances may influence the issue of reliance ... [and] reliance and detriment are often intertwined ... Moreover the fundamental principle that equity is concerned to prevent unconscionable conduct permeates all the elements of the doctrine. In the end the court must look at the matter in the round.

18.3.1.1 *The representation*

This may well, of course, be made in express terms, as it was in *Re Basham* [1986] 1 WLR 1498, and in some of the other cases which we will consider in Chapter 20. It may however be made more indirectly, as for example by encouraging a course of action which it would not be sensible for the claimant to undertake unless he was to be granted some interest in the property—thus raising the expectation that such a grant is to be made.

An old example of this approach, though not expressed to be decided on this basis, is *Dillwyn* v *Llewellyn* (1862) 4 De G F & J 517 in which a son was 'given' land by his father and thereafter built a house upon the land. No formal conveyance of the estate was ever made. Despite the usual rule that equity will not assist a volunteer (one who acquires property without giving value) and accordingly will not perfect an imperfect gift, the court held that the son was entitled to a con-veyance of the fee simple because he had expended his own money on building, in reliance on his father's representation.

A modern example of the same principle, and one which was expressly decided on the basis of estoppel, is *Inwards* v *Baker* [1965] 2 QB 29. Here a son, acting on a suggestion of his father, built a bungalow on his father's land (partly at his own expense). Thereafter, the son occupied the bungalow in the belief that he would be able to remain there for his lifetime. However, when his father later died, the son discovered that the estate in the land had been left to other people. The Court of Appeal held that the son had a licence (i.e., permission) entitling him to remain in the property as long as he wished, because he had altered his position to his detri-ment in reliance on a belief induced by his father's conduct. In this case Lord Denning MR suggested that the operation of the rules of estoppel gave rise to 'an equity' in favour of the son, and that this equity should be satisfied by the grant of a suitable remedy, in this case a licence for life. (For a contemporary comment on this decision, see Maudsley [1965] 81 LQR 183.)

Finally, as we have seen in the quotation from Lord Carnworth in *Ramsden* v *Dyson* [1866] LR 1 HL 129, representations can be made by conduct, including complete silence, as where an owner stands by and watches another mistakenly building on his land and does nothing to correct the mistake.

18.3.1.2 *Reliance on representation*

It is an essential element in establishing estoppel that the claimant has relied on the represention, in the sense of being influenced or induced by it to act in a particular way. There are statements in earlier decisions which suggest that it is for the claimant to prove reliance, and this approach appears to have been adopted by Oliver J in *Taylors Fashions Ltd* v *Liverpool Trustees Co.* [1982] 1 QB 133 at p. 156. However, the contrary view finds strong expression in *Greasely* v *Cooke* [1980] 1 WLR 1306 at p. 1311 (the facts of which are outlined in 20.3.4), in which Lord

Denning MR repeated a statement he had made in an earlier judgment (*Brikom Investments Ltd* v *Carr* [1979] QB 467 at pp. 482–3):

Once it is shown that a representation was calculated to influence the judgement of a reasonable man, the presumption is that he was so influenced.

In *Gillet* v *Holt* [2001] Ch 210 the Court of Appeal accepted without question that reliance would be presumed, citing *Greaseley* v *Cooke* as authority for this.

The burden is thus on the person who made the representation and is now contesting the estoppel, to show that the claimant did not rely upon it.

In seeking to do this, it may well be suggested that the claimant acted as he did for a variety of reasons, and was not influenced solely by the representation made to him. This problem of mixed motives was considered recently by the Court of Appeal in *Campbell* v *Griffin* [2001] EWCA Civ 990 [2001] W&TLR 981, the facts of which were as follows.

The claimant, Mr Campbell had lived for many years as a lodger in a house jointly owned by an elderly couple, Mr and Mrs Ascough. As the Ascoughs became increasingly frail, they depended upon Campbell for practical help, and as time went by he gradually took on the role of an unpaid carer, preparing meals for them and helping them to wash and get to bed. At various times over the years he received assurances from them that he had a home for life. An attempt was in fact made by Mr Ascough to give effect to this assurance in his will, but by the time he did this his wife was suffering from senile dementia and was no longer capable of altering her own will to the same effect. Mr Ascough died before his wife, who took the whole property by right of survivorship (see 16.3.1.3), with the result that at her death the whole house passed to those entitled under her will. In these circumstances, the executors of the couple's wills were obliged to oppose Mr Campbell's subsequent claim of estoppel. In the course of the trial, the claimant admitted that he had been influenced by feelings of affection and responsibility towards the elderly couple, who had treated him as one of the family, and that he would have acted as he did even without an expectation of receiving an interest in the property. In the light of this, the trial judge held that Mr Campbell had not acted in reliance on the assurances, and that in consequence no estoppel was established.

On appeal, the court considered the position of a claimant who realises that he had several reasons for incurring the detriment on which he relies. In the words of Robert Walker LJ (at para. 29):

It would do no credit to the law if an honest witness who admitted that he had mixed motives were to fail in a claim which might have succeeded if supported by less candid evidence.

His Lordship quoted with approval the words of Balcombe LJ in *Wayling* v *Jones* (1993) 69 P&CR 170 at 173:

The promises relied upon do not have to be the sole inducement for the conduct: it is sufficient if they are an inducement.

The Court of Appeal accepted that the assurances given by the Ascoughs were among the inducements which led Mr Campbell to act as he did, and in consequence found that he was entitled to equitable relief.

18.3.1.3 *Claimant must act to his detriment*

While reliance on the representation may be presumed, the detriment resulting from that reliance must be proved by the claimant (*Gillett* v *Holt* [2001] Ch 210 at p. 232, rejecting the suggestion that the detriment could be presumed).

The detriment relied upon may often involve the expenditure of money (for example on property in which one believes one has or will have an interest—see for example *Pascoe* v *Turner* [1979] 1 WLR 431), but it does not necessarily have to do so. In *Crabb* v *Arun DC* [1976] 1 Ch 179 the detriment consisted of the plaintiff's selling off part of his land without reserving a right of way over it. In *Greasely* v *Cooke* [1980] 1 WLR 1306 a former maid had continued to live in the house and look after the family 'when otherwise she might have left and got a job elsewhere' (at p. 1312). In *Re Basham* [1986] 1 WLR 1498 the plaintiff and her husband had looked after her stepfather, providing meals for him and working in his house and garden, and had continued to live in the neighbourhood rather than moving away, so that they could continue to care for him.

In *Gillett* v *Holt* [2001] Ch 210, the Court of Appeal identified a wide range of matters which in its view constituted detriment: the claimant had left school without academic qualifications at the request of the defendant; he and his wife had subordinated their wishes to those of his employer in a number of ways, most notably in connection with their sons' education; they had sold their own house (and so had 'stepped off' the property ladder) and had lived as rent-paying tenants in a farmhouse owned by Holt, on which they had spent a good deal of their own money. In addition, by remaining in Holt's employment, Gillett had deprived himself of the chance to try to better himself in some way—although the court also accepted that he might have done less well with a different employer.

A difficulty sometimes experienced in seeking to establish detriment is that the claimant may appear to have derived considerable benefit from the arrangements to which he was a party. Thus, in situations such as those in *Dillwyn* v *Llewellyn* and *Inwards* v *Baker*, the claimants had had the advantage of occupying land without paying rent, while Gillet had found Holt to be a generous employer, and had benefited from gifts to the family and substantial help with the school fees. While things were going well between the two men, it would not have appeared that Gillett was acting to his detriment, and it was this that apparently led the trial judge to consider that the necessary element of detriment had not been established. However, the Court of Appeal was at pains to point out that

The issue of detriment must be judged at the moment when the person who has given the assurance seeks to go back on it (p. 232).

In elaborating this point, the court quoted with approval (at pp. 232–3) a passage from the judgment of Dixon J in the Australian case of *Grundt* v *Great Boulder Pty Gold Mines Ltd* (1937) 59 CLR 641 at 674–5):

The real detriment or harm from which the law seeks to give protection is that which would flow from the change of position if the assumption were deserted that led to it. So long as the assumption is adhered to the party who altered his situation upon the faith of it cannot complain. His complaint is that when afterwards the other party makes a different state of affairs the basis of an assertion of right against him then, if it is allowed, his own original change of position will operate as a detriment.

18.4 **Satisfying the equity**

You may have noted from our account of various decisions, that the estoppel, when established, is said to give rise to an 'equity', by which we understand the courts to mean that the claimant has a right to some form of remedy in equity. Once the equity is established, the courts have to consider how to 'satisfy' it, i.e., to decide what relief should be given.

Over the years the courts have drawn on a range of remedies, including restraining the owner from exercising his rights, or requiring him to pay compensation or grant the claimant some interest in the land. In deciding what remedy to give, the courts seek to achieve 'the minimum equity to do justice to the plaintiff' (*per* Scarman LJ in *Crabb* v *Arun DC* [1976] 1 Ch 179 at p. 198), a statement repeated with approval in a range of judgments over the years.

In some cases the court has decided that the equity can be satisfied only by giving effect to the expectations which the representation has encouraged. Thus in *Re Basham* [1986] 1 WLR 1498 the plaintiff received the estate she had expected to inherit, and in *Crabb* v *Arun DC* [1976] 1 Ch 179 the landowner was granted the rights of access and way on which he had relied. In *Greasely* v *Cooke* [1980] 1 WLR 1306 the former maid was allowed to remain in the house as long as she wished, and similarly in *Inwards* v *Baker* [1965] 2 QB 29 the son was in effect given a licence for life. The most generous way of satisfying the equity is perhaps that to be found in *Pascoe* v *Turner* [1979] 1 WLR 431, in which, in rather exceptional circumstances, the fee simple owner was required to transfer the estate in the house to his former mistress (see further 20.2.4).

In other cases, however, it has been either impossible or, in the view of the court, inappropriate to satisfy the expectations of the claimant in full. In *Gillett* v *Holt* [2001] Ch 210 there could be no question of giving effect to the full expectations encouraged by Holt, since they were to take effect on his death and he was still very much alive! The court described its task of satisfying the equity in this case as presenting unusually difficult problems, but having regard to the extent of the property involved ordered that the farmhouse and farm currently occupied by the Gilletts should be transferred to them, together with a payment of £100,000.

In *Campbell* v *Griffin* [2001] EWCA Civ 990, Robert Walker LJ commented (at para. 34) that:

Mr Campbell has a moral (and, as I see it, a legal) claim on the property, but it is not so compelling as to demand total satisfaction, regardless of the effect on other persons with claims on the Ascoughs' estate.

The court also took into account that the life interest which Mr Campbell had expected to receive would necessarily take effect under a trust of land, with resulting legal expenses and that there could well be disputes about the maintenance of the house. It accordingly favoured the 'clean break' approach, which would enable those with other interests in the property to benefit from them without delay, and therefore ordered the sale of the house and the payment to Mr Campbell of £35,000. It accepted that this would not be sufficient to buy him a home, but considered that it would be a reasonable contribution to the cost of doing so.

Another similar question, and on similar facts, arose in *Jennings* v *Rice* [2003] 1 P&CR 8, p. 100. For many years, Mr Jennings had worked, originally as a gardener, for an elderly and wealthy widow, who gradually came to depend upon him as her carer. After a time she no longer paid him for his work, but assured him that he had no need to worry and that 'this will all be yours one day'. Despite this, she died without making a will, leaving an estate which was valued at over £1 million. At first instance the trial judge accepted that Mr Jennings had acted to his detriment in reliance on the assurances and that it was unconscionable for the deceased to go back on her word. In deciding how to satisfy the equity that had arisen, he rejected Mr Jennings's claim that he was entitled to the whole estate, holding that the claimant was unaware of the true extent of the deceased's wealth and therefore could not have expected to receive her whole estate. He also rejected the alternative claim to the house and furniture (valued at £435,000), considering that the house was not suitable for Mr Jennings to live in on his own and also that a reward of such value would be excessive. He took into account the fact that the cost of full-time nursing care would have been in the region of £200,000 and that Mr Jennings could probably buy a suitable house for £150,000, and accordingly awarded the claimant the sum of £200,000. On appeal by Mr Jennings, who sought a greater award, the Court of Appeal upheld the lower court's decision.

The interest of the Court of Appeal's judgment in this case lies in its review of the various approaches which may guide a court in its search for an appropriate remedy, and we will look in more detail at this below. First, however, we must note a slightly earlier decision, *Sledmore* v *Dalby* (1996) 72 P&CR 196, in which the court refused to give any relief at all to the applicant.

In *Sledmore* v *Dalby* the plaintiff sought possession of a house which she owned, and which the defendant, her son-in-law, had occupied for over 30 years, initially in exchange for rent but subsequently on a rent-free basis. The defendant relied on proprietary estoppel, claiming that during his wife's lifetime he had been led to believe that the house would be left to her on her parents' death, and that at that period he had made various improvements to the house at his own expense. He had remained in the house for some 12 years after his wife's death, and assumed that he would be allowed to live there rent-free for the rest of his life. At first instance, the court gave effect to this expectation, refusing the plaintiff's application for possession and declaring that the defendant had a personal licence to occupy the house during his life, so long as he wished.

The Court of Appeal, however, took into account the relative circumstances of the two parties. The defendant's children were grown up, and had either left home or were capable of doing so; he was in employment; and he had the use of alternative accommodation, spending much of his time away from the house and using it on only one or two nights each week. By contrast, the plaintiff was an elderly woman who could no longer afford to remain in her present home, and accordingly needed the house to live in. The court emphasised that in applying the equitable doctrine of proprietary estoppel

... it is necessary to consider the extent of the equity created and what is, in the circumstances, the equitable way in which to give effect to it (at p. 207).

The court referred to a discussion of the law of estoppel to be found in a decision of the High Court of Australia (*Commonwealth of Australia* v *Verwayen* (1990) 170 CLR 394), and (at p. 208) quoted with approval the statement of Mason CJ that:

A central element of [the doctrine of estoppel] is that there must be a proportionality between the remedy and the detriment which [it] is its purpose to avoid.

Having regard to these principles, and to all the circumstances of the case, the English Court of Appeal considered that it was no longer inequitable to allow the expectation raised some 18 years earlier to be defeated, and accordingly made an order for possession against the defendant. For a critical consideration of this decision, see Adams [1997] Conv 458.

18.4.1 How does the court decide on appropriate relief?

The decisions considered above illustrate the range of approaches which the court may be asked to adopt in giving relief. While the claimant hopes that the court will give full effect to his expectations, those opposing the claim may suggest that it would be enough to compensate him for the detriment he has suffered. Thus, if a situation similar to *Pascoe* v *Turner* were to arise again, the claimant would hope for ownership of the house, while the other side might argue that it would be sufficient to repay the money spent on improvements to the property. Yet again, where the detriment in question consists of the performance of personal services it might be thought that the equity would be satisfied by payment for those services, plus if necessary reimbursement of out-of-pocket expenses.

In *Jennings* v *Rice* [2003] 1 P&CR 8 at p. 100, the Court of Appeal discussed these various approaches, emphasising that while each might be appropriate in some situations, there was no one approach which would apply to all circumstances. The court stressed that the guiding principle must be the need to do justice, or, as Robert Walker LJ put it (at p. 116):

The essence of the doctrine of proprietary estoppel is to do what is necessary to avoid an unconscionable result.

The court drew attention to the flexibility of this form of relief and the importance of considering all the circumstances of each individual case. Further the judges emphasised the long-established principle that the relief given must be 'the minimum equity to do justice'. In some cases, such as *Pascoe* v *Turner*, the minimum required may be to give full effect to the claimant's expectations, but that is because this is what in needed in the circumstances of the case—not because there is any rule that the award *must* satisfy the expectation (see pp. 107–8). In each case, the court must go no further than is necessary to prevent unconscionable conduct and, as was said in *Sledmore* v *Dalby* (1996) 72 P&CR 196, must ensure that there is proportionality between the benefit and the detriment. As Hobhouse LJ explained in that case (at p. 209):

This is to say little more than that the end result must be a just one having regard to the assumption made by the party asserting the estoppel and the detriment which he has experienced.

Thus again and again in *Jennings* v *Rice* the Court of Appeal returned to the point that there is no one correct formula by which a court can identify the relief to be given: it is a matter for the court's discretion, and the relief must be tailored to the specific facts of each case. In dealing with such applications the court will undertake a detailed consideration of all the circumstances, and you may like to note the following passage (at p. 115) in which Robert Walker LJ outlines some of the matters which a court might take into account:

It would be unwise to attempt any comprehensive enumeration of the factors relevant to the exercise of the court's discretion, or to suggest any hierarchy of factors. In my view they include . . . factors [such as the] misconduct of the claimant . . . or particularly oppressive conduct on the part of the defendant. To these can safely be added the court's recognition that it cannot compel people who have fallen out to live peaceably together, so that there may be a need for a clean break; alterations in the benefactor's assets and circumstances . . . ; and (to a limited degree) the other claims (legal or moral) on the benefactor or his or her estate. No doubt there are many other factors which it may be right for the court to take into account in particular factual situations.

18.5 Nature of the equity arising from estoppel

As we have seen, the equity which arises from proprietary estoppel entitles the claimant to some form of equitable relief. What happens if the landowner who made the representation and so is subject to the equity transfers his property to another person after the equity arose, but before the claimant seeks relief in the courts? Is the equity a purely personal right, enforceable only against the original owner or does it have the character of a proprietary right, binding those who take the land from him?

There are a number of decisions relating to licences of *unregistered* land in which the equity arising from estoppel has been held to bind third parties, and we will tell you about these in Chapter 20. Until recently, there was little authority on the status of the equity in relation to *registered* land, although it appeared that it was the practice of the Registrar to allow the protection of such an equity by means of a notice or caution on the register (see Ruoff and Roper, *The Law and Practice of Registered Conveyancing*, R.18 Jan. 2001, para. 8–02). There were also suggestions that the equity was capable of taking effect as an overriding interest under LRA 1925, s. 70(1)(g) (rights of person in actual occupation), and this is now supported by two recent decisions: *Habermann* v *Koehler (No. 2)* [2000] TLR 825 (see 20.3.4.1(2)) and *Lloyd* v *Dugdale* [2002] 2 P&CR 13 p. 167.

In *Lloyd* v *Dugdale* (the facts of which are to be found towards the end of 3.4.2), the trial judge held that the claimant's right arising from estoppel bound the purchaser as an overriding interest under LRA 1925 s. 70(1)(g). The Court of Appeal reversed this decision, holding that the claimant was not in actual occupation of the registered property at the relevant time. However, the court appeared to accept, without any discussion, that if actual occupation had been established, the equity would have been an overriding interest and bound the purchaser.

Shortly before the two decisions noted above, the position of the equity in relation to registered land was considered by the Joint Working Party of the Law Commission and the Land Registry, which developed the proposals for reform of registered title discussed in Chapter 5. The Working Party emphasised the increasing importance of the doctrine of proprietary estoppel, which in its view had become:

one of the principal vehicles for accommodating the informal creation of proprietary rights (*Consultative Document*, 1998, Law Com No. 254, para. 3.33).

The status of the equity arising from estoppel was uncertain, but such authority as there was indicated that the equity was of a proprietary nature capable of binding successors, rather than a personal right against the original owner. It was desirable to clarify the status of the equity in relation to registered land, and during the consultation process it emerged that similar clarification was needed in respect of 'mere equities' (for which, see 1.6.4 and Report, Law Com No. 271, paras. 5.32–36).

Accordingly LRA 2002, s. 116 provides:

It is hereby declared for the avoidance of doubt that, in relation to registered land, each of the following—

(a) an equity by estoppel, and

(b) a mere equity

has effect from the time the equity arises as an interest capable of binding successors in title (subject to the rules about the effect of dispositions on priority).

It seems therefore that the case law development discussed above has now been overtaken by statute, and that the equity arising from estoppel is capable of binding a purchaser of registered land if it is protected by an entry on the register or takes effect as an overriding interest under LRA 2002 Sch. 3, para. 2 (interests of persons in actual occupation).

18.6 Situations in which there is 'no room' for proprietary estoppel

We must now briefly mention two cases in which a party who already had an equitable interest in the property sought to rely in addition on proprietary estoppel.

In *Lloyds Bank* v *Carrick* [1996] 4 All ER 630 (for facts, see 4.4.5.4), the defendant's equitable interest under an estate contract was void against the mortgagee because it had not been registered as a land charge. She sought, therefore, to rely on proprietary estoppel arising from representations made to her by her brother-in-law. This was rejected by the Court of Appeal for a number of reasons, including the fact that there was 'no room for the application of the principles of proprietary estoppel' (at p. 641) when, at the relevant time, the defendant already had interests in the property arising from the estate contract.

A similar statement is to be found in the more recent decision in *Birmingham Midshires Mortgage Services Ltd* v *Sabherwal* (2000) 80 P&CR 256. The facts here were very similar to those in *City of London Building Society* v *Flegg* [1988] AC 54 (see 5.10.4.5(1)). Mrs Sabherwal had an equitable interest in the family home under a resulting trust which arose from her previous contributions to the cost of acquisition. This interest was overreached by a mortgage transaction in which the lender paid the mortgage money to her two sons as the registered proprietors. Mrs Sabherwal tried to resist possession proceedings by claiming that she also had rights to the property by virtue of an estoppel, arising from her sons' promises to provide a home for her, and that estoppel rights were not capable of being overreached. The

Court of Appeal however, took the view that her earlier financial contributions gave her an interest under a trust and that (p. 263):

Such a trust, however labelled, does not then leave room for a separate interest by way of equitable estoppel . . . To do so would cause vast confusion in an area which is already quite difficult enough.

Despite holding that proprietary estoppel was not relevant in this case, the Court of Appeal considered briefly whether such rights, if they had existed, could have been overriding under LRA 1925, s. 70(1)(g), and, if so, whether they would have been overreached by the mortgage. The court assumed, without hearing argument on the point, that such rights could be overriding, thus providing further support to the view discussed above that the equity rising from estoppel is capable of binding successors in title. The court also considered that such rights would be capable of being overreached; equitable interests under a trust are overreachable and (p. 262):

it would [be] a remarkable result if these more precarious rights were incapable of being overreached.

For a note on these points, and on the other aspects of this decision which we have already considered in 13.11.8, see Harpum (2000) 116 LQR 341.

18.7 Relationship between proprietary estoppel and constructive trusts

While reading this account of proprietary estoppel you have probably been reminded of some aspects of the rule in *Gissing* v *Gissing* [1971] AC 886: the need for detrimental reliance in establishing an estoppel is reminiscent of the requirement that the party claiming a share under a common-intention constructive trust must show that he acted to his detriment in reliance upon the agreement between the parties. We have already noted the link between the two concepts made by Lord Bridge in *Lloyds Bank* v *Rosset* [1991] 1 AC 107 at 132 (see 17.5.4), but should also draw your attention to a passage from the judgment of Browne-Wilkinson VC in *Grant* v *Edwards* [1986] 1 Ch 638 at pp. 656–7. In this case the Vice-Chancellor specifically based his decision on the existence of a constructive trust (at p. 657), as did the other members of the Court of Appeal, but at p. 656 he suggested that:

in other cases of this kind, useful guidance may in the future be obtained from the principles underlying the law of proprietary estoppel which . . . are closely akin to those laid down in *Gissing* v *Gissing* [1971] AC 886. In both, the claimant must to the knowledge of the legal owner have acted in the belief that the claimant has or will obtain an interest in the property. In both, the claimant must have acted to his or her detriment in reliance on such belief. In both, equity acts on the conscience of the legal owner to prevent him from acting in an unconscionable manner by defeating the common intention. The two principles have been developed separately without cross-fertilisation between them: but they rest on the same foundation and have on all other matters reached the same conclusions.

The Court of Appeal recently expressed similar views again in *Yaxley* v *Gotts* [2000] Ch 162 (see 3.4.2), in which Robert Walker LJ commented that although there are large areas where the concepts of constructive trust and proprietary estoppel do not overlap:

in the area of a joint enterprise for the acquisition of land . . . the two concepts coincide. . . . A [common intention] constructive trust is closely akin to, if not indistinguishable from, proprietary estoppel (at pp. 176 and 180).

The relationship between these two equitable doctrines forms the subject matter of a lively academic debate. We must leave you to pursue the details of this for yourself, if you wish to do so, but we think that it might be helpful to mention briefly that despite the similarities between the two concepts, there are also certain differences. Thus, the *Gissing* v *Gissing* type of constructive trust depends on agreement or common intention between the parties, whereas estoppel arises from a representation by one party inducing a mistaken belief by the other. Again, the interest under a trust arises when the trust itself comes into existence, at the time when the claimant acts to his detriment. Under such a trust, the claimant has a beneficial interest in the property and this recognised equitable interest will bind later purchasers in accordance with established rules. By contrast, the equity arising from proprietary estoppel, although it also comes into existence when the claimant acts to his detriment, gives only a right to a remedy, the nature of which is at that stage uncertain. Moreover, as we have seen above, there used to be doubt as to whether this right binds successors in title, although it now appears that it does. Even so, the right is only to such remedy as the court may decide. It may be that some time in the future the court will order the grant of an interest in the land, but equally it may award only an irrevocable licence or the payment of a sum of money.

A more detailed consideration of the whole question, together with details of the relevant literature will be found in Pawlowski, *The Doctrine of Proprietary Estoppel*, 1996, pp. 10–16; see also Megarry and Wade, *The Law of Real Property*, 6th edn., paras. 10–30 and 13–036.

FURTHER READING

Land Registration for the Twenty-First Century: A Consultative Document, 1998, Law Com No. 254, paras. 3.33—3.36.

Land Registration for the Twenty-First Century: A Conveyancing Revolution, 2001, Law Com No. 271, paras. 5.29–5.36.

Gardner, 'The Remedial Discretion in Proprietary Estoppel', (1999) 115 LQR 438.

Megarry and Wade, *The Law of Real Property*, 6th edn., Sweet & Maxwell, 2000, Chapter 13 (Proprietary Estoppel).

Gillett v *Holt*

Thompson, 'Estoppel: A Return to Principle' [2001] 65 Conv 78

Wells, 'The Element of Detriment in Proprietary Estoppel' [2001] 65 Conv 13.

Campbell v *Griffin*

Thompson, 'Estoppel, Reliance, Remedy and Priority' [2003] 67 Conv 157.

Jennings v *Rice*

Thompson, 'The Flexibility of Estoppel' [2003] 67 Conv 225.

Relationship between constructive trusts and proprietary estoppel

Ferguson, 'Constructive Trusts—A Note of Caution' [1993] Conv 114.

Hayton, 'Equitable Rights of Cohabitees' [1990] Conv 370.

Hayton, 'Constructive Trusts of Homes—A Bold Approach' (1993) 109 LQR 485.

Smith, 'Oral Contracts for the Sale of Land: Estoppels and Constructive Trusts' [2000] 116 LQR 11.

PART V

....

Licences

Introduction

We have now considered the two legal estates in land and the way in which they may be put in trust. Before we turn to consider the legal and equitable interests in land, we must look at the law relating to licences. Licences to use land are unusual in the sense that, although they are rights which concern the use of land, theoretically they create neither an estate nor an interest in land. Indeed the term 'licence' covers a diversity of rights to use land. Some of the problems which arise in this area are better illustrated if we look at some practical examples, before attempting to examine the law in detail.

Trant Way

Number 1 Trant Way has a small front garden with a short path leading to the front door, on which there is a door-knocker. Every day the postman, milkman and the paper-boy walk up to the front door in order to make deliveries.

Barbara Bell has completed the purchase of **3 Trant Way** (see Chapter 4) and has moved into the property. Her father, Bob Bell, has come to live in the 'granny flat' on the top floor. Mr Bell has his own separate front door and Barbara has given her father the only set of keys to the flat. She never enters her father's flat unless he invites her in. When Mr Bell moved in Barbara told him, 'You need never worry again, you will have a home here with me for as long as you live'. Since moving in, Mr Bell has used some of his savings to make improvements to the flat.

The fee simple estate of 8 Trant Way belongs to Mildred Mumps, who bought it in 1980. The basement is a self-contained flat **(8A Trant Way)** which has been occupied by Laura Lymeswold since 1985. Miss Lymeswold pays Mrs Mumps £120 a week for the use of the flat. However, Mrs Mumps was keen to ensure that Laura did not obtain any statutory protection, and has always refused to give her a written lease. She has always told Laura, 'You only have a licence, dear. You must go if I say so.' Mildred has kept a key to the front door of the flat and lets herself in once a month to empty the gas and electricity meters and to check that the flat is clean and in good order.

legal title *Henry No chance of selling anything*

Mrs Mumps occupies the rest of **8 Trant Way** herself, together with Henry Mumps. In fact Mildred and Henry are not married, but have lived together as husband and wife ever since Mildred first bought the property. They have two children, now grown up. Mildred has a very highly paid job and so, whilst she has always worked (apart from brief maternity leave when the children were born), Henry stayed at home to look after the children and still does all the cooking and cleaning. Henry is very clever at 'do-it-yourself' and, whilst he has never contributed financially to the purchase of the property or to the family living expenses, he has made considerable improvements to the property. Recently Mildred and Henry's personal relationship has been under some strain and now Mildred appears to be having an affair with another man. Henry is very worried that soon Mildred may tell him that she wants to end their relationship.

Cross Reference to p.64 24.2.1 24.2.2

These four situations are very different in nature, but each may well be regarded by a court as giving rise to a licence. One, the 'licence' of Laura Lymeswold, may cause considerable problems if considered by the courts, since it is likely that Laura will allege that the arrangement is not a licence at all but a lease which gives her extensive rights under the Rent Acts. Two of the situations, those concerning the positions of Bob Bell and Henry Mumps, look like family arrangements which would only come before a court should the family relationships break down. The other situation, the front path, is one with which we are all familiar. Yet normally, when we walk on to someone else's land, we do not consider the nature of our right to do so.

In addition to these examples, there are many other types of rights which can amount to a licence to use land, for example, a licence to walk across another's property (which may look very like an easement) or a licence to run the sweet counter in a cinema foyer. These assorted rights give rise to three main problems:

(a) What is the nature of a licence, and how can it be distinguished from other rights?

(b) Are these licences enforceable against the original grantors, or may they be revoked at will?

(c) Are these licences enforceable against successors in title of the original grantors?

We will deal with the first of those questions in Chapter 19, and will then consider both aspects of enforceability in Chapter 20.

19

Nature of a licence

19.1 Introduction

The starting point for any consideration of the nature of a licence is the classic statement made by Vaughan CJ in *Thomas* v *Sorrell* (1673) Vaugh 330 at p. 351, that:

A dispensation or licence properly passeth no interest, nor alters or transfers property in any thing, but only makes an action lawful, which without it had been unlawful.

(Oddly enough this case concerned the granting of alcohol licences and had nothing to do with land law, yet ever since it has been regarded as crucial to any discussion of licences to use land.) Put more simply, this means that a licence does not give the licensee an estate or interest in the land but does make his presence on the property authorised, so that he is not a trespasser.

If we look at our four initial examples (pp. 397–8) it is clear that Bob Bell, Laura Lymeswold and Henry Mumps could not possibly be regarded as trespassers; obviously they have permission to be on the properties concerned. What about the postman, and others, who use the footpath leading to the front door of 1 Trant Way? In this case the owners of 1 Trant Way have not expressly given permission to each caller to walk up to the front door, but they have impliedly done so by providing the path and by putting a knocker on the door. Thus someone who walks up to the front door and knocks would not be a trespasser, though a visitor who went further and prowled about the rest of the garden would have gone beyond the limits of the implied licence and would be trespassing. It is also open to the estate owner to limit the implied licence, e.g., by putting up a sign saying 'No salesmen' at the garden gate, and then any person who is a salesman and who fails to observe the restriction would also be a trespasser.

Once one has established that a person who is on the land is not a trespasser, one then has to establish whether that person has an estate or interest in the land. If the person has no property ('proprietary') interest giving him *the right* to be on the land, then it is usually true to say that he is there by *permission* and is a licensee of some kind. (Since the decision of the House of Lords in *Bruton* v *London & Quadrant HT* [2000] 1 AC 406 there is the further possibility that he may be a tenant under a non-proprietary lease, but this is a new and unfamiliar concept, which we will explain later when we consider the decision in *Bruton*—see 19.2.4.4).

The rights which are most commonly confused with licences are leases and easements and we will now consider these separately.

19.2 **Distinguishing a lease from a licence**

19.2.1 **Nature of the problem**

Sometimes it can be very difficult indeed to distinguish a lease from a licence. The agreement relating to 8A Trant Way is a good example of the type of arrangement which may give a considerable amount of difficulty to the lawyer who is asked to classify it. As we have already explained (at 8.5.1), the tenant's right to security of tenure under, for example, the Rent Acts is very considerable and landlords/licensors, like Mrs Mumps, have sought to avoid the application of these rules by trying to grant licences, which have little protection, rather than leases, which are fully protected under the Acts.

Another source of difficulty is the fact that families such as the Bells often make informal arrangements without taking advice or considering the legal consequences of what they are doing. It is not until things go wrong between them, or one of them dies, that any thought is given to the nature of the interest which has been created (see for example *Errington* v *Errington* [1952] 1 KB 290, or *Nunn* v *Dalrymple* (1989) 59 P&CR 231).

19.2.2 **Significance of distinction between a lease and a licence**

The nature of a lease is essentially very different from that of a licence. In general, with the rare exception of the non-proprietary lease (see 19.2.4.4), a lease, if made in the proper form, creates a legal estate in the land, binding on both the landlord and his successors. The tenant has a property interest in the land, with which he can deal. He is able to sell or mortgage his estate, dispose of it on his death, and create lesser interests out of it, by granting subleases (see 8.2.4.1).

By contrast, the licensee has a mere permission to be on the land; he does not own a property interest in it, and therefore has nothing which he can sell or give to others. In general his rights, if any, are against the licensor, and are unenforceable against the licensor's successors, although there are exceptions to this, which we consider in Chapter 20.

In addition to these essential differences, resulting from the nature of the lease and the licence, there are many situations in which the distinction between the two is of considerable significance. As we have already indicated, one of the most important consequences of the distinction relates to the provisions for tenants' security of tenure under the Rent Acts, which do not apply to licensees. The statutory protection afforded to tenants of residential accommodation under leases granted on or after 15 January 1989 is by no means as great as it was under the Rent Acts, but the distinction between leases and licences is still important in determining the process by which the landlord may recover possession (see, for example, *Gray* v *Taylor* [1998] 1 WLR 1093). It is also highly relevant to the protection of business tenants under the Landlord and Tenant Act 1954, and to the imposition of the landlord's statutory duty to repair under the Landlord and Tenant Act 1985.

There are, however, many other areas in which the distinction is important. In a land law context, the question of whether a tenant has granted a sublease or a licence would be relevant in considering whether he had broken a covenant against subletting (see 9.2.2.2; *Brent LBC* v *Cronin* (1997) 30 HLR 43). Similarly the need for a written contract under the Law of Property (Miscellaneous Provisions) Act 1989, s. 2 (see Chapter 3) would apply in the case of a lease, but not to a licence. (See *Wright* v *Stavert*, 1860 2 E & E 721 on the earlier requirements as to form contained in the Statute of Frauds (1677).) Under the relevant statutory provisions, compensation for compulsory acquisition of land is payable to an occupier with a legal or equitable interest in the land, but not to a licensee (*Rochester Poster Services* v *Dartford BC* (1991) 63 P&CR 88); and accelerated procedures for recovering possession of land are available against licensees but not against tenants (*Crancour Ltd* v *Da Silvaesa* [1986] 1 EGLR 80; and *Esso Petroleum Co. Ltd* v *Fumegrange Ltd* [1994] 2 EGLR 90).

The distinction between leases and licences can also be of importance in branches of law which you might think were well removed from your study of land law. Thus, in the field of tort, the traditional view is that claims in respect of torts to land, such as trespass and nuisance, can be brought only by an occupier with a property interest in the land (such as a lease), and not by a mere licensee. Recent decisions show signs of relaxing this requirement (see, for example, *Manchester Airport plc* v *Dutton* [2000] 1 QB 133 with reference to trespass; and the speeches of some members of the House of Lords in *Hunter* v *Canary Wharf Ltd* [1997] AC 655, when considering a claim in nuisance), but the distinction remains relevant to an understanding of the older case law.

A particularly interesting example of the distinction in a tort-based claim is to be found in *Appah* v *Parncliffe Investments Ltd* [1964] 1 WLR 1064. The plaintiff occupied a room in a rooming-house. The lock on her door was defective, and as a result property was stolen from her room. She sued the proprietors, claiming damages for negligence, and the outcome of the action depended on the nature of her occupation. If she was a tenant, the defendant owed her no duty of care; but if she was a licensee, the defendant was under an obligation to take reasonable care of her property. After a detailed consideration of the nature of her occupation (for which see 19.2.3.1(1)), the Court of Appeal held that she was a licensee and accordingly entitled to recover damages for negligence.

Thus, although many of the cases which we consider in this chapter arise under the Rent Acts, it is important to remember that there are many other settings in which the distinction between a lease and a licence may be of crucial importance.

19.2.3 How to distinguish between a lease and a licence

The first step is to consider whether the arrangement between the parties satisfies the essential requirements for the existence of a lease.

19.2.3.1 *Requirements for a lease: certainty and exclusive possession*

We have already considered this topic in Chapter 8, and in particular have noted that a lease must be for a certain period, and give the tenant exclusive possession. If either of these requirements is not met, the arrangement cannot be a lease and must be a licence. Since *Prudential Assurance Co. Ltd* v *London Residuary Body* [1992] 2 AC 386 the need for certainty does not present any particular problem, but it can be difficult to decide whether or not an occupier has exclusive possession, and so we need to consider this matter in a little more detail.

(1) *Exclusive possession* Exclusive possession involves the right to use the premises to the exclusion of all others, including the landlord himself. As Lord Templeman explained in *Street* v *Mountford* [1985] AC 809 at p. 816:

The tenant possessing exclusive possession is able to exercise the rights of an owner of land, which is in the real sense his land albeit temporarily and subject to certain restrictions. A tenant armed with exclusive possession can keep out strangers and keep out the landlord.

Clearly someone who occupies a hotel room or lives in someone else's house as a lodger or paying guest cannot be said to have exclusive possession in this way, and so cannot have a tenancy. To quote Lord Templeman again (at p. 818):

The occupier is a lodger if the landlord provides attendance or services which require the landlord or his servants to exercise unrestricted access to and use of the premises. A lodger is entitled to live in the premises but cannot call the place his own.

The difficulty of applying this test for exclusive possession arises of course in borderline cases, such as *Appah* v *Parncliffe Investments Ltd* [1964] 1 WLR 1064, where only a minimum level of service was provided, and the judgment in that case is a useful example of the level of detail which a court may have to consider in deciding whether an occupier has exclusive possession. In *Appah* the plaintiff had an agreement under which she occupied a room in a house in which 17 such rooms were separately occupied. Each room had some cooking facilities but the bathroom was shared. The agreement provided that (a) no notice was required if an occupant wished to leave; (b) the fee simple owner retained the right to enter the room to empty gas and electricity meters and to clean; and (c) rules were made specifying that guests had to leave by 10.30 p.m. and otherwise regulating the use of the premises. The court held that this agreement must amount to a licence, since the licensee did not have exclusive possession of the room: she had no right to exclude the landlord, and the making of rules concerning her use of the premises also indicated that she did not have a proprietary right amounting to a lease.

(2) *Exclusive occupation* Before leaving the topic of exclusive possession, we should draw your attention to the apparently similar phrase, 'exclusive occupation', which may cause you some confusion.

We suggest that the two phrases are best used to describe two different situations. A hotel guest will expect to have *exclusive occupation* of his room, in the sense that he will not be required to share it with another guest; he will not, however, have *exclusive possession*, in the sense of being able to exclude the proprietor and his agents, since they will have access to the room for cleaning and the provision of other services.

The same distinction can be made in the case of longer-term residential accommodation. Clearly an occupier who did not have exclusive occupation (because, for instance, he was required to share with other occupiers selected by the owner) could not claim to have exclusive possession; but the fact of sole or exclusive occupation would not mean that the occupier automatically had exclusive possession in the sense of controlling the property and being able to exclude the owner.

We are emphasising this point because some confusion between the two phrases has arisen from their use by Lord Templeman. In *Street* v *Mountford* he referred throughout to 'exclusive possession', save for one occasion when he substituted the phrase 'exclusive occupation' (at p. 822). In a later decision, however (*AG Securities* v *Vaughan* [1990] 1 AC 417 at p. 455), he explained that:

Exclusive possession means either exclusive occupation or receipt of rents and profits.

He then used the phrase 'exclusive occupation' throughout the rest of his speech in apparently the same sense in which he had spoken of 'exclusive possession' in *Street* v *Mountford*. Although other members of the House of Lords in *AG Securities* v *Vaughan* continued to speak of 'exclusive possession', Lord Templeman's usage has sometimes been adopted in later cases, for example in *Family Housing Association* v *Jones* [1990] 1 WLR 779, where Balcombe LJ (at p. 788) emphasised the fact of sole *occupancy* as bringing the agreement within the terms of *Street* v *Mountford*. Despite this, however, we suggest that you should follow the language of *Street* v *Mountford* and in general use the phrase 'exclusive possession'.

19.2.3.2 *Certainty and exclusive possession are not conclusive signs of a lease*

Although a lease cannot exist unless there is a certain term and exclusive possession, it does not follow that an arrangement which satisfies these requirements necessarily creates a lease: the occupier may have exclusive possession for a fixed period and still be only a licensee:

There can be no tenancy unless the occupier enjoys exclusive possession; but an occupier who enjoys exclusive possession is not necessarily a tenant (*Street* v *Mountford* [1985] AC 809 at p. 818).

At one time it was true to say that if an agreement did give exclusive possession then it was necessarily a lease (see *Lynes* v *Snaith* [1899] 1 QB 486) but this is no longer true for, from the 1950s onward, there has been a number of decisions in which it has been held that, despite exclusive possession, the occupant is only a licensee. Early examples are to be found in *Foster* v *Robinson* [1951] 1 KB 149, in which a former farm worker was allowed to remain rent-free in his cottage after retirement, and *Errington* v *Errington* [1952] 1 KB 290, in which a young married couple occupied a house belonging to the husband's father (see further 20.3.3). An arrangement whereby a homeless family was given exclusive possession of a house rent-free has also been held to create only a licence (*Heslop* v *Burns* [1974] 1 WLR 1241), and the same result is to be found in respect of exclusive possession of a room in an old people's home (*Abbeyfield (Harpenden) Society Ltd* v *Woods* [1968] 1 WLR 374).

The common theme in most of these cases of licences with exclusive possession was summarised as follows by Denning LJ in the case of *Facchini* v *Bryson* [1952] 1 TLR 1386 at p. 1389:

In all the cases where an occupier has been held to be a licensee there has been something in the circumstances, such as a family arrangement, an act of friendship or generosity, or such like, to negative any intention to create a tenancy.

This statement draws attention to two issues: first, some act of generosity and, second, the intention of the parties to the arrangement. The importance of the intention of the landlord and tenant, or licensor and licensee, has been emphasised in other cases, such as *Marcroft Wagons Ltd* v *Smith* [1951] 2 KB 496, where the landlord, as an act of kindness, had allowed the daughter of the former tenant to remain in the property after her mother's death, but had refused to grant her a tenancy. In that case the court took notice of the fact that it was clearly not the intention of the owner to create a tenancy and that accordingly the agreement was a licence and not a lease.

19.2.3.3 *Grantor's intention not conclusive*

This emphasis on the grantor's intention can, however, give rise to difficulties, because in recent years landlords/licensors have always wished to grant licences in order to prevent the Rent Acts applying to the agreement. Thus in nearly every case the intention of the grantor would be to create a licence, whilst the recipient would probably wish to receive a lease. As a result there are a number of cases in which the courts have held an agreement to be a lease, even where it is expressly described as a licence. An early example is to be found in *Facchini* v *Bryson* [1952] 1 TLR 1386, in which the Court of Appeal held that an agreement created a tenancy, although it expressly provided that it was not to do so. The court emphasised that it would look at the nature of the relationship created between the parties, and at their respective rights, not merely at the words they used. In the words of Denning LJ, to do otherwise 'would drive an articulated vehicle through the Rent Acts' (at p. 1390). In the same way, an arrangement for the use of a tennis court has been held to amount to a business tenancy even though it purported to be a licence (*Addiscombe Garden Estates Ltd* v *Crabbe* [1958] 1 QB 513).

Similarly, in *Street* v *Mountford* [1985] AC 809 the House of Lords held that a written agreement which stated that it was a licence and which referred to the payment of a licence fee rather than rent, was nonetheless a lease. It was agreed by all concerned that the agreement gave exclusive possession to Mrs Mountford (the occupier) but that, when it was signed, both parties expressed the intention to create a licence (Mrs Mountford signed a declaration to this effect). Lord Templeman said, however (at p. 819):

If the agreement satisfied all the requirements of a tenancy, then the agreement produced a tenancy and the parties cannot alter the effect of the agreement by insisting that they only created a licence.

To put it another way:

The manufacture of a five-pronged implement for manual digging results in a fork even if the manufacturer, unfamiliar with the English language, insists that he . . . has made a spade (at p. 819).

In other words, the *apparent* intention of the parties, expressed in the words they use, cannot alter the effect of the agreement. That effect depends upon their *real* intention, as shown by their conduct and the circumstances of the case.

Although giving exclusive possession prima facie indicates an intention to create a tenancy, there might on occasion be exceptional circumstances which would negative that intention. For example, it might be that the parties did not intend to enter into legal relations at all; or exclusive possession might be explicable by reference to some other legal relationship (such as vendor and purchaser); or again the owner might have no power to grant a tenancy (p. 821).

19.2.3.4 *Summary of approach in* Street v Mountford

Lord Templeman's speech in *Street* v *Mountford* provides a useful guide to the approach adopted by the courts in considering whether an agreement creates a lease or a licence. His account of earlier decisions is very full and can perhaps be slightly confusing. It may therefore be helpful to note the summary to be found towards the end of his speech (at p. 826):

Sometimes it may be difficult to discover whether, on the true construction of an agreement, exclusive possession is conferred. Sometimes it may appear from the surrounding circumstances that there was no intention to create legal relationships. Sometimes it may appear from the surrounding circumstances that the right to exclusive possession is referable to a legal relationship other than a tenancy. [A further possibility, omitted from this summary but included at p. 821 of the report is that it may appear that the owner had no power to grant a tenancy] . . . But where . . . the only circumstances are that residential accommodation is offered and accepted with exclusive possession for a term at a rent, the result is a tenancy.

This summary gives rise to the following questions which you could ask yourself when considering whether an arrangement creates a lease or a licence.

(1) *Does the occupier have exclusive possession?*   As we have seen, this must be the starting point for any enquiry; if exclusive possession does not exist, there cannot be a lease, and the enquiry is at an end.

(2) *If the occupier has exclusive possession, was there an intention to create legal relations?*   The existence of exclusive possession does not automatically indicate the existence of a tenancy, because it may have been given for some family or charitable motive, with no intention to create legal relations. The earlier decisions, summarised by Lord Denning in *Facchini* v *Bryson* remain alive and well after the decision in *Street* v *Mountford*, and it is necessary to consider whether the parties intended to give rise to a legal relationship. Further, even if they did, the relationship need not be that of landlord and tenant: there are a number of other circumstances in which an occupier may have exclusive possession.

(3) *What are the circumstances giving rise to the occupier's exclusive possession?*   Lord Templeman suggests a wide range of situations in which an occupier could have exclusive possession but not be a tenant. He might be an owner in fee simple; a trespasser; a mortgagee in possession (see Chapter 21); a purchaser allowed into possession of the property before completion; or a service occupier (i.e., an employee, such as a housekeeper or gardener who occupies residential accommodation belonging to his employer for the better performance of his duties). As recognised by Pill LJ in *P. Dunwell* v *Hunt* (1996) 72 P&CR D6, this list is not exhaustive, and the Court of Appeal has recently added to it the relationship between a beneficiary and the trustees who allow him to occupy trust property (see *Gray* v *Taylor* [1998] 1 WLR 1093).

(4) *Does the grantor have the power to grant a tenancy?*   There is only a brief reference to this point in *Street* v *Mountford* (at p. 821), supported by the example of a requisitioning authority. The matter was explored further by the Court of Appeal in *Bruton* v *London & Quadrant Housing Trust* [1998] QB 834 at p. 843, in which Millett LJ considered whether this exception is limited to cases where the grantor has no capacity to grant a tenancy (because for example such a grant is outside its statutory powers), or whether it extends as well to cases where the grantor has no estate or interest in the land. The House of Lords' decision in this case ([2000] 1 AC 406)

adopts the more limited interpretation and confines the exception to lack of capacity (see further at 19.2.4.4).

A recent example of a situation in which the grant may be outside the grantor's powers is to be found in *Gray* v *Taylor* [1998] 1 WLR 1093. Here the Court of Appeal accepted the view of the trial judge that granting a tenancy of accommodation in an almshouse would be outside the powers of the trustees, because it might infringe the objects of the charity by permitting the grantee to remain in occupation although he had ceased to satisfy the conditions for residence.

(5) *Are there any other exceptional circumstances in the case which might negative the intention to create a tenancy?* The situations described by Lord Templeman are only examples, and there may well be other circumstances which would displace the intention. For attempts to establish these in some later cases concerned with housing for the homeless, see 19.2.4.2.

Asking the five questions we have considered above should enable you to see whether the arrangement you are considering could be said to fall outside the rule in *Street* v *Mountford*. Unless it does so, however, the position is clear: the grant of exclusive possession for a term at a rent creates a tenancy. In such circumstances, neither the parties' intentions, nor the label they attach to the transaction, will persuade the court to regard the arrangement as creating only a licence.

Thus, unless Mrs Mumps (see p. 397) could persuade a court that her retention of a key and her monthly visits to the flat have prevented Miss Lymeswold acquiring exclusive possession (as to which, see 19.2.3.1), it seems very likely that she would be found to have granted a tenancy of the basement flat, despite her insistence that she has given Laura only a licence.

19.2.4 **Leases and licences since *Street* v *Mountford***

In the years since *Street* v *Mountford*, many cases on the lease/licence distinction have come before the courts. In general they involve no more than an application of the *Street* v *Mountford* principles to the facts of a particular arrangement, although even this can be difficult when it involves deciding whether or not the occupier has exclusive possession (a problem which did not arise in *Street* v *Mountford* where this point was conceded by the landlord). In the aftermath of *Street* v *Mountford* landlords wishing to avoid the security of tenure provisions went to great lengths to make it appear that the occupier did not have exclusive possession, and many cases involve the courts in deciding whether the written agreement represents the true state of affairs between the parties. Even where there was no intention to avoid the Rent Acts, the question of whether an occupier has exclusive possession can present difficulties, for example in relation to housing for the homeless and to shared accommodation.

19.2.4.1 *Attempts to avoid the Rent Acts*

Following *Street* v *Mountford*, the courts were required to consider a number of agreements designed to prevent the occupier acquiring exclusive possession and being able to claim a lease. Typical devices included: the retention of a key by the landlady, coupled with the reservation of her right to enter the premises at any time (*Aslan* v *Murphy (Nos. 1 and 2)* and *Duke* v *Wynne*, both reported at [1990] 1

WLR 766); the limitation of the hours at which the occupier might use the property (use excluded between 10.30 a.m. and noon each day—*Crancour Ltd* v *Da Silvaesa* [1986] 1 EGLR 80 and *Aslan* v *Murphy (Nos. 1 and 2)* [1990] 1 WLR 766); and provisions that the landlord himself might share the premises with the occupier, or permit others to do so (*Hadjiloucas* v *Crean* [1988] 1 WLR 1006; *Antoniades* v *Villiers* [1990] 1 AC 417). In considering these various provisions, the courts followed *Street* v *Mountford* in seeking to identify the true nature of the agreement between the parties and to disregard terms which the landlord had no real intention of enforcing but had inserted as a pretence to avoid statutory protection.

This approach is well illustrated by the comments of Lord Donaldson MR in *Aslan* v *Murphy* [1990] 1 WLR 766 at p. 773, on the retention of keys by the landlord/licensor. The fact that the owner retains a key does not by itself prevent the occupier having exclusive possession and holding a tenancy. The court must consider the purpose for which the key is retained. If it is to allow the owner to enter in an emergency, or to read the meters, or to do repairs, this would not by itself prevent the occupier from holding a tenancy; conversely if the purpose of having keys is to provide genuine services such as frequent cleaning and daily bed-making it could be inferred that the occupier was a lodger rather than a tenant. Having considered the circumstances in *Aslan* v *Murphy*, the Court of Appeal found that although the keys were retained so that the owner could provide services, no services were in fact provided, and in consequence the court held that the occupier was a tenant, not mere licensee.

19.2.4.2 *Housing for the homeless*

The status of occupiers in hostels or other accommodation provided for the homeless has been considered by the courts in a number of cases.

In *Family Housing Association* v *Jones* [1990] 1 WLR 779, the appellant, who was homeless, was given a flat in premises operated by a housing association. The association itself held the premises as a licensee of the local authority, which owned the property, and the association's agreement with the appellant was described as being for the use of temporary accommodation and was expressed to be a licence. The housing association kept a set of keys in order to enter the premises to offer help to the occupier, to give her advice and to inspect the condition of the premises. The Court of Appeal found that the occupier had the right of 'sole occupation' (as to which, see 19.2.3.1(2)) for a term on payment of an accommodation charge, and applying *Street* v *Mountford* held that this arrangement created a lease and not a licence. Following its earlier decision in *Aslan* v *Murphy* the court considered that the retention of a key by the housing association was not decisive; in this case it had been done to assist the occupier, and did not prevent a tenancy from arising. In holding that the occupier was a tenant, the Court of Appeal rejected the suggestion that the housing association's role in providing temporary accommodation for the homeless should be considered as 'exceptional circumstances' which took the case outside the rule in *Street* v *Mountford*.

In *Westminster City Council* v *Clarke* [1992] 2 AC 288, the House of Lords adopted a similar approach, but reached a different conclusion on the facts. The council provided hostel accommodation for homeless single men under a licence agreement, which included the provision that an occupier could be required to change rooms or to share his room with another occupant. The House of Lords accepted that these provisions were genuine, being necessary for the proper management of the hostel, and were not included for the purpose of avoiding the Rent Acts. Accordingly, the occupier did not have exclusive possession of his room, and was a licensee and not a tenant. If you read the report of this case, you may note that the headnote describes the decision as overruling *Family Housing Association v Jones*; however, this does not appear to be entirely accurate, since the House of Lords considered only one aspect of the decision in *Jones*. Moreover, the decision in *Jones* has recently been approved by the House of Lords in *Bruton v London & Quadrant Housing Trust* [2000] 1 AC 406, a case in which the court again refused to accept that the provision of housing for the homeless involved special circumstances which could negative the intention to create a tenancy (see further at 19.2.4.4).

19.2.4.3 *Shared accommodation*

A number of cases since *Street v Mountford* have involved the shared occupation of accommodation. As we have seen in Chapter 16, it is possible for a legal estate to be held by several people in a form of co-ownership known as 'joint tenancy', and it is open to a couple, or a group of friends, to take jointly a lease of property which they plan to occupy together. However, joint tenancy of a legal estate can exist only if certain requirements, known as the 'four unities', are satisfied (see 16.3.1.1). In general terms, this means that all the co-owners must be entitled to possession of the whole property (unity of possession), rather than having it divided up between them, and their interests in the property must start at the same time (unity of time), be derived from the same document (unity of title), and be identical as to nature and duration (unity of interest). This last requirement, of unity of interest, 'imports the existence of joint rights and obligations' (*Mikeover Ltd v Brady* [1989] 3 All ER 618 at p. 627), and means that each co-owner is both jointly and severally (i.e., individually) liable for any duties imposed by the estate. Thus, in a joint tenancy of a lease, each tenant is liable for the full rent due for the property, even although in practice he pays only his share of it.

It was against this background that the House of Lords considered two flat-sharing agreements, which came before it in 1988. In *AG Securities v Vaughan* [1990] 1 AC 417 the landlord/licensor owned premises comprising a flat which had four bedrooms together with other normal living accommodation, such as a kitchen and bathroom. The flat was occupied by four people who were selected by the owner and who did not know one another. Each had arrived at a different time and each paid a different amount for the use of the flat. Each had the use of one bedroom and the use of the other rooms in common with the other three. The owner did not dictate which room each occupier should have: that was agreed between the current occupiers. If an occupier left, the owner replaced him with a new occupier of the owner's choice but then left it to the four occupiers to settle between them the new room allocation. It was held that this arrangement constituted a licence because the occupiers did not (even jointly between themselves) have exclusive possession of the property. Lord Oliver of Aylmerton (at p. 471) said:

The landlord is not excluded for he continues to enjoy the premises through his invitees, even though he may for the time being have precluded himself by contract with each from withdrawing the invitation.

In *Antoniades v Villiers*, also reported at [1990] 1 AC 417, a couple took a one-bedroom flat under written agreements which were described as 'licence agreements'. Each signed a separate agreement and each agreement provided that the 'licensor' might also occupy the premises or might license others to occupy jointly with the 'licensees'. The House of Lords held that this arrangement was clearly a lease and that the terms allowing for occupation by the landlord or others were simply pretences. It would be ridiculous to contemplate that the landlord intended to share the young couple's bed or that he genuinely intended to send others to do this.

It is clear that in *AG Securities* v *Vaughan* the unities required for a joint tenancy were in no way satisfied. The interests of the individual occupants arose at different times, and under different agreements; their individual obligations varied, and there was no sense in which each was jointly and severally liable, for example, for the payment of a rent due on the whole property. On the other hand, in *Antoniades* v *Villiers* both occupiers entered into identical agreements at the same time. The couple was originally quoted a single rent for the flat, but, on entering the agreements, each person was required to assume liability for half of that rent. In these circumstances the House of Lords considered that the written agreements did not give effect to the true intentions of the parties, and was able to hold that the occupiers were joint tenants of a lease, despite the apparent absence of the necessary joint obligations.

By contrast, in *Mikeover Ltd* v *Brady* [1989] 3 All ER 618, on facts very similar to *Antoniades* v *Villiers*, the Court of Appeal was satisfied that terms providing for the payment of separate rents were genuine agreements, representing the true intention of the parties that the monetary obligations of each occupier were to be entirely independent. Accordingly, the agreements were incapable of creating a joint tenancy, because there was no unity of interest, and the parties held only as licensees.

The factors to be taken into account when applying the decisions in *Vaughan* and *Villiers* were also considered by the Court of Appeal in *Stribling* v *Wickham* [1989] 2 EGLR 35. The court said that agreements for flat sharing of this type had to be construed in the light of all the surrounding circumstances, which would include the relationship between the sharers, the course of negotiations, the nature and the extent of the accommodation provided and the intended and actual mode of occupation. It was emphasised once again that it was the function of the courts to determine the true nature of 'the substance and reality' of the transaction.

19.2.4.4 Bruton *v* London & Quadrant Housing Trust *[2000] 1 AC 406*

This is the most recent consideration by the House of Lords of the lease/licence distinction. It deals with the interesting question of the relationship between *Street* v *Mountford* and the principles of tenancy by estoppel (see 8.10.4), but, as you will see, the House of Lords' decision also has far-reaching consequences for our understanding of the nature of a lease.

The facts of the case were as follows. The trust held various properties (which were awaiting redevelopment) as a licensee of Lambeth Council, and used them to provide short term housing for the homeless, entering into licence agreements with the individual occupiers. One of the occupiers, Mr Bruton, subsequently claimed that he had exclusive possession of his self-contained flat and that, despite the wording of the agreement, he was therefore a tenant under the principles of *Street* v *Mountford*. His purpose in doing this was to bring himself within s. 11 of the

Landlord and Tenant Act 1985, which imposes a repairing obligation on landlords in respect of certain tenancies, but does not apply to licences. The trust itself had no estate in the land, and so could not grant a tenancy, but it was alleged that it was estopped from denying that it had done so. In other words, the occupier sought to combine the principles of *Street* v *Mountford* and the doctrine of tenancy by estoppel.

The occupier's claim was rejected by the Court of Appeal (see [1998] QB 834). At this stage, it seems to have been accepted by both parties that the trust could not have granted a tenancy because it had no estate in the property. In other words, it could not give what it had not got. It is in such circumstances that a tenancy by estoppel may arise, and it was a tenancy of this nature that the occupier claimed.

The Court of Appeal however considered that the situation in this case did not give rise to a tenancy by estoppel. In the words of Millett LJ (at pp. 842–3) such a tenancy is based on the principle that:

A man who purports to grant a tenancy is not permitted to deny that he has done so by asserting his own want of title. If he has none, the grant creates a tenancy by estoppel.

In this case, the trust did not purport to grant a tenancy, because it was aware of its lack of title and specifically granted a licence. There was thus no purported grant which the trust could be estopped from denying, and accordingly no tenancy by estoppel arose.

The decision of the Court of Appeal was reversed by the House of Lords ([2000] 1 AC 406), which held that a tenancy had been created between the parties. On the facts of the case, the occupier had exclusive possession for a term at a rent; this raised a prima facie conclusion that he was a tenant, and the House of Lords did not agree that the special nature of the trust (as a charitable body providing short-term accommodation) was sufficient to take it out of the rule in *Street* v *Mountford*.

In holding that the occupier held a lease and was not just a tenant by estoppel, the House of Lords rejected the argument that the trust could not create a lease because it had no estate in the land. Lord Hoffmann explained that the creation of an estate is the usual but not essential consequence of a lease, and that an agreement which creates a landlord and tenant relationship is a lease, even though the landlord is unable to grant an estate to the tenant. In the words of Lord Hoffmann (at p. 415):

. . . the term 'lease' or 'tenancy' describes a relationship between two parties who are designated landlord and tenant. It is not concerned with the question of whether the agreement creates an estate or other proprietary interest which may be binding on third parties. A lease may, and usually does, create a proprietary interest called a leasehold estate or, technically, a 'term of years absolute'. This will depend upon whether the landlord had an interest out of which he could grant it. *Nemo dat quod non habet* [no-one can give what he has not got]. But it is the fact that the agreement is a lease which creates the proprietary interest. It is putting the cart before the horse to say that whether the agreement is a lease depends upon whether it creates an proprietary interest.

A similar view was expressed by Lord Hobhouse (at p. 418):

The present case does not depend upon the establishing of an estoppel nor does any problem arise from the fact that the housing trust did not have a legal estate. The [appellant's] case depends upon his establishing that his agreement with the housing trust has the legal effect of creating a relationship of tenant and landlord between them. That is all. It does not depend upon his establishing a proprietary title good against all the world.

Thus, although the trust could not create a proprietary interest, the agreement between the parties satisfied the requirements of *Street* v *Mountford* and created a lease within the meaning of s. 11 of the Landlord and Tenant Act 1985.

We should note at this point that the House of Lords also took the opportunity to explain the operation of tenancy by estoppel. In what follows, their Lordships were presumably referring to the form of tenancy by estoppel which arise from the purported grant of a lease, rather than from the landlord's representation as to title (see 8.10.4.2), since it is clear from the facts that the trust had made no such representation. To quote Lord Hoffmann once more (at p. 415):

> I think Millett LJ [in the court below] may have been misled by the ancient phrase 'tenancy by estoppel' into thinking that it described an agreement which would not otherwise be a lease or tenancy but which was treated as being one by virtue of an estoppel. In fact . . . it is not the estoppel which created the tenancy, but the tenancy which created the estoppel. The estoppel arises when one or other of the parties want to deny one of the ordinary incidents or obligations of the tenancy on the ground that the landlord had no legal estate. The basis of the estoppel is that having entered into an agreement which constitutes a lease or tenancy, he cannot repudiate that incident or obligation.

And again (p. 416):

> . . . it is the fact that the agreement between the parties constitutes a tenancy that gives rise to an estoppel and not the other way round. It therefore seems to me that the question of tenancy by estoppel does not arise in this case. The issue is simply whether the agreement is a tenancy.

19.2.4.5 *Implications of the decision in* Bruton

Although Lord Hoffmann speaks as though his analysis of the nature of a lease is well established and, indeed, obvious, it came as a considerable surprise to many lawyers. When considering tenancies at will (8.10.3), we have seen that it is possible to have the relationship of landlord and tenant without the creation of an estate, but this appeared to be an unusual but useful way of explaining an anomalous situation. Historically, of course, the lease did begin as a purely contractual relationship between the parties which gave no interest in the land, but once the notion of the leasehold estate had developed, it was generally thought that a lease inevitably created such an estate or interest. As Millett LJ put it in the Court of Appeal in *Bruton* ([1998] QB 834 at 845): 'A tenancy is a legal estate'.

In the light of the House of Lords' decision, however, it seems that we now have to divide leases into two categories; the proprietary lease, which creates an estate or interest in the land, and the contractual or personal lease—which does not. Lord Hoffmann makes it clear that leases will usually create a proprietary interest, but the possibility of a non-proprietary lease, even if rare, raises a number of questions. These include:

(i) *When may a non-proprietary lease be created?*
Does it rise only where the grantor has no title, or may it be created in other circumstances?

(ii) *How is a non-proprietary lease to be created?*
The requirement of a deed in the case of leases for more than three years is imposed by the general rule in LPA 1925, s. 52(1) that a deed must be used for the conveyance or creation of a legal estate. Since no estate is created by a non-proprietary

lease, it presumably can be created orally or in writing, whatever its length, and a contract for such a lease would not need to be made in writing.

(iii) *In what circumstances will a court find a tenancy by estoppel?*
If the agreement between the parties creates a non-proprietary lease, their rights and obligations must surely arise from that lease, and not from any estoppel. It is at first sight difficult to envisage the future use of tenancy by estoppel or, indeed, to understand why the concept has been used in the past if the non-proprietary lease has always been available to the courts.

Yet while the non-proprietary lease may be sufficient to determine the parties' rights and duties between themselves, its effect on third parties is far from clear. As we have seen (8.10.4), tenancies by estoppel bind and benefit not only the parties, but their successors. Will the non-proprietary lease by itself have the same effect, and will the benefit and burden of obligations under it run to the parties' successors? Presumably, rights under the tenancy could be assigned, but the transfer of burdens would be ruled out by the privity of contract rules. We have already noted (9.6.1.6(2)) the considerable difficulties the courts have had in dealing with the running of covenants in equitable leases, where at least the landlord has an estate in the land and the agreement is capable of specific performance, and a non-proprietary lease seems likely to pose even greater problems. Such problems might be resolved, however, if the parties to the contractual lease were estopped from denying the existence of a proprietary lease and the estoppel bound and benefited successors in the established way. This does not, however, explain why courts in the past have needed to rely on the concept of estoppel in dealing with the rights and duties of the original parties to the agreement.

These questions, and a number of others, are posed in various case notes in the legal journals, and we give references to some of them in the section on further reading at the end of this chapter. Although writers may speculate on the nature and characteristics of what one author describes as 'a beast long thought extinct' (Dixon [2000] CLJ 25 at p. 27), there are unlikely to be any answers to these questions until *Bruton* is considered and interpreted in later decisions. It may be that, with hindsight, the immediate reactions to *Bruton* will be seen as 'making a mountain out of a molehill', but it has to be said that at present it appears to be a somewhat startling decision and we can only wait and see what courts will make of it in the future.

19.2.5 **Tenancies at will and licences**

The distinction between a licence and this particular type of tenancy may cause you some difficulty. We have already described the characteristics of the tenancy at will (8.10.3), and you may remember that although it gives rise to a landlord-tenant relationship, it is thought that it does not create a legal estate, thus, at least before *Bruton* v *London & Quadrant Housing Trust* [2001] 1 AC 406, increasing its apparent similarity to a licence. Gray describes the tenancy at will as occupying 'an obscurely defined no-man's land between the periodic tenancy and the mere licence' (Gray and Gray, at p. 411), and it is certainly not easy to explain the distinction between this form of lease and a licence.

A significant difference between the two used to be found in the Limitation

Act 1939; under s. 9, a tenancy at will was deemed to end after one year, so that time would start to run against the landlord (see Chapter 6), whereas a licensee's occupation remained permissive, so that he could never rely on the rules of adverse possession. It was this distinction between the two which provided the setting for *Heslop* v *Burns* [1974] 1 WLR 1241, and is essential to an understanding of that case; but it did not survive the Limitation Act 1980, which repealed s. 9 of the 1939 Act and did not replace it. Thus the present position is that time does not start to run in favour of a tenant at will until his tenancy has been brought to an end, and on this point therefore the distinction between tenancies at will and licences is no longer of great significance.

Gray and Gray note what is described as one vital difference between the two: the tenant at will is regarded as being in possession of the land, and is therefore able to sue a third party for trespass to the land (p. 413); but even this distinction seems to be eroded by the recent decision in *Manchester Airport plc* v *Dutton* [2000] 1 QB 133, allowing a licensee to maintain a claim in trespass.

For a further consideration of tenancies at will and licences, see the note by Bridge in [1991] CLJ 232.

19.3 Distinguishing an easement or profit from a licence

If A walks across B's land and it is clear from the circumstances that A is not a trespasser, then one must establish whether A has an easement (a *right* to walk across the land—a right of way) or a licence (he has *permission* to walk across the land). A similar question arises when C fishes in D's lake: does C have a profit or a licence? Once again one has to distinguish between the ownership of a proprietary right and the existence of a permission which merely prevents A from being a trespasser. The distinction may well be very important, because the grant of an easement or profit creates a right which cannot be revoked, whereas often the permission given in a licence can be withdrawn. Moreover, if a third party interferes with the enjoyment of an easement or profit, the person entitled has a right of action for this infringement, whereas a licence would at best be enforceable against the licensor.

Unfortunately, there is no simple method of distinguishing between an easement or profit and a licence. The only method of approach that can be adopted is to establish first whether the right claimed is capable of being an easement or profit (see Chapter 22), for if not, it can be only a licence. An illustration of this is to be found in *Hill* v *Tupper* (1863) 2 Hurl & C 121, in which it was held that the right to put pleasure boats on a canal could only be a licence and not an easement, because it did not benefit the claimant's land and thus failed to meet one of the criteria for establishing an easement (see further 22.2.1.3). Second, even if the arrangement is capable of giving rise to an easement or profit, it will amount to no more than a licence if the intention to create an interest in land is missing (see *Fitzgerald* v *Firbank* [1897] 2 Ch 96). An example of the operation of this second principle is to be found in *IDC Group Ltd* v *Clark* [1992] EGLR 187, in which an agreement for a fire escape route through a neighbouring flat was held to create only a personal licence and not an easement binding on successors in title.

FURTHER READING

Hill, 'Shared Accomodation and Exclusive Possession' (1989) 52 MLR 408.

Landlord and Tenant: Reform of the Law, 1987, Law Com No. 162, paras. 4.4–11.

Street, 'Coach and Horses Trip Cancelled? Rent Act Avoidance after *Street* v *Mountford*' [1985] Conv 328.

Bruton *v* London & Quadrant HT

Bright, 'Leases, Exclusive Possession, and Estates' (2000) 116 LQR 7.

Dixon, 'The Non-Proprietary Lease: The Rise of the Feudal Phoenix' [2000] CLJ 25.

Routley, 'Tenancies and Estoppel—After *Bruton* v *London & Quadrant HT*' [2000] MLR 424.

20

Enforcement of a licence

20.1 Introduction

Originally, since a licence gave no right in law and was a mere permission, it could be revoked at any time at the will of the licensor (with one exception, see 20.2.1). However, over the years a number of different types of licence have been recognised by the courts and it appears now that not all licences are so easily withdrawn by the licensor. There are also some decisions which suggest that licences may sometimes be enforceable against the licensor's successors, and this raises the question of whether it is really still true to say that a licence creates no interest in land.

Before considering these issues, however, we must give a brief description of the various types of licence.

20.1.1 Types of licence

20.1.1.1 *Licences coupled with an interest*

Sometimes licences do not stand alone but are coupled to some other right. An example would be the grant of a profit allowing A to cut wood on B's land. Obviously a licence must be implied into this agreement because A cannot exercise his right to cut wood, unless he is permitted to go on B's land to do so. Another example of the operation of the rule is given in *Doe d Hanley* v *Wood* (1819) 2 B & Ald 724, at p. 738, in which it was said that if a man sells hay standing on his land he cannot later prevent the purchaser from entering the land to collect it (sees also *Wood* v *Manley* (1839) 11 Ad & El 34 and *James Jones & Sons Ltd* v *Earl of Tankerville* [1909] 2 Ch 440).

20.1.1.2 *Contractual licences*

As the name suggests, a licence is a contractual one if it is conferred by contract, and this is so even if the right to enter land is only a secondary part of the contract *(Hounslow LBC* v *Twickenham Garden Developments Ltd* [1971] Ch 233). In most of the cases we will be considering, however, the primary purpose of the contract is to grant the licence in return for consideration; everyday examples are to be found in the purchase of tickets for rail travel or for cinema and theatre visits. Longer term contractual licences are to found in the licences to occupy premises, which we considered in the previous chapter. These are most usually commercial arrangements, granted in exchange for what is described as 'rent' or a licence charge, and are an important type of contractual licence.

Contracts giving rise to contractual licences will usually be expressly created, but you should notice that there have been occasions on which the courts were prepared to infer a contractual agreement giving rise to the licence. Thus, in *Tanner* v *Tanner* [1975] 1 WLR 1346 a contractual licence was inferred in favour of a woman who had given up a protected tenancy in order to move into a home provided by her lover and there to care for the children of the relationship. Lord Denning MR said that the court should infer a contract that the woman should remain in the property for so long as the children were of school age and accommodation was reasonably required. A contractual licence was similarly found in *Chandler* v *Kerley* [1978] 1 WLR 693 in which a man had bought a house from his mistress and her husband at less than the market price on the understanding that he and the woman would live there together and that eventually they would marry. When the relationship ended soon after the purchase, the Court of Appeal held that the woman had a contractual licence to remain, which could be terminated only on reasonable notice (a year in this instance). A contractual licence was also inferred between a mother and daughter-in-law in *Hardwick* v *Johnson* [1978] 1 WLR 683.

Other cases, however, show that the courts will not always be willing to accept the existence of a contract in such cases. Indeed it seems unusual to construe arrangements of this nature as demonstrating the intention to create legal relations which is necessary in the law of contract. Thus, in *Horrocks* v *Forray* [1976] 1 WLR 230 a woman failed to establish that a contractual licence existed on the basis of a claim that she had subordinated her choice of residence and mode of life to the will of her former lover in return for a promise that she should have a permanent home. The Court of Appeal rejected her case on two grounds: first, the parties had no intention to enter into a legally binding agreement and, second, she had provided no consideration. (It should be recalled that the courts will not recognise consideration which they regard as being 'immoral' in character.) The situation in *Tanner* v *Tanner* was distinguished on the ground that in that case, '[T]he man and the woman were making arrangements for the future at arm's length' (at p. 745).

20.1.1.3 *Bare licences*

Bare licences may be seen as a sort of residuary category: permission to enter another's land may be described as a bare licence if it does not fall into any other category. These licences are essentially gratuitous, since if any charge was made for them, they would be regarded as contractual. A good example of a bare licence is the implied licence to walk up the garden path to the front door of 1 Trant Way (see p. 397). Most of us spend a large part of our lives as bare licencees, for every time we visit a friend's house, for example, or enter a shop we are acting as licencees (see *Davis* v *Lisle* [1936] 2 KB 434 at p. 440).

20.1.1.4 *Licences by estoppel*

In certain situations, which we consider later, an owner may be estopped (pre-cluded) by his own representations from denying that another person has a licence to be on his land or from revoking a licence already given. These situations are sometimes described as creating a distinct type of licence (licences by estoppel or estoppel licences), but they may equally well be seen as operating on the existing categories of bare and, possibly, contractual licences, which we have already mentioned. To some extent this is no more than a question of presentation: what is important is that you are familiar with the relevant decisions and can recognise the occasions on which an estoppel is likely to arise. We have already dealt with some of the relevant decisions in Chapter 18, and will look at the application of estoppel to licence situations in 20.2.4 and 20.3.4 below.

20.2 Enforcement against the licensor

The question we have to consider here is whether the licensee can continue to enjoy his licence over another's land, even if the owner changes his mind and purports to revoke or withdraw that licence. As we shall see, the answer to this question depends very much on the type of licence which has been granted.

20.2.1 Licences coupled with an interest

This type of licence is not revocable as long as the proprietary interest (the profit) continues.

20.2.2 Bare licences

A bare licence may be revoked at any time. Once the licence is revoked the former licensee must be given a reasonable period in which to leave and once that period has elapsed will become a trespasser if he remains on the property. In *Robson* v *Hallet* [1967] 2 QB 939 some police officers went up to the door of a house and knocked. In doing this they were licensees and within their rights. However, in the absence of a search warrant or other authority permitting the officers to insist on remaining, their licence could be revoked, although the householder had to give them reasonable time to leave the property.

20.2.3 Contractual licences

Originally, when considering revocation by the licensor the courts do not appear to have distinguished between bare licences and those which were granted for consideration. Thus, in *R* v *Inhabitants of Horndon-on-the-Hill* (1816) 4 M & S 562 a licence to build a cottage on a piece of land, the licensee making an annual payment for the right, was held nonetheless to be revocable at the will of the licensor.

The same view was taken in the famous case of *Wood* v *Leadbitter* (1845) 13 M & W 838, in which a racegoer was ejected by force from a racecourse even though he had paid one guinea (£1.05) for the right to enter the premises and view the racing. The racegoer was unsuccessful when he sued the race steward for damages for battery and false imprisonment, because the court said that his licence was revocable at the will of the licensor, despite the fact that this was in breach of contract. Since he had refused to leave when told to go, the racegoer had become a trespasser and reasonable force could be used to remove him. The licensor might be acting in breach of contract, but while common law would award damages against him for breach it would not compel him to perform his contract. This rigid view of the inherent revocability of any type of licence continued at least until the passing of the Supreme Court of Judicature Acts 1873 and 1875, after which time the availability of equitable remedies in all courts appears to have produced a considerable change in attitudes to the licence.

In *Hurst* v *Picture Theatres Ltd* [1915] 1 KB 1 a situation arose which was very similar to that in *Wood* v *Leadbitter*. In this case a cinema-goer was asked by the management to leave the premises because it was believed, incorrectly, that he had not paid for his ticket. When he refused to leave, the cinema-goer was ejected with the use of force and later sued for assault and false imprisonment. In this case the court found for the licensee cinema-goer. It was explained that since the licensee had a contract with the cinema to watch the film, the equitable remedy of an injunction to restrain breach or an order for specific performance of the contract would have been available to prevent the breach of contract, had it been possible to obtain the remedy in the short time before the breach actually occurred. Accordingly in equity the licensee did have a right to remain for the whole contractual period. In consequence he was not a trespasser and his removal was unjustified; and he was entitled to damages for assault and false imprisonment. Buckley LJ distinguished *Wood* v *Leadbitter* on the ground that the case had been heard in a court of law before the Supreme Court of Judicature Acts 1873 and 1875.

A rather surprising aspect of the majority judgment in *Hurst* v *Picture Theatres Ltd* (Phillimore LJ dissented) is that it treated the licensee's contractual right to view a spectacle (such as a film show or a race) as amounting to an 'interest'. The licence to enter the premises for this purpose was regarded as coupled to this interest, thus producing an irrevocable licence under the rules relating to licences coupled with a grant, which we considered above. Understandably, this approach has been much criticised; see for example the observations of Latham LJ in *Cowell* v *Rosehill Racecourse Co. Ltd* (1937) 56 CLR 605. However, although this approach forms the major part of the judgment in *Hurst* v *Picture Theatres*, Buckley LJ did offer another reason for the decision: the licence to view the spectacle contained an implied term that the permission would not be withdrawn before the end of the show, and equity would restrain revocation in breach of this term. It is this approach which has been developed in later cases, so that a contractual licence is now regarded as enforceable against the original grantor according to its terms. Thus, a contractual licence for a specified period cannot be revoked by the grantor until the contractual period has expired (*Hounslow London Borough Council* v *Twickenham Garden Developments Ltd* [1971] Ch 233). Should the licence be for an unspecified period, a term will be implied that the licence can be terminated upon reasonable notice (*Winter Garden Theatre (London) Ltd* v *Millennium Productions Ltd* [1948] AC 173).

If the licensor should purport to revoke the licence in breach of contract, the licensee may seek an injunction to restrain the breach or, in appropriate cases, an order for specific performance of the contract (as in *Verrall* v *Great Yarmouth BC* [1981] 1 QB 202).

20.2.3.1 *Limited statutory protection*

Where a licence constitutes a 'periodic licence' of a dwelling, s. 5(1A) of the Protection from Eviction Act 1977 (inserted by the Housing Act 1988) requires that the licence may not be terminated otherwise than after four weeks' notice in writing, such notice to be in the prescribed form. In addition s. 3(2A) and (2B) now provide that in the case of such licences the licensor may only recover possession of the property by court order. By these amendments the Housing Act 1988 has conferred a limited protection upon certain licensees and given them some of the rights enjoyed by tenants. The term 'periodic licence' is not defined but is likely to be construed as covering those licences which resemble periodic leases. It is not clear whether the term extends to cover bare licences or only relates to contractual licences. However, the provisions are likely to be used largely in relation to those contractual licences that closely resemble tenancies, save perhaps that the licensee does not have exclusive possession. Sections 3 and 5 do not apply to 'excluded licences', the largest category of these being licences under which the licensee shares facilities with the licensor.

20.2.4 Licences by estoppel

In Chapter 18 we explained how the principles of proprietary estoppel may prevent an owner relying on his strict legal rights when he has encouraged another in the mistaken belief that he has or will have rights in the property. This principle has been used in a number of cases to prevent a licensor revoking a licence (usually a gratuitous or bare one) and recovering possession from a licensee who has been led to believe that he will be allowed to remain in the property.

An early example of estoppel preventing the revocation of a licence is provided by *Plimmer* v *Wellington Corporation* (1884) 9 App Cas 699. Plimmer occupied part of the foreshore of Wellington Harbour as a 'licensee at will' of the Crown. With the encouragement of the government, and indeed at its request, he incurred expenditure in first erecting and later extending a jetty on the land. At a later stage, when questions as to the nature of his interest arose, he was held by the Privy Council to have acquired an irrevocable licence, because his dealings with the government:

were sufficient to create in his mind a reasonable expectation that his occupation would not be disturbed (at p. 714).

Nearly a hundred years later, *Pascoe* v *Turner* [1979] 1 WLR 431 shows the Court of Appeal applying a very similar approach. The plaintiff and defendant had lived together as man and wife, in houses owned by the plaintiff, for almost ten years. When the relationship ended, the plaintiff moved out of their current house, telling the defendant that she had nothing to worry about: the house and its contents were hers. In reliance on this, she stayed in the house thinking that it belonged to her, and expended a considerable proportion of her small savings on repairs and improvements. In fact, the plaintiff did nothing to convey the property to her, so that she remained in occupation as a licensee; a couple of years later he gave her notice to terminate the licence and sought possession of the property.

At first instance, the judge considered that these events gave rise to a constructive trust, but the Court of Appeal did not agree. Instead, it identified the case as one of proprietary estoppel, holding (at p. 436) that the estoppel arose:

from the encouragement and acquiesence of the plaintiff, when, in reliance upon his declaration that he was giving and, later, that he had given the house to her, she spent a substantial part of her small capital upon repairs and improvements to the house.

The court then had to decide how the equity, arising from the estoppel, was to be satisfied (see 18.4). The choice lay between granting the plaintiff a licence for life, and requiring the transfer to her of the fee simple. Having regard to the plaintiff's apparent determination to evict the defendant, and to the precarious nature of the licence ('she may find herself ousted by a purchaser for value without notice'—at p. 439), the court considered that it must compel the plaintiff to give effect to the defendant's expectations, and convey the fee simple to her.

A more recent example of the licensee being restrained from revoking a bare licence is to be found in *Matharu v Matharu* (1994) 68 P&CR 93, in which a licensor was estopped from recovering possession of a house from his daughter-in-law. The facts of the case were that the plaintiff owned a house which had been occupied by his son and daughter-in-law as their matrimonial home. He sought to recover possession from the daughter-in-law after the breakdown of the marriage and the death of his son. The Court of Appeal held that the defendant could establish an estoppel, arising from her mistaken belief, known to her father-in-law, that the house belonged to her husband, on which she had acted to her detriment in a number of ways. However, the court rejected the woman's claim that this entitled her to a beneficial interest in the property and held that she had no more than a licence to remain in the house 'for her life or such shorter period as she may decide' (at p. 103). Moreover, this limited right was subject to a requirement that she take on responsibility for some repairs to the property and for financial outgoings on it (including the mortgage repayments). Although there have been other decisions in which the equity recognised by the court has been satisfied by giving the licensee a mere right to remain in the property, this has not usually been coupled with such requirements, and it seems somewhat strange that the licensee here was required to pay off the mortgage debt without having any chance to acquire some share in the beneficial interest in the property.

There are a number of other decisions which make use of estoppel in the context of licences, but they involve enforcement against the licensor's successors, and so we will postpone consideration of them until 20.3.4.

20.3 Enforcement against successors of the licensor

As we have already seen in *Binions v Evans* [1972] Ch 359 (17.3.2.2), it may well happen that a licensor will sell his estate to a third party, leaving the licensee with the problem of whether his licence can be enforced against the new owner, or whether he is likely to face eviction from the property. Similar questions arise when the licensor becomes bankrupt or dies, and his trustee in bankruptcy or those entitled under his will or on intestacy seek possession of the property. In the case of some of the various types of licence that we have described above, these questions can be answered quite briefly. In the case of others, the law does not provide such clear answers. Again we will consider each type of licence separately.

20.3.1 **Bare licences**

With the bare licence there is no problem: since these licences can be revoked at will by the grantor they can certainly be revoked at any time by a successor in title of the licensor.

20.3.2 **Licences coupled with an interest**

These licences will bind a successor in title of the licensor if he is bound by the interest to which the licence is coupled. As long as the licensee can enforce that interest, he can insist on the continuance of his licence. Accordingly, the enforceability of these licences depends on issues outside the scope of this chapter, and the rules applicable will vary as the nature of the coupled interest varies.

20.3.3 **Contractual licences**

Hurst v *Picture Theatres Ltd* [1915] 1 KB 1 established that a contractual licence was enforceable just as any other contract is enforceable. This suggests that a contractual licence would not bind a successor to the original licensor, because such a person would not be a party to the original contract. It is part of standard contractual principles that whilst the benefit of a contract can be assigned to a third party the burden, or obligation, under the contract cannot be transferred. Indeed in two cases this rule has been applied to contractual licences. In *King* v *David Allen & Sons (Billposting) Ltd* [1916] 2 AC 54 the licensee had a contractual agreement under which it could display posters on the wall of a cinema. The House of Lords held that this contract could not bind a tenant who took a lease of the cinema from the licensor. In reaching this conclusion the court applied the normal rule that a contract creates a personal obligation enforceable only against the original parties. The Court of Appeal accepted the same principle in *Clore* v *Theatrical Properties Ltd* [1936] 3 All ER 483 and thus, whilst agreeing that the benefit of a licence could be assigned to a third party, said that the burden of the contract would not pass. Unfortunately for the licensee, this means that any contractual obligation to allow the licence to continue cannot bind a successor in title to the licensor.

This at least was the accepted position until the case of *Errington* v *Errington* [1952] 1 KB 290. A father bought a house in order to provide a home for his son and daughter-in-law. The property was conveyed to the father, but it was agreed that if the son and his wife paid all the mortgage instalments he would then convey the property to them. In due course the father died and the property vested in his widow as executrix (she was also beneficiary under the will). Thereafter the son went to live with his mother whilst the daughter-in-law remained in the property and continued to pay the mortgage instalments. At this point the mother attempted to revoke her daughter-in-law's licence. The Court of Appeal held that this licence was not revocable by the new owner, even though she was a third party to the original agreement. Denning LJ said that the original contractual arrangement gave rise to an 'equity' in favour of the daughter-in-law which was enforceable against a third party according to the notice rules (it certainly is not a land charge). Since the new owner was a volunteer, having acquired the property as a gift, she was bound by the contract. This decision can be criticised on the grounds that it flies in the face of normal contractual rules and is contrary to the decisions in two earlier, and binding, authorities. Furthermore, since at the date of the action the mother was still acting as executrix of her husband's estate and held the land in that capacity, she was *not* a third party at all but was bound as executrix by obligations which bound her husband's estate. The case, however, came to be regarded as authority for the proposition that in certain circumstances a contractual licence will bind a third party who acquires as a volunteer, or even one who buys the property with notice. In the view of Denning LJ (at p. 299):

neither the licensor nor anyone who claims through him can disregard the contract except a purchaser for value without notice.

Errington v *Errington* was followed by a number of decisions in which a contractual licence was held to bind the licensor's successors. In *Binions* v *Evans* [1972] Ch 359, the majority of the Court of Appeal based its decision on the existence of a Settled Land Act settlement, but Lord Denning MR regarded the arrangement as giving rise to a contractual licence, which would bind the purchaser with notice in accordance with the principle he had articulated in *Errington* v *Errington* (at p. 367). In addition, the fact that the plaintiff had expressly taken subject to the defendant's licence and accordingly paid a reduced price would justify the imposition of a constructive trust.

The use of a constructive trust in the particular circumstances of *Binions* v *Evans* would appear to be fully justified, but relying upon that decision Lord Denning MR then developed the idea that constructive trusts arose in all cases involving contractual licences (see *DHN Food Distributors* v *Tower Hamlets LBC* [1976] 1 WLR 852).

The consequences of imposing a constructive trust were considered in some detail by Browne-Wilkinson J in *In re Sharpe* [1980] 1 WLR 219. The facts here were that a nephew bought a house, the bulk of the purchase money being lent to him by his elderly aunt, who was to live with him and his wife and be cared for by them. Unfortunately, the nephew subsequently went bankrupt, and the property vested in his trustee in bankruptcy, who sought possession of the house. The aunt claimed a right to remain in the house, at least until the loan was repaid.

In giving judgment, Browne-Wilkinson J confessed to feeling some uncertainty about the Court of Appeal decisions which spelt out irrevocable licences from informal family arrangments. He referred to decisions on both proprietary estoppel and contractual licences; in his view, the aunt had the right, as against her nephew, to remain in the property:

whether it be called a contractual licence or an equitable licence or an interest under a constructive trust (p. 224).

The more difficult question, however, was whether that right was enforceable against the nephew's trustee in bankruptcy. In general, the trustee steps into the debtor's shoes, and takes his property subject to all rights and equities affecting it; he is, however, free to break any merely contractual obligations of the debtor. On which side of this line did the rights of the aunt fall: were they merely contractual obligations or did she have some interest over the property? In considering this question, the judge found guidance in *DHN Food Distributors Ltd* v *Tower Hamlets LBC* [1976] 1 WLR 852. If the licence was to be regarded as creating an interest in land, the use of a constructive trust was essential, since by virtue of LPA 1925, s. 40 (see 3.3.1), an enforceable interest in relation to land could not arise simply under an oral contract. Here the aunt's contractual or equitable licence did confer an interest under a constructive trust, which accordingly bound the trustee in bankruptcy.

In reaching this conclusion, Browne-Wilkinson J made it clear that he had considerable reservations about the current state of the law, describing it (at p. 226) as:

very confused and difficult to fit in with established equitable principles.

Similar doubts about the decision in *Errington* v *Errington* and subsequent developments were expressed by a number of judges and academics, as for example by Russell LJ in *National Provincial Bank Ltd* v *Hastings Car Mart Ltd* [1964] Ch 665 at pp. 696–7. However, the House of Lords when considering the appeal in that case (under the name of *National Provincial Bank* v *Ainsworth* [1965] AC 1175) declined to express any final view on the matter, which accordingly remained unresolved for some considerable time.

The matter was, however, considered at some length by the Court of Appeal in *Ashburn Anstalt* v *Arnold* [1989] 1 Ch 1. Unfortunately all the remarks of the court upon this subject constitute *obiter dicta* because in the case the agreement under consideration was held to be a lease and not a licence. Nonetheless, having heard lengthy argument upon the *Errington* problem, the court felt it proper to express its views upon this subject. After a detailed consideration of the authorities, Fox LJ concluded (at pp. 21–2):

It must, we think, be very doubtful whether this court's decision in *Errington* v *Errington* . . . is consistent with its earlier decisions in *Daly* v *Edwardes* (1900) 83 LT 548; *Frank Warr & Co.* v *London County Council* [1904] 1 KB 713 and *Clore* v *Theatrical Properties Ltd* [1936] 3 All ER 483. That decision cannot be said to be in conflict with any later decision of the House of Lords, because the House expressly left the effect of a contractual licence open in the *Hastings Car Mart* case. But there must be very real doubts whether *Errington* can be reconciled with the earlier decisions of the House of Lords in *Edwardes* v *Barrington* (1901) 85 LT 650 and *King* v *David Allen & Sons (Billposting) Ltd* [1916] 2 AC 54. It would seem that we must follow those cases or choose between the two lines of authority. It is not, however, necessary to consider those alternative courses in detail, since in our judgment the House of Lords cases, whether or not as a matter of strict precedent they conclude this question, state the correct principle which we should follow . . .

Before *Errington* the law appears to have been clear and well understood. It rested on an important and intelligible distinction between contractual obligations which gave rise to no estate or interest in the land and proprietary rights which, by definition, did. The far-reaching statement of principle in *Errington* was not supported by authority, not necessary for the decision of the case and *per incuriam* in the sense that it was made without reference to authorities which, if they would not have compelled, would surely have persuaded the court to adopt a different *ratio*. Of course, the law must be free to develop. But as a response to problems which had arisen, the *Errington* rule (without more) was neither practically necessary nor theoretically convincing.

As a result it seems most unlikely that in future it will be possible to argue that a contractual licence is binding on a third party to the contract and the contractual licence has been returned to its true place, which appears simply to be as part of the law of contract. The Court of Appeal did, however, accept that there might be cases in which the facts justified the imposition by the court of a constructive trust. It was emphasised that the courts will not take this step where the evidence is 'slender' and that the issue for the court in such cases is: 'whether the [third party] has acted in such a way that, as a matter of justice, a trust must be imposed . . .' (at p. 27). The court agreed that the imposition of a constructive trust was justified by the facts of *Binions* v *Evans* [1972] Ch 359, where the purchaser had acted in breach of the term in his contract that he would take the property subject to the occupier's rights. You may like to note though that were a similar situation to arise today, an appropriately worded contract might enable the occupier to enforce the term against the purchaser under the Contracts (Rights of Third Parties) Act 1999, without having to seek the imposition of a constructive trust.

The remarks of the Court of Appeal in *Ashburn Anstalt* v *Arnold*, although theoretically only of persuasive authority, are helpful in clarifying the law on this issue, and were welcomed by Browne-Wilkinson V-C in *IDC Group Ltd* v *Clark* [1992] EGLR 187 at p. 189 as:

[putting] what I hope is the quietus to the heresy that a mere licence creates an interest in land . . . [and] to the heresy that parties to a contractual licence necessarily become constructive trustees.

As we have seen (8.2.3.1), the decision in *Ashburn Anstalt* v *Arnold* was criticised (although not in relation to its comments on contractual licences) and overruled by the House of Lords in *Prudential Assurance Co. Ltd* v *London Residuary Body* [1992] 2 AC 386. However, this does not seem to have affected the persuasive force of its views on *Errington* v *Errington*.

In *Habermann* v *Koehler* (1996) 73 P&CR 515 at 523, the Court of Appeal referred to the case as being the decision which governs contractual licences, and more recently in *Lloyd* v *Dugdale* [2002] 2 P&CR 13 p.167 at 183 Sir Christopher Slade cited *Ashburn Anstalt* v *Arnold* as authority for the principle that:

Notwithstanding some previous authority suggesting the contrary, a contractual licence is not to be treated as creating a proprietary interest in land so as to bind third parties who acquire the land with notice of it, on this account alone.

20.3.4 Licences by estoppel

In a number of cases in which the licensor would be estopped from revoking the licence, the courts have had to deal with the additional question of whether his successors in title are subject to that estoppel.

Two cases we have already noted, *Dillwyn* v *Llewellyn* (1862) 4 De G F & J 517 and *Inwards* v *Baker* [1965] 2 QB 29 (see 18.3.1.1), arose after the death of the licensor and involved questions about the extent to which those inheriting the deceased's property took subject to the licence. In both cases they were held to be bound by the rights which the licensee could have asserted against the licensor.

Similarly, in *Greasely* v *Cooke* [1980] 1 WLR 1306 the action to recover the property from the licensee was brought by family members who had inherited the property from the original licensor. The licensee, Miss Cooke, had lived in the house for nearly 40 years, having started work as a maid with the family when she was just 16. Over the years she came to be regarded as one of the family, living as the wife of one of the brothers, and caring for other members, including an invalid daughter. After the first ten years she was no longer paid for her services, but was assured that she could regard the property as her home for the rest of her life. When her partner died, the younger generation, who inherited the house, sought to recover possession from her.

The Court of Appeal held that the various elements of proprietary estoppel were established in this case (see 18.3.1), and that the claimant had an equity arising from that estoppel, which, as in *Inwards* v *Baker* should be satisfied by allowing her to remain in the house for as long as she wished. This was enforced against the new owners, taking by inheritance, who were not able to evict her.

We have already considered the decision in *In re Sharpe* [1980] 1 WLR 219, but think it is worth mentioning here as well. Parts of the judgment suggest that the circumstances could give rise to an estoppel, and so the case could be seen as illustrating the enforcement of such an equity against the owner's trustee in bankruptcy.

20.3.4.1 *Enforcement against purchaser for value*

So far the decisions we have considered involve enforcing the estoppel licence against successors who are volunteers or who for some other reason are regarded as stepping into the shoes of the licensor. The really interesting question about the enforcement of these licences arises when the licensor's successor is a purchaser for value: can the equity be enforced against him?

It happened that the first cases in which this question was considered all involved unregistered land, and we will deal with these now and then go on to look at the position with regard to registered title.

(1) *Unregistered land*

In *Inwards* v *Baker* [1965] 2 QB 29 at p. 37 Lord Denning MR stated that:

any purchaser who took with notice would clearly be bound by the equity

but this must be considered as merely *obiter dicta*, since no purchaser was involved in the case.

In *Hopgood* v *Brown* [1955] 1 WLR 213, the Court of Appeal held that a purchaser for value was bound by an estoppel which had been binding on his vendor. However there was little discussion of this point, and in part at least the court seemed to argue by analogy from the legal doctrine of tenancy by estoppel rather than relying on the equitable concept of proprietary estoppel.

There is, however, one major decision, *E. R. Ives Investment Ltd* v *High* [1967] 2 QB 379, in which an equity arising from estoppel was enforced against a purchaser for value. The facts of this case were as follows. A building company, whilst erecting a block of flats, mistakenly allowed the foundations of the new building to encroach on to land belonging to a neighbour. When the neighbour objected, he was persuaded to accept a right of way across the courtyard of the new block (allowing access to his back garden from the road) in compensation for the continuing trespass. Thereafter, he built himself a garage, access to which was only possible via the courtyard. Later the owner of the block of flats sold the property and it was eventually resold to the plaintiffs. They bought it subject to the neighbour's right of way but subsequently claimed that since this right amounted to an unregistered D(iii) land charge (an equitable easement) it was not binding on them. The Court of Appeal held that the neighbour's right to cross the courtyard did bind the plaintiffs.

This decision appears to be reached on two separate grounds. The first ground is that it is a basic rule of law that one cannot take the benefit of an agreement without accepting a related burden. (This principle is discussed further in Chapter 23 in relation to covenants relating to freehold land and the decisions in *Halsall* v *Brizell* [1957] Ch 169—see 23.5.1.) Thus, as long as the plaintiffs wished to maintain their foundations on the neighbouring land they could not revoke the neighbour's right of way. This analysis causes few problems. It is the second reason given for the decision in this case which causes concern: that the actions of the original owner in allowing the neighbour to build his garage gave rise to an estoppel or, as Lord Denning MR put it, 'an equity arising out of acquiescence'. It was held that this 'equity', which is not a land charge and therefore was not void for non-registration, would bind a purchaser who bought with notice, as had the plaintiffs in this case. The decision is thus a rare example of the enforcement of an estoppel licence against a purchaser for value, and seems to elevate the licence by estoppel into some kind of quasi-interest in land.

This departure from traditional ideas about licences led to criticism (see Crane (1967) 31 Conv NS 332) and it must be said that since the dispute in *E. R. Ives Investment Ltd* v *High* could have been resolved on the point of the related benefit and burden alone, the discussion of the 'equity' arising from estoppel was quite unnecessary. The case, however, stands as authority for the proposition that licences in respect of unregistered land can bind third parties, including a purchaser for value, and the decision as a whole was referred to with approval by the Court of Appeal in *Thatcher* v *Douglas* (1995) 146 NLJ 282. It is also worth noting *obiter dicta* in *Lloyds Bank plc* v *Carrick* [1996] 4 All ER 630, in which Morritt LJ, referring to counsel's argument that proprietary estoppel cannot give rise to an interest in land capable of binding successors in title, observed that it was hard to see how that argument 'can surmount the hurdle created by the decision of this court in *E. R. Ives Investments Ltd* v *High*' (at p. 642).

(2) *Registered land*

As we saw in 18.5, there was, until recently, little authority on whether an equity arising from estoppel would bind a purchaser of registered land, and none at all in the context of licences.

At last, however, in 1996, the question of the overriding effect of this equity was raised before the Court of Appeal in the case of *Habermann* v *Koehler* (1996) 73 P&CR 515. The facts were as follows. The defendants' employer was the registered proprietor of a house which he made available to the defendants, giving them an oral promise that they could live there rent-free for the rest of his life, and could buy the property from him at a reduced price. The defendants moved into the house on the strength of the arrangement, and for some time worked without payment for their employer. The property was then mortgaged, and some 10 years later was sold to the mortgagee to meet the mortgage debt. The purchaser sought possession of the property from the defendants, who in their defence relied on proprietary estoppel. It seemed that at last all the unanswered questions about estoppel licences, on which, as the Court of Appeal observed, 'there is much controversy', would arise in an appellate court for decision. Tantalisingly, however, the Court of Appeal considered that too many relevant factual questions had not been dealt with at first instance and, accordingly, remitted the case for a new trial.

At that further trial, the judge held that the option to buy the property could not be enforced against the purchaser under LRA 1925, s. 70(1)(g) because the occupier had not disclosed it on enquiry. However, it appears that the licensee's right to remain in the property was held to bind the purchaser. The court ordered the execution of a declaration of trust giving effect to the occupiers' right to remain in occupation of the property for the lifetime of the previous owner (that is, the occupiers' previous employer, who had created the licence). This first instance decision is recorded in the report of *Habermann v Koehler (No 2)* [2000] TLR 825, in which the occupiers appealed, unsuccessfully, against the decision that their option was unenforceable. The purchaser did not appeal against the decision on the right to occupy, and accordingly there is no reference to that part of the first instance decision in the Court of Appeal's judgment. Nevertheless, it does appear that an equity arising from proprietary estoppel in a licence situation was held binding on a purchaser for value of registered land, albeit at first instance only (see further 20.4.3).

20.3.5 Could a contractual licensee rely on estoppel?

This is a question to which there is no clear answer and it has generated a certain amount of academic debate. As Pawlowski puts it in *The Doctrine of Proprietary Estoppel*, 1996, at p. 8:

There are conflicting views as to whether a contractual licence and proprietary estoppel can overlap.

The question of whether there could be such an overlap seems to be of particular importance in the context of enforcing a licence against the licensor's successor. Following *Ashburn Anstalt v Arnold* [1989] 1 Ch 1 it is generally accepted that a contractual licence will not bind a third party (unless, of course, there are special circumstances which lead the court to impose a constructive trust). By contrast, as we have seen, the equity arising from proprietary estoppel now appears to be enforceable against successors in title and, as in *Habermann v Koehler (No. 2)* [2000] TLR 825, can result in a licence being enforced against a purchaser for value. If a contractual licensee could establish that he has acted to his detriment in reliance on a representation by the licensor—for example that the licence would not be revoked—could any resulting equity make that licence enforceable against a third party?

It seems that as yet there is no direct authority on this point. Megarry and Wade, p. 748, is of the opinion that:

there is no reason why both a claim in contract and to an equity by proprietary estoppel should not normally arise from the same facts

and the same view is put forward by Thompson [1983] Conv 50. For the contrary view, see Briggs [1981] Conv 212 and [1983] Conv 285.

20.4 Are licences becoming interests in land?

At the start of this chapter we referred to the traditional idea that licences are mere permissions and do not constitute interests in land. Having looked at the modern case law, it is worth considering whether this is still true, or whether modern decisions mean that the licence has become, or is becoming, an interest in land.

20.4.1 What is an interest in land?

The authorities seem to suggest that the crucial factor, in deciding whether a right amounts to an interest in land, is whether the right is enforceable against third parties. A right which cannot be enforced against a successor in title is clearly *not* an interest in land. However, since the answer to the question, 'What rights bind successors in title?' appears to be, 'Those which are interests in land', this definition seems to be somewhat circular in nature (see Gray and Gray pp. 107–9). It is nevertheless the best that can be offered, and so, in considering whether a right creates an interest in land, attention centres on whether it binds third parties, and in particular the purchaser for value.

The other essential characteristic of an interest in land is that it is capable of being transferred to another person, passing either by itself, or on the transfer of the land to which it is attached. Thus, in considering whether licences can be regarded as interests in land, we need to ask not only whether they bind the licensors' successors but also whether they are transferable.

20.4.2 Is a licence transferable?

There is not a great deal of authority on this in English law, although it would seem that rights arising under a contract are usually assignable, subject, of course, to the specific terms of the contract. The question of whether the benefit of an estoppel could be assigned was considered and answered affirmatively in the Australian case of *Hamilton* v *Geraghty* (1901)1 SRNSW Eq 81 (see Cheshire and Burn, p. 659). In *E. R. Ives Investment Ltd* v *High* [1967] 2 QB 379, Lord Denning described such an equity as being available also to the claimant's successors in title (at p. 395), although, as Gray comments, it is not entirely clear what was meant by this (see Gray and Gray, p. 775). However, Lord Denning's statement is, so far, the best authority on the point in English law.

20.4.3 Does a licence bind the licensor's successor?

As we have seen, it did appear at one time that contractual licences were to be regarded as binding everyone except the purchaser for value without notice (*Errington* v *Errington* [1952] 1 KB 290). The 1984 edition of Megarry and Wade, *The Law of Real Property*, 5th edn., at p. 808 stated that 'all the indications now are that contractual licences are capable of binding successors in title as equitable interests', adding that 'the courts appear to be well on their way to create a new and highly versatile interest in land'. This was, of course, written before *Ashburn Anstalt* v

Arnold [1989] 1 Ch 1, and since the Court of Appeal's disapproval of *Errington* v *Errington* it seems unlikely that contractual licences will any longer be regarded as binding on the licensor's successor. There is still the possibility that in situations similar to that in *Binions* v *Evans* [1972] Ch 359 a constructive trust might be imposed, but the purchaser would then be bound by the beneficial interest under the trust, a recognised property interest, rather than by any right arising directly from the contractual licence.

As far as estoppel licences go, we have noted both the decisions in which the equity has been enforced against the licensor's successors and the new more general statutory provision relating to registered land that an equity by estoppel has effect 'as an interest capable of binding successors in title' (LRA 2002, s. 116— see 18.5). It would seem now that licences by estoppel are being accorded the status of interests in land, but you may like to note the contrary view expressed in Megarry and Wade (p. 733) that:

although an equity arising by estoppel is probably best regarded as a species of equitable proprietary right, it is questionable whether an estoppel licence can do so (*sic*).

The correctness of describing an estoppel licence as an equitable proprietary right is described as 'open to doubt', mainly because LPA 1925 appears to prohibit the creation of new equitable interests (s. 4(1) proviso), and there is no decision pre-dating the Act in which an estoppel licence had been held to bind a third party. Moreover (at p. 734):

it is not obvious that a licence declared to be irrevocable by reason of estoppel should create an equitable interest in land when a contractual licence does not.

On this point, see also Megarry and Wade, p. 1057, and Pawlowski, *The Doctrine of Proprietary Estoppel*, 1996, p. 9. It remains to be seen whether the courts will regard these views as persuasive.

20.5 Trant Way

The matters we have been discussing in this chapter could be relevant to two of the licensees described on pp. 397–8. Henry Mumps and Bob Bell are each living as licensees in property owned by another member of their family.

20.5.1 8 Trant Way

Henry is already worried about his position, fearing that Mildred wants to end their relationship, and possibly to turn him out of the house. If he could establish that he is entitled to a share of the beneficial interest under a common-intention constructive trust, he would have the right to remain in occupation, as well as a right to a share in the capital value of the house. However, as we have seen at 17.5, the chances of doing this are slight in the absence of any direct contribution to the cost of acquiring the property.

If he cannot establish such a trust, he will be left trying to show that he has an irrevocable licence to remain in the house. Decisions on implied contractual licences (such as *Tanner* v *Tanner* [1975] 1 WLR 1346) might be thought to give him some comfort, but as we have seen the courts have not always been willing to adopt this approach (see 20.1.1.2). Even if Henry could establish such a contract, since *Ashburn Anstalt* v *Arnold* [1989] 1 Ch 1 he would be at risk from anyone to whom Mildred might sell or mortgage the house.

The other possibility for Henry would be to seek to establish an estoppel, but for this he would need to show that Mildred led him to believe that he would be allowed to remain in the house, and that he had acted in reliance on this to his detriment.

Failing all else, Henry does have a limited statutory right to occupation under the Family Law Act 1996, and we will deal with this and consider Henry's position more generally in Chapter 24.

20.5.2   **3 Trant Way**

Although relations between Bob Bell and his daughter Barbara seem happy at the moment, it is worth noting that he might have a licence by estoppel which could be enforced against his daughter. Bob has spent money on his flat in reliance on her statement that he has a home for life. It is possible that if a dispute arose a court could hold that Bob had an irrevocable licence for life although the court would be free to satisfy the equity arising from estoppel in whatever way it thought best, and might choose to make only a money award, to compensate Bob for his expenditure.

FURTHER READING

Battersby, 'Contractual and Estoppel Licences As Proprietary Interests in Land' [1991] Conv 36.

Crane, 'Estoppel Interests in Land' (1967) 31 Conv 332.

Everton, ' "Equitable Interests" and "Equities"—In Search of a Pattern' (1976) 40 Conv 209.

Moriarty, 'Licences and Land Law: Legal Principles and Public Policies' (1984) 100 LQR 376.

PART VI

Third-party rights

Introduction

In this Part we move on to look at the major third-party rights in land. This group of rights includes mortgages and charges (Chapter 21), easements and profits à prendre (Chapter 22) and covenants affecting freehold land (Chapter 23). As you have already seen (1.4 to 1.7) these rights are capable of existing as interests in land and you should already be familiar with the rules relating to the question of whether such rights will bind any later acquirer of an estate or interest in the land. However, in each chapter, as well as explaining the nature of the rights in great detail, we will also explain how the rules as to later acquirers operate in relation to each interest. As you will see, in some cases this can produce quite complex problems, which can be difficult for practitioners and are much beloved of examiners!

21

Mortgages and charges

21.1 Background

Very few individuals or companies have sufficient liquid assets to pay for the purchase of property outright. The normal method of financing such a purchase is to obtain a loan from a building society, bank or finance house. Since large sums of money are involved, the lender will seek security for the money advanced and this will normally take the form of a mortgage of the property to be purchased. Accordingly, a large proportion of real property in this country is mortgaged. In addition to such mortgages for purchase, it is also common to offer a mortgage of land as security for any sizeable loan. Such a loan might be taken in order to improve the land (e.g. to install central heating) or for purposes unconnected with the land (e.g. to finance the owner's business ventures).

Thus far, we have mentioned only mortgages. 'Mortgage' is the traditional name for the arrangement by which property becomes security for a debt but, as we shall see, the correct modern term is normally 'charge'. In practice, however, the two terms are often used interchangeably. You should also note that land is not the only form of property that can be used as security. It is not at all uncommon for valuable chattels also to be used as security for a debt and thus chattel mortgages are perfectly possible. Ships, aeroplanes and fleets of cars are often mortgaged as a way of financing their acquisition. The rules for chattel mortgages are not identical to those for mortgages of land or interests in land, though there are similarities. However, we deal here only with mortgages that relate to land.

In this chapter we examine the types of mortgages or charges of land and interests in land which may be created and consider the rules regarding their administration and their protection against later acquirers of interests in the land.

21.2 Introduction

When they purchased **1 Trant Way**, the Armstrongs were able to pay their own removal expenses and legal fees, and provided 10 per cent of the purchase price of the property from their own resources. They obtained the remaining 90 per cent of the house price by way of a loan from the Double Gloucester Building Society (DGBS). As security for the loan, the society took a charge by deed over 1 Trant Way. This charge was registered at the same time as the transfer to the Armstrongs.

Henry Harding, who is buying a 99-year lease of the maisonette at **2 Trant Way**, also needs to raise money by way of a mortgage. He plans to borrow 95 per cent of the price from his bank, the Wensleydale Bank plc.

Mildred Mumps wishes to borrow a large sum of money from her bank (the Royal Windsor Bank), in order to start her own business. The bank has insisted on security for the loan. **8 Trant Way** is already mortgaged to the Red Leicester Building Society but Mildred has offered her bank a second mortgage on the property, as security for her business loan. Mildred has not told Henry of her plans.

Nigel Neep, the owner in fee simple of **14 Trant Way**, has asked his bank manager for overdraft facilities for one month. The bank manager has said that this is possible but has suggested that the bank take Mr Neep's title deeds and hold them as security for the loan. Mr Neep bought the property in 1980, raising the bulk of the purchase price by a loan secured by a mortgage. He finished repaying that debt in 1995. He is happy to deposit the title deeds (which are normally stored for safe-keeping by his solicitor) with the bank as suggested.

21.3 What is a mortgage or charge?

In *Santley* v *Wilde* [1899] 2 Ch 474 a mortgage was described as 'a conveyance of land . . . as security for the payment of a debt or the discharge of some other obligation'. The purpose of a mortgage or charge is to provide a lender of money with security for the debt. Then, if the borrower fails to repay the debt, the lender can use the property to recover the sum advanced and any interest allowed for under the agreement. The usual way in which this is done is for the lender to take the property that has been used as security and to sell it and to use the proceeds of sale to repay the sums due under the agreement.

It is worth stopping here for a moment and considering the terminology that is used in relation to mortgages and charges, since it often causes confusion. In a mortgage the mortgage is granted by the property owner (the borrower), who is thus called the mortgagor. The lender, who receives the benefit of the security provided by the mortgage is called the 'mortgagee'. It is thus not the building society or bank that grants the mortgage, although in common parlance we often speak as though this is the case. In the case of a charge, the correct terms are chargor (the owner who borrows) and chargee (the lender) but the terms 'mortgagor' and 'mortgagee' are normally used even where the arrangement is technically a charge rather than a mortgage.

21.3.1 Types of mortgage or charge

There are a number of different types of mortgage or charge that can be created, although in modern times with the registration of title one form has come to be by far the most common. That form is usually called the 'registered charge' and we will look at it in more detail below. Some of the older methods of creating mortgages are no longer commonly used, particularly those that relate only to unregistered land but we will note them because in relation to mortgages an understanding of how the forms of mortgage or charge developed can make some of the modern rules easier to follow.

As is the case with many interests in land, mortgages and charges can be either legal or equitable, although recent changes to the law have made equitable mortgages or charges of legal estates much less common. It is also possible to use nearly any interest in land as security and not just a legal estate. Thus, the holder of an equitable lease could mortgage or charge his or her equitable interest as security for a loan. However, as this is a mortgage of an equitable interest, the mortgage or charge can only take effect in equity. Thus, while a legal estate or interest can be the subject of a legal or an equitable mortgage or charge, an equitable interest can only be the subject of an equitable mortgage or charge. In the days of the large settled estates, it was not at all uncommon for an heir to mortgage his equitable future interest in the property. However, in modern times, equitable mortgages of equitable interests are much less common.

21.3.2 The traditional method of creating a mortgage

The traditional form of mortgage is no longer possible in relation to a legal estate but it is nonetheless important to understand how it operated, both in order to see why some of the modern rules developed and also to understand some of the older cases. This method was abolished in 1926 (as a consequence of ss. 85–87, LPA 1925).

Originally, a mortgage was created by the mortgagor (the borrower) transferring his (in those days the owner was usually male) legal estate in the land to the mortgagee (lender) as security for the loan. Thus, if the mortgagor defaulted on his debt (failed to pay) the mortgagee, as legal owner of the property, could sell or let the property in order to reimburse himself. The agreement made between the parties did, however, provide for the estate to be re-conveyed to the mortgagor if he repaid the loan in full (usually on a specified date).

There were a number of problems with this arrangement. One that arose early in the history of the mortgage was that lenders often tried to prevent the mortgagor being able to repay on the contractual date. This abuse was dealt with by Equity developing the principle that the mortgagor did nonetheless have an equitable right to repay ('redeem the mortgage') after the contractual date. Another flaw was that it was impossible for the mortgagor to create two mortgages over the same piece of property because the first mortgage conveyed the whole legal estate to the mortgagee. This problem was circumvented by the mortgagor granting a mortgage over his equitable right to redeem but since that mortgage was of an equitable interest, the second mortgage itself had to be equitable. These are just two illustrations of how the pre-1926 rules caused unnecessary complications, which became unacceptable in a modern commercial world.

21.3.3 The LPA 1925 reforms

The LPA 1925 replaced the older form of legal mortgage with new forms that did not involve the conveyance by the mortgagor of his estate to the mortgagee. Instead, security was provided by either granting the mortgagee a long lease of the premises (ss. 85 and 86, LPA 1925) or by the mortgagor creating a charge over the property that gave the mortgagee the same rights as though he had been granted a long lease (s. 87, LPA 1925). It is the latter arrangement that has become the modern charge and is the form that has for many years been used by most banks and building societies. It is also, since the coming into force of the LRA 2002, now the only form of mortgage or charge of a registered legal estate that is possible. The s. 85 and 86 mortgages thus may still be encountered but are relatively rare. We will now look at the legal mortgages in more detail and then consider the equitable forms of mortgage.

21.4 Legal mortgages

21.4.1 Legal mortgage of a fee simple under LPA 1925, s. 85

Under the provisions of LPA 1925, s. 85, the mortgagor, instead of transferring the fee simple, grants a long lease of the property to the mortgagee. This lease will be expressed to be terminable when the loan is repaid: it is said to be subject to 'cesser on redemption'. This method has the advantage that the mortgagor retains his estate in the land, but the mortgagee also has an estate (the lease) which gives him certain rights in relation to the land. In order to ensure that the lease will not end before the debt is repaid, it is normal to grant an extremely long term of years. Indeed the statute provides that should one try to create a mortgage by the old method of transferring the fee simple this will automatically be converted into a grant of a lease for a term of 3,000 years from the date of the mortgage (s. 85(2)), and those drafting mortgages in accordance with s. 85 usually adopted a similar period of lease.

   This method of creating a legal mortgage had an advantage over the older form of mortgage. It allowed the creation of a second legal mortgage over the same land, by giving the second mortgagee a lease which is longer than the lease of the first mortgagee. This creates a leasehold reversion in the second mortgagee, giving him the landlord's rights in relation to the first tenant (mortgagee). (As we have already explained, it is possible to grant several leases which take effect at the same time in the same piece of land—see 8.10.5.) It would not, in fact, matter if the leases given to the various mortgagees were all the same length, but it was usual to give a slightly longer term to each successive mortgagee.

21.4.2 Legal mortgage of a term of years under LPA 1925, s. 86

Before 1926, mortgages of leases were also created by assigning the whole term of years to the mortgagee. However, LPA 1925, s. 86, provided for such a mortgage to be created by granting a sublease to the mortgagee. Again, the mortgagee was thereby given an estate in the land, while the mortgagor retained his own estate. Should an attempt be made to use the old method of mortgaging, the disposition would be converted into a sublease. The period of the sublease would be the unexpired period of the mortgaged lease, less 10 days (s. 86(2)). The 10-day gap allowed the creation of a second mortgage of the same lease, made by granting a sublease that is a day longer than the first sublease. Once again this allowed for the creation of two or more legal mortgages of the same term of years.

21.4.3 **Charge by deed by way of legal mortgage under LPA 1925, s. 87**

The third method of creating a legal mortgage is the method in normal use today. Instead of granting a lease or sublease to the mortgagee, the mortgagor merely executes a deed which declares that he is charging his land by way of legal mortgage with the repayment of the sums specified. This form of 'charge' may be used for both freehold and leasehold estates. LPA 1925, s. 87, provides that the effect of such a mortgage is to give the mortgagee 'the same protection, powers and remedies' as if the mortgage had been made by lease or sublease (whichever is relevant). Thus, the mortgagee is treated as though he had a lease or sublease, although in fact no such estate is created. The effect of this provision is illustrated by *Grand Junction Co. Ltd* v *Bates* [1954] 2 QB 160, in which leasehold property had been charged by way of legal mortgage under s. 87. Later, the landlord began forfeiture proceedings under s. 146 for breach of covenant by the tenant. Had he succeeded, the mortgagee's security for the loan would have been totally destroyed, for the lease ceases to exist on forfeiture. If the mortgage had been made by sublease, the mortgagee would have been able to apply for relief as a subtenant under s. 146(4) (see Chapter 10), but the question arose whether a chargee could do this since he had no legal estate in the property. However, the court held that the provisions of s. 87 gave him a right to apply for relief, just as though he held a mortgage by sublease.

The charge by way of legal mortgage does have several advantages over the other methods of creating a legal mortgage. It enables an owner to mortgage his freehold and leasehold property in one document and, in the case of leasehold property, has the further advantage that, since no actual sublease is created, the grant of such a charge will not amount to breach of a covenant against subletting (see *Grand Junction Co. Ltd* v *Bates* per Upjohn J at p. 168).

As a result of its simple form (a brief example is given in LPA 1925, Sch. 5, form No. 1), and the fact that it can be used to mortgage either of the legal estates, the legal charge has become in modern times the most usual method of mortgage. The mortgages of both 1 and 2 Trant Way are likely to take this form. The sample format of such a charge given in the LPA 1925 does not, however, give a true picture of the type of document which one would expect to see today. Most modern charges add to the statutory skeleton a long list of covenants between the mortgagor and mortgagee (e.g., preventing the mortgagor from granting leases or taking lodgers). There will also be detailed provisions concerning repayment of the sum advanced, together with interest, usually by instalments (and normally spread over a period of 20–25 years in the case of domestic mortgages). The modern mortgage is accordingly a very much longer document than the Act might suggest.

21.4.3.1 *Registered land*

The legal charge is also used when one is dealing with registered land. Section 23(1)(a), LRA 2002 expressly says that the powers of an owner in relation to a registered estate include the power to make any disposition permitted by the general law *except* a mortgage by demise or subdemise (see above 21.4.1 and 21.4.2), thus the legal charge will be the only correct form of mortgage to use for registered land. In line with the general policy applying to registered land, the completion of the deed does not, by itself, create a legal mortgage. It is the registration of the charge which perfects it (ss. 4 and 27, LRA 2002).

Note that it is clear that in relation to registered land a legal charge may be created (subject to the necessary formalities, such as the need for a deed) by the simple use of words that make it clear that the land is to be regarded as charged with the repayment of a loan. Thus, in registered land, it is not necessary to include the words 'by way of legal charge' in the deed, if the intention to charge is clear. This position in relation to the wording used in the LRA 1925, s. 25(2), was confirmed in *Cityland and Property (Holdings) Ltd* v *Dabrah* [1968] Ch 166, 171 and now is governed by s. 25, LRA 2002 and r. 103, Land Registration Rules 2003. Since r. 103 says that 'A legal charge of a registered estate may be made in [the form provided]', rather than that it must ('shall') be made in that form, it would appear that any wording that is clearly intended to create a legal charge will do.

21.4.4 Grant of legal mortgage as a trigger for first registration

The creation of a legal mortgage or charge of an unregistered estate may itself trigger a requirement to register the estate charged and the mortgage or charge. Under s. 4(1)(g) LRA 2002, the creation of a 'protected first legal mortgage' of a qualifying estate gives rise to the requirement of registration. The 'protected first legal mortgage' is defined by s. 4(8) as follows:

> (8) For the purposes of subsection (1)(g)—
>
> (a) a legal mortgage is protected if it takes effect on its creation as a mortgage to be protected by the deposit of documents relating to the mortgaged estate, and
>
> (b) a first legal mortgage is one which on its creation, ranks in priority ahead of any other mortgages then affecting the mortgaged estate.

You will recall from our earlier discussion of land charges (see 4.4) that, in unregistered land, only mortgages that are not protected by deposit of title deeds can be protected as land charges. The effect of s. 4, LRA 2002 is that the creation of a legal mortgage in which the title deeds *are* deposited will lead to a requirement to register the estate charged, unless the mortgage is not a first mortgage (which is very unlikely). Section 6(2) makes it quite clear that it is the charged estate that must be registered and not just the mortgage or charge. Thus, the land will become registered land and then all charges must be protected in accordance with the land registration provisions. Thus, if Mr Neep, the owner of 14 Trant Way, has to create a legal mortgage of his property as security for his bank loan, rather than using the informal method suggested by the bank manager, he will have then to register his fee simple estate.

Once the estate is registered, any legal mortgage or charge over that estate must itself be registered (s. 27(2)(f)). Once registered, the mortgage or charge will take effect as a charge by deed by way of legal mortgage, even if originally created as a different type of legal mortgage (s. 51, LRA 2002). Thus, if Mr Neep did create a new legal mortgage of his premises but used the s. 85 LRA 1925 method (the grant of a lease), the effect would be that the s. 85 mortgage will be transformed into a charge by deed by way of legal mortgage (the s. 87 form) once it is registered.

All of this produces a constant movement towards all estates being registered and all legal mortgages of those estates becoming legal charges. However, even in future there will for some time still be cases in which registration is not triggered. Notably, these include the creation of a second legal mortgage of unregistered land and the creation of an equitable mortgage of unregistered land. Equitable charges of registered land are, of course, also possible but unlike legal charges are not protected by registration of the charge itself. We will look at this in more detail once we have considered how equitable mortgages and charges can arise.

21.5 Equitable mortgages

21.5.1 Contract to create a mortgage

Under the principle that 'Equity regards as done that which ought to be done', a contract to create a legal mortgage will be regarded as giving rise to an equitable mortgage from the date of the contract. Of course, since the introduction of s. 2 of the Law of Property (Miscellaneous Provisions) Act 1989, the contract itself must be made in writing. Reliance on the equitable rule is also dependent upon the contract being one which the courts would enforce by an order for specific performance (*Tebb* v *Hodge* (1869) LR 5 CP 73). A defective legal mortgage (e.g., one which has been signed but not witnessed) will be similarly treated, as long as specific performance is available. This is similar to the rule for defective leases (see *Walsh* v *Lonsdale* (1882) 21 ChD 9 and Chapter 8). However, specific performance will not be available in any of these cases unless the mortgage money has actually been advanced, for traditionally equity has declined to force someone to make a loan. In such cases, the mortgagor could fall back on his common law remedy of damages.

21.5.2 Informal mortgage by deposit of deeds

In the past, the willingness of equity to recognise and protect any transaction in which it was clear that an estate owner had intended to charge his property with the repayment of a loan meant that many informal arrangements were regarded as equitable mortgages because equity regarded what had taken place as evidence of a contract to grant a mortgage. The classic example of the protection afforded by equity arose where an estate owner deposited his land certificate or title deeds with the lender in return for the loan. This was recognised as creating an equitable mortgage of the property in *Russel* v *Russel* (1783) 1 Bro CC 269, and continued in modern law under the saving provisions of LPA 1925, s. 13. For this type of mortgage, until 1989, no written record of any kind was necessary, for the deposit of title deeds was regarded not only as constituting the contract to make the mortgage, but also as amounting to part performance for the purposes of LPA 1925, s. 40(2). Moreover, the deposit and receipt of the deeds were regarded as part performance by each party respectively, so whichever side wished to rely on the doctrine might do so. Despite this, however, a written record was desirable in order to provide clear evidence of the nature of the transaction. These mortgages were convenient and cheap where a short-term loan was envisaged.

The law relating to these informal mortgages was, however, changed by the Law of Property (Miscellaneous Provisions) Act 1989, s. 2, because that provision relates to:

A contract for the sale or other disposition of an interest in land . . .

Accordingly, for an equitable mortgage to be enforceable it is now necessary to show that the agreement was *made* in writing. It will not do merely to have a later deed which states that the agreement exists (as was previously common practice) because that deed would merely purport to record an existing contract which would not satisfy s. 2, and accordingly would not amount to a contract at all. This effect of s. 2 (which may well have been unforeseen) was confirmed by the Court of Appeal in *United Bank of Kuwait plc* v *Sahib* [1997] Ch 107. This prevents the creation of the most informal old type of mortgage, in which deposit of deeds was used without anything more being done. Therefore, Nigel Neep's bank will be wise to insist that his mortgage is made by a written agreement which satisfies s. 2. If a mortgage is ineffective due to s. 2, the loan will become immediately repayable because the security has failed. However, old informal mortgages created before the 1989 Act are not affected by s. 2 and thus a few may still exist.

21.5.3 Equitable charge

An equitable charge arises when a chargee appropriates specific property to the repayment of a sum of money in such circumstances that a legal charge does not arise. This type of arrangement is rare and would normally require a written document. For an old example see *Matthews* v *Goodday* (1861) 31 LJ Ch 282.

21.5.4 Equitable mortgage of an equitable interest

One obviously cannot grant a legal mortgage of an interest that is recognised only in equity. This rule dates from the days of separate courts with separate jurisdictions. Common law did not recognise the equitable interests developed in the Chancellor's courts, and accordingly would not enforce any legal dealings with them. Therefore, any mortgage of an equitable interest in land, such as that of a life interest under the old settlement, had to be equitable in character. The method of creating such mortgages was not changed in 1925 and thus they continue to be made by a transfer of the entire interest to the mortgagee, subject to an agreement that it will be returned to the mortgagor on repayment of the loan. The transfer must be made, at the least, by writing, in order to pass the equitable interest to the mortgagee under LPA 1925, s. 53(1)(c). (Note that this is a transfer and not an agreement to transfer.) Normally thereafter, the mortgagee should give notice of the transfer to the trustees of the trust under which the interest exists (see 21.13.2).

21.6 Rights of the mortgagor

Having examined the methods of creating a mortgage we must turn our attention to the position of the parties after a mortgage has been made. We will look first at the rights of the mortgagor.

21.6.1 **Right to redeem**

The primary right enjoyed by the mortgagor is the right to *redeem* the mortgage on repayment of the loan and payment of any interest provided for by the charge.

21.6.1.1 *Right to redeem at law*

At law the right to redeem is a matter of contract: the mortgagor can redeem on the date or dates and in the manner provided for in the mortgage. Thus, should the agreement provide that the mortgage should be redeemed on a particular date, the mortgagor has, at law, a right to redeem on that date only. The legal rules do not allow him to insist on redeeming the mortgage either before or after the contractual date: see the discussion in *Kreglinger* v *New Patagonia Meat & Cold Storage Co. Ltd* [1914] AC 25 at p. 35. At common law, if he did not pay on the contractual date, the mortgagor at one time forfeited the land to the mortgagee *and* could still be sued in contract for the repayment of the debt. Accordingly the legal right to redeem was, and is, very limited.

21.6.1.2 *Right to redeem in equity*

Fortunately, equity took a very different view of the situation, particularly as there were examples of mortgagees absenting themselves so that it became impossible for the mortgagor to repay on the contractual date. As the purpose of the agreement was merely to provide the mortgagee with security for the loan, equity took the view that, as long as the advance and any interest was paid, the mortgagee should not be able to object to redemption. Originally equity intervened only in cases of fraud by the mortgagee but soon came to recognise a general right to redeem in all cases (*Salt* v *Marquess of Northampton* [1892] AC 1). Thus, equity allows the mortgagor to redeem even after the date fixed by the mortgage agreement for repayment has passed. Of course, since this right is enforceable in equity only, it is subject to the general principle that equitable remedies are discretionary in nature and all the equitable maxims (particularly the 'clean hands' doctrine) will apply. Furthermore, in deciding whether redemption is possible, equity will look at the substance of the agreement, not its form. Accordingly, a mortgage which is drafted to look like an outright transfer of the property, rather than the creation of an interest by way of security, will still be subject to the equitable right to redeem, if the facts are such as to indicate that only a grant by way of security was intended (*Darby* v *Read* (1675) Rep t Finch 226).

21.6.1.3 *Instalment mortgages*

So far, we have spoken as though the full sum owed becomes payable on one date. The modern mortgage is more likely to provide for repayment by instalments, spread over a number of years. However, it usually will contain a provision that if the mortgagor defaults on the payment of one instalment the whole sum will become due. In law, the mortgagor will then have to redeem the mortgage or lose his property for ever, but equity will moderate the rigour of this in the way already described.

21.6.2 **The equity of redemption**

Obviously a legal mortgagor retains his legal estate in the land but subject to the rights of the mortgagee (see below). In equity the mortgagor is described as owning the 'equity of redemption'. This must be distinguished from the equitable right to redeem which is mentioned above. The equity of redemption is the mortgagor's equitable interest in the property and it consists of *the sum total* of the mortgagor's rights in relation to the land (including, *inter alia*, the right to redeem). The equity of redemption is therefore an interest in land (*Pawlett* v *Attorney-General* (1667) Hardres 465, at p. 469) and can be dealt with like any other equitable interest.

21.6.3 **No clogs on the equity of redemption**

Equity is so protective of the mortgagor's equity of redemption that it will not tolerate any arrangement which either prevents or deters the mortgagor from exercising his right to redeem. Similarly, any burdens imposed by the mortgage on the mortgaged property that may continue after the date of redemption are generally regarded with disfavour. They derogate from the principle that the mortgage should provide security only and that on redemption the mortgagor should recover the property without further fetter. In restricting the contents of mortgage agreements in this way, equity recognised the fact that the mortgagor is often unable to dictate the terms of the mortgage because of his need for the mortgage advance. It was therefore appropriate that he should be afforded some protection by the courts. However, in some cases this approach has been taken to undesirable lengths.

Equity's approach is summed up in the rule that there must be no clogs (restrictions) on the equity of redemption and this is applied to a number of situations, some of which we must now consider.

21.6.3.1 *Prevention of redemption*

Any provision in a mortgage which would operate to prevent the mortgagor from redeeming will be disregarded by equity and will be void. Thus a mortgagee cannot include in a mortgage a term that, should a specified event occur, the land would become his absolutely (*Toomes* v *Conset* (1745) 3 Atk 261). This rule has, however, been taken to extremes, so that it is not possible to give a mortgagee a valid option to purchase the estate as part of the mortgage transaction. The option, if exercised, would extinguish the mortgagor's right to redeem and is accordingly void. The original rationale for this rule was sound. As Lord Henley put it in *Vernon* v *Bethall* (1762) 2 Eden 110 at p. 113:

there is great reason and justice in this rule, for necessitous men are not, truly speaking, free men, but to answer a present exigency will submit to any terms that the crafty may impose upon them.

However, in *Samuel* v *Jarrah Timber & Wood Paving Co. Ltd* [1904] AC 323 the House of Lords applied (albeit reluctantly) the same rule to an 'arm's-length' commercial transaction. Lord Linley referred to the old axiom, 'Once a mortgage always a mortgage' (meaning that the agreement could not covertly become something greater), and said (at p. 329):

The doctrine . . . means that no contract between a mortgagor and a mortgagee made at the time of the mortgage and as part of the mortgage transaction, or, in other words, as one of the terms of the loan, can be valid if it prevents the mortgagor from getting back his property on paying off what is due on his security. Any bargain which has that effect is invalid, and is inconsistent with the transaction being a mortgage.

It was suggested that granting the option in a separate document might avoid the rule, but it seems that even this may not avail the mortgagee, unless the option is granted some time after the mortgage (this gives the mortgagor a chance to refuse an unfair agreement once he has received his loan): *Lewis* v *Frank Love Ltd* [1961] 1 WLR 261; but see also *Reeve* v *Lisle* [1902] AC 461 in which an option was upheld. The issue of whether a transaction made later could be acceptable was further considered by the Court of Appeal in *Jones* v *Morgan* [2002] 1 EGLR 125 and, in the particular circumstances of that case, a later transaction was nonetheless held to be a clog on the equity of redemption and thus invalid, probably because a transaction carried out three years after the initial creation of the mortgage amounted to a complete reconstruction of the debt arrangements, rather than being a separate transaction. The judgment of Chadwick LJ usefully provides a short history of the doctrine (see paras. 50–73). However, the case is perhaps chiefly notable for the acerbic comment of Lord Phillips MR that, '. . . the doctrine of a clog on the equity of redemption is, so it seems to me, an appendix to our law which no longer serves a useful purpose and would be better excised' (para. 86).

21.6.3.2 *Postponement of redemption*

Any provision in a mortgage that attempts to postpone redemption to such an extent that the right to redeem becomes illusory may also be rendered void. The equitable right to redeem arises only once the contractual, legal date for redemption has passed. There is no general right in equity to redeem earlier (but see the Consumer Credit Act 1974, ss. 94 and 173, for rare cases of small mortgages which may be redeemed at any time). Accordingly, one way by which a mortgagee may try to obtain an irredeemable mortgage is to postpone the contractual date for redemption.

(a) *Freehold cases* In *Knightsbridge Estates Trust Ltd* v *Byrne* [1939] Ch 441 a company had mortgaged its freehold property to an insurance company on terms that the mortgage would be repaid over 40 years. Later the mortgagor wished to redeem the mortgage before that period had expired, but the mortgagee objected. The court held that the term postponing redemption for 40 years was valid. The agreement was a commercial one made by businessmen and the mortgaged property was a fee simple. Due to the great duration of the freehold estate (effectively it is perpetual), the company would recover an estate of equivalent worth when it did redeem the mortgage. The effect of this case is not, however, to make any postponement for a similar period valid. Were a domestic mortgage to be made irredeemable for such a long period, the court might still regard the bargain as oppressive and unconscionable. In fact most modern domestic mortgages expressly allow for early redemption, usually on payment of an extra sum (at least during the early years) to compensate the mortgagee for the production of the necessary paperwork.

(b) *Leasehold cases* Postponement of the date of redemption is rather more serious when one is concerned with a mortgage of leasehold property, for a lease is inherently of finite duration and therefore a wasting asset. In *Fairclough* v *Swan Brewery Co. Ltd* [1912] AC 565 the residue of a leasehold term of 20 years was mortgaged; the agreement being that the mortgage was not to be redeemed until a date six weeks before the lease was to end. Three years later the mortgagor sought to redeem early and the court upheld his right to do so. In this case, had the postponement been valid, the mortgagor would on redemption have recovered an estate which was nearly valueless and very different in character from that which had been mortgaged. In the case of leases, accordingly, postponement of the contractual date for redemption is likely to be rather more objectionable, even where the mortgage is a commercial bargain made between businessmen.

21.6.3.3 *Collateral advantages for the mortgagee*

The final type of clog on the equity of redemption that is commonly encountered is the creation of further advantages for the mortgagee, which are collateral to the mortgage. These are common in certain types of commercial mortgage. Thus, breweries will often advance money on mortgage to the licensees of public houses, provided that the mortgagors agree that they will buy their beer from the mortgagee-brewery (subject to recent amendments of the law allowing 'guest beers', arising from concerns about competition policy), and similar arrangements are made between petrol companies and garage owners (on this see the discussion in relation to similar provisions in leases at 9.2.2.3). Such collateral advantages, if they are not unconscionable, are valid whilst the mortgage continues (*Biggs* v *Hoddinott* [1898] 2 Ch 307). They will not, however, normally endure once the mortgage is redeemed (even if the mortgagor has accepted a term that they shall continue beyond redemption), for otherwise the mortgagor would recover an estate encumbered in a manner that the estate he mortgaged was not (see also *Bradley* v *Carritt* [1903] AC 253). An advantage will not, however, invariably end once the mortgage is redeemed. In *Kreglinger* v *New Patagonia Meat & Cold Storage Co. Ltd* [1914] AC 25 a meat company mortgaged its property to a wool-broker (the mortgage was in the form of a floating charge, a special type of mortgage granted by companies). It was a term of the mortgage that the mortgagor would, for five years, offer its sheepskins (a by-product of its meat business) to the mortgagees for purchase. The mortgage was redeemed after two years but the House of Lords held that the mortgagor was obliged to continue to offer the mortgagees first refusal on the skins for the full five-year period. The option was regarded as being reasonable in its terms (it was for a short period and at the best price) and was to be regarded as a separate agreement not really forming part of the mortgage. It was also, of course, a commercial transaction which had been agreed to by businessmen with 'open eyes'. It seems unlikely that such a collateral advantage could validly continue after redemption of a domestic mortgage.

Collateral advantages may also be held to be invalid, even during the continuance of the mortgage, if they are unconscionable or oppressive. Thus in *Cityland & Property (Holdings) Ltd* v *Dabrah* [1968] Ch 166 an agreement which imposed an extremely high premium, rather than requiring payment of interest, was rewritten by the court. In this case the mortgagor was allowed to redeem on repayment of the loan together with interest at a rate approved by the court. It is not, however, sufficient to show that the terms are unreasonable (certainly in a commercial bargain), even if they are extremely advantageous to the mortgagee. The agreement must be 'unfair and unconscionable' and imposed by the mortgagee 'in a morally reprehensible manner, that is to say, in a way which affects his conscience' (see *Multiservice Bookbinding Ltd* v *Marden* [1979] Ch 84, p. 110 per Browne-Wilkinson J).

The issue is not, however, confined to commercial mortgages and charges. The extension of the range of services provided by lenders has led to concerns that mortgagors may be forced into agreements which require them to use a prospective mortgagee to provide, for example, removal vans or estate agency services. The mortgagor might be told that unless he took such other items from the mortgagee the rate of interest on his mortgage would be higher. This problem was addressed by the Courts and Legal Services Act 1990, ss. 104–7 ('tying-in provisions'). These provisions have never been brought into force, but could be were 'tying-in' to become common. Another approach some mortgagees have adopted is to apply unduly heavy rates of interest imposed if the mortgagor is ever late in making payment. In *Falco Finance Ltd* v *Michael Gough*, a County Court case (see *Solicitor's Journal*, 22 January 1999, p. 72 for details), the terms of the mortgage were that if the mortgagor made any repayment late by even a day, the advertised rate of interest on the mortgage (8.99 per cent) was to rise by a further 5 per cent for the whole of the remainder of the term. The County Court judge struck down the additional 5 per cent provision on two grounds: first, that it was an unfair penalty and unenforceable under the Unfair Terms in Consumer Contracts Regulations 1994; and, secondly, that the additional interest payments required 'grossly contravene ordinary principles of fair dealing' and thus constituted an 'extortionate credit bargain' under the Consumer Credit Act 1974, s. 138. More recently, the Office of Fair Trading has issued guidance to banks and building societies as to the rates of interest that properly can be charged to those who are 'locked into' mortgages (usually by means of high charges made on early repayment of the mortgage).

21.6.4 **Right to grant leases**

Having already granted a lease or sublease (or being in a similar position in the case of a charge by way of legal mortgage), the mortgagor would be unable, on general principles, to grant further leases of the same property which could bind himself and his mortgagee. Any further lease he did create would operate as a lease of the reversion, and would not give the tenant any right to possession of the land which he could assert against the mortgagee. However, this caused difficulty, particularly in the case of large estates, where the mortgagor remained in possession of the land and continued to manage it, needing to grant new leases to, for example, tenant farmers and estate workers. The mortgagor is therefore given a statutory power by LPA 1925, s. 99: where he is still in possession of the land he may create both leases and contracts for leases which will be binding on the mortgagee. Section 99 sets out a number of detailed requirements for the form and content of such leases, but we do not propose to consider them here, for in practice most mortgages will exclude the mortgagor's statutory power of leasing altogether, unless the mortgage is security for a business loan designed to allow the acquisition of a property for the purpose of letting it. This is because, in general, the mortgagee does not want the land to be burdened with a sitting tenant, for this will reduce its value if the mortgagee needs to realise his security (obviously different arrangements are made for the management of large estates and in commercial cases where the plan is to let the property).

The statutory power of leasing will almost certainly be excluded in any domestic mortgage, such as that of the Armstrongs at 1 Trant Way, though mortgagees do sometimes agree to waive this exclusion in the case of approved tenants. Interestingly, in *Citibank International plc* v *Kessler* (1999) EGCS 40 a mortgagor tried to argue that such an exclusion was contrary to Article 48 of the Treaty of Rome as inhibiting the free movement of workers. However, unsurprisingly this claim failed, even in this instance in which a German worker had returned to Germany and could not sell the house in question because it had structural defects that would prevent anyone else obtaining a mortgage on the property.

Should the right to grant leases be excluded, any lease granted will nonetheless bind the mortgagor and tenant (a lease by estoppel) but will be void as regards the mortgagee and his successors (*Iron Trades Employers Insurance Association Ltd* v *Union Land & House Investors Ltd* [1937] Ch 313). In *Starling* v *Lloyds TSB Bank plc* [2000] 2 EGLR 101, a mortgagor tried to argue that, where permission to lease had been sought, the mortgagee should be under a duty to consider that request properly. However, this claim was dealt with robustly by the Court of Appeal, who struck out the cause of action because there was no suggestion in the papers that the mortgagee had acted dishonestly or due to any improper motive. The court regarded as impractical the argument that the bank should, on receiving such a request, indulge in a balancing exercise between the interests of the mortgagor and the bank's interests.

It should be noted that the mortgagor has power under LPA 1925, s. 100, to accept surrenders of leases as well. This may be done, however, only in order to replace the surrendered lease with a fresh lease and the new lease must be made within one month of the termination of the old.

21.6.5 Right to sue

In some cases the rights of the mortgagor to sue in relation to the land might be hampered by the fact that his estate is subject to the rights of the mortgagee. Any such problems are remedied by LPA 1925, s. 98, which allows a mortgagor in possession, who has not been notified that the mortgagee intends to take possession, to sue in a number of situations in which there might otherwise be difficulties. Generally, therefore, the mortgagor is free to bring any necessary action in relation to the land.

21.7 Rights of the mortgagee

21.7.1 Rights to title deeds or charge certificate

Under the pre-1926 type of mortgage the mortgagee necessarily had a right to hold the title deeds to the property, since the grant of the mortgage conveyed the legal estate to the mortgagee. Under the modern system, however, the mortgagee at most has only a lease or sublease and it is not normal for a tenant to hold his landlord's deeds. It is nonetheless desirable for the mortgagee to take the deeds, since this will usually prevent the creation by the mortgagor of later interests in the same property without the knowledge of the mortgagee (see 21.12). Accordingly, ss. 85(1) and 86(1) specifically provide that a first mortgagee has the *right* to take the title deeds from the mortgagor. A mortgagee under a charge by way of legal mortgage is expressly given similar rights (s. 87(1)). In practice all banks and building societies, and any private mortgagee who takes proper advice, will insist on exercising this right. Of course, the mortgagor may well need upon occasion to see the deeds: he may, for example, need to check them to settle a dispute about the boundary line of the property. Accordingly LPA 1925, s. 96(1), gives the mortgagor the right to inspect the deeds and make copies, as long as this is done at a reasonable time and any costs incurred by the mortgagee are paid.

The equitable mortgagee has a similar equitable right to the deeds but, since the most common form of equitable mortgage was that which involved deposit of the deeds, this was rarely a problem.

In the case of registered land a legal charge is created only when the charge is substantively registered. Section 27(2)(f), LRA 2002, provides that the grant of a legal charge is a disposition that is required to be completed by registration. On the application being made, the registrar will enter the chargee in the register as the proprietor of the charge. Before the 2002 Act, such a registration would then have led the registrar to issue a new certificate in relation to the charged estate: a Charge Certificate. This was held by the chargee (rather like holding the title deeds of unregistered land). Now, however, such certificates are no longer issued, though you may still encounter old ones.

21.7.2 **Right to possession of the land**

Since a legal mortgagee has a lease or sublease (or is treated as though he had) he has a right to possession of the land from the moment that the mortgage is created (see *Four-Maids Ltd* v *Dudley Marshall (Properties) Ltd* [1957] Ch 317 at p. 320 and *National Westminster Bank plc* v *Skelton* [1993] 1 WLR 72). This right may well be restricted by a term in the mortgage deed that possession will not be taken whilst the mortgagor makes regular payments (see, e.g., *Birmingham Citizens Permanent Building Society* v *Caunt* [1962] Ch 883).

Usually, the taking of possession is only normal as a preliminary to the remedy of sale and is not otherwise generally exercised. However, at some points in recent years, it became more common for lenders to seek possession of a property in order to let it. This may cause problems for a mortgagor because the interest under the mortgage will continue to mount. In *Palk* v *Mortgage Services Funding plc* [1993] Ch 330, the Court of Appeal said that where sale was preferable in the mortgagor's interests a sale would be ordered instead (see further below on foreclosure for the court's power to order sale). The taking of possession must, in any event, be exercised peaceably (e.g., one may not break into premises) and this may necessitate an application to the court. However, if peaceable re-entry is possible without resort to the court this is perfectly acceptable (see *Ropaigealach* v *Barclays Bank plc* [1999] 1 QB 263). However, it should be noted that the case proceeded on the assumption that the bank had taken possession peaceably but without those facts ever being established. In practice it may be difficult or impossible to regain possession peacefully in the absence of an application to the court. Where it is possible, it will be attractive to the mortgagee because it is a means of avoiding the protection available to the mortgagor when a court order for possession is sought (see 21.8.1.5). See also 10.3.1 for a discussion of potential human rights issues in relation to peaceable re-entry.

21.7.3 Insuring at the mortgagor's expense

Normally, the mortgagee will wish to ensure that the property is properly insured, since should it be damaged the value of the mortgagee's security will be diminished. Accordingly, most mortgages include express terms concerning the maintenance of insurance. If there is no express agreement, LPA 1925, s. 101(1)(ii), implies into every mortgage made by deed a term allowing the mortgagee to insure the property against loss or damage by fire. The premiums paid become a charge on the property in addition to the mortgage advance. The amount of the insurance and the mode of application of any sums arising from the policy are further regulated by LPA 1925, s. 108.

21.7.4 Right to lease

A mortgagee who has taken possession has always had a right to grant leases. These, however, would be subject to the rule that there must be no clog on the equity of redemption and so would not survive redemption by the mortgagor, were it not for the statutory power to lease under LPA 1925, s. 99(1), which gives rights similar to those of the mortgagor described above. Any lease created under the statutory power will also bind the mortgagor. Since possession by the mortgagee was normally only a preliminary to sale, such leases used to be rare but have occurred on occasion in recent years.

21.7.5 Right to tack further advances

This right is relevant only when there is a dispute about priorities, and so we will consider it in the section on priorities (21.16).

21.7.6 Right to consolidate mortgages

This right applies when one mortgagee has vested in him two or more mortgages which were both made by the same mortgagor. This might occur if Henry Harding (2 Trant Way) had already granted a mortgage of, say, his business premises at 15 High Street, Mousehole to the Wensleydale Bank plc. The Bank would have the right to consolidate the two mortgages if, as is normal, this is expressly provided for in the mortgage (LPA 1925, s. 93).

The effect of the right is to allow the mortgagee to refuse to allow the mortgagor to redeem one of the mortgages without also redeeming the other. In the case of Mr Harding's mortgages, this right might prove important to the bank should the value of 15 High Street fall below the sums outstanding on the mortgage of that property. If Mr Harding chose to redeem the mortgage on 2 Trant Way, rather than the mortgage of his business premises, the mortgagee bank would be left with a mortgage for which the security is defective. By consolidating, the Bank can insist that Mr Harding redeems *both* mortgages.

The right to consolidate is an equitable one, and is an unusual example of equity permitting a clog or fetter on the equity of redemption. It may be seen as the 'price' which equity exacts for allowing the mortgagor to redeem the mortgage when he could no longer do so at law. Accordingly, the mortgagee has this right only *after* the contractual date for redemption has passed, when the mortgagor is relying on his equitable right to redeem. If the mortgagor should in fact repay the debt on the contractual date, the mortgagee would not be able to require him to pay off the other debt as well. The doctrine can affect subsequent purchasers if they buy land subject to the mortgage. Thus, if someone bought 2 Trant Way from Mr Harding subject to the mortgage and then sought to redeem it, he or she would find that the bank's right to consolidate still applied, and that the mortgage on 15 High Street would also have to be redeemed. Fortunately, it is extremely rare for estates to change hands without any mortgages first being discharged.

We have tried to give a relatively simple account of the doctrine of consolidation, illustrating it with a situation in which both mortgages are granted to the same mortgagee. This is not in fact an essential requirement: provided the mortgages are granted by the same person it does not matter that they are granted to different people. The rules governing the various different situations which may arise as a result of this are complicated, and beyond the scope of this book, but if you are interested you will find them fully discussed in Megarry and Wade, pp. 1217–23.

21.8 Mortgagees' remedies

The whole purpose of a mortgage is to provide security which the mortgagee can realise if the mortgagor fails to repay the loan. Obviously the mortgagee, like any lender, can always sue in contract for the repayment of the loan, but this may be a long process in which enforcing payment, even once judgment is obtained, can be difficult. The advantage of the mortgage is that it allows the mortgagee to use the charged land to repay the loan, often without the need for any court proceedings at all. At one time the special remedies available to a mortgagee were of such import-ance that it was rare in the extreme for mortgagees to bother to sue for repayment as a simple matter of contract. However, fluctuations in property prices have made it more common, in appropriate cases, for mortgagees simply to seek a money judgment (since in cases of 'negative equity' the price realised by enforcement against the property will not repay the loan in full) or to use this remedy in addition to the special remedies available to a mortgagee. Despite this change, the additional protection provided by the security of a charge on property still makes mortgagees' remedies of crucial importance.

21.8.1 **Remedies available to a legal mortgagee**

21.8.1.1 *Foreclosure*

Foreclosure was the traditional remedy by which a mortgage was enforced. However, today it is rarely used.

Although equity would allow a mortgagor to redeem after the contractual date, there would come a time in many cases when it was obvious that the mortgagor would never have the means to repay the debt. Foreclosure proceedings in equity were therefore the means whereby 'the court simply removed the stop it had itself put on' (*Carter* v *Wake* (1877) 4 ChD 605 at p. 606) and enabled the mortgagee to realise his security. For this reason foreclosure cannot be sought before the contractual obligation to repay has been broken (*Williams* v *Morgan* [1906] 1 Ch 804). A court order is required for foreclosure (*Re Farnol Eades Irvine & Co. Ltd* [1915] 1 Ch 22) and its effect is to vest the mortgagor's estate in the mortgagee in full settlement of the debt (LPA 1925, ss. 88(2) and 89(2)). Should the property be worth more than the debt, the mortgagee is not liable to pay the balance in value to the mortgagor. Since this is normally the case, foreclosure is a remedy which is often unfair to the mortgagor (and to any subsequent mortgagees, who lose their security). Accordingly, on hearing an application for foreclosure, the court will give the mortgagor a period in which he can redeem the mortgage (and will allow later mortgagees the chance to protect their security by redeeming the prior mortgage). Generally, the mortgagor is in financial difficulties and is unable to repay the loan and redeem. Accordingly he is given the right to ask for an order for sale instead of foreclosure (LPA 1925, s. 91(2)). This is an advantage because on sale the mortgagee may keep only the portion of the proceeds that represents the debt, plus interest and costs. The balance must be returned to the mortgagor, or paid to anyone else entitled, such as later mortgagees. Sale may also be appropriate in any case in which it produces a better financial result for the mortgagor (see *Palk* v *Mortgage Services Funding plc* [1993] Ch 330).

Another reason foreclosure is an unpopular remedy (but this time from the mortgagee's point of view) is that even once a foreclosure order has been made the court may reopen the whole situation and allow the mortgagor to redeem the property after all. *Campbell* v *Holyland* (1877) 7 ChD 166 (in which an order for foreclosure was reopened three months after it had been made absolute) sets out the various matters which the court will take into account in considering such an application. These include: the speed of the mortgagor's application; his reasons for failing to redeem before foreclosure; and the nature of the property.

As might be expected, the court would be less willing to reopen foreclosure if the mortgagee had already sold the property to someone else, although even in that case this could, in theory, still be done.

21.8.1.2 *Possession and sale*

We have already discussed the basic rules relating to possession. Generally this right of the mortgagee is only used as a remedy and normally is a prelude to sale. The mortgagee might, however, take possession so that he can repay his debt from the income produced by the premises (e.g., if the premises are let to a tenant). However, in such cases it is more common to appoint a receiver instead so that, as we shall see below, the mortgagee is not personally liable for any mismanagement of the land. The chief purpose of taking possession is therefore to ensure that on a subsequent sale the mortgagee will be in a position to give vacant possession to the purchaser. The power for the mortgagee to sell the land is implied into every mortgage made by deed by LPA 1925, s. 101(1)(i). This power *arises* when the mortgage money has become due (for instance, on the contractual date of redemption) but does not become *exercisable* until one of the conditions prescribed by LPA 1925, s. 103, has been met. These are that:

(a) a notice requiring payment has been served on the mortgagor and the default has continued for three months thereafter; or

(b) some of the interest payable is at least two months in arrear; or

(c) there has been breach of a covenant in the mortgage deed (other than that relating to the payment of money) or of some provision of the LPA 1925.

A purchaser must satisfy himself that there is power to sell under the mortgage (that is, that it was made by deed and that the power has arisen), but he does not have to check that one of the conditions for exercise of the power ((a) to (c) above) has been met (see *Bailey* v *Barnes* [1894] 1 Ch 25 at p. 35).

Sale has the advantage over foreclosure that it is generally not necessary to apply for a court order. The sale may be negotiated in any suitable manner (e.g., by auction or by private contract) and may be made subject to such conditions as the mortgagee sees fit (s. 101(1)(i)). As we shall see, the mortgagee may be liable to the mortgagor, and others, for any loss caused through his negligence in conducting the sale.

However, an order for possession (as a prelude to sale) may be delayed for a time if the court believes that the mortgagor may obtain a higher price if he sells himself. (See *Target Home Loans Ltd* v *Clothier* [1994] 1 All ER 439.)

This possibility was also explored in *Palk* v *Mortgage Services Funding plc* [1993] Ch 330 and in *Barrett* v *Halifax Building Society* (1995) 28 HLR 634, and in these cases the courts seemed to take a generous approach to the use of the power under LPA 1925, s. 91(2) to direct sale of the property 'on such terms as it thinks fit', in order (for example) in the *Barrett* case to enable the mortgagor to carry out the sale himself. The reasoning was that the mortgagor is likely to get a better price for the property than the mortgagee (in practice this is almost inevitably the case). However, this approach was criticised in *Cheltenham & Gloucester plc* v *Krausz* [1997] 1 All ER 21, in which the Court of Appeal said that these powers and those under the Administration of Justice Act 1970, s. 36 (see 21.8.1.5) should not be used unless it is clear that the result will be that the mortgage debt will be repaid in full. Where the mortgagor is still faced by a debt greater than the value of the property (a 'negative equity' in common parlance) the mortgagee will still be entitled to immediate possession and sale. (See also Kenny, 'No Postponement of the Evil Day' [1998] Conv 223.)

When considering the possibility of sale, you should also bear in mind that where the land in question is held under a trust of land (which will be the case in all co-owned property which is not the subject of a SLA 1925 settlement) the mortgagee can also apply for sale under TOLATA 1996, s. 14, because the mortgagee has an interest in the property subject to the trust. For an example of this (in which sale was ordered despite the existence of a pre-existing overriding interest) see *Bank of Baroda* v *Dhillon* [1998] 1 FLR 524. However, in the cases since TOLATA 1996 the courts have expressed differing views as to the weight to be given to the interests of the mortgagee when carrying out the balancing exercise under ss. 14 and 15. See, for example, *Mortgage Corporation* v *Shaire* [2001] Ch 743 and *Bank of Ireland Home Mortgages Ltd* v *Bell* [2001] 2 FLR 809.

It is worth noting when reading these cases that the mortgagee's remedies are cumulative and that, as a last resort, the mortgagee can also sue for repayment of the debt and (if necessary) make the mortgagor bankrupt. Due to the interaction of the various different legal principles and rules, such as s. 36 of the Administration of Justice Act 1970, the effects of TOLATA 1996, the possibility of undue influence (on which see para. 21.17 below) and the law of insolvency (which allows the trustee in bankruptcy to obtain a charge over the bankrupt's home—see s. 313, Insolvency Act 1986 and s. 261, Enterprise Act 2002), the law in this area is complex. A wise mortgagee takes great care before deciding on the exact approach to the issue in any case that is not entirely straightforward and most certainly in any case in which the sale of the property is unlikely to repay all the sums due under the mortgage.

21.8.1.3 *Effect of sale*

On sale, the mortgagee will convey to the purchaser a good estate or interest (for example, the fee simple) free of the interests of the mortgagor and of any estates, interests or rights to which the mortgage has priority, but subject to any estates or interests having priority to the mortgage (LPA 1925, s. 104(1)). Thus, if 1 Trant Way were subject to two mortgages:

(a) to the Double Gloucester Building Society; and

(b) to the Mousehole Bank plc

then on a sale by the DGBS the purchaser would take a title free of the second mortgage to the MB plc, but on a sale by the MB plc the purchaser would take an estate subject to the first mortgage to the DGBS.

It is perhaps worth emphasising that on sale the purchaser obtains the full estate belonging to the mortgagor, not just the long lease or sublease which was granted to the mortgagee (LPA 1925, ss. 88(1) and 89(1)).

21.8.1.4 *Disposition of proceeds of sale*

The selling mortgagee becomes a trustee of the proceeds of sale of the property (LPA 1925, s. 105), and should apply the proceeds in the following order:

(a) in payment of any sums needed to discharge any encumbrance prior to the mortgage and to which the sale was not made subject;

(b) in payment of the costs, charges and expenses properly incurred in arranging the sale;

(c) in discharge of the mortgage debt, including interest and other sums due; and

(d) any balance should be paid to the mortgagor or the other person 'entitled to the mortgage property'.

Thus, in the example given in 21.8.1.3, were the DGBS to sell 1 Trant Way, it would first pay the costs of sale (e.g., legal expenses), and then would pay its own mortgage debt, interest and costs. Thereafter, the balance of the proceeds of sale should be paid to the MB plc, which at the time of sale was next entitled to the property (*British General Insurance Co. Ltd* v *Attorney-General* (1945) 12 LJNCCR 113). The MB plc will in turn become trustee, and after repaying itself, should (if anything remains) pass the balance of the proceeds of sale to the mortgagors.

Should the sale not realise sufficient funds to repay the mortgagee, he may still sue in contract for the balance of the debt (*Rudge* v *Richens* (1873) LR 8 CP 358). Since the property itself may well have been the mortgagor's only valuable asset, it may prove difficult to obtain satisfaction of any judgment but in recent years there have been cases in which mortgagors voluntarily 'handed back' their property to permit sale by the mortgagee but were then sued some years later for sums not recovered on sale. Two recent examples of this are to be found in *Bristol and West* v *Bartlett* [2003] 1 WLR 284 and *Scottish Equitable plc* v *Thompson* [2003] HLR 48, which establish that any such action is subject to a 12-year limitation period.

21.8.1.5 *Protection for the mortgagor*

There are circumstances in which it would be unfair for the mortgagee to be allowed to sell the property. Thus, if the mortgage interest is only a few months in arrears and the mortgagor can show that he will be in a position to pay his debts very shortly it would be undesirable to allow the mortgagee to insist on sale. Accordingly the following means of protection is provided for the mortgagor.

As we have seen, the first step towards sale is for the mortgagee to obtain possession. The mortgagee may not do this by means of any force (e.g., by breaking a window) since this would constitute a criminal offence (Criminal Law Act 1977, ss. 5 and 6). Normally, therefore, an application to the court for possession will have to be made. This in itself will give the mortgagor extra time to pay and the court has inherent jurisdiction to postpone possession, although this power will be exercised sparingly (see *Cheltenham & Gloucester plc* v *Krausz* [1997] 1 All ER 21).

If the land is or includes a dwelling-house, further protection is given to the mortgagee by the Administration of Justice Act 1970, s. 36. Under this provision the court may, on hearing an application for possession, adjourn the proceedings, stay or suspend judgment or postpone the date for delivery of possession, if it appears that 'the mortgagor is likely to be able within a reasonable period to pay any sums due under the mortgage'. This permits the court to give the mortgagor a 'second chance' to pay but will not be exercised where the mortgagor cannot make payments which will clear the debt within a reasonable time (whilst continuing to pay current instalments: see *First National Bank plc* v *Syed* [1991] 2 All ER 250).

As originally drafted, these provisions proved unsatisfactory when dealing with instalment mortgages, in which it is normal to provide that should one instalment be unpaid the whole sum becomes due. If the mortgagor has to pay 'any sums due' in such a case this would include the *whole* advance and few mortgagors could comply with this requirement (see *Birmingham Citizens Permanent Building Society* v *Caunt* [1962] Ch 883). Accordingly, an amendment was introduced by the Administration of Justice Act 1973, s. 8, and now in the case of instalment mortgages the 'sums due' are only those payments which are in arrear and a clause requiring repayment of the whole loan can be disregarded by the court when exercising its discretion under s. 36 of the 1970 Act. The 1973 Act also extends the powers of the court to foreclosure actions even where possession is not also sought: s. 8(3). Note that if peaceable re-entry can be effected without the need for an order for possession (if, for example a dwelling is standing empty), s. 36 does not come into play: *Ropaigealach* v *Barclays Bank plc* [1999] 1 QB 263. The court's powers under s. 36, Administration of Justice Act 1970, are also not available if the mortgagor has voluntarily given up possession but later realises that it would be in his or her best interests to delay sale. This is illustrated by *Barclays Bank plc* v *Alcorn* [2002] All ER (D) 146, in which the court said that in such a case it had no jurisdiction to exercise its discretion under s. 36(2). The case was also one in which, even had the court had powers under s. 36(2) it would not, on the facts, have exercised those powers in favour of the mortgagor because the mortgagor had failed to establish that she would be likely to pay the debts within a reasonable time.

The question of what is a 'reasonable period' to allow the mortgagor is a matter which is determined in the light of the circumstances of each case: see *National and Provincial Building Society* v *Lloyd* [1996] 1 All ER 630. In the case of a domestic instalment mortgage, the Court of Appeal indicated in *Cheltenham and Gloucester Building Society* v *Norgan* [1996] 1 WLR 343 that it would, in assessing what was a reasonable period, be appropriate for a court to take as its starting point the whole of the outstanding term of the mortgage. Indeed that is an arrangement which had often been proposed voluntarily by mortgagees, where arrears were not too great.

At one time it was thought that the mortgagee owed no duty to the mortgagor when exercising the power of sale (other than the duty not to act fraudulently). However, it is now clear that the courts do consider in such cases that the mortgagee is under a duty to 'obtain a proper price'. This is a duty that arises in equity rather than in contract but is analogous to a duty of care in negligence (see *Raja* v *Lloyds TSB Bank plc* (2001) Lloyds Rep Bank 113). For this reason, a mortgagee may elect to appoint a receiver rather than sell himself because then the duty of care will fall on the receiver, provided that the appointment itself is not unreasonable. (See para. 21.10 for more on the duties of receivers and mortgagees.)

21.8.1.6 *Power to appoint a receiver*

A receiver is a person who is appointed to take charge of the mortgaged land and either manage it (in order to produce an income to repay the debt) or sell it. Receivers are not commonly appointed in respect of mortgages of domestic property but are very frequently used in commercial mortgages.

The power to appoint a receiver may be granted expressly by the mortgage but in addition, provided the mortgage is created by deed, the right to appoint will be implied by LPA 1925, s. 101(1)(iii). The power arises and becomes exercisable in exactly the same way as the statutory power of sale.

The receiver is appointed by a written document executed by the mortgagee (LPA 1925, s. 109). The receiver appointed under the power in LPA 1925, s. 101, becomes an agent of the mortgagor (and not of the mortgagee who appointed him) and thus the mortgagee will not be liable for any negligence of the receiver (but see 21.10). Where a receiver obtains income from the land he should apply it in the following order:

(a) in payment of any outgoings in respect of the land (e.g., rates, and instalments on mortgages which have priority to that under which he was appointed);

(b) in payment of insurance premiums in respect of the land and his own commission (fees);

(c) in payment of interest on the loan;

(d) in payment of capital if the mortgagee agrees; and

(e) payment of any balance should be made to the mortgagor (or other person entitled to income).

21.8.2 Problems regarding remedies when the mortgage is equitable

In describing the remedies available to the mortgagee we have, so far, concentrated on the position of the legal mortgagee. It is, however, important to note that in a number of ways an equitable mortgagee may not be in such a strong position. In several instances he may, in the end, obtain the same remedy as a legal mortgagee, but he will often do this only after the trouble and expense of obtaining a court order, whereas the legal mortgagee may make use of such remedies without applying to the court. It must also be remembered that, in any event, remedies given by the court in protection of an equitable mortgagee will always be discretionary in character because of the basic nature of the equitable jurisdiction.

We will now consider each remedy in turn.

21.8.2.1 *Foreclosure*

This causes little difficulty since it requires a court order in any event and being an equitable remedy applies to equitable mortgages just as it does to legal ones.

21.8.2.2 *Possession*

There appears to be no reason why an equitable mortgagee should not be regarded as having a right to possession in equity. It has, however, been said that the equitable mortgagee has no such right (see *Barclays Bank Ltd* v *Bird* [1954] Ch 274 at p. 280). By contrast, other authorities suggest that he may be so entitled (see *Ex parte Bignold* (1834) 4 Deac & Ch 259 and the article by Wade (1955) 71 LQR 204 and the decisions discussed in it).

The weight of academic opinion certainly seems to be that an equitable mortgagee does have the right to possession (see Megarry and Wade, p. 1214).

It should be noted that the issue under discussion here is whether an equitable mortgagee has the right to take possession *without a court order*, for it is certainly possible for him to do so on an order from the court (*Barclays Bank Ltd* v *Bird*). These days, few mortgagees would risk taking possession without a court order, even when they are entitled to do so and so the whole question, although interesting, does seem largely a theoretical one.

Finally, it seems to be the case that a chargee under an equitable charge will have no right to possession, since he cannot be regarded as having a contract for a lease or sublease, as can other equitable mortgagees (*Garfitt* v *Allen* (1887) 37 ChD 48). However, even this might be questioned if the equitable charge is regarded as a contract to create a charge by deed by way of legal mortgage, under which the chargee certainly does have a claim to possession.

21.8.2.3 *Sale*

The statutory power of sale under LPA 1925, s. 101(1)(i), applies only to mortgages made by deed, and therefore an equitable mortgagee will have no automatic power of sale unless he can rely on such a deed. In consequence, an equitable mortgagee normally required execution by the mortgagor of a memorandum under seal evidencing the transaction, which would be sufficient to satisfy the statutory requirements. Today it is likely that such a mortgage will be made by deed (at which point one might as well opt for a legal charge).

Even if the mortgagee has obtained such a deed he may still experience problems, since it has been held that he is not able to convey the legal estate because he has only an equitable interest in the property (*Re Hodson and Howes's Contract* (1887) 35 ChD 668). Although this view may be supported by the principle that no one can give more than he has, the same argument might appear to apply to the legal mortgagee, who has only a lease but is enabled by statute to convey the full estate (LPA 1925, ss. 88(1) and 89(1)). It is difficult to see why the equitable mortgagee, selling in exercise of the statutory power, cannot rely on these provisions in the same way, and in *Re White Rose Cottage* [1965] Ch 940 Lord Denning MR expressed the view that there was no reason why he should not be able to convey the legal estate (at p. 951).

Uncertainty on the point, however, persists and mortgagees continue to avoid any possible trouble by relying on the device traditionally used of inserting in the deed a declaration of trust or a power of attorney.

In the case of an equitable mortgage created without the formality of a deed the mortgagee may still apply to the court for an order for sale under LPA 1925, s. 91(2).

21.8.2.4 *Appointing a receiver*

The statutory power to appoint a receiver under LPA 1925, s. 101(1)(iii), applies only to equitable mortgages which are made by deed. However any equitable mortgagee may apply to the court for the appointment of a receiver (Supreme Court Act 1981, s. 37).

21.8.3 **Disadvantages of equitable mortgages**

From what we have said above, it can be seen that a mortgagee who accepts an equitable mortgage not made by deed may find the remedies available to him less satisfactory than those of a legal mortgagee. To some extent, although not entirely, these disadvantages may be overcome by the use of a deed.

Given the need for a deed to enable the equitable mortgagee to take advantage of the statutory remedies, a lender may regard it as being altogether easier to create a charge by way of legal mortgage (using a deed), and thereby avoid all the problems. In the case of the planned mortgage by deposit of deeds by Mr Neep of 12 Trant Way, his bank manager may well feel, on consideration, that, following the decision in *United Bank of Kuwait plc* v *Sahib* [1997] Ch 107, the best course as far as the bank is concerned will be to insist on taking a legal charge, rather than adopting a more informal method of creating a mortgage: writing will now be necessary to create an equitable mortgage (save perhaps in rare cases based on estoppel) and very little more effort is required to produce a deed. However, now the grant of such a charge will trigger a requirement to register the fee simple: s. 4(1)(g), LRA 2002. Accordingly, Mr Neep may be able to persuade the bank to accept an equitable mortgage made by means of a written contract.

21.9 **Right of certain third parties to redeem**

The mortgagor and the mortgagee are not the only people who may have rights in respect of a mortgage, for others may be entitled to exercise the right to redeem. This arises because *any* person who has a right in the equity of redemption is also allowed to redeem (of course by repaying the sums secured by the mortgage) (*Peace* v *Morris* (1869) LR 5 ·Ch App 227). Thus, if Henry Mumps manages to establish that he has an interest in 6 Trant Way, he will be entitled to redeem any mortgage of the property should he choose to do so. A spouse who has a right to occupy the matrimonial home under the Matrimonial Homes Act 1983 (see further on this para. 24.3.3.1) has also been held to have a sufficient interest in the equity to allow him to redeem under this rule (*Hastings & Thanet Building Society* v *Goddard* [19701] 1 WLR 1544). This rule is expressly recognised in the case of married couples by the Family Law Act 1996, s. 30(3), in favour of a spouse with a right to occupy a dwelling.

A second or later mortgagee is also a person who has an interest in the equity of redemption and he may also claim to redeem a superior mortgage. This reference to 'later' and 'superior' mortgages brings us to the notion of priorities, which we must briefly explain. Where there are several mortgages of the same property, those mortgages are ranked in order, with the mortgagees being entitled to receive the money owed to them according to their place in that ranking. Thus, if the property is not worth the full amount of the debts secured on it, those ranking first take their money in full and those coming later may receive nothing. The rules which determine the order of priorities will be explained later but for the moment it is enough to know that mortgages are ranked in this way.

Where a later mortgagee wishes to redeem an earlier mortgage and this can be arranged by agreement, there is no difficulty. It may be, however, that the earlier mortgagee refuses to accept payment, either because there is a dispute about what is owed or because he is relying on his right to consolidate. In this case, the person wishing to redeem will have to seek a court order, and in doing this will find that he is subject to the rule that he should 'Redeem up and foreclose down'. This is best explained by reference to the following illustration.

Assume that land is subject to mortgages in favour of different lenders, A, B, C, D and E, the mortgages ranking for priority in that order. If D wishes to redeem the mortgage to B by court action, he is obliged to redeem also the intervening mortgage to C (redeem up). He does not have to redeem A's mortgage which simply keeps its priority. He is also required to bring foreclosure proceedings, which will extinguish the rights of E and the mortgagor. This apparently harsh provision comes about because B will be required to account for any payments he has already received and show what is still owed to him. The later mortgagees and the mortgagor are all interested in this, because if D redeems B's mortgage he will take over B's position, and be entitled to recover that amount of money from the value of the property in priority to all those who rank after B. They therefore have to be made parties to the action between D and B, so that they can protect their own interests and be bound by the court's decision about the amount owed to B. However, it was felt to be unreasonable to put all these people to the expense of coming to court simply to watch the proceedings, and therefore the rule developed that, while they were there, their claims on the property must be dealt with as well. Therefore, as well as redeeming B's mortgage, D must take the opportunity to quantify and pay off the debts due to any intervening mortgagees (here, C), and must also take foreclosure proceedings to vest the property in himself, free from the rights of later mortgagees (here E) and the mortgagor. Of course, if E or the mortgagor can pay off the debt owed to D, one or other of them can prevent his foreclosing. If neither of them has the resources to do that, it may be worth their while asking the court to order sale instead of foreclosure in the hope that sale will produce enough money to pay off all the earlier mortgages and still leave enough for E and the mortgagor.

21.10 Liability of mortgagees, receivers and valuers for fraud or negligence

As we have seen, a mortgagee has extensive powers to enter the property and to dispose of it. Alternatively, he will often choose to appoint a receiver to take charge of the property and conduct any disposition. Inevitably, over the years the issue has arisen as to what liability the mortgagee or receiver has to the mortgagor should the property be mismanaged or should the sale price be lower than expected. In some instances, the question of the liability of a valuer employed by the mortgagee or receiver has also arisen and whether a mortgagee or receiver who has innocently relied on a negligent valuation is liable to the mortgagor for any loss. The slump in the property market in the 1990s led to many cases in which sale of a property either did not repay the entire debt or realized far less than the mortgagee had expected. Unsurprisingly therefore, there have been a number of important developments in the law in this area in recent history.

The leading case is now the Court of Appeal decision in *Silven Properties v Royal Bank of Scotland plc* [2004] 1 WLR 997, in which in giving judgment Lightman J summarised nearly all the case-law on this issue. The case involved 34 properties owned by two family property companies, all of which had been charged to the bank to secure extensive borrowing by the companies. In 1996 the total debt was nearly £5 million and the bank in that year appointed receivers in relation to all the properties, which were then sold over an 18-month period. The mortgagors complained that many of the properties were sold at an undervalue, though by the time of the appeal the issue was restricted to complaints in relation to only six of the sales, in relation to which the complaints were that—

(1) in some cases, a far better price would have been obtained had the receivers or mortgagees first obtained planning permission for development (initially permission had been sought but the receivers later decided to sell without waiting for it to be granted); and

(2) in other cases, a better price would have been obtained had possible leases of vacant property been completed before sale.

In some instances the properties were sold by the receivers and in some cases by the mortgagees. Thus, helpfully, in giving judgment the court considered the duties of both. We will now look at each in turn.

21.10.1 **The duties of mortgagees**

21.10.1.1 *Mortgagee can elect not to exercise powers*

In *Silven* Lightman J first restated the basic principle that a mortgagee is under no obligation to exercise any of his powers: 'He is entitled to remain totally passive.' Thus, the mortgagee cannot be forced to take possession or sell, even if the mortgagor would benefit were this to happen.

21.10.1.2 *Mortgagee in possession must take reasonable care of premises*

If, however, the mortgagee chooses to take possession of the property, he becomes its manager and thereby assumes a duty to take reasonable care of the premises: on this see *Downsview Nominees Ltd* v *First City Corporation Ltd (No 1)* [1993] AC 295 at p. 315A. See also the older cases, *White* v *City of London Brewery Co* (1889) 42 ChD 237 and *Hughes* v *Williams* (1806) 12 Ves Jr 493, which show that this concept is far from new.

21.10.1.3 *Mortgagee is not a trustee of his powers*

Second, Lightman J reiterated the time-honoured expression 'A mortgagee is not a trustee of the power of sale for the mortgagor' (which also applies to the mortgagee's other powers). This means that the mortgagee may sell when he chooses and may select the time of sale without regard to whether a different time may be more beneficial to the mortgagor: see *Raja* v *Austin Gray (a firm)* [2002] EWCA Civ 1965 (which also contains a useful summary of the basic rules), *China & South Sea Bank Ltd* v *Tan Soon Gin* [1990] 1 AC 536 and *Tse Kwong Lam* v *Wong Chit Sen* [1983] 1 WLR 1349 at p. 1355B. This principle can be traced back at least as far as *Nash* v *Eads* (1880) 25 Sol J 95 and *Warner* v *Jacob* (1882) 20 ChD 220, but note that these older cases proceeded on the basis that a mortgagee could only be liable for fraud (see also, for example, on the older approach *Davey* v *Durrant* (1857) 1 De G&J 535). In *Silven*, Lightman J. expressly rejected the suggestions made (*obiter dicta*) by Lord Denning MR in *Standard Chartered Bank Ltd* v *Walker* [1982] 1 WLR 1410 at pp. 1415G–H and 1416A that there might nonetheless be some restriction on the mortgagee, who therefore probably could not elect to sell at the worst possible time.

21.10.1.4 *The mortgagee may sell the property as it is*

Third, in relation to the claims that the mortgagees should have taken steps to improve the position before selling, Lightman J said, 'The mortgagee is entitled to sell the mortgaged property as it is. He is under no obligation to improve it or to increase its value.' While accepting that there was a duty to *preserve* the property (see the first point above) the Court of Appeal in *Silven* declined to extend this to a duty to *improve*, whether by obtaining planning permission, granting leases or in any other way. The mortgagee is free to take such steps if he so chooses but is not even obliged to continue with any steps that he has started to take.

You may wonder what protection the mortgagor has. Lightman J indicated that should the mortgagor wish to impose any such obligations on the mortgagee he should do so when entering into the mortgage or charge as part of its terms. This is, save in commercial transactions and perhaps not even there, likely to be impossible because the lender is likely to be in the position of dictating the terms of the agreement to the borrower. Thus, save in rare cases, this possibility is theoretical rather than practical. Lightman J also says that, should he feel himself at risk if the mortgagee exercises his rights, it is open to the mortgagor to redeem the mortgage. Since the issue is only likely to arise in a case in which the mortgagor is already unable to make repayments on the mortgage, this is again an option that is not likely to be a real one.

21.10.1.5 *Duty to obtain market value*

However, the mortgagee is not without any duties because, fourthly, the decision in *Silven* confirms that when he does sell, the mortgagee is under a duty in equity to take reasonable precautions to obtain the 'fair' or 'true market value' or 'proper price' for the property at the date of sale. In the conduct of the sale, the mortgagee must not unduly rush the transaction or sell at a low price that will simply cover the mortgage debt: *Palk* v *Mortgage Services Funding plc* [1993] Ch 330 at pp. 337–8. Lightman J says in *Silven*: 'He must take proper care, whether by fairly and properly exposing the property to the market or otherwise, to obtain the best price reasonably obtainable at the date of sale.'

In the circumstances in *Silven* this would include taking reasonable care to obtain any extra value that would arise as a consequence of drawing the attention of prospective purchasers to the possibility of obtaining planning permission or granting the leases that were under negotiation, but that is the full extent of the duty.

In *Standard Chartered Bank Ltd* v *Walker* Lord Denning MR seemed to suggest that this was a duty in negligence. The same approach was taken in the modern case that really started the concept of the possibility of liability in negligence for certain matters other than choice of time of sale: *Cuckmere Brick Co* v *Mutual Finance Ltd* [1971] Ch 949 at p. 969G. In that case the property had the benefit of one planning permission for houses and a second (an alternative scheme) for flats. Subsequently, there was a problem with meeting mortgage payments and the mortgagee moved to sell. The property was widely advertised but the adverts failed to mention that there was planning permission for flats. The mortgagor asked for the sale to be delayed and better details advertised but the mortgagees went ahead with the sale. The property realised £44,000, although the mortgagor had a valuation saying that with permission for flats it was worth £75,000. When the matter came before the Court of Appeal it was held that, while a mortgagee was not a trustee of the power of sale for the mortgagor and, where there was a conflict of interests, he was entitled to give preference to his own over those of the mortgagor (notably in deciding on the timing of the sale), when exercising the power of sale the mortgagee was not merely under a duty to act in good faith but also to take reasonable care to obtain whatever was the true market value of the mortgaged property at the moment he chose to sell it. This was a clarification of the law at the time and the decisions appears to be based on the concept of liability in negligence, although a curtailed liability due to the nature of the mortgagee's rights. However, the most recent cases have clearly said that this approach is incorrect and the liability is not in tort for negligence but arises from a duty in equity. Thus, the correct remedy is not for damages for negligence but that the mortgagee account to the mortgagor for the sums that would have been raised had the mortgagee complied with his duty. Also, it is a duty owed not just to the mortgagor but also to anyone who has an interest in the equity of redemption. This includes a later mortgagee or indeed a later acquirer of the estate, who takes subject to the mortgage (see *Freeguard* v *Royal Bank of Scotland plc*, *The Times*, 25 April 2002).

21.10.2 **The duties of receivers**

It is normal for a mortgagee to ensure that any receiver who is appointed is appointed as an agent of the mortgagor. This both enables the receiver to manage or sell in the capacity of agent but also avoids the mortgagee becoming liable for any fault on the part of the receiver (unless the mortgagee 'inter-meddles' with the receiver's actions in some way). However, the supposed agency relationship has over the years given rise to a suggestion that the duties of the receiver to the mortgagor may differ from those owed by a mortgagee who elects to act in person. This issue was also discussed in *Silven*, in which it was argued that as agent of the mortgagors the receiver should have acted in their interests when selling.

21.10.2.1 *Duty of receiver same as that of mortgagee when selling*

In *Silven* the Court of Appeal confirmed the long line of cases that establish that a receiver when selling property owes the same equitable duty to obtain the market value as does a mortgagee. On this point see also the Court of Appeal decision in *Medforth* v *Blake* [2000] Ch 86.

21.10.2.2 *Receiver may not be passive*

Since the receiver is appointed to manage or sell, he or she is under a duty not to remain passive, if to do so would be damaging to the mortgagor or anyone else interested in the equity of redemption. The receiver must be active in the protection and preservation of the property.

21.10.2.3 *Otherwise duties are the same as those of a mortgagee*

In *Silven* the Court of Appeal recognised that, while the receiver may, due to the terms of appointment, be an agent, the agency in question is very unusual in form. The main differences are:

(1) the mortgagor does not appoint the receiver and cannot give instructions to or remove the receiver;

(2) there is no contractual relationship and no duty in tort between mortgagor and receiver but only a relationship in equity;

(3) the receiver also owes a duty to the mortgagee and thus the relationship is tripartite;

(4) the duty owed to the mortgagor is in fact a duty to the whole class of persons who have an interest in the equity of redemption;

(5) the receiver's primary responsibility is to produce a situation in which the mortgage debt is repaid, rather than just to manage the property; and

(6) really the receiver is managing the security that is the property of the mortgagee for the mortgagee's benefit (in *Silven* this is regarded as a separate point but really seems to be an element of point (5)).

After reviewing all the case law, and considering a very influential article by the then Peter Millet QC in which he pointed out that the so-called agency was not really a true agency (see *The Conveyancing Powers of Receivers After Liquidation* (1977)

41 Conv (NS) 83 at p. 88), Lightman J concluded that the duties of receivers in respect of the exercise of the power of sale were the same as those of mortgagees. Accordingly, in *Silven* the receivers were not liable for not having obtained planning permission or granted leases prior to sale.

21.10.3 Setting aside sale in cases of fraud

While the remedies of a mortgagor are restricted in cases of negligence, the position is very much better where a sale of property is conducted fraudulently. In such a case the sale can normally be set aside, allowing a further sale to take place in a proper manner: see *Farrar* v *Farrars Ltd* (1888) 40 ChD 395. However, it is frequently difficult to establish fraud and, as we have seen above, a mere sale at an undervalue will not suffice, since it may arise simply due to negligence or the choice of the time of sale. Furthermore, not even the existence of some deception coupled with a sale at an undervalue will necessarily suffice. In *Corbett* v *Halifax Building Society* [2003] 1 WLR 964, a sale to the uncle of an employee of the Society at an undervalue and subsequent sub-sale to the employee, in breach of the terms of his employment, did not suffice to allow the transactions to be set aside. In this case the mortgagor was left to his remedy in damages.

21.10.4 Valuers

One of the ways in which both mortgagees and receivers endeavour to ensure that they comply with the duty to sell for the market value is to ensure that they take an independent valuation of the property before selling. It had been assumed that provided that reliance had been placed in a competent, qualified valuer the receiver or mortgagee would have done all that was necessary. However, the Court of Appeal decision in *Raja* v *Austin Gray (a firm)* [2002] EWCA Civ 1965 demonstrates that this is not the case, essentially because the liability of either receiver or mortgagee is not in the tort of negligence but is an equitable duty. The case also illustrates that the valuer owes no duty of care to the mortgagor.

21.11 Terminating a mortgage

Obviously, apart from a termination by use of one of the remedies set out above, a mortgage normally ends when the mortgagor repays his debt. At that point any estate granted to the mortgagee will terminate automatically (cesser on redemption). However, the mortgagor will require evidence that he has repaid the mortgage sums, so that future purchasers can be assured that the land is free of any encumbrance.

In the case of registered land, the aim will be to remove the registered charge from the register, so that it is clear that the title has been freed of the charge. The procedure in the new system is governed by rr. 114 and 115 of the Land Registration Rules 2003 and the accompanying forms (which include an acknowledgement by the lender that the property is no longer charged as security for the repayment of sums due under the registered charge). The registrar will on receipt of the appropriate documents then exercise his wide power under Sch. 4, para. 5, LRA 2002, to bring the register up to date by removing the entry relating to the registered charge.

In unregistered land the necessary evidence of discharge is provided by asking the mortgagee to execute a memorandum of discharge, which is usually endorsed on the back of the mortgage deed itself.

21.12 **Priorities**

Often, when a person is asked to lend money on the security of a mortgage, or when he later comes to enforce that mortgage, he will discover that there are a number of people who have interests in the property. When Mildred's bank is considering her request for a loan secured by a mortgage of 8 Trant Way, it will have to take into account the claims of: (a) the first mortgagee, the Red Leicester Building Society (see 21.2); (b) Laura Lymeswold's lease/licence (see Chapter 19); and (c) Henry's possible rights arising from contribution (see Chapter 17). The bank will be concerned with these other rights, because it wants to be sure that if Mildred fails to repay the loan it will be able to sell the property (or exercise its other remedies) without any difficulty, and that the proceeds of sale will be sufficient to repay the debt. The bank therefore will need to consider:

(a) The amount of the loan secured by the first mortgage. If the property was sold, and the debt to RLBS discharged first, would there be enough left to repay the bank?

(b) The nature of Laura's interest. If she has a lease, this would decrease the value of the property, because a purchaser is unlikely to pay as much for a house with a sitting tenant as he would for one with vacant possession. If Laura has a licence enforceable against third parties, this would, of course, decrease the value of the property in the same way.

(c) Whether Henry has any rights arising from contribution, such as an irrevocable licence or an interest under a resulting or constructive trust. Either of these might give him a right to remain in the property, which would effectively prevent sale; and if he had an interest under a trust, the bank might find that the mortgage attached only to Mildred's share of the beneficial interest.

The existence of other interests in the property is therefore of considerable importance to mortgagees. The mortgagee needs to know which interests he can largely ignore because they are *postponed* to his rights, and which interests he must take into account because they have *priority* to his mortgage.

The rules on priorities are in the main merely a practical application of the rules on the enforceability of legal and equitable interests against third parties, which we discussed in Chapters 4 and 5. However, these rules often appear rather confusing when applied to mortgages, because there are so many rules and there seem to be so many different situations to consider. In fact, if you can work out which situation is presented by the facts before you, you should find that applying the relevant rule is not too difficult.

21.12.1 **Start with chronological order**

We suggest that when dealing with a question of priorities, you begin by arranging the competing mortgages in chronological order, that is, according to their date of creation. The final order of priorities may be very different from this, but it at least provides a starting-point and a basis from which to apply the rules. Having done that, we think you will find it helpful to ask yourself a series of questions, in a prescribed order, which we work through in the following pages, and which are set out in Figures 21.1–21.4. Figure 21.4 provides a diagrammatic representation of the rules as a whole but you will find greater detail in the separate Figures 21.1–21.3, which contain elements of 21.4.

21.12.2 **Application to other interests**

In what follows, we usually refer to competing *mortgages*, but in general the same principles will apply where questions of priority arise between a mortgage and any other interest (such as that of a purchaser of the fee simple).

21.12.3 **What has been mortgaged?**

Begin by asking yourself:

What is the nature of the property which is subject to the mortgage: is this a mortgage of the legal estate or of an equitable interest (such as a beneficiary's interest under a trust)?

We will deal with mortgages of the equitable interest straight away, because the rules can be stated relatively shortly, and we can then concentrate for the rest of the chapter on mortgages of the legal estate.

21.13 **Priorities of mortgages of an equitable interest**

21.13.1 **Where the equities are equal**

We have already seen that any dealing with an equitable interest must itself be equitable, so we are concerned here only with successive equitable mortgages. Where there is a competition between equitable interests, the general rule is expressed in the maxim: 'Where the equities are equal, the first in time prevails'.

Therefore the interests will rank chronologically, according to the date of creation, provided each mortgagee has, in equity's view, acted fairly in regard to those who come after him.

21.13.2 **The rule in *Dearle* v *Hall***

However, where the property which is mortgaged consists of a beneficial interest under a trust, questions of priorities are regulated by special rules.

Competing assignments of the beneficial interest are regulated by the rule in *Dearle* v *Hall* (1823) 3 Russ 1, as applied to trusts of land by LPA 1925, s. 137. This rule applies to all successive assignments of the beneficial interest, and provides that priority of competing assignments (which include mortgages) depends on the order in which notice of the assignments is received by the trustees. Therefore, in the following situation:

(a) mortgage to A,

(b) mortgage to B,

(c) B gives notice,

(d) A gives notice,

B would normally gain priority over A. However, since one is dealing with the equitable jurisdiction, B is not allowed to gain priority by giving notice first if he knew of the existence of A's mortgage when the second mortgage was created, for to allow this would be patently unfair. Thus, only a second mortgagee without notice can improve his priority under the rule (*Re Holmes* (1885) 29 ChD 786). If B had no notice at the date when his mortgage was created, but learned of A's mortgage before giving notice, B may still obtain priority by giving notice first (*Mutual Life Assurance Society* v *Langley* (1886) 32 ChD 460). It is important to note that the crucial time for the operation of the rule is the date at which the trustee *receives* the notice, rather than the time at which notice is given. Accordingly, a mortgagee who posted a notice through the trustee's letter-box one evening, was held not to have given notice until the following day when the notice was opened and read (*Calisher* v *Forbes* (1871) LR 7 Ch App 109).

When giving notice under *Dearle* v *Hall* the assignee of the equitable interest should take care to give notice to the correct persons. Usually the trustees to be served will be the persons, or person, in whom the legal estate is vested. However, in the case of land which is settled under the SLA 1925, notice should be given to the trustees of the settlement and not to the tenant for life, in whom the estate is vested. Great care should be taken to give notice to *all* the trustees, whatever the type of trust. If this is done, the notice is effective for priority purposes even if later those trustees who received the notice retire, or die in office, and leave their successors without any knowledge of the notice which was given (*Re Wasdale* [1899] 1 Ch 163). However, if, where there are several trustees, notice is given to one only, that notice becomes invalid when that trustee retires or dies, unless that trustee had told the others that he had received notice (*Timson* v *Ramsbottom* (1836) 2 Keen 35, but see also *Ward* v *Duncombe* [1893] AC 369). If giving notice proves unduly difficult or expensive a 'purchaser' (this includes a mortgagee) can require that a memorandum be endorsed on the document which created the trust and under LPA 1925, s. 137(4), this is effective in place of giving notice to the trustees.

LPA 1925, s. 137(3) provides that, 'A notice, otherwise than in writing, . . . shall not affect the priority of competing claims of purchasers in that equitable interest'. The meaning of this provision is not entirely clear: it may mean that all notices for the purpose of *Dearle* v *Hall* must since 1925 be in writing, or it may be that an oral notice is sufficient to maintain an assignee's existing chronological priority, although inadequate to give him priority over an earlier assignee.

Where the subject matter of the trust was registered land, the priority of assignments of the beneficial interest used to depend upon the order in which the assignments were entered in a special index called the Index of Minor Interests (LRA 1925, s. 102(2)). Relatively little use was made of the Index and therefore it was abolished by LRA 1986, s. 5: from that time the rule in *Dearle* v *Hall* has applied to interests in both registered and unregistered land.

The principles for mortgages of an equitable interest are summarised in Figure 21.1.

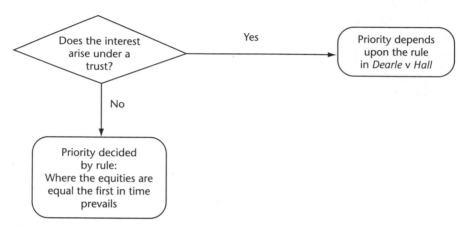

Figure 21.1 Priorities of mortgages of an equitable interest

21.14 Priorities of mortgages of the legal estate

Where it is the legal estate which is subject to the mortgage, one begins by asking:

Is title to the estate registered or unregistered?

21.14.1 Registered title

In the case of registered title, the LRA 2002 has codified and, to some extent, modified the various rules relating to the priority of interests in the land. Whereas the LRA 1925 did not cover all these rules expressly, and some not even impliedly, the new Act provides a comprehensive statement of the rules on priority. The result is a general statement of principle in s. 28, LRA 2002 and the provision of modifications that apply in certain cases, which are listed in ss. 29 and 30. The overall result is, in general, to provide a simplification of the rules.

First, however, you should note the requirement in s. 27(1) and (2)(f), LRA 2002 to complete *legal charges* by registration. The creation of the charge takes effect only in equity until this is done. On registration, the chargee will be entered on the register as proprietor of the charge (Sch. 2, para. 8). This entry is made in the charges section of the register entry for the estate that has been registered. Any *equitable charges* will have to be protected by the entry of a notice in the register: s. 32(1). Any notices entered under the provisions of the LRA 1925 will continue to have effect for the purposes of LRA 2002.

21.14.1.1 *The basic principle*

The effect of s. 28, LRA 2002, is that the priority of competing interests in registered land is determined by the order in which they were created. Thus, the section says that a disposition of the registered estate will not affect the priority of an existing interest in that estate. It further says that it makes no difference for the purpose of the section whether or not the earlier interest or disposition has been registered. To apply this rule to two competing charges one therefore simply asks which was created first and that charge has priority even if it was not registered when the second charge was created.

21.14.1.2 *The exceptions to the basic principle*

However, ss. 29 and 30 provide cases in which the basic s. 28 rule is not to apply and, in practice will mean that the simple 'first created get priority' rule will not apply in a large number of cases. Section 29 is relevant where there is a registrable disposition of a registered estate. Section 30 applies where there is a registrable disposition of a registered charge. Note that you will normally be considering cases under s. 29 because usually you will be concerned with a later disposition made by the owner of the freehold or leasehold estate that is registered. Section 30 only applies in relation to dealings with the charge itself (e.g., a transfer for value of the charge from one lender to another lender) and we will not deal with that issue further.

Section 29 applies where there is a registrable disposition of a registered estate and that disposition is then registered. Where this happens, the rights of any person who has an interest affecting the estate before the registrable disposition is created (the first interest) are postponed to those of the owner of the interest conferred by the registered disposition (the second interest) unless the priority of the first interest had been protected by the time that the second interest is registered. Thus, if an estate owner creates two registrable charges of the land in the order Charge 1 and then Charge 2, the basic rule in s. 28 is that they will rank for priority in the order: (1) Charge 1; and (2) Charge 2. If, however, Charge 1 is not itself registered when Charge 2 is registered, Charge 1 will lose its priority and they will rank in the order: (1) Charge 2; and (2) Charge 1. This is a simple example involving two registrable charges and in such a case the charges each have to be protected by registration in order to maintain priority. However, this is not the only possibility and s. 29(2) lists the ways in which various forms of interest must be protected. It provides:

. . . the priority of an interest is protected—
  (a) in any case, if the interest–
    (i)   is a registered charge or the subject of a notice in the register,
    (ii)   falls within any of the paragraphs of Schedule 3, or
    (iii) appears from the register to be excepted from the effect of registration; and
  (b) in the case of a disposition of a leasehold estate, if the burden of the interest is incident to the estate.

In essence, the effect of this is that in most cases to keep its priority a first interest must be (1) protected by registration where it is a registrable charge (legal charge); or (2) in the case of all other interests must be protected by entry of a notice in the register *unless* it is (3) in the Schedule 3 class of unregistered interests which override (and has not been the subject of a notice—see s. 29(3)).

Thus, in the case of registered title the first question to ask is—

Is the later disposition for value?

If not, the usual rule is that the disposition will not gain priority over any earlier interest. If the disposition is for value, assume that s. 28 applies. Then go on to ask—

Is any earlier interest (1) a registered charge, (2) protected by a notice or (3) listed in Schedule 3 (overriding)?

If the answer is 'Yes', the earlier interest retains its priority. If the answer is 'No', the earlier interest loses its priority to the later interest (s. 29, LRA 2002).

Note that these new rules change significantly the position prior to LRA 2002, under which the priority between two competing equitable interests was determined by the maxim 'Where the equities are equal, the first in time prevails'.

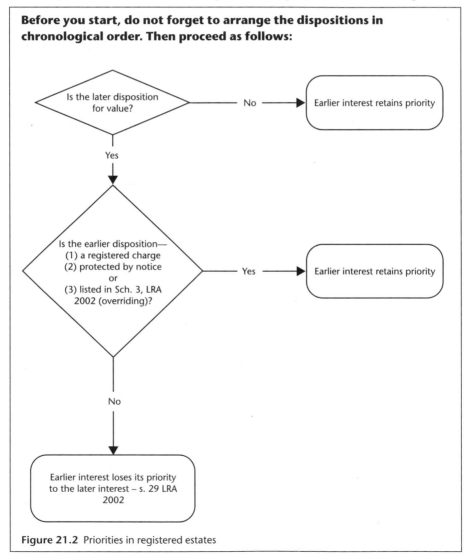

Before you start, do not forget to arrange the dispositions in chronological order. Then proceed as follows:

Is the later disposition for value? — No → Earlier interest retains priority

Yes

Is the earlier disposition—
(1) a registered charge
(2) protected by notice
or
(3) listed in Sch. 3, LRA 2002 (overriding)? — Yes → Earlier interest retains priority

No

Earlier interest loses its priority to the later interest – s. 29 LRA 2002

Figure 21.2 Priorities in registered estates

Under that rule, there were instances in which the circumstances (particularly the conduct of one of the parties) could disrupt the order of priority. Under s. 28, even between competing equitable interests, time of creation is all that matters and ss. 29 or 30 cannot change the priority. In addition, the complexities in unregistered land in relation to any equitable right arising from estoppel or any 'mere equity' is removed by s. 116, LRA 2002, which treats both as interests capable of binding successors in title.

This approach is designed to produce an admirable simplicity in the rules on priorities in registered land. However, it will be interesting to see how the rules are interpreted by the courts. One also needs to consider the extent to which the impact of these rules is changed by other areas of law: see in particular the material below on undue influence (para. 21.17.2).

21.14.2 Unregistered title

The first question to ask in the case of unregistered title is:

Does the mortgagee hold the title deeds to the property?

Taking the title deeds is a standard precaution to prevent the mortgagor from making further dispositions of the property, and has the effect of ensuring that anyone dealing with the mortgagor is alerted to the fact that the land is already encumbered. Although cases could be imagined in which a fraudulent mortgagor could divide his title deeds in such a way as to be able to give a convincing set of deeds to more than one mortgagee, the general position will be that only one mortgagee can take the deeds, and that any other mortgagee will not have that protection.

21.14.2.1 *Position where the mortgagee does not hold the title deeds*

If the mortgagee does not take the title deeds when the mortgage is created, his mortgage is a registrable land charge. Such a mortgage, if legal, is known as a 'puisne mortgage' and should be registered as a class C(i) land charge, while if it is equitable, it is a general equitable charge and registrable in class C(iii) (LCA 1972, s. 2(4)(i) and (iii)). Registration constitutes actual notice (LPA 1925, s. 198) and so all later mortgagees, whether legal or equitable, will take subject to a mortgage which is protected in this way.

What happens if a registrable land charge is not registered? You will remember that some classes of land charge, if unregistered, are void only against the purchaser of the legal estate, while others are void against the purchaser of any interest (legal or equitable) in the land. Class C(i) and (iii) land charges, with which we are concerned here, fall into the second category, and thus any later mortgagee, whether legal or equitable, will take free of an earlier unregistered mortgage, or, in other words, will gain priority over it.

The basic position we have just described is quite straightforward, but there are two possible problems associated with it of which you should be aware:

(a) *Later return of deeds*   Writers have asked what would happen if a mortgagee took the title deeds at the creation of the mortgage, which was therefore not a registrable land charge, but later returned them to the mortgagor. Does the mortgage then become registrable? The general view seems to be that it does not become registrable. This is based partly on considerations of convenience (for otherwise the mortgage would fluctuate between being registrable or non-registrable as the title deeds moved backwards and forwards between the parties), but also derives support from the wording of the relevant sections. These refer to a '*deposit*' of deeds, the rather than to a 'retention', and so it is thought that an initial deposit of deeds is sufficient to make the mortgage unregistrable for the rest of its life (see further, Megarry (1940) 7 CLJ 243).

(b) *Two or more registrable charges* The second problem could arise only where there is more than one mortgage which is not protected by a deposit of deeds, and consequently there are two or more registrable land charges. In such a case, a conflict could arise between two statutory provisions: LCA 1972, s. 4(5) and LPA 1925, s. 97.

In general, there will probably be no difficulty about the operation of these two provisions. If the first mortgage is not registered, the second mortgagee will take free of it, and if he then registers his own mortgage as a land charge no complications can arise. There may, however, be a conflict between the two provisions if transactions occur in the following order:

    (i)   registrable mortgage A created;

    (ii) registrable mortgage B created;

    (iii) mortgage A registered; and

    (iv) mortgage B registered.

According to LCA 1972, s. 4(5), B should take priority, because A was not registered when B was created. However, if you apply LPA 1925, s. 97, then A should take priority because it was registered as a land charge before B was registered.

Many have suggested solutions to this problem (see, for example, Megarry (1940) 7 CLJ 243 at p. 255; Hargreaves (1950) 13 MLR 533 at p. 534; Sir Robert Megarry and H. W. R. Wade, *The Law of Real Property*, 5th edn., pp. 999–1001; and note that the earlier articles refer to LCA 1925, s. 13, which was in exactly the same terms as the present provision in the 1972 Act). Some writers favour the provisions of the LCA 1925, others support LPA 1925, s. 97. A third approach suggests that there is really no conflict between the two sections: s. 97 is seen as a signpost, pointing on to the LCA 1925 and saying, in general terms, that the priority of these mortgages shall depend upon the detailed provisions of that Act.

The point is a fascinating academic conundrum, on which each reader may form his or her own views. It is, however, perhaps worthy of note that there has been no reported decision on the point in the 77 years since the two conflicting provisions were first enacted.

21.14.2.2 *Position where the mortgagee does hold the title deeds*

In this case, one needs to begin by asking:

Is the mortgage legal or equitable?

(1) *Legal mortgages* In general, the legal mortgagee with the title deeds can rely on the basic principle that legal rights bind the whole world. This means that anyone who later acquires an estate or interest in the land will take it subject to an earlier legal right. This is so even if the later purchaser did not know of, or could not discover, the existence of that right, although in the case of a mortgage he or

she will usually be forewarned by the fact that the mortgagor cannot produce his title deeds. Thus a legal mortgage will take priority over all mortgages, legal or equitable, which are created after it, *unless the first legal mortgagee acts in such a way as to lose the natural priority*.

Loss of legal mortgage's natural priority due to mortgagee's fraud, misrepresentation or gross negligence

(a) *Fraud.* If a mortgagee colludes with the mortgagor in some kind of fraud on a later acquirer, it would be manifestly unjust to allow him later to depend upon the natural priority of his own mortgage. Neither law nor equity will assist a cheat, and in such a case the fraudulent mortgagee will lose his priority to the person whom he has deceived. In this way even a legal mortgage can be postponed to a later equitable interest (*Peter* v *Russel* (1716) 1 Eq Cas Abr 321).

(b) *Misrepresentation.* Similarly, a mortgagee who enables the mortgagor to make some false representation to a later purchaser will be prevented from claiming a priority which conflicts with the representation made. Thus allowing the mortgagor to recover the deeds (or, before 1926, to retain them) in order to create a later mortgage is regarded as holding the mortgagor out as being able to mortgage the property. In such a case, the second mortgagee will get priority if he did not know of the first mortgage, and thus even an equitable mortgagee may take priority over an earlier legal mortgage. In *Perry Herrick* v *Attwood* (1857) 2 De G & J 21, the legal mortgagees left the title deeds in the hands of the mortgagor, so that he could raise a further loan of a prescribed amount, secured by a mortgage which, it was agreed, should take priority over the earlier mortgage. In fact, the mortgagor then created two further mortgages, for a greater amount than was intended, and it was held that in these circumstances the first legal mortgagees lost their priority to both later mortgagees.

(c) *Gross negligence.* The suggestion that it is possible to lose one's priority due to gross negligence in the protection of one's own interests causes rather more difficulties.

In *Northern Counties of England Fire Insurance Co.* v *Whipp* (1884) 26 ChD 482 a mortgagee company, which allowed the mortgagor access to a safe in which his deeds were stored, was held not to have lost its priority when the mortgagor recovered the deeds and created a second mortgage. Oddly, the court held the first mortgagee's action to be merely careless, and said that priority could only be lost in a case of gross negligence. In *Walker* v *Linom* [1907] 2 Ch 104, a purchaser of the legal estate, who asked for the title deeds but failed to check that all had been delivered to him, was held to take the land subject to a later equitable mortgage. It may be that the purchaser in this case was regarded as having been grossly negligent because he was a solicitor and accordingly should have been aware of the need to check the deeds carefully. A contrary decision was reached in *Cottey* v *National Provincial Bank of England Ltd* (1904) 20 TLR 607. However, also see *Hunt* v *Elmes* (1860) 2 De G F & J 578, where a solicitor mortgaged two properties, A and B, to a client. The client-mortgagee received a parcel bearing a label which stated that the deeds of both properties were enclosed. In fact the deeds of property B were missing, and the solicitor later sold that property to a third party. In this case the mortgagee was held not to have lost his natural priority because he was entitled to rely on the solicitor mortgagor. It was accepted that the mortgagee had been imprudent, but not so imprudent as to lose his priority.

(2) *Equitable mortgages*   In the case of an equitable mortgage with deposit of title deeds, the first question to ask is:

What is the nature of the later competing mortgage—legal or equitable?

(a) *Position where the competing mortgage is legal.*   This situation, of an earlier equitable mortgage and a later legal one, would seem likely to turn on a straight-forward application of the doctrine of notice. If the purchaser for value of a legal estate has actual or constructive notice of an earlier equitable interest (that is, knows or ought to know of it) he will be bound by it, whereas if he does not have that notice he will take free of the interest. Here, the later mortgagee is a 'purchaser for value of the legal estate' (*Brace* v *Duchess of Marlborough* (1728) 2 P Wms 491), and one would expect that the mortgagor's inability to produce the title deeds would give the later mortgagee actual or constructive notice of the earlier equitable mortgage which is protected by deposit of those deeds.

There are, however, a number of decisions which do not deal with the matter in these terms, but are instead concerned with whether the legal mortgagee has been so *negligent* in investigating title that he should be postponed to the earlier equitable mortgagee. Thus, in *Hudston* v *Viney* [1921] 1 Ch 98, in which a legal mortgagee did not investigate the mortgagor's title for the full statutory period and therefore failed to discover an earlier equitable mortgage, Eve J said that something more than mere carelessness was necessary to make the legal purchaser subject to the equitable interest:

[I]t must at least be carelessness of so aggravated a nature as to amount to the neglect of precautions which the ordinarily reasonable man would have observed and to indicate an attitude of mental indifference to obvious risks.

Several cases in which the decision is based on negligence rather than notice are concerned with the situation in which the legal purchaser has asked for the title deeds and has been given some excuse by the owner for their non-production. In *Oliver* v *Hinton* [1899] 2 Ch 264, a purchaser who accepted the excuse that the deeds related also to other property was held to be guilty of gross negligence, and post-poned to an earlier mortgagee, Lindley MR specifically saying: 'I do not base my judgment upon constructive notice of the charge' (at p. 273). In *Hewitt* v *Loosemore* (1851) 9 Hare 449, however, a mortgagee who accepted the rather weak excuse that the mortgagor was busy and would produce the deeds at a more convenient time, was allowed to take free of an earlier equitable mortgage; the court saying that a legal mortgagee was not to be postponed to an earlier equitable one 'unless there be fraud or gross or wilful negligence on his part' (at p. 590). This decision may, however, have been affected by the fact that the mortgagor was a solicitor, whilst the mort-gagee was a farmer and the mortgagor's cousin. A later acquirer was also protected in *Agra Bank Ltd* v *Barry* (1874) LR 7 HL 135, when he accepted the excuse that the deeds were in Ireland, which, since the land was in Ireland, may well have appeared reasonable, at least in the context of gross negligence. One cannot help but feel, though, that these excuses should have put the legal mortgagees on their guard and they might well have been deemed to have had constructive notice, had the courts been employing the doctrine of notice rather than the concept of negligence.

It was for this reason that we mentioned earlier, when comparing the position of legal and equitable mortgagees, that the equitable mortgagee might also find himself at a disadvantage on questions of priority. In the days before 1926, when these cases were decided, there was nothing more that equitable mortgagees could do to protect themselves. Today, however, they might perhaps be better advised not to take the title deeds, for without them they have a registrable land charge, registration of which gives actual notice to all later purchasers.

(b) *Position where the competing mortgage is equitable.* Here there will be two competing equitable mortgages, and accordingly the principle we have already mentioned will apply: where the equities are equal, the first in time prevails. Thus, equitable mortgages rank for priority in chronological order, unless the earlier mortgagee loses his priority through fraud, misrepresentation or negligence in failing to retain the title deeds. The general principles involved are very similar to those discussed in connection with the postponement of a legal mortgage, although there have been suggestions that an equitable mortgagee will be postponed by a lesser degree of negligence than is needed in the case of a legal mortgagee. However, we know of no decision in which an equitable mortgagee has been postponed for anything less than gross negligence, and in *Taylor* v *Russell* [1891] 1 Ch 8 the court expressed the view that the same standard should apply to both.

The rules relating to mortgages of unregistered land are shown in Figure 21.3.

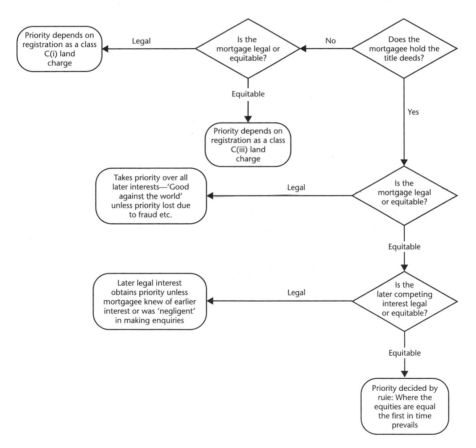

Figure 21.3 Priorities of mortgages of legal estate—unregistered land

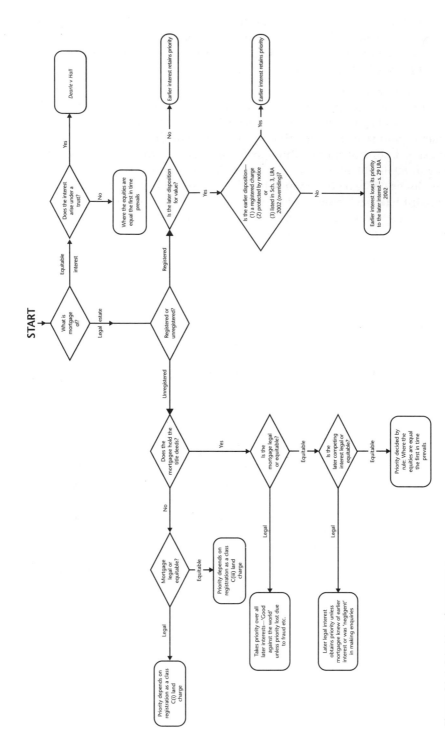

Figure 21.4 Priorities of mortgages

21.15 **Priorities of three or more mortgages**

So far, we have described the rules about priorities as though we were concerned only with a competition between two mortgages. It is, however, possible to have three or more mortgages of the same estate, and you may therefore have to deal with questions of priorities in such a situation. We suggest that you should continue to apply the approach adopted so far: begin by listing the mortgages according to their date of creation, and then consider the earliest one in relation to each successive mortgage. When you have done this, take the next one to be created, and consider it in relation to each one that follows it. If you proceed in this way, considering each pair separately, you will often find that at the end you can list all the mortgages in order of priority.

21.15.1 **A simple example**

Take, for example, three mortgages of a legal estate, title to which is not registered, which have been created in the following order:

(a) legal mortgage to A, who takes the title deeds;

(b) legal charge to B, who registers a class C(i) land charge; and

(c) equitable mortgage to C.

Now compare the mortgages in pairs:

(a) *A and B*. A has a mortgage protected by deposit of title deeds, which is therefore not a registrable land charge. He has a legal mortgage, so his right is good against the world, and there is no suggestion of any conduct on his part which would deprive him of his priority.

Result: A before B.

(b) *A and* C. The position is exactly the same as in the case of A and B.
Result: A before C.

(c) *B and C*. B has a legal mortgage not protected by deposit of title deeds. It is therefore a registrable class C(i) land charge, and having been registered as such will bind all those who take a later interest in the property including C.
Result: B before C.

On this occasion, then, this method of approaching the problem produces a clear and simple set of answers:

A before B
A before C
B before C

and the mortgages can be sorted into a neat straight line of priority:

A first
B second
C third

In registered land it should normally be possible to 'sort' charges in a fairly straight-forward manner. However, there has historically been a more complex possibility in relation to unregistered land.

21.15.2 A more complex possibility

It is possible to think of cases in which the order of priorities does not resolve itself so readily. For example, after applying the priorities rules to a set of mortgages in pairs (as shown above) you might theoretically come up with the following order of priorities, which produces a circle:

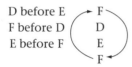

D before E
F before D
E before F

   How you break into this circle is unclear, because the point has never come before the courts. Two possible solutions are: (a) that all the mortgagees should bear an equal loss (for there is only a problem if the value of the property is less than the sums outstanding on all three mortgages), or (b) that the mortgages should rank in the order in which they were created. Some authorities have suggested applying the rules of subrogation, but this produces a manifestly unfair result. (See Megarry and Wade, p. 1275, and Gilmore (1961) 71 Yale LJ 53.) Happily, the circular priority problem is now rarely likely to arise in practice, because, as we have seen above, a mortgage supported by deposit of title deeds will trigger a need for first registration of title. Thus, this possibility, though interesting is very unlikely to occur in future.

21.15.3 Is that the end of the matter?

Once one has sorted out priorities according to the rules given above, that is not however the end of the matter because there remain rules which cause the standard pattern of priorities to be disrupted (such as the rules relating to undue influence). We deal with a number of these issues at the end of this chapter, when we look at the position of Henry Mumps in more detail (see para. 21.17).

21.16 Mortgagee's right to tack further advances

As we have seen, 8 Trant Way is already subject to a first mortgage to the Red Leicester Building Society (RLBS), and a second mortgage may soon be created in favour of the Royal Windsor Bank (RWB). At some later date, after the creation of the second mortgage, Mildred, the owner of No. 8, might return to the RLBS and ask whether it would extend her mortgage to cover an additional advance. If the building society considers doing this, it will wish to know whether the fresh advance is effectively a third mortgage, ranking for priority after the RWB's mortgage, or whether it can 'tack' (add on) this further advance to the first mortgage, so as to gain priority for the later advance.

Again, the need to tack further advances will often arise where a mortgage has been given to a bank to secure the mortgagor's overdraft. As each cheque is presented for payment, the bank makes a further loan to the mortgagor, but it is obviously desirable, from the bank's point of view, that all these loans should rank for priority with the original mortgage.

The circumstances in which further advances may be tacked are governed by different statutory provisions in the case of registered and unregistered title.

21.16.1 **Registered title**

Under the LRA 2002, the rules on tacking in relation to registered land changed. LRA 2002, s. 49 provides that the proprietor of a registered charge may make a further advance that ranks in priority to any later charge, if he has not received notice of the subsequent charge from the subsequent chargee. This places the onus on a new chargee to give notice to any earlier chargee of the creation of the new charge. A further advance may also be made with priority over *any* later charges if the advance is made in pursuance of an obligation and that obligation has been entered on the register (s. 49(3)), or if the parties to the earlier charge have agreed a maximum for which the charge is security and that agreement is entered on the register (s. 49(4)). Section 49(4) is an entirely new provision but you should note that rules may be made to make certain variations to the position under s. 49(4): see 49(5). However, this power has not yet been used. In any other case, it is only possible to take and gain priority if the chargee of the later charge agrees: s. 49(6).

21.16.2 **Unregistered title**

The rule is that under LPA 1925, s. 94, a mortgagee has the right to tack further advances in three situations:

(1) Where all the subsequent mortgagees agree. This is unlikely to happen.

(2) Where the mortgagee seeking to tack did not have notice of the existence of the subsequent mortgage at the date at which the further advance was made.

It may be thought that this second category would be of little use to the earlier mortgagee if the later mortgage was registered as a land charge, since registration constitutes notice. However, under s. 94(2), the first mortgagee is not deemed to have notice of the second mortgage merely because it has been registered as a land charge, provided that:

(i) the first mortgage was expressly made for the purpose of securing further advances; and

(ii) the second mortgage was not registered at the date when the first mortgage was created or when the first mortgagee last searched the register, whichever is the later.

Therefore, if a later mortgagee wants to prevent tacking in these circumstances, he must give express notice of his position to the earlier mortgagee.

(3) Where the first mortgage obliges the mortgagee to make further advances. Here he may tack even if he has notice of the later mortgage. Thus, should a mortgagee agree to finance the building of a new estate, it might be agreed

that the advance should be paid in stages as each house is finished. In such a case the mortgagee can tack the separate loans together, even if he has knowledge of a later mortgage.

21.17 Interests prior to the mortgage: a cause for concern to the mortgagee

21.17.1 8 Trant Way

Finally, before we leave mortgages, we need to look again at the position at 8 Trant Way. Mildred is seeking a loan from the Royal Windsor Bank (RWB) on the security of a second mortgage of No. 8, and the bank will need to consider the extent to which it will be bound by the existing interests in the property. The title is unregistered.

The RWB must first consider the earlier legal mortgage to the Red Leicester Building Society (RLBS). If the RLBS has the deeds (as is normal) and has not done anything to forfeit its natural priority, it will take priority over any second mortgage to the RWB. Should the RLBS not have the deeds, its mortgage still takes priority if it is registered as a class C(i) land charge. If it does not have the deeds, and its mortgage is not registered when the second mortgage is created, the second mortgagee will gain priority, even if the RWB knew of the earlier mortgage (*Midland Bank Trust Co. Ltd* v *Green* [1981] AC 513). Accordingly, before making any advance, the RWB should check the situation with regard to the RLBS mortgage. Thereafter, it will need to have 8 Trant Way valued, and should ensure that it does not lend more than the balance of the value after deduction of the sums due to the RLBS.

The RWB needs also to consider the situation of Laura Lymeswold, who has a licence or lease of 8A Trant Way (see Chapter 19). If she has a lease (as is very possible after *Street* v *Mountford* [1985] AC 809), the RWB will take a mortgage *subject to* the pre-existing legal estate vested in her. It should ensure that its valuation takes account of the existence of a sitting tenant. Should Laura have only a licence, it appears that it will not bind the bank (and a later purchaser on sale by the mortgagee) for the licence would be contractual: see *Ashburn Anstalt* v *Arnold* [1989] Ch 1 (overruled in *Prudential Assurance Co. Ltd* v *London Residuary Body* [1992] 2 AC 386, but no criticism was made of the analysis of the position relating to licences).

The greatest problem for the RWB would be the uncertain position of Henry Mumps. If Henry were to have an equitable interest in the property due to his contribution, this will bind the RWB, unless the bank could claim to be a bona fide purchaser for value of a legal estate without notice. Since Henry is in occupation of the premises the bank would be likely to have notice under the rule in *Hunt* v *Luck* (see Chapter 4). (For the position if the title to No. 8 were registered, see *Williams & Glyn's Bank Ltd* v *Boland* [1981] AC 487, and note the overriding interest which Henry might seek to rely on pursuant to LRA 2002, Sch. 3, para. 2.) The existence of such a binding interest would mean that the bank's mortgage would attach only to Mildred's interest in the property and not to Henry's share. Thereafter, since as an equitable co-owner Henry would have a right to reside in the property until sale

(TOLATA 1996, s. 12) and as the mortgage would not affect his interest, Henry might be able to prevent the second mortgagee selling the property (see *Williams & Glyn's Bank Ltd* v *Boland*). This would prevent realisation even of the partial security with which the bank would be left. However, note the decisions in *Bank of Baroda* v *Dhillon* [1998] 1 FLR 524 and *Bank of Ireland Home Mortgages Ltd* v *Bell* [2001] 2 FLR 809 which demonstrate that, even where an overriding interest does exist, it may be possible to obtain an order for sale of property held on trust (in the earlier case under LPA 1925, s. 30 but in the latter under TOLATA 1996, s. 14). The possibility of such interests arising has accordingly created a minefield for the building societies and banks. One solution to the problem would be for Mildred to appoint another trustee to join with her in receiving the mortgage money, so that Henry's interest would be overreached and attach only to the mortgage advance (*City of London Building Society* v *Flegg* [1988] AC 54) and, where no capital moneys (mortgage advance) arise, see also *State Bank of India* v *Sood* [1997] Ch 276). Note that any mortgage granted will *not* trigger registration of the title because it will not be a first legal charge: s. 4, LRA 2002.

21.17.2 Undue influence

Of recent years, the professional mortgagees (e.g., building societies and banks) have been increasingly concerned about the position of people such as the mortgagor's family and friends, who occupy the property with him at the date of the mortgage and may have rights to the property which can be enforced against the mortgagee. Accordingly the practice has grown up of asking a spouse or anyone else the mortgagee identifies as being resident in the premises to sign a document postponing his or her rights to those of the mortgagee. Also, where there are co-owners the mortgagee will have to seek the signatures of all involved (typically a husband and a wife or a couple who are living together). However, in recent years, those who have signed in this way only later to discover that a loan was being used for a purpose they had not anticipated (for example, to invest in a business rather than for home improvements), or where later there has been a default on the mortgage, have often sought to argue that they are not bound by the mortgage *despite* having signed the mortgage or some document acknowledging the mortgagee's priority.

The basis on which such claims are made is the equitable concept known as 'undue influence'. This is not a rule which is specific to land law but is a general principle that arose as part of the equitable jurisdiction to see that there was fair play between the parties. Accordingly, it might more properly be regarded as being better dealt with in a text on equity and trusts rather than land law. However, in recent years its importance in the law of mortgages particularly (and in relation to some other interests in land) has become so considerable that we think that it is appropriate to give some explanation here of the operation of the equitable principles. In addition, this area of law provides an interesting example of the inter-action between various aspects of land law and equitable principles, in that it is necessary first to establish what rights (if any) parties have in relation to the land in question, then to determine the normal order of priorities and then to decide whether that normal order is in some way disrupted by the application of the equitable principles relating to undue influence (and, as we see below, the extent to which the various parties to a transaction are implicated in any undue influence that may have gone on).

This equitable concept grew up in order to supplement the common law defence of duress, which originally was restricted to quite extreme cases (such as where a signature was obtained only by threat of serious personal violence). The basic idea behind the doctrine of undue influence is that a person should not be held to a transaction if he has been induced to enter into that transaction due to the exercise of power over him by someone with whom he had a relationship of confidence or trust. Traditionally, this doctrine has often been brought into play when a husband persuaded his wife to enter into a transaction which was to the benefit of the husband but not of the wife. This is, however, far from being the only situation in which this issue arises and it could be relevant in some instances in the case of an unmarried couple like the Mumps. Another example may be where an elderly person is persuaded to a transaction by relatives upon whom he is dependant. In *Langton* v *Langton* (1995) *The Times*, 24 February 1995, the transfer of his estate in his home made by a man of 80, who had recently had two serious operations, to his son and daughter-in-law who had lived with him was set aside on the basis of undue influence. The case is somewhat unusual because an extra factor that had led to the transfer was that the son had earlier served 13 years in prison for the murder of his mother and had only recently been reconciled with his father, following the son's release from prison. The circumstances taken as a whole were regarded as such as to place the son and daughter-in-law in a position in which they had an unusual sway over the decisions of the father.

21.17.3 When does undue influence arise?

In the case of *Allcard* v *Skinner* (1887) 36 ChD 145, Lindley LJ indicated that there were two key elements to undue influence: these were a relationship of trust and some evidence of abuse of that trust. Thus, he indicated that, in the case of a gift, the mere evidence of a gift between the parties would not be enough, there must be something in the facts to suggest that the gift could not be accounted for as an act of friendship or according to some other ordinary motive. In *Allcard*, the gift was of nearly all the property of a nun and it was made to her Mother Superior. The court viewed this relationship and the nature of the gift as in themselves suggestive of undue influence.

In modern times the catalyst for an outburst of undue influence cases was *Barclays Bank* v *O'Brien* [1994] 1 AC 180. The facts involve the fairly typical situation in which the O'Brien's matrimonial home was in joint names but Mr O'Brien wanted to use the property as security for an overdraft facility for his business. Mrs O'Brien attended the bank's premises and signed the needed paperwork but subsequently, when the mortgage repayments were not being met and the bank wished to enforce its security, claimed that the mortgage was not binding upon her interest in the property because she had been induced to sign the paperwork either as a consequence of undue influence or misrepresentation and the bank had actual or constructive notice of the position. In fact the case was decided upon the basis of misrepresentation but in it Lord Browne-Wilkinson set out in detail the rules that he regarded as relevant to undue influence. He also categorised types of undue influence into classes:

Class 1—cases of actual undue influence

Class 2—cases of presumed undue influence, which he sub-divided further into:

Class 2(A)—cases in which the relationship between the parties was such that the presumption of undue influence was raised as a matter of law (such as the doctor–patient relationship);

Class 2(B)—cases in which undue influence was presumed if the complainant established that there was a relationship existed under which the complainant usually reposed trust and confidence in the other party (cases such as husband and wife fell into this category).

This categorisation has been subsequently heavily criticised but you will need to note the concepts because many of the cases refer to the Lord Browne-Wilkinson's classes at length and because they may still be of importance at least in part. However, for some time the case-law developed by means of piling refinement upon refinement upon this class structure. A notable example of this tendency is to be found in *Bank of Credit and Commerce International SA* v *Aboody* [1990] 1 QB 923.

Following *Barclays Bank plc* v *O'Brien* there was a considerable increase in the number of cases in which wives, unmarried partners, children and others in situations of confidence sought to argue that they had signed away their rights under the influence of another. Over a relatively short time, there were a number of cases in which the courts attempted to apply the principles laid down in *O'Brien*. Unfortunately, however, those decisions did not always seem consistent and it was clear that there remained confusion about the law on this issue. This led to the major step of the House of Lords hearing, as conjoined appeals, a total of eight cases in which undue influence had been alleged and seeking to establish some clear principles for the future. These landmark decisions will form the basis of this area of law for the future: see *Royal Bank of Scotland* v *Etridge* (and conjoined cases) [2002] 2 AC 773. At paragraphs 34–37 Lord Bingham of Cornhill stated the essence of the modern problem that gave rise to these cases:

34. The problem considered in *O'Brien*'s case and raised by the present appeals is of comparatively recent origin. It arises out of the substantial growth in home ownership over the last 30 or 40 years and, as part of that development, the great increase in the number of homes owned jointly by husbands and wives. More than two-thirds of householders in the United Kingdom now own their own homes. For most home-owning couples, their homes are their most valuable asset. They must surely be free, if they so wish, to use this asset as a means of raising money, whether for the purpose of the husband's business or for any other purpose. Their home is their property. The law should not restrict them in the use they may make of it. Bank finance is in fact by far the most important source of external capital for small businesses with fewer than ten employees. These businesses comprise about 95 per cent of all businesses in the country, responsible for nearly one-third of all employment. Finance raised by second mortgages on the principal's home is a significant source of capital for the start-up of small businesses.

35. If the freedom of home-owners to make economic use of their homes is not to be frustrated, a bank must be able to have confidence that a wife's signature of the necessary guarantee and charge will be as binding upon her as is the signature of anyone else on documents which he or she may sign. Otherwise banks will not be willing to lend money on the security of a jointly owned house or flat.

36. At the same time, the high degree of trust and confidence and emotional interdependence which normally characterises a marriage relationship provides scope for abuse. One party may take advantage of the other's vulnerability. Unhappily, such abuse does occur. Further, it is all too easy for a husband, anxious or even desperate for bank finance, to misstate the position in

some particular or to mislead the wife, wittingly or unwittingly, in some other way. The law would be seriously defective if it did not recognise these realities.

37. In *O'Brien*'s case this House decided where the balance should be held between these competing interests. On the one side, there is the need to protect a wife against a husband's undue influence. On the other side, there is the need for the bank to be able to have reasonable confidence in the strength of its security. Otherwise it would not provide the required money. The problem lies in finding the course best designed to protect wives in a minority of cases without unreasonably hampering the giving and taking of security. The House produced a practical solution. The House decided what are the steps a bank should take to ensure it is not affected by any claim the wife may have that her signature of the documents was procured by the undue influence or other wrong of her husband. Like every compromise, the outcome falls short of achieving in full the objectives of either of the two competing interests. In particular, the steps required of banks will not guarantee that, in future, wives will not be subjected to undue influence or misled when standing as sureties. Short of prohibiting this type of surety-ship transaction altogether, there is no way of achieving that result, desirable although it is. What passes between a husband and wife in this regard in the privacy of their own home is not capable of regulation or investigation as a prelude to the wife entering into a suretyship transaction.

Although all eight of the *Etridge* conjoined cases concerned wives who had given up their rights at the instance of their husbands, the court recognised that this issue arose equally for unmarried couples, including gay couples (see para. 47). All these are instances of cases in which in particular instances undue influence is possible. However, they are also all cases of relationships in which an adult might reasonably make a decision that was not entirely in her or his best interests in order to provide support to a partner. Thus it was emphasised that the *Etridge* principles apply to all non-commercial transactions where there may be a relationship of trust (see, for example, Lord Nicholls at para. 87). Hence the need for great care in balancing the conflicting interests of a lender and a person who has been disadvantaged by a document he or she has signed.

In *Etridge* Lord Clyde mounted a strong attack on the attempt to classify cases of undue influence. He said (paras. 92 and 93):

92. I question the wisdom of the practice which has grown up, particularly since *Bank of Credit and Commerce International SA* v *Aboody* [1990] 1 QB 923 of attempting to make classifications of cases of undue influence. That concept is in any event not easy to define. It was observed in *Allcard* v *Skinner* (1887) 36 Ch D 145 that 'no court has ever attempted to define undue influence' (Lindley LJ, at p. 183). It is something which can be more easily recognised when found than exhaustively analysed in the abstract. Correspondingly the attempt to build up classes or categories may lead to confusion. The confusion is aggravated if the names used to identify the classes do not bear their actual meaning. Thus on the face of it a division into cases of 'actual' and 'presumed' undue influence appears illogical. It appears to confuse definition and proof. There is also room for uncertainty whether the presumption is of the existence of an influence or of its quality as being undue. I would also dispute the utility of the further sophistication of subdividing 'presumed undue influence' into further categories. All these classifications to my mind add mystery rather than illumination.

93. There is a considerable variety in the particular methods by which undue influence may be brought to bear on the grantor of a deed. They include cases of coercion, domination, victim-isation and all the insidious techniques of persuasion. Certainly it can be recognised that in the case of certain relationships it will be relatively easier to establish that undue influence has been at work than in other cases where that sinister conclusion is not necessarily to be drawn with such ease. English law has identified certain relationships where the conclusion can

prima facie be drawn so easily as to establish a presumption of undue influence. But this is simply a matter of evidence and proof. In other cases the grantor of the deed will require to fortify the case by evidence, for example, of the pressure which was unfairly applied by the stronger party to the relationship, or the abuse of a trusting and confidential relationship resulting in for the one party a disadvantage and for the other a collateral benefit beyond what might be expected from the relationship of the parties. At the end of the day, after trial, there will either be proof of undue influence or that proof will fail and it will be found that there was no undue influence. In the former case, whatever the relationship of the parties and however the influence was exerted, there will be found to have been an actual case of undue influence. In the latter there will be none.

However, the other Lords of Appeal did not appear to be prepared to discard the whole classification: Lord Hobhouse said (at para. 99) that the essential structure was sound although there was a need for some clarification. The key clarification appears to be that the Class 2(B) 'presumption' is not really a presumption at all (see also Lord Scott of Foscote at para. 161). It is for the person alleging undue influence to prove it. However, having raised sufficient evidence to establish a prima facie case, he or she may elect to sit back and invite the other party to adduce evidence to displace that case (though it would be best to make the strongest case possible, in case the other party can manage to challenge any aspects of the evidence).

21.17.4 The need for manifest disadvantage

In some of what have been described as Class 2 cases the courts have suggested that in order to establish undue influence it is necessary to show that the trans-action in question is to the manifest disadvantage of the 'innocent' party. This test is not relevant to a Class 1 case because there actual undue influence must be proved and although manifest disadvantage in the transaction might be useful as supporting evidence that there has been actual abuse of a position of trust, it is the abuse of trust itself that is the key element. In *Bank of Credit and Commerce International SA* v *Aboody* [1990] 1 QB 923 the Court of Appeal had suggested that manifest disadvantage must also be established in a Class 1 case but in *CIBC Mortgages plc* v *Pitt* [1994] 1 AC 200 Lord Browne-Wilkinson (at pp. 208–9) said that he had no doubt that manifest disadvantage did not apply in a case of actual undue influence.

The issue of manifest disadvantage had previously been considered by the House of Lords in *National Westminster Bank plc* v *Morgan* [1985] AC 686 in terms that might be taken to suggest that it was relevant to Class 1 cases but in *CICB* v *Pitt* Lord Browne-Wilkinson said that that case should not to be taken to indicate that there was a general rule applicable to all cases of undue influence, whether actual or presumed, and that it should clearly not be requisite in the cases of actual undue influence, which was akin to fraud and which thus entitled the innocent party to have the transaction set aside, whatever its actual disadvantages or benefits to that party.

In *CICB* v *Pitt* Lord Browne-Wilkinson also seems to be questioning whether manifest disadvantage must always be established even in Class 2 cases (presumed undue influence). While this seemed to be the view clearly taken in *National Westminster Bank plc* v *Morgan*, in *CICB* v *Pitt* (at p. 209) Lord Browne-Wilkinson said that, 'the exact limits of the decision in *Morgan* may have to be considered in the future'.

The claim in *Morgan* was that Mrs Morgan had been induced to give security to the bank by the undue influence of one of the bank's managers. The case was not one in which actual undue influence was argued and Mrs Morgan relied on Class 2, presumed undue influence. On the facts the House of Lords held that the relationship between the bank manager and Mrs Morgan had not been such as to establish that he had assumed such a position as to give rise to a relationship of such close trust that undue influence could be assumed. However, their Lordships went on to indicate that Mrs Morgan's case also failed because she had not established that the transaction was manifestly unjust.

Fortunately, the decisions in *Royal Bank of Scotland plc* v *Etridge* gave the House of Lords the opportunity to review the apparent conflict between earlier decisions of that court in relation to the need or otherwise for manifest disadvantage when attempting to establish a case of undue influence. Manifest disadvantage was, of course, the second of the two elements of undue influence mentioned in *Allcard* v *Skinner* (1887) 36 ChD 145 (the first being a relationship of trust). Lindley LJ said (at p. 185):

. . . if the gift is so large as not to be reasonably accounted for on the ground of friendship, relationship, charity, or other ordinary motives on which ordinary men act, the burden is upon the donee to support the gift.

It involves something in the facts that would make an ordinary person stop and think whether the gift or other act (such as signing mortgage papers) seemed surprising. In *Etridge* the court was asked to abandon the need for this second element in undue influence cases and thus to depart from the House of Lords' decision in *National Westminster Bank* v *Morgan*. Lord Nicholls of Birkenhead rejected this approach and confirmed that such an element was needed. He said (at para. 27) that this principle:

. . . is good sense. It is a necessary limitation upon the width of the first prerequisite [the need for a relationship of trust]. It would be absurd for the law to presume that every gift by a child to a parent, or every transaction between a client and his solicitor or between a patient and his doctor, was brought about by undue influence unless the contrary is affirmatively proved. Such a presumption would be too far-reaching. The law would out of touch with everyday life if the presumption were to apply to every Christmas or birthday gift by a child to a parent, or to an agreement whereby a client or patient agrees to be responsible for the reasonable fees of his legal or medical adviser. The law would be rightly open to ridicule, for transactions such as these are unexceptionable. They do not suggest that something may be amiss. So something more is needed before the law reverses the burden of proof, something which calls for an explanation. When that something more is present, the greater the disadvantage to the vulnerable person, the more cogent must be the explanation before the presumption will be regarded as rebutted.

However, he criticised the use of the term 'manifest disadvantage' used by Lord Scarman in *Morgan* as having been applied in a way not originally intended and advised that rather than concentrating on the term, in future greater attention should be given to the test as outlined by Lindley LJ in *Allcard* v *Skinner* and set out above. It is also worth noting that Lord Nicholls of Birkenhead was clear that manifest disadvantage was not an essential element in every case of undue influence. He said (at para. 12):

In *CIBC Mortgages Plc* v *Pitt* [1994] 1 AC 200 your Lordships' House decided that in cases of undue influence disadvantage is not a necessary ingredient of the cause of action. It is not essential that the transaction should be disadvantageous to the pressurised or influenced person, either in financial terms or in any other way. However, in the nature of things, questions of undue influence will not usually arise, and the exercise of undue influence is unlikely to occur, where the transaction is innocuous. The issue is likely to arise only when, in some respect, the transaction was disadvantageous either from the outset or as matters turned out.

Perhaps the proper approach is to say that where any disadvantage that arises is not very great it may be easier to produce evidence to overturn the prima facie case of undue influence made out, but that this will be extremely difficult where the nature of the transaction itself is such that it 'shocks' the conscience of the court: see *Credit Lyonnais Bank Nederland NV* v *Burch* [1997] 1 All ER 144, at p. 152. It is also possible that there may be cases (Class 1 cases in *O'Brien* terms) in which there is actual undue influence proved on the facts, even though the transaction in question does not appear on its face to be in any way suspicious. However, such cases are likely to be extremely rare.

21.17.5 Displacing evidence of undue influence

In cases of alleged Class 1 (actual) influence, the issue of displacing evidence does not arise because one is dealing with an established fact of undue influence and not a presumption. It would be for the applicant to establish that something has occurred that amounts to actual undue influence and the burden of proving this will be heavy, due to the quasi-fraudulent nature of such an event. Any evidence as to the absence of the undue influence will merely go to the heart of the claimant's case.

In *O'Brien* it was indicated that once evidence had been brought to establish a relationship of trust, there arose a rebuttable presumption of undue influence and that thereafter the burden of proof passed to the alleged influencer, who had to bring evidence to rebut that presumption. This approach is strongly criticised in *Etridge*, in which it is made clear that this is not a matter of presumptions but of evidence and that it always lies on the person alleging undue influence to raise a prima facie case. However, the distinction may in most cases be a fine one because normally the courts will be prepared to draw inferences from the fact of the relationship of trust and the apparently surprising nature of the transaction in question (this is where manifest disadvantage can play its part). Lord Bingham of Cornhill said (at paras. 13 and 14):

13. Whether a transaction was brought about by the exercise of undue influence is a question of fact. Here, as elsewhere, the general principle is that he who asserts a wrong has been committed must prove it. The burden of proving an allegation of undue influence rests upon the person who claims to have been wronged. This is the general rule. The evidence required to discharge the burden of proof depends on the nature of the alleged undue influence, the personality of the parties, their relationship, the extent to which the transaction cannot readily be accounted for by the ordinary motives of ordinary persons in that relationship, and all the circumstances of the case.

14. Proof that the complainant placed trust and confidence in the other party in relation to the management of the complainant's financial affairs, coupled with a transaction which calls for explanation, will normally be sufficient, failing satisfactory evidence to the contrary, to discharge the burden of proof. On proof of these two matters the stage is set for the court to infer that, in the absence of a satisfactory explanation, the transaction can only have been

procured by undue influence. In other words, proof of these two facts is prima facie evidence that the defendant abused the influence he acquired in the parties' relationship. He preferred his own interests. He did not behave fairly to the other. So the evidential burden then shifts to him. It is for him to produce evidence to counter the inference which otherwise should be drawn.

Thus, while not all of their Lordships in *Etridge* seemed disposed to discard the whole of the *O'Brien* approach, it does seem that the distinction between Class 1 and Class 2 cases seems to be reduced to a matter of the strength of the evidence. The distinction may be most relevant in a case in which a relationship of trust clearly exists, but the transaction on its face is not in any way unusual. In such a case, the courts will not be ready to draw an inference of undue influence and thus the only chance of success arises if the person claiming to have been influenced can produce clear evidence that the apparently unexceptional transaction was in fact induced by actual undue influence. In other cases, where there is a relationship of trust and something unusual in the transaction, the courts are likely to be prepared to conclude, on the evidence, that undue influence arose in the case unless the alleged influencer can produce clear evidence to the contrary. The strongest expression of this is to be found in Lord Clyde's short speech at para. 93 (quoted above at para. 21.17.3).

The difference between Class 1 and Class 2 cases (if after *Etridge* it remains proper to use such classifications at all) may still have real effects, however, because in practice allegations of undue influence are most often made in cases in which the parties are the person claiming to have been influenced and a third party (usually a lender) such as a bank. In such a case, unless the alleged influencer can be produced as a witness and proves credible, the other party may be at a disadvantage when seeking to produce evidence to counter a prima facie case raised by the person saying she or he has been improperly influenced. In such cases, the inference drawn from the unusual (disadvantageous) nature of the transaction may suffice to decide the matter. To that extent the classification into at least Class 1 and Class 2 cases may remain of assistance when seeking to analyse a case involving an allegation of undue influence.

21.17.6 Unconscionable bargains

If you read the *Langton* case mentioned in 21.17.2 you will also find an interesting discussion of a second equitable principle which is related to undue influence. This is a principle that is sometimes described as being that of the 'unconscionable bargain'. This arises where there is some benefit to the person making the disposition but the transaction is so unfair (for example, the price paid is so low) that it can be regarded as the unconscientious exploitation of the weakness of a person in order for the recipient to obtain an undeserved benefit. You will realise that not all bargains at an undervalue can be attacked in this way because in general the law of contract is not interested in the adequacy of consideration. However, it may be brought into play where the facts indicate that there is some element of exploitation involved in the bargain made. In *Fry* v *Lane* (1889) 40 ChD 312, at p. 322, Kay J said:

. . . where a purchase is made from a poor and ignorant man at a considerable undervalue, the vendor having no independent advice, a Court of Equity will set aside the transaction.

This case does date, however, from a time of less public education and the courts will not be so ready to apply the principle today where someone has simply made a bad deal, but it may come into play in appropriate circumstances. A modern example might be, for example, if the other party to the transaction is aware of some mental incapacity of the person in question and takes advantage of the position. *Hart* v *O'Connor* [1985] 1 AC 1000 (PC) indicates that knowledge by the other party of the incapacity is essential if the doctrine is to be established. This is because equity is intervening as a matter of conscience. See also *Boustany* v *Pigott* (1995) 69 P&CR 298, in which the Privy Council's decision may have been influenced by the facts: (1) that the person making the disposition was an elderly lady, whose affairs were generally managed by a relative because of her age and because (as the witnesses described it) she was 'slow', and (2) that the terms of the lease that she herself had granted were manifestly at odds with the explanation she had given herself for making the transaction. (See further Capper, 'Undue influence and unconscionability: a rationalisation' (1998) 114 LQR 479.)

21.17.7 Why does a mortgagee need to be concerned?

If undue influence can be established, the complainant will have the right to have any transaction set aside as against the wrongdoer. However, the complainant's rights as against a mortgagee would normally be determined by the rules set out above (21.13 and 21.14) as to priorities between competing interests in land. Why then does the mortgagee need to worry if it has either obtained a release of that priority or if the complainant appeared to act as a full party to the transaction (Mrs O'Brien actually signed the charge over her home as one of two co-owners and in all eight of the conjoined *Etridge* cases some document had been signed by the wife)? The answer is that the courts have taken the view that the undue influence (where established) gives rise to 'an equity' in favour of the complainant (not, note, an equitable interest but rather a right to a remedy against the wrongdoer (1.6.4)). They have also said that such an equity is binding on the mortgagee if it has notice of the equity. In unregistered land, the issue is one of the conscience of the affected party. To this extent this area remains one in which the general equitable concept of doing justice between the parties can come into play and disrupt the operation of more specific rules (such as those relating to overreaching—see *O'Brien* itself). However, in relation to registered land this is an area in which the LRA 2002 has made a notable difference. Prior to that Act, since here one has an equity and not an equitable interest in land, the notice rule was still applied (see *Barclays Bank plc* v *Boulter* [1998] 1 WLR 1). However, for the future in registered land an equity is treated like an equitable interest (s. 116) and thus should be protected by means of a notice (unless it can be an overriding interest under Sch. 3, para. 2).

   Where one is dealing with a Class 2(A) case, as long as the nature of the relationship (such as solicitor–client) is known to the mortgagee, the mortgagee must be taken to be aware of the undue influence because it is presumed as a consequence of the relationship. In other cases the question will be whether there is anything in the circumstances to suggest that the mortgagee had notice. One therefore has to consider what will constitute sufficient notice, to affect the third-party mortgagee. Since we are dealing with conscience, actual knowledge by the mortgagee of undue influence will clearly mean that the mortgagee cannot enforce against the person influenced, where the influencer would be unable to do so himself. However, such cases are uncommon because usually a mortgagor will have no personal contact with the person influenced. In such cases Lord Browne-Wilkinson in *O'Brien* relied on the concept of constructive notice, but applied in a slightly innovative way in order to cover the instances that actually arise, which are where a mortgagee is aware of the relationship of trust (for example the parties are married) and there is something sufficiently unusual in the circumstances as to put the mortgagee on enquiry or even to do more and to take reasonable steps to ensure that the person influenced is acting of his or her own free will. However, this application of a wide version of constructive notice was challenged following *O'Brien* and, accordingly, in the conjoined *Etridge*, cases the House of Lords reviewed the position once again and gave guidance as to the steps that a mortgagee should take in order to protect itself. You should note that, in doing so, they made some criticism of the idea that this was properly a matter of applying the notice rules and, in essence, urged a common-sense approach to the facts in each case.

One of the results of *O'Brien* had been that mortgagees took care to avoid any personal contact with a wife or other person in a relationship of trust, in order to rely on the argument that that person had had independent advice or that the mortgagee had reasonably believed that such independent advice had been given to that person. This, in essence, 'passed the buck' to a legal adviser who signed a statement for the mortgagee saying that the person in question had had such advice and had decided to authorise the transaction. Unfortunately, as is illustrated by some of the conjoined *Etridge* cases, even where such statements had been obtained no proper advice had been given. In *Coleman* (see *Etridge*, para. 130), the solicitor's clerk concerned had given a written statement to the bank that, 'I confirm that [the relevant document] was signed in my presence and that the full effect of its contents have been explained to and were understood by Miriam Mara Coleman, and that she has signed this document of her own free will.' Mrs Coleman later gave evidence (which was accepted at first instance) that all that the clerk had done was to ask her, in her husband's presence, whether her husband had explained the documents to her, without making any genuine attempt to ascertain whether she really knew what she was signing and what were its implications. The case also illustrates another common problem, in that the firm of solicitors in question were not acting for Mrs Coleman, but for her husband. Since it is normal for a solicitor to act for both husband and wife, should the bank insist on a separate solicitor for the wife or can it rely on the veracity of the statement made by the lawyer (who is subject to his or her own professional duties and who could be sued by the wife were he or she to be in breach of them)? In *Samson*, the solicitor was acting for the bank rather than the husband or wife at the relevant point and only attested the wife's signature, having given no advice to her (see *Etridge*, para. 264). In *Gill*, the solicitor did quite properly give full advice to the wife on the nature and effect of the document she was signing but both the solicitor and Mrs Gill were unaware that the charge would in fact secure a much larger loan than appeared to be the case from what they had been told. In that case the bank was, of course, aware of the full amount that would be covered by the security. In a separate case, *National Westminster Bank plc* v *Amin* [2002] 1 FLR 735, heard by the House of Lords a little while after *Etridge*, a husband and wife were persuaded to allow their property to be used as security for an advance to their son. The bank had relied on a statement signed by a solicitor saying, 'I confirm that I have explained the terms and conditions to Mr and Mrs Amin'. However, Mrs Amin alleged this was impossible because neither she nor her husband spoke any English. In all these cases, the issue arises as to whether the mortgagee can claim to rely on the statement made by the lawyer in question, or whether the facts are such that the bank should be tainted by the behaviour of the influencer because there is something in the circumstances to give rise to the possibility or likelihood that the transaction has not been agreed to freely by the person influenced.

Once it can be shown that the mortgagee had actual or constructive notice of the undue influence, the transaction may also be set aside as against the mortgagee. Accordingly, were Mildred Mumps to approach her bank for an advance, even were Henry to be prepared to sign a document giving up any priority he may have as against the bank, this would not guarantee that the bank was safe in making the advance. The facts of co-habitation might in themselves give rise to a potential undue influence as between Henry and Mildred, if Henry were to be in the habit of placing trust and confidence in Mildred. Were Mildred to have resorted to threats, actual undue influence might be in play. However, all this would, of course, only be relevant were Henry to have rights in the property. In these circumstances a wise bank would not want to take risks because it would not know enough about what has gone on between Mildred and Henry in order to be sure: (a) whether Henry has rights in the property; and (b) whether the relationship does give rise to undue influence; or (c) whether actual undue influence has occurred. The question is what the bank can do to protect itself, because numerous cases demonstrate that getting Henry to sign away his rights would not, in itself, suffice.

21.17.8 What can a mortgagee do to protect himself?

As we can see from *O'Brien* it is not enough to rely for example on the overreaching provisions in the property legislation (see 13.9.3) because the innocent party may have signed while acting as a consequence of undue influence. What the mortgagee must do, in any case in which undue influence might be possible, is either to ensure that there is no undue influence or that, if there is, the circumstances are such that the undue influence cannot be attributed to him in any way.

21.17.8.1 *Not safe to rely on mortgagor*

If a mortgagee relies on the actual borrower to obtain the signature of the other party or parties this will usually *not* be safe for the mortgagee because it is easy for the borrower to misrepresent to the other party or parties what is intended: for an example of this see *TSB Bank plc* v *Camfield* [1995] 1 WLR 430. The duty imposed on the mortgagee is to take reasonable steps to ensure that any undue influence which may exist is counteracted by ensuring that other parties are aware of the consequences of signing a mortgage or a waiver of rights.

21.17.8.2 *The* Etridge *'rules'*

In *Barclays Bank plc* v *O'Brien* the House of Lords seemed to be laying down a very detailed and specific set of steps to be taken by all lenders in order to ensure that they afforded themselves sufficient protection against a later claim of undue influence. Lord Browne-Wilkinson suggested in his speech that the lender will have satisfied the requirement to take reasonable steps to ensure that it does not have constructive notice of rights if it insists that the wife (the case assumes it is dealing with a wife) attends a private meeting with a representative of the lender; that the husband is not present at that meeting; and that at the meeting the wife is warned of the extent of her liability should there be default, warned of the risk she is running and urged to take independent legal advice.

However, later cases did not seem to require that these steps necessarily be taken but appeared to place more value on the wife actually taking legal advice, in which case the courts seem now to be prepared to leave it to the legal adviser to ensure that there is no conflict of interests and that the wife is properly advised.

The safest course for a mortgagee appeared to be to get the other party to sign in the presence of a solicitor and then to require the solicitor to sign a declaration that, before the other party had signed, the purpose and effect of the document had been explained to him: see *Banco Exterior Internacional SA* v *Thomas* [1997] 1 WLR 221.

Due to the considerable confusion about what did or did not constitute sufficient protection for the lender (the examples given above are simply a few of the complications that have arisen), the House of Lords returned to the issue of rules for lenders in *Etridge*. The essential principle to be applied is enunciated by Lord Nicholls of Birkenhead at para. 54:

> The furthest a bank can be expected to go is to take reasonable steps to satisfy itself that the wife has had brought home to her, in a meaningful way, the practical implications of the proposed transaction. This does not wholly eliminate the risk of undue influence or misrepresentation. But it does mean that a wife enters into a transaction with her eyes open so far as the basic elements of the transaction are concerned.

He considered that there was no obligation on a bank to see the wife (or other person in a relationship of trust—in what follows, references to 'the wife' include any such persons) itself (para. 55), and that ordinarily it will be reasonable to rely on a confirmation given by a solicitor, acting for the wife, that he has advised the wife appropriately. However, despite this, the lender was still at risk if he knew the advice had not been given or knew facts from which he should have realised that appropriate advice had not been received (paras 56 and 57). Furthermore, Lord Nicholls approved a statement made by Fletcher Moulton LJ in *In re Coomber* [1911] 1 Ch 723 at p. 730, in relation to persons who are competent to form an opinion of their own:

> All that is necessary is that some independent person, free from any taint of the relationship, or of the consideration of interest which would affect the act, should put clearly before the person what are the nature and the consequences of the act. It is for adult persons of competent mind to decide whether they will do an act, and I do not think that independent and competent advice means independent and competent approval. It simply means that the advice shall be removed entirely from the suspected atmosphere; and that from the clear language of an independent mind, they should know precisely what they are doing.

He was content that the solicitor should act both for a husband and the wife and that it was for the solicitor to determine whether any conflict of interest actually arose and to decline to act for one party if so (para. 74). In order to ensure safety, Lord Nicholls said (para. 79):

> (1) Since the bank is looking for its protection to legal advice given to the wife by a solicitor who, in this respect, is acting solely for her, I consider the bank should take steps to check

directly with the wife the name of the solicitor she wishes to act for her. To this end, in future the bank should communicate directly with the wife, informing her that for its own protection it will require written confirmation from a solicitor, acting for her, to the effect that the solicitor has fully explained to her the nature of the documents and the practical implications they will have for her. She should be told that the purpose of this requirement is that thereafter she should not be able to dispute she is legally bound by the documents once she has signed them. She should be asked to nominate a solicitor whom she is willing to instruct to advise her, separately from her husband, and act for her in giving the necessary confirmation to the bank. She should be told that, if she wishes, the solicitor may be the same solicitor as is acting for her husband in the transaction. If a solicitor is already acting for the husband and the wife, she should be asked whether she would prefer that a different solicitor should act for her regarding the bank's requirement for confirmation from a solicitor.

The bank should not proceed with the transaction until it has received an appropriate response directly from the wife.

(2) Representatives of the bank are likely to have a much better picture of the husband's financial affairs than the solicitor. If the bank is not willing to undertake the task of explanation itself, the bank must provide the solicitor with the financial information he needs for this purpose. Accordingly it should become routine practice for banks, if relying on confirmation from a solicitor for their protection, to send to the solicitor the necessary financial information. What is required must depend on the facts of the case. Ordinarily this will include information on the purpose for which the proposed new facility has been requested, the current amount of the husband's indebtedness, the amount of his current overdraft facility, and the amount and terms of any new facility. If the bank's request for security arose from a written application by the husband for a facility, a copy of the application should be sent to the solicitor. The bank will, of course, need first to obtain the consent of its customer to this circulation of confidential information. If this consent is not forthcoming the transaction will not be able to proceed.

(3) Exceptionally there may be a case where the bank believes or suspects that the wife has been misled by her husband or is not entering into the transaction of her own free will. If such a case occurs the bank must inform the wife's solicitors of the facts giving rise to its belief or suspicion.

(4) The bank should in every case obtain from the wife's solicitor a written confirmation to the effect mentioned above.

The effect of these rules will be to ensure that wives either obtain proper advice or are at least made aware that it is in their best interests to have independent advice. Any advisor used by the wife will be under a professional duty to advise properly and could be sued by the wife if he or she did not do so. This approach is summarised by Lord Hobhouse in *Etridge* as follows (at para. 120):

The central feature is that the wife will be put into a proper relationship with a solicitor who is acting for her and accepts appropriate duties towards her. Likewise the bank or other lender must communicate directly with the wife to the end that that relationship is established and that any certificate upon which it may seek to rely is the fruit of such a professional relationship.

Lord Scott took the matter further and set out the obligations that will fall on the wife's adviser (by reference to the case of a wife acting as a surety, though the principles should be applicable to most undue influence cases) as follows (para. 169):

Normally, however, a solicitor, instructed to act for a surety wife in connection with a suretyship transaction would owe a duty to the wife to explain to her the nature and effect of the document or documents she was to sign. Exactly what the explanation should consist of would obviously depend in each case on the facts of that case and on any particular concerns that the wife might have communicated to the solicitor. In general, however, the solicitor should, in my opinion:

(i) explain to the wife, on a worst case footing, the steps the bank might take to enforce its security;

(ii) make sure the wife understands the extent of the liabilities that may come to be secured under the security;

(iii) explain the likely duration of the security;

(iv) ascertain whether the wife is aware of any existing indebtedness that will, if she grants the security, be secured under it;

(v) explain to the wife that he may need to give the bank a written confirmation that he has advised her about the nature and effect of the proposed transaction and obtain her consent to his doing so.

In *Etridge* the House of Lords indicated that it was laying down the steps to be taken in future. The decision in *Governor and Company of the Bank of Scotland* v *Hill and Tudor (No. 2)* [2002] 29 EG 152 (NS), illustrates that in the case of a mortgage created before *Etridge* was decided the courts will be more liberal in relation to the steps taken by the chargee to protect himself. See also *UCB Corporate Services Ltd* v *Williams* [2002] 19 EG 149 (NS), which emphasises that a bank cannot rely simply on the fact that a person in Henry's position may have had legal advice (here the same solicitor acted for a husband and the wife, who later claimed to have been the subject of undue influence) and *Charter* v *Mortgage Agency Services Number Two Ltd* [2003] 15 EG 138 (NS), in which undue influence was established but the bank was not affected by it because there had been nothing in the facts to put it on notice. For other cases but of gifts, rather than charges, created as a consequence of alleged undue influence see also: *Jennings* v *Cairns, The Times,* 16 November 2003, and *Pesticcio* v *Huet* (2003) 73 BMLR 57.

If the RWB want to be sure that any rights Henry may have will not interfere with the RWB's rights to enforce their mortgage they would be well advised to advise Henry to take independent advice and to insist that they have a certificate from his lawyer confirming that the nature and effect of the mortgage have been explained to him. It should also be noted that, in the case of registered land, a signed release from a person in actual occupation may be of limited assistance in any event for reasons which have nothing to do with undue influence: see further on this *Woolwich Building Society* v *Dickman* (1996) 72 P&CR 470.

If you read the report in *Etridge* you will see how the court applied the principles set out in the report to each of the sets of facts in the eight conjoined cases. The case also provides a useful review of the recent case law on this area. The interaction of the various aspects of law and equity certainly makes this topic a popular subject with legal examiners.

FURTHER READING

Bently, 'Mortgagee's Duties on Sale—No Place for Tort' [1990] Conv 431.

Cousins and Clarke, 'Law of Mortgages', 2nd edn., 2001, Sweet & Maxwell.

On the *Etridge* conjoined cases, see the case note by Thompson, in [2002] 66 Conv 174.

22

Easements and profits à prendre

22.1 Introduction

The title 'easements and profits à prendre' may make you imagine that this chapter is concerned with strange rights known only to land lawyers and having archaic names. In fact both easements and profits are commonly encountered and most of us use such rights every day of our lives: for example, when we walk across the courtyard in the block of flats in which we live, or enjoy the continuing support of our houses that is provided by walls belonging to our neighbours. Once you have read this chapter you can, on your next train journey, play a variant on a childrens' game, and spot from the train windows the situations in which easements and profits are likely to arise. Is the woman driving up a shared driveway exercising an easement (a right of way)? Is the little girl leading her pony into that field exercising a profit (grazing)? Does the path across the back gardens of those terraced houses indicate an easement (right of way on foot)? From this you can see that the interests discussed in this chapter are often quite straightforward and some are essential to our daily life. The common strand to all these arrangements is that they are all rights exercised over land which belongs to another person, and so come into the category of third-party interests in land.

22.1.1 Trant Way

22.1.1.1 *14–16A Trant Way*
The plan of 14, 15, 16 and 16A Trant Way in Figure 22.1 may assist you when reading this chapter.

In 1947 the then owner of 15 Trant Way decided to install modern drains in the property. The nearest main drain was in Gouda Grove. After discussion the then owner of 16 Trant Way agreed that the drains could be laid across his front garden into Gouda Grove. A deed was drawn up which contained the following words:

The grantor [the owner of 16] as beneficial owner hereby grants unto the grantee [the owner of 15] full right and liberty to use the sewer or drain marked [with a dotted line] on the plan attached hereto for the passage or conveyance of sewage water and soil from the said 15 Trant Way to the public sewer.

The current owner of 15 Trant Way is Charles Chive.

The current owner of 14 Trant Way (Nigel Neep) keeps a goat which he grazes on Fieldy Farm (to the rear of 14). Fieldy Farm is owned in fee simple by Farmer George.

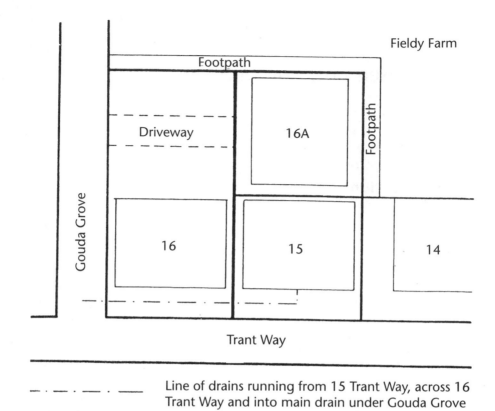

— · — · — · — Line of drains running from 15 Trant Way, across 16
Trant Way and into main drain under Gouda Grove

Figure 22.1 Nos. 14, 15, 16 and 16A Trant Way

There is a footpath leading from the back of 14 Trant Way to Gouda Grove. This
path runs across Farmer George's land. The path has been in regular use by the
owners of 14 Trant Way for many years.

For the last 50 years the fence separating 14 Trant Way from Fieldy Farm has been
maintained by Farmer George or his father (who was his predecessor in title).

At one time 16 and 16A formed one plot of land. In 1980 the then owner of
16 Trant Way (Marjorie Marjoram) sold the freehold of the property now known
as 16A Trant Way to Basil Borage. The only access to 16A is across the driveway on
16 Trant Way (see figure 22.1) but this fact was not mentioned in the conveyance to
Basil Borage. In 1996 Miss Marjoram sold 16 to Dan Dill (who has made a first
registration of title). Mr Dill dislikes Mr Borage and wants to prevent his use of the
driveway.

At present 16 Trant Way enjoys an uninterrupted view of fields to the rear of the
property over Fieldy Farm. Farmer George has just obtained planning permission to
erect a corn silo on the farm and Dan Dill believes that this will spoil his view.

22.1.1.2 *Basement flat: 2 Trant Way*

You will recall from Chapter 8 that Fingall Forest, the fee simple owner of 2 Trant
Way, has granted a tenancy of the basement flat at No. 2 to his friend Gerald

Gruyère. When Mr Gruyère first moved in he had only an oral lease. At that time he asked Mr Forest if he could keep his dustbin in the back garden of 2 Trant Way (which Mr Forest retained for his own use) and Mr Forest agreed. About two months ago the two friends decide to formalise their arrangement, and Mr Gruyère was given a written lease of the flat for a period of two years. The agreement was recorded in a written document which did not mention the right to keep the dustbin in the garden.

22.2 **What is an easement?**

Easements are rather like elephants: easy to recognise but very difficult to define. We are easily able to identify rights which are commonly accepted as being easements, for example, rights of way and rights of light. However, the label 'easement' covers such a wide range of interests that it may be difficult to discern any similarity between them. One might, as a result, be inclined to ignore the difficulties of definition and merely construct a list of rights which have been recognised as easements. However, although this may be helpful, it is not sufficient, for the courts have recognised that the list of easements is not closed and that the need for new easements will be met as the circumstances of life change (*Dyce* v *Lady James Hay* (1852) 1 Macq 305). For example, an easement allowing the erection of a satellite dish is obviously a modern addition to the list. We must accordingly address the question of a standard against which a claim to a new right can be tested.

This standard is provided in the judgment of the Court of Appeal in *Re Ellenborough Park* [1956] Ch 131 which, although it does not define an easement, provides rules for its recognition.

22.2.1 **The rules in *Re Ellenborough Park***

The original owners of Ellenborough Park also owned the surrounding land, which they sold off in plots for building purposes. Each conveyance granted to the purchasers the right to use the park, subject to an obligation to make a contribution towards the cost of maintaining it. The plaintiffs in the case acquired the park itself from the original owners, and intended to build upon it. The owners of the surrounding plots claimed the right to use the park and to be able to prevent the proposed building. The Court of Appeal upheld these claims, saying that the rights to use the park were legal easements. Since these rights were legal interests in land, they bound the purchasers of the park, and thus prevented them from building upon it. The court approved four rules of recognition for an easement:

(a) there must be a dominant tenement and a servient tenement;

(b) dominant and servient owners must be different persons;

(c) the easement must accommodate the dominant tenement; and

(d) the right claimed must 'lie in grant'.

We will now look at these rules and their application in greater detail.

22.2.1.1 *Need for a dominant and servient tenement*

An easement is a right enjoyed over one piece of land (the 'servient tenement') for the benefit of another piece of land (the 'dominant tenement'). In the case of the easement of drainage given in our practical examples, 16 Trant Way is burdened and is the servient tenement, whilst 15 Trant Way is benefited and is the dominant tenement.

It is essential that there is a dominant tenement, for an easement cannot exist 'in gross', that is, without being attached to a particular piece of land which derives benefit from it. It is this which distinguishes, for example, an easement of way from a public right of way: in the latter, anyone may use the way, whereas the easement is available only to those connected in some way with the dominant tenement.

Accordingly, when a claim is made to an easement, the two pieces of land must be readily identifiable and, therefore, when an easement is being created, care must be taken to ensure that the two properties are clearly identified. This is particularly important in the case of the servient tenement and, in our example of the right to drainage, the burdened land is clearly identified by the dotted line showing the line of the drain as it passes under 16 Trant Way. In a properly drafted document, the dominant tenement should also be clearly defined, thus the use of words such as 'for the benefit of the land known as 15 Trant Way' is desirable. However, it is not fatal if such an express mention is omitted as long as it is clear from the deed which land is to be benefited (see *Thorpe* v *Brumfitt* (1873) LR 8 Ch App 650). A power to nominate land to be benefited will not suffice for this purpose because the land must both exist as a separate estate and be identified before the time of the grant (*London and Blenheim Estates Ltd* v *Ladbroke Retail Parks Ltd* [1994] 1 WLR 31).

22.2.1.2 *Dominant and servient owners must be different persons*

This is how the rule is stated in *Re Ellenborough Park*, but it is perhaps easier to understand if one says that the two tenements must not be both owned and occupied by the same person. An easement is essentially a right over another's land for the benefit of one's own, and one cannot exercise a right against oneself. Thus, if a person owns two pieces of land and walks across one piece in order to reach another, he cannot be exercising an easement (*Roe* v *Siddons* (1888) 22 QBD 224 at p. 236). Sometimes, however, such a situation is said to give rise to a 'quasi-easement': this is, as we shall see, a potential easement which could develop into an easement if the plots came into separate hands.

We have emphasised the requirement that the same person must not own *and* occupy the two tenements, because it is possible for a tenant to have an easement over other land belonging to his landlord, and equally for the landlord, during the period of the lease, to have an easement over land occupied by the tenant. Thus, in the case of Fingall Forest and Gerald Gruyère at 2 Trant Way it is perfectly possible for Mr Gruyère to have an easement in respect of the land owned and occupied by Mr Forest, although Mr Forest owns the fee simple of both dominant and servient tenements.

Should one person acquire both the servient and the dominant tenement this will extinguish a pre-existing easement, if at the same time the two properties come into common occupation. If, at some future date, the same person were to buy and occupy both 15 and 16 Trant Way, this would bring the easement over 16 Trant Way to an end. This is because one cannot have rights as against oneself, unless one is acting in different capacities (for example, as a trustee in one case).

22.2.1.3 *The easement must accommodate the dominant tenement*

This rule requires that the right must confer an advantage on the dominant land. It is not sufficient for the right to confer a merely personal advantage on the current owner. Such a personal right is said to be an interest 'in gross' and, as we have seen, it is not possible to have an easement in gross. All easements must be 'appurtenant', that is, they must benefit identifiable land. In *Re Ellenborough Park* the right to use the park was held to benefit the surrounding plots of land because a domestic property is always improved in character by the availability of a garden. Unfortunately it is sometimes difficult to distinguish between personal benefits and benefits conferred on land, though, if it can be shown that the right increased the value of the land or its saleability, this would be sufficient. It may help to consider whether *any* possible owner of the property would regard the right as advantageous. Obviously any owner would regard the availability of drainage into the main drains as an advantage.

A problem may arise where the right claimed tends to confer an advantage, not on the land itself, but rather on some trade or business which is being carried on upon the land. In *Hill* v *Tupper* (1863) 2 Hurl & C 121 the right claimed as an easement was the right to put pleasure-boats on the canal which bordered the 'dominant' land. It was held that this right did not amount to an easement, because it did not benefit the land. Rather it benefited the business which Mr Hill happened to be running upon his land. The fact that the right benefits a business is not necessarily fatal, however, to a claim that the right is an easement. In *Moody* v *Steggles* (1879) 12 ChD 261, a right to hang on neighbouring land a sign pointing towards a public house was held to be capable of being an easement. This may well be because it is common for land used as a public house to remain in such use for prolonged periods, sometimes for centuries, so that the business run on the land and the land itself become inextricably linked.

The requirement that benefit be conferred on the land does, however, mean that the servient tenement and the dominant tenement must be reasonably close together. Normally the two properties will adjoin one another (as is the case in all our practical examples) but this is not absolutely necessary (*Pugh* v *Savage* [1970] 2 QB 373). The two pieces of land must, however, be close enough to support a claim that the dominant land receives an actual benefit from the right, and thus one could not have an easement exercisable over land at the other end of the country (*Bailey* v *Stephens* (1862) 12 CB NS 91 at p. 115). The easement does not, however, benefit other neighbouring land not covered by the grant (see, for example, *Peacock* v *Custins* [2002] 1 WLR 1815).

The requirement for benefit to land has given rise to other issues, notably (1) 'What happens if the benefited land changes its character over time, so that the impact of the easement on the burdened land changes?', and (2) 'What if the owner of the dominant tenement tries to use the easement to benefit other land he owns?'.

The first issue was considered in *Attwood* v *Bovis Homes Ltd* [2001] Ch 379, in relation to an easement of drainage. Here the land having the benefit of the drainage had ceased to be agricultural land and was being developed. It is important to note that here the easement had been obtained by long use (prescription) and not by reason of an express grant. Thus, the owner of the dominant land argued that the easement should be restricted to the benefit conferred on land as it had been while the right was being acquired. This argument was rejected. However, as you will see from the decision and the older cases cited in it, a different result might be reached if the changed use of the dominant tenement led to a substantial increase in the burden or changed the nature of the burden (see also *British Railways Board* v *Glass* [1965] Ch 538). In *Attwood* it was accepted that the drainage had not been increased by the change in use. It appears that the court did consider that it was more likely to be accepted that there was a substantial increase or change in nature where the easement was a right of way. For an example of this, see *Wimbledon and Putney Commons Conservators* v *Dixon* (1875) 1 Ch D 362.

On the second issue, in *Peacock* v *Custins* [2002] 1 WLR 1815 a farmer wanted to use a right of way in order to gain access to a field that was not part of the land expressed to be the benefited land in the conveyance creating the easement but which he farmed with the benefited land. The Court of Appeal held that the right of way could not be used to gain access to the extra field and confirmed that the right was determined by reference to the land mentioned in the conveyance. In *Das* v *Linden Mews Ltd* [2003] 2 P&CR 4, the same rule was applied to prevent a right to drive across a private mews being used to gain access to a car-parking area that the owners of the dominant properties (houses on either side of the mews) had added by acquiring new land at the end of the mews. You will appreciate that this rule, while generally sensible in order to prevent increase in the burden of an easement, may cause a problem in some cases, if the user of a right of way has a primary purpose of reaching the dominant land but once there may decide to move on to the extra land. This issue was considered in *Macepark (Whittlebury) Ltd* v *Sargeant* [2003] 1 WLR 2284, in which it was indicated that access to such extra land was acceptable but that the right of way could not be used substantially for that purpose and that the access to the extra land had to be merely ancillary to the proper main use of the easement in relation to the benefited land. The same approach was adopted by the Court of Appeal in *Massey* v *Boulden* [2003] 1 WLR 1792.

22.2.1.4 *The easement must be capable of forming the subject-matter of a grant*

Easements are interests in land which can be legal interests, and as such they must 'lie in grant'. This means that a right must be capable of being granted by deed if it is to be recognised as an easement. A number of rules result from this requirement, the first of which is that the right claimed must be specific and definable, for it would have to be carefully defined if included in a deed. This can be a problem if the right claimed involves issues of taste, since such matters cannot be defined. Thus one cannot claim a right to a prospect (a fair view) as an easement, for one cannot define such a right (*William Aldred's Case* (1610) 9 Co Rep 57b—'the law does not give an action for such things of delight'). Accordingly, Dan Dill at 16 Trant Way cannot complain about Farmer George's silo on the basis of an easement for a view. He should have made his complaints at the stage at which the farmer applied for planning permission (though he might not have been able to prevent the grant of permission). The vague nature of the right claimed may also result in its failing this test. Thus, in *Mounsey* v *Ismay* (1865) 3 Hurl & C 486, a claim to use land for general recreational purposes was held to be too vague to amount to an easement, although a right to use a garden for similar purposes was upheld in *Re Ellenborough Park* itself. In *Chaffe* v *Kingsley* [2000] 79 P&CR 404, a claim to a right of way failed because the conveyance by which it was alleged the right was granted was insufficiently specific as to the area of land affected. Accordingly, care must be taken when drafting an easement to be as specific as possible about the right granted.

The second important consequence of the rule that easements lie in grant is that, at the date at which the right arose, there must have been two persons who were capable respectively of granting and receiving the easement. This is of importance where easements are acquired otherwise than by express grant and will accordingly be discussed later when we consider methods of acquisition.

22.2.2 Some examples of easements

It is not possible for us to list all the rights which have been recognised as amounting to easements, but we will mention some of the most common.

22.2.2.1 *Rights of way*

The right of way is an easement that you are likely to have encountered frequently in your daily life: it involves a right to pass over the servient land. It can be general (passage by any means) or limited (for example, on foot only). See *Borman* v *Griffith* [1930] 1 Ch 493 at p. 499 for comment on the right of way.

22.2.2.2 *Right to light*

This must be a specific right, so that light is claimed for particular windows or skylights, and there cannot be a general claim for light over the whole piece of land (*Colls* v *Home & Colonial Stores Ltd* [1904] AC 179). The amount of light which one can claim is that which is necessary according to the ordinary notions of mankind. This rule relates to and in essence is derived from the rule in nuisance that the damage must be such as, 'materially to interfere with the ordinary comfort of human existence': *St Helen's Smelting Co. Ltd* v *Tipping* (1862) 11 ER 1483 and see *City of London Brewery Co. Ltd* v *Tenant* (1873) LR 9 Ch App 212. The amount of light to be expected will also vary depending upon the nature of the property. Thus this right would be infringed were the light so obstructed that in a dwelling the electric light had to be lit all day but this might not be objectionable were the premises in question to be a warehouse (see *Colls* above). A mere diminution in the light is not sufficient, nor can one claim extra light because of the activities carried on on the land, unless the special use contemplated was known to the owner of the servient land at the time at which the easement was acquired.

22.2.2.3 *Rights to water*

One has no general right to water which percolates through the soil, but an easement may exist in respect of water in a defined channel, e.g., a pipe or stream. On this see *Race* v *Ward* (1855) 4 El & Bl. 702 and *Dickinson* v *Grand Junction Canal Co. Ltd* (1852) 7 Exch 282 at p. 301.

22.2.2.4 *Right to drainage*

This is a common and important easement (see the example in para. 22.1.1.1). For a further discussion see *Atwood* v *Bovis Homes Ltd* [2001] Ch 379 and para. 22.2.1.3.

22.2.2.5 *Rights to air*

Once again there is no general right to the passage of air (*Webb* v *Bird* (1861) 10 CB (NS) 268) but a claim to air owing in a de ned channel can amount to an easement. This might include, for example, rights in respect of ventilation ducts (*Wong* v *Beaumont Property Trust Ltd* [1965] 1 QB 173).

22.2.2.6 *Rights to storage*

This is now a well-accepted easement, provided that the right is suf ciently de nite (*Wright* v *Macadam* [1949] 2 KB 744). A vague right or one which excludes the servient owner from the use of his own land is not, however, acceptable (*Copeland* v *Greenhalf* [1952] Ch 488 and *Grigsby* v *Melville* [1974] 1 WLR 80). Mr GruyËreís right to keep his dustbin in the garden of 2 Trant Way seems to qualify as an easement in this category.

22.2.2.7 *Right to support*

This right is very important where one is dealing with a semi-detached or terraced house. In such a case the boundary frequently runs down the centre of the connecting wall. Were one owner to remove his half, the remaining portion would probably soon collapse. Accordingly an easement of support is recognised in this, and other similar cases (*Dalton* v *Angus & Co.* (1881) 6 App Cas 740); this right is limited, however, so that whilst the servient owner may not pull his wall down he may let it fall down for lack of repair (*Jones* v *Pritchard* [1908] 1 Ch 630 at p. 637). The right to support is not, however, con ned to walls (see *Jordeson* v *Sutton, Smithcoates & Drypool Gas Co. Ltd* [1898] 2 Ch 614, which related to quarrying at the bottom of a hill that resulted in part of the land in a neighbouring fruit farm being dislodged). This area of law interacts with the tort of nuisance: see *Holbeck Hall Hotel* v *Scarborough BC* [2000] QB 836.

22.2.2.8 *Use of facilities*

Common examples include the use of a lavatory (*Miller* v *Emcer Products Ltd* [1956] Ch 304), of a letter-box (*Goldberg* v *Edwards* [1950] Ch 247) or a kitchen (*Haywood* v *Mallalieu* (1883) 25 ChD 357).

22.2.2.9 *Parking*

A popular modern claim is to an easement of parking. In a sense this is really only an extension of the easement of storage and the dif culty with it may be the extent to which the servient owner is excluded from the use of his own land (see *Handel* v *St Stephen's Close* [1994] 1 EGLR 70 and *London & Blenheim Estates Ltd* v *Ladbroke Retail Parks Ltd* [1992] 1 WLR 1278 at p. 1288BñC, *Batchelor* v *Marlow* [2003] 1 WLR 764 and 22.2.3.1). All in all, the easement of parking appears to have occupied a considerable amount of court time in recent years. The conclusion seems to be that it is possible to have an easement of parking and that if it is granted expressly the courts may be less inclined to investigate whether it disrupts the use of the servient land to the extent that it cannot be used: see *Stonebridge* v *Bygrave* [2001] All ER

(D) 376. However, even in the *Blenheim Estates* case and *Batchelor* v *Marlow* the courts were sufficiently uncomfortable with the idea to wonder whether parking might take effect as some sort of right other than an easement. Where the right that is claimed would have to arise by long use (prescription), the courts seem more inclined to find that it is not an easement because the owner of the servient tenement is excluded from the use of his land.

22.2.2.10 *Fencing?*

This easement obliges the owner of the servient tenement to maintain a fence between the servient and dominant tenements. This is unusual, because easements do not usually impose expense on the servient tenement. There is no requirement, for example, to make up or maintain a road or track across one's land, and similarly we have just seen that there is no duty to repair a wall which is supporting one's neighbour's house. For this reason, the easement of fencing has been described as a spurious easement, but its existence was recognised by the Court of Appeal in *Crow* v *Wood* [1971] 1 QB 77.

Farmer George's habit of fencing off 14 Trant Way may possibly fall into this category (see also *Egerton* v *Harding* [1975] QB 62). However, you should note that fencing as an easement seems to be rare and the courts may well be reluctant to extend the use of this 'spurious' category. Such cases as have arisen appear to have done so in purely rural settings and thus such a claim might not succeed in a more developed area, such as Trant Way. Gray and Gray, p. 476 suggests that such an easement could not arise otherwise than by prescription though, logically, this produces an odd result.

The types of easements described above merely provide some examples, and reference should be made to C. J. Gale, *Gale on Easements*, 17th edn., pp. 38–40, if you want a more detailed list.

22.2.3 **Establishing a new easement**

If one wishes to establish a claim to a hitherto unknown easement, one must first show that the right claimed satisfies the four rules of recognition adopted in *Re Ellenborough Park*. Thereafter it is necessary to satisfy the court that the claim to a new type of easement is justified. This is considerably easier if one can show that the nature of the right claimed is analogous to that of some existing easement. Thus, Mr Gruyère might wish to show that his claim to store a dustbin is similar in character to the right to store coal which was accepted in *Wright* v *Macadam* [1949] 2 KB 744. In addition there are certain other rules which should be considered.

22.2.3.1 *Must not exclude use by servient owner*

The courts will never accept as an easement a right which has the effect of excluding the servient owner from his own use of the land. An easement is by nature a limited right, and if the dominant owner seeks to oust the servient owner he is claiming a right which is considerably greater than that conferred by an easement (see *Grigsby* v *Melville* [1974] 1 WLR 80). This is a common problem in claims to an easment of parking: see above para. 22.2.2.9.

be legal: s. 27(1) and (2)(d). However, an easement or profit granted due to the effect of LPA 1925, s. 62 is expressly excluded by s. 27(7) (see para. 22.7 for the effects of s. 62). When registering the benefit, the registrar will now automatically enter a notice on the register for the burdened land.

In relation to the burden of easements and profits as overriding interests, the position under LRA 2002 differs between first registration of title and subsequent dispositions. On first registration, all legal easements and profits are overriding interests: Sch. 1, para. 3. Section 27 and Sch. 3, para. 3 deal with the situation on later dispositions of the registered estate and they limit considerably the easements and profits that can be overriding. Due to s. 27, most legal easements and profits will not now be capable of being overriding interests because expressly created legal interests must be registered to be protected. An easement or profit will only be overriding if it is a legal interest arising by implied grant or reservation, or by prescription, or under LPA 1925, s. 62 *and* if one of the following applies

(a) it is registered under the Commons Registration Act 1965; or

(b) the acquirer actually knew of its existence; or

(c) the acquirer did not know of it but it would have been obvious on a reasonably careful inspection of the land over which it is exercisable; or

(d) even if it does not fall within (a) to (c) above, it has been exercised within the period of one year ending with the date of the disposition in question.

This will make the registration of burdens far more important than was previously the case, since the burden of many legal easements and profits will have to be entered on the register of the servient land if an acquirer is to be bound.

An easement or profit that is overriding can also be protected by a notice and s. 37 gives the registrar power to enter the notice himself (see Sch. 1, para. 3). The intention is that the registrar will exercise this power so that, over time, the register will be a more complete record of all the interests affecting land and fewer and fewer interests will operate as overriding interests, which can be a trap for an unwary purchaser of burdened land. Once a notice is entered against the servient tenement, the interest ceases permanently to be an overriding interest; see s. 29(3). The Land Registration Rules 2003 require anyone applying for registration of an estate to inform the registrar of any interests of which he is aware. Rule 35 requires the registrar to enter any burdens he discovers on first registration. This will lead to the entry of a notice on the register of the burdened land. Section 33 gives him power on first registration to enter benefits on the register of title relating to the benefited land. Where the land is already registered, the person obtaining the benefit will wish to ensure its validity for the future by registering the benefit under s. 27 (to ensure it is enforceable at law and not just in equity) and applying for a notice to be entered on the register relating to the burdened land (to ensure it binds anyone acquiring that land or an interest in it). All this is in line with one of the purposes of the LRA 2002, which was to make the Land Register a more complete record of the title to, and interests in, registered land (see further 5.2.5).

Equitable easements and profits must be entered on the register by way of notice on the register for the servient land if they are to bind a subsequent acquirer: the entry would be made pursuant to ss. 32 and 33.

In the unregistered land system, a legal easement or profit is enforceable against any purchaser, under the principle that legal rights bind the whole world. Equitable easements in unregistered land are registrable as land charges if created on or after 1 January 1926 (LCA 1972, s. 2), though some passages in *E. R. Ives Investment Ltd* v *High* [1967] 2 QB 379 suggest that some equitable easements may be binding without registration but this point has not been further developed. Equitable easements and profits in relation to unregistered land and which were created before 1926 are subject to the old equitable rules of notice.

22.5 Acquisition by express grant or reservation

The story of the installation of the drains of 15 Trant Way, given at the beginning of this chapter, shows that an easement or profit can arise by agreement between two owners who already hold separate properties. In such a case, the owner of the land which is to become the servient tenement executes a deed granting the easement to his neighbour.

Very often, however, easements or profits are created when land is divided on sale. The vendor may sell only part of his land, keeping the rest for himself (as happened with 16 and 16A Trant Way), and he and the purchaser may each want to enjoy rights over the other's property. Where the purchaser is to be given easements or profits, they are granted by deed, usually by the same deed which conveys the legal estate to him. Where the vendor wishes to retain certain rights over the land he is selling, he must 'reserve' those rights in the conveyance. The purchaser takes his rights by express grant, while the vendor obtains his by express reservation.

The reservation of an easement requires care because the document will be construed strictly against the vendor/grantor (*Cordell* v *Second Clanfield Properties Ltd* [1969] 2 Ch 9).

22.6 Acquisition by implied grant or reservation

In certain cases in which a conveyance of land makes no mention of the grant or reservation of an easement or profit, it may be possible to say that one arises by implication. As we shall see, it is easier to establish an implied grant, in favour of the purchaser, than it is to set up an implied reservation on behalf of the vendor.

22.6.1 Implied grant

Traditionally, it was said that easements, and in some cases profits, can arise by implied grant in the following cases:

(a) easements of necessity;

(b) intended easements and profits;

(c) easements under the rule in *Wheeldon* v *Burrows* (1879) 12 ChD 31.

However, *Nickerson* v *Barraclough* [1981] Ch 426 suggests that the first two of these are not really separate categories, and that easements of necessity are really a form of intended easement.

22.6.1.1 *Easements of necessity*

An easement of necessity is an easement which is so essential to the enjoyment of the land that the land cannot be used without the easement. It used to be said that such easements would be implied into a transaction because to hold otherwise would be to allow the grantor to derogate from his grant. The classic example of such an easement arises in the case of 'the land-locked close'. This is land which, like 16A Trant Way, is totally inaccessible, unless an easement to permit access is implied into the conveyance or transfer. On this basis an easement of way would have been implied in the conveyance of 16A Trant Way by Marjorie Marjoram to Basil Borage, as otherwise Mr Borage would have acquired a useless estate. In *Nickerson* v *Barraclough* [1981] Ch 426, however, which did involve land-locked land, it was held that this method of acquisition also depended upon the intentions of the parties. Thus, an easement of necessity could not be implied where the original vendor had expressly stated that no right of access was being granted. (For a useful plan which assists the understanding of this case see (1980) 130 NLJ 204.) In such a case, the purchaser has simply bought a bad deal (and might well sue his or her conveyancer).

The overlap between necessity and intention can be illustrated by the older case of *Wong* v *Beaumont Property Trust Ltd* [1965] 1 QB 173, in which basement premises had been let upon the express understanding that the property was to be used as a restaurant. Later, after assignment by the original tenant, the assignee was required to improve ventilation if the restaurant business were to continue. The assignee claimed an implied easement for passage of air through a duct to be constructed on the landlord's property, and was successful on the ground that this was necessary if the contemplated use of the premises were to continue. On the facts, one can see that the case might have been similarly decided by implying that the parties *intended* all rights which permitted the use of the premises as a restaurant. Another important case in this area of the law is *Liverpool City Council* v *Irwin* [1977] AC 239 (see 22.2.3.4) in which easements were implied giving the right to use rubbish chutes, stairs and lifts in a multi-storey block of flats. In addition the grant of a flat was held to include an implied right to have the facilities maintained in a reasonable state of repair. Again, is this a matter of intention or is it that a lessee cannot make any real use of a flat at the top of a tall block unless there is a lift, kept in working order?

22.6.1.2 *Intended easement and profits*

As we have seen above, it may be that rights which are necessary for the use of the land are to be presumed to be within the intention of the parties unless expressly excluded. This second category, however, includes more than easements of necessity, for under this heading a grantee may claim a profit or any easement, even though not necessary to the enjoyment of the property, provided he can show that both parties intended to grant it. An example of this is found in *Cory* v *Davies* [1923] 2 Ch 95, where a row of terraced houses had been built with a drive at the front and an exit to the road at each end. One of the owners barred the exit at his end of the terrace, requiring all traffic to go the other way. There was no express grant of an easement in favour of all the house owners over all parts of the drive, but the court found that the original parties had a common intention that the drive should be used in this way, and thus an intended easement was implied.

Stafford v *Lee* (1992) 65 P&CR 172, is a more recent case which shows how the question of the intention of the parties was addressed in a case of 'land-locked' land and which therefore might properly appear to fall into the area of easements of necessity. Here the defendant's predecessor in title had conveyed an area of woodland and a pond to the plaintiffs' predecessors. The land fronted a drive but no right of way over the drive to the nearby highway was conferred. The plaintiffs wished to build a house on part of the land but the defendants said that there could be no right of way over the drive for residential purposes (including construction work). The court accepted that it was appropriate to infer an easement to give effect to the intentions of the original parties, but indicated that this could only be done in cases in which the parties intended that the dominant land should be used in some definite and particular manner. In this case because the plan on the relevant conveyance showed other neighbouring buildings the court was ready to infer that the woodland would be used for similar purposes. Accordingly, the claim to an easement for domestic purposes succeeded.

22.6.1.3 *The rule in* Wheeldon v Burrows

In order to understand this rule, it is necessary to remind ourselves about quasi-easements (see 22.2.1.2). Although a landowner may derive benefit from one piece of his own land in favour of another, he cannot be said to have an easement, because there are no separate tenements. For example, if he enjoys the uninterrupted passage of light over his garden to his windows, he cannot say he has an easement of light, although, if the garden were in separate ownership he might very well have such a right. This situation is sometimes described as giving rise to a quasi-easement.

(1) *The rule* The rule in *Wheeldon* v *Burrows* (1879) 12 ChD 31 provides that if, in such a situation, the owner sells that part of his land which is benefited (e.g., the house) and retains the land which is burdened (e.g., the garden), the purchaser may acquire an easement over the land retained by the vendor. Thus, in the example given above, the quasi-easement would become a true easement of light.

In *Wheeldon* v *Burrows*, Thesiger LJ stated the principle as follows (at p. 49):

[O]n the grant by the owner of a tenement of part of that tenement as it is then used and enjoyed, there will pass to the grantee all those continuous and apparent easements (by which, of course, I mean *quasi* easements), or, in other words, all those easements which are necessary to the reasonable enjoyment of the property granted, and which have been and are at the time of the grant used by the owners of the entirety for the benefit of the part granted.

(2) *Elements of the rule* There seem to be three elements of this rule, for the quasi-easement must be:

(a) 'continuous and apparent';

(b) 'necessary to the reasonable enjoyment' of the land sold; and

(c) in use at the time of the sale.

If all three requirements are satisfied then a grant of a legal easement is implied into the conveyance or transfer of the portion of the land which is sold. In *Wheeldon* v *Burrows* itself, requirements (a) and (b) appear to have been regarded as alternatives.

However, it was suggested in *Ward* v *Kirkland* [1967] Ch 194 at p. 224, by Ungoed-Thomas J, that requirement (a) applied to positive easements (e.g., a right of way) and requirement (b) applied to negative easements (e.g., a right to light). The best view appears to be that (a) and (b) are alternatives, though in a number of cases the court appears to have discovered both.

The words 'continuous and apparent' have sometimes been construed widely, so that a right of way which can be in regular but hardly 'continuous' use, has been held to satisfy the test (*Borman* v *Griffith* [1930] 1 Ch 493 at p. 499).

The requirement that the right be 'apparent' arises because this rule is based on the principle of non-derogation from grant. On inspecting the land a purchaser may see visible signs of a quasi-easement and assume that he will obtain the benefit of the right. In the case of 16A Trant Way, if there was a house on the property when Mr Borage bought it and a driveway across 16 leading to it, the driveway would render apparent the quasi-easement being used by the vendor.

The requirement that an easement should be 'necessary for the reasonable enjoyment of the land' does *not* produce a test as strict as that for easements of necessity. All that is needed for *Wheeldon* v *Burrows* is that the right claimed should facilitate the reasonable enjoyment of the property. However, in *Wheeler* v *J. J. Saunders Ltd* [1996] Ch 19, a second access route to premises was held by the Court of Appeal *not* to be necessary for the reasonable enjoyment of the land, even though it was convenient, because the alternative route would 'do just as well'.

22.6.2 Implied reservation

In general the courts will not readily accept a claim to the acquisition of an easement or profit by implied reservation because of the rule that documents are to be construed strictly against the grantor. This is because it is presumed that the grantor is in a position of strength, and is able to reserve any rights which he chooses to retain. Should he fail to reserve these rights he has only himself (or his conveyancer) to blame. Moreover, it can be said that an implied reservation derogates from the grant, for the grantor has apparently given the grantee an unencumbered estate and is then trying to burden it with an easement or profit.

However, there are a few cases in which easements or profits may be claimed by implied reservation, and the rules relating to easements of necessity and intended easements or profits can apply to reservations as well as to grants. Thus, an easement giving a right of access to land-locked land may be acquired by implied reservation (*Pinnington* v *Galland* (1853) 9 Exch 1), as may an easement of support (*Richards* v *Rose* (1853) 9 Exch 218). In *Re Webb's Lease* [1951] Ch 808, a landlord owned a three-storey property and ran a business on the ground floor, while letting the two upper floors. He displayed advertisements for his business on the exterior of the upper floors before and after the grant of the relevant lease. The tenant claimed the landlord had reserved no easement allowing him to display signs on the demised premises. The court found for the tenant. While the signs were clearly visible, and although this was evidence of an intention that the landlord should have an ease-ment, this was not the only possible explanation. The court said that the facts must not be (reasonably) consistent with any explanation other than that the parties must have intended the landlord to have an easement. This was considered further by the Court of Appeal in *Peckham* v *Ellison* [2000] 79 P&CR 276, in which a succes-sor to a council that had sold some properties under the 'right to buy' scheme, while retaining other neighbouring property, claimed that the council must have reserved a right of way by implication. Perhaps surprisingly, the Court of Appeal held that on the particular facts of the case, the judge at first instance had been entitled to conclude that there was no other possible explanation of the circum-stances other than that the council and purchasers had intended that the council should reserve the easement. The case emphasises that the matter is one to be decided on the facts of each case. The issue was further considered in *Chaffe* v *Kingsley* [2000] 79 P&CR 404, where a claim to a reserved easement failed because the alleged common intention was insufficiently clear as to the exact area covered by the right of way sought and the period within which that right could be exercised. This illustrates the point that the common intention must be in relation to all the necessary requirements for an easement.

There is, however, no possibility of an implied reservation under the rule in *Wheeldon* v *Burrows*, for the court in that case rejected the vendor's claim to an easement over the land he had sold. (It is interesting to note that the rule which takes its name from this case is in fact derived from *obiter dicta*, for the court was not dealing with any question about implied grant.)

22.7 Acquisition by express grant by virtue of LPA 1925, s. 62

22.7.1 Section 62

LPA 1925, s. 62(1), provides that:

A conveyance of land shall be deemed to include and shall . . . operate to convey, with the land, all buildings, erections, fixtures, commons, hedges, ditches, . . . liberties, privileges, easements, rights, and advantages whatsoever, appertaining . . . to the land, . . . or, at the time of conveyance, . . . enjoyed with . . . the land.

At first reading the subsection appears to be nothing more than a word-saving provision, designed to make it clear that on the conveyance of an estate in land the grantee obtains the benefit of houses, fences and other things upon the land and any rights, interests and privileges existing for the benefit of the estate, without any express mention of them being made in the conveyance. However, the section has been interpreted in such a way that it is capable of creating new legal easements and profits in favour of a purchaser, as well as transferring those which already exist.

22.7.2 **Conversion of licence into legal easement**

An examination of the case of *Wright* v *Macadam* [1949] 2 KB 744 illustrates how this may occur. While in possession as a protected tenant under the Rent Acts, Mrs Wright was given permission by her landlord, Mr Macadam, to store coal in a garden shed, which was retained by the landlord. Later a fresh lease of one year was made (by an unsealed document in accordance with LPA 1925, s. 54(2)) which did not refer to the shed. After some time, Mr Macadam tried to charge for the use of the shed and Mrs Wright refused to pay, claiming that she had an easement of storage. It was held, by the Court of Appeal, that the creation of the fresh lease was a 'conveyance' within the meaning of LPA 1925 and that it operated to grant Mrs Wright a legal easement of storage. Thus, by virtue of s. 62, a conveyance can convert a pre-existing licence into a legal easement. A further example is found in *Goldberg* v *Edwards* [1950] Ch 247, where a permissive use (licence) of an alternative route of access was regarded as becoming a legal easement on the grant of a lease. It is not easy to see why s. 62 should have this effect, for the words of the section would suggest that the licence should pass as a licence, rather than changing into a legal right. However, this interpretation was first adopted in nineteenth-century decisions on similar provisions in earlier statutes and it is now well accepted and has been expressly recognised in LRA 2002, s. 27(7).

22.7.3 **Application of the rules**

If we now consider the situation of Mr Forest and Mr Gruyère at 2 Trant Way, it appears that Mr Gruyère has acquired the legal easement of storing his dustbin in the garden by virtue of s. 62. The right to store is capable of being an easement and the creation of a legal lease (even in the absence of a deed, which is not necessary in this case to create a legal lease) provides the necessary 'conveyance' for the operation of s. 62: see *Wright* v *Macadam* itself. In order to prevent such a development, a landlord who is granting a fresh lease should either revoke any licences he has previously given, or include a term in the lease which will exclude the operation of s. 62.

22.7.4 **Is separate occupation required?**

In both the cases we have mentioned so far the two properties were in separate occupation before the date of the relevant conveyance, and the owner had given a permissive right to the occupier of the dominant land. What if the land had been previously owned and occupied by the same person (as was the case, for example, with 16 and 16A Trant Way)? In *Long* v *Gowlett* [1923] 2 Ch 177 it was said that in such a case there was no 'privilege, easement or advantage' being exercised at the date of such a conveyance, for the owner-occupier of both plots could not be exercising rights against himself. In such a case there are no rights which can mature into easements on the conveyance. This view is confirmed by *obiter dicta* of Lord Wilberforce in *Sovmots Investments Ltd* v *Secretary of State for the Environment* [1979] AC 144, in which his Lordship said (at p. 169):

The reason is that when land is under one ownership one cannot speak in any intelligible sense of rights, or privileges, or easements being exercised over one part for the benefit of another. Whatever the owner does, he does as owner and, until a separation occurs, of ownership or at least of occupation, the condition for the existence of rights, etc., does not exist.

(But see the articles by Jackson (1966) 30 Conv NS 342, and Smith [1978] Conv 499.)

This issue was considered further by the Court of Appeal in *Payne* v *Inwood* (1996) 74 P&CR 42. This case involved two houses in a terrace of three: No. 1 was the corner house and access to the rear of the house could be obtained by passing up the side of the house; No. 1A was the next house in the terrace and originally access to the rear of No. 1A could only be obtained by passing through the house itself. Both No. 1 and No. 1A had yards at the rear of the house which adjoined one another and in about 1964 the then owner of No. 1 had allowed the construction of a gate between the two rear yards (largely because the owners of the two properties were close friends and this permitted easy access between the houses). Thereafter it was possible to gain access to the rear of No. 1A by walking up the side of No. 1, across the back yard of No. 1 and through the gate into the yard of No. 1A. The evidence was that generally, from about the early 1970s, this method of access had been used, although there had been some periods during which the gate between the two yards seems to have been blocked by stored goods. In 1971 No. 1A was owned by a Miss Cutler and it appears that she used the route via No. 1 to have coal delivered to her property. Miss Cutler decided, however, that she preferred No. 1 to her own property and thus on 1 October 1971 she bought No. 1 and on 8 October 1971 she sold No. 1A. Over the years No. 1A was sold again several times and eventually came into the hands of the respondents. In 1989 Miss Cutler sold No. 1 to the appellants. When the appellants claimed that the respondents had no right of access to their rear yard via No. 1, the respondents started County Court proceedings and at first instance succeeded in establishing that they had an easement by virtue of s. 62: the judge deciding that in essence the Court of Appeal had been in error in *Sovmots* because it had not been referred to a case on an easement of light (*Wardle* v *Brocklehurst* (1860) 1 El & El 1065) and that here accordingly the common ownership of the properties by Miss Cutler in 1971 did not destroy the claim to an easement on the disposal of No. 1A by Miss Cutler in 1971.

In the Court of Appeal reliance was placed also on *Broomfield* v *Williams* [1897] 1 Ch 602 as authority for the proposition that separate ownership was not required for s. 62 to operate. However, the Court of Appeal confirmed the view expressed in *Sovmots* that at least separate occupation (if not ownership) is necessary prior to the relevant conveyance if s. 62 is to operate. In *Wardle* v *Brocklehurst* there had been common ownership but separate occupation because one property had been let to a tenant and, in any event, the case had not been based on s. 62 or its predecessor, s. 6(2) of the Conveyancing Act 1881. It was accepted that *Broomfield* did provide a genuine exception to this approach but it was said (at p. 50) that the exception arose because it concerned a claim to a right to light and that such an easement is unusual because its use is genuinely continuous (at least during daylight hours). However, in *P & S Platt Ltd* v *Crouch* [2004] 1 P&CR 18, the Court of Appeal said that separate occupation was not needed if the use was continuous and apparent.

In general, therefore, it appears that *Broomfield* will be confined to cases of truly continuous easements, of which there are likely to be few. Indeed, the right to light maybe the only example. In this context it seems that 'continuous' is likely to be taken fairly literally. However, the reason for the distinction seems as difficult to understand as does the reason why s. 62 should ever have been construed as having the effect of changing the nature of the privilege or advantage in question into that of an easement, rather than simply transferring the thing (usually a licence) that actually exists. This seems, quite simply, to amount to a piece of statutory magic. (See further Tee [1998] Conv 115, Harpum [1989] Conv 113 and Thompson [1997] Conv 453.)

22.7.5 Acquisition of profits

Profits, as well as easements, may be acquired by the s. 62 method, where a right capable of amounting to a profit has been given and thereafter a conveyance satisfying s. 62 has been made (*White v Williams* [1922] 1 KB 727 (grazing sheep)).

22.7.6 Express grant

Since s. 62 operates by importing certain words into the conveyance, it has the effect of making an *express*, not implied, grant of the easement or profit (*Gregg v Richards* [1926] Ch 521). The fact that the section works through a conveyance in this way means that it is subject to a number of limitations. For example, it will not operate on a contract to convey or create a legal estate, for this does not constitute a conveyance (*Re Peck's Contract* [1893] 2 Ch 315) (we have already mentioned (see 8.3.4) that this is one way in which a contract for a lease is not as good as a lease). Nor can it convert into an easement or profit a right which does not satisfy the tests for such rights (*Phipps v Pears* [1965] 1 QB 76 (claim to easement of protection from weather)). It is also probable that a short lease granted informally under LPA 1925, s. 54(2) will only amount to a conveyance for these purposes if there is a document making the grant. Although an oral lease will be legal under s. 54(2) if it is for not more than three years, in *Rye v Rye* [1962] AC 496 it was held that the definition of conveyance in LPA 1925, s. 205 requires there to be an instrument. This case was in fact a decision in relation to LPA 1925, s. 71 but there is no reason why the same reasoning should not apply to cases under s. 62, so that the wording of this section would be taken to cover only those grants made by some form of document. A claim under s. 62 will also fail where the express words of the conveyance manifest a contrary intention.

22.7.7 Comparison of the rule in *Wheeldon* v *Burrows* and LPA 1925, s. 62

Space does not permit us to make a detailed comparison, and indeed it will be more useful to you to make this for yourself, but we will indicate briefly the main differences:

(a) *Wheeldon* v *Burrows* relates only to easements, whilst s. 62 applies to both easements and profits.

(b) *Wheeldon* v *Burrows* operates where, before the conveyance, the two pieces of land have been occupied by the same person, whereas diversity of occupation is required for s. 62. This distinction is not one which, however, can be given without the warning that not all writers upon land law are agreed that s. 62 can only apply when before the date of the relevant conveyance the two plots of land were at least in separate occupation. Indeed the leading texts on this area of the law dispute this view (see Jackson, *The Law of Easements and Profits* (1978), p. 100 and Gale, *Easements*, 17th edn. (2002), p. 157). Accordingly the matter should not be regarded as settled. However, support for the view that s. 62 only applies where there has been diversity of occupation can be found in *Long* v *Gowlett* [1923] 2 Ch 177; *Ward* v *Kirkland* [1967] Ch 194, 228, and in the decision of the House of Lords in *Sovmots Investments Ltd* v *Secretary of State for the Environment* [1979] AC 144, in which this view was expressly stated (by Lord Wilberforce at p. 169 and by Lord Edmund-Davies at p. 176). Obviously an express statement of this type cannot be ignored but Jackson points out that the remarks in *Sovmots* are no more than *obiter dicta* and were made without full consideration of the authorities. A number of cases did suggest that diversity of occupation is not essential (*James* v *Plant* (1836) 4 Ad & El 749; *Berkshire* v *Grubb* (1881) 18 ChD 616; *Broomfield* v *Williams* [1897] 1 Ch 602; *Wright* v *Macadam* [1949] 2 KB 744, 748; but see *Payne* v *Inwood* (1996) 74 P&CR 42 (see 22.7.4)), which resolves the issue in favour of a need for diversity.

(c) The types of easements which can pass under *Wheeldon* v *Burrows* are restricted by the three requirements of the rule, whereas there are no such restrictions in the case of s. 62.

(d) *Wheeldon* v *Burrows*, unlike s. 62, is apparently not limited to conveyances. Thus it seems that a contract to grant a lease may be sufficient to create an easement in favour of the tenant under *Wheeldon* v *Burrows* (*Borman* v *Griffith* [1930] 1 Ch 493).

22.8 Acquisition by prescription

Both easements and profits may be acquired as the result of long use, as well as by the means of grant and reservation described above. This method of acquisition is called 'prescription', of which there are three forms:

(a) common law prescription;

(b) the fiction of lost modern grant; and

(c) under the Prescription Act 1832.

All these types of prescription will give the acquirer a legal easement or legal profit, even though there has in fact been no grant by deed. With the exception of one of the forms of prescription under the Act, all these methods are based on the fiction that such a grant has been made at some time in the past, and long use is regarded merely as evidence of that grant. Some of the rules about prescription which may seem strange will be more easily understood if you remember that they are designed to maintain this pretence.

22.8.1 **Basic rules for prescription**

There are three basic rules which apply to all the methods of prescription and we will discuss these first and then consider each of the three forms of prescription in turn.

22.8.1.1 *Use must be as of right*

It is essential for the claimant to establish that, throughout the period of use, he or she has enjoyed the right claimed 'as of right'. The use (and that of any predecessors in title, if relevant) must be consistent with the fiction that the right was granted at some time in the past, and that the owner of the dominant land has been acting in reliance on this. Any inconsistent behaviour will be taken to show that the claimant does not have such a right. It appears that it is irrelevant that the claimant of the easement has been exercising the right in the mistaken belief that it has in fact been granted (*Bridle* v *Ruby* [1989] QB 169). On the concept of 'user as of right' see the articles by Riddal [1977] Conv 199 and Simpson [1998] Conv 442.

The traditional formulation of the test of whether the use is as of right is that the use must be *nec vi, nec clam, nec precario*.

(1) *Nec vi* This means that the right claimed must not have been exercised by force. Thus, if Farmer George were to have erected a gate blocking access to the footpath on his land, Mr Neep would be using the path by force if he broke down the gate, or even if he simply climbed over it. Even a protest by the servient owner can prevent user as of right, for ignoring a protest is regarded as use by force (*Eaton* v *Swansea Waterworks Co.* (1851) 17 QB 267). The rule prevents people obtaining interests in land by use of 'strong-arm' tactics. It was said at one time that acting illegally also prevented acquisition of an easement: *Hanning* v *Top Deck Travel Group Ltd* [1993] 68 P&CR 14. However, the House of Lords took the opposite view in *Bakewell Management Ltd* v *Brandwood* [2004] 2 WLR 955.

(2) *Nec clam* The right must not be exercised secretly, for such use prevents the servient owner from objecting to the acquisition of the right and appears inconsistent with a claim of right. In *Liverpool Corporation* v *Coghill & Sons Ltd* [1918] 1 Ch 307 a claim to an easement of drainage was unsuccessful because the claimant's drain had entered the general sewer below ground and it was impossible for the corporation to ascertain that one more load of effluent had been added to its general burden. Thus, if Mr Neep had used the farmer's path only at dead of night and in a manner designed to conceal his use, he would be regarded as not having exercised an easement of way as of right.

(3) *Nec precario* This means that the right must not be enjoyed precariously, i.e., by permission. If the servient owner has given the claimant permission, the right is a licence and not an easement or profit and (unless contractual, or binding due to an estoppel) is revocable at the will of the licensor. Thus, if Farmer George has given Mr Neep permission to use the path, the use is not made 'as of right'. Of course, if permission was given very far in the past it may be deemed to have lapsed in time, so that the more recent use may be regarded as not being by permission (*Arkwright* v *Gell* (1839) 5 M & W 203). On permission, see further below at para. 22.8.8.

22.8.1.2 *The right must be acquired by a fee simple owner against a fee simple owner*

Again, this rule originates in the pretence that the right has been properly granted at some time in the past, for the only way to explain its continuance is that it was granted in fee simple, rather than for a limited period of years. This implies a grant by a fee simple owner to a fee simple owner. Thus, even if the use in question is by a tenant, any easement or profit acquired as a result will attach to the fee simple in the dominant land, rather than to the tenant's lease (though of course the tenant will still have an interest in claiming).

Prescription by and against a tenant

As a result, it is never possible for a tenant of dominant land to acquire rights by prescription against his own landlord (*Gayford* v *Moffat* (1868) LR 4 Ch App 133), for such a tenant can only claim to acquire an easement on behalf of the landlord, and the landlord cannot have rights against himself (*Ivimey* v *Stocker* (1866) LR 1 Ch App 396). It is emphasised that what we are saying is only that a tenant cannot acquire easements against his landlord by *prescription*, for we have already seen that he may acquire such rights by express or implied grant. Similarly it was held in *Simmons* v *Dobson* [1991] 1 WLR 720 that a tenant could not obtain by prescription against another tenant of the same landlord (see also on this point *Wheaton* v *Maple* [1893] 3 Ch 48 and *Kilgour* v *Gaddes* [1904] 1 KB 457).

Where an easement is acquired by prescription it binds the fee simple estate in the servient land. If that land is let to a tenant during the prescription period it seems unfair to allow the dominant owner to claim the acquisition of an easement or profit by prescription. The tenant on the servient land may well not be concerned about the exercise of the right, whilst the fee simple owner may not be aware of the user since he has given exclusive possession of the land to his tenant. It is therefore the rule that there should be no tenancy of the servient land at the start of the prescription period. If, however, the fee simple owner is in possession when the use begins, he has the opportunity to discover what has happened and, if he subsequently lets the land, can make enquiries of his tenant in order to ascertain whether the use is continuing. Thus, in *Pugh* v *Savage* [1970] 2 QB 373 an easement was acquired by prescription even though the servient land had been let for 10 years in the middle of the prescription period. If, however, the land is let when the use began, the prescription period will only start when the fee simple owner re-enters (*Daniel* v *North* (1809) 11 East 372).

22.8.1.3 *The use must be continuous*

The infrequent use of a right is not sufficient if one is claiming an easement or profit by prescription. Thus, if Mr Neep had used Farmer George's path on only three occasions in the last 12 years this would not support a claim to an easement by prescription (see *Hollins* v *Verney* (1884) 13 QBD 304). As we have mentioned previously, the exercise of a right of way can never be continuous in a literal sense, but in such cases regular usage will suffice. Also the right exercised should not generally be varied during the period for prescription, although in the case of *Davis* v *Whitby* [1974] Ch 186 it was regarded as acceptable if a minor variation was made for the sake of convenience (here the alteration was to the exact path used in the case of a right of way).

22.8.2 **Prescription at common law**

In order to establish a claim to an easement or profit by prescription at common law, it is necessary to establish that the interest has been enjoyed, as of right, since *time immemorial* or, to use the traditional phrase, 'from time whereof the memory of man runneth not to the contrary'. You may, however, be amused to discover that lawyers have a very definite view on when the 'memory of man' started. Under the Statute of Westminster the First (1275), c. 39, the date of legal memory is 1189 and this date has never been amended. Therefore this method of prescription requires that the right in question was in existence before that date.

You will appreciate that it is practically impossible to establish positively such a long period of use. Accordingly, the rule has developed that proof of use during living memory will raise a presumption that the right has been enjoyed since 1189. Originally user during living memory was established by asking the oldest inhabitants of the area whether the right had been exercised as long as they recalled. Today all that is needed is evidence that the right has been used for at least 20 years (*Darling* v *Clue* (1864) 4 F & F 329).

However, the presumption raised by the 20-year use is a rebuttable presumption, and the claim to prescription at common law can be destroyed by evidence which shows that the right claimed must have begun later than 1189. Thus if the claim were to an easement of light, proof that the building on the dominant tenement had been built after 1189 would destroy the claim at common law (*Bury* v *Pope* (1588) Cro Eliz 118). Similarly, if the dominant and servient tenements have been in common ownership at any time since 1189 this claim at common law will fail. Even if the right had been granted before 1189, it would have come to an end when the two pieces of land came into the same hands (see 22.2.1.2), and any grant when they separated again would be after the date of legal memory (*Keymer* v *Summers* (1769) Bull NP 74). Thus, were Nigel Neep to claim his right to use the footpath on Farmer George's land by common law prescription, he would be able to raise the presumption of use since 1189 if he and his predecessors in title had used the path for 20 years, but his claim would easily be defeated if Farmer George could prove that 14 Trant Way and Fieldy Farm were once owned by one person (which is very likely to be the case). As a result claims by prescription under the pure common law rule are rarely successful today, although, as we shall see, some assistance is provided by the Prescription Act 1832.

22.8.3 **Lost modern grant**

Because it was so difficult to obtain an easement or profit under the general common law rules, the courts eventually developed a second method of prescription at common law, known as the fiction of the lost modern grant. This requires that the claimant should first establish user during living memory (for at least 20 years). Once this has been established the court is prepared to presume that the right is being exercised as the result of a modern grant by deed, *but that the grant has been lost*. This is recognised as a complete fiction (see *Dalton* v *Angus & Co.* (1881) 6 App Cas 740). It appears that the presumption cannot be rebutted by proving that no grant *has* been made but it will destroy the claim if the servient owner can show that, at the date at which it is alleged the grant occurred, there was no person capable of making the grant (for example, because the land was subject to a strict settlement, under which no grant could be made—this will become less likely over time because of the wide powers of trustees of trusts of land). Similarly the claim may be opposed by showing that at the relevant time the dominant and servient tenements were in common ownership (see *Neaverson* v *Peterborough Rural District Council* [1902] 1 Ch 557).

This method of prescription, based on a blatant fiction, was disliked in the nineteenth century, and it was hoped that the changes introduced by the Prescription Act 1832 would make it unnecessary to use it. However, as we shall see, this Act has proved to be most unsatisfactory, and so the method of the lost modern grant is still in use today.

The extent of the fiction is well illustrated by *Bridle* v *Ruby* [1989] QB 169. There a developer built and sold a number of houses. Originally it was intended that the purchaser of plot 12 was to be granted an express right of way over a drive. In fact the relevant clause was deleted from the conveyance so that the grant of the right was never made. The purchaser and his successors, in the mistaken belief that they had the right to do so, used the driveway for 22 years. Here the Court of Appeal held that the right could be claimed on the basis of lost modern grant. The fact that the relevant clause had been deleted from the original conveyance did not prevent the operation of the theory that, at a later date, a grant had been made. It was even irrelevant that the owners of plot 12 had used the right believing that the right to do so arose from the original conveyance. This case clearly demonstrates that the legal fiction is alive and well today. For a further illustration see *Mills* v *Silver* [1991] Ch 271, in which the Court of Appeal considered at length the issue of permission in relation to the doctrine of lost modern grant. (Also, see further 22.8.5.3(2).)

The usual common law rules apply to lost modern grant, thus for example it applies only by a fee simple owner against a fee simple owner (see *Simmons* v *Dobson* [1991] 1 WLR 720).

22.8.4 Prescription Act 1832

The Prescription Act 1832 may very well have the dubious honour of being the worst drafted Act of Parliament on the statute book. Indeed it is even generally presumed that there is a serious misprint in s. 8 of the Act and lawyers have accordingly adopted the habit of reading the section as though the misprint did not exist (thereby substituting the word 'easement' for the word 'convenient' where it appears in s. 8). The Act was intended to remove the difficulties which arose with the common law forms of prescription; however, it did not abolish the common law forms, so that the three forms now exist alongside one another. Furthermore, the Act introduced fresh complexities of its own.

The Act divides the easement of light from all other easements and profits and deals with it separately. Furthermore it creates two different prescription periods (a 'short period' and a 'long period'), with different effects, for profits and easements other than light. The provisions relating to the short period merely assist a person claiming under the common law rules, but those relating to the long period introduce a form of statutory prescription, which does not depend on any fiction.

22.8.5 **Profits and easements other than light under the Prescription Act 1832**

22.8.5.1 *Short period*

The short period for easements is 20 years (Prescription Act 1832, s. 2), and for profits is 30 years (s. 1). The Act provides that, where use can be shown for the appropriate period, no claim to prescription at common law shall be defeated by showing that the right 'was first enjoyed at any time prior to such period'. The effect of this provision is quite simple but understanding why the statutory words have this effect is not so easy. The explanation is as follows. Legal memory does not go back before 1189, so, if the right was first enjoyed before that date, it would not be possible to show when it started. Thus the fact that one *can* show when it started means that that beginning must be *after* 1189, which would be fatal to a claim at common law. Therefore the Act is saying, in a roundabout way, that once the period had been completed, common law prescription cannot be defeated merely by showing that the use began after 1189.

The claim can still be defeated in any other way that would defeat common law prescription, such as showing that the use is not as of right, or that the right claimed lacks the characteristics of an easement or profit. Accordingly, if permission has been given, orally or in writing, at any time, this will prevent a claim under the short period because the right would have been exercised precariously. For more on permission see para. 22.8.8 below. (If the permission were of considerable antiquity it may be disregarded as lapsed, particularly if it is oral: see below.) In much the same way in *Diment* v *Foot Ltd* [1974] 1 WLR 1427 a claim to an easement of way based on 36 years use failed because the use was not known to the servient owners (*'clam'*). A similar result was caused by secret use in *Union Lighterage Co.* v *London Graving Dock Co.* [1902] 2 Ch 557, in which the claimed easement of support was being exercised secretly, below water level.

More recently, the House of Lords has indicated that, even in the absence of express permission, a claim to acquire by prescription by means of 20 years' use can theoretically be displaced by evidence of implied permission; see *R (Beresford)* v *Sunderland City Council* [2003] 3 WLR 1306 (this cannot work for the long period— see para 22.8.5.2). When you look at the case you will see that it did not concern an easement but it was about public rights to use a recreational area. However, this is an area of law in which the same concept of user as of right applies and thus the case is also useful in relation to easements and profits. Lord Bingham said (at para. 5):

I can see no objection in principle to the implication of a licence where the facts warrant such an implication. To deny this possibility would, I think, be unduly old-fashioned, formalistic and restrictive.

However, he also emphasised that mere inaction of the landowner at a time at which he had knowledge of the use being made of his land would not suffice to establish that permission had been given. Here it was argued that because the Council had mown the grass and provided seating it had impliedly consented to the use being made (and thus given permission). The House of Lords did not, however accept this view of the facts and held that the public use during the 20-year period had not been by permission and thus was user as of right.

Deductions

In order to provide some protection for a servient owner who is subject to a legal disability, s. 7 of the Act provides that certain periods should be deducted when one computes the 20 or 30-year short period. The effect of these provisions, as modified by later reforms of the law, is that one should deduct any period during which the servient owner was:

(a) an infant;

(b) a patient under the Mental Health Act 1983 (or the Acts which preceded it); or

(c) a tenant for life.

Thus, if Nigel Neep had exercised his right of way for 35 years but for 20 of those years the owner of Fieldy Farm had been incapable (e.g., Farmer George's father had suffered from dementia for 20 years before his death) Mr Neep can only claim 15 years of user for the purposes of the short period. He can, however, add together the use before the old man's illness overcame his mental capacity and the use after Farmer George inherited on his father's death. He does *not* have to restart the period once the disability is removed (*Pugh* v *Savage* [1970] 2 QB 373).

22.8.5.2 *Long period*

The long period is 40 years for easements (s. 2) and 60 years for profits (s. 1). The benefit of proving use for the longer period is that the right claimed 'shall be deemed absolute and indefeasible, unless it shall appear that the same was enjoyed by some consent or agreement expressly given or made for the purpose by deed or writing'. This is the statutory form of prescription, and does not depend on the common law rules, nor on any fiction.

(1) *Consents* It is clear from the statutory provisions we have quoted that written consent can destroy a claim under the long period, whether it was given before the period started or during the period. At first reading this may seem to imply that purely oral permission cannot destroy the claim. However, this is not the case for it is still necessary for the dominant owner to show that his use of the easement or profit during the 40- or 60-year period has amounted to use as of right. As we have seen already, if the servient owner has given oral permission the use is precarious and *not* as of right. Accordingly oral permission given *during* the long period will destroy the claim but oral permission given *before* the period can be ignored.

(2) *Does the use have to start against a fee simple owner?* As we have said, at common law the prescription period could not start at a time when the servient land was let to a tenant. In *Davies* v *Du Paver* [1953] 1 QB 184 the Court of Appeal appeared to apply the same rule to a case brought under the Prescription Act 1832. However, in the earlier case of *Wright* v *Williams* (1836) 1 M & W 77 (which was not cited in *Davies* v *Du Paver*) it was held that the common law rule did not apply because of the positive wording of the Act. It would appear that the better view is that the rule *does not* apply, particularly as in s. 8 special provision is made for deduction of periods during which the servient land is subject to a lease (see Megarry (1956) 72 LQR 32).

(3) *Deductions* Deductions from the long period are governed by s. 8. It should be noted that these rules bear no real relation to the deductions from the short

period prescribed by s. 7. Assuming that the word 'convenient' in s. 8 is a misprint for 'easement', s. 8 provides for the deductions from the long period of any term during which the servient land was:

(a) held by a tenant for life;

(b) held by a tenant under a lease for more than three years.

However, the s. 8 deductions may only be made if the servient owner resists the claim to acquisition by prescription within the three years following the end of the life interest or lease.

(4) *Application of rules* The following example may make this clearer:

1 January 1962	The then owner of 14 Trant Way started to use the footpath on Fieldy Farm.
1 January 1990	Lease of Fieldy Farm for 10 years granted.
31 December 1999	Lease ends.
31 December 2001	40 years' use of right of way.

In this example, if Mr Neep had claimed under the longer period on 1 January 2002, Farmer George would have been able to claim a deduction from the period of use, under s. 8. For in these circumstances the servient tenement, Fieldy Farm, would have been subject to a lease for more than three years (10 years) and that lease would have ended less than three years before the date of the action. (Action started on 1 January 2002 and lease ended two years earlier on 31 December 1999). If, however, the use continues, but no action had been brought until 2003, more than three years would have elapsed since the end of the lease, and Farmer George would accordingly not be entitled to make any deduction. Thus, if the matter came to court in 2002 Nigel Neep would only have a claim based on 30 years' use (40 years' actual use, less 10 years during which the servient land was let), whilst if the case started in or after 2003 Nigel Neep can claim 41 years' use (no deduction is permitted). This result may seem odd at first sight but one should remember that the purpose of s. 8 is to provide limited protection for the reversioner who takes action swiftly on recovering the land. This may be particularly important to the freehold reversioner or a remainderman, following on after a tenant for life, who should accordingly make immediate enquiries about such matters as soon as his interest vests in possession.

22.8.5.3 *Rules common to both short and long periods*

Certain rules are common to both the long and the short periods.

(1) *User as of right* We have already seen that the Prescription Act 1832 does not exclude the common law requirement that the user relied upon must be as of right during the period claimed, and this has been held to mean not only that the use should be *nec vi, nec clam,* and *nec precario*, but also that use must be by and against fee simple owners (*Kilgour* v *Gaddes* [1904] 1 KB 457).

(2) *Period must be 'next before some suit or action'* Under s. 4, the period relied upon must be 'next before some suit or action wherein the claim or matter to which such period may relate shall have been or shall be brought into question'. Thus, a period of use which ceased some time before the commencement of an action cannot be relied upon for the purpose of statutory prescription, although it may be effective

to support a claim to prescription at common law. Thus, in *Tehidy Minerals Ltd* v *Norman* [1971] 2 QB 528 claims based upon user which had ceased in 1941 (when the land was requisitioned by the army) were ineffective under the Act, although some claimants succeeded in establishing their rights under the principle of lost modern grant (see also *Mills* v *Silver* [1991] Ch 271). Another effect of s. 4 is that no right to the easement or profit can exist under the statutory rules until some action is started, regardless of the length of use involved (*Hyman* v *Van den Bergh* [1908] 1 Ch 167). Of course, in order to secure his interest in the land, the dominant owner has only to apply to the court for a declaration that an easement or profit has been secured under the Act.

(3) *There must have been no interruption*   A claim based on either period may be destroyed by proof that there has been some 'interruption' to the claimed interest and that the dominant owner has acquiesced in that interruption for the period of one year. An 'interruption' is any action which interferes with the right claimed. In the case of the footpath on Fieldy Farm, Farmer George could create an interruption by erecting a gate, or other barrier, preventing access to the path. Thus, in *Davies* v *Du Paver* [1953] 1 QB 184, the servient owner erected a fence in order to exclude the dominant owner's sheep and thereby to prevent the acquisition of a profit. This case illustrates, however, that there must not only be an obstruction but that the obstruction must be *acquiesced in* for one year by the claimant. In *Davies* v *Du Paver* the dominant owner immediately protested at the erection of the fence, but did not issue proceedings to establish his claim to a profit until 13 months later. The Court of Appeal found that he had not acquiesced in the interruption for one year because his initial protest must have been effective for some period (at least a month) in which case at the start of the action there had been less than one year's acquiescence. However, mere discontent which is not sufficiently communicated cannot amount to sufficient action to indicate a lack of acquiescence (*Dance* v *Triplow* [1992] 1 EGLR 190).

As a result of this provision about acquiescence, it is not possible to rely on an interruption to prevent the claimant succeeding under the Act once 19 years and 1 day have passed with respect to the short period (29 years and 1 day for profits) and 39 years and 1 day (59 years and 1 day for profits) for the long period. For, if an interruption were made, for example, to an easement after it had been used for 39 years and 1 day, the dominant owner could still issue proceedings 364 days later, as soon as the 40-year term is up, and claim that he had not acquiesced in the interruption for a year. By protesting at the interruption, he can extend the time still further. Thus, once usage has entered the last year of one of the periods, a servient tenement owner who objects to the use should commence proceedings immediately for trespass, for until the period is completed his opponent will not be able to rely on the existence of an easement or profit by prescription by way of defence. For more on acquiescence, see para. 22.8.8.

22.8.6 **Right to light under the Prescription Act 1832**

22.8.6.1 *One period only*

The right to light is dealt with by the Prescription Act 1832 in a different way from its treatment of all other easements. There is only one period (not a 'short' and a 'long' period) and that requires user for a period of 20 years. Section 3 of the Act provides that if the 'use of light' to 'any dwelling-house', workshop, or other building' has been 'actually enjoyed . . . for the full period of 20 years without interruption, the right thereto shall be deemed absolute and indefeasible'. There are a number of differences between this provision and those relating to other easements and profits. In particular s. 3 does not require the satisfaction of the common law requirements for prescription. Accordingly, the use need not be as of right, nor is it necessary for the use to be by a fee simple owner against a fee simple owner. Thus, a tenant can acquire an easement of light by prescription against his landlord, or against a fellow tenant holding from the same landlord.

22.8.6.2 *Interruption*

The rules on interruption, however, do apply to easements of light in the same way as they apply to other rights claimed under the Act, and it has also been held that the 20-year period relied on must be next before suit or action, even though s. 3 does not specifically mention this (*Hyman* v *Van den Bergh* [1908] 1 Ch 167).

22.8.6.3 *Preventing acquisition of right*

It can be seen that it is far easier to acquire an easement of light than any other easement or profit. Accordingly, a 'servient' owner may well wish to take action to prevent his neighbour acquiring such a right. Unfortunately, in order to do this he or she would need to interrupt the use of the right and the erection of some structure (e.g., a hoarding) in order to do this will probably be contrary to the planning regulations applicable to the property. As a result, the Rights of Light Act 1959 was passed in order to provide a simple means by which a claim to light can be interrupted. Under this Act, instead of building a hoarding, a servient owner may, after taking certain preliminary steps, register a notice in the Local Land Charges Register specifying the size and position of the obstruction which he would other-wise have erected. Notice of this entry should be given to the dominant owner unless the case is one of exceptional urgency (s. 2). The entry upon the register operates as though a real obstruction had been built and therefore if the dominant owner takes no action for a year he will be deemed to have acquiesced in the interruption. In the case of registered land, r. 36 of the Land Registration Rules 2003 provides that the registrar may enter a notice on the title register where it appears that there is any agreement that prevents the owner of that estate from acquiring the benefit of a right to light. This is even though it is not strictly speaking a burden on that estate. However, this applies only to an agreement. As the registration of a notice under the 1959 Act is of a *local* land charge, it is effective in relation to both registered and unregistered land. In the case of registered land, local land charges are overriding interests, both on first registration and on any later disposition (see Sch. 1 and Sch. 3, LRA 2002).

22.8.7 **How to apply the three forms of prescription**

We have now looked at a bewildering variety of rules, and you must wonder how they fit together and which method to use. At one time it was thought that the courts in modern times would generally be unwilling to accept a claim based on a lost modern grant, but the decision in *Tehidy Minerals Ltd* v *Norman* [1971] 2 QB 528 produced a rehabilitation of the doctrine (see also *Bridle* v *Ruby* [1989] QB 169 and *Mills* v *Silver* [1991] Ch 271).

There are thus still three main methods to consider, and it appears that they should be applied in the following order. Begin with the long period under the Prescription Act 1832. If there is not a sufficient period of use, or it is not 'next before the action', or for some other reasons that method does not succeed, apply the common law rules, assisted if possible by the short-period provisions of the Act. If that is not successful, as a last resort you should apply the doctrine of the lost modern grant. This is in effect the order in which the various forms of prescription were considered in *Tehidy Minerals Ltd* v *Norman*. This judgment of the Court of Appeal does provide a very good example for anyone who has to deal with a problem of this kind and so we will end this section with an account of that case.

The plaintiffs owned an area of downland on which local farmers had grazed their animals since the nineteenth century. For some time during and after the Second World War the down was requisitioned, and when grazing was resumed it appeared to be by permission. The plaintiffs fenced the down and tried to exclude the farmers, but they broke the fences. The plaintiffs alleged trespass and the defendants claimed that they had a profit of grazing.

It was not possible to make the claim under the long period of the Act, for the period of requisitioning and permissive use broke into this. The long use, dating back to the nineteenth century did, however, enable some farmers to raise a presumption that the right had existed from time immemorial, and they succeeded at common law. The other defendants, however, could not rely on the common law, because their farms and the down had been in common ownership at some time after 1189. They were not assisted by the shorter period under the Act because it was interrupted by the requisitioning. They were, however, able to show over 20 years' use before the war, and the Court of Appeal held that this was sufficient to raise a presumption of a lost modern grant and found that they had acquired a profit by this means.

Prior to *Tehidy* v *Norman* it had been suggested that the doctrine of lost modern grant was dead after the Prescription Act. However, *Tehidy* rehabilitated the fiction and it has been in regular use as a basis of claim ever since. For another case in which a claim under the short period in the Act failed but the claimant won by relying on lost modern grant, see *Smith* v *Brudenell-Bruce* [2002] 2 P&CR 4.

22.8.8 Acquiescence and permission

Often those dealing with prescription find it difficult to distinguish between a permission (licence), which prevents an easement or profit being acquired by prescription, and acquiescence, without which prescription is impossible. It is therefore worth pausing at this point to look again at the two concepts.

Since one cannot claim by prescription unless the servient owner has known of the use being made of the land and has not tried to stop it, for a claim by prescription to succeed it is said that the servient owner must have *acquiesced* in the use. In essence, the servient owner has put up with the use and this is construed as acceptance that the person claiming the easement or profit has been using as a right. The need for acquiescence means that the use made must not be secret (e.g., sneaking across a path at dead of night) because an owner cannot acquiesce in a use of which he or she is unaware. See on this: *Dalton* v *Angus & Co* (1881) 6 App Cas 740; *Mills* v *Silver* [1991] Ch 271; *R* v *Oxfordshire CC, ex parte Sunningwell* [2000] 1 AC 335; and *R (Beresford)* v *Sunderland City Council* [2003] 3 WLR 1306.

However, if before or during the use the servient owner has given *permission* for the land to be used by the claimant or his or her predecessors in title, that establishes that the claimant is not using the right because he has an easement or profit: rather, it shows that the user has a licence *(permission)* to make use of the land. Giving permission therefore bars a successful claim to an easement or profit because the servient owner can say, 'You were using the land because you had a licence to do so. Therefore there is reason for your use that establishes that you were not using my land as of right: you were using it because I let you do so and not because you had a right (an easement or profit) to do so'. On permission, see *Ironside* v *Cook* (1978) 41 P&CR 326; *Gardner* v *Hodgson's Kingston Brewery Co. Ltd.* [1974] 1 WLR 1427; and note that an old permission may lapse, allowing use to become as of right in time, *Arkwright* v *Gell* (1839) 5 M&W 203.

22.9 Remedies

We will now consider briefly the remedies which may be used to protect an easement or profit.

22.9.1 Abatement

Theoretically If any obstruction to the lawful exercise of a profit or easement is erected, the dominant owner may exercise a 'self-help' remedy and may simply 'abate' (remove) the obstruction. This may be done without informing the servient owner (*Perry* v *Fitzhowe* (1846) 8 QB 757) but the right should be used with care. The dominant owner must not use unreasonable force, nor may he injure any person in attempting to enforce his rights. It would, however, be permissible to break down a fence or gate. In general, however, it is inadvisable for the dominant owner to rely upon self-help, and indeed in *Lagan Navigation Co.* v *Lambeg Bleaching, Dyeing & Finishing Co. Ltd* [1927] AC 226 at p. 245 Lord Atkinson indicated that the law preferred that a remedy be sought through the courts, and that abatement should only be used in cases of extreme urgency.

22.9.2 Action

Normally, a person claiming that his or her easement or profit has been infringed will apply to the courts for a suitable remedy. Obviously, it is possible to seek a declaration to clarify the rights of the parties (useful where a right is claimed by prescription). The claimant may, however, go further and seek damages to compensate for any loss caused by the infringement but, if this is done, must establish some serious interference with the rights, rather than some trivial incident (*Weston* v *Lawrence Weaver Ltd* [1961] 1 QB 402). Generally, the remedy which will be sought is that of an injunction restraining the interference of which the dominant owner complains. Once again, the courts will not intervene where the act complained of is only a trivial interference with the dominant owner's rights (*Cowper* v *Laidler* [1903] 2 Ch 337). However, there is no right to alter the terms of an easement even where the dominant owner could not reasonably object to the change. Thus, it would not be a defence to a complaint of interference with a private right of way that a reasonable substitute had been provided (*Greenwich Healthcare National Health Service Trust* v *London and Quadrant Housing Trust* [1998] 1 WLR 1749). The relevant question is not whether the use left to the person with the benefit of the right is reasonable, but whether it was reasonable for that person to insist on all he or she had bargained for: see *Celsteel Ltd* v *Alton House Ltd* [1985] 1 WLR 204 at p. 217. In relation to a claim for damages for interference with a right to light it should be noted that the issues are so complex that the College of Estate Management has published a guide to the subject (*The Valuation of Rights to Light*, J. Anstey).

22.9.2.1 *Claim in nuisance*

One must also note that the inability to enforce an easement may not mean that a complainant has no remedy at all because in some cases a claim in nuisance may be available. This may be particularly important in cases which, at first, seem to involve the easement of support. As we have noted above (22.2.2.7), the easement of support does not require the servient owner to maintain his premises in order to ensure that adequate support is provided. He may instead allow his premises to collapse, should he so wish: *Jones* v *Pritchard* [1908] 1 Ch 630 at p. 637. However, the owner of the dominant premises is not obliged simply to sit around and watch the servient premises (for example, a party wall) collapse; he can enter the servient premises and take the necessary steps to ensure that the support continues by effecting repairs to the part of the servient premises that provides the support: *Bond* v *Nottingham Corporation* [1940] Ch 429, per Greene MR at pp. 438–9. This is the right of abatement explained above. However, *Bradburn* v *Lindsay* [1983] 2 All ER 408 suggests that another right maybe available even where abatement has not been practicable. In *Bradburn*, Mr and Mrs Bradburn owned 55 Kennerley Road, Stockport and Mrs Lindsay owned 53 Kennerley Road. In fact the premises formed one building with a party wall (providing two semi-detached houses) but which were not divided in any way in the loft space. In 1972 Mr Bradburn complained that dry-rot had taken hold in the party wall between the premises. Mrs Lindsay's premises at No. 53 were becoming derelict and appeared abandoned, although there was evidence of some transient occupation (possibly by trespassers). By 1975 the council had become involved and there was evidence of extensive dry-rot and damage at No. 53. In 1976 the council made a demolition order in relation to No. 53 due to its dangerous condition and the premises of No. 53 (other than No. 53's half of the party wall) were demolished in 1977. The Bradburns, whose half of the house was left unsupported, bought a claim in nuisance and negligence. A claim based on the easement of support should not in this case (at least theoretically) have succeeded since Mrs Lindsay had merely allowed the dereliction to occur and the pulling down of the house had been carried out by the council under statutory powers. However, the court held that the Bradburns' claim could succeed. The decision appears to be based in part in nuisance and in part in negligence. Judge Blackett-Ord V-C said that the considerable dry-rot at No. 53 constituted a nuisance, that Mrs Lindsay should have appreciated the risks to

No. 55 and accordingly should have taken steps to prevent the damage. Accordingly the Bradburns were able to recover the costs of works to strengthen and support No. 55. It may be that this case does not conflict with the traditional view of the easement of support because, on a careful reading of the case, it seems that the decision is based on the principle that allowing spread of dry rot falls within the ambit of nuisance and goes further than simply allowing a structure to fall down. However, in practice the two may typically run together and thus nuisance may provide a useful alternative when the law relating to easements fails to provide a remedy (see also *Nuisances* by Gordon Wignall, 1998 (Sweet & Maxwell)).

There are two other cases that adopt this approach. In *Holbeck Hall Hotel* v *Scarborough BC* [2000] QB 836, it was said that a duty may arise in tort but this extends only to damage that is reasonably foreseeable. In *Holbeck* it could only have been foreseen had there been geological investigation and the defendant was not obliged to carry out such an investigation.

Rees v *Skerrett* [2001] 1 WLR 1541 concerned two terraced houses, one of which was demolished. As a consequence the party wall between the properties became unstable and it also was exposed to the weather. The instability was clearly a breach of the easement of support and the court held so. However, the owner of the affected (dominant) property had suffered additional loss due to the penetration of rain through the wall, which had caused damp in his house. This loss was not attributable to the loss of support. It was accepted that no easement could be claimed in relation to protection from the weather (*Phipps* v *Pears* [1965] 1 QB 76). However, the court held that the servient owner did owe an additional duty to take care when demolishing his house, to the extent necessary to prevent consequential damage to the dominant property. Thus a claim in relation to the damp could succeed.

22.10 Extinguishment of easements and profits

Once easements and profits have arisen they will, as interests in land, endure through successive ownerships of the land. Indeed they may well endure for very long periods. We must therefore consider the means by which such rights are brought to an end.

22.10.1 Dominant and servient tenements coming into the same hands

Because a person cannot have rights against him or herself, an easement, or a profit appurtenant to land, will be extinguished if the dominant and the servient tenements come into common ownership and possession. It is essential that *both* ownership and possession become common, and that both tenements are acquired for an estate in fee simple (*R* v *Inhabitants of Hermitage* (1692) Carth 239). Thus if the fee simple owner of one tenement takes a lease of the other this does not extinguish the easement or profit. All that happens is that the exercise of the easement or profit as a *right* is suspended for a period of the lease and will revive when it ends (*Simper* v *Foley* (1862) 2 John & H 555). If, however, the two tenements do come into common ownership the easement or profit will be completely extinguished and will not revive if the plots are separated again at a later date.

22.10.2 Release

An easement or profit may be 'released' (given up) by the dominant owner at any time. Obviously, at law such a release should be effected by deed, but equity will recognise an informal release if it would be inequitable to allow the releasing owner to go back on his word (e.g., *Waterlow* v *Bacon* (1866) LR 2 Eq 514). The effect of a release is to return the easement or profit to the servient owner, at which point it merges with his or her estate and is thereby extinguished.

22.10.3 Implied release: abandonment

In general the mere lack of use of an easement or profit, once it has been acquired, will not lead to the extinguishment of the right (*Seaman* v *Vawdrey* (1810) 16 Ves Jr 390), for one is never obliged to exercise the rights which one may have. However, a prolonged non-use may be adduced as evidence that the dominant owner has impliedly abandoned a right. It should, however, be noted that if the dominant owner explains the non-use he or she may still be regarded as not having abandoned the right. Thus, in *James* v *Stevenson* [1893] AC 162 a right was not lost due to a long period of non-use because the dominant owner explained that he had simply had no occasion to exercise the right (but presumably might wish to in the future). In *Benn* v *Hardinge* (1992) 66 P&CR 246 the Court of Appeal said that non-use, even for 175 years, was not enough on its own to indicate an intention to abandon. The Court also commented that the abandonment of such a right would not be lightly inferred.

If, however, the dominant tenement has been altered in such a way that the right claimed becomes unnecessary or impossible to exercise, then the alteration may be regarded as evidence of an intention to abandon the right. This presumption may be rebutted by evidence that the original character of the land may be restored in the future and that the need for the easement or profit would revive. Thus, in the case of a right to light, the easement will not be extinguished merely because the house on the dominant land is destroyed, as long as it is intended to erect another building in its place (*Ecclesiastical Commissioners for England* v *Kino* (1880) 14 ChD 213).

22.11 Law reform

22.11.1 The need for reform

By this point you may well have concluded that the law relating to easements and profits is sadly in need of reform. It may be of some comfort to know that the authors agree with this conclusion. The existence of three methods of prescription is in itself an unnecessary complication and the nightmarish quality of the Prescription Act 1832 has been a cause of complaint for generations. Indeed in 1966 the Law Reform Committee recommended that all the existing rules on prescription should be abolished and replaced by one simpler method of prescription providing for a single period of 12 years (14th Report, Cmnd 3100) In addition it has been recommended that a more far-reaching reform be contemplated in order to bring the law relating to easements and freehold covenants in line with one another (Law Commission Working Party, Working Paper 1971, No. 36). The Law Commission is currently working further on the reforms needed to the law of easements, with a view to bringing forward one coherent scheme on land obligations that is consistent with the new rules on commonhold. We will consider possible reforms at greater length once we have explained the rules relating to freehold covenants (see Chapter 23) but will mention at this point two small reforms which have already taken effect.

22.11.2 Access to Neighbouring Land Act 1992

In the absence of an easement giving access, in the past there has been no right for a neighbour to gain access to his neighbour's premises in order to enable the carrying out of maintenance work to his own premises. Thus, if one bought an estate in premises which were build right up to the boundary of the land concerned, it was essential to check that express rights had been provided in order to allow access to neighbouring property for the purpose of pointing brickwork, repairing windows or doing any other work which could only be carried out from the neighbour's premises. This was no problem where due care had been taken by those building premises which extended right to the boundaries of their land but in some cases caused undesirable problems. It was, of course, always possible to enter the neighbour's property with his permission (by licence). However, should such permission be refused, even if such refusal were unreasonable, nothing could be done. A limited change in the law was made by the Access to Neighbouring Land Act 1992.

22.11.2.1 *Access orders*

Although the 1992 Act does allow access in certain cases in order to carry out works which are 'reasonably necessary for the preservation of the whole or any part of the dominant land', it does *not* create a form of statutory easement. It does not give rise to a new interest in land but merely gives a right to access, which right can be enforced against certain persons concerned with the 'servient' land. Nor is the right one to which the person seeking access has an immediate claim: the right only arises where a court makes an access order in favour of an applicant. An order can only be made where the works are reasonably necessary to preserve land and where they cannot be carried out, or would be substantially more difficult to carry out, without the access (s. 1(2)). Even where these requirements can be established, an order will not be made where the court concludes that it would be unreasonable to make an order due to the degree of interference caused to the neighbour's use or enjoyment of the land or due to any hardship which would be caused to the neighbour or anyone in occupation of the 'servient' land. Nonetheless, this rule will allow access for a wide number of works to be carried out: for example, clearing drains and sewers, repairing buildings or any part of a building, replacing windows, felling trees and so on. The Act does not restrict the type of works for which an access order may be sought; all that matters is that the works should be reasonably necessary for the preservation of the land, though certain types of work ('basic preservation works') are taken to be reasonably necessary (s. 1(4)).

Where an order under the Act is granted it may include conditions as to the days on and times at which work may be done and may include a wide range of other provisions (for example, specifying who must carry out the work and providing for payment to be made for any damage caused to the 'servient' land) (s. 2(4)). Where the premises to which the work is to be carried out do not comprise residential land, the court may require a 'fair and reasonable' payment to be made for the right of access (s. 2(5)).

22.11.2.2 *Who is bound by an order?*

One problem with the access order is that it only has effect to require the respondent(s) to the application to allow the applicant the necessary access in order to carry out work. As you are already aware, it is perfectly possible for a number of different persons to have coterminous rights to one piece of land and this means that the applicant must try to ensure that he joins as respondents to his action all persons who might have a right to prevent him gaining access to the neighbouring land. This might give rise to difficulties if, for example, the current occupant of the neighbouring land is a licensee (without exclusive possession) or if the portion of the land to which access is sought is subject to third-party rights (for example, a right of way in favour of another neighbour which would be interrupted by the access conferred by the order). However, once an order is made, it will be binding on anyone acquiring an estate or interest from or under the respondent after the making of the order. Accordingly, whilst the order does not confer an interest in land it does create a right which, to an extent, runs to bind later acquirers and thus has some of the characteristics of an interest in land. Accordingly the 1992 Act provides for the registration of orders made under it and any such right may, and should, be protected by entry of a notice in the case of registered land (s. 5(2)) or, in the case of unregistered land, by registration of the order as a 'writ or order affecting land' (s. 5(1)).

22.11.3 **Party Walls Act 1996**

A further limited reform has been made by the Party Walls Act 1996 which extends to the whole country rules which previously only applied to properties in Inner London (under the London Building Acts (Amendment) Act 1939). The Party Walls Act 1996 gives certain special rights in relation to 'party walls' and 'party structures'. Party walls are walls which either separate buildings in different ownership or which are part of a building and which stand on lands in different ownership. The commonest examples are likely to be the central walls which separate the properties in semi-detached or terraced houses. Party structures are things like floor partitions or other structures which separate buildings or parts of buildings which are approached by separate staircases or separate entrances. The Act gives the owner of a building rights to enter the adjoining building to carry out certain works to party walls or party structures. The works covered are matters such as repairing or rebuilding walls or even demolition. However, the Act contains protection for the owner of the adjoining premises by requiring the person doing the works to safeguard the position of the adjoining owner, to provide adequate weatherproofing if the adjoining owner's property becomes exposed, and to pay compensation. Generally, no action under the Act may be taken unless notice has first been served on the adjoining owner. These rights are quite complex and it is necessary to check their precise parameters before assuming that any particular works can be carried out. However, in appropriate cases they will solve some of the problems which arise from the law relating to easements and they will supplement the rights available under the Access to Neighbouring Land Act 1992.

22.11.4 The 'right to roam'

We cannot end without mentioning a further reform, but one which does not really give rise to an easement but merely prevents the person's entry onto the land constituting a trespass (and thus properly amounts to a limited statutory licence). However, since it is akin to a right of way, we mention it here. It is the right, under Part I of the Countryside and Rights of Way Act 2000, to have access on foot, for open-air recreation, to land that is mountain, moor, heath, down or registered common land. This right is very limited and does not, for example, extend to land that is improved or semi-improved grassland (essentially land used for fairly intensive grazing or to produce crops such as hay for fodder). The right will accordingly not apply in relation to land on which crops are grown or most land used for grazing (except moors used for open grazing). It is thus very unlikely that, for example, any of Fieldy Farm in Mousehole would be caught.

FURTHER READING

Bickford Smith and Francis, *Rights of Light: The Modern Law*, 2000, Jordans.

Gale, *Easements*, 17th edn., 2002, Sweet & Maxwell.

Gray and Gray, *Elements of Land Law*, 3rd edn., 2002, Butterworths, pp. 476–81 (supposed rule against possessory easements).

Land Registration for the Twenty-First Century A Consultative Document, 1998, Law Com No. 254, Part X: Adverse Possession and Prescription, paras. 10.79–94.

Wignall, *Nuisance*, 1998, Sweet & Maxwell.

Zif and Litman, 'Easements and Possession: An Elusive Limitation' [1989] Conv 296.

23

Covenants relating to freehold land

23.1 Introduction

We saw in Chapter 9 that it is usual for covenants to be included in leases. Similarly, covenants are quite commonly made in respect of freehold property, particularly if land is divided and the vendor wishes to ensure that his new neighbour does not behave in an inconvenient or disturbing manner. In the case of a new estate, the developer may well wish to impose covenants upon all the purchasers, in order to ensure that the estate is maintained in good order. Thus, covenants are frequently imposed upon freehold estates. However, while the covenants made will be binding between the original parties as a matter of the law of contract, once the land burdened with the covenant is sold, the question will arise whether the covenant is binding upon the purchaser of the property. Over the years, special rules have developed in order to settle the question of which covenants can run with freehold land. These rules have some links with the rules governing covenants in leases but the two systems are not the same and should not be confused with one another. In many cases a covenant by a freehold owner will not bind a purchaser from him, although a similar covenant, if contained in a lease, would bind the tenant's assignee.

23.2 Trant Way

23.2.1 17 and 18 Trant Way

In 1988, Nos. 17 and 18 Trant Way were both owned in fee simple by Olive Orange. Miss Orange occupied 17 Trant Way, whilst No. 18 was let to a tenant. When the tenant left the property at the end of the lease, Miss Orange decided to sell 18 Trant Way. She sold the fee simple estate in the property to Robert Raspberry and, because she was concerned that her new neighbour should not inconvenience her, or alter the character of the neighbourhood, she insisted that Mr Raspberry should enter into a number of covenants in the conveyance. The covenants were:

(a) not to use No. 18 'for business purposes';

(b) to keep the exterior of No. 18 in good repair;

(c) to contribute one-half of the cost of maintaining the driveway shared with No. 17; and

(d) not to sell No. 18 to a family with children (Miss Orange was elderly and found the noise of children at play disturbing).

In 1995, Miss Orange died, and her executors sold 17 Trant Way to Paul Peach.

In 1998, Mr Raspberry sold 18 Trant Way to Silvia Strawberry. Mrs Strawberry has proved to be rather a difficult neighbour to Mr Peach and causes him considerable trouble. As a piano teacher, she gives lessons at home and the noise of children playing their scales throughout the day and early evening disturbs Mr Peach greatly. Furthermore, Mrs Strawberry has failed to repair the outside of No. 18, which has become something of an eyesore, and when Mr Peach had repairs made to the joint driveway she refused to contribute to the cost.

23.2.2 **19 Trant Way**

19 Trant Way was the old rectory, which had a very large garden and an orchard. In 1999, a development company, Big Builders plc, bought the old rectory, demolished it and built a new crescent of six bungalows. The gardens of the properties were landscaped and are 'open plan' in style. The six bungalows have now been sold, and the new owners of the fee simple estates have been registered as proprietors at HM Land Registry. The crescent is called Rectory Crescent, and the bungalows have been numbered 1 to 6, and were sold in that order. 1 Rectory Crescent was bought by Alfred Alpha, and 6 Rectory Crescent was bought by Oscar Omega. On each sale, the purchaser covenanted with Big Builders plc not to fence the garden of the plot being purchased.

We now need to consider the extent to which the covenants we have just described are enforceable, not only between the original parties but also between their successors in title.

23.3 **Enforceability of covenants: original parties**

23.3.1 **Covenantor and covenantee: burden and benefit**

When Olive Orange sold 18 Trant Way to Robert Raspberry in 1988, the covenants contained in the conveyance to Mr Raspberry constituted a contract between the parties. We have already explained that a covenant is a promise by deed (1.6.2.4). Here, Mr Raspberry is the 'covenantor', and assumes the 'burden' under the covenant, and Miss Orange is the 'covenantee', and takes the 'benefit'. If Mr Raspberry had broken a covenant, Miss Orange could have sued for damages for breach of contract or sought an injunction restraining the breach. In this situation the basic rules of the law of contract apply.

The first point to note is that, as with any contract, it is important when drafting a covenant to make its exact limits entirely clear. However, *Dano Ltd* v *Earl Cadogan* [2003] 2 P&CR 10, provides an interesting example of a case in which the court seemed to accept that the exact meaning of a covenant might change over time. Here the covenant restricted use of premises to 'the housing of the working classes', it was accepted that the interpretation of this covenant might change to mean (in modern times) those whose income was sufficiently low that they required inexpensive accomodation. However, an alternative approach to construction mentioned was that if one could find some persons who still clearly fell within the restriction it was not necessary to be able to identify every person who did so. However, in a later Court of Appeal decision on another issue in the same case (see *The Times*, 2 June 2003) it was held that since the document creating the covenant, when read as a whole, envisaged that the covenant lasted only as long as the benefited land remained settled and that had ceased to be the case, the covenant was not in fact enforceable.

23.3.2 **LPA 1925, s. 56**

It is easy enough to see that Miss Orange and Mr Raspberry had a contractual relationship with one another, for both executed a deed which contained their agreement. However, it is possible for someone to take the benefit of such a covenant, even though he was not a party to the deed or perhaps did not even know that the contract had been concluded. In the case of 6 Rectory Crescent, Mr Omega clearly has entered into a contract with Big Builders plc, for both parties have correctly executed the transfer (which was made by deed). If, however, Big Builders plc had put a clause in the transfer saying that the covenant not to fence the garden of No. 6 was made with Big Builders plc and with 'the owners for the time being of land forming part of Rectory Crescent', then Mr Alpha (and the owners of plots 2–5) would also be able to enforce the covenant made by Mr Omega. This effect is produced by LPA 1925, s. 56(1), which provides that, 'A person may take . . . the benefit of any condition, . . . covenant or agreement over or respecting land, . . . although he may not be named as a party to the conveyance or other instrument'.

In *Re Ecclesiastical Commissioners for England's Conveyance* [1936] Ch 430, it was held that the effect of s. 56 was that a person, expressed in the conveyance to be one for whose benefit the covenant was made, was to be regarded as an original covenantee, even though he was not a party to the deed. As a result, the covenant may confer enforceable benefits on other persons, even though they may have been unaware that such a covenant had been made! Accordingly, *Re Ecclesiastical Commissioners for England's Conveyance* seems to suggest that if Mr Omega broke the covenant not to fence, Mr Alpha could sue him for breach of contract, provided that he could satisfy the court that the covenant did purport to be with him as covenantee, although he was not a party to the agreement (*Re Foster* [1938] 3 All ER 357 at p. 365).

However, in *Amsprop Trading Ltd* v *Harris Distribution Ltd* [1997] 1 WLR 1025, Neuberger J said that s. 56 was only effective in a case in which the covenant purported to be made *with* the person seeking to enforce and not where the covenant merely purported to be made for the benefit of that person. This appears to draw undesirable conclusions based upon the exact wording used in the covenant in the case but this maybe unsurprising in a situation in which a statutory provision appears to be being stretched beyond what would appear to be its intended ambit. It may also be of importance that the case involved an attempt to circumvent the standard rules relating to covenants in leases. You may recall that we considered this case in Chapter 9 (9.8.2) and that it concerned a covenant in a sublease which the head landlord, rather than the tenant/landlord of the sublease itself, was seeking to enforce. The head landlord could not use the leasehold rules to enforce the covenant because there is no privity of estate or contract between the head landlord and the subtenant. However, the covenant in the sublease was expressed to give the head landlord power to enforce the covenant and thus he claimed to be able to enforce the covenant under the general covenant rules because the covenant was clearly intended to benefit the head landlord. Neuberger J held that, on the construction of the sublease in question, the covenant was not expressed to be made with the head landlord, although it was clearly intended to benefit him. In such a case, it was held that s. 56 did not operate to permit the head landlord to enforce the covenant.

One reason for the decision may have been that, were this interpretation not to be adopted, it would be easy to circumvent the standard leasehold rules and to allow enforcement of covenants by persons who have no privity of estate or of contract with the tenant in question. Unfortunately, however, the effect may be merely to make the result in such cases depend entirely upon the drafting approach.

23.3.3 The 'mischief' addressed by statute

In trying to decide what s. 56 will or will not do, it can be helpful to consider the mischief that the statutory provisions appear to have been addressing, even if to do so does require a short historical digression. The 'mischief' was the effect of the common law rule that a person could not sue on a deed unless he was actually named in that deed: a description which identified the person in question but did not *name* him would not do. Accordingly, if in an old deed one described one of the parties as 'the owner for the time being of 21 Trant Way', that would not have sufficed to enable the owner of that property at the time the deed was made to enforce the covenants in that deed. This was true even though the actual person involved was readily identifiable and where there was no doubt as to who was intended by the description given. This rule was first modified by s. 5 of the Real Property Act 1845 and then by s. 56. Accordingly, courts might have been expected to view s. 56 as only removing the problem created by the common law rule so that a person who was described in a document as a party but not named and who clearly was a contracting party could benefit. However, as can be seen from the discussion above, the courts have in fact gone further than this in their use of s. 56. The main limitation on s. 56 seems to be simply that the persons covered by the description in question can only benefit if they are existing and identifiable at the date that the covenant was made. The statutory provision does not (as some originally suggested) have the effect of setting aside altogether the principles of privity of contract (see the discussion in *Smith and Snipes Hall Farm Ltd* v *River Douglas Catchment Board* [1949] 2 KB 500 at p. 514 and *Beswick* v *Beswick* [1966] Ch 538 at p. 556).

23.3.4 An alternative

In addition to s. 56, it may be possible to rely on the general contractual provisions in the Contracts (Rights of Third Parties) Act 1999, which were designed to relieve some of the problems connected with the rules on privity of contract. The benefits and obligations conferred by that Act are in addition to those provided by s. 56 (see s. 7(1) of the 1999 Act), but are similar in many ways and normally use of s. 56 will suffice for land cases. However, you should remember this as a possible alternative approach.

23.4 Enforceability of covenants: successors of the original parties

In time, the benefited and burdened pieces of land will change hands, and pass to new owners. We must now consider whether the new owner of the benefited land obtains the right to enforce the covenants, and whether the duties under these covenants bind the new owner of the burdened land. In other words, do the benefits and burdens of the covenants run with the respective pieces of land?

23.4.1 Position after sale by the covenantee: does the benefit pass to the new owner?

In 1995 Olive Orange, the original covenantee in relation to the covenants burdening 18 Trant Way, died and her executors sold her fee simple estate in No. 17 to Paul Peach. At this time, the original covenantor, Robert Raspberry, was still the owner of 18 Trant Way. If Mr Raspberry had broken one of the covenants contained in the 1988 conveyance to himself, could Mr Peach have enforced the covenant against him?

Obviously there is no privity of contract between Mr Peach and Mr Raspberry, but common law does allow the benefit of such a covenant to pass to a successor in title of the original covenantee, if four conditions are met:

(a) the covenant must 'touch and concern' the land of the covenantee;

(b) at the time when the covenant was made, it must have been the intention of the parties that the benefit of the covenant should run with the land to the covenantee's successors in title;

(c) at the time when the covenant was made, the covenantee must have held the legal estate in the land to be benefited; and

(d) the claimant must derive his title from or under the original covenantee (this is the common law rule as amended by LPA 1925, s. 78).

We will look at each of these requirements in greater detail.

23.4.1.1 'Touching and concerning' the land of the covenantee

Common law rules do not allow the successor of the original covenantee to claim the benefit of a covenant unless, at the date when the covenant was made, the covenantee had land which was benefited by the covenant. This emphasises the fact that only the benefit of covenants which are appurtenant to land can be claimed under these rules although no such connection is required where the original contracting parties are concerned.

In addition, the covenant must 'touch and concern' the covenantee's land. The purpose of the rule is to distinguish between covenants which confer a benefit upon land and those which confer a purely personal benefit upon the covenantee.

In *P. & A. Swift Investments* v *Combined English Stores Group* [1989] AC 632 at p. 642, Lord Oliver of Aylmerton provides a useful working test designed to ascertain whether a covenant 'touches and concerns' land. The first element of the test is that the covenant must benefit the estate owner for the time being and that it would cease to be of benefit to the covenantee were it to be separated from the ownership of the benefited estate. Second, the covenant must affect the nature, quality, mode of use or value of the benefited land. Third, even if it satisfies the first two elements of the test, a covenant will not be regarded as 'touching and concerning' benefited land if the benefit is in some way expressed to be personal to the covenantee (this last element accordingly raises the issue of the intention of the parties). In the case of 17 Trant Way we may well feel that the covenant not to sell No. 18 to anyone with children was purely for the personal benefit of Miss Orange. Such a covenant does not seem to confer any benefit upon 17 Trant Way itself: the test here is the same as that used in relation to leases made before 1 January 1996 (the test in *Spencer's Case* (1583) 5 Co Rep 16a). The other covenants made by Mr Raspberry do, however, appear to confer a benefit upon No. 17.

23.4.1.2 *The parties must have intended the benefit to run*

This condition requires proof that, when the covenant was made, the parties intended that it should run to benefit successors of the covenantee. Evidence of such an intention can be provided by the covenantor covenanting with 'the covenantee, his successors in title, and those deriving title under him'. These words are, however, now deemed to be contained in the covenant, by virtue of LPA 1925, s. 78(1):

A covenant relating to any land of the covenantee shall be deemed to be made with the covenantee and his successors in title and the persons deriving title under him or them, and shall have effect as if such successors and other persons were expressed.

23.4.1.3 *At the time when the covenant was made, the covenantee must have held the legal estate in the land*

At common law, covenants attach to the legal estate and pass with it, and so it is essential that, at the time the covenant was made, the covenantee was the owner of the legal estate in the land on which the benefit is to be conferred (*Webb* v *Russell* (1789) 3 TR 393).

23.4.1.4 *The successor claiming to enforce the covenant must derive title from or under the original covenantee*

At one time, a successor claiming the benefit of a covenant at common law had to show that he had acquired the same estate as had been held by the original covenantee, for common law regarded the covenants as attaching to the estate, so that only a person who took the estate could obtain the benefit of the covenants. Thus, a purchaser of the fee simple from the covenantee could enforce a covenant, whilst a tenant acquiring a term of years (even if it were for 999 years) could not do so. Today, however, a tenant may claim the benefit of a covenant which is attached to the freehold estate in the land of which he is a tenant, for in *Smith and Snipes Hall Farm Ltd* v *River Douglas Catchment Board* [1949] 2 KB 500 it was held that LPA 1925, s. 78, has the effect of extending the right to enforce a covenant to such a person. In this case the original owner of the benefited land had sold it to a purchaser and that purchaser had granted a lease of the premises to a tenant. The Court of Appeal took the view that the effect of s. 78(1) was that the benefit of the covenant was enforceable not only by the successor in title to the freehold estate but also by the tenant, who derived title under that freeholder. Section 78 appears to have been intended to be merely a word-saving provision, but here and elsewhere has been held to create important substantive changes in the law. In this instance it was said that, because the section refers to persons 'deriving title under' the covenantee, it extends the benefit of such covenants to tenants, who derive their title *under* the covenantee (or his successors). Were such persons incapable of obtaining a benefit under the legal rules, the inclusion of the reference to them in s. 78 would be meaningless and thus the section has been interpreted as creating an amendment to the law.

The benefit of a covenant amounts to a chose in action and thus it is possible for the holder of the benefit to assign it to any third party in accordance with the ordinary rules of law. Under LPA 1925, s. 136, any such express assignment should be made in writing and notice of it should be given to the covenantor.

23.4.1.5 *Application of the rules*
One can see from these rules that when Miss Orange's executors sold 17 Trant Way to Paul Peach, he would have obtained the benefit of all Mr Raspberry's covenants, except perhaps that of the covenant not to sell No. 18 to a family with children, which appears to be purely personal in nature. Apart from this, the benefit of all the covenants, both positive and negative, would pass with the estate to the new owner, for at common law the benefit of both types of covenant can run to a successor of the covenantee.

23.4.2 Position after sale by covenantor: does the burden pass to the new owner?

In 1998, Mr Raspberry sold the fee simple in 18 Trant Way (the burdened land) to Silvia Strawberry, and it appears that Mrs Strawberry is in breach of a number of the covenants originally made between Mr Raspberry and Miss Orange. The current owner of the benefited land, Mr Peach, needs to know whether Mrs Strawberry is in fact bound by these covenants.

23.4.2.1 *Burdens do not run at common law*
Unfortunately for Mr Peach, the basic rule is that the burden of covenants does not run at common law. Common law dislikes restraints being placed on your use of your own estate, and accordingly applies the strict rule of privity of contract in such cases. The leading decision on this issue is *Austerberry* v *Corporation of Oldham* (1885) 29 ChD 750, in which it was held that, at common law, the obligation to make up a road and keep it in good repair could not pass to the successor in title of the original covenanter. This position was re-affirmed by the House of Lords in *Rhone* v *Stephens* [1994] 2 AC 310, in the case of a covenant to maintain a roof. Thus, Mrs Strawberry will not be liable *at law* for breach of any of the covenants made in respect of 18 Trant Way. This is in line with the general principles of the law of contract, which allow the benefit of a contract to be transferred to a third party but not the burden. The rule arose principally because of the concerns at law to keep

land freely alienable and to prevent it becoming burdened with incumbrances which might hinder sale. However, in the increasingly complex modern world, such a rule can be inconvenient since in many cases it may be quite reasonable to wish to impose restrictions when one sells, for example, part of one's property and to wish to ensure that those restrictions apply to anyone subsequently acquiring the part sold.

23.4.2.2 *The burden of certain covenants can run in equity*

The common law rule caused considerable inconvenience, because the owner of benefited land could find that covenants became unenforceable merely because the burdened land changed hands. Equity took note of this difficulty and, through applying general equitable principles, arrived at the conclusion that where a purchaser acquired the burdened land with knowledge of the covenants it was quite fair that he should be bound to observe them. The enforceability of the burden of certain covenants against a successor in title to the covenantor was settled finally in the famous case of *Tulk* v *Moxhay* (1848) 2 Ph 774. In this case, the burdened land formed the centre of Leicester Square in London, and the original covenantor had covenanted with the owner of adjacent property that he would maintain the square as an ornamental open space. Later the square was sold, and the purchaser, relying on the common law rule that burdens do not pass on sale, intended to build on the property. It was held that the owners of the neighbouring benefited land had a right *in equity* to enforce the covenant against the purchaser of the burdened land, because he had known of the restriction when he acquired his estate.

In taking this view of the position the court attached great importance to the inequity of a purchaser who acquired with notice simply disregarding the restriction in question. Lord Cottenham in *Tulk* v *Moxhay* seems to be taking a fairly liberal view (for the period) of the power of the court to intervene in an inequitable case. However, the reasoning adopted may not be that strong because, if before *Tulk* v *Moxhay* the burden of covenants had not run (see *Keppell* v *Bailey* (1834) 2 My & K 517), a purchaser would surely be entitled to assume that although he knew of the covenant it would have no impact upon him. The decision to alter the law may have been a surprising result. Lord Cottenham seems also to have thought that if one bought at a reduced price due to the covenant, one should in conscience be bound by it. However, surely if the law (or rather equity) were clear that burdens did *not* run, then normally the vendor could sell at a higher price because he knew that the purchaser would not be bound by the covenant. If the vendor failed to claim a higher price in this way, the loss is the vendor's and that of the owners of the benefited land: the vendor loses solely due to his ignorance of the law. It is difficult to see in such a case how the purchaser's conscience is affected. Accordingly, while the decision in *Tulk* v *Moxhay* proved to be an essential step towards the introduction of a more modern approach to the planning of land use, one wonders to what extent the reasoning in the case stands up to close scrutiny. In essence the decision is an early example of an attempt to introduce land-use planning by non-statutory means. (The Leicester Square covenants were again the subject of litigation in *R* v *Westminster City Council, ex parte Leicester Square Coventry Street Association* (1989) 87 LGR 675.)

Since 1848 the courts have, in later cases, identified the rules which must be satisfied before equity will regard the burden of a covenant as passing under the

Tulk v *Moxhay* doctrine. These rules are derived from *Tulk* v *Moxhay* but are not (apart from the last of them) expressly mentioned in the case. To a certain extent they amount to a stepping back by the courts from the very liberal and reforming approach taken in *Tulk* v *Moxhay*, in the interests of certainty and some restriction on the liberality of that approach. In their modern form, the rules may be stated as follows:

(a) the covenant must be negative;

(b) at the date of the covenant, the covenantee must have owned land which was benefited by the covenant;

(c) the original parties must have intended that the burden should run to bind successors; and

(d) as the rule is equitable, general equitable principles (and the need for notice or its modern equivalent) apply.

(1) *The covenant must be negative*   This rule may seem odd when one remembers that the covenant in *Tulk* v *Moxhay* was to maintain Leicester Square as an ornamental open space. However, it is the substance of the covenant which matters, and not the form in which it is expressed. Thus, the effect of the covenant in *Tulk* v *Moxhay* was that the owner should keep the square in an open state and *not* erect buildings. In the case of the covenants relating to 18 Trant Way, the covenants to keep the exterior in good repair and to contribute to the cost of maintaining the driveway are both positive, and thus cannot run to bind Mrs Strawberry under the rule in *Tulk* v *Moxhay*. This can produce rather inconvenient results, and reform of the law has been recommended (see 23.8.3). Indeed, some writers have argued that *Tulk* v *Moxhay* makes no mention of such a requirement, and that in the past positive covenants had been enforced against the covenantor's successors (see Bell [1981] Conv 55). However, this limitation on the rule has been accepted since the case of *Haywood* v *Brunswick Permanent Benefit Building Society* (1881) 8 QBD 403, in which Lindley LJ said that 'only such a covenant as can be complied with without expenditure of money will be enforced' against a successor in title. Thus, a covenant 'not to allow the premises to fall into disrepair' would be regarded as a positive covenant, even though it is worded in a negative form, because compliance with the covenant will require action, and expenditure, on the part of the owner of the burdened land.

The difference between positive and negative covenants was summarised by Cotton LJ in *Austerberry* v *Corporation of Oldham* (1885) 29 ChD 750 at pp. 773–4 in a passage in which it was explained that a covenant requiring someone to 'lay out money':

. . . is not a covenant which a court of equity will enforce: it will not enforce a covenant not running at law when it is sought to enforce that covenant in such a way as to require the successors in title of the covenantor to spend money, and in that way to undertake a burden upon themselves. The covenantor must not use the property for a purpose inconsistent with the use for which it was originally granted: but in my opinion a court of equity does not and ought not to enforce a covenant binding only in equity in such a way as to require the successors of the covenantor himself, they having entered into no covenant, to expend sums of money in accordance with what the original covenantor bound himself to do.

the covenants. In such a case, it would be inequitable for the court to assist the person who is in breach of the agreement.

More importantly, the fact that the burden of the covenants runs only in equity means that one must bear in mind the need to protect the right to the covenant by entry on the register in the case of registered land or registration of a land charge in unregistered land. As we have seen, *Tulk* v *Moxhay* was decided primarily on the basis that the purchaser of Leicester Square bought with notice of the covenant restricting the use of the land. Where one is dealing with unregistered land and with restrictive covenants created *before* 1 January 1926 the old equitable doctrine of notice will still apply. You should not assume that such old covenants can be ignored, for they are still frequently encountered and can still be enforced where the rules in *Tulk* v *Moxhay* are satisfied. Where the title to the land is unregistered, and the covenant was created on or after 1 January 1926, it requires registration as a class D(ii) land charge (LCA 1972, s. 2(5)). If such a covenant is not registered, it will be void against a purchaser of a legal estate for money or money's worth, regardless of notice (LCA 1972, s. 4(6)). The date by which the covenant must have been registered is the date on which the burdened land was conveyed to the purchaser. In the case of 18 Trant Way, Mrs Strawberry will *not* be bound by the restrictive covenants relating to the property unless they were registered as land charges before she bought the fee simple in 1998 (the land had not been sold since Mousehole became an area of compulsory registration in 1990).

When she acquired the property, Mrs Strawberry was obliged to register her title to the land with HM Land Registry (see Chapter 2), because Mousehole became a compulsory registration area on 1 December 1990 (see 2.2.3.1.). On any such registration, the purchaser must tell the registrar of any pre-1926 covenants of which he has notice and present to him a land charges search, which will reveal any registered covenants made after 1925. When the estate is registered, the registrar will also enter on the register notice of any such encumbrances. At the time Mrs Strawberry purchased, this requirement arose from the Land Registration Rules 1925, r. 40; LRA 1925, s. 50(1). Today the requirement on the registrar arises from the Land Registration Rules 2003, r. 35. These burdens on the land will affect a purchaser only if entered on the register relating to the burdened land. Usually the registrar will insert a full copy of the terms of the covenant in the charges section of the register.

Any covenants created after the title becomes registered must also be entered against the burdened estate. Most new covenants are created on transfer of the estate, and in the transfer deed. These covenants will be entered automatically on the register by way of notice. In the case of a covenant created at another time, the person with the benefit of the covenant should apply to have his interest noted on the register of the burdened land (under LRA 2002, s. 32) by way of notice.

23.4.3 Where the burden runs in equity, the benefit must be made to run in equity

Having established that Mrs Strawberry may be bound by certain covenants burdening 18 Trant Way, it must still be established that Mr Peach has a right to enforce the covenants. Where he has to argue that Mrs Strawberry is bound *in equity* by the covenants, he must also establish that he has obtained the benefit of the covenants according to *equitable* rules: it is not enough to show that the benefit passes at common law. However, in general the equitable rules are more generous to the person claiming the benefit and thus one would not wish to use the legal rules.

In equity, there are three ways in which a purchaser of the benefited land can acquire the right to enforce the covenant:

(a) by annexation (which maybe express, implied or statutory);

(b) by express assignment of the benefit of the covenant; and

(c) under the special rules relating to building schemes.

23.4.3.1 *Express annexation*

Where 'words of annexation' are used, the benefit of the covenant is annexed or attached to the land, so that for ever after it passes automatically with the land to the new owner. In order to achieve express annexation, it is necessary that the words of the covenant should show that the original parties intended the benefit to run, and one way of doing this is to state expressly that the covenant is made 'for the benefit of' named land (*Rogers* v *Hosegood* [1900] 2 Ch 388). Another method which will have the same effect is for the covenant to be made with the covenantee as 'estate owner', that is, describing him as the owner of the land to be benefited. For example, Mr Raspberry may have covenanted with Miss Orange as 'the owner for the time being of 17 Trant Way', and these words would have the effect of attaching the benefit of the covenants to No. 17. It is not enough, however, for the covenant to be made with the covenantee and his 'heirs, executors administrators and assigns' (or any similar set of words), for such a phrase does not link these people with the benefited land (*Renals* v *Cowlishaw* (1878) 9 ChD 125).

Where a claimant seeks to establish express annexation, a problem will arise if the wording of the deed creating the covenant purports to annex it to an area of land which is so large that it cannot reasonably be said that the covenant confers actual benefit on the whole property. In *Re Ballard's Conveyance* [1937] Ch 473, a covenant was said to be for the benefit of the whole of a large estate (approximately 690 hectares). In fact, the covenant could confer a benefit on only a small portion of that estate. Here the court said that, since the covenant did not confer a benefit on the whole estate, it could not run on a sale of the estate. Nor would it run when a part of the estate which *was* benefited was sold, because the court would not sever the covenant and attach it to parts of the land where the express wording of the deed did not allow for this (but see also *Earl of Leicester* v *Wells-next-the-Sea Urban District Council* [1973] Ch 110). As a result, when one drafts a covenant and wishes to attach it to a large area of land, it is wise to say that the covenant is for the benefit of 'the whole or any part of the named land'; this will allow the covenant to run with any part of the large estate which is actually benefited, and will also allow the benefit to be divided between several plots if the estate is ever sold off in that way (*Marquess of Zetland* v *Driver* [1939] Ch 1; and see *Morrells of Oxford Ltd* v *Oxford United Football Club Ltd* [2001] Ch 459).

23.4.3.2 *Implied annexation*

Where words of express annexation are lacking, some cases suggest that it may still be possible for the court to identify the benefited land by looking at the sure that it benefited his land, because this would not be clear from the documents creating the covenant.

23.4.3.4 *Assignment*

Even where the benefit of a covenant has not been expressly annexed to land, it has always been the case that the covenantee could transfer that benefit by express assignment. The benefit of a covenant, like the benefit of any other contract, is a *chose in action* and can be assigned at will. If one relies on this method it is, however, necessary to show that there is an unbroken chain of assignments, so that on each sale of the benefited land the benefit has been passed to the new owner and has finally come to the person who now seeks to enforce the covenant (*Re Pinewood Estate* [1958] Ch 280). It is also essential that the right should be assigned to the purchaser of the estate at the time of the conveyance to him: an assignment made after the estate has been transferred is not acceptable (*Re Union of London & Smith's Bank Ltd's Conveyance* [1933] Ch 611 at p. 632).

23.4.3.5 *Building schemes*

Some of the rules discussed above would cause difficulty when applied to the development of a new estate, such as Rectory Crescent. As we have seen, each purchaser entered into covenants with the developer, but now the estate is completed Big Builders plc will move on to work elsewhere and will not be concerned with enforcing these covenants. What the purchasers want is to be able to rely on a sort of 'local law' for the area (*Re Dolphin's Conveyance* [1970] Ch 654 at p. 662), which each householder can enforce directly against his neighbours if he needs to do so. To a large extent, this could be achieved by the existing rules, but this would be complicated and would depend on knowing the exact order in which the plots had been sold.

(1) *Rectory Crescent: the position without a building scheme*   In our example, plots 1 to 6 Rectory Crescent were sold in that order. If some time in the future, the successor of the original purchaser of No. 3 should fence his garden in breach of the covenant, those holding plots sold after No. 3 (i.e., 4 to 6) could claim that they held land retained by the developer at the time of the sale of No. 3. The benefit of that purchaser's covenant would therefore be annexed to the retained land (assuming of course that the covenant had been drafted correctly), and it would have passed to them, or their predecessors in title, when the later plots were sold. Those who bought before the sale of No. 3 (i.e., 1 and 2) might be able to rely on LPA 1925, s. 56, if the covenant purported to be with the owners of those plots and provided that, if they are not the original purchasers, they can show that the benefit has passed to them under the usual rules.

Proceeding in this way may not seem too difficult, but that is because we have simplified matters by saying that plots 1 to 6 were sold in that order. In real life, the houses on a new estate may be sold in no particular order, as purchasers present themselves and make their choices, and after 50 years or so it could be quite difficult to know, in respect of a particular breach, who could proceed under s. 56 and who could rely on annexation.

There is, further, the problem we mentioned earlier: because Big Builders plc retained no land when the last plot was sold, an essential rule for the running of the burden is not satisfied on the sale of that plot and so the successor to the original purchaser of No. 6 would take free of the covenant.

However, all these difficulties are avoided if it can be established that the development satisfies the legal requirements of a 'building scheme'.

(2) *Requirements for a building scheme*   The traditional requirements for a building scheme were established in the Edwardian case of *Elliston* v *Reacher* [1908] 2 Ch 374, in which a building society had laid out an area for development in separate plots and had sold these using identical conveyances and imposing identical covenants upon each purchaser. The court held that the covenants were enforceable against a successor to the original covenantor and set out four rules to be satisfied in order to establish a building scheme (sometimes called a 'scheme of development'):

(a) the purchasers must derive their titles from a common vendor;

(b) before selling, the vendor must have laid out his land in lots (or plots);

(c) on sale, the same restrictions must be imposed on all the plots, and it must be clear that those restrictions are intended to be for the benefit of all the plots sold; and

(d) each purchaser must have acquired his plot on the understanding that the covenants were intended to benefit all the other plots in the scheme.

(3) *Developments after* Elliston *v* Reacher   In later cases, however, it has been established that these four rules provide only guidance, and that what is crucial is the intention of the parties to create a building scheme. Accordingly, a scheme was found in *Baxter* v *Four Oaks Properties Ltd* [1965] Ch 816, even though the whole area had not been divided into lots in advance of the first sale. In this case the developer had wished to allow purchasers to choose lots of varying sizes. Again, in *Re Dolphin's Conveyance* [1970] Ch 654, a single scheme was established, even though the purchasers had not acquired from a common vendor. The first sales were made by two co-owners, but later the land came into the hands of their nephew, who continued the sale of plots and imposed covenants identical to those imposed by his aunts. The court considered that this satisfied the essential requirement, since it was quite clear the the various vendors did intend to create a local law for the area. If, however, a common intention cannot be established, for example because the covenants vary between the plots of land, a building scheme will not exist (see *Emile Elias & Co. Ltd* v *Pine Groves Ltd* [1993] 1 WLR 305).

(4) *Advantages of establishing a building scheme*   Once a scheme has been established, and Rectory Crescent would appear to be a clear example of such a scheme, it is necessary to consider what benefits will accrue. The first is that, although it is still necessary to establish that the rules in *Tulk* v *Moxhay* have been satisfied, these rules are modified slightly in one respect, so that the burden *will* run with the last plot sold (here, No. 6) despite the fact that the developer does not retain any land capable of being benefited. With this exception, though, all the basic rules have to be observed: so there is no question of the burden of positive covenants being enabled to run under a building scheme, and the usual registration or protection by entry on the register is needed if successors of the covenantors are to be bound.

The second benefit of a building scheme is that all purchasers of plots in the scheme are enabled to enforce the covenants between themselves, irrespective of the date on which they, or their predecessors in title, bought their plots. There is

Ives Investment Ltd v *High* [1967] 2 QB 379, and *Tito* v *Waddell (No. 2)* [1977] Ch 106 at p. 290). For the rule to apply, the burden and benefit do have to be related to one another in some way. Comments by Megarry V-C in *Tito* v *Waddell (No. 2)*, which suggested that the benefits and burdens did not have to be inter-related provided that they were part of the same transaction, were expressly disapproved by the House of Lords in *Rhone* v *Stephens* [1994] 2 AC 310, in which Lord Templeman said (at p. 322):

> It does not follow that any condition can be rendered enforceable by attaching it to a right nor does it follow that every burden imposed by a conveyance may be enforced by depriving the covenantor's successor in title of every benefit which he enjoyed thereunder. The condition must be relevant to the exercise of the right. In *Halsall* v *Brizell* there were reciprocal benefits and burdens enjoyed by the users of the roads and sewers.

Accordingly, under this rule only related burdens can be enforced and, where there is no necessary relationship between the benefit exercised and the burden for which enforcement is sought, the courts will not act. The problems that this approach can produce when dealing with modern estate housing is illustrated very clearly by *Thamesmead Town Ltd* v *Allotey* (1998) 37 EG 161. Here the original covenantor had covenanted to pay a service charge to maintain roads, sewers and landscaped and communal areas on an estate. Mr Allotey acquired a property from the original covenantor and was held not to be liable to make payments in relation to the landscaped and communal areas because he had obtained no entitlement to benefit from these areas. He did, however, have to pay the service charge in relation to the roads and sewers, which he had a right to use and did use. The possible arguments that may arise where someone argues that they never use a facility and thus are not going to pay for it can be imagined, though, if they have a right but do not choose to use it, this argument should fail.

The principle in *Halsall* v *Brizell* may assist the current owner of 17 Trant Way, in compelling Mrs Strawberry to contribute to the cost of the repairs recently made to the shared driveway. The rule is also frequently of considerable importance when one is dealing with a building scheme in which positive covenants for the maintenance of shared facilities may be necessary.

23.5.2 Evasion of the rules by techniques of drafting

There are a number of ways in which the burden of a positive covenant can be imposed on a later acquirer of burdened land.

23.5.2.1 *Granting leases*

Where a lease is granted, covenants in the lease which fall within the rule in *Spencer's Case* or pass under the Landlord and Tenant (Covenants) Act 1995 will bind the tenant's assignees (see Chapter 9). In such cases, the law makes no distinction between positive and negative obligations, and covenants to contribute to the cost of maintenance or to an insurance premium are common. As a result, a vendor may well choose to grant a long lease of property, rather than selling the fee simple estate. You will remember from our discussion of commonhold in Chapter 11 that in the case of blocks of flats, where the enforcement of positive obligations may be crucial, it is exceptionally rare for the flat owners to hold estates in fee simple, and leases are the norm. In such cases, the purchaser may well pay as much as he would have paid to acquire a freehold estate, but will obtain only a wasting asset. In addition his ownership will be subject to the landlord's rights of re-entry and to a continuing obligation to pay ground rent. He may also encounter the difficulty that mortgagees are often less willing to lend money on the security of a leasehold property. All this is quite a high price to pay to enable the vendor to ensure that the burden of positive covenants passes to the successors in title of the covenantee. The new commonhold system is designed to meet these problems but it remains to be seen whether it will prove popular in practice.

23.5.2.2 *Indemnity covenants*

Another method of circumvention is to impose upon the covenantor an obligation to require an indemnity covenant from his successor. Should the covenant be broken, the covenantee can then sue the original covenantor, who remains liable on the covenant; *he will* sue his successor, and so on down the line. This method is not, however, very effective, because it is dependent on the maintenance of an unbroken chain of indemnity covenants. In the case of *Thamesmead Town Ltd* v *Allotey* (23.5.1) this approach broke down on the first transfer. In addition, after some years it may prove impossible to find the original covenantor in order to enforce against him.

23.5.2.3 *Creating estate rentcharges*

Another possible method is for a vendor to require the purchaser to grant him an estate rentcharge over the land. You will remember that a rentcharge imposes a duty on the current estate owner to make regular payments of money to the person entitled to the charge (see Chapter 1), and so a rentcharge can be useful where it is wished to impose an obligation to contribute to the cost of maintenance; it might, for example, have been used in relation to the shared driveway at 17 and 18 Trant Way. However, in addition to this, the rentcharge can be used to enforce other positive obligations beyond the mere payment of money, for the owner of the charge has a legitimate interest in maintaining the value of the land, and so can require the estate owner, when he grants the rentcharge, to enter into covenants for repair and maintenance. The rentcharge, and its associated obligations, run with the land to bind successive owners. The right of re-entry which supports the rentcharge enables the owner of the charge to enter on the land and do the work himself, if the estate owner fails to do so.

The estate rentcharge was exempted from the general bar on the creation of rentcharges imposed by the Rentcharges Act 1977 (see s. 2), and so may still be created. It takes effect as a legal interest in land. In the case of registered land, the rentcharge must be substantively registered in order to be legal. Where a rentcharge is granted in relation to a registered estate its creation does not operate at law until the registration requirements are met: LRA 2002, s. 27. If the rentcharge is granted for a term of years of up to and including seven years' duration, the requirement is to enter a notice on the register of the burdened land (LRA 2002, s. 27(4) and Sch. 2, para. 7). In the case of any other rentcharge the person granted the charge must be registered as proprietor of the rentcharge and a notice must be entered against the register relating to the estate that has been charged (LRA 2002, s. 27(4) and Sch. 2,

These possibilities are well illustrated by *Gafford* v *Graham* (1998) 77 P&CR 73, in which the servient owner, in breach of covenant, between 1986 and 1989 constructed and ran, on the servient land, a riding school. The covenants binding the land permitted only a bungalow and livery yard and stable and prohibited other building without the consent of the dominant owner (which had not been obtained). The building works in question comprised the conversion of the bungalow into a two-storey house, an extension to a barn and the provision of an indoor riding school for the purpose of riding instruction. The first complaint of the breaches had been a solicitor's letter, written three years after the first of the breaches commenced. Nourse LJ held that in relation to the alterations to the house and the barn the delay (three years) in making a complaint was such that the dominant owner's rights to any relief for breach were entirely barred. The complaint in relation to the construction and operation of the riding school was much closer to the events of which complaint was made and in relation to these the dominant owner was not taken to have acquiesced. However, the dominant owner had not sought an immediate (interlocutory) injunction to prevent the building work continuing but had waited until the full hearing of the action and sought there a final injunction (which would have required the removal of the riding school). Nourse LJ concluded that in these circumstances it was not appropriate to grant the injunction sought in relation to the riding school. However, he did award £25,000 damages for the breach of covenant involved in its construction and operation. The sum awarded as damages was to be calculated by reference to the amount that might reasonably have been expected in payment for an agreement to relax the covenant permanently in relation to the riding school.

The message for the aggrieved dominant owner is accordingly not to be tolerant of breaches and to seek a remedy swiftly, obtaining interim relief as appropriate. In such a case, where the servient owner acts flagrantly in breach of covenant and ignores warnings the court may require any building constructed to be demolished (*Wakeham* v *Wood* [1981] 43 P&CR 40) but will not do so as an invariable principle (see 23.6.1). For an older example of acquiescence defeating a claim see *Sayers* v *Collyer* [1885] 28 ChD 103, where a complainant lost his case in respect of a beershop that had been constructed in breach of covenant because of evidence that he had made regular use of the premises!

23.6.3 Declaration under LPA 1925, s. 84(2)

In many cases, the real problem with a covenant is not in enforcing it, but in establishing whether it is binding on a particular person, or whether the person seeking to enforce it is entitled to do so. Suitable relief in the case of such a dispute is provided by LPA 1925, s. 84(2) as amended by LPA 1969, s. 28(4), which allows an applicant to ask the court to declare whether or not land is affected by 'a restriction imposed by an instrument' and 'the nature and extent' of the restriction. In addition, a declaration may be sought 'whether the same is or would in any given event be enforceable and if so by whom'. For an excellent summary of the remedies available and some of the difficulties encountered in enforcement see the article by Professor Martin on this subject in [1996] Conv 329.

23.7 **Discharge of covenants**

23.7.1 **Common ownership**

A covenant will be extinguished automatically should the burdened and benefited land come into common ownership and occupation (*Re Tiltwood, Sussex* [1978] Ch 269) but remember the special rule relating to plots within a building scheme (*Texaco Antilles Ltd* v *Kernochan* [1973] AC 609). Otherwise it is open to the parties affected to agree to discharge the obligation (the discharge itself being made by deed). Apart from these methods, a covenant would continue to affect land in perpetuity, under the rules of common law and equity. This causes considerable inconvenience, where after the passage of many years the covenant has become redundant or unreasonable. As a result, a statutory method has been provided whereby certain covenants may be discharged or varied.

23.7.2 **Application to Lands Tribunal**

Under LPA 1925, s. 84, as amended by the LPA 1969, an application to discharge or modify, 'any restriction arising under covenant or otherwise as to the user [of land] or the building thereon' may be made to the Lands Tribunal, which may modify or discharge the restrictive covenant in whole or in part. The party who is applying must establish one of four grounds on which he seeks discharge or modification of the covenant.

First, he may show that the restriction has become obsolete due to 'changes in the character of the property or the neighbourhood' or to other relevant circumstances. This would apply, for example, to a covenant to use premises only as a dwelling, if the surrounding area had come into business or mixed use. Second, it may be established that the covenant impedes a reasonable user *and* either does not provide any practical benefit of substantial value to any person or is contrary to the public interest and, in either case, money would be adequate compensation for the loss or disadvantage (if any) that would be suffered due to the discharge or modification. Third, it may be established that those entitled to the benefit have agreed, expressly or impliedly 'by their acts or omissions' to the discharge or modification. Finally, the claimant may succeed if he can establish 'that the proposed discharge or modification will not injure the persons entitled to the benefit of the restriction'. In considering applications for discharge, the Lands Tribunal must take into account the development plan for the area and any declared or ascertainable pattern for the grant or refusal of planning permission (s. 84(1B)). *In re University of Westminster* [1998] 3 All ER 1014 indicates the approach that should be adopted by the Lands Tribunal on any application made under s. 84. For a selection of cases on s. 84, see the short article by H. Wilkinson in [2000] NLJ 1623.

If the Tribunal agrees to discharge or modify a covenant on any ground, it may require the payment of compensation to the owners of the benefited land. It should be noted that the wording of s. 84 is such that the powers of the Lands Tribunal do not apply to positive covenants.

23.7.3 **Housing Act 1985, s. 610**

A further statutory power to discharge a covenant requiring property to be kept as a *single* dwelling exists under Housing Act 1985, s. 610. This permits a county court to authorise an alteration of the property in breach of a covenant (for example, into several flats) if the property cannot be disposed of readily as one unit due to a change in character of the neighbourhood. The aim of this provision is to prevent land falling into disuse because of a limitation imposed by a covenant, and thereby to prevent a diminution in the number of dwellings available for occupation.

23.8 **Reform of the law relating to burdens running with the land**

After reading the last two chapters, you may well be left with the impression that the rules relating to burdens running with the land are in considerable need of reform. This is a generally accepted opinion.

23.8.1 **Some proposals for reform**

The rules relating to the running of covenants have been particularly heavily criticised and have been the subject of three major reports over the years: (a) the Law Commission, *Report on Restrictive Covenants* (Law Com No. 11, 1967); (b) the Wilberforce Committee, *Report on Positive Covenants Affecting Land* (Cmnd 2719, 1968); and (c) the Law Commission, *Report on the Law of Positive and Restrictive Covenants* (Law Com No. 127, 1984). The last of these reports was a detailed attempt to make some sense of the confusion of the rules relating to easements and covenants. The position regarding positive covenants was particularly criticised, since such covenants do not run to bind a subsequent owner, and accordingly the original covenantor, who remains liable on his contract, can find himself being held responsible for the acts of some later owner long after his own interest in the land has ceased (para. 4.3 of the Report). This problem has now been addressed in relation to covenants in leases (see 9.5.2) but no reform has yet been made of the law in relation to freehold covenants. In 1998 the Lord Chancellor announced that the Law Commission Report of 1984 (No. 127) would not be implemented but said that the issues it raised would be considered further by the Law Commission in the light of other proposals for reform. The law of easements is currently under consideration by the Law Commission, with a view to producing a coherent scheme of land obligations and easements that is compatible with the LRA 2002 and commonhold.

23.8.2 **Problems of the current rules**

The horrors of the rules regarding restrictive covenants were cogently summarised in para. 4.9 of the 1984 report:

The burden of a restrictive covenant does not run at all at law, but it does run in equity if certain complicated criteria are met. The benefit, by contrast, runs both at law and in equity, but according to rules which are different. These rules are, if anything, more complicated than the rules about the burden, and some of them are particularly technical and hard to grasp: as examples one may cite the rules about 'annexation' and those about 'building schemes'.

For some years now there has been further pressure to reform the rules about covenants, as part of a wider campaign for changes in the law to facilitate the sale of flats as freehold rather than as leasehold properties. We have noted the development of these proposals for change in Chapter 11 and it is hoped that the commonhold system, once established, will be successful and facilitate the sale of freehold flats and similar units of property. However, sales of individual properties, such as the sale by Mrs Orange to Mr Raspberry, will not be affected by this change. Thus, the problem of later enforcement of positive covenants will continue to arise in some cases even after the introduction of commonhold.

23.8.3 **What reforms are possible?**

23.8.3.1 *Land obligations*
The 1984 Law Commission report took the view that the existing rules on covenants should be abolished and a new class of rights, 'land obligations', should be created to replace them. Such rights would be subject to rules similar to those applying to easements (which the Commission regarded as more satisfactory), and should subsist as legal interests in land, binding on successive owners under normal rules. After sale, the original parties would lose their contractual rights and obligations, thus destroying the present continuing contractual liability of the original covenantor (see para. 4.22 of the Report). Under such a scheme, no distinction would be made between positive and negative covenants.

23.8.3.2 *Easements*
The 1984 Report accepted that in general the law relating to easements is preferable to the rules on covenants. Whilst this may be true with respect to expressly created easements, the law on implied grant, the provisions of LPA 1925, s. 62, and the law on prescription are also sorely in need of reform. In 1971, the Law Commission Working Paper, *Transfer of Land: Appurtenant Rights* (Working Paper No. 36), recognised the difficulties in this area, and made a number of recommendations. In particular it was suggested that certain important easements (for example, the right to support) should become automatic statutory rights (para. 50 of the Paper). Further recommendations were made in relation to acquisition of easements by other methods. In particular, it was suggested that the prescription period should be reduced to 12 years in order to bring it into line with the limitation period for actions in respect of land (para. 101 of the Paper). In 1966 the Law Reform Committee, when considering easements and profits (Cmnd 3100), had been divided on whether prescription should be abolished in its entirety, but was unanimous in agreeing that, if retained, the law required drastic reform.

23.8.3.3 *Commonhold*
The various suggested reforms were, to some extent, drawn together in the consultation paper on 'Commonhold' presented to Parliament in November 1990

(Cmnd 1345 (1990)) and, thus far, the reforms discussed in Chapter 11 are the only changes that have been made but, as noted earlier, the Law Commission is currently working further on easements issues with a view to producing one coherent scheme.

FURTHER READING

Gravells, 'Enforcement of Positive Covenants Affecting Freehold Land' (note on *Rhone* v *Stephens*) (1994) 110 LQR 346.

Hayton, 'Revolution in Restrictive Covenant Law?' (1980) 43 MLR 445.

Newsom, 'Universal Annexation' (1981) 97 LQR 32 (see also Newsom (1982) 98 LQR 202).

Todd, Case note on *Roake* v *Chadha* [1984] Conv 68.

Todd, 'Annexation After Federated Homes' [1985] Conv 177.

Wade, Case note on *Halsall* v *Brizell* [1957] CLJ 35.

Wade, 'Covenants—A Broad and Reasonable View' [1972B] CLJ 157 (see pp. 171–5: 'What is wrong with section 78?').

PART VII

In conclusion

24

The family home

/

24.1 Introduction

The purpose of this chapter is to pull together some matters about the family home which we have mentioned at various points in the book, and to give you a little more information about certain statutory rights which members of a family may have in respect of their homes.

24.1.1 Trant Way

There are three inhabitants of Trant Way who are particularly relevant to this chapter: Henry Mumps and Bob Bell, whom we met on pp. 397–8, and Sally Mould, who made her first appearance in 17.1.1. Although the circumstances of each may be very different, they all have one thing in common. Each of them is living in a house owned by another member of the family; none of them has the legal title to the property he or she regards as home. This can give rise to a number of problems if things go wrong, and this is what we want to focus on in this chapter. We will not concern ourselves with Mr and Mrs Armstrong, although they too occupy a family home, because they are both registered as legal owners of 1 Trant Way (see 16.2), and the position of legal joint tenants has been explored sufficiently in Chapter 16.

Good to look @ Section A

24.1.2 What might go wrong?

It is always possible that relationships may break down, ending in divorce if the parties are married or in separation if they are cohabiting. Similarly, home-sharing arrangements between different generations within a family sometime become unhappy and are no longer workable. We need to consider the position which Henry, Sally and Bob would find themselves in if this happened to them. Could they go on living in their homes if they wanted to, and, even more important, could they claim a share in the capital value of the property which they could use to acquire alternative accommodation?

Even if all these characters are lucky enough to enjoy successful relationships (and Henry is already worried about his), a further possibility we have to consider is that their families may encounter financial problems. We do not know how the Moulds and Barbara Bell financed the purchase of their houses (although they may very possibly have had to borrow money to do so), but we do know that Henry's home is already mortgaged to the Red Leicester Building Society, and that his partner, Mildred, is planning to create a second mortgage to raise money for her business (see 21.2). If Mildred was unable to meet repayment obligations under a mortgage, the mortgagee would have the right to seek possession of the house and to sell it. We need to consider therefore what rights Henry might have in such a situation, and whether his position would differ in any way from that which Sally and Bob would face if their houses were subject to repossession by a mortgagee.

24.2 Right to a share in the value of the house

24.2.1 Against a spouse or partner at the end of the relationship

We have already seen that spouses and cohabitants are in very different positions when their relationships come to an end. On divorce, the courts are empowered to make property adjustment orders, and can take into account a wide range of matters, including the needs of the respective parties and the contribution which each has made to the marriage (see 17.4.1.1). If Sally Mould's marriage were to end in divorce, she could rely on these provisions, so as to receive a fair share of what she probably regards as the 'family assets'. If there are children of the marriage, she might well be allowed to remain with them in the family home until they are grown up.

By contrast, there are no legal provisions governing arrangements when a relationship between cohabitants comes to an end. These days, couples planning to live together are advised to discuss in advance what would happen if their relationship ended, and to draw up formal cohabitation contracts which would provide for matters such as the division of property. It used to be thought that such contracts were illegal, as conducing to immorality, but it seems that the judges have kept pace with social change, and it is unlikely that any court today would refuse to recognise such a contract. This view has recently received support from *obiter dicta* in *Sutton* v *Mishcon de Reya* (2004) *The Times* 28 January 2004, in which Hart J stated that there was nothing to prevent cohabitors from entering into perfectly valid legal relations concerning their mutual property rights. 'Such a contract would not be a contract of cohabitation [that is, a contract for sexual relations outside marriage, which would be void] but a contract between cohabitors.'

However, couples at the start of a relationship are understandably unwilling to contemplate that it may not succeed. As Waite LJ commented in *Midland Bank plc* v *Cooke* [1995] 4 All ER 562 at p. 575:

for a couple embarking on a serious relationship, discussion of the terms to apply at parting is almost a contradiction of the shared hopes that have brought them together

and it is likely that in practice most couples will give no thought to such matters until it is too late.

Henry and Mildred were probably not even aware of cohabitation contracts when they set up home together in 1970. If they have not made any specific arrangement, any claim to a share of the property which Henry might want to make would have to satisfy the requirements of *Gissing* v *Gissing* [1971] AC 886 and *Lloyds Bank plc* v *Rosset* [1991] 1 AC 107 (see 17.4). Thus he would have to show a common intention between himself and Mildred that he was to have a share; in the absence of express agreement, this would have to be inferred from conduct, and it seems that he has not made the sort of direct contribution to the cost of acquiring the house which the courts would require.

Sadly, it is clear from *Burns* v *Burns* [1984] 1 Ch 317 that his years of devoted 'house husbandry' would count for nothing. As the decision in that case shows, where an unmarried couple is involved in a separation, only financial contributions are effective, and long-term commitment to the family and its welfare counts for nothing. By contrast, where a marriage ends in divorce, the court considering applications for property adjustment orders is specifically authorised (by the Matrimonial Causes Act 1973, s. 25(2)(f)) to take into account:

the contributions which each of the partners has made . . . to the welfare of the family including any contributions by looking after the home or caring for the family.

However, as well as running the household, Henry has made considerable DIY improvements to the property, and these may well have increased the value of the house. Could they entitle him to a share? Again, he will find himself at a disadvantage compared with a married man.

Under s. 37 of the Matrimonial Proceedings and Property Act 1970 a husband or wife who contributes in money or money's worth to the improvement of real or personal property belonging to the other spouse may claim a share (or an increased share) in that property. The contributions must be 'of a substantial nature'. You should note that this section only applies to contributions to improvements and *not* to purchase. Where such a contribution is made it will be presumed that the parties intended the contributor to obtain a share, or an enlarged share, in the premises. (This presumed intention may be displaced by express agreement to the contrary.) The court is given a general discretion to assess the amount of the share thus obtained.

The improvements which Henry Mumps has made to 8 Trant Way would have allowed him to claim under s. 37 were it not for the fact that he is not married to Mildred. This emphasises once again that unmarried couples are at a disadvantage in this type of situation. However, Henry's improvements, if more than routine maintenance which either party might do on the house (*Pettit* v *Pettit* [1970] AC 777, could be relevant to any claim he might make on the basis of a constructive trust. However, he must prove in any such proceedings that there was an agreement that he would obtain an interest in the property. Were he married that intention would be implied.

The only other way in which Henry might succeed in claiming a share would be through the doctrine of proprietary estoppel. If he could show that Mildred, by words or conduct, had led him to believe that he would have a share, and that in reliance on this he had acted to his detriment, this would, by analogy with *Pascoe* v *Turner* [1979] 1 WLR 431, give rise to an equity which the court could satisfy by requiring Mildred to hold the legal title in trust for herself and Henry, or by awarding any other remedy which the court considered to be appropriate.

24.2.2 Against a mortgagee on a claim for possession

When a claim to a share in the beneficial interest is being asserted against a mortgagee, it makes no difference whether the parties to the relationship are married or unmarried. Both Sally and Henry would have to establish their claims by virtue of a common intention trust or proprietary estoppel: the spouse's rights on divorce have no application against a third party during the course of the marriage.

If the claimant's interest arose under a trust, its enforceability against the mortgagee would depend on the usual rules: notice in the case of unregistered land (*Kingsnorth Finance Co. Ltd* v *Tizard* [1986] 1 WLR 783), and entry on the register or enforcement as an overriding interest by virtue of actual occupation in the case of registered land. You should remember, however, that in practice the beneficiary may have waived these rights expressly in order to enable the owner to obtain a mortgage; where there is no express waiver, the court may yet imply one where the beneficiary knew that a mortgage advance was needed in order to purchase the property (see 5.10.4.5(2) and (3)).

If Henry or Sally was to base a claim on proprietary estoppel, rather than on a common intention trust, the position would most probably be the same, since it now appears reasonably certain that an equity arising from estoppel will be enforced against purchasers of both registered and unregistered land (18.5 and 20.3.4.1).

From what we know about Bob's story, it seems unlikely that he would be in a position to claim a share in his daughter's house, but he might very well need to assert a right to remain in occupation if Barbara tries to bring their arrangement to an end, and we will consider this in the following section.

24.3 Right to remain in occupation

24.3.1 As a beneficiary under a trust

If Henry or Sally could establish a claim to a share in the beneficial interest, he or she would, as a beneficiary under a trust of land, have a right to occupy the property (TOLATA 1996, s. 12—see 13.7.1). This right would be enforceable against both the legal owner (Mildred or Mark), and against third parties such as mortgagees, on the principles we have noted above. However, as we have seen in *Mortgage Corporation* v *Shaire* [2001] Ch 743 and *Bank of Ireland Home Mortgages Ltd* v *Bell* [2001] 2 FLR 809, the secured creditor (and, indeed, the owner) has the right under s. 14 of the Act to apply to the court for an order for sale, and the beneficiary may be ordered to give up occupation so that the property can be sold and the proceeds divided between those entitled. Further, even if the court refuses to order sale, the creditor may adopt the alternative route of suing for the money owed and bankrupting the debtor if he cannot pay, so that eventually the property will be sold under the provisions of the Insolvency Act 1986.

24.3.2 Under a contractual licence or by proprietary estoppel

In Chapter 20 we noted a variety of ways in which the courts have intervened to prevent licensors from revoking licences which arise from family arrangements. We will not repeat what we said there, except to remind you that in Lord Denning's day, Henry Mumps might have been advised to try to establish an implied contractual licence (by analogy with *Tanner* v *Tanner* [1975] 1 WLR 1346), but that today both he and Bob Bell would be better advised to rely if necessary on the doctrine of proprietary estoppel.

Spouses are not usually regarded as occupying the matrimonial home as licensees (see *National Provincial Bank* v *Ainsworth* [1965] AC 1175 at pp. 1223–4), and Sally has in fact a statutory right to occupation, which would serve her better, provided she takes the necessary steps to protect it (as to which, see below).

24.3.3 Under a statutory right of occupation

This is another area of the law in which a spouse is in a very much better position than a cohabitant or anyone else seeking to remain in occupation of the family home.

24.3.3.1 *Matrimonial Home Rights*

In 1965 the House of Lords held in *National Provincial Bank Ltd* v *Ainsworth* [1965] AC 1175 that a wife who had no proprietary interest in the matrimonial home had no occupation rights which she could enforce against a purchaser. She did have a common law right to be supported and provided with a home, but this was a personal right enforceable against her husband only. Thus a husband could desert his wife and family, and sell or mortgage the house in which they lived, leaving them homeless.

The decision in *Ainsworth* brought to an end an interesting development associated with Lord Denning MR, who had pioneered the concept of the 'deserted wife's equity', i.e., a right to remain in the matrimonial home which bound purchasers from her husband.

Although the House of Lords was unable to accept the existence of such a right, the earlier decisions by the Court of Appeal which had developed the concept had drawn attention to the wife's need for protection. Following the House of Lords' decision, a new statutory right was created in 1967, which is now to be found in the Family Law Act 1996 (FLA 1996). Section 30 confers the following rights on one spouse where the other spouse is entitled to occupy a dwelling by virtue of a beneficial estate or interest or contract or has a right to remain in occupation of the dwelling by virtue of any enactment:

(a) a right not to be evicted or excluded if already in occupation; and

(b) a right, with the leave of the court, to enter and occupy if not already in occupation.

The rights conferred by FLA 1996, s. 30 are described as 'matrimonial home rights' and by virtue of s. 31 they constitute a charge on the estate or interest of the other spouse. In the case of registered land this charge should be protected by the entry of a notice on the register (s. 31(10)(a)) and cannot constitute an overriding interest (s. 31(10)(b)). In the case of unregistered land, where the interest of the 'owning' spouse is a legal estate, the matrimonial property rights of the other spouse should be registered as a land charge, Class F (s. 31(13) and LCA 1972, s. 2(7) as amended by FLA 1996, Sch. 8, para. 47). Where the right is protected in this way, it will bind anyone who acquires the legal estate in the property.

Where a spouse has matrimonial home rights, FLA 1996, s. 33, gives the court power to make an 'occupation order', which can be used for various purposes including requiring the owning spouse to let the other into the premises, regulating the occupation of the premises or even excluding the owning spouse from the property. In reaching any decision on the exercise of these powers the court is entitled to take into account the needs and resources of the parties and any child living with one of them (or who might be expected to live with one) and the likely effect of any decision on the health, safety or well-being of the parties or any such child (s. 33(6)).

Matrimonial home rights only arise in relation to premises which have been a matrimonial home of the couple or which were intended to be a matrimonial home (s. 31(7)).

Accordingly, Sally does have a statutory right to remain in occupation of 11 Trant Way, but she should be advised to protect it by entering a notice on Mark's registered title, and should be warned as to the consequences of not doing so.

24.3.3.2 *Cohabitants' occupation rights*

Henry too has certain statutory rights of occupation under the Family Law Act 1996, but they are very much more limited than those enjoyed by Sally. The Act defines cohabitants as 'a man and a woman, who, although not married to each other, are living together as husband and wife' (s. 62(1)(9a)).

Section 36 of the Act permits a court to make an order against a cohabitant giving the other (or a former) cohabitant:

(a) a right not to be evicted or excluded (s. 36(3)); or

(b) a right to enter and occupy (s. 36(4)).

An order may also be made excluding the owning co-habitant from the property (s. 36(4)).

Section 36(6) provides a long list of matters to which a court is to have regard before making an order under s. 36. These matters include the nature and duration of the relationship, whether there have been children and the needs and resources of the cohabitants and any children. However, s. 41(2) specifically provides that as far as the nature of the parties' relationship is concerned, the court, 'is to have regard to the fact that [the cohabitants] have not given each other the commitment involved in marriage'.

Even in those cases in which an order can be obtained under s. 36, the rights conferred are far less than those provided to a spouse by ss. 31 and 33, because whereas a spousal occupation order can be made for an indefinite period or a period of any duration (s. 33(10)), an order under s. 36 can only be made for a period of six months, subject to only one extension for another six months. Accordingly, the maximum period of security provided by s. 36 is one year. However, from Henry Mumps's point of view, even this limited protection would be of value if Mildred told him to go.

The s. 36 powers can only be used in relation to a property in which the co-habitants 'lived together as husband and wife' or which they intended so to occupy (s. 36(1)(c)). This provision, taken with the definition of 'cohabitant' in s. 62(1) means that s. 36 cannot be used by parties to a homosexual relationship or by relatives or others who have been sharing a house.

24.3.3.3 *Associated persons*

Bob, as a father living in his daughter's house, has no right to an occupation order under the Family Law Act 1996. A few provisions of the Act apply to what it terms 'associated persons', who are defined (in s. 62(3)) as including not only spouses and cohabitants, but also relatives and those who live or have lived in the same household (thus including homosexual cohabitants). The Act confers a limited range of rights on associated persons (in the case of spouses and heterosexual partners these are, of course, in addition to those we have noted above). Under s. 42 the court may make a non-molestation order, which prevents a person from molesting another associated person or a child living with either of them. These provisions replace and extend the earlier provisions of the Domestic Violence and Matrimonial Proceedings Act 1976, which applied only to couples who were married or were living together as man and wife.

Accordingly, if family relationships deteriorate seriously, both Henry and Bob could seek protection from domestic violence under s. 42 of the Act, but this by itself will not help them to deal with the very real problem of losing their homes.

24.3.3.4 *Homosexual cohabitants*

As we noted above, a same-sex partner has no occupation rights under s. 36 of the Family Law Act 1996. In considering this limitation, you may like to note two decisions in which the courts have given a wide interpretation to similarly limited provisions in the Rent Act 1977. In general, the statutory protection of tenants is outside the scope of this book, but we will consider these decisions here because they are possibly of wider significance.

Schedule 1, paras. 2 and 3 of the Rent Act 1977 provide that when a tenant protected under the Act dies, a person who has been living with that tenant in the property may have the right to remain there. Under para. 2(1), the surviving spouse of the tenant may remain as a *statutory tenant*, and para. 2(2) provides that for the purpose of that provision:

a person who was living with the original tenant as his or her wife or husband shall be treated as the spouse of the original tenant.

In other words, a heterosexual cohabitant receives the same protection under the Act as would a spouse. Under para. 3(1), where there is no spouse or cohabitant, a member of the tenant's family who has lived with the tenant for a prescribed minimum period is entitled to remain as an *assured tenant*.

We suggest that you do not concern yourself with the differences between statutory and assured tenancies, but simply note that the cases we are considering proceed on the basis that there is greater security of tenure under a statutory tenancy than under an assured tenancy.

In *Fitzpatrick* v *Sterling Housing Association Ltd* [2001] 1 AC 27, a case which had arisen before the Human Rights Act 1998 came into force, the House of Lords held that the survivor of a stable homosexual relationship, who had lived for many years with the deceased Rent Act tenant, was a member of the tenant's family and entitled to an assured tenancy under Sch. 1, para. 3(1). At the time this was seen as a very considerable move forward in the recognition of same-sex relationships, and involved reversing the decision of the Court of Appeal which, while sympathetic, had considered itself unable to extend the concept of 'family' in this way. However, while the House of Lords was willing to take this step, it was not ready to go any further, and accordingly rejected the claim to a statutory tenancy under para. 2(2). In the words of Lord Clyde (at p. 47):

The language [in para.2(2)] plainly indicates a biological distinction between the sex of the original tenant and that of the successor . . . [and points] to a heterosexual relationship. . . . the sub-paragraph does not in my view include a homosexual relationship.

Interestingly, the question of whether this result might discriminate against same sex couples in comparison with heterosexual couples was identified by Lord Slynn as something which might have to be considered when the Human Rights Act 1988 was in force (see p. 34).

In fact it was exactly this question which arose for consideration by the Court of Appeal in *Ghaidan* v *Godin-Mendoza* [2003] 2 WLR 478. On facts very similar to *Fitzpatrick*, the defendant to possession proceedings sought a declaration that he was entitled to a statutory tenancy under para. 2(2). At first instance this was refused, the judge holding instead that the defendant was entitled to an assured tenancy. On appeal against this decision, the defendant claimed that providing a statutory tenancy to the survivor of a heterosexual relationship when the survivor of a homosexual relationship was limited to the less beneficial assured tenancy constituted discrimination on grounds of sexual orientation, and thus infringed Art. 14 of the Convention. The Court of Appeal considered in detail the possible justification for discriminating between the survivors of such relationships in this way, but concluded that there was no objective and reasonable justification for the difference.

Accordingly the court considered that para. 2(2) as interpreted by the House of Lords in *Fitzpatrick* did infringe Art. 14. Under the Human Rights Act 1998 s. 3 , the court must, so far as possible, read Sch. 2, para. 2 in such a way that its provisions are rendered compatible with Convention rights. In the court's view this could be done:

by reading the words '[living with the original tenant] as his or her wife or husband' to mean 'as *if they were* his or her wife or husband' (see p.491).

This interpretation was accordingly adopted by the court, which in consequence held that on the death of the original tenant his partner succeeded to a statutory tenancy.

Returning to the question of occupation rights under s. 36 of the Family Law Act 1996, it is interesting to speculate whether we may in time see a similar approach to the interpretation of that section, although much will depend on the outcome of the appeal to the House of Lords in *Ghaidan* v *Mendoza*, for which leave has been given.

24.4 **Reform**

The provisions of the Family Law Act which we have noted take a step in the right direction by extending protection against domestic violence to a wider range of people who are likely to be sharing a home. However, there is still a great difference between the positions of a married person like Sally, with her long-term statutory right of occupation and the opportunity to seek an adjustment of property on divorce, and of a cohabitant like Henry, who has only a limited right of occupation under the Family Law Act, and who has to satisfy strict property law rules if he is to obtain a share in the family home. If his relationship with Mildred does break down and she tells him to move out, he will find himself in a very difficult position. As Waite J noted in *Hammond* v *Mitchell* [1991] 1 WLR 1127, the lack of any legal process to deal with the ending of a relationship can, due to property disputes, give rise to even greater stress than that which arises on the breakdown of a marriage.

Parties to other long-term relationships have, as yet, no statutory right of occupation, and face the same difficulties in claiming a share of the home.

Law Commission review

In 1994, the Law Commission embarked on a review of the property rights of home-sharers, a move which was welcomed by members of the judiciary who have to deal with the very difficult problems created by the present law (see Waite LJ in *Midland Bank plc* v *Cooke* [1995] 4 All ER 562 at pp. 564–5, and Peter Gibson LJ in *Drake* v *Whipp* [1995] 28 HLR 531 at p. 533). However, the project proved to be unsuccessful, and in 2002 the Law Commission issued a discussion paper, in which it explained that it had been unable to devise any recommendations for statutory reform (see 'Sharing Homes: A Discussion Paper', July 2002—available in electronic form on **www.lawcom.gov.uk**).

This is a disappointing outcome, but the discussion paper is of interest for the accounts which it gives of the current law and of the difficulties which the Law Commission encountered in trying to develop proposals for change. The Commission explained that it sought to develop a property-based scheme, which would be suitable for all home-sharers, without reference to the nature of their relationship. Thus the same rules would apply to any situation in which the home was owned by one person and shared with another or others, irrespective of whether they were sexual partners (of the same or opposite gender), members of a family, or simply friends. The non-owner would 'earn' a share in the family home through contributions to its acquisition, improvement, or retention, or to the parties' joint lives (para. 3.5). These contributions would include not only direct and indirect financial payments, but also home-making services of the type provided by Mrs Burns (see 17.5.3 above). The share acquired by the non-owner would take effect through a statutory trust, and the discussion paper gives examples of how the contributions, and the resulting shares, would be quantified. There would be provision for the property owner to 'contract out' of the statutory trust by means of a formal notice, but unless this was done the trust would be imposed without any reference to the parties' intentions. This would end the search by the courts for the inferred 'common intention', but it would also exclude all reference to any actual intentions which might have existed.

The Law Commission was, however, unable to devise rules for valuing and attributing contributions which would be regarded as fair in their application to all homeshares: it appears from the examples given in the paper that what would be recognised as 'fair' in one type of relationship would seem unfair in different circumstances. The Commission also came to recognise that the parties' real intentions might be very significant and could not be left out of account. Moreover it became apparent to those working on the project that the current law, with all its defects, still has certain advantages to offer. As the discussion paper put it in para. 1.3:

It has, indeed, become clear that the current law offers a degree of flexibility which is positively desirable in that it can respond with some sophistication to different factual circumstances and to different personal relationships.

In conclusion, the Commission recommended that the courts should adopt a more flexible approach both in giving credit for indirect financial contributions and in quantifying the share which arises from the contribution (see paras. 4.6 and 4.7). It made no other recommendations and emphasised that the home-sharing project was now at an end (para. 5.5 and Part VI), but it recognised the need for further consideration of:

the adoption, necessarily by legislation, of new legal approaches to personal relationships outside marriage (Part VI (7)).

Meanwhile the Government announced in November 2001 that it would undertake a review of 'civil partnerships'. We can only hope that eventually this will result in statutory provisions for some form of property adjustment when relationships between unmarried partners (whether of the same or opposite gender) come to an end, but so far the only outcome has been the Civil Partnerships Bill, the benefits of which, if enacted, will be confined to homosexual partnerships.

FURTHER READING

Deech, 'The Case Against Legal Recognition of Cohabitation' [1980] Int. Comp. Law Quart, 480.

Jackson, 'People Who Live Together Should Put Their Affairs In Order' (1990) 20 Fam Law, 439.

Law Commission, 'Sharing Homes: A Discussion Paper', July 2002 (available on: **www.lawcom.gov.uk**).

Thompson, 'Home Sharing—Reforming the Law' [1996] Conv., 155.

25

What is land?

25.1 The statutory definition

Thus far we have said very little about the definition of land. At first it may seem odd that there should be any question about the matter at all: surely everybody knows what land is? However, as we will see, the word 'land' to a lawyer means far more than it does when the word is used in normal speech. As well as defining 'land', we will also consider some of the other terminology which is applied to estates and interests in land, as this is relevant to the rather complex statutory definition of land.

25.1.1 LPA 1925, s. 205

'Land' is defined in LPA 1925, s. 205(1)(ix), as follows:

'Land' includes land of any tenure, and mines and minerals, whether or not held apart from the surface, buildings or parts of buildings (whether the division is horizontal, vertical or made in any other way) and other corporeal hereditaments; also . . . a rent and other incorporeal hereditaments, and an easement, right, privilege, or benefit in, over or derived from land . . .

This definition is, of course the one that is used in the LPA 1925. The SLA 1925 has the same definition in s. 117(1)(ix) and the same words appear in s. 68(6) of the TA 1925 and s. 3(viii) of the LRA 1925. Accordingly, this provides the general rule when you are dealing with the 1925 legislation. Section 25(2) of TOLATA 1996 adopts the LPA 1925 definitions but you should note that Sch. 4 to TOLATA 1996 repealed some words that used to appear at the end of s. 205(1)(ix) ('but not an undivided share in land'). Those words are no longer relevant after the introduction of the new trust of land rules and the changes made to the doctrine of conversion by s. 3 of the 1996 Act, because a beneficial interest under a trust of land is an interest in land, unlike an interest under a trust for sale, which was in money (see para. 12.2.2.1). As a consequence of all these provisions, when you are dealing with any of the main property statutes mentioned in this book you will be using the same definition of land.

25.1.2 Interpretation Act 1978

If, however, you are construing other legislation you may need to refer to the definition in Sch. 1 to the Interpretation Act 1978 (but note that this only applies to statutes passed on or after 1 January 1979):

'Land' includes buildings and other structures, land covered with water, and any estate, interest, easement, servitude in or over land.

Note that both the LPA 1925 and the Interpretation Act definitions are merely inclusive and not exclusive and thus it would remain theoretically possible for other things also to constitute land (if one could think of an example of such a thing).

25.1.2 Other definitions

Were you to be construing a document other than an Act of Parliament you would, of course, have to look to see whether a special definition had been provided for that document and in drafting any such document yourself you might need to provide a definition (perhaps by expressly adopting the LPA 1925 definition).

You can see that there is a relationship between the two definitions given above and both contain similar terms. Here, because we are primarily concerned with the property legislation, we will concentrate on the LPA 1925 definition. That definition requires some thought and so we will now consider its individual parts.

25.2 Earth, minerals, buildings and fixtures

25.2.1 The basic rule

It is easy to accept that 'land' includes the earth beneath our feet and any minerals contained therein. However, the legal definition of land goes further and includes in the definition plants growing on the land *and* any other thing which is actually fixed to the land. 'Buildings' and 'parts of buildings' are actually mentioned in s. 205(1)(ix), and, after a moment's thought, it is not altogether surprising that they are included in the term 'land'. It is perhaps more surprising, at first thought, when one discovers that any item affixed to the land becomes land itself. Thus in *Buckland* v *Butterfield* (1820) 2 Brod & Bing 54, it was held that a conservatory which was attached to a house by eight cantilevers, each 9 inches long, formed part of the land. This is important, because should one wish to retain and remove such a fixture when selling the freehold estate in the land, one must specifically contract to exclude the fixture from the sale. Thus, should a vendor intend to remove the rose bushes from the garden of a house which he is selling, he should provide for this when the contract is made. *Buckland* v *Butterfield* also illustrates the point that since the house is land, because it is fixed to the earth, anything fixed to the house also becomes land. However, something which is merely placed upon the land, and not fixed to it, will not be regarded as forming part of the land, however heavy it is and even if it would be very difficult to move it. In *Berkley* v *Poulett* (1976) 242 EG 39, a large statue, made of marble and weighing nearly half a ton, was not regarded as part of the land, because it was not fixed down in any way.

The basic rule is therefore that anything annexed to land *is* land. However, the courts have long accepted that something which is affixed merely to facilitate its display, or in order to steady it, is *not* to be regarded as becoming part of the land. Thus in *Leigh* v *Taylor* [1902] AC 157, a tapestry tacked to strips of wood, which were then affixed to the wall, was not regarded as being part of the land. The degree of annexation in this case was merely that which was necessary for the display of the tapestry. In *Hulme* v *Brigham* [1943] KB 152, printing machines weighing between 9 and 12 tons were not regarded as fixtures, even though they were attached to motors which were fixed to the floor. In this case the degree of annexation was slight and was necessary merely to render the motors stable.

25.2.2 Items not fixed to the land

In rare circumstances something which is not actually fixed to the land but which appears to form an integral part of it, may be regarded as forming part of the land for legal purposes. The best example of this is *D'Eyncourt* v *Gregory* (1866) LR 3 Eq 382, in which stone statues, seats and garden vases were held to be part of the land, even though they were free-standing, as were certain tapestries and pictures hanging upon the walls. The basis of the decision is that the ornaments formed an integral part of the architectural design of the house on the property. Thus it appears that the existence of a 'master plan' concerning the property may render items part of the land, even though there is no real annexation. Another illustration was supplied by Blackburn J in *Holland* v *Hodgson* (1872) LR 7 CP 328 at p. 335, when he explained that a pile of stones lying in a builder's yard would obviously not form part of the land upon which it lay. However, were the same stones to be constructed into a drystone wall (which uses no mortar and no method of fixing the wall to the ground) on a farm, the wall obviously would form part of the land of the farm. A more recent example is provided by *Elitestone Ltd* v *Morris* [1997] 1 WLR 687, which concerned a chalet bungalow, which had been placed on concrete blocks but which was not attached to them in any way. The blocks were attached to the land. The land was occupied by the defendants under an agreement which purported to be a licence but which the court of first instance held to be a lease. However, for the defendants to have Rent Act protection the bungalow itself had to be land and the landlord argued that this was not the case because the building was not fixed to land in anyway but merely rested on the blocks. The case was finally decided in the House of Lords, who concluded that in this the bungalow *was* land despite the absence of annexation. Lord Lloyd of Berwick said (at pp. 692–3):

Many different tests have been suggested, such as whether the object which has been fixed to the property has been so fixed for the better enjoyment of the object as a chattel, or whether it has been fixed with a view to effecting a permanent improvement of the freehold. This and similar tests are useful when one is considering an object such as a tapestry, which may or may not be fixed to a house so as to become part of the freehold. . . . These tests are less useful when one is considering the house itself. In the case of the house the answer is as much a matter of common sense as precise analysis. A house which is constructed in such a way so as to be removable, whether as a unit, or in sections, may well remain a chattel, even though it is connected temporarily to mains services such as water and electricity. But a house which is constructed in such a way that it cannot be removed at all, save by destruction, cannot have been intended to remain as a chattel. It must have been intended to form part of the realty.

This decision emphasises that what is of primary importance is the 'intention' involved. However, Lord Clyde (at p. 698) indicated that the use of this word may be misleading because it is the purpose which the object in question is serving which matters and not the intention or purpose of the person who put it there. Thus, Lord Clyde said that the test was objective and not subjective. The relevant issue is whether the object is 'designed for the use or enjoyment of the land or for the more complete or convenient use or enjoyment of the thing itself'. Although this may sound complicated, the case in fact indicates that the courts are really applying a common-sense test, rather than relying on technical arguments about the degree of annexation. These principles were applied in *Chelsea Yacht and Boat Club Ltd* v *Pope* [2000] 1 WLR 1941 in which the attachment of a houseboat to pontoons, and to the river bed and banks by means of an anchor and rings, were held to be insufficient to make the boat real property, rather than a chattel. However, by way of contrast see also *Cinderella Rockerfellas Ltd* v *Rudd* [2003] 3 All ER 219, in which a permanently moored vessel was regarded as forming part of a hereditament for the purposes of rateable valuation. You should, however, note that in giving the judgment of the court Potter LJ appears not to be saying that the vessel in question was land but that it was a chattel which was, for rating purposes, sufficiently connected to the land to be capable of being regarded as part of the rateable property. Accordingly, the apparent conflict with the *Chelsea* case is not a real conflict: the vessel is a chattel but can be taken into account in assessing the rates payable in respect of the land (which includes the water above the land on which the vessel floats as well as the bank to which it is moored).

25.3 Hereditaments

25.3.1 LPA 1925 definition

Before 1926, 'hereditaments' were those rights which were capable of passing to heirs by way of inheritance. The term is defined in LPA 1925, s. 205(1)(ix), as 'any real property which on an intestacy occurring before the commencement of this Act might have devolved upon an heir'. This includes the estates and interests in land which we have discussed in this book, and which are not purely personal rights. Thus a licence is not a hereditament because it was a personal permission and not an interest which would have passed to an heir.

25.3.2 Corporeal and incorporeal hereditaments

Having defined 'hereditaments' as 'inheritable interests', the common law went on to distinguish between 'corporeal' and 'incorporeal' hereditaments. Corporeal hereditaments are physical objects: the physical land and its attachments. Incorporeal hereditaments are rights, not things, and there is a fixed list of such hereditaments, which includes rentcharges, easements and profits.

This traditional classification may cause you some surprise, for the two groups, corporeal and incorporeal, seem strangely unrelated, though they are supposed to be subdivisions of one category. To paraphrase Austin (*Jurisprudence*, 5th edn., vol. 1, p. 362): one class consists of intangible rights over objects (incorporeal), and the other of physical objects over which rights may be exercised (corporeal). Further, the notion of corporeal hereditaments seems to conflict with the basic principle of English land law, which we emphasised in chapter 1, that one cannot own the land itself, but only an estate in it. No provision for estates in land seems to be made in this classification: they are certainly not within the accepted list of incorporeal hereditaments, but one cannot describe them as corporeal because they are intangible rights rather than tangible objects.

This is a classification which has always caused difficulty and debate and we would not trouble you with it if it were not for the fact that you will see references to 'hereditaments' in the statutory definition of land. It is also important that you should realise that easements, profits and rentcharges are not merely interests in land but are themselves 'land' within the statutory definition. We suggest, though, that it is enough to note the meaning of the terms and that you should not spend too much time on this rather difficult point until your studies of land law are very advanced.

The statutory definition of 'hereditaments' includes the term 'real property' and this leads us to the next set of technical terms.

25.4 Real and personal property (or, realty and personalty)

25.4.1 The meaning of 'real'

Often you may see references to 'real property' which suggest that this term is synonymous with 'land' (e.g., in the book title, *Cheshire and Burn's Modern Law of Real Property*). This is not, however, entirely true, for, as we shall see, some interests in land do not amount to real property.

The distinction between real and personal property is an ancient one and is still of importance today. The term 'real' property refers to that property which the early courts would protect by a 'real' action (an action *in rem*). In this context the adjective 'real' does not have its usual meaning of 'genuine' but is used in a technical sense. The word 'real' derives from the Latin word *res* (thing). A 'real action' was one in which the court would order that the property itself (the *res*) be restored to an owner who had been dispossessed, rather than giving the defendant the choice of returning the property or paying damages to compensate for the loss. If someone takes your table, a remedy in damages will usually suffice, for you may take the money and buy another table. However, land is unique in its character and, at a time when status in society depended upon one's relation to land, it was felt that where land was lost it was essential that it should be recovered. Thus, there was a distinction between 'real' property (where the property could be recovered by an action *in rem*) and 'personal' property, so called because it could be protected only by an action *in personam* (an action against the person of the wrongdoer). Where an action *in personam* was concerned the wrongdoer would in general pay damages rather than return the property. Thus the history of English forms of action has led to a labelling of property which is still used today.

25.4.2 **Exceptions**

Most of the rights considered in this book amount to real property because they are rights in land which would have been subject to an action *in rem*. There have been, however, two main exceptions.

25.4.2.1 *Rights of beneficiaries under trusts*

The first of these was the right of a beneficiary under a trust for sale. Since the doctrine of conversion notionally transformed the trust property into money (a form of personal property) the beneficiaries' interests under the trust were seen to be interests in personalty. The doctrine of conversion was abolished in relation to trusts for sale by TOLATA 1996 and now the interests of beneficiaries under the trusts of land, which replaced trusts for sale, *will* be interests in land.

25.4.2.2 *Leases*

The other exception is not so obvious and results once again from the manner in which the law has developed. When leases first came into common use, they were regarded as commercial contracts creating rights *in personam* between the parties. Unlike freehold estates they did not affect the tenant's position on the feudal ladder, and were not subject to one of the real actions. If the tenant were dispossessed by his landlord, he could not recover the land but would only be awarded damages for breach of contract. Since it was protected only by an action *in personam* the lease came to be regarded as personal property. After a time, the tenant was enabled to recover the land by action, whether he was dispossessed of the land by his landlord or by some third party, but by this time it was too late to alter the classification of the lease. A lease was therefore a 'chattel' (another name for personal property, derived from a French word from which 'cattle' is also derived, livestock being an important form of personal property). However, recognition of the rather special nature of the lease led to the rather paradoxical nomenclature of 'chattel real', which emphasises its hybrid nature.

Leases remain personal property to this day and the distinction can sometimes prove to be of importance. Thus if a testator were to make the following disposition in his will: 'All my real property to my son Alfred and all my personal property to my son Bernard', Alfred would receive any freehold property owned by his father, but Bernard would be able to claim any leasehold property, together with (in the past) any equitable interests his father might have had in a trust for sale, and all his father's chattels. In this case the freehold property is obviously an estate *in land*. It should be recalled, however, that the lease, whilst being personal property, is also an estate in land (LPA 1925, s. 1(1)). The equitable interest behind a trust for sale, however, not only *was* personal property but also *was not* an interest in land, although in *Williams & Glyn's Bank Ltd* v *Boland* [1981] AC 487 the House of Lords did accept that it was an interest in relation to land. The abolition of the trust for sale and of the doctrine of conversion as a result of TOLATA 1996 removed this oddity. Today, beneficial interests in land held on a trust of land are interests in land.

25.5 **Flying freehold**

25.5.1 **The extent of ownership**

It is often said that a freehold owner owns the land up to the skies and down to the centre of the earth. This theory is usually expressed in the Latin maxim *Cuius est solum eius est usque ad coelum et ad inferos* (which colourfully refers to the heavens and the depths). However, in practice this theory is far from true and in any event lawyers throughout the centuries, while espousing this theory, appear to have had problems with some of the logical consequences.

You will realise that there must be some restrictions on this theory, as otherwise every plane that passes over an owner's land would be committing a trespass, whereas this is not the case. Also, while the title to the land may be vested in the freehold owner, this does not mean that all the elements of the physical land are his to use. One example will suffice to illustrate this point but in fact there are many others. While there are limited cases in which it is possible for a landowner also to own the title to the coal in his land, normally the freehold title to coal is vested in the Coal Authority, regardless of who owns the freehold to the surrounding land (see the Coal Industry Act 1994, s. 7(3)). Thus, the law recognises that the general theory set out above can be disrupted in some cases and also that it appears that land can be owned in layers. Thus, it appears perfectly possible for the freehold title to land to be vested in A down to a certain depth and for the title to the land below that depth to be vested in B. This, is confirmed in s. 205(1)(ix) of the LPA 1925 (see 25.1.1) which expressly says that both horizontal and vertical division of land is possible. Accordingly, it should follow that it would be possible for layers above ground level to be similarly divided and thus for a freehold to be conveyed, for example in a flat above ground level, without the owner also having to own the fee simple in the land at ground level. Surprisingly, however, this seems to be a concept that lawyers have over the centuries found hard to accept, although it should follow logically from the maxim given above.

25.5.2 **The problems of a 'flying freehold'**

One could argue for a long time over why the concept of what is usually called a 'flying freehold' has given problems. However, one explanation is that, despite the theory of estates, early land law was very much centred upon physical land, the control of physical land and the relationships within society that were built upon the foundation of tenure of land. Interestingly, the idea of a leasehold estate in a stratum above the ground does not appear to have given the same problems. The reason for this may be rooted in the fact that early leases were viewed solely as commercial agreements that did not give rise to the same tenurial incidents as the freehold estate or have the same impact upon the owner's place in society. Accordingly, while many seem to have struggled with the possibility of a freehold estate in 'thin air', the law of leases accepted that if a tenant had a lease of a upper floor and the building burned down, the lease continued and rent had to be paid: *Cricklewood Property and Investment Trust Ltd* v *Leighton's Investment Trust Ltd* [1945] AC 221 (but see above at 8.6.1 for the modern rule as to frustration and leases). It is this reasoning, as well as the benefits of a lease in relation to running of positive covenants (see Chapter 9), that has made it standard practice for the estate granted in flats to be a leasehold estate rather than a freehold estate, with the freehold of the whole property being vested either in the owner of the ground floor flat or in some other person (sometimes to be held upon trust for all the leaseholders but often as a commercial investment in its own right).

This approach to the freehold estate seems, however, to be an unnecessary complication and it has been pointed out for centuries that there is no real justification for the view that there is some difficulty involved in creating a flying freehold. The same approach does not apply elsewhere; for example, Scottish law appears to have no difficulty with the concept of the Scottish equivalent to freehold in a flat and this can prove beneficial to the owner, since a major defect of a lease is that it is a time-limited estate. Although the disadvantage of the time limitation can be overcome by giving the leaseholder the right to renew the lease when it expires the wish to avoid the use of the flying freehold has, in recent history when tenurial relationships are unimportant, probably arisen solely from the practical problems that can arise because of the freehold rules on running of covenants (see Chapter 23). If the difficulty of ensuring compliance with suitable covenants, including positive covenants where necessary, could be overcome, there seems to be no genuine reason for English law not to accept that a flying freehold can be a useful concept in practice. One of the very real problems in the past has been that there has been no means of requiring a freehold owner to maintain his building in a proper state of repair. While it is a nuisance if your neighbour allows his house to become derelict (and may even affect the value of your neighbouring property), the problem is not severe if your property does not depend upon his for support. Where support was crucial, the law developed a limited right to support by means of an easement (see 22.2.2.7) but still did not oblige the neighbour to keep his property in good repair. This difficulty becomes acute if the safety of your own property depends upon that neighbour keeping his own premises in good repair (which would be true if his property were a lower flat and yours an upper flat) and thus there was a tendency to adopt the known path of granting leaseholds, with the benefit that, in a lease, positive covenants could be imposed that would bind later acquirers of the estate. However, even in the past, in particular circumstances, this issue was found not to be impossible of solution and it is perhaps amusing to note that one example of the use of flying freeholds has been in relation to some of the properties forming part of Lincoln's Inn in London. It appears that barristers were less troubled by the concept than other lawyers, or perhaps that they were happier to rely on the careful drafting of agreements in order to ensure that the flying freeholds did not cause insuperable problems.

Having said that flying freehold should not cause insuperable difficulties to the careful, it is perhaps worth looking at a case that illustrates how things can go wrong if insufficient thought is given when a flying freehold is created. In *Abbahall Ltd v Smee* [2003] 1 All ER 465, a house had been separated so that the upper two floors constituted a flying freehold owned by Miss Smee, while the ground floor was owned by Abbahall Ltd. Miss Smee had allowed some parts of the property to fall into disrepair and water thus leaked onto the ground floor and there was a danger of falling masonry. Abbahall therefore obtained a court order allowing it to enter Miss Smee's premises in order to repair the roof. It then brought further proceedings to recover the costs of the repairs from Miss Smee, on the basis that the roof must form part of her premises. At first instance the judge found that the two parties were both responsible for the roof but, in deciding how much each should pay towards the repairs, he took account of Miss Smee's poor financial position and ordered that she should only have to pay one quarter of the costs of repair. On appeal, the Court of Appeal agreed that both parties were responsible for the roof but that their liability to pay depended on the extent of the benefit to each. On the facts of the particular case, they determined that the parties should each be responsible for half of the costs of the repairs. The case therefore leaves much room for dispute in any future case in which it is not clear to what extent each party benefits from the element of the property in question.

25.5.3 'Commonhold'

Interestingly, the concept of commonhold advanced by the Law Commission in its Report *Commonhold: Freehold Flats and Freehold Ownership of Other Independent Buildings* (Cm 179, July 1987) decided not to build solely upon the idea of flying freeholds but on an adaptation of the existing model used for flats, where each flat owner has a lease of the flat and is a member of a management company, which owns the freehold. As we have seen in para. 11.2, the commonhold scheme provided by the Commonhold and Leasehold Reform Act 2002 involves each flat owner owning the freehold estate in his or her flat and being a member of a company, the commonhold association, which owns the freehold of the common parts of the building. It will be interesting to see to what extent this new approach proves popular once the commonhold provisions are brought into force. Bear in mind that there can be no 'flying commonhold' (see para. 11.2.2), thus the issues mentioned in para. 25.5.2 cannot arise.

25.5.4 A practical approach to land law

This whole area of law provides an excellent example of how lawyers are affected by both society and custom (the early influence of tenurial incidents and relationships) and practicalities (making covenants work) rather than by absolute theories. The practising lawyer, while being a person who has to understand and apply concepts and theories that are often extremely complex, is mainly driven by the need to find a practical solution to a problem. Where there is doubt, the lawyer will usually prefer a proven solution to the risks of experimenting with uncertainties. The push for growth or reform comes when existing approaches no longer meet all the practical needs of those affected.

We said at the start of this book that it was our intention to avoid a discussion of purely historical matters. However, you will have found that historical issues have intruded rather often into this last chapter. The reason for this is that modern land law is still, to a certain extent, tied to its past. The 1925 property legislation was not a complete break with the past but rather reformed and built upon the existing law, which had developed over the centuries. The relationship between land law ancient and modern is particularly noticeable when dealing with the technical definition of 'land' because in this area the 1925 statutes attempted no radical reforms. Accordingly, we feel that, although a knowledge of the historical development of land law is not essential to the modern student, it may be of interest and assistance to those who wish to deepen their understanding of the subject. We hope that this book has shown you that land law is a fascinating and lively subject and that we have encouraged you to extend your reading into such areas.

FURTHER READING

Cheshire and Burn's Modern Law of Real Property, 16th edn., 2000, pp. 172–83 (The Legal Position of a Tenant in Fee Simple).

Lawson and Rudden, *The Law of Property*, 3rd edn., 2002, Chapter 2 (The Classification of Things).

Smith, *Property Law*, 4th edn., 2003, pp. 7–10 (Some Basic Distinctions).

Gray, 'Property in Thin Air' [1991] CLJ 252 (on flying freeholds).

BIBLIOGRAPHY

Abbey and Richards, *A Practical Approach to Conveyancing*, 5th edn., Oxford University Press, 2003.

Austin, *Jurisprudence*, 5th edn., Murray, 1885.

Cheshire and Burn, *Cheshire and Burn's Modern Law of Real Property*, 16th edn., Butterworths, 2000.

Fry, A *Treatise on the Specific Performance of Contracts*, 6th edn., Stevens, 1921.

Gale, *Gale on Easements*, 17th edn., Sweet & Maxwell, 2002.

Gray and Gray, *Elements of Land Law*, 3rd edn., Butterworths, 2001 (4th edn. due autumn 2004).

Hanbury and Martin, *Modern Equity*, 16th edn., Sweet & Maxwell, 2001.

Lawson and Rudden, *The Law of Property*, 3rd edn., Oxford University Press, 2002.

Maitland, *Equity*, Cambridge University Press, 1936.

Megarry and Wade, *The Law of Real Property*, 6th edn., Sweet & Maxwell, 2000.

Morris and Leach, *The Rule against Perpetuities*, 2nd edn., Stevens, 1962.

Oakley, *Constructive Trusts*, 3rd edn., Sweet & Maxwell, 1997.

Pawlowski, *The Doctrine of Proprietary Estoppel*, Sweet & Maxwell, 1996.

Pearce and Stevens, *The Law of Trusts and Equitable Obligations*, 3rd edn., Butterworths, 2002.

Preston and Newson, *Restrictive Covenants Affecting Freehold Land*, 9th edn., Sweet & Maxwell, 1998.

Rook, *Property Law and Human Rights*, Blackstone Press, 2001.

Ruoff and Roper, *Registered Conveyancing*, Sweet & Maxwell, looseleaf edn.

Smith, *Property Law*, 4th edn., Longman, 2003.

Woodfall, *Law of Landlord and Tenant*, Sweet & Maxwell, looseleaf edn.

GLOSSARY

abatement A 'self-help' remedy by which the owner of the dominant tenement may remove an obstruction to the exercise of an easement.

absolute interest An interest which is not determinable or conditional (see 7.3), i.e., it is not granted on such terms that it is liable to end prematurely on the occurrence of some specified event.

administrators See 'personal representatives'.

adverse possession (acquisition of title by). The process of acquiring title to land by dispossessing the previous holder and occupying the land until: (1) the owner's right to recover it is time-barred under the Limitation Act (unreg.land); (2) the adverse possessor is registered as proprietor (reg.land).

alienation The act of disposing of one's property, i.e., passing it from one owner to another.

annexation The procedure of attaching the benefit of a restrictive covenant to the land of the covenantee, so that it will run automatically with that land, without any need for the benefit to be assigned (transferred) to the new owner when the land changes hands.

appurtenant See 'profit à prendre'.

assent A disposition by personal representatives, by which property is vested in the person entitled under the deceased's will or on his intestacy.

assignment A transfer of property (used particularly in respect of the transfer of a lease or a reversion).

barring the entail See 'disentailing'.

base fee The interest created when the holder of an entailed interest tries to transfer it to another person, without satisfying the requirements for 'disentailing' (converting the interest into a fee simple). The recipient takes only a base fee, which lasts as long as the entailed interest would have lasted, and ends when the original grantor becomes entitled to enforce his reversion.

caution, inhibition, notice, restriction Methods of protecting interests in registered land by entry on the register under LRA 1925; under LRA 2002 only notices and restrictions are used.

caveat emptor Let the buyer beware.

cesser on redemption The process by which a mortgage automatically comes to an end when the obligation which it secures is performed.

charge An encumbrance securing the payment of money.

charge by way of legal mortgage See 21.4.3.

chattels real Leases—see 25.4.2.2.

choses in action See 1.9.2.2.

choses in possession See 1.9.2.1.

clog (on the equity of redemption). Any restriction imposed by the mortgage on the mortgagor's right to redeem the mortgaged property.

commonhold See Chapter 11.

conditional interest See 7.3.1.

consolidate (right to). The right of the mortgagee to refuse to allow the mortgagor to redeem one mortgage unless some other mortgage is redeemed at the same time.

co-ownership A form of ownership in which two or more people are entitled to possession of the property at the same time. See 'joint tenancy' and 'tenancy in common'.

concurrent lease See 'lease of the reversion'.

conversion A change in the nature of property, from realty to personalty, or vice versa. Actual conversion of this kind occurs when land is sold, so that the purchaser's property changes from money into land, and that of the vendor changes from land into money. Under the equitable doctrine of conversion, this change notionally takes place at an earlier stage, as soon as the contract to sell is concluded (see 12.2.2.1). This doctrine was abolished by TOLATA 1996 in relation to trusts for sale.

conveyance An instrument (other than a will) which transfers property from one owner to another.

corporeal hereditament See 25.3.2.

covenant A promise made by deed.

covenantee The person with whom a covenant is made, who takes the benefit of the covenant and has a right to enforce the promise.

covenantor The person who makes a covenant, and has the burden or duty of performing the promise.

deed A document which is signed in the presence of a witness as a deed and is then delivered (see 1.6.2.3(1)).

deed of discharge See 13.9.4 and 14.10.6.

determinable interest See 7.3.2.

disentailing The procedure by which an entailed interest is converted into a fee simple (see 12.2.1).

disponee A person to whom a disposition is made.

disponer A person who makes a disposition.

distress (to levy distress, to distrain). The legal seizure of chattels in order to satisfy some debt or claim; in particular, may be used by the landlord against the tenant in respect of unpaid rent.

dominant tenement A piece of land which is benefited by some right (see 'easement').

easement A right enjoyed over one piece of land (the 'servient tenement') for the benefit of another piece of land (the 'dominant tenement'), e.g., rights of way, rights of drainage, rights of light. See also 'quasi-easement'.

encumbrance A liability burdening property.

entail See 'entailed interest'.

entailed interest An interest in land inheritable only by the issue (child, grandchild, etc.) of the original grantee; existed only as an equitable interest after 1925 and can no longer be created after TOLATA 1996.

en ventre sa mère Literally, 'in one's mother's womb', i.e., conceived but not yet born.

equity of redemption The mortgagor's interest in the property during the continuance of the mortgage.

estate An interest in land which entitles its owner to exercise proprietary rights over that land for a prescribed period.

estate contract A contract to sell or grant an estate in land. Both parties are bound by the contract, so that either can enforce against the other. The statutory definition of estate contracts which are registrable as class C(iv) land charges (LCA 1972, s. 2(4)(iv)) includes two further rights, the option to purchase and the right of pre-emption, but these do not create the reciprocal rights and duties of the full estate contract.

An **option** (to purchase an estate or to renew a lease) gives the person entitled the right to compel the owner to sell or grant the estate, but does not impose on him any duty to buy. He is free to exercise the option or not, as he chooses.

A **right of pre-emption** (or right of first refusal) gives the person entitled a right to be offered the property if the owner decides to sell, but does not impose any duty to sell on the owner, nor any duty to buy on the person entitled.

estate rentcharge A rentcharge (q.v.) created to ensure that the owner of the land, subject to the charge, contributes to maintenance costs or performs some other positive obligation (see 23.5.2.3).

executors See 'personal representatives'.

fee simple absolute in possession The larger of the two legal estates in land (the other being the term of years absolute: LPA 1925, s. 1) which will last indefinitely, as long as there are persons entitled to take the property under the will of the previous owner or on his intestacy.

fee tail See 'entailed interest'.

fine A premium, sometimes payable on the grant or assignment of a lease.

fixed-term tenancy See 8.1.2.

foreclosure The procedure by which a mortgagee asks the court to extinguish the mortgagor's equitable right to redeem, and his other rights to the property, and to permit the mortgagee to take the property in satisfaction of the debt or other obligation for which it is security.

freehold estate Fee simple absolute in possession.

hereditament See 25.3.1.

incorporeal hereditament See 25.3.2.

infant A minor; a person who has not attained the age of majority, being under the age of 18.

in gross See 'profit à prendre'.

inhibition See 'caution'.

in possession Denotes that an interest so described gives a right to present enjoyment of the property, rather than to enjoyment that will not commence until some time in the future.

instrument A legal document whereby a right is created or confirmed or a fact recorded.

intestacy The condition of dying without having made a will.

inter vivos Literally, 'among the living'; the phrase denotes that a disposition so described takes effect during the lifetime of the grantor, rather than under his will (which takes effect at death).

joint tenancy The form of co-ownership in which each owner is entitled to the whole property, rather than to an undivided share in it. The right of survivorship (*jus accrescendi*) applies here, so that the last surviving tenant becomes solely entitled to the whole property, while those joint tenants who predecease him have no share in the property to pass with their estates. (Compare 'tenancy in common'.)

lease The second legal estate in land ('term of years absolute', LPA 1925, s. 1(1); an interest which gives the person entitled exclusive possession of the land for a fixed period of time, usually but not essentially in consideration of the payment of rent. The term 'lease' is used to describe both the estate and the document creating it. (See also 'tenancy'.)

leasehold estate The term of years absolute.

lease of the reversion (or concurrent lease). A lease which is created where a landlord grants a second lease in respect of property which is already subject to a lease granted by him (distinguish 'reversionary lease').

lessee Tenant under a lease.

lessor Landlord under a lease.

licence Permission (in this context, usually permission to use land).

limitation of actions The procedure whereby the right to bring an action is barred after the lapse of a prescribed period of time.

mesne profits The profits lost to the owner of land by reason of his having been wrongfully dispossessed of his land.

minor interest An interest in registered land which required protection by an entry on the register (LRA 1925). The term is not used in LRA 2002.

mortgage The grant of an interest in property as security for the payment of a debt or the discharge of an obligation.

mortgagee The person to whom a mortgage is granted and the interest in the mortgaged property conveyed (see 'mortgage').

mortgagor The person who creates the mortgage and conveys an interest in his property as security for the payment of a debt, etc. (see 'mortgage').

nec vi, nec clam, nec precario Literally, 'not by force, nor by stealth, nor by permission'. The phrase describes the way in which one who claims an easement or profit by prescription must have acted during the prescription period.

notice 1. See 'caution'. 2. Knowledge. (a) **actual notice**—real knowledge; (b) **constructive notice**—knowledge which a person is deemed to have, usually because he failed to make the necessary enquiries and is taken to know what they would have revealed; (c) **imputed notice**—notice belonging to an agent which is ascribed to his principal.

notice to quit The method whereby landlord or tenant may end a periodic tenancy.

option See 'estate contract'.

overreaching The statutory procedure which enables a purchaser to take the legal estate free from certain equitable interests (arising, for example, under a Settled Land Act settlement or trust of land), provided the purchase money is paid to two trustees or a trust corporation.

overriding interest An interest in registered land, which does not require protection by entry on the register and binds the registered proprietor and all who acquire later interests in the land (LRA 2002).

partition The physical division of land between several co-owners, so that each becomes the sole owner of a separate plot.

periodic tenancy See 8.1.2.

perpetually renewable lease See 9.2.1.3.

personal property (personalty). See 25.4.

personal representatives Persons authorised to administer the estate of a dead person. There are two types: **executors**, who are appointed by will; and **administrators**, who are appointed by the court in cases of intestacy (i.e., where the deceased leaves no will), or where there is no executor willing or able to act.

personalty See, 'personal property'.

possibility of reverter The right of a grantor to recover the land if a determinable interest comes to an end (see 7.3.2).

pre-emption (right of). See 'estate contract'.

prescription A method of acquiring easements or profits by long use.

profit à prendre The right to take something (such as sand, wood, pasture) from land belonging to another. A profit may be **appurtenant** to a piece of land, that is, it may benefit that land and run with it; or it may be **in gross**, that is, it may belong to an individual without being attached to a specific piece of land which is benefited by it.

puisne mortgage A legal mortgage of unregistered land which is not protected by the deposit of the title deeds with the mortgagee, and so is registrable as a class C(i) land charge (LCA 1972, s. 2(4)).

purchaser A person who takes an estate or interest by act of parties rather than by operation of law (1.7.3.2). When used as a technical term, the word does not have its colloquial meaning of 'buyer', and so one who buys has to be described as 'a purchaser for value'.

quasi-easement A potential easement. The term is used to describe the situation in which land, which is owned and occupied by one person, is used in a way which would constitute an easement if the land was divided into two tenements which were separately owned or occupied (see 22.2.1.2).

real property (realty). See 25.4.

registered proprietor The person registered as the owner of a legal estate in registered land.

remainder An interest in land granted under a settlement to take effect after some previous interest (e.g., to A for life, **remainder** to B in fee simple). A remainder gives a right to possession of the land in the future and so, since 1925, exists only in equity.

rentcharge A right entitling the holder to receive a periodic sum of money from the owner of land charged with that payment. Provision may be made, for example, for the payment of annuities in this way. See also 'estate rentcharge.' A rentcharge should be distinguished from **rent service**—the rent due from a tenant to a landlord under a lease.

rent service Payments (generally in money, although sometimes in goods or services) made to a landlord by a tenant holding under a lease.

reservation A method of creating an easement or profit, whereby a grantor retains these rights over the land which he conveys to the grantee.

restriction See 'caution'.

reversion The right remaining in a grantor after he has granted some interest shorter in duration than his own. The term is used in respect of both settlements and leases. 1. Settlements: the owner of a fee simple, for example, who grants a life interest or (before they were abolished by TOLATA 1996) an entailed interest, has not disposed of his full estate, and therefore retains a right to the land when the interests he has granted come to an end (the property will 'revert' to the grantor). A reversion gives a right to possession of the land in the future and so, since 1925, exists only in equity. 2. Leases: an estate owner who grants a lease retains his own legal estate in the land (fee simple or superior lease) throughout the duration of the lease. This interest in the land, which includes the right to receive rents and profits, if any, during the lease, and to recover the physical possession of the land at the end of the term, is called the 'landlord's reversion'.

reversionary lease A lease creating a term which will begin at a future date (distinguish a 'lease of the reversion', which arises where a landlord grants concurrent leases of the same property).

rights *in personam* Rights enforceable against only certain categories of persons, e.g., the right of a beneficiary under a trust.

rights *in rem* Rights in respect of a piece of land which are enforceable against any person who acquires an estate or interest in that land, e.g., in the case of unregistered land, a legal easement or a legal lease.

seisin Possession (historically, the type of possession enjoyed by the holder of a freehold estate).

servient tenement A piece of land which is burdened by some right (see 'easement').

settlement A disposition of property, made inter vivos or by will, whereby the settlor (the estate owner making the settlement) creates a series of successive interests in the property, e.g., a grant to A for life, remainder to B in fee simple.

severance The procedure by which a joint tenant converts his relation with the other co-owners into that of a tenant in common, so that he has a notional undivided share in the property and is no longer affected by the right of survivorship. Distinguish 'words of severance'.

socage The surviving form of tenure, by which land in England and Wales is held of the Crown.

statutory owners A person who acts where there is no tenant for life of a Settled Land Act settlement (14.3).

sublease A lease granted by a landlord who is himself a tenant of a superior estate owner.

tack (right to). The right to add a further advance (i.e., a later loan) to an earlier debt secured by a mortgage, so that the additional loan shares the priority of the earlier debt and thus takes priority over any intervening mortgages.

tenancy A lease; the two terms, 'tenancy' and 'lease', are used interchangeably throughout the book.

tenancy at sufferance See 8.10.2.

tenancy at will See 8.10.3.

tenancy by estoppel See 8.10.4.

tenancy in common The form of co-ownership in which each owner has a notional, although undivided, share in the property, which passes with his estate at his death; the right of survivorship does not apply to this form of co-ownership. Compare 'joint tenancy'.

tenant for life The beneficiary under a Settled Land Act settlement who has the right to present (current) enjoyment of the property. Under the Act, the tenant for life holds the legal estate and has statutory powers of management over the settled land.

tenure The set of conditions on which a tenant held land from his feudal lord; today all land is held in 'socage' tenure.

terms of years absolute A lease.

title A person's right to property, or the evidence of that right.

transfer The deed used to pass the legal estate in registered land from one owner to another.

trust corporation The Public Trustee or a corporation either appointed by the court in any particular case to be a trustee or entitled by rules made under Public Trustee Act 1906, s. 4(3), to act as a custodian trustee (LPA 1925, s. 205(1)(xxviii)).

trust for sale A trust which imposes a duty to sell the property. Under TOLATA 1996 this form of trust now takes effect as a trust of land.

trust instrument See 14.5.1.1.

trust of land The new form of trust relating to land introduced by the Trusts of Land and

Appointment of Trustees Act 1996. Any trust in which some or all of the trust property is land constitutes a 'trust of land'.

undivided shares in land The interests of tenants in common; sometimes used as another name for tenancy in common.

usual covenants A term of art, denoting a fixed list of covenants to be included to a lease (see 9.3.3).

vesting deed See 14.5.1.2.

volunteer A person who takes property without giving value for it.

waste (liability for). The liability of a limited owner, such as a tenant under a lease or a tenant for life of settled land, for any act or omission which alters the state of the land whether for better or worse.

words of severance Words in a grant of property to co-owners, which indicate an intention that the grantees should hold as tenants in common and not as joint tenants.

INDEX

Abandonment of easement/profit 529
Abatement remedy 526
Absolute freehold title 76–7
Absolute leasehold title 78–9
Access to neighbouring land 530–1
Access to premises 186
Accumulation of income, rules against 340–2
Acquisition of estate
  adverse possession *see* Adverse possession
  buying a house *see* House purchase
Action, choses in action 19
Actual notice 17
Adoption 331
Adverse possession 113–35
  establishment of 116–22
  fact of possession 117
  future interests and 123–4
  human rights issues 133–5
  importance of possession in land law 113
  intention and 117–18, 122
  justification for 115–16
  land reserved for specific purpose 120–1
  limitation periods 114–15, 122–4
    effect of completion of period 125–6
    squatter's rights during 124–5
  owner's state of mind 118
  registered land 81, 127–33
    application of existing rules 127–8
    defence to proceedings for possession 132
    first application by adverse possessor for
      registration 130–2
    legislation of 1925 127–9
    legislation of 2002 130–3
    purchasers and 133
    reform proposals 128–9
  tenants 119–20, 126, 128
  terminology 116–17
  unregistered land 81, 122–7
    effect of completion of limitation period
      125–6
    rights of squatter during limitation period
      124–5
    time 122–4
Agreement to grant a lease 156
Air, rights to 500
Alteration of register 105–6
Annexation of covenants
  express 545
  implied 545–6
  statutory 546–8
Annuities 53, 58
Assignment
  covenants 548
  leases 161–2
    covenant not to assign 189–94

enforcement of covenants and 204–5,
  209–11, 210, 211, 215, 216, 218
express 161
forfeiture for breach of covenant 232
by operation of law 161–2
Associated persons 569
Assured tenants 569
Auctions 36
Authorised guarantee agreement 203

Bankruptcy
  deeds of arrangement 59
  register of petitions 58
  severance of joint tenancy and 355
  trusts of land and 284
Bare licences 416, 417, 421
Base fee 307
Behaviour, imposition of constructive trust and
  368–70
Beneficiaries under trusts
  equitable interests 11
  rights of 279–82, 578
  trusts of land
    appointment and retirement of trustees and
      268–9, 299
    consultation and consents 273–5, 299, 300
    conveyance of land to 271–2
    nature of interests 299
    occupation by 279–82, 300, 566
    rights of 279–82
Bona fide purchaser 16–17
Breach of contract
  remedies for 46–8, 156
  repudiatory 171–2
Breach of covenants 185–6, 187–8
  liability for 200–2
  remedies 221–37, 555–6
    general contractual remedies 221–4,
      555
    landlord's remedies against defaulting
      tenant 225–37
    tenant's remedies against defaulting
      landlord 224–5
  waiver of 227
Break clauses 147, 164
Building schemes 548–50
Buildings, included in definition of land 574

Car parking 500–1
Care, general duty of 197
Cautions in register 74, 84–5
Charge certificate, mortgagee's right to
  446–7
Charges
  land charges *see* Land charges

mortgages *see* Mortgages
Chattels real 19, 578
Children and minors
  illegitimacy 331
  settled land 307, 322
  trusts of land and 293
Choses in action 19
Choses in possession 19
Civil partnerships 572
Class gifts 331–3
Cohabitation
  licences by estoppel and 419–20
  resulting and constructive trusts and 371–2,
    375–6
  right to remain in occupation 566, 568–70
  right to share in value of house and 564–5
  same-sex partners 569–70
Collateral advantages for the mortgagee 444–5
Common, tenancy in 348–9
  differences in law and equity 349, 350
Common intention trusts 372, 373–4
Common ownership, discharge of covenants
    and 557
Commonhold estate 3, 4, 238–53, 552–3,
    559–60, 581
  advantages 251
  commonhold association 242
  commonhold scheme 240–4
  community statement 242–3
  compared with long leaseholds 253
  creation of 244–6
    conversion of property 245–6
    extinction of existing leases 164, 246
    new development 244–5
  disadvantages 251–3
  ending 250–1
    by court 250–1
    by voluntary winding-up 250
  insolvency and 252
  land 241
  managing property 246–7
    restrictions on dealing with freehold estate
      248–9, 252
  need for 238–40
  positive covenants and 554
  unit holders 242
    nature of interest 247–9
Completion of house purchase 28
  registered land 108–9
Compulsory first registration 71–2
Concurrent leases 181
Condition of property 186
Conditional interests 140–1, 144
  compared with determinable interests 141–2
  perpetuities rules and 326–7
Conditions in lease 182–3
Conscience, equitable interests and 14
Consent, landlord's consent to assign or sublet
    190–3
Constructive notice 17

contracts for creation or operation of 36
  searches to avoid constructive notice 60–2
Constructive trusts 11, 31, 368–70
  arising from contribution 371–3
  contracts for sale of land and 43
  establishing claim to share in beneficial
    interest 373–9
  fraud/unconscionable behaviour and 368–70
  inequitable conduct and 370
  nature of 368
  proprietary estoppel and 43, 394–5
  quantifying share 379–81
Contingent interests 307–8
  perpetuities rules and 326–7, 328
Continuing purpose, doctrine of 287–8
Contracts
  auctions 36
  cohabitation and 564
  contractual licences 415–16, 417–19, 421–4,
    566–7
  contractual remedies for breach of covenants
    221–4, 555
  to create mortgage 439
  for creation or operation of trusts 36
  equitable interests in land and 11–12
  estate contracts 53
  Financial Services Act and 36
  house purchase 27, 29–48
    by correspondence 34–5
    effect of contract 45–6
    electronic conveyancing and 110
    exchange 34–5
    incorporation of expressly agreed terms
      31–3
    made before 27 Sept 1989 37–40
    made on or after 27 Sept 1989 29–37
    oral contract 37–8
    part performance 37, 38, 39–41
    passing of equitable interest 45–6
    remedies for breach 46–8
    signature 35–6, 38
    written 29–37, 156
  leases 160
    contractualization of leases 173–4
    determination by discharge of contract
      168–72
    frustration 169–71
    repudiatory breach 171–2
    short leases 36
  privity of 14
  remedies for breach of contract 46–8, 156
Contribution, constructive trusts and 371–3
Conversion
  notional conversion of property 46
  trusts for sale and 260–1
Conveyancing process 26–8
  completion 28
  contract 27, 29–48
    by correspondence 34–5
    effect of contract 45–6

exchange 34–5
incorporation of expressly agreed terms 31–3
made before 27 Sept 1989 37–40
made on or after 27 Sept 1989 29–37
oral contract 37–8
part performance 37, 38, 39–41
passing of equitable interest 45–6
remedies for breach 46–8
signature 35–6, 38
written 29–37
electronic conveyancing 67–8, 109–11
formalities 109–10
simultaneous registration 110–11
investigating title 27–8, 74
pre-contract 26–7
registered land 66–112
alteration of register 105–6
discovering encumbrances 83–5, 102–3
electronic conveyancing 109–11
indemnity 106
need for reform 66–9
transfer and completion 107–9
what can be registered 69–71
unregistered land 50–65
application for first registration 63–5
checking for encumbrances 51
conveyance 63
land charges 51–9
other legal or equitable interests 59–63
ownership of estate 50–1
searches 63
Co-ownership 345–65
commonhold estate 242
coparceny 346
imposition of statutory trusts 350–1
joint tenancy 346–8
determination of lease by 172–3
differences in law and equity 349
severance 347–8, 352–7
survivorship 348, 363–4
occupation right 361–2
partitioning property 363
purchaser and 363–5
relationship between co-owners 358–63
rent to other co-owners 362–3
selling 358–60, 363–5
tenancy by entireties 346
tenancy in common 348–9
differences in law and equity 349, 350
trusts
imposition of statutory trusts 350–1
number of trustees 351
trusts for sale 261–2
types 346
Coparceny 346
Corporeal hereditaments 576–7
Correspondence, contracts by 34–5
Courts
trusts of land and 282–8, 302

winding up commonhold scheme 250–1
Covenants 182–3
annexation of 545–8
assignment 548
breach of 185–6, 187–8
liability for 200–2
remedies 221–37, 555–6
waiver of 227
building schemes and 548–50
enforcement 199–220
examples 214–16
freehold land 534–51
new law governing new leases 202–5, 213–14
old law governing old leases 200–2, 207–12
position of new landlord and/or tenant after transfer of lease and/or reversion 207–14
position of original parties after transfer of lease and/or reversion 200–7
provisions applying to old and new leases 205–7
sublease and 216–20
equitable interests and 14
leases 159–60
express 183, 185–95
landlord's 185–9, 195
tenant's 189–95
freehold land 533–60
discharge 557–8
enforceability 534–51
positive covenants 541, 551–5
reform of law 558–60
remedies 555–6
implied 160, 183, 195–8
indemnity 553
letting schemes 551
positive covenants 541, 551–5
restrictive *see* Restrictive covenants
usual 183, 198–9
Crown
intestacy and 5
ownership of land and 4
Curtain principle 312–13

Damage, tenant's liability for 197–8
Damages 11, 46
Debentures 36
Declaration remedy 47–8, 556
Deeds
charge by deed by way of legal mortgage 437–8
constructive notice by examination of 61
creation of easement/profit by 505
creation of lease by 154
delivery of 13
discharge of trusts of land 291
formal requirements 12–13
identification of 13
informal mortgage by deposit of 439–40
mortgagee's right to title deeds 446–7
surrender of lease and 167

vesting deed for settled land 311–12
Derogation, covenant not to derogate from grant 187–8, 196
Determinable interests 141–2, 307
Disclaimer of lease 168
Disrepair, tenant's liability for 197–8
Distress remedy 225–7
Divorce, property adjustment orders 371
Drainage rights 500

Easements 493, 495–502
    acquisition
        express grant or reservation 507, 511–15
        implied grant 507–10
        implied reservation 510–11
        prescription 515–26
    creation 92–3, 501–2, 505
    enforcement 505–7
    equitable 14, 63
    examples 499–501
    extinguishment 528–9
    in law and equity 504–7
    law reform 529–32, 559
    legal 8–9
    licences distinguished from 413
    meaning 495
    as overriding interests 92–3
    period 504–5
    perpetuities and 340
    prescribed period 504–5
    remedies for protection 526–8
    rules of 495–9
Electronic conveyancing 67–8, 109–11
    formalities 109–10
    simultaneous registration 110–11
Encumbrances, checking for 51
Enforcement
    covenants 199–220
        examples 214–16
        freehold land 534–51
        new law governing new leases 202–5, 213–14
        old law governing old leases 200–2, 207–12
        position of new landlord and/or tenant after transfer of lease and/or reversion 207–14
        position of original parties after transfer of lease and/or reversion 200–7
        provisions applying to old and new leases 205–7
        sublease and 216–20
    easements 505–7
    equitable interests in land 59–63
        against later acquirers 62–3
        against purchaser of legal estate 59–62
        equitable leases 158–9
    legal interests in land 59
    licences 415, 417–30
        against licensor 417–20
        against successors of licensor 420–7, 428–9

profits à prendre 505–7
Enlargement of lease 168
Enquiries see Searches and enquiries
Entailed interest 6–7, 139–40, 259–60, 306
    attempt to create 293–4
Entry
    rights of 10, 140
    tenant's obligation to allow landlord's entry 198
Equitable interests in land 10–15
    beneficiaries under trust 11
    contract and passing of 45–6
    contracts and 11–12
    creation of 10–11
    discretionary nature of equity 15
    doctrine of notice 16–18, 59–62
        acquiring legal estate 17
        bona fide purchaser 16–17, 62
        giving value 17
        notice of equitable interest not given 17–18, 62
        reducing dangers of 59–60
        registered land 104–6
        searches to avoid constructive notice 60–2
        today 60
    easements 14, 63, 504–7
    enforcement 16, 59–63
        against later acquirers 62–3
        against purchaser of legal estate 59–62
        equitable leases 158–9
    estoppel 15
        as replacement for part performance 41–5
    leases
        covenants 159–60
        creation 156–60
        enforcement 158–9
        enforcement of covenants and 211–12
    legal interests compared 15–18
    mere equities 14
    mortgages 435, 439–40
        disadvantages 456
        priorities 464–6
        remedies 455–6
    not created formally 12–13
    priorities 111–12
    profits 504–7
    registered land 111–12
    resulting from statutory reform 14
    traditional 11–14
Estate, privity of 207–9
Estate contracts 53
Estate rentcharges 9, 553–4
Estates in land 3, 4–7
    tenure and 4
    see also Commonhold estate; Freehold estate (fee simple); Leasehold estate
Estoppel 31
    equitable 15
    first registration by adverse possessor and 131
    by grant 179

licences by 416–17, 419–20, 424–7
promissory 382
proprietary *see* Proprietary estoppel
as replacement for part performance 41–5
by representation 179
tenancy by 15, 178–80, 412
Estovers, profit of 503
Exchange of contracts 34–5
Expectation as to future rights 383–5
Expiry of lease 164

Facilities, right to use of 500
Family arrangements 293
Family/matrimonial property 563–72
    problems 563–4
    reforms 570–2
    resulting and constructive trusts
        arising from contribution 371–3
        establishing claim to share in beneficial
            interest 373–9
        quantifying share 379–81
    right to remain in occupation 566–70
    right to share in value of 564–6
    tenancy by entireties 346
    see also Co-ownership
Fee tail *see* Entailed interest
Fences 501, 554
Fertility assumptions 330–1, 336–7
Feudal system 4
Financial contribution, constructive trusts and
    371–3
First registration 63–5, 71–3
    by adverse possessor 130–2
    cautions against 74
    compulsory 71–2
    failure to apply for first registration 72, 142
    registering title 73–82
    triggering events 71–2
    voluntary 25, 73
Fitness for purpose, covenants on 196
Fixed-term tenancies 145–6
    expiry 164
Fixtures, included in definition of land 574
Flying freehold 579–82
Foreclosure of mortgages 450, 455
Forfeiture
    lease 168, 227–37
        for breach of other covenants 228
        for non-payment of rent 228
        protection for mortgagees 234
        protection for subtenants 234, 236
        reform proposals 236–7
        relief from 233
        self-help 232–3
        statutory restrictions 234
    severance of joint tenancy and 357
Formal requirements 12–13
    creation of trusts of land 297–8
    electronic conveyancing 109–10
    equitable interests not created formally 12–13

written contracts 29–37, 156
Franchises 71
Fraud 63
    constructive trusts and 368–70
    mortgage priority and 471
    mortgagee's liability for 458, 459–61
    receiver's liability for 458, 461–2
    valuer's liability for 458, 462
Freehold estate (fee simple) 3, 4, 5–6, 139–44
    buying a house *see* House purchase
    classes of title 76–8
    covenants 533–60
        discharge 557–8
        enforceability 534–51
        positive covenants 541, 551–5
        reform of law 558–60
        remedies 555–6
    effect of 1925 legislation 6–7
    flying freehold 579–82
    legal mortgage of 436
    public policy and 143–4
    registration 69
    restrictions on dealing with freehold estate in
        commonhold scheme 248–9, 252
    upgrading title 79–80
Frustration of contracts 169–71
Furnished lettings, covenants on fitness for
    purpose 196
Future interests 142
    adverse possession and 123–4
    contingent interests 307–8
    expectation as to 383–5
    reversionary lease 147–8

General equitable charge 52–3
Glossary of terms 584–9
Good faith duty 16–17
Good leasehold title 79
Grant, estoppel by 179
Guarantors, enforcement of covenants and
    205–6

Harassment 185–6, 225
Hardship, liability for breach of covenants and
    201
Heirs 5, 139
    entailed interest 6
Hereditaments 576–7
Homelessness, hostel accommodation 407–8
Homosexual partners 569–70, 572
Hostel accommodation 407–8
House purchase 23–8
    completion 28, 108–9
    contracts 27, 29–48
        by correspondence 34–5
        effect of contract 45–6
        electronic conveyancing and 110
        exchange 34–5
        incorporation of expressly agreed terms
            31–3

made before 27 Sept 1989 37–40
made on or after 27 Sept 1989 29–37
oral contract 37–8
part performance 37, 38, 39–41
passing of equitable interest 45–6
remedies for breach 46–8
signature 35–6, 38
written 29–37
conveyancing process 26–8
completion 28
contract 27
investigating title 27–8
pre-contract 26–7
registered land 66–112
unregistered land 50–65
notional conversion of property 46
risk 45
two systems of title 23–6
registered 24–6
unregistered 24, 26
what buyer wants to know 23
which system applies 24–6
Human rights issues 19–20
adverse possession 133–5
conditional interests and 144
landlord's remedies and 226, 232

Illegitimacy 331
Implied covenants 160, 183, 195–8
Implied trusts 11, 257, 258
contracts for creation or operation of 36
Imputed notice 17–18
Incorporeal hereditaments 576–7
Incorrect names, land charges and 54
Indemnity
breach of covenant 201–2
indemnity covenants 553
registered land 106
Informal mortgage by deposit of deeds
439–40
Inheritance
entailed interest 6
heirs 5
intestacy 5
Inhibitions in register 85
Injunctions 47
Inland Revenue, land charges and 53
Insolvency, commonhold scheme and 252
Instalment mortgages 441
Insurance
covenants to insure 195
mortgagee's insurance at mortgagor's expense
448
Intention
adverse possession 117–18, 122
common intention trusts 372, 373–4
creation of lease and 154–5, 404, 405
distinguishing licences from lease and 404,
405
resulting trusts and 367

Interests in land 3, 7–18
conditional interests 140–1, 144
compared with determinable interests 141–2
perpetuities rules and 326–7
contingent interests 307–8
perpetuities rules and 326–7, 328
determinable interests 141–2, 307
entailed interest 6–7, 139–40, 259–60
attempt to create 293–4
future interests 142
adverse possession and 123–4
contingent interests 307–8
interests of persons in actual occupation 90,
92–101
comparison of new and old system 94–6
meaning of actual occupation 96–7
purchaser taking free of occupier's rights
100–2
several people in occupation 99–100
statutory provisions 93
temporary absence 98–9
time of occupation 97–8
which rights override 90–2
licence coupled with 415, 417, 421
licences developing into 428–9
life interests 139, 260
overriding interests 67, 77, 80, 88–92
proprietary estoppel and 392–3
protected by entries on register 84–7
successive 292–3
vested interests, perpetuities rules and 326–7
see also Equitable interests in land; Legal
interests in land
Intestacy 5
Investigating title 27–8, 74
Investment
contracts 36
trustees of settled land 323

Joint tenancy 346–8
determination of lease by 172–3
differences in law and equity 349
severance 347–8, 352–7
survivorship 348, 363–4

Keep-open covenants 221–3
Knowledge, non-registration of land charges
and 57

Land
buying a house *see* House purchase
definition 573–4
earth, minerals, buildings and fixtures 574–6
estates in *see* Estates in land
glossary of terms 584–9
inspection of 104
constructive notice 61
interests in *see* Interests in land
items not fixed to 575–6
multiplicity of rights 18

Land charges 51–9
  classes 52–4
  local 27
  nature of 51–2
  other registers maintained by Land Charges
      Department 58–9
  registration of 54–5, 59
    effect of non-registration 56–8
    effect of registration 55–6
Land obligations 559
Landlords
  obligations of 182–220
    express covenants 185–9, 195
    implied covenants 196–7
  remedies against defaulting tenant 225–37
  tenant's remedies against defaulting landlord
      224–5
Lands Tribunal, discharge of covenants and 557
Leasehold estate 3, 4, 7, 145–81, 578
  adverse possession and 119–20, 126, 128
  agreement to grant a lease 156
  assignment of lease 161–2
    covenant not to assign 189–94
    enforcement of covenants and 204–5,
        209–11, 210, 211, 215, 216, 218
    express 161
    forfeiture for breach of covenant 232
    by operation of law 161–2
  classes of title 78–9
  commonhold estate 253
  concurrent leases 181
  conditions in lease 182–3
  contracts 160
    contractualization of leases 173–4
    determination by discharge of contract
        168–72
    frustration 169–71
    repudiatory breach 171–2
    short leases 36
  covenants in leases see Covenants
  creation of lease 153–60
    express grant 153–4
    grant of legal lease 153–5
    implied grant 154–5
    intention 154–5, 404, 405
    leases in equity 156–60
    non-compliance with requirements for legal
        grant 155–6
    tenancies at will 178
  definition of lease 148
  determination 162–73
    common law rules 163–8
    by discharge of contract 168–72
    disclaimer 168
    effect on subtenant of determination of
        head lease 174–6
    enlargement 168
    expiry 164
    extinction and conversion to commonhold
        164, 246

    forfeiture 168
    frustration 169–71
    by joint tenants 172–3
    merger 168, 175
    notice to quit 164–7
    repudiatory breach 171–2
    statutory protection for tenants 162–3
    surrender 15, 167–8, 175
    tenancies at will 178
  disposition 160–2
  equitable leases
    covenants 159–60
    creation 156–60
    enforcement 158–9
    enforcement of covenants and 211–12
  fixed-term see Fixed-term tenancies
  forfeiture of lease 168, 227–37
    for breach of other covenants 228
    for non-payment of rent 228
    protection for mortgagees 234
    protection for subtenants 234, 236
    reform proposals 236–7
    relief from 233
    self-help 232–3
    statutory restrictions 234
  formalities not observed 13
  leasehold reversion 151
    sale of 162
  legal mortgage of 436
  letting schemes 551
  licence distinguished from lease 400–13
  mortgagee's right to grant leases 448
  mortgagor's right to grant leases 445–6
  non-proprietary lease 411–12
  overriding interests 89–92
  periodic tenancies see Periodic tenancies
  registration 69–70, 154
  renewal of leases 188–9
  requirements for lease 148–53, 401–3
    determinate term 149–50, 401
    exclusive possession 148–9, 402–3,
        405
    rent 152–3
    term less than that of grantor 151–2
  restrictions on leasing in commonhold
      scheme 248–9
  reversionary lease 147–8
  short leases
    contracts 36
    covenants to repair 196
    creation by express grant 153–4
  special types of lease 176–81
  subleases see Subleases
  surrender 167–8
  tenant for life's power to grant lease
      315
  terminology 145–8
  underleases 151–2
  upgrading title 80
  see also Tenants

Legal action
  mortgagor's right to sue 446
  protection of easement/profit by 526–8
Legal interests in land 8–10
  contracts to create 11–12
  easements 504–7
  enforcement of 59
  equitable interests compared 15–18
  legal leases 153–5
  legal mortgages 10, 435, 436–9, 437–8
    priorities 466–74
  profits 504–7
  registration 70–1
Legal parol leases, enforcement of covenants and
    211
Letting schemes 551
Licences
  bare 416, 417, 421
  contractual 415–16, 417–19, 421–4, 566–7
  conversion into legal easement 512
  coupled with interests in land 415, 417, 421
  developing into interests in land 428–9
  distinguished from easement or profit 413
  distinguished from lease 400–13
  enforcement 415, 417–30
    against licensor 417–20
    against successors of licensor 420–7, 428–9
  by estoppel 416–17, 419–20, 424–7
  implied 120
  nature of 399–413
  transferability 428
  types 415–17
Life, lease for 150
Life interests 139, 260
  see also Tenant for life
Light, right to 499, 523–4
Limitation periods, adverse possession 114–15,
    122–4
  effect of completion of period 125–6
  squatter's rights during 124–5
Limited owner's land charge 52
Local authorities, enforcement of positive
    covenants and 555
Local land charges 27
Lost modern grant, prescription and 518–19

Maintenance see Repair and maintenance
Marriage
  lease until marriage 150
  property granted on condition of marriage 143
  see also Family/matrimonial property
Mere equities 14
Merger of lease 168, 175
Minerals 574
Misrepresentation, mortgage priority and 471
Mistake, adverse possession and 115
  first registration by adverse possessor 131–2
Mixed trusts 266
Mortgages 433–92
  consolidation of 448–9

constructive trusts and 372
creation 435
  contract to create 439
default 435
equitable 435, 439–40
  disadvantages 456
  priorities 464–6
  remedies 455–6
forfeiture of lease and 234
informal mortgage by deposit of deeds
    439–40
instalment mortgages 441
interests prior to 478–92
legal 10, 435, 436–9, 437–8
  priorities 466–74
mortgagee
  claim for possession against 565–6
  collateral advantages for 444–5
  interests prior to mortgage and 478–92
  liability for fraud and negligence
    458–62
  remedies 449–56
  rights 446–9, 476–8
mortgagor
  interests prior to mortgage and 478–92
  protection from mortgagee's right to sell
    453–4
  rights 440–6
priorities 463–76
  equitable mortgages 464–6
  legal mortgages 466–74
  three or more mortgages 475–6
puisne mortgage 52
redemption 435, 462
  collateral advantages for mortgagee
    444–5
  equity of redemption 442–5
  postponement 443–4
  prevention of 442–3
  right to redeem 441
  third parties and 457–8
reforms of 1925 435–6
severance of joint tenancy and 355
tacking further advances 448, 476–8
tenant for life's power 316
termination 462–3
types 433–5
unconscionable bargains 486–7
undue influence and 479–86
Multiplicity of rights 18

Names, land charges and 54–5
Necessity, easement of 508
Negligence
  mortgage priority and 471
  mortgagee's liability for 458, 459–61
  receiver's liability for 458, 461–2
  valuer's liability for 458, 462
Neighbouring land, access to 530–1
Noise 185, 186

Non-payment of rent
  distress remedy 225–7
  forfeiture for 228, 235–6
Non-proprietary lease 411–12
Notice
  categories of 17–18
  equitable doctrine of 16–18, 59–62
    acquiring legal estate 17
    bona fide purchaser 16–17, 62
    giving value 17
    reducing dangers of 59–60
    registered land 104–5
    searches to avoid constructive notice
      60–2
    after 1925 60
  to quit 164–7
  severance of joint tenancy by 352–4
Notices in register 84, 85–6
Nuisance 527–8

Occupation
  beneficiaries' right 279–82, 300, 566
  co-ownership and 361–2
  exclusive 402–3
  interests of persons in 92, 94–103
    comparison of new and old system
      96–8
    meaning of actual occupation 98
    purchaser taking free of occupier's rights
      102–3
    several people in occupation 101–2
    statutory provisions 94–5
    temporary absence 99–101
    time of occupation 98–9
    which rights override 95–6
  licence for *see* Licences
  shared 408–9
  by spouses/cohabitants 61–2, 566–70
  see also Adverse possession
Options
  to purchase 189, 215
  to renew leases 188–9
  tenant for life's power to grant 316
Oral agreements
  house purchase and 37–8
    part performance and 38, 39–40
    written evidence of 38
  legal parol leases and enforcement of
    covenants 211
  short leases 153
Overreaching
  protection of purchasers 59, 60, 100–1,
    288–92, 301–2
  tenant for life of settled land (strict
    settlements) 314–15
Overriding interests 67, 77, 80, 88–96
  proprietary estoppel and 392–3
Overriding lease, right to 206–7
Ownership
  extent of 579

joint *see* Co-ownership
passing of 45
unregistered land 50–1

Parking 500–1
Part performance, contracts for house purchase
    and 37, 38, 39–41
  replacement for 41–5
Party walls
  right to support 500, 527–8
  special rights for 531–2
Pasture, profit of 503
Pension schemes, perpetuities and 340
Periodic tenancies 145–6
  grant of legal lease 153–4
    express grant 153–4
    implied grant 154–5
  notice to quit 164–7
  term 146–7, 149–50
Perpetually renewable leases 188–9
Perpetuities 215, 326–40
  class gifts 331–3
  common law rules 326–33, 337
  easements and restrictive covenants 340
  legislation of 1964 334–8
  options and pre-emption rights 339
  period 328–31, 334–6
  powers of trustees and 338–9
  reform proposals 342–4
  reforms made in 1925 333–4, 337
Personal property 18, 19, 577
Personam, rights in 16, 577
Piscary, profit of 503
Positive covenants 541, 551–5
Possession
  adverse *see* Adverse possession
  choses in possession 19
  covenant not to part with 189–94
  elements of 117–18
  exclusive
    leases and 148–9, 402–3, 405
    licences and 403–4
  fee simple estate and 6
  importance in land law 113
  joint *see* Co-ownership
  leasehold estate and 147
  mortgagee's right to 447–8, 450–2, 455
  quiet enjoyment covenant 185–7, 196
Possessory freehold title 78
Possessory leasehold title 79
Prescription, acquisition of easements/profits by
    515–26
  acquiescence and permission 525–6
  application 524–5
  basic rules 516–17
  common law 518
  long period 521–3
  lost modern grant 518–19
  short period 520–1, 522–3
  statute 519–24

Priorities
  equitable interests in land 111–12
  mortgages 463–76
    equitable mortgages 464–6
    legal mortgages 466–74
    three or more mortgages 475–6
Privileges, legal 8–9
Privity of contract 14
Privity of estate 207–9
Profits à prendre 9, 71, 493, 503–4
  acquisition
    express grant or reservation 507,
      514
    implied grant 507–10
    implied reservation 510–11
    prescription 515–26
  appurtenant 503–4
  creation 91–2, 505
  enforcement 505–7
  examples 503
  extinguishment 528–9
  gross 503
  in law and equity 504–7
  law reform 529–32
  licences coupled with 415
  licences distinguished from 413
  as overriding interests 91–2
  period 504–5
  prescribed period 504–5
  remedies for protection 526–8
Promissory estoppel 382
Property
  classification of 18–19
  condition of 186
Property adjustment orders 371
Proprietary estoppel 44, 379, 382–95, 566–7
  constructive trusts and 43, 394–5
  essential elements 385–8
  expectation as to future rights 383–5
  nature of 382–5
  nature of equity arising from 392–3
  satisfying equity 389–92
  situations where 'no room' for 393–4
Public auctions 36
Puisne mortgage 52
Purchaser
  bona fide 16–17
  buying a house *see* House purchase
  protection of purchasers by overreaching 59,
    60, 100–1, 288–92, 301–2
  for value 17

Qualified freehold title 77–8
Qualified leasehold title 79
Quiet enjoyment, covenant to allow 185–7,
  196
Quit, notice to 164–7

Rates, covenant to pay 197
Real property 18, 577

Receiver
  appointment of 454–5, 456
  liability for fraud and negligence 458, 461–2
Rectification remedy 47
  alteration of register 105–7
Registered land 24–6
  adverse possession 81, 127–33
    application of existing rules 127–8
    defence to proceedings for possession 132
    first application by adverse possessor for
      registration 130–2
    legislation of 1925 127–9
    legislation of 2002 130–3
    purchasers and 133
    reform proposals 128–9
  aim of registration 66
  alteration of register 105–6
  areas of compulsory registration 24
  buying house with registered title 83–4
  classes of title 76–80
  conveyancing process 66–112
    alteration of register 105–6
    discovering encumbrances 80–1, 102–4
    electronic conveyancing 67–8, 109–11
    indemnity 106
    need for reform 66–9
    transfer and completion 107–9
    what can be registered 69–71
  dealings with registered estate 82
  electronic conveyancing 67–8, 109–11
  evidence of registration 81
  finding out if title is registered 25–6
  first registration 63–5, 71–3
    by adverse possessor 130–2
    cautions against 74
    compulsory 71–3
    failure to apply for first registration 72, 142
    legal mortgage as trigger for registration
      438–9
    registering title 73–81
    triggering events 71–2, 438–9
    voluntary 25, 73
  form of register 74–5
  grant of long leases on 154
  interests of persons in actual occupation 90,
    92–101
    comparison of new and old system 94–6
    meaning of actual occupation 96
    purchaser taking free of occupier's rights
      100–1
    several people in occupation 99–100
    statutory provisions 93
    temporary absence 98–9
    time of occupation 97–8
    which rights override 94
  interests protected by entries on register 84–7
  investigating title 74
  legal mortgage 437–8
  licences by estoppel and 426–7
  mortgage priorities 466–9

non-registration of land charges compared
   with 58
overriding interests 67, 77, 80, 88–92
proprietary estoppel and 392
purchasers of other interests 111–12
recording encumbrances 80
sale of freehold reversion 161
searches 103–5
termination of mortgage 462–3
upgrading title 79–80
vesting deed for settled land 312
voluntary registration 25, 73
Registration of land charges 54–5, 59
   effect of non-registration 56–8
   effect of registration 55–6
Registration of leases 69–70, 154
Release of easement/profit 529
Rem, rights in 16, 577
Remainders 142–3
Renewal of leases, option for 188–9
Rent 152–3
   co-ownership and 362–3
   covenant to pay 189, 197
   low rent and covenants on fitness for purpose
      196
   non-payment
     distress remedy 225–7
     forfeiture for 228, 235–6
   restriction of liability for 206
Rentcharges 9, 140, 308
   estate rentcharges 9, 553–4
Repair and maintenance
   covenants to repair 195, 196, 197
     remedies for breach 223–4, 225
   tenant's liability for disrepair 197–8
Representation
   estoppel by 179
   proprietary estoppel and 383, 385, 386–8
Repudiatory breach of contract 171–2
Rescission remedy 47
Restrictions in register 84, 86–7
Restrictive covenants 14, 53
   enforcement against subtenant 217–18
   perpetuities and 340
Resulting trusts 11, 366–7
   arising from contribution 371–3
   contracts for creation or operation of 36
   establishing claim to share in beneficial
      interest 373–9
   examples 367
   intention and 367
   quantifying share 379
Reversion 142–3
   covenant to sell to tenant (option to purchase)
      189, 215
   enforcement of covenants and 210–11
   entailed interest and 6
   freehold reversion 151
     sale of 161
   leasehold reversion 151

   sale of 162
   leases of (concurrent leases) 181
Reversionary lease 147–8
Rights, legal 8–9
Risk, house purchase and 45
Roam, right to 532
Root of title 50–1
Royal lives clause 328–9

Sale
   co-ownership and 358–60, 363–5
   houses *see* House purchase
   leases 160–2
   mortgagee's remedy 450–4, 455–6, 459–60
   public policy and restrictions on 143
   setting aside in cases of fraud 462
   tenant for life's power of 315
   trust for *see* Trusts for sale
Scotland 3
Searches and enquiries
   to avoid constructive notice 60–2
   enquiries before contract 26, 51
   land charges 56
   registered land 102–3
   search certificate 56
   unregistered land 63
Security *see* Mortgages
Seisin 113
Service charge, restriction of liability for 206
Settled land (strict settlements) 258, 267,
      304–25
   basic form 305
   compared to trusts of land 296–302
   creation 297, 310–14
     after 1996 313–14
     curtain principle 312–13
     inter vivos 310–12
     paralysing section 313
     trust instrument 310–11
     vesting deed 311–12
     by will 312
   defective dispositions 319–21
   derivative settlement 313–14
   end of 324, 325
   existing settlements 304
   historical background 259–60
   need for reform 261
   tenant for life 309
     consent for exercise of powers 317–18
     end 323–4
     notice of exercise of powers 317
     powers 314–17, 318–19
   trustees 309–10
     role 321–4
   trusts of land in place of 292–4
   types 306–8
Shared accommodation 408–9
Shops, keep-open covenants 221–3
Signature of house purchase contracts 35–6, 38
Specific performance remedy 11–12, 13, 47

keep-open covenants 221–3
repairing covenants 223–4
Spouses
    right to remain in occupation 61–2, 566,
        567–8
    right to share in value of house 564–5
    tenancy by entireties and 346
    undue influence and mortgages 479–86
Squatting *see* Adverse possession
Statutory trusts 258
Storage, rights to 500
Strict settlement *see* Settled land (strict
    settlements)
Subleases 151–2
    covenant not to sublet 189–94
    effect on subtenant of determination of head
        lease 174–6
    enforcement of covenants and 216–20
    forfeiture of head lease and 234, 236
    mortgage as 436
Successive interests in land 292–3
Sue, mortgagor's right to 446
Sufferance, tenancy at 177
Support, right to 500
Surrender of lease 15, 167–8, 175
Survivorship, joint tenancy 348, 363–4

Taxes, covenant to pay 197
Tenant for life (settled land/strict settlements)
    309
    consent for exercise of powers 317–18
    end 323–4
    notice of exercise of powers 317
    powers 314–17, 318–19
Tenants
    adverse possession against 126, 128
    adverse possession by 119–20
    assignment of lease by 161–2
    assured 569
    by estoppel 15, 178–80, 412
    joint tenancy 346–8
        determination of lease by 172–3
        differences in law and equity 349
        severance 347–8, 352–7
        survivorship 348, 363–4
    joint tenants, determination of lease by
        172–3
    landlord's remedies against defaulting
        tenant 225–37
    notice to quit 164–7
    obligations of 182–220
        express covenants 189–95
        implied covenants 197–8
    prescription by and against 517
    quiet enjoyment right 185–7, 196
    remedies against defaulting landlord 224–5
    rent *see* Rent
    statutory protection for 162–3, 569
    subletting *see* Subleases
    at sufferance 177

tenancy by entireties 346
tenancy in common 348–9
    differences in law and equity 349, 350
    at will 177–8, 411, 412–13
Tenure, estates in land and 4
Third parties
    breach of quiet enjoyment covenant and
        186–7
    enforcement of equitable leases against 158–9
    redemption of mortgages by 457–8
Title 23–6
    investigating title 27–8, 74
    relative nature of 114
    root of 50–1
    see also Registered land; Unregistered land
Trustees
    co-ownership trusts 351
    perpetuities rules and powers of 338–9
    settled land (strict settlements) 309–10
        role 321–4
    trusts of land 298
        appointment of 267–9, 299
        beneficiaries' occupation right and 280–1
        consents and consultation 273–5, 299,
            300
        delegation by 276–8, 300
        duties 276, 298–9
        limitation of powers 272–6
        number of 267
        powers 270–6, 298
        retirement and discharge 268–9, 299
Trusts
    beneficiaries *see* Beneficiaries under trusts
    common intention trusts 372, 373–4
    constructive *see* Constructive trusts
    contracts for creation or operation 36
    co-ownership
        imposition of statutory trusts 350–1
        number of trustees 351
        trusts for sale 261–2
    creation of 257–8
    first registration of title and 77
    historical background 259–62
    implied 257, 258
    of land *see* Trusts of land
    nature of 257
    perpetuities rules *see* Perpetuities
    rentcharges and 9
    resulting *see* Resulting trusts
    for sale *see* Trusts for sale
    settlements *see* Settled land (strict settlements);
        Trusts for sale
    statutory 258
Trusts for sale 258–9
    compared to trusts of land 296–302
    conversion into trusts of land 266, 267,
        294–5
    historical background 260–1
    need for reform 261–2
Trusts of land 262–3, 264–303

beneficiaries
  appointment and retirement of trustees and
    268–9, 299
  consultation and consents 273–5, 299, 300
  nature of interests 299
  rights of 279–82, 566
children and minors and 293
comparison of old and new law 296–302
conversion of trusts for sale into 266, 267,
  294–5
court's powers 282–8, 302
deed of discharge 291
definition 266–7
doctrine of continuing purpose 287–8
formalities for creation 297–8
future 303
protection of purchasers 288–92, 301–2
settlor's powers 300–1
trustees 298
  appointment of 267–9, 299
  beneficiaries' occupation right and 280–1
  consents and consultation 273–5, 299, 300
  delegation by 276–8, 300
  duties 276, 298–9
  limitation of powers 272–6
  number of 267
  powers 270–6, 298
  retirement and discharge 268–9, 299
trusts of proceeds of sale of land 291–2
when trust arises 292–6
Turbary, profit of 503

Unconscionable bargains 486–7
Unconscionable behaviour, constructive trusts
  and 368–70
Underleases 151–2
Undue influence, mortgages and 479–86
Unit trusts 36
Unmarried couples *see* Cohabitation
Unregistered land 24, 26, 50–65
  adverse possession 81, 122–7
    effect of completion of limitation period
      125–6

    rights of squatter during limitation period
      124–5
    time 122–4
  application for first registration 63–5
  checking for encumbrances 51
  conveyance 63
  grant of long leases on 154
  land charges 51–9
  legal mortgage as trigger for registration
    438–9
  licences by estoppel and 425–6
  mortgages
    priorities 469–74
    right to tack further advances 477–8
  other legal or equitable interests
    59–63
  ownership of estate 50–1
  proprietary estoppel and 392
  sale of freehold reversion 161
  searches 63
  termination of mortgage 463
  vesting deed for settled land 311–12
Upgrading title 79–80
User as of right 522
Usual covenants 183, 198–9

Value, purchaser for 17
Valuers, liability for fraud and negligence 458,
  462
Vested interests, perpetuities rules and
  326–7
Vesting deed for settled land 311–12
Voluntary first registration 25, 73

Waste 197–8
Water, rights to 499
Way, rights of 499
Widows, unborn 330, 337
Will, tenancy at 177–8, 411, 412–13
Wills
  creation of settled land by 312
  revoking 384